W9-CQS-091

ARCTIC

RUSSIAN FEDERATION

NORWAY
SWEDEN
FINLAND
DENMARK
ESTONIA
LITH.
RUS.
LATVIA
GERMANY
POLAND
BELARUS
CZECH REP.
SLVK.
UKRAINE
AUS.
HUNG.
MOLDOVA
SLO.
ROMANIA
CRO.
BOS.
BULG.
ITALY
MAC.
GEORGIA
KAZAKHSTAN
MONGOLIA
GREECE
TURKEY
ARM.
AZER.
UZBEKISTAN
KYRGYZSTAN
TUNISIA
MALTA
CRETE
CYPRUS
LEB.
SYRIA
TURKMENISTAN
TAJIKISTAN
N. KOREA
JAPAN
ISR.
IRAQ
IRAN
AFGHANISTAN
S. KOREA
CHINA
LIBYA
EGYPT
JORDAN
KUWAIT
BAHRAIN
PAKISTAN
NEPAL
BHUTAN
PACIFIC
ERIA
SAUDI
ARABIA
QATAR
U.A.E.
OMAN
BANGLADESH
TAIWAN
OCEAN
NIGER
CHAD
SUDAN
ERITREA
YEMEN
DJIBOUTI
INDIA
MYANMAR
(BURMA)
VIETNAM
NIGERIA
CENTRAL
AFRICAN REPUBLIC
ETHIOPIA
SRI
LANKA
THAILAND
CAMB
PHILIPPINES
NORTHERN
MARIANAS (U.S.)
MARSHALL
ISLANDS
CAMEROON
UGANDA
SOMALIA
MALDIVES
GUAM (U.S.)
GUINEA
CONGO
(ZAIRE)
GABON
RWANDA
KENYA
BRUNEI
MALAYSIA
FEDERATED STATES
OF MICRONESIA
NAUHU
KIRIBATI
MÉ &
NCIPE
CONGO
BURUNDI
SINGAPORE
INDONESIA
PAPUA
NEW
GUINEA
INDIAN
TANZANIA
MALAWI
SEYCHELLES
COMOROS
SOLOMON
ISLANDS
ANGOLA
ZAMBIA
ZIMBABWE
MADAGASCAR
OCEAN
VANUATU
FIJI
NAMIBIA
MOZAMBIQUE
MAURITIUS
NEW
CALEDONIA
(FR.)
BOTSWANA
SOUTH
AFRICA
SWAZILAND
LESOTHO
AUSTRALIA

NEW
ZEALAND

ANTARCTICA

UNDERSTANDING
THE POLITICAL WORLD

Understanding the Political World

A Comparative Introduction to Political Science

SEVENTH EDITION

James N. Danziger
University of California, Irvine

PEARSON
Longman

New York   San Francisco   Boston
London   Toronto   Sydney   Tokyo   Singapore   Madrid
Mexico City   Munich   Paris   Cape Town   Hong Kong   Montreal

To Lesley, Nick, and Vanessa

Vice President and Publisher: Priscilla McGeehon
Executive Editor: Eric Stano
Acquisitions Editor: Ed Costello
Senior Marketing Manager: Elizabeth Fogarty
Media and Supplements Editor: Kristi Olson
Senior Media Editor: Patrick McCarthy
Production Manager: Ellen MacElree
Project Coordination, Text Design, and Electronic Page Makeup: Electronic
    Publishing Services Inc., NYC
Cover Designer Manager: John Callahan
Cover Photos: (Top): Photo by Carolyn Cole. Copyright, 2005, Los Angeles Times. Reprinted with
    permission. (Bottom, both): Photo courtesy of Getty Images, Inc.
Photo Researcher: Photosearch, Inc.
Senior Manufacturing Buyer: Al Dorsey
Printer and Binder: Hamilton Printing Company
Cover Printer: Phoenix Color Corp.

For permission to use copyrighted material, grateful acknowledgment is made to the copyright holders on page 515, which are hereby made part of this copyright page.

On the Cover:
(Top) Election day in Rwanda. As developing countries attempt to institutionalize democracy, the military musch achieve the delicate balance of maintaining order and protecting democratic practices without taking control of the government during the inevitable periods of instability.
(Bottom left) School days in China. In an isolated region of China, the state uses a school as an agent of socialization and modernization, introducing preteens of the Dong minority people to a Chinese view of the world, and drawing them away from their traditional culture, unique religion, barter economy, and unwritten, singing language.
(Bottom right) The logo of the United Nations.

Library of Congress Cataloging-in-Publication Data
Danziger, James N.
   Understanding the political world : a comparative introduction to political science / James N.
Danziger.— 7th ed.
       p. cm.
   Includes bibliographical references and index.
   ISBN 0-321-21610-5
   1. Political science. 2. Comparative government. I. Title.
   JA66.D36 2005
   320—dc22   2004004647

Please visit our website at http://www.ablongman.com

ISBN 0-321-21610-5

1 2 3 4 5 6 7 8 9 10—HT—07 06 05 04

Contents

Boxed Features

Preface

In these early years of the twenty-first century, there are especially good reasons why we should attempt to enhance our understanding of the political world. For Americans, the shocking attacks on September 11, 2001, the subsequent "war on terrorism," and the attempt at "nation-building" in Iraq brought into sharp relief what many others around the world were already experiencing: that the post–cold war period, despite expectations that it would usher in a benign "new world order," is neither orderly nor benign. Moreover, while increased globalization has resulted in new levels of prosperity and interdependence, it has also heightened antagonisms and exacerbated conflicts within and between countries.

At this time, there are a variety of "more than ever" situations that intersect with politics. There are more electoral democracies than at any time in history. The power of transnational/multinational actors, whether the European Union or a large corporation, is at its highest point ever. The political world has never been characterized by as many countries or as many ethnic groups attempting to establish new states that correspond to their identity group. Potent technologies, ranging from those manipulating information to those capable of mass destruction, are more prevalent and pervasive than ever. The political economies of individual countries have never been as interdependent. At no time have larger numbers of people lived in such material abundance and/or have so many suffered from relative deprivation in the distribution of resources.

These circumstances are indicative of a period that is extraordinary and that poses fascinating challenges to those of us who attempt to use information and the concepts of political science in order to understand better the real world of politics.

Objectives

Addressing such challenges is at the heart of this book. The main objective is, as the book's title indicates, to help the reader better understand the political world. It attempts to link the central analytic concepts of political science that have emerged over decades of research to the realities of the political world in the early twenty-first century. Using contemporary and some historical evidence, the emphasis is on empirical research that illuminates the processes and structures of politics. The level of analysis ranges from the individual's political beliefs and actions through the politics of groups and states to the dynamics of the international system.

This book asks the reader to assess whether it is possible and useful to develop generalizations about political phenomena. It combines attention to systematic descriptive analysis—the *what* questions—with efforts to explain underlying patterns—the *why* and *how* questions. And readers are continually reminded that they must consider the important normative questions that are embedded in most issues about politics. Many topics are also presented in a manner that encourages the reader to think as a political scientist—to structure questions and assess evidence in order to make inferences.

Features

This seventh edition has retained most key features of the earlier editions:

- A strong, comparative framework
- Coverage of micropolitics, macropolitics, and international relations
- A focus on political economy, including a complete chapter on this important topic
- Thorough analyses of key political processes
- An engaging, readable style
- Presentation of current data to facilitate analysis and comparisons on many topics
- The instructive use of political cartoons and photographs.

In addition, the book features 62 boxed discussions that offer rich, memorable examples of key concepts and issues, such as the different paths of political activism taken by Gandhi and Osama bin Laden, the rational choice perspective on why a person should not vote, the role of microcredit in the development process, Russia's struggles to establish democratic politics and a market economy, the political impacts of television, the effects of colonialism and neocolonialism on Congo, the different policies for dealing with population growth in developing countries, the extensive social control exercised by the state in Singapore, and the American imposition of a constitution on Japan.

New to This Edition

Given the extraordinary rate of change in the political world, many examples have been updated. In addition, there are the following significant differences from the previous edition:

- The implications of the expanding "war on terrorism" and the U.S.-led war against Iraq are explored.
- Chapter 11, previously called "Politics Between States" has been reformulated as "Politics Across Borders" to focus greater analytic attention on the actions of non-state actors, such as intergovernmental organizations, NGOs, and transnational corporations, as well as on the actions of states.
- There is consideration of the increasing challenges to sustaining and deepening democratization that face many transitional and developing countries.

- With the further blurring between conventional war and other forms of political violence, the treatment of all forms of interstate conflict is now integrated into Chapter 12's discussion of political violence.
- There is explication of the integration of most countries in Central and Eastern Europe into the European Union.
- The remarkable economic development of China from Mao to now is examined.
- The historical relationship of the Palestinians and Jews is detailed to provide a context for understanding the current conflict.
- The role of the World Trade Organization as the key intergovernmental actor shaping globalization is detailed.
- "On the Web"—a list of particularly useful and relevant Internet sites at the end of each chapter—has been updated and substantially expanded.

Organization

The seventh edition retains the conceptual framework of the sixth edition, focusing on micropolitics and macropolitics.

- Chapter 1 and the Appendix introduce students to the logic of political science and the methods of political analysis.
- Chapters 2 through 4 examine political behavior at the individual and group levels, describing and explaining the causes of individual political beliefs and actions.
- Chapters 5 through 8 emphasize the structural and institutional elements of political systems, offering analytic frameworks for characterizing the different ways in which people organize themselves politically.
- Chapters 9 through 12 analyze interesting and important political processes, such as decision making and the exercise of power, political and economic development, politics across borders, and political violence.
- Chapters 13 through 15 explain in detail how certain groups of countries try to achieve their broad goals of prosperity, stability, and security within the complex international environment. Specific analysis is provided for the developed countries, the developing countries, and two sets of transitional countries—the post-communist developed countries and the newly industrializing countries.
- Chapter 16 concludes the book with a prospective assessment of the major political challenges in the early twenty-first century.

Audience

This book is written for anyone who wants to enrich his or her basic understanding of the political world and to learn how political scientists attempt to describe and explain politics. One might be in an introductory course in political science or comparative politics, but the book would also be useful for those taking a "capstone" course that integrates their political science studies. Readers might also be those who want to think about the fascinating and confusing world of politics in a more informed and systematic way.

Supplements for Instructors

Instructor's Manual with Test Bank to Accompany *Understanding the Political World*, Seventh Edition. Written by James N. Danziger (me!), the *Instructor's Manual with Test Bank* includes up-to-date chapter summaries, multiple-choice questions, essay questions, and discussion questions.

Supplements for Students

Longman Atlas of World Issues (from the Penguin Atlas Series) ISBN 0-321-22465-5. Introduced and selected by Robert J. Art of Brandeis University, and sampled from the acclaimed Penguin Atlas Series, the new *Longman Atlas of World Issues* is designed to help students understand the geography and major issues facing our world today. These thematic, full-color maps examine forces shaping politics today at a global level. Explanatory information accompanies each map to help students better grasp the concepts being shown and how they affect our world today.

Discounted Subscription to *Newsweek* Magazine. Students can receive 12 issues of *Newsweek* at an 80 percent savings off the regular subscription price. An outstanding way to engage students and get them involved in the most current events and issues in politics today. Contact your local Allyn & Bacon/Longman rep for ordering information.

Acknowledgments

Many sources of ideas and information constitute the basis of *my* understanding about politics. Broadly, you should know that I was born and have primarily been educated in the United States. I have studied, lived, and/or spent significant periods in North America, Western and Eastern Europe, Asia, the Middle East, and Africa. The people I met and the events I experienced in these places have certainly influenced my perceptions about politics.

More direct contributions to this book have come from my colleagues in political science and from the many students and others in the political world with whom I have interacted. I have drawn deeply and often from the ideas of these groups.

By the publication of a seventh edition, the layers of contributions and ideas to the construction of this book are deep, rich, and indescribable. In every edition, there is a list of people who added positively to that edition, and I continue to be grateful to them all. Explicit guidance and advice regarding the writing of this particular edition have come from several valuable sources: the cadre at Longman Publishers, including the executive editor, Eric Stano, and the acquisitions editor, Ed Costello; Jim Hill at Electronic Publishing Services; scholarly colleagues who have offered useful suggestions; and students who have provided specific material for the book, especially Jacqueline Chattopadhyay, Cyrus Ameri, and Stephanie Domzalski. The reviewers, who offered very thoughtful and constructive commentaries for this edition, are: William Kelly, Auburn University; David Van Heemst, Olivet Nazarene University; Isaac Endeley, St. Cloud State University; and M.J. Peterson, University of Massachusetts–Amherst.

I am very grateful for the help provided by all these (and many unnamed) sources. Regarding the roads not taken and the missteps in this book, the responsibility is mine.

James N. Danziger

To the Reader

The aim of this book is revealed by its title: It is meant to help you understand the political world. It assumes that you are willing to think about politics. It does not assume that you have substantial knowledge about politics or political science, nor does it assume that you know the difference between politics and political science. I hope that when you complete the book (especially if it is complemented by instruction about politics from a teacher), you will feel that you have increased your knowledge about the contemporary political world.

The study of politics is full of fascinating questions. First are the questions about *what is,* such as: Who exercises political power, and what values and purposes guide them? Why do people accept political authority? How do people organize themselves politically? What causes individuals and groups to take political action? A second set of questions concerns *what ought to be:* Who should exercise political power, and what values should they pursue? Why should people accept political authority? How should political structures be organized? Why should individuals and groups act politically? People disagree sharply about answers to both these descriptive (what is) and normative (what ought to be) questions. In addition, the study of politics provokes a third set of questions regarding *what we can actually know* about the political world. Here also there are major disagreements about the appropriate methods for describing and understanding politics.

Although this book cannot resolve the underlying disputes, it offers you the basis for making sense out of politics at all three levels. As author, I make some basic assumptions: that you can think systematically about politics and make general statements about how politics works; that you will learn more about politics by considering the politics of many different places; that every observer of politics (certainly including you and me) has biases, only some of which can be understood; that you need a variety of sources of ideas and information before you can make informed and sensible decisions about the value disagreements pervading politics; and that this book is one such source that can be helpful to you. My efforts will be successful to the extent that *you* ultimately judge my assumptions to be correct (especially the last one . . .).

It is inevitable that you will be frustrated with the treatment of politics at some (many?) points in this book. I would say: Reader, be merciful! The study of politics is very complex. Gather bits of understanding where you can find them.

About the Author

James N. Danziger is a professor and former chair of the Department of Political Science at the University of California, Irvine, where he also has served as campuswide Dean of Undergraduate Education and Director of the Center for Research on Information Technology and Organizations. He is recipient of many honors and awards, including a Marshall Scholarship (to Great Britain), a Foreign Area Fellowship, Phi Beta Kappa, and an IBM Faculty Award. He received the first UC Irvine Distinguished Faculty Lectureship Award for Teaching in 1987 and the UC Irvine Distinguished Service Award in 1997. His research has received awards from the American Political Science Association and the American Society for Public Administration. He has published extensively, particularly on information technology and politics, and he is on the editorial board of *Local Government Studies*. He has been an active participant in local politics and especially enjoys playing sports, travel, music, and cinema.

UNDERSTANDING
THE POLITICAL WORLD

CHAPTER 1   **Politics and Knowledge**

ON POLITICS

Fang Zheng, who lost the use of both legs in 1989, is one of China's out-standing disabled athletes. Yet in September 1994, the Chinese government refused to allow him to represent China in the international games for disabled athletes. The government's refusal is deeply embedded in politics. Can you think of a political reason why the Chinese government would prevent him from participating?

Stop for a moment. I encourage you to reflect on this question for 20 to 30 seconds, rather than rushing ahead in order to complete your reading. Questions like this appear throughout this book. Your responses to these brief "reflections" should help you to clarify your own thinking on the subject under discussion. As novelist E. M. Forster said, "How do I know what I think until I see what I say?" So, can you think of a political reason for stopping Fang?

Fang had been a senior at Beijing Physical Education College in 1989. He was among the many students who, despite their state-provided education, rejected the Chinese political leadership and political institutions. In a series of dramatic protest demonstrations, the students and other citizens demanded that China establish a democratic government. In turn, the Chinese political authorities rejected these demands and used the military to suppress the demonstrations. In the violent confrontation between demonstrators and the military in Beijing's Tiananmen Square, a tank crushed Fang's legs. It is for this reason that the government judges Fang to be an unfit representative of China in international sports competition. It is not prepared to allow Fang to be the focus of attention and have the cause of his disability revealed.

This incident captures some of the crucial themes that relate to politics. **Politics** is defined in a variety of ways. (The **bold type** indicates that the concept is included in the Glossary beginning on page 495.) Some of the most widely used definitions of politics are:

Politics is the exercise of power.

Politics is the public allocation of things that are valued.

Politics is the resolution of conflict.

Politics is the competition among individuals and groups pursuing their own interests.

Politics is the determination of who gets what, when, and how.

All of these definitions share the central idea that *politics is the process through which power and influence are used in the promotion of certain values and interests.* Politics operates at many levels in the Fang example. When Fang decides that his government is undemocratic and that he should publicly protest against his leaders and their programs, he is engaging in politics at the individual level. When Fang joins with other students and workers to demonstrate against the government in Tiananmen Square, that is an example of group-level politics. At the societal level, the government uses its political power to allocate benefits to Fang when it provides him with a free university education. But the government also uses its powers to withhold benefits when it prevents him from participating in the international games for the disabled. And the government has exercised its political powers even more dramatically when it sends troops to stop the protests by force, a government action that resulted in Fang losing his legs.

As individuals, groups, and governmental actors make decisions about what is good or bad for society, and as they try to implement their decisions, politics is at work. For our purposes, politics is associated with those aspects of life that have *public* significance. Other aspects of life, in contrast, are understood to be private and thus are beyond the domain of politics. However, we shall see that what is considered "public" in one country may be considered "private" in another. Even your choice about the job you take, the religion you practice, or the music you listen to can be either a private choice or one within the public domain. Can you see why a government might conclude that these choices have public significance? Within each country, there is a constant debate about the appropriate areas for governmental action and the domains of life that should remain private and unrestrained by political action. Sometimes the term "politics" is used even more broadly than in this book to refer to competition over values in domains that are not truly public, such as the "politics of the family" or "office politics."

In almost every contemporary society, the area that is subject to politics is very large. Politics, usually via government, determines how much education you must have and what its content will be. Politics establishes the words you cannot utter in a public place, how much of your hard-earned income you must give to government, and how various governments spend that money to provide different groups with a vast range of benefits (e.g., education, roads, fire protection, subsidized health care, safe food, and so on). Politics determines whether you are allowed to use a certain drug, the amount of pollutants that your car can emit, how secure you feel against violence by others within your neighborhood and within the global system, and whether you receive unequal treatment in the allocation of benefits because of your ethnicity, gender, ideology, or some other factor.

TYPES OF POLITICAL KNOWLEDGE

Clearly, politics can impact our lives in many ways. Yet people differ greatly in their understandings about the nature of politics, the uses of political power, and the distribution of political benefits and burdens. If you have discussed politics with your friends, you probably have noticed that they differ in how much they know about politics and in their opinions about what constitutes good and bad political actions. Your understandings about politics and your decisions about whether to undertake specific political actions are grounded in your knowledge of politics. But what are the sources of your political knowledge? How do you make sense out of the many conflicting issues and statements about the political world that confront you each day?

Here, for example, are three political statements:

A "single-payer" system is the best way to solve the United States' many health care problems.

In a democracy, men are more likely to vote than women.

The United States is the most peaceful, least warlike nation in modern history.

When you hear or read a statement like one of these, you might

Ignore it

Accept that it is correct

Reject it

Try to assess it

If you decide to assess it, you would probably ask questions such as these: Is it based on accurate information? Is it consistent with other things that I know about politics? Are its assertions persuasive? Does it influence any political actions I might take?

When you begin to ask assessment questions, and especially when you try to answer them, you are performing political analysis. At its core, **political analysis** is *the attempt to describe (to answer the* what *questions) and then to explain (to answer the* why *and* how *questions regarding) politics.* This book attempts to enhance your ability to do political analysis, to answer the *what, why,* and *how* questions about politics.

Suppose a group of people is instructed to give each of the three preceding statements a "truth score," ranging from 100 percent (absolutely true) to 0 percent (absolutely false). Do you think anyone would give all three statements a score of 100 percent? 0 percent? What truth score would you give these statements? Did you give every statement a score of either 100 percent or 0 percent? Do you expect that most other people will report scores close to your own? Why?

It is reasonable to assume that few people, if any, believe that all the things they hear about politics are absolutely accurate and true. One reason to be suspicious of statements about politics is that they usually reflect the values and interests of the source of the statement.

The first statement is by the Physicians for a National Health Program (2003), a not-for-profit organization of physicians, medical students, and other health care professionals. The second statement was made by political scientists Lester Milbrath and M. L. Goel (1982: 116) in a book summarizing the research on political participation. And the third was made by Ronald Reagan, president of the United States from 1981 to 1989, during his nomination acceptance speech to the Republican Party in 1984. Unless you view all these sources as equally reliable, your knowledge of who made the statements might alter your truth score in some cases. If it does, can you explain why?

There are many sources of statements about politics—family, friends, television, books, newspapers, teachers, politicians. Such sources can provide information about politics, but the information can be unclear, contradictory, or wrong. You are surrounded by competing claims regarding the political world. How are you to determine what you do know about politics?

Political science is one way of attempting to establish such knowledge. As you will discover in reading this book, **political science** is a *set of techniques, concepts, and approaches whose objective is to increase the clarity and accuracy of our understandings about the political world.* You will learn how some political scientists try to think systematically about political phenomena in order to describe "political reality" and explain how politics works. You will also be introduced to some of the findings about politics that have emerged from the work of political scientists and other social scientists.

It was noted earlier that people have very different views about politics. Your friends probably differ in how much they know about such things as the names of the leaders of various countries, do not agree on such questions as how easy it is for a president to get a law passed, and have significant differences of opinion on political issues such as whether there should be a system of "free" health care for all citizens. An individual's understanding of politics is composed of three general types of political knowledge: (1) descriptions of political facts, (2) explanations of how and why politics occurs as it does, and (3) prescriptions of what should happen i

Description

Many bits of political knowledge focus on *what* questions, which require a descriptive response based on one or more "facts." They can be answered with relatively straightforward political facts, such as the ones below:

> The date the Soviet Union ceased to exist: December 25, 1991, with the resignation of Mikhail Gorbachev.
>
> The number of states in Nigeria: 36.
>
> The country with the highest gross domestic product (GDP) per capita in the world in 2004: Luxembourg.

But on many questions about the political world, there are no indisputable answers. On some questions, it is difficult to get precise information. Suppose you want to know the number of countries with operational nuclear weapons. Seven countries acknowledge having operational nuclear devices (China, France, India, Pakistan, Russia, the United Kingdom, and the United States). Experts believe that two other countries (Israel and North Korea) have nuclear weapons, and at least one additional country (Iran) is suspected of having secret nuclear weapons programs. Several others (Algeria, Argentina, Belarus, Brazil, Iraq, Kazakhstan, Libya, South Africa, and Ukraine) had or were close to having nuclear weapons but are now assumed to have backed away from nuclear ambitions (Federation of American Scientists 2004). Even the experts cannot reach consensus on the straightforward issue of which countries belong to the "nuclear club." Box 1.1 asks you an important question about these countries. Is your answer yes?

On other questions about politics, description requires assessments that raise complicated issues about power, interests, and values making it difficult to reach agreement about the facts. Here are two examples:

> Do nonwhites and whites in the United States enjoy equal treatment before the law?
>
> Can a country legally invade another country that has not used military force against it?

 ## BOX **1.1**

Where in the World?

The section on "Description" briefly refers to 21 countries (and 1 country that no longer exists) on 5 continents. Do you have a clear sense of where they are?

There will be detailed discussions of many countries in this book. Knowing the location of a country and its geographic relation to certain other countries is sometimes extremely important for an understanding of its political choices and actions. When such discussions occur, you are strongly encouraged to locate the country on a map. For this purpose, there is a world map on the front inside cover of this book.

Several recent studies have shown that American students are more ignorant of world geography than are students in most other countries. If that characterization applies to you, help change the situation by referring frequently to the map.

Explanation

Many questions about politics are even more difficult to answer because they ask *why* something happens and require political knowledge in the form of explanation.

Why is one in eight families "poor" in the wealthy United States? What causes a country (e.g., Congo) to have inflation of more than 500 percent in a single year? Why does revolutionary violence overthrow the government in one country (e.g., Nicaragua) but not in another (e.g., El Salvador)? These kinds of questions require explanation, not mere descriptive facts. Such questions can be among the most fascinating in politics, but adequate explanation is often difficult because patterns of cause and effect can be extraordinarily complex.

Prescription

Statements about politics often include claims or assumptions that certain choices and actions are more desirable than others. These represent a third form of political knowledge, prescriptions. A prescription is a value judgment that indicates what *should* occur and *should* be done. Thus a prescription deals with "normative" political knowledge—answers to questions about what ought to be, not merely description and explanation of what is.

For example, there are many possible prescriptive responses to this question: What should the government's role be in the provision of health care? Answers vary from the viewpoint that government should take absolutely no action that interferes with the private provision of health care to a viewpoint that government employees should meet the full range of health care needs at no direct cost to the patient. You can probably think of many positions between these two extremes.

The position you select is an element of your **normative political knowledge—** your value judgments. Notice that normative political knowledge combines three levels of understanding: (1) your descriptive knowledge of certain facts (e.g., the alternative forms of health care that are available in a particular society); (2) your explanatory knowledge about why certain outcomes occur (e.g., the causes of unequal health care); and most importantly, (3) your priorities among competing values (e.g., how much you prefer equality, lower taxes, personal responsibility).

SOURCES OF POLITICAL KNOWLEDGE

Each individual's political knowledge is a unique combination of descriptive facts, explanations, and prescriptions about politics. What is the basis of such knowledge? This section describes three important sources: (1) authority, (2) personal thought, and (3) science.

Authority

The method of **authority** involves *the appeal to any document, tradition, or person that is believed to possess the controlling explanation regarding a particular issue.* Knowledge about politics can be based on three kinds of authority sources: (1) a specific authority, (2) a general authority, or (3) "everyone."

Specific authority sources.   A particular individual (but few others) might place great confidence in the knowledge he derived about politics from a specific authority source, such as a parent, teacher, friend, or famous person. Young people and those minimally interested in politics are especially likely to rely on specific authorities for much of their political knowledge. Chapter 4 will argue that specific authority sources powerfully influence some important political beliefs of most individuals. Can you think of a significant piece of your own political knowledge that is derived primarily from a parent, an influential teacher, or a public figure you admire?

General authority sources.   A general authority source is one that has substantial influence on a large proportion of people in a society. Examples are constitutions, revered leaders, widely respected media or books, and religious teachings. General authorities are especially evident as a basis for normative political knowledge. (See Box 1.2 on the role of women in politics.)

"Everyone" as authority.   Sometimes we are convinced that something is true because it is a belief strongly held by many other people. If virtually "everyone"

 BOX **1.2**

General Authorities and Normative Knowledge: The Role of Women in Politics

General authorities are particularly powerful in providing normative knowledge. It can be extremely difficult to decide how to judge political issues, and in such cases, it can be helpful to find a widely accepted authority for guidance. For example, consider the question, "What is the role of women in a country's politics?" While some people see this as a straightforward question of fact, others view it as a normative question about what the role of women should be. In some societies, there is disagreement about this question, and many look to an authority source to provide the answer.

In the United States, the crucial source of authority for such questions is the Constitution. The U.S. Constitution does not mention women. For nearly 150 years, this omission was interpreted to mean that women should be excluded from any political role, even from voting. Finally, political pressure resulted in a formal change within the source of authority, with the passage of the Nineteenth Amendment in 1920, which added language to the Constitution granting women voting rights (and, implicitly, all political rights exercised by men).

In Iran, as in the United States, the key source of authority on women's political rights is a document; but in Iran, it is a religious document, the Koran. During the political regime of Shah Reza Pahlavi (1941–1979), women were encouraged to participate more fully in politics than a strict interpretation of the Koran might suggest. However, when the Ayatollah Khomeini (in power 1979–1989) replaced the shah, he insisted on a strict interpretation, and the political roles of women were

(continued)

BOX **1.2** (CONTINUED)

significantly limited. Since Khomeini's death, more moderate leaders have again extended the political rights and activities of Iranian women, and there are numerous female participants in the political process, including female members of the national government. However, there is continuing disagreement and debate in Iran about the appropriate political behavior of women, and some of the most "modern" Iranian women continue to be frustrated by constraints on that behavior.

In contemporary China, it has been the authoritative pronouncements of a person, Mao Zedong (who ruled from 1949 to 1976), that established the contemporary political rights of women. Prior to the revolution of 1949, the role of women in China was defined by the religious traditions of Confucianism. Most women were essentially the property of men, and they had few political rights. As part of Chairman Mao's efforts to transform Confucian tradition, he granted women full equality under the law, and women were encouraged to participate actively in all aspects of political life.

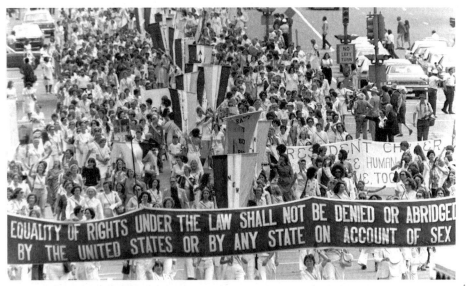

Tens of thousands march in Washington, D.C., in support of an amendment to the U.S. Constitution that would guarantee equal rights for women.

(i.e., the reference group to which you look for information and knowledge) seems to agree on a "fact" about politics, there is little reason for you to disagree or challenge that fact. One reason to place confidence in a belief strongly held by many people is the assumption that it is unlikely so many people will be incorrect. Such knowledge has stood the test of time, since it could have been challenged and repudiated in the marketplace of ideas. For example, you will probably find that virtually everyone you know agrees that political terrorism is bad.

However, there are fundamental problems with this method of authority as a way of knowing. This should be most obvious with *specific authorities*. You might think that your parent or best teacher or favorite celebrity has the correct view on an important political issue, but few of the other 6 billion people in the world have any confidence in this source of your political knowledge.

And, although "everyone knows that *X* is true," there is no guarantee that *everyone* is correct. First, as "Honest Abe" Lincoln observed, you can fool all of the people some of the time. Indeed, a political belief that is widely held might be particularly immune to careful assessment. Experiments in psychology have revealed the extent to which a person's beliefs can be altered by the beliefs of others. For example, if a subject hears several respondents (collaborating with the experimenter) all give identical wrong answers to a question, the subject can thereby be persuaded to change his mind about what he knows, even when he is correct. Second, "everyone" often consists mainly of people whose cultural background we share. When reexamining the above example about terrorism with a different "everyone," it is unlikely that virtually everyone living under an oppressive political regime believes that political terrorism is bad.

It is common for citizens in most political systems to believe that the citizens of rival political systems have been brainwashed. We know that some beliefs of our rivals are incorrect. Is it not likely that they are equally convinced that some of our strongly held beliefs are wrong?

There are even problems with *general authorities*. Sometimes, as when they are listing the countries with nuclear weapons or explaining why poverty exists, even the most competent general authorities might not have access to crucial information or might disagree about how to interpret the available data. And sometimes, even when a people accepts a single authority, there can be ambiguities and problems of interpretation. Consider again the normative issue of the political role of women discussed in Box 1.2:

> In the United States, all branches of government continually interpret and apply the rather limited framework outlined in the Constitution. The strong political agitation for an "equal rights" amendment indicates that many people feel that the Constitution, even with the Nineteenth Amendment, still fails to ensure women of political rights equivalent to those enjoyed by men.

> Women's political and civil rights in Iran have been extended somewhat since Khomeini's death, and especially after the election of a reformist president (Khatami in 1998, reelected in 2001) and legislature (in 2000). Women have become more active in Iranian politics, and a female vice president was selected in 1998. However, powerful positions of authority in Iranian society, such as the judiciary and the Council of Guardians, continue to be dominated by those who share Khomeini's views regarding women's political rights. Consequently, the appropriate role of women in Iran's politics remains a highly contested issue. Indeed, there is considerable difference of opinion within the Muslim world regarding how to interpret the Koran's authoritative prescriptions regarding women's roles in political life. In some Muslim countries, such as Saudi Arabia and Sudan, women's roles are greatly restricted. Yet Bangladesh, the "Islamic Republic of Pakistan," Indonesia, and

Turkey are Muslim-majority countries that selected female heads of government (prime ministers) in recent years.

In China, some people in rural areas never accepted the changes Mao introduced regarding women's roles in political and social life, preferring to follow the traditional Confucian norms. The Chinese leadership since Mao's death has continued to support his view on the equality of women in politics, although the leadership has rejected Mao's views on many other subjects, especially on economic matters.

In short, it is common, and perhaps inevitable, for authority sources to offer inconsistent or conflicting knowledge claims about the political world. It is extremely difficult to differentiate between alternative authorities or even to establish widespread agreement on precisely what political knowledge a particular authority source provides.

Personal Thought

Have you ever insisted that some fact is correct because it seemed so "obvious" to you? It is possible to feel confident that you know something on the basis of your own reason, feelings, or experiences. This second source of knowledge does not rely on outside authorities; rather, it assumes that the individual can use his own powers of thought to determine what he knows about the political world. Such knowledge can be based on rationality or intuition or be grounded in personal experience.

Rationality. First, an individual can rely on his own rational thought as a means for deciding that something is correct. On occasion, you probably have decided that a certain fact is true because it is logical or obvious—it just "makes sense." The underlying assumption is that such a knowledge claim is verified because it will seem self-evident to all reasonable people and needs no further justification. For example, the Preamble to the American Declaration of Independence claims that there are "self-evident" truths—that all men are created equal and that they have inalienable rights to life, liberty, and the pursuit of happiness.

Intuition. A second form of personal thought is intuition. Here, one's knowledge is based on feeling, on a sense of understanding or empathy, rather than on reason. You have probably been convinced that something is correct because it *feels* right. For example, the key slogan of Barry Goldwater, the Republican presidential candidate in 1964, was an explicit appeal to intuition: "In your heart, you know he's right!"

Personal experience. Third, you can be convinced that something is true because of your own personal experiences. For example, you might be convinced that government bureaucracies are inefficient because a specific agency handled your inquiries so ineptly. Or you might believe that different ethnic groups can live together in harmony based on your own positive experience in a multiethnic setting. Personal involvement in a dramatic event, such as witnessing a handgun murder or being physically harassed by the police, can have a particularly powerful impact on one's political beliefs.

A major problem with all three forms of personal thought as a source of knowledge is that there is no method for resolving "thoughtful" differences of opinion among individuals. This is most obvious with personal experience—because people have quite different personal experiences, they are unlikely to reach the same conclusions about what is true. Similarly, there is no reason to assume that different people will share the same intuitive feelings regarding what is true. Goldwater's poor electoral showing (he received only 39 percent of the vote) suggests that many people concluded (intuitively?) that he was not right, or perhaps they decided (rationally?) that he was too far right, ideologically.

Even rational thought will not necessarily enable people to agree on political facts. We do not all employ the same logic. Consider again the key knowledge claim cited earlier: "We hold these truths to be self-evident—that all men are created equal." This seems a clear appeal to rationality, a political fact that is self-evident to all thinking people. But what exactly does this claim mean? Do all men have equal physical or mental traits at birth? Do they grow up with equal opportunities? Are they equal before the law, regardless of the quality of legal help they can purchase? Are all women created equal too? Many legal and political struggles in the United States during the more than two centuries since this "self-evident" truth was proclaimed have concerned precisely what equal rights *are* assured to every person in the American political system, with particular regard to race, gender, and age.

Science

In contrast to the two other sources of knowledge, science uses explicit methods that attempt to enable different people to agree about what they know. The goal of any science is to describe and explain—to answer *what, why,* and *how* questions. There are four essential characteristics of the scientific method:

1. Science entails a *search for regularities* in the relationships among phenomena.
2. Science is *empirical* in the sense that it is concerned with phenomena that can be observed, or at least measured.
3. Science is *cumulative* because it tentatively accepts previously established knowledge on a subject as the foundation for development of further knowledge. One can challenge existing knowledge, but it is not necessary to reestablish the knowledge base every time.
4. The method of science is *testable.* Its practitioners, "scientists," specify the assumptions, data, analytic techniques, and inference patterns that support their knowledge claim. They look for some analysis or evidence that would invalidate ("falsify") the claim. Other scientists can evaluate all aspects of the claim and can repeat the analysis to ensure that everyone reaches the same conclusion.

POLITICAL SCIENCE

Most contemporary political scientists attempt to use the scientific method to establish shared knowledge about the political world. Box 1.3 demonstrates how to apply the scientific method to one of the knowledge claims listed near the beginning of

BOX **1.3**

Gender and Voting: Applying the Scientific Method to Politics Using the Appendix

Our analysis of gender and voting is typical of one form of political analysis employed by political scientists. As you read through it, ask yourself whether you understand how to interpret Table 1.1, whether you know the kinds of data that would strengthen the analysis, and whether you think this is a functional or relational analysis (see page 15). If you understand these terms and feel confident in answering such questions, you have a strong analytic basis for discussions later in the book. If you feel that you could use a bit more background on such issues, read the Appendix before you continue. It explains some of the major analytic approaches that are used in applying the scientific method to the study of politics, the types of empirical data that are employed, and the means of reaching conclusions through use of such data. Even those readers with some analytic background will find the Appendix helpful as a review and as a means of checking their understanding.

Is it true that men are more likely than women to vote in a democracy? Let us briefly consider how you might analyze this claim by means of the scientific method. Remember that applying the scientific method entails formulating a question with precision, gathering and analyzing empirical evidence that is relevant to the question, and then proposing a generalization or conclusion.

1. *Examine existing evidence* that is relevant to the issue you are analyzing. In this example, it would be sensible to look in various sources for studies of voting by political scientists or other social scientists (e.g., *Political Behavior of the American Electorate* by Flanigan and Zingale [2002], www.gendergap.com, and "Explaining the Gender Gap in Voting" by Studlar, McAllister, and Hayes [1998]).

2. With this background, you *state the issue* you are examining in a precise manner. This particular issue is already stated in the form of a hypothesis (i.e., a proposition about a political fact): In a democracy, men are more likely to vote than women.

3. *"Operationalize" key concepts.* This means that you specify exactly what each concept means and how it might be measured. Defining political concepts such as democracy can be extremely difficult (as you will see in Chapter 7). In this example, let us tentatively propose that a political democracy is "a state with periodic elections in which most adult citizens are allowed to vote in order to select among genuine alternative candidates for public office." The probability of voting is operationalized as "the percentage of those eligible to vote who actually do vote on a major political office."

4. *Gather appropriate data.* You need a strategy for collecting evidence that is *valid* (i.e., it measures what it is supposed to measure) and *reliable* (i.e., it is accurate). You also decide what specific cases you are going to analyze. In this example, choose one or more democracies and certain specific elections for which you are going to gather data. You might gather the relevant data

BOX **1.3** (CONTINUED)

from books or reports, or you might need to go "into the field" to measure the phenomena yourself. For this example, suppose you select the United States as the democracy, the presidential election as the vote on a major public office, and 1976 and 2000 as the elections for which you actually gather data. Do you think these are reasonable choices with which to assess the question? The survey data are displayed in Table 1.1. (Regarding the data in Table 1.1: These data are individuals' own reports, after the election, on whether or not they voted. The data were gathered for a carefully selected national sample of voters in a survey designed by academic researchers. Can you think of any problems with the validity of such data? How might more valid data be gathered?)

TABLE 1.1

Participation of Eligible Voters in the U.S. Presidential Election, by Gender

	1976		2000	
	%Men	%Women	%Men	%Women
Voted	77	6/	53	56
Did not vote	23	33	47	44

5. *Analyze the evidence.* According to the 1976 data in Table 1.1, men do vote at a substantially higher rate than women (77 percent versus 67 percent). In 2000, however, the voting rate for women (56 percent) is slightly higher than that for men (53 percent).

6. *Decide what, if any, inferences can be made* about the issue on the basis of your evidence. This is where your analytic skills must be especially rich. The Appendix illustrates a statistical technique that can help you judge whether the difference in the data for women and men is greater than might be expected by chance. In the absence of such statistics, what do you think?

Is the evidence sufficient? Can you have confidence in a generalization about gender and voting in the United States based on only two elections? Table 1.1 probably would lead you to observe that you cannot generalize with any confidence until you have more data. In fact, if you did get comparable data for other presidential elections, you would discover that women have voted at a higher rate than men in every U.S. presidential election since 1980, and at a lower rate in every election prior to 1980. What is your inference now?

Among the reasons that the study of politics is so fascinating are that things are rarely straightforward and can change (sometimes quite rapidly). For the political analyst, this means that generalizations must be made with care and with attention to longitudinal patterns (i.e., patterns over time). If you wanted to establish a broad generalization about gender and voting, you would need voting data from several democracies, not just the United States.

(continued)

BOX **1.3** (CONTINUED)

Even with data from more elections, you still must assess whether you have analyzed the evidence correctly. Have you overlooked some other important variable that might affect the relationship between gender and voting? To deal with this possibility, identify the factors that might affect voting rates among men and women. Many other explanatory factors might seem relevant: age, ethnicity, education, party identification, attitudes on key policy issues, and so on. By analyzing the relationships among various factors, you can gain a clearer understanding about the importance of gender in explaining varying rates of voter turnout. As an example of the kinds of subtle relationships that exist among different explanatory factors, the Appendix reconsiders the 1976 data. The analysis reveals that the apparent relation between gender and voting in the 1976 data is virtually eliminated when the voter's education level is considered.

7. Ideally, the final stage of your analysis is to *offer a tentative conclusion* regarding the issue. Defensible conclusions in analyses of politics often require extensive data, thorough analysis, and consideration of several alternative explanations. Sometimes the phenomena are so complicated or the evidence is so mixed that no generalization is possible. In our example, the data seem too contradictory to support any clear generalization about gender and voting. Rather, more data and more thoughtful analysis are required. If anything, this brief analysis seems to support the conclusion that, in recent U.S. elections at least, men are not more likely to vote than women.

the chapter: that in a democracy, men are more likely to vote than women. This example reveals how political scientists structure the search for regularities and the methods that they use. This book will offer many examples of generalizations and empirical findings about politics that are based on the scientific method.

Within the framework of the scientific method, there are different ways of undertaking political analysis. (Some of the most important are explained in detail in the Appendix.) Each mode of analysis is distinct in terms of its assumptions, methods, use of data, and inference structures. However, all modes share a fundamental commitment: to discover regularities among political phenomena using approaches that are empirical, cumulative, and testable.

In the example of political analysis in Box 1.3, as in any scientific study, one's conclusions, as well as one's concepts, data, and methods, are subject to scrutiny and challenge by others. An analyst's conclusion is presumed to be correct until there is compelling criticism or contrary evidence that undermines it. Because many knowledge claims about politics concern complex phenomena, it is often difficult to establish with precision what we do know, even when we use the scientific method. Nonetheless, the scientific method does help people to identify more clearly the points on which they agree or disagree and, ultimately, to develop generalizations about politics.

Political science is composed of certain subfields that are usually defined by their specific subject matter, rather than by their mode of analysis. While there are different ways to categorize the subfields, four are prominent:

1. **Comparative politics** focuses on similarities and differences in political processes and structures. Comparison might be cross-national (e.g., comparing the legal systems of Iran and Taiwan or comparing the voting patterns in 40 countries) or it might compare actors within a single country (e.g., comparing the welfare policies of the 50 American states). (While U.S. politics is sometimes treated as a separate subfield, it is best classified as a part of the subject matter of comparative politics.) Comparative politics covers a huge domain within political analysis, and it has many sub-subfields (e.g., public administration, political parties, development, individual political behavior, and public policy).

2. **International relations** examines the political relations between countries, the behavior of transnational actors, and the dynamics within the worldwide system of states. Subjects within international relations include war, interstate conflict resolution, international law, globalization, regional alliances, colonialism, and international organizations. The study of foreign policy is also within this subfield.

3. **Political theory** (or, more precisely, political philosophy) focuses on the ideas and debates dealing with important political questions. Some of this work attempts to characterize and interpret the writings of major political theorists (e.g., Plato, Thomas Hobbes, Karl Marx, John Rawls), whereas other works are original explorations of the political questions themselves (e.g., What is the nature of a just society? Why is there conflict between groups?). Political theory is the source of many of the normative knowledge claims produced by political scientists. Much of the work in political theory is based on the methods of rationality or authority or on an appeal to moral truths, rather than on the scientific method.

4. **Boundary-spanning subfields.** Political science is an eclectic field that often links with other fields of inquiry or, at least, that borrows and adapts ideas from other disciplines. Some work actually spans the boundary between political science and another discipline. While the subject matter of much of this work fits within one of the preceding three major subfields, we could list these hybrids as components of a fourth subfield, which would include political anthropology, political economy, political psychology, political sociology, and biopolitics.

POLITICAL "SCIENCE"?

Criticisms of Political Science as a "Science"

Not everyone agrees that it is appropriate and desirable to apply the scientific method to politics. Four different kinds of criticism have been aimed at political science.

It is not a "real" science.   The first criticism is that political science is not "scientific" in comparison with "real" natural and applied sciences (e.g., chemistry, physics, engineering). Stimulated by Thomas Kuhn's (1996) book, *The Structure of Scientific Revolutions,* this view posits that there is general agreement on the four key elements that provide organization and direction within a fully developed science: (1) central *concepts,* which identify and name crucial phenomena (specifically, such as "Iraq War," or generally, such as "war"); (2) *theories,* which are sets of systematically related generalizations that provide explanations and predictions about the linkages between certain concepts (in the form, "If A, then B under conditions C, D"); (3) *rules of interpretation,* which indicate the methods that will establish whether the explanations and predictions posited by the theory are right or wrong; and (4) a list of questions or *issues* that are worth solving within the area of inquiry.

These four key elements are well developed and widely shared within the research communities of every natural and applied science. In contrast, researchers in political science (and other social sciences) have not agreed upon a coherent set of concepts, theories, and rules of interpretation. As you will discover throughout this book, there are many different methods used in political science. There is disagreement regarding the important issues that ought to be solved, little consensus on what theories or generalizations have been proven, and even great difficulty in operationalizing key concepts, such as "power" and "democracy."

Its subject matter defies generalization.   The second criticism is the assertion that it is impossible to develop a science of politics because of the subject matter. In this view, the political world is far too complex and unpredictable for systematic generalizations. Politics is based on the actions and interactions of many individuals, groups, and even countries. Politics occurs in the midst of many changing conditions that can influence those actions. The range of variation in what people might do and in the conditions that might exist is so vast that clear "if A, then B" statements about politics are impossible. Thus it is not surprising that political analysts cannot precisely explain the causes of war, or why women vote differently from men, or what effect a law banning private handguns will have on crime rates.

Its "scientists" cannot be objective.   The third criticism is that the analysis of politics cannot be objective in the way assumed by the scientific method. The issues chosen for study and the manner in which variables are defined, measured, and analyzed are all powerfully influenced by the analyst's social reality (e.g., by his culture, ideas, life experiences). In this view, no person (whether Sunni Muslim or agnostic, rural Nigerian or cosmopolitan Parisian, international lawyer or migrant farm worker) can be totally objective and unbiased in the way he tries to analyze political phenomena. (See Box 1.4)

Its practice diverts attention from normative questions.   Finally, the fourth criticism faults the scientific method itself for not helping to answer the crucial normative questions of politics. Since the time of Aristotle (384–322 B.C.E.), classical political theorists have insisted that the ultimate aim of political analysis is to discover "the highest good attainable by action." In this view, political analysis is a noble endeavor because it helps determine what government and individuals

BOX 1.4

How's Your Bias?

In its idealized form, the method of science might be value free. But in the analysis of politics, it is impossible for the analyst to describe and explain without being influenced by his own values. You should remember this fact as you consider the arguments and information in this book. It is likely that most readers (including the author) have lived primarily in Western democratic countries. As you will see in Chapter 4 and as you should recognize when you react to the claims throughout the book, your attitudes and judgments are biased by your experiences and your political socialization.

As I wrote this book, I attempted to be sensitive to my own political biases (I recognize some of them, but others are subconscious) and to be fair in describing, analyzing, and generalizing about different political systems. But throughout the book, value judgments are embedded in every choice about what content is included and how it is presented. There is likely to be material that is at variance with your own views.

It is most appropriate for you to assess whether the basis of the claims in this book seems sound and to consider what biases affect the discussion. The chapters are based on my study of social science research (mainly in the English language) and on my personal experiences, which have occurred in many parts of the world. I am aware that my writing includes many explicit or implicit evaluations and that it might reflect political reality or my biases (as an American, a male, etc.). It is important that you assess issues of bias whenever you encounter claims about politics, from any source.

It will take far more than this book to help you make your own judgments regarding political reality. As you read, try to become more conscious of *your* biases, which will undoubtedly influence your ultimate assessments of politics and even your openness to any claims made about the political world.

---

should do so that valued goals (e.g., democratic politics, a good life, a just society) can be achieved.

However, even many of those who use the scientific method to study politics do not assume that it can achieve such goals. Max Weber (1864–1920), the influential German social scientist, argued that the scientific method is useful for describing and categorizing political and social reality. But, Weber added, it cannot provide answers to fundamental normative questions about goals and appropriate means. Weber (1958a: 152–153) approvingly quoted Russian novelist Leo Tolstoi's assertion that science can provide no answer to the essential question, "What shall we do, and how shall we arrange our lives?" According to this fourth critique, then, political science becomes an arid enterprise if its reliance on the scientific method discourages attempts to address essential questions about political values and political good (Strauss 1959; Wolin 1960).

Political Science as a Means of Understanding the Political World

These four main criticisms of a science of politics are important; you should assess them throughout this book. In general, this book will make the case that, despite the complexity of politics, generalizations are possible—each political phenomenon is not *sui generis,* a unique thing. If political "science" means the attempt to apply the scientific method in order to understand the political world better, it is desirable to use such systematic and analytic thinking. And if we are to share *any* knowledge about the political world, we need methods to reach some interpersonal agreement about political facts. Although political science lacks precise concepts and theories, it does enable us to develop better concepts, improved methods, and sound generalizations, and thereby it makes the study of the political world an exciting intellectual challenge.

This book assumes that understanding politics is extremely important. As Austrian philosopher of science Karl Popper (1963: 227) suggests, "We must not expect too much from reason; argument rarely settles a [political] question, although it is the only means for learning—not to see clearly, but to see more clearly than before." In the face of fundamental value conflicts and the potential for massive political violence among individuals, groups, and countries, political knowledge might reduce our misunderstandings and misconceptions. Thus, it can be the grounds for greater tolerance and wiser value judgments about normative political issues. Moreover, enhancing *what* we know about politics should make us more effective in knowing *how* to behave politically—as voters, political activists, and political decision makers. Thus the study of the political world is of crucial importance to the creation of humane social life. Ultimately it is up to you, as you read this book, to decide what can be known about politics and whether you think political "science" is feasible.

WHERE IS THIS BOOK GOING?

Just as there are different approaches to political science, there are different ways to introduce you to the political world. This book is organized to lead you along one route to understanding. But there are other routes, including reading the book in a different order than beginning at Chapter 1 and finishing with Chapter 16 (for example, I think it would be helpful for you to read the Appendix now; it has also been suggested that Part Two could be read after Parts Three and Four).

"Man is the measure of all things," observed the ancient Greek philosopher Protagoras (c. 490–421 B.C.E.). In that spirit, this book begins its exploration of the political world at the most personal and individual level. It initially examines what individual men and women think about politics and how they act politically (Part Two). The book then focuses primarily on the politics of large collectivities of people that we call states and that are organized politically as governments. Thus, Parts Three, Four, and Five offer perspectives and explanations from political science regarding how states and governments are organized for political action, how political processes occur, and how countries are attempting to fulfill their political goals in the challenging conditions of the early twenty-first century.

Part Two, "Political Behavior," begins (Chapter 2) with an assessment of the kinds of *political beliefs* that people hold and the way in which those beliefs fit (or do not fit) into a more general framework of ideas. It continues (Chapter 3) with a consideration of the *political actions* that people and groups undertake. Chapter 4 moves from description to explanation: Can we explain *why* people seem to think and act in certain ways?

Part Three, "Political Systems," is about the politics of large numbers of people—about how the political world is organized and about *the structures of government.* Chapters 5 through 8 address such issues as: What is a state? How are the political system and the economic system linked? What features distinguish democracies or dictatorships? What are the responsibilities of such political structures as the bureaucracy or the legislature?

Part Four, "Political Processes," emphasizes *key dynamics of politics.* Chapter 9 details three major explanations for how political power is distributed and how political decisions are made. Chapter 10 explores the important processes of political change and development. The vital issues of politics across borders and the manner in which states and other transnational actors cooperate and compete are central to Chapter 11. The various forms and causes of political violence are analyzed in Chapter 12.

Part Five, "Politics among States," focuses on the actions and challenges facing *countries in the contemporary political world.* Chapters 13 through 15 consider countries at different stages of development as they pursue the general goals of prosperity, security, and stability in the complicated, global system. Finally, Chapter 16 summarizes the key themes of the book. The Appendix explains major concepts in political science, including four important frameworks for engaging in political analysis.

Whatever the order in which you read the sections of this book, I hope it will enhance *your* understanding of the political world.

KEY CONCEPTS

authority as a knowledge source (pg.8)
concept
description (pg. 7)
explanation
normative knowledge (pg.8)
political analysis (pg 6)

political science (pg- 6)
politics (pg.3)
prescription
the scientific method (pg. 17)
theory

FOR FURTHER CONSIDERATION

1. What do you think is the most serious obstacle to a "science" of politics?
2. Which authority have you relied on most extensively as a source of your knowledge about politics? What is the biggest shortcoming of this source?
3. What is the most important question that political science should attempt to answer? What might prevent political scientists from answering this question adequately?

4. Many people insist that most of their political knowledge is based on their own rational thought processes. What might be wrong with this claim?

5. Do you think political scientists can play an important role in government or are they just intellectuals who can only stand on the sidelines and analyze politics?

6. Which statement about the political world proposed within this chapter do you think would receive the greatest variations in "truth scores" among citizens in your society? Which statement would receive the greatest score variations between your society and another one that you identify? Why do you expect variation in the assessment of these statements?

FOR FURTHER READING

Almond, Gabriel. (1989). *A Discipline Divided: Schools and Sects in Political Science.* Newbury Park, CA: Sage. One of the major scholars of comparative politics assesses the diversity of approaches to political science and the possibility of a science of politics.

Goodin, Robert, and Hans-Dieter Klingemann, Eds. (1996). *A New Handbook of Political Science.* New York: Oxford University Press. Articles by well-known political scientists discuss the central concepts, institutional issues, and recent empirical research in many important subfields.

Kuhn, Thomas. (1996). *The Structure of Scientific Revolutions.* 3d ed. Chicago: University of Chicago Press. A short, understandable, and enormously influential discussion of how sciences develop and overturn paradigms, first published in 1962.

Manheim, Jarol B., Richard Rich, and Lars Willnat. (2002). *Empirical Political Analysis: Research Methods in Political Science.* 5th ed. New York: Addison Wesley Longman. A very effective and understandable presentation of the primary methods that political scientists utilize in the attempt to understand politics and develop defensible generalizations.

Popper, Karl R. (1968). *The Logic of Scientific Discovery.* London: Hutchinson. A major and widely respected statement of the philosophy and application of the scientific method.

White, Louise G. (1994). *Political Analysis: Technique and Practice.* 3d ed. Belmont, CA: Wadsworth. A readable introduction to the methods of doing research and of gathering and analyzing data in empirical political science, emphasizing engaging, do-it-yourself examples.

ON THE WEB

http://www.apsanet.org/

This website for the American Political Science Association, the major organization for political scientists in the United States, provides links to a variety of activities and opportunities associated with political science professionals, including online papers from the national conference and articles from *PS: Political Science & Politics*.

http://www.psqonline.org/

Political Science Quarterly is America's oldest continuously publishing political science journal and brings you the world of politics.

http://www.etown.edu/vl/

The rich and extensive set of links on this website, "WWW Virtual Library: International Affairs Resources," includes numerous sites for each region as well as links to key international topics as varied as international organizations, environmental issues, world religions, media resources, health, and human rights.

http://www.library.ubc.ca/poli/

The Political Science Net Station, provided by the University of British Columbia library, contains a comprehensive listing of political science resources available on the Internet.

http://www.lib.umich.edu/govdocs/polisci.html

The University of Michigan library has compiled an in-depth listing of political science resources, including a compilation of government-related sites.

http://www.psr.keele.ac.uk/

Richard Kimber's Political Science Resources page includes an extensive listing of sites focusing on international relations and European politics.

Drawing by Dick Wright © Tribune Media Services, Inc. All Rights Reserved. Reprinted with permission.

CHAPTER 2 Political Beliefs

You stop at a Burger King to eat. While ordering your food, you see some acquaintances motioning you to join them. As you sit down, someone you don't know is saying "The U.S. invasion of Iraq was totally immoral. The United States had no right to cause all that suffering, and it cost America billions of dollars that should be spent dealing with poverty at home!" She looks directly at you. What would you do in this situation?

Many reactions are possible. You might feel anxiety, admiration, or even anger. You might be silent and act as if this has nothing to do with you. You might change the subject or say you have no opinion. You might indicate that you agree with her, or you might heatedly dispute her assertions.

Your responses to this incident offer interesting evidence about your reactions to the political world. Some of your responses might involve beliefs and others might involve actions. This combination of your political beliefs and actions is the essence of the domain of political science called *political behavior,* or **micropolitics.** It is called *micro*politics because the key object of study is the smallest political unit—the individual as a thinker and actor in the political world. Micropolitics can also include study of the political beliefs and actions of groups, such as families, committees, and juries.

Part Two of this book explores themes in the study of micropolitics. This chapter focuses on *political beliefs.* Initially, it develops a taxonomy of an individual's orientations toward the political world. Second, it describes configurations of beliefs held by individuals, a cluster called a *political belief system.* Third, it attempts to characterize the dominant patterns of political behavior for an entire society—its *political culture.* Finally, it characterizes some fundamental systems of beliefs, called *political ideologies.* Chapter 3 will then undertake a similar examination of individual political action and of the activities of groups in the political world. Chapter 4 assesses alternative explanations of the sources of people's political beliefs and actions.

INDIVIDUAL POLITICAL BELIEFS

Some of your reactions to the incident described at the beginning of this chapter might involve your factual *knowledge* about the political world: for example, why the United States sent troops into Iraq, how much the military effort cost, the level of poverty in the United States, and so on. Other reactions might involve your *feelings:* for example, antagonism or indifference to this strong criticism of the United States' actions. And some reactions might engage your powers of *assessment:* for example, an attempt to judge whether the action was, in fact, immoral and whether it was appropriate to spend billions of dollars on either a war against Iraq or a war on poverty. These different reactions typify the three types of orientations that constitute our political beliefs. The following paragraphs describe these cognitive, affective, and evaluative political orientations.

A person's *cognitive orientations* include what she believes are political "facts." Such facts might be correct and accurate or they might be totally wrong. (Recall our discussion of "truth scores" in Chapter 1.) A person might know many things about the politics of her locality, region, and country as well as some things about the broader political world. This knowledge might include such facts as the names of political leaders; the policies supported by particular politicians, political groups, or nations; events in political history; the features of constitutions; or the procedures and actions of a governmental agency.

Affective orientations include any feelings or emotions evoked in a person by political phenomena. For example, what (if any) feelings are stimulated in you when you come across the following:

You see someone burning your national flag?

You read about a deadly terrorist attack?

You are faced with the option of voting in an election and you don't like the candidates?

You are present at a political demonstration supporting a policy of which you strongly approve?

The nature and intensity of your feelings in these kinds of situations are instances of your affective orientations.

Finally, an *evaluative orientation* involves your synthesis of facts and feelings into a judgment about some political phenomenon. If you become aware that your government has proposed a policy that restricts the right of a woman to have an abortion, this might stimulate many different thoughts—your knowledge about the constitutional rights of an individual to freedom of action and of the state to limit those rights; your religious, moral, or scientific beliefs about the status of a fetus; your personal knowledge of the experiences of people who have been involved in decisions about abortions; your assessment of the arguments made by spokespersons for and against the proposed policy. In short, your judgment about a political issue can be grounded in many different kinds of cognitive and affective orientations that are combined into an evaluation. Ultimately, many of the political attitudes that you would identify as your "fundamental beliefs" are likely to be evaluative orientations.

There are several stages in building our conceptual understanding of political beliefs. If we want to understand one person's political orientations, we might begin by identifying one or a few specific beliefs she holds. Does she know the name of the country's chief executive? How does she react to news that her state's governor has just prevented the execution of a convicted murderer? What is her opinion on a proposal to reduce the number of nuclear weapons stockpiled by her country? (Note that some political analysts distinguish among opinions, attitudes, beliefs, and orientations, with each successive category being more stable, general, and deeply held. In our discussion, we will not make this distinction, although the emphasis is on those understandings about politics that are more general and stable.)

A similar analytic strategy can be used to determine what many people think about a specific issue. When the attitudes of many people are gathered, aggregated, and summarized, they constitute the most widely available data about people's political orientations: *public opinion polls.* Virtually every day, the media provide data on the percentage of people who hold a certain opinion regarding a political issue. For example, a public opinion poll might report data on the question, "Do Germans oppose further immigration of non-Europeans into Germany?" On the basis of this poll, you might decide you know what Germans think about the issue. This information seems a stronger basis for a knowledge claim than a discussion with a few German friends or even a statement by a German political leader.

However, public opinion polls should be interpreted with care. In assessing the information, you should consider such questions as these: Did those who conducted the poll have a bias toward a particular result? Were the questions or the possible responses worded in a way that might distort people's opinions? Were those asked for an opinion a representative sample of the group to whom the opinion is attributed? Are different interpretations of the data possible? Even when the pollsters are unbiased, there are numerous instances in which their estimates are inaccurate (e.g., there can be errors in their predictions of how the population will vote in an election).

BELIEF SYSTEMS

Beyond the identification of specific beliefs of individuals, other interesting analyses can focus on the array of their political beliefs. The term **political belief system** refers to *the configuration of an individual's political orientations.* A related concept used by political psychologists is a person's "opinion schema." This is a network of cognitive, affective, and evaluative orientations that serves as a basic framework, guiding a person as she organizes her existing political knowledge and processes new information in order to establish an opinion on a particular subject (Hastie 1986; Niemi and Weissberg 2001).

To examine a person's belief system, you can ask a series of questions:

1. What is the *content* of the beliefs—that is, the subject matter and the nature of the beliefs?
2. What is the *salience* of the beliefs—that is, the importance or significance the person attaches to the beliefs?
3. What is the level of *complexity* of the beliefs?
4. What level of *consistency* is there among the belief(s) held by the person?
5. How *stable* are the beliefs over time?
6. Do the beliefs *motivate* the person to undertake any political action(s)?

Some empirical research on the nature of belief systems has focused on the belief systems of the political elite or of the "mass public"—that is, of ordinary people in the society. The most intensive, analytical research has focused on belief systems in the United States, and this work has been particularly influenced by the analyses of Philip Converse (1964). In general, Converse argues that a belief system has two levels of information. One level includes relatively straightforward *facts or opinions,* such as the opinion that American public schools should not allow Christian prayers during class time. The second level is *constraint knowledge,* in which more abstract and overarching concepts (such as liberalism and conservatism) operate to shape and link ideas. In the school prayer example, a person might base her opinion on constraint knowledge about the constitutional separation of church and state or about free speech issues.

Belief Systems among Mass Publics

On the basis of his empirical analyses of (American) individuals' belief systems, Converse (1964) concludes that there are important and predictable differences between the elite and the mass publics in the nature and structure of their belief systems. As you might expect, the belief systems of individuals in the mass public are simpler and narrower, and they are organized far less by constraint knowledge, than are those of members of the elite. Within the mass public, Converse distinguishes five gradations in the level of conceptualization in people's belief systems. Only about 15 percent of members of the mass public have substantial constraint knowledge in their belief system. And almost half of the U.S. public is characterized by the two lowest levels—extremely simplistic political beliefs and "political ignorance."

While there has been continuing debate regarding the precise nature of political belief systems among mass publics (Rosenberg 1988; 2002; Sniderman 1993), most researchers agree on certain generalizations about the citizens of Western democracies (i.e., the United States, Canada, and the Western European and Scandinavian countries). Like nearly every other generalization about politics, the following six generalizations are broadly accurate for "most people" but are subject to many qualifications and some exceptions:

1. Political issues have low salience in relation to other concerns in people's lives. Although Aristotle termed the citizen *homo politicus*, or "political man," most people do not locate political issues in the center of their interest and attention space.

2. People tend to focus attention on concrete issues and have minimal grasp of the abstract political concepts that serve as constraint knowledge.

3. Interest and knowledge are greater on immediate, short-term issues than on longer-term ones.

4. While people's fundamental beliefs are relatively stable, there can be considerable volatility in their short-term political opinions, which tend to shift when subjected to modest changes in political information. This volatility might be due to limited interest or to the sheer difficulty of trying to understand complicated political questions.

5. Significant inconsistencies can exist across political beliefs, in the sense that a person can hold contradictory positions. (For example, an American might express support for the First Amendment right to free speech but deny the right of a Communist to speak at a public meeting or the right of the Ku Klux Klan to hold a public rally.)

6. The content of beliefs is often inaccurate. (In one survey, for example, half the Americans questioned did not know how many U.S. Senators serve their state, and less than one in six knew who William Rehnquist is. You know the correct answers . . . don't you?)

The basic ideas of Converse (1964) and others have been challenged by those who acknowledge that the mass public might have a minimal grasp of political information and ideas but argue that people *are* able to fashion reasonable political opinions. In this view, members of the mass public use simple rules of thumb to make sense of issues; focus most of their attention on some issue areas (e.g., foreign policy, race relations, and economic concerns) and have little knowledge of other issue areas; and receive considerable guidance from information provided by the elite and the media (Sniderman 1993; see also Chapter 4).

Another challenge to the view that most people have simplistic belief systems is the viewpoint that individuals develop different structured ways of thinking about the world. Thus it is argued that the analyst must first study and understand how people think, not merely ask questions about their specific beliefs, and then look for a pattern in their responses. When the analyst specifies a person's structure of thinking, her political attitudes might be generally consistent and coherent within this structure (Rosenberg 1988; 2002). This is an intriguing, alternative way to analyze the mass public's political beliefs that could change our unflattering picture of most people's belief systems, but there is not much empirical support for it. Moreover, even with these refinements, most research continues to reveal a mass public whose political belief systems are neither rich nor sophisticated.

Belief Systems among Elites

The **political elite** is a term for *those who have relatively high levels of interest and involvement in political life.* Some actually hold positions of political responsibility, and most communicate their knowledge and beliefs about politics to others. The belief systems of the elite are regarded as particularly important because the elites are presumed to have a major role in politics and because they can strongly influence the beliefs of the mass public.

Overall, Converse (1964) and others conclude that generalizations regarding the belief systems of the elites are the opposite of those for the mass public on each of the six points listed in the previous section. For the most part, their belief systems are characterized by relatively high levels of abstraction, accuracy, complexity, stability, and breadth. Constraint knowledge is well developed and influences most specific opinions. Despite the emphasis on consistency among beliefs, individuals in the elite can support core values that are in conflict. In contrast to those in the mass, those with an elite belief system can reconcile differences within their constraint knowledge. This enables them to integrate conflicting information as they generate political opinions (Tetlock 1984).

All individuals with sophisticated belief systems do not necessarily share the same core beliefs. For example, some people might have a coherent system of beliefs that support the protection of an individual's civil liberties, while other people's constraint knowledge and specific opinions consistently support the right of the government to limit individual liberties substantially in the protection of social order (Sniderman et al. 1991). Several important systems of beliefs, termed "ideologies," are characterized later in this chapter; others are explored in Parts 4 and 5.

Research has attempted to specify the central elements of belief systems among elites. For example, studies of the belief systems of the elite responsible for U.S. foreign policy during the 1980s identified three distinctive perspectives among most members of that elite. Each perspective was based on different assumptions about the nature of the international political environment, the source of the major threats to national security, and the most appropriate policy responses to those threats (Rosenau and Holsti 1986):

- The "cold-war internationalists" focused on the dangerous superpower conflict between the United States and the Soviet Union and emphasized the need for continual military buildup.

- The "post–cold-war internationalists" worried mainly about how huge inequalities between the world's rich countries and poor countries would produce global instability and argued that the superpowers had mutual interests in stabilizing the developing countries.

- The "semi-isolationists" concluded that America's domestic problems, such as unemployment, crime, and racial conflict, were the most serious threats to the country's stability and that dealing with these internal problems was the top priority.

Empirical research concluded that most members of the U.S. foreign policy elite in the early 1980s shared the cold-war internationalist belief system (Rosenau and Holsti 1986). However, at the beginning of the twenty-first century, the cold war is over and the international system is dramatically different (these changes are described in Chapters 11–16). The U.S. foreign policy elite is attempting to formulate a new belief system that incorporates such key challenges as global economic competition, international terrorism, and the proliferation of weapons of mass destruction. Given the powerful role of elites in most societies (see Chapter 9), the study of elite belief systems remains important and intriguing.

POLITICAL CULTURE

Some analysts attempt to identify broadly shared patterns of political orientations that characterize a large group of people. The objective is to develop generalizations about the political culture of the group. **Political culture** is normally defined as *the configuration of a particular people's political orientations*—that is, as the generalized belief system of many. For this reason, political culture is not precisely a topic in micropolitics, but it is examined here because it is embedded in individual-level analyses.

Most commonly, it is the political culture of a country or of a major (ethnic or religious) community within a country that has been studied. The composition of the group that is studied depends on the interests of the researcher. It might be the people of a geographic community (e.g., Londoners, English, British, or Europeans) or of a community of shared identity (e.g., Sikhs in the Indian state of Punjab, Sikhs in the Indian subcontinent, or all Sikhs in the world) or of a community of shared meaning (e.g., French Canadians or all French-speaking peoples).

National Character Studies

A traditional approach that attempts to capture the essence of a people's political culture involves "national character" studies (Inkeles 1997). When someone is described as being "soooo French," you might think of her as being sophisticated, romantic, and volatile. At one level, we recognize immediately that such a characterization is a stereotype that does not fit the majority of individual subjects. Yet most of us, including people in the political world, use these kinds of labels (at least occasionally) as a shorthand method of describing groups or nations. Indeed, Franklin Delano Roosevelt (U.S. president from 1933 to 1945) observed that "the all-important factor in national greatness is national character."

Some political analysts have tried to specify the national character of certain countries and then to predict or explain their political behavior on the basis of such characteristics. Typically, these studies do not claim that everyone fits the national character profile, but they maintain that the profile is accurate for the politically relevant strata. Thus the top ruling group in Britain has been defined in terms of English national character—control of emotions, a sense of propriety, a belief in class and national superiority, and reliance on "old boy" connections. This national character has supposedly been nurtured by a shared upper-/upper-middle-class background and training at a public school (in Britain, this actually means an elite private school) followed by attending university at Oxford or Cambridge. Interestingly, the key prime ministers of the past three decades (Margaret Thatcher, John Major, and Tony Blair) have not fit this class and early educational profile, although the description of the English national character does fit Margaret Thatcher quite well. While the backgrounds of those in the British political elite in Parliament and the higher civil service are becoming more varied, the national character profile is still evident in the orientations and behavior of many in this leadership elite.

In another example, Ervand Abrahamian (1993) analyzes what he terms the "paranoid style of Iranian politics." He describes the constant tendency of the political leaders and the mass public to fear foreign plots and conspiracies meant to subvert the culture and create societal chaos. He traces this political belief system to a "national culture" characterized by pessimism, subservience, egotism, dishonesty, and distrust of others. While he acknowledges that colonial dealings with the British and Americans provide Iranians with ample grounds to distrust foreigners, Abrahamian argues that the character of the population is excessively paranoid. He details how this has resulted in disastrous consequences, undermining the Iranians' capacity to develop cooperative internal politics based on coalition building, the ability to compromise, and tolerance for domestic opposition.

A controversial recent analysis based on broad notions of supranational character is Samuel Huntington's (1996) description of nine global "civilizations." These civilizations are the highest level of cultural identity among humans, with the nine groups differing in history, language, culture, and especially religion. The groups, which are also somewhat regionally based, are: African, Buddhist, Confucian, Hindu, Islamic, Japanese, Latin American, Orthodox (Russian), and Western. Huntington predicts that clashes among these civilizations are increasingly the fundamental source of international political conflict and will be the most likely cause of the next global war.

National character studies are criticized by many analysts as impressionistic and loaded with gross generalizations that greatly oversimplify political reality. Consequently, most scholars dismiss national character studies as caricatures with little capacity to account for the complex actual political behaviors within a country. However, the more thoughtful analyses of national character, based on dominant patterns of beliefs and behaviors, can provide fascinating insights into both the political culture and the political actions taken in a society, and such culture-based explanations have been widely employed in recent research (see Box 15.4 in Chapter 15).

Survey Research

There is a more systematic and scientifically acceptable method for establishing the nature of a political culture—the use of survey research. This involves taking a carefully selected sample of the population and then asking each person a series of questions that aims to tap individual political beliefs and actions. The researcher then aggregates each person's responses, searching for patterns or configurations that profile the political culture of the sample and, by inference, that characterize the political culture of the population from which the sample is taken.

The first major study of this type is still the most famous one: *The Civic Culture*, by Gabriel Almond and Sidney Verba (1963). Lengthy interviews were conducted with a large sample of citizens in each of five countries. The data were then aggregated and analyzed in a diversity of ways to provide rich descriptions of each country's political culture. Numerous comparisons between the five political cultures were also presented. Because *The Civic Culture* is a landmark in survey research on political culture, revealing both virtues and shortcomings in such analyses, it is detailed in Box 2.1.

 BOX 2.1

Using Survey Research to Characterize Political Culture: The Civic Culture

Political scientists Gabriel Almond and Sidney Verba selected Italy, Mexico, the United Kingdom, the United States, and West Germany for the first large-scale empirical and comparative study of political culture. Based on survey research techniques, their analyses were reported in *The Civic Culture* (1963).

In each country, a sample of about one thousand respondents was asked many questions about their individual political beliefs and actions, such as:

Can you identify the national leaders of the principal political parties (in your country)?

Suppose a regulation was being considered by your local government that you considered very unjust or harmful. What do you think you could do?

How would you feel if your son or daughter married a supporter of the (opposition) political party? Would you be pleased, would you be displeased, or would it make no difference?

How often do you talk about public affairs to other people?

Thinking about the national government, how much effect do you think its activities, the laws passed, and so on have on your day-to-day life?

Almond and Verba postulated a taxonomy of three "ideal-type" political cultures, as represented in Table 2.1. Each successive ideal type entails more extensive

TABLE 2.1
Ideal-Type Political Cultures

Political Culture Type	Orientations Toward			
	Political System	Political Outputs	Political Inputs	Self as Political Participant
Parochial	0	0	0	0
Subject	+	+	0	0
Participant	+	+	+	+

Note: 0 means little or no explicit orientation; + means positive orientation.
Source: Adapted from Almond and Verba 1963.

(continued)

BOX **2.1** (CONTINUED)

involvement between individuals and the political order. In fact, after analyzing all the empirical data, only one of the five countries in *The Civic Culture* was actually classified as one of the three ideal types: the United States was termed a "participant" political culture. Italy was "alienated," Mexico was "alienated but aspiring," West Germany had "political detachment and subject competence," and the United Kingdom was a "deferential civic culture."

Important criticisms were raised about the methodology of *The Civic Culture* (Almond and Verba 1980). For example, in Mexico only urban citizens were interviewed, a clearly inadequate basis for generalizing about the political culture of what was then a predominantly rural society. In addition, the findings were very time-specific, with many responses contingent upon the country's political context at the point the survey was completed.

Perhaps the most serious fault with *The Civic Culture* was Almond and Verba's ideological biases. The authors praised the British political culture because its citizens had very positive attitudes toward the outputs they received from the government but were not highly active participants in political processes. Almond and Verba worried that a highly participant political culture, such as the United States, might not remain stable and democratic under the constant pressure of extensive citizen involvement and demands (Pateman 1980). Yet despite its shortcomings, *The Civic Culture* is a pathbreaking attempt to undertake a systematic, empirical, and comparative study of political cultures, and as such it has influenced virtually all subsequent work on the subject.

Most survey research on political culture has attempted to improve our understanding of the political orientations of citizens in "democratic" societies. One major study found widespread similarities in the social and political concerns among citizens in many countries. Personal desires for a happy family life, a decent standard of living, and good health were most important, and political concerns centered on fears about war and political instability (Cantril 1965). In research on Western societies, Ron Inglehart (1989, 1997; see also Dalton 2002) suggests that the central sociopolitical values held by citizens have recently changed for many, especially the younger generations. Inglehart concludes that older adults emphasize "materialist" values for strong defense, order maintenance, and economic growth; in contrast, many young adults stress "postmaterialist" values for a more esthetically satisfying environment, for freedom of expression, and for more personal power in social and political life. In some cultures, there has been a substantial increase in the proportion of citizens classified as postmaterialists since the early 1980s. For example, the percent of postmaterialists has tripled among Germans from the former West Germany (increasing to 44 percent) and has doubled in others (e.g., Argentina to 29 percent, Britain to 22 percent, and Mexico to 16 percent). In some societies, the proportion has remained quite stable (e.g., Finland at about 28 percent, South Korea at about 7 percent, and Hungary at 2 percent). And postmaterialist orientations have declined in some countries facing harsh economic and social transitions (e.g., Russia, Poland) (*World Values Survey* 2001). The range among Western democracies is from 39 percent (Netherlands) to 17 percent (Norway) (Dalton 2002: table 5.2).

The extensive empirical research on political culture, as it has become more precise in its methods and more cautious about cultural biases, has revealed the considerable variability within political cultures across individuals, between groups, and over time. Chapter 4 will examine some of the factors that might account for differences in the political beliefs of individuals within a society. But it is also evident from the survey research that many societies do have a political culture—a general configuration of political beliefs that distinguishes them from certain other societies.

POLITICAL IDEOLOGY

You have probably heard certain people described by their political perspectives as "liberals" or "conservatives." Such a general belief system can be termed a political ideology. A **political ideology** is *a comprehensive set of beliefs about the political world—about desirable political goals and the best ways to achieve those goals.*

Three points can help to clarify the different ways in which the term "political ideology" is used. First, a political ideology can be composed of the political beliefs of a single person or of a group of any size—from a small set of friends to millions of people around the world. In this sense, "ideology" is used synonymously with "belief system," as discussed previously. Second, it is usually assumed that a political ideology displays high coherence, complexity, and salience, but it could be low on any of these dimensions. Third, the label "political ideology" is typically applied to one of a few comprehensive and widely held sets of beliefs. Most of these are "isms," such as those cited in the next paragraph. However, any relatively complete bundle of political beliefs could be termed a political ideology.

The objective in this section is to introduce you to the basic tenets of some of the Western world's most general ideologies: conservatism, liberalism, and several variations of socialism, including communism. Elements of these sets of ideas influence the political thinking of large numbers of people. Many other "isms," such as fascism (Box 2.2), have also mobilized populations and had substantial impact.

Key Issues

Ideologies can include a description of political reality, but they are primarily a normative expression of what ought to be. Each major ideology has its own internal logic, and each is based on assumptions and value judgments about the individual and her human nature, about the proper relationship between the individual and society, and about the desirability of establishing certain kinds of equality among individuals.

Individual human nature.   The "nature versus nurture" debate centers on disagreements about whether a person's fundamental beliefs and behaviors are determined primarily by innate needs and values with which she is born, or whether those beliefs and values are mainly a product of her environment and experiences. The implications of nature and nurture for political beliefs and actions will be assessed in Chapter 4. In this section, our focus is on the key assumptions that political ideologies make about an individual's innate nature (e.g., the extent to which individuals are selfish or sharing, violent or nonviolent, emotional or rational) and about the adaptability of individuals (the extent to which they can be taught or induced to act and think in a way that is against their innate nature).

Individual and society.   What is the proper relationship between the individual and society? One view is that the highest value in social arrangements is individual freedom of action. Alternatively, the collective good is seen as paramount, and individual freedom must be constrained to achieve that collective good.

 # BOX 2.2

From the "Ism" File I: Fascism

Fascism is one of the other political ideologies that had a major impact on twentieth-century history. Nazism, its variant in Germany, was the pivot of the most devastating war in the century (World War II). **Fascism** *places fundamental importance on the unity and harmony of government and society and is defined particularly by its opposition to forces that might weaken that collective unity.* In particular, fascism is: (1) antisocialist—it opposes the egalitarian ethic, the idea that there might be persistent violence and struggle among groups in society, and the seizure of private property by the state; and (2) antidemocratic—it views competitive, multiparty politics as divisive and destabilizing.

Fascism shares with conservatism the idea that the society and the government should be unified into a single, organic whole. All groups should enthusiastically coordinate their social and economic activities to achieve the good of the entire nation. Fascism further assumes that the top leader is the embodiment of the national will and that all individuals and groups must obey the will of the leader. The ideology also usually distinguishes between a superior racial or ethnic group that forms the nation and other, inferior groups that are reviled and persecuted (on the "nation," see Chapter 5).

While several twentieth-century regimes included strong elements of fascism, this political ideology is most closely associated with the regimes of Adolf Hitler in Germany (1932–1945) and Benito Mussolini in Italy (1922–1943). Hitler's particular version of fascism, emphasizing nationalistic fervor and virulent racism, effectively mobilized the German people to support a war that spread across 3 continents, causing more than fifty-one million deaths (17 million military and 34 million civilian), and being particularly marked by the brutal extermination of more than six million Jews and other "undesirables" in the concentration camps of Europe.

In the 1990s, variations of fascism reemerged as a strong political force in Europe. While some "neo-Nazi" groups, such as skinheads and the American Ku Klux Klan, have continued to have small followings, there has been significant electoral support for neofascist parties such as Jean-Marie Le Pen's National Front in

BOX **2.2** (CONTINUED)

France, Georg Haider's Freedom Party in Austria, and Vladimir Zhrinovsky's Liberal Democratic Party in Russia. There were strong protests in Austria and by Austria's European Union partners when the Freedom Party became a key participant in a coalition government in 2000. As in earlier periods, these neo-Nazi groups appeal to strong antiforeigner sentiment, particularly against immigrant groups, whose ethnicity and culture are dramatically distinctive from the dominant groups in the society. They also promise to use government power aggressively to eliminate crime and disorder in the society. Some analysts predict that a severe crisis, such as a prolonged economic or health crisis, could spawn a dramatic increase in support because "the fascist ideology appeals to our deepest longings for community, for solidarity, for safety in the face of a seething world" (Segre 1993: 296).

Fascism in Germany under Adolf Hitler was among the most effective and destructive mass-mobilization ideologies in modern history.

Equality.   To what extent should there be equality in terms of what individuals do and the benefits they acquire? One position is that there should be legal equality—that every person should be equal before the law, have equal political rights, and enjoy equality of opportunity. A contrasting position is that there should be material equality—that every person deserves a comparable level of benefits and goods. This second position places high value on equality of conditions, adding social and economic equality to legal equality. A third position posits that people and situations are intrinsically unequal and that it is neither possible nor desirable to attempt to legislate any kind of equality.

While there is broad agreement regarding the general perspective of each major ideology, be aware that each ideology is subject to varying interpretations across groups and especially across cultures. This variation is particularly evident for the term "liberalism," which has both a traditional meaning (described later in this section) and a very different meaning at the beginning of the twenty-first century. Similarly, the ideology of socialism in its Marxist–Leninist form is quite distinct from its democratic socialist form.

Conservatism

Conservatism *attempts to prevent or slow the transition away from a society based on traditional values and social hierarchy.* As the word suggests, the essence of conservative ideology is to conserve the many valued elements of the system that already exists. What the conservative wishes to preserve varies with the time and place, but certain underlying elements are highly valued. Particular importance is placed on stability, tradition, and loyalty to God and country. The relation of the individual to society and an antipathy to egalitarianism (i.e., equality of conditions) are at the core of conservatism.

The individual.   Conservatism makes two key assumptions about human nature. First, it is posited that individuals are not consistently rational. In many situations, people are emotional and are unable to reason clearly. Thus individual rationality is not usually a sound basis for decisions about appropriate social or political behavior. Second, individuals are inherently unequal in intelligence, in skills, and in status. Some individuals and groups are superior to others, and it is clearly preferable that those from the superior groups should be in positions of power in society and in government.

Individual and society.   Individuals have a basic need for order and stability in society. They belong to different groups that are unequal in power, status, and material possessions. Social harmony is maintained when these various groups work cooperatively together. Traditional values and ethics provide the guidelines for group cooperation and individual behavior. And it is the role of institutions such as the family and the church, as well as government, to communicate and enforce these values.

Individual liberty is valued, but only within a framework of mutual responsibility. No majority or government should have sufficient power to abridge the rights of others. But, even more importantly, no individual or group has absolute freedom to do whatever they want; rather, each should behave in a manner consistent with society's traditional values. The superior groups should be allowed to enjoy the benefits and exercise the responsibilities associated with their position; but they also should protect the weak from severe hardships, a responsibility that the French term *noblesse oblige*—"the obligations of the nobility."

Existing values and social organization have evolved slowly and have survived the test of time. Tradition and religion, rather than reason, are viewed as the most reliable sources for guiding society, since they support stability and temper change. In the words of one British conservative, "The accumulated wisdom and experience of countless generations gone is more likely to be right than the passing fashion of the moment" (Hearnshaw 1933: 22).

Equality.   Since inequality is viewed as a natural aspect of society, it is considered foolish and even dangerous to seek egalitarianism. Forced equality is unwise because

Edmund Burke

it disrupts the natural, cooperative hierarchy among groups and causes social conflict and endangers the fundamental goal of order and stability. Attempts to force equality are also unacceptable because they directly undermine individual liberty, which is of greater importance than equality.

Edmund Burke (1729–1797), a British member of Parliament, is perhaps the most articulate spokesperson for conservatism. Other important advocates were British Prime Ministers Benjamin Disraeli and Winston Churchill and, to a lesser extent, American Founding Fathers James Madison and Alexander Hamilton. Many who are now called conservatives or neoconservatives are really more closely aligned to the philosophy of classical liberalism (discussed in the next section).

In those contemporary situations where government has become strong, and especially where government uses its power to equalize wealth and status, conservatism argues for a return to traditional values, for a contraction of government, and for the individual freedom to be unequal. Many of the contemporary political actors who come closest to the spirit of conservatism are in certain countries in Asia and the Middle East (e.g., Brunei, Kuwait, Nepal, and Saudi Arabia) where social hierarchy, order, and traditional values are celebrated. Most contemporary conservatives are pragmatic and recognize that a return to eighteenth-century society is impossible. They accept some of the government policies implemented in their societies to equalize status and income. But even here the rationale is to change in order to preserve, as the British Conservative Party has put it. The conservative perspective is sympathetic to government intervention if the goal is to maintain or return to traditional values, such as patriotism, family, morality, and piety. Thus a conservative government might actively expand its military power to influence other countries, support a state religion, or make abortion illegal.

Classical Liberalism

The ideology of **classical liberalism** *places the highest value on individual freedom and posits that the role of government should be quite limited.* In part, this ideology emerged (in the sixteenth through eighteenth centuries) as a response to rigid, hierarchical societies, such as those in feudal Europe. Intellectual and commercial actors, among others, desired to be free from the constraints imposed by the dominant political, economic, and religious institutions in their society. They articulated a view centering on the idea that each person should be allowed to act with minimal constraints from such institutions. While each person should be responsible for her actions, she should also be allowed to enjoy fully the benefits of her efforts and to live in the manner dictated by her beliefs.

The individual. John Locke (1632–1704), a primary theorist of classical liberalism, describes individuals in a "state of nature," prior to the existence of government. Each person enjoys natural rights to life, liberty, and property. Moreover, each person is rational and has the ability to use her reason to determine the sensible rules

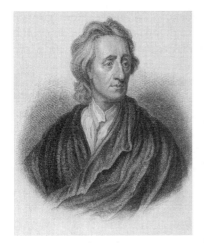

John Locke

(the "laws of nature") that shape how she should live. Essentially, every individual is capable of deciding rationally how to pursue her own needs and to avoid harming others. Notice two important contrasts with conservatism: (1) each person is rational and responsible and is the best judge of what is in her self-interest; and (2) there is no higher value in classical liberalism than the freedom of the individual to pursue her natural rights.

Individual and society.   A person's full capabilities can be realized only if she is not limited by a social order in which tradition and hierarchy are dominant. Such a social order would not only restrict individual freedom but also stifle progressive change and growth. And no one is forced to accept the authority of government. Individuals can consent to be governed—choosing to "contract" with a minimal government, the main roles of which are limited to clarifying the laws of nature and enforcing the occasional violations of those laws. (See Box 2.3 if you are wondering why all this doesn't sound "liberal.")

For similar reasons, classical liberals celebrate a laissez-faire economy (i.e., one unconstrained by government regulations) that is guided by enlightened self-interest and the "invisible hand" of the market. (This vision of the "market political economy," associated with the writings of Adam Smith [1723–1790], will be explained in detail in Chapter 8.) Each person should be free to pursue her economic goals by means of any legal activity and to amass as much property and wealth as possible.

Equality.   While equality before the law (equality of opportunity) is important, government should not attempt to create material equality (equality of outcomes). People pursue their interests in different ways and with different levels of success. Even in situations of hardship, government action is undesirable because it can undermine individual initiative and independence. Thus government should have no significant role in addressing inequalities.

Among the many political thinkers associated with classical liberalism in addition to John Locke and Adam Smith are Jeremy Bentham (1748–1831) and John Stuart Mill (1806–1873). More contemporary advocates of classical liberalism (some of whom are labeled "neoconservatives") include economists F. A. Hayek and Milton Friedman and political commentator William F. Buckley. Part Five of this book will reveal that many contemporary political regimes are powerfully influenced by classical liberalism. Its emphases on limited government, individual liberty, and laissez-faire economics are among the central themes in many debates about policy and government action.

Socialism

For **socialism,** *the most important goal is to provide high-quality, relatively equal conditions of life for everyone, with an active state assisting in the achievement of*

BOX 2.3

Whither Liberalism? Is That Liberal or Conservative?

If you are an American, you probably have noticed that the description of classical liberalism given in this chapter, emphasizing limited government, is quite different from the political beliefs currently termed "liberal" in the United States. In the political language of today, a liberal in America is understood as someone who supports substantial government intervention and policies that increase equality of condition, not merely equality of opportunity.

This confusion of terminology is partly due to developments during Franklin Delano Roosevelt's tenure as U.S. president (from 1933 to 1945). Faced with a devastating economic depression, Roosevelt argued for a "New Deal" in which the central government had a clear duty and responsibility to assist actively in economic recovery and in social action. While not proposing the expansive government role in the economy and the egalitarianism of socialism, he did insist that government must be very active in solving economic and social problems. Among other things, government must actively regulate business, create jobs, and distribute extensive welfare services to the citizens, including cash payments and increased public provision of education, housing, health care, and so on.

To avoid the politically negative label of socialism, Roosevelt termed himself and his policies "liberal," contrasting them with the "conservative" policies of others (mainly Republicans, such as the previous president, Herbert Hoover) who emphasized limited government, laissez-faire economics, and individual freedom. Notice that in the general language of political ideology, what Roosevelt was terming conservatism was really classical liberalism, and what he was proposing himself was a very modest version of democratic socialism.

Eventually, Roosevelt's terminology was widely adopted in the United States, and thus political discourse in the United States is characterized as a debate between liberals and conservatives, even though the ideologies of both groups combine, in different amounts, elements of classical liberalism and democratic socialism. In this book, the traditional ideology of liberalism will be termed "classical liberalism" to distinguish it from the current understanding of liberalism as an ideology of big government and egalitarianism.

this goal. Many were still impoverished and exploited in the nineteenth-century world, despite the emergence of industrialization and democracy. Socialism evolved as a distinctive ideology among those who were concerned about the plight of people with relatively little economic, social, or political power and who were displeased that neither conservatism nor classical liberalism revealed particular concern for these groups. Socialism articulated a vision through which economic and political power could be directed to benefit all groups in society.

The individual. In the socialist perspective, people are not innately selfish and aggressive. If anything, humans are social and caring by nature. To a large extent, individuals' attitudes and behaviors are determined by the environment in which they live and learn, not by invariant features of human nature. Consequently, it is considered crucial to create an environment that encourages individuals to place the highest value on cooperation and sharing and to believe that the most important goal for each person is to increase the collective good of all.

Individual and society. While individual rights and freedom are valued, the most important value is identified as the good of the society as a whole. Thus the individual's interests must be subordinated to, or at least coordinated with, the overall interests and needs of everyone in the society. All groups, from national organizations (e.g., trade unions) to local organizations (e.g., social clubs) to the family, must encourage these attitudes of cooperation and service to the common good.

The government has a crucial role, both through education and civic training and through policies that provide every citizen with good material living conditions and security. Thus government must take an expansive role, ensuring that every citizen has access to quality education, shelter, health care, jobs, and financial security against economic uncertainty.

Equality. Both the organic, hierarchical world of conservatism and the individualistic, self-serving world of classical liberalism result in societies in which there exist huge disparities of material conditions, status, and power. From the socialist perspective, these disparities cause misery, deep alienation, and pervasive conflict in the society.

Thus the ideology of socialism centers in a deep commitment to use the power and policies of the state to increase the material as well as the social and political equality of all its members. Such equality is believed to transform people into fulfilled, happy citizens who willingly contribute to the common good.

There are significantly different variations within the ideology of socialism. Among these, two major variations should be distinguished: Marxist–Leninist socialism and democratic socialism.

Marxist–Leninist socialism. The Marxist–Leninist variant of socialist ideology begins with three assumptions regarding the changes necessary to produce equality and social justice. First, the old socioeconomic order will resist change by every means available, and thus change will require violent overthrow of the old order. Second, the transformation to socialism will be complex and difficult. To achieve the desired equality of conditions, a powerful government must be installed. Among the government's most important tasks is the restructuring of the economic system, with public ownership of all the major resources in the society and the production and distribution of goods and services for human need (see Chapter 8 on the command political economy for a fuller discussion of this point). And third, a small, dictatorial leadership group must be empowered to manage the government and to effect the complex changes in the economy and society. When relative equality is achieved, both the small leadership group and the powerful government support-

Karl Marx

ing it can be eliminated. They will be replaced by a decentralized, citizen-run politics and an efficient administration.

The core elements of this version of socialism are the theories of Karl Marx, and its modified practical applications by V. I. Lenin in the Soviet Union and Mao Zedong in China. These variations of socialism are often termed communism, Marxism, or revolutionary socialism, as well as Marxist–Leninist socialism. In the last sixty years this version of socialism has been attempted in more than sixty countries, ranging from A (Albania, Angola, Algeria) to Z (Zimbabwe). Most of the major regimes that implemented Marxist–Leninist socialism have since abandoned it (see especially Chapter 15 on the post-communist countries).

Democratic socialism.   The other major variation within socialist ideology is democratic socialism. This variant also treats egalitarianism as its primary goal, but it assumes that the changes can be effected by a government that comes to power and rules by democratic means, not by violence and repression. This government's authority is derived from consent of the governed in elections. In democratic socialism, the state's policies emphasize the substantial reduction of inequalities in material conditions, power, and status, but they do not attempt to achieve complete equality of material conditions. The approach to change is gradual, placing continued importance on the protection of individual rights and freedoms, even as it transforms the socioeconomic order. The government might own some of the major economic resources in the society and it strongly regulates much of the economic system, but it does not attempt to plan and control all aspects of the economic system (Przeworski 1985, 1993).

The ideology of democratic socialism is rooted in such Utopian socialists as Thomas More (1478–1535), Robert Owen (1771–1856), and Claude-Henri St. Simon (1760–1825); in Fabian socialists such as George Bernard Shaw (1856–1950) and Sydney (1859–1947) and Beatrice (1858–1943) Webb; and in revisionist Marxists such as Karl Kautsky (1854–1938). The ideology has been partially implemented in the contemporary "social market systems" present in such countries as Denmark, Germany, Great Britain, and Sweden (see Box 13.1 in Chapter 13). It is also advocated by some of the political elites in the post-communist countries of Central and Eastern Europe (see Chapter 15).

One vision of democratic socialism was articulated by the British economist Sir William Beveridge in a major policy statement to the British government in 1941. Beveridge argued that there are five tragic effects on some people in a society operating according to the tenets of classical liberalism. Thus the government should act as a "welfare state," implementing policies to overcome each of these five effects:

1. *Disease:* to be combated by public provision of subsidized or free health care services, including doctors, treatment, hospitals, and medicines.

2. *Want:* to be eliminated by public provision of sufficient money and other services to raise people above poverty.

3. *Squalor:* to be reduced by state provision of publicly owned and subsidized housing affordable to all.

4. *Ignorance:* to be eliminated by universal, free public education.

5. *Idleness:* to be overcome by government policies that ensure meaningful work for every person.

Some Further Points about "Isms"

This section has identified three major political ideologies that characterize the political belief systems of many citizens in Western countries. There are many other significant political ideologies in the contemporary political world, at least some of which are "isms." Box 2.4 briefly characterizes the essence of some of the political

---

BOX 2.4

A Brief Primer on Political "Isms"

In politics and political theory, there are many "isms"—systems of beliefs that address how societies should function, how people should live and what they should value, and how political systems should operate. Entire books are devoted to each of the "isms" that follow, but here they are characterized in 40 words or less to give you a (dangerously simplified?) orienting idea about the core vision regarding any "ism" with which you are unfamiliar. The references in parenthesis indicate where some of these "isms" receive greater attention in other chapters in this book.

Anarchism—a moral–political ideal of a society that is untouched by relations of power and domination among human beings; there is an absence of organized government.

Authoritarianism—a system in which the political rights and interests of individuals are subordinated, usually by coercion, to the interests of the state. (Chapter 7)

Capitalism—linking politics to the political economy, it is a system dominated by a (laissez-faire) market economy in which economic actors are generally free from state constraints. (Chapter 8)

Collectivism—a doctrine holding that the individual's actions should benefit some kind of collective organization such as the state, a tribe, or the like, rather than the individual herself.

Communism—based on the theories of Karl Marx, the essential goal of this system is the socialization of societal resources, with the state owning land, labor, and capital and using them to promote the equal welfare of all citizens. (Chapters 8 and 15)

Conservatism—a belief in the virtue of preserving traditional values and social institutions and of promoting loyalty to country, reliance on family, and adherence to religion.

Corporatism—a political economy in which there is extensive economic cooperation between an activist state and a few groups that represent such major economic actors as large industry, organized labor, and farmers. (Chapter 8)

BOX **2.4** (CONTINUED)

Environmentalism—advocacy of the planned management of a natural resource or of the total environment of a particular ecosystem in order to prevent exploitation, pollution, destruction, or depletion of valuable natural resources.

Fascism—a system in which the unity and harmony of government and society are of central importance, and forces that might weaken that unity are repressed; a top leader is usually viewed as the embodiment of the natural will, and all individuals are expected to obey the leader's will.

Feminism—a diverse social movement promoting equal rights and opportunities for women in their personal lives, their economic activities, and politics.

Liberalism—an emphasis on the primacy of the freedom and rights of the individual, relative to any constraints imposed by the state.

Libertarianism—an extreme version of liberalism, advocating the right of individuals to act freely and unconstrained by the state as long as they do not harm other people.

Marxism—a set of ideas based on the writings of Karl Marx, who argued, inter alia, that society is composed of competing classes, based on economic power; that class struggle and change are inevitable; and that the desirable goal is the equal distribution of welfare in the society. (Chapter 9)

Nationalism—a deep commitment to the advancement of the interests and welfare of the core group (based on location, ethnicity, or some other crucial factor) with which an individual identifies powerfully. (Chapter 5)

Pacifism—a belief that the highest political and social value is peace and the absence of violence.

Socialism—a system committed to utilizing the state, the economy, and public policy to provide a high-quality, relatively equal standard of living for all and, usually, to support democratic political processes. (Chapters 9 and 13)

Totalitarianism—a system in which the state possesses total control over all aspects of people's lives, including their economic, social, political, and personal spheres. (Chapter 7)

"isms" that you might encounter. There are also broader systems of religious-social beliefs that have great political importance, including Islamic fundamentalism, Confucianism, and Hinduism. Many of these other "isms" will be detailed at some point in this book, where they are particularly relevant to a topic. To advance your understanding of these kinds of belief systems, you might take a course in political theory, political ideology, or world religions, or pursue the "ism" of interest at the library or via the Internet.

In the contemporary political world, few individuals adhere absolutely to any one of these political ideologies. Almost no one has a complete grasp of the details and subtleties of any ideology, and even fewer are prepared to accept without reservation every element of an ideology. Some "true believers" do adhere almost totally to a particular ideology, and these people are the genuine ideologues. There is a larger set of people who are substantially influenced by one or more ideologies. They have developed their own system of political beliefs, which is a combination of basic principles of particular ideologies with ideas from other sources. And, as was noted earlier in the discussion of the beliefs of mass publics, in most societies, many people have only rudimentary and inconsistent political beliefs that are shaped by perceptions of underlying principles of one or more political ideologies.

LOOKING AHEAD

Chapter 2 has begun our exploration of micropolitics. It has introduced you to issues about political beliefs—what individuals know and think about politics. Analysis can focus on a single person or on a group, and it can assess a single belief or an array of beliefs across many issues. While examining specific beliefs can be quite interesting, political analysis contributes most when it attempts to generalize about the belief system of a person or a group. A belief or belief system can be analyzed in terms of its cognitive, affective, and evaluative components. The balance among these emphases and the composition of the group sharing a belief system, as well as the content of the beliefs, vary considerably when one is examining political ideologies, political cultures, mass belief systems, or elite belief systems.

The next step in micropolitical analysis is to move beyond description and develop explanations of political behavior (Chapter 4). However, we must first look at the second general form of political behavior, political actions. Thus the focus of Chapter 3 is the array of political actions in which an individual or group can engage.

KEY CONCEPTS

affective orientation	national character studies
belief system	political belief
classical liberalism	political culture
conservatism	political ideology
cognitive orientation	postmaterialism
evaluative orientation	public opinion polls
fascism	socialism
micropolitics	survey research

FOR FURTHER CONSIDERATION

1. What are your general beliefs about human nature? Are these beliefs consistent with your most important beliefs about how people ought to behave and do behave politically?

2. What do you think is the most sensible assumption and the most questionable assumption of conservatism? Of classical liberalism? Of socialism?

3. Can you characterize your own political belief system? For example, what are your three to five most salient political beliefs? Do they deal with the same general content area?

4. If you were to analyze the political belief system of another person on the basis of five questions, what questions would you ask?

FOR FURTHER READING

Almond, Gabriel, and Sidney Verba. (1963). *The Civic Culture.* Princeton, NJ: Princeton University Press. As described in the chapter, this is the landmark empirical, comparative study of the political cultures of different countries.

Ebenstein, William, and Alan Ebenstein. (1991). *Great Political Thinkers: Plato to the Present.* 5th ed. Fort Worth, TX: Harcourt Brace. This collection includes extensive excerpts from many major political theorists, supplemented by very helpful editors' introductions.

Fromm, Erich, Ed. (1965). *Socialist Humanism.* New York: Doubleday. Prominent social scientists and political philosophers expound the virtues of socialism.

Griffin, Roger, Ed. (1998). *International Fascism: Theories, Causes and the New Consensus.* New York: Oxford University Press. A diverse and thorough selection of writings on fascism, by both fascists and antifascists, exploring the strong appeal of this ideology to many individuals and groups during the mid-twentieth century and also at the beginning of the twenty-first century.

Huntington, Samuel P. (1996). *Clash of Civilizations and the Remaking of the World Order.* New York: Simon & Schuster. As described in this chapter, the author offers a sweeping and controversial analysis of major cultural groupings at the global level, where identity, especially religious and cultural, is the dominant force shaping the beliefs and actions of individuals.

Inglehart, Ronald. (1997). *Modernization and Postmodernization: Cultural, Economic and Political Change in Forty-Three Nations.* Princeton, NJ: Princeton University Press. Building on his important earlier work (Inglehart 1989), the author further elaborates his thesis about the conditions under which there is a shift in political culture toward less materialistic values, especially in the more prosperous countries.

Love, Nancy S., Ed. (1998). *Dogmas and Dreams: A Reader in Modern Political Ideologies.* 2d ed. New York: Seven Bridges Press. A solid reader that includes important writings by many key theorists of the three major "isms" as well as anarchism, fascism, and feminism.

Mayer, Lawrence, and Erol Kaymak. (1998). *The Crisis of Conservatism and the Rise of the New Right in Western Democracies: Populist Revolt in the Late Twentieth Century.* Armonk, NY: M. E. Sharpe. An interesting exploration of the activities of ideologically driven and rather alienated populist groups that have their roots in traditional conservatism but have diverged substantially from it in both their attitudes and their political styles.

Murray, Charles. (1997). *What It Means to Be a Libertarian.* New York: Broadway Books. A brief, readable application of libertarian ideology to many contemporary issues (e.g., abortion, education, drugs, economic regulation, free speech), written by one of America's most controversial social critics.

Nisbet, Robert. (2001). *Conservatism: Dream and Reality.* Piscataway, NJ: Transaction Publishers. A short, illuminating discussion that traces the development of conservative thought and its significance in contemporary politics.

Putnam, Robert D. (1993). *Making Democracy Work: Civic Tradition in Modern Italy.* Princeton, NJ: Princeton University Press. Using communities in northern and southern Italy as his cases, the author develops a significant, and widely cited, argument about the role of political culture in sustaining democracy, and especially about the crucial importance of "social capital"—the citizens' willingness to engage and interact with each other.

Pye, Lucian W. (1985). *Asian Power and Politics: The Cultural Dimensions of Authority.* Cambridge, MA: Belknap Press. The author presents an intriguing account of the varying political cultures in East Asia. See also Pye's *The Mandarins and the Cadre: China's Political Cultures* (Ann Arbor: University of Michigan Press, 1988) .

Sniderman, Paul M., Richard Brody, and Philip E. Tetlock. (1991). *Reasoning and Choice: Explorations in Political Psychology.* New York: Cambridge University Press. A careful assessment of the extent to which Americans in the mass public actually do reason about political choices, focusing on such issues as racial attitudes, poverty, civil liberties, and AIDS.

Spencer, William. (1995). *Islamic Fundamentalism in the Modern World.* Brookfield, CT: Millbrook Press. A sensitive and informative discussion of the diverse ideologies and approaches associated with those generally termed Islamic fundamentalists.

Tucker, Robert, Ed. (1978). *The Marx–Engels Reader.* New York: Norton. An extensive selection of the important writings, with commentaries, from the major theorists of revolutionary socialism, Karl Marx and Friedrich Engels.

ON THE WEB

http://www.nationalgeographic.com

National Geographic has offered rich information and photographs from locations around the world for nearly a century. Some of this material is informative about culture and society in many places, including insights about political culture.

http://jkalb.freeshell.org/web/trad.php

This site offers an interesting and very diverse array of links to materials associated with "traditionalist conservatism worldwide." Links range across political perspectives from various countries to conservatism in many of the world's religions to extreme-right fringe groups.

http://free-market.net

This is the portal of the libertarian belief system and provides many sources that are guided by this ideology.

http://internationalsocialist.org

The site of the International Socialist Organization, an association promulgating the Marxist–Leninist perspective, and publisher of the *Socialist Worker* newspaper and the *International Socialist Review* journal.

http://socialist.org

The site of the international democratic socialist movement, it contains information about the people, ideas, and events important to the movement.

http://www.independent.org/archive/pol_ideology.html

The Political Ideology Link Archive, produced by the Independent Institute, provides access to a comprehensive list of various online opinion articles and book reviews tied to political ideology.

http://www.fordham.edu/halsall/mod/modsbook18.html

The Internet Modern History Sourcebook includes a number of links related to important works on both liberalism and feminism.

http://www.liberal-international.org/

This web site serves as the electronic home of Liberal International, a worldwide federation of liberal political parties.

http://www.feminist.com/

Feminist.com is an online community designed to promote feminism and women's rights. The site contains a number of articles and speeches related to feminist thought.

CHAPTER 3 Political Actions

Help us get drunk drivers off the road so you and I can drive without fear. Please don't leave it up to the "other guy." We need you. . . . My husband was nearly killed because of a drunk driver. The driver of a pickup truck crossed the center line and struck us head-on. My husband suffered a broken arm and severe head injuries. As a result of a concussion he contracted spinal meningitis and almost died. I had broken bones myself.

After the crash, I was angry and hurt. But rather than sitting back and feeling sorry for myself, I turned my energies toward working against this problem of drinking and driving. I joined the Mothers Against Drunk Driving crusade because MADD fights to make our roads safe . . . for you, me and our loved ones.

Since our founding in 1980, we've made a great deal of progress— Congress passed a national Minimum Drinking Age Act . . . judges nationwide now impose stiffer drunk driving sentences . . . and government is taking drunk driving more seriously. Yes, we've made progress. But there's so much more to be done. . . . Please help us continue our fight.

—Micky Sadoff, MADD solicitation letter

Chapter 2 considered the nature of people's political beliefs. Ultimately, the more important issues regarding the individual in politics might be questions about what people *do* politically, not merely what they think. For instance, in the incident at Burger King described at the beginning of Chapter 2, the most relevant questions from the perspective of the political world would be, "What did you *do*? What did you *say* to the woman?" In this chapter, we examine the prominent modes of actual political behavior that people engage in. Moreover, many individuals, such as Micky Sadoff, decide that they can be more effective politically if they act with others rather than alone. Thus, instead of engaging in a lonely act of protest, a person could join a huge demonstration; instead of writing a letter requesting a change in public policy, a person could join an organization that speaks for thousands of people.

Broadly, **political participation** is the term that is applied to *all of the political actions by individuals and groups.* The explicit objective of most political participation is *to influence the actions or selection of political rulers* (Nelson 1993: 720). What is the range of behaviors that a person might undertake in the political world? At one extreme are people who are obsessed with politics, see political implications in most of life's actions, are constantly involved in political discussion and action, and want to make political decisions for others. At the other extreme are people who have absolutely no interest in politics, pay no attention to political phenomena, and engage in no politically relevant actions. (In some instances, such as not voting in an election to indicate dissatisfaction, not doing something can also be a type of political participation.) The first half of this chapter focuses on individual political action in the context of the range of actions between the two extremes just described.

An individual acting alone can engage in virtually the same political actions as a member of a group. The actions of groups can be analyzed on some additional dimensions because of their size and structure. Thus the second half of this chapter considers the activities and types of the two major forms of political groups—interest groups and political parties.

INDIVIDUAL POLITICAL ACTIONS

Modes of Political Activity

Table 3.1 lists various modes of individual political action, with specific examples of action given for each mode. Broadly, the modes are ranked on the basis of the effort or costs required to perform that type of political action, and the examples within each mode are ranked according to the frequency with which Americans tend to perform them (see Milbrath and Goel 1982: 17–20). Some of the most extensive empirical and crossnational analyses of political participation, by Sidney Verba and his colleagues (Verba and Nie 1972, 1975; Verba, Nie, and Kim 1978), have emphasized four broad categories of political participation: (1) voting; (2) campaign activities (e.g., attending rallies, working on the campaign, contributing funds); (3) personalized contacts (e.g., communicating with a politician via letter, e-mail, meeting); and (4) communal activities (e.g., participating in a group or club that tries to promote civic and community life).

There have been two important changes in the recent empirical studies of political participation. First, it has become clear that political action should not be treated as a single dimension. Most early studies of political participation assumed that political actions were hierarchical—that is, that a person who performs a more difficult act, such as communal contacting, will also perform all less difficult acts, such as voting. The richer empirical studies, however, have indicated that there are different dimensions of political participation. Thus a person high (or low) on one mode of political action is not necessarily high (or low) on another. While there is some overlap, the campaign activists, communal activists, and those making personalized contacts are not necessarily the same people, and many people specialize in one or another mode. Also, protesters might not engage in any of the other activities, or they might engage in all of them (Dalton 2002: ch. 3, 4; Rueschemeyer, Rueschemeyer, and Wittrock 1998; Verba, Schlozman, and Brady 1995: ch. 3).

TABLE 3.1
Modes of Political Action

Actor Type	Characteristic Actions
Revolutionaries/protesters	Undertake violence against the political order
	Riot
	Engage in civil disobedience
	Join in public protest demonstrations
	Attend protest meetings
	Refuse to obey unjust laws
	Protest verbally if government does something morally wrong
Government activists	Candidates for/hold public office
Partisan activists	Contribute money to party, candidate, issue
	Attend meetings, rallies
	Actively work for party, candidate, issue
	Persuade others how to vote
	Join and support party
Community activists	Active in community organization
	Form group to work on local problems
	Contact officials on social issues
	Work with others on local problems
Communicators	Write letters to media
	Send support or protest messages to political leaders
	Engage in political discussions
	Keep informed about politics
Contact specialists	Contact local, state, or national officials on particular problems
Voters	Vote regularly in elections
Supporters and patriots	Show patriotism by flying flag, attending public parades, etc.
	Express love of country
	Pay all taxes
Inactives	No voting, no other political activity
	No patriotic inputs

Source: Most categories adapted from Milbrath and Goel 1982, figure 1.1.

Second, there is increasing recognition of the significant level of unconventional political action, such as demonstrations, protests, and rioting, in both democratic and nondemocratic countries. Whereas Verba and his colleagues gathered data only on conventional forms of political action, analysts today often include unconventional modes of political action in their research (Dalton 2002: ch. 4). This trend is reflected in Table 3.1 in the "revolutionaries/protesters" category, as well as in Table 3.3 . Indeed, some analysts conclude that group protest activities have become so widespread that they are now an accepted and institutionalized form of participation in many democratic countries (Meyer and Tarrow 1997).

"I didn't protest this war, but I'll try to protest the next one."

Political Activists

Although the more routine modes of political action (listed in the middle and bottom of Table 3.1) constitute the vast majority of actual political behavior, most of us are particularly interested in the extraordinary actions of the few political activists who seem to "live politics." They might hold government office, spend many hours furthering a political idea or leader, or even risk their freedom and life in the pursuit of a dramatic change in the political order. At least three different types of political activists can be identified: foot soldiers, extremist-activists, and political leaders.

Foot soldiers.   *Foot soldiers* are those activists who do the basic work of politics. They link the government and the top political leadership to the masses by performing such tasks as raising money for candidates or political issues, working in the local offices of political leaders, communicating the views of top leaders to citizens, and regularly voicing their opinions to political leaders. In most countries, foot soldiers are members of political parties or groups with a political mission, although such membership is not necessarily synonymous with political activism.

Extremist-activists.   *Extremist-activists* are outsiders who are willing to engage in extensive political action in pursuit of their vision of an ideal political world, which would require a dramatic shift in the nature of the existing system. "Extremism" is a subjective and relative concept; a person is politically extreme only in comparison with some standard position, typically the broad center of the existing political order. Like foot soldiers, extremist-activists might engage in some conventional political activities inside the system. However, they more often engage in intensive modes of political action, ranging from organizing grassroots movements to guerrilla warfare, that are on the edge of or outside the system.

Political analysts have focused considerable attention on individual extremist-activists, especially revolutionary leaders. (Two examples are featured in Box 4.4.) A *revolutionary* is a person who desires to overthrow the existing political order and to replace it with a quite different one, using political violence if necessary (see Chapter 12). Some revolutionaries, such as Mao Zedong (China), Fidel Castro (Cuba), Ayatollah Khomeini (Iran), and Nelson Mandela (South Africa), eventually achieved leadership roles in their political system after years or even decades of struggle. Others, including Che Guevara (Cuba, then Bolivia) and Steve Biko (South Africa), have died in the struggle and become martyrs to those committed to revolutionary change. The largest number of revolutionary leaders have acted in relative obscurity, eventually burning out, being captured by the state, or dying as a result of political violence.

In addition to the focus on leaders, there is also increasing analytic attention on those who become members of extremist-activist groups with revolutionary goals. Contemporary examples include the people who join Osama bin Laden's worldwide Al-Qaeda ("The Base") network, the "soldiers" of the Zapatista National Liberation Army (EZLN) in the Chiapas area of Mexico, and the followers of Aum Shinrikyo in Japan. Other individuals can also be classified as extremist-activists if their political goals or tactics locate them on the margins of the existing political system and political culture. Members of environmental activist groups such as Earth First! in the United States and the violent, antiforeigner activists in many countries in Western and Eastern Europe are examples.

Political leaders. Many of us are fascinated with such ultimate political activists as Fidel Castro, Winston Churchill, Adolf Hitler, Nelson Mandela, and Saddam Hussein. These top political leaders are distinctive because they succeed in capturing supreme political power within a government and using it with extraordinary energy and effect (whether good or bad). Their titles vary by country and level of government and include chairman, chancellor, dictator, governor, king, mayor, president, prime minister, and supreme leader, among others. A top political leader might put his substantial political power and position to admirable purposes, might implement reprehensible policies, or might accomplish virtually nothing. These political leaders have been the subject of more descriptions, analyses, and evaluations than any other type of actors in the political world. They will frequently be a subject in this book.

Political Participation Studies

Once categories of political action are established, a basic research question is: How many people participate in each category, both within and across various national political contexts? In studying participation, Milbrath and Goel (1982) argue that

Political leaders who capitalize on celebrity and media attention can be formidable.

only a small proportion of the population can be termed "gladiators"—those people who are active in the most demanding forms of political action, such as protest and extensive partisan political work. They concluded that only about 5 percent of the adults in the United States were gladiators and more than half of the adults were either "observers" or "apathetics." More recent empirical research reports that about one in five adults in the United States engages in no political activity and another one-fifth do little more than vote. This research also suggests that only about 5 percent of the population engage in a significant level of political activism (Verba, Schlozman, and Brady 1995: 50–54, 72–74).

Some empirical data compare levels of participation across many countries. The most reliable of these comparative data measure voting in national elections. Table 3.2 provides these data for selected countries. The most striking observation about these figures is the huge variation in voting level, ranging from a reported 98 percent in Vietnam to only 41 percent in Singapore. Notice the very high voter turnout in countries such as Cuba and North Korea (which reports voting participation at about 99 percent). In such countries, voting is primarily a symbolic act that is supposed to express support for the existing political leadership, not an action in which citizens select their leaders. Unlike Vietnam and Cuba, nearly every country in Table 3.2 does now offer the voters a choice among candidates. However, there is considerable variation in the extent to which the choice is genuine and the votes really do determine the top leadership. There are some countries (e.g., Singapore, Zimbabwe) where one group is virtually assured of victory and other countries (e.g.,

TABLE 3.2
Voting Participation in Selected Countries: Percentage of Eligible Adults Voting in
Most Recent Major National Election

| | Election | | | Election | |
Country	Percentage	Year	Country	Percentage	Year
Vietnam	98	2002	Ukraine	70	2002
Cuba	96	2003	Nigeria	69	2003
Australia	95	2001	Israel	68	2003
Indonesia	93	1999	Costa Rica	67	2002
Denmark	89	2001	Iran	67	2001
South Africa	89	1999	Mexico	64	2000
Cambodia	82	2003	Canada	63	2000
Mongolia	82	2001	Ireland	63	2002
Italy	81	2001	Syria	63	2000
Brazil	80	2002	Portugal	62	2002
France	80	2002	Poland	61	2000
Netherlands	80	2003	Haiti	60	2000
Palestine (territory)	80	1996	Japan	60	2003
Sweden	80	2002	United Kingdom	59	2001
Taiwan	80	2004	India	58	2004
Turkey	79	2002	Kenya	56	2002
Sri Lanka	76	2001	Russia	56	2003
Bangladesh	75	2001	Zimbabwe	54	2002
Greece	75	2000	Guatemala	54	2003
Norway	75	2001	United States	51	2003
Slovakia	74	1999	Colombia	47	2002
Hungary	71	2002	Algeria	46	2002
South Korea	71	2002	Pakistan	42	2002
Spain	71	2000	Singapore	41	2001

Source: Elections Around the World (http://www.electionworld.org), 2004.

Algeria, Myanmar) where the top leadership or the military has repudiated the elections if it does not approve of the electoral results. These variations regarding the act of voting alert us to a general problem in crossnational analyses of micropolitical data—the same action or belief might have a quite different meaning and significance in different settings.

It is even more difficult to do empirical, crossnational comparisons between other modes of individual political participation. Even more than with voting, the same act can vary in meaning in different political and cultural environments. For example, the significance and potential personal risk of a public political protest is far greater for a person in North Korea than in South Korea, and greater in both those countries than for someone in Sweden.

The most consistent finding in virtually all recent comparative research on participation in democracies is clear: Most people do not regularly engage in high levels of political activity (Dalton 2002; Rueschemeyer, Rueschemeyer, and Wittrock 1998; *World Values Survey* 2001; see also the earlier studies, such as Verba, Nie, and Kim 1978). Apart from voting, which *is* a political act completed by many/most citizens (Table 3.2), high levels of persistent political activity tend to be uncommon in most political systems. For example, Dalton (2002: tables 3.3 and 3.5) finds that fewer than one in ten citizens engages in active, partisan activities in the four Western democracies in his study.

A second broad finding is that some citizens are willing to engage occasionally in more activist modes of political participation. While very few citizens participate in violent protests against people or property, Table 3.3 indicates that a significant number of people perform certain less-conventional political acts, including some actions that require considerable effort or risk. In about half of the countries listed in the table, 15 percent or more of the citizens have engaged in at least one "challenging act" (e.g., a lawful demonstration, boycott, or building occupation). The photograph that opens this chapter depicts citizens engaged in a demonstration against government policy, while other citizens protest against their protest. Skinheads and Ku Klux Klan members march in opposition to the celebration of Mar-

"I'M HAVING SECOND THOUGHTS ABOUT THE ELECTION... I'M NOT SURE I VOTED AGAINST THE RIGHT PERSON."

Drawing by Dunagin. © Tribune Media Services, Inc. All Rights Reserved. Reprinted with permission.

TABLE 3.3
Level of Less-Conventional Political Actions in Selected Countries

| Country | Mode of Political Action | | | |
	Sign Petition	Boycott	Lawful Demonstration	Occupy Building
Australia	78%	21%	18%	2 %
Belarus	9	3	19	0.3
Brazil	47	6	25	3
Bulgaria	6	2	9	1
Canada	76	22	20	3
Chile	16	2	14	2
Denmark	50	10	27	2
France	51	11	31	7
Ghana	7	3	7	3
Great Britain	75	14	13	2
Hungary	25	3	9	0.2
India	17	11	8	1
Italy	44	10	34	4
Mexico	28	9	10	4
Nigeria	4	5	9	5
Japan	51	7	9	0.1
Poland	19	5	9	2
Russia	9	2	20	0.5
South Africa	13	11	10	2
South Korea	40	16	14	2
Sweden	71	33	30	0.8
Turkey	19	9	9	0.7
United States	71	18	15	2
Uruguay	34	4	4	7

Note: About 1,500 respondents in each country indicated whether they had engaged in the action.
Source: World Values Survey, 1995–1997, 2001.

tin Luther King, Jr.'s birthday in Tennessee, flanked by African-Americans who mock them with fascist salutes.

These crossnational differences underscore the third broad observation based on these empirical participation studies. There is substantial variation, from country to country, in the proportion of citizens who undertake various forms of conventional and unconventional political action. In the data in Table 3.3, the difference in rates of activity (from highest to lowest) between countries is often a ratio of 3 : 1

or higher (except for voting). For example, three out of four Canadians have signed a petition, whereas fewer than one in twenty Nigerians has done so. And about one in three Italians and Swedes have participated in a lawful demonstration, compared with about one in twenty Uruguayans. In some countries, there can be an explosion of protest behavior and political violence against the regime during periods of unsatisfactory political or economic conditions. Such political behavior can manifest itself in strikes, violent demonstrations, insurrections, and revolutionary action.

In democratic countries, about which we have the most systematic empirical data, the evidence generally supports the conclusion that most people employ the conventional modes of voting and contacting public (elected or appointed) officials as the key means of achieving political objectives. But data such as those in Table 3.3, which reveal a notable level of unconventional modes involving protest or political violence, have revealed that individuals' choices of political action might not conform to the democratic model. It is also clear that many people continue to rely on nongovernmental channels to achieve objectives that could be pursued by contacting public officials.

Although systematic, comparative data on less democratic and nondemocratic countries are limited, it seems that the reliance on nongovernmental channels and the incidence of unconventional political behavior are greater (and vary more substantially) there, relative to democratic systems. In some less democratic countries, state repression deters the great majority of citizens from participation. And there are also countries characterized by "de-participation," as the political leadership has weakened or even eliminated the mechanisms that enable citizens to engage in political actions (Nelson 1987: 116–120).

GROUP POLITICAL ACTIONS

Recall the letter from Micky Sadoff of MADD at the beginning of this chapter. Rather than suffer privately, Sadoff decided to take political action. She became a leader, and ultimately the president, of MADD. This group has developed into an effective, nationwide organization in the United States. MADD recruits members and solicits contributions and then uses its resources to lobby politicians to pass more aggressive policies for punishing drunk drivers.

Sadoff's story is quite dramatic, but it illustrates the most common reason why people join political groups. A person might want to influence the actions of his government but might believe that his individual actions will not make any difference. People tend to feel that they are relatively powerless in politics when acting alone—but there might be strength in numbers. If a person joins with many others in a political group, it is possible that the group can exercise influence in the political world because of the group's numbers, organization, and capabilities.

Although a few political activists can have a major impact on politics, most individuals, most of the time, have a minimal effect on political decisions and actions. Even in democracies, casting a vote is their primary political act. But if huge numbers of votes are cast (more than 100 million votes are cast in a U.S. presidential contest), one person's vote is politically insignificant.

To have a greater impact, an individual's best strategy is to combine his political actions with those of others through a political group. Groups are extremely important in politics because they are often the major mechanism through which individuals are linked to the political system; hence their label as "linkage institutions." Some political groups, such as a major political party, can have wide-ranging goals and a huge membership. Other groups, such as MADD, are more narrowly focused in their objectives and have limited membership. And extremist groups, such as Al-Qaeda, might have few members but can still pursue extensive, radical agendas. The rest of this chapter describes the nature and activities of various kinds of political groups and political parties.

As an analytic concept, a group can be defined as *an aggregation of individuals who interact in order to pursue a common interest.* It is the pursuit of a common interest that is most crucial to this definition, since the individuals do not necessarily interact directly with one another. The factor that distinguishes a **political group** from other groups is that the common interest which the group pursues is a political objective—an interest in a particular policy or action that might be taken.

A distinction is usually made between political interest groups and political parties, although both types fit under our general definition of political group. A political group enters the special category of *political party* when the group seeks not merely to influence political decisions but also to place its members in the actual roles of government, such as chief executives and legislators. Although this distinction can become rather fuzzy among the most politically active groups, we shall treat political parties as a category different from other types of political interest groups.

POLITICAL INTEREST GROUPS

Activities of Political Interest Groups

All political interest groups share the common objective of attempting to influence the allocation of public values. But such groups can employ a variety of strategies to achieve this purpose.

Political action. The most direct methods to achieve political objectives involve some form of political action. Such action might be taken by all group members or by some members who formally or informally represent the entire group. Depending on the political system, this might entail voting and campaign activities to influence the selection and action of political authorities. Or the group might attempt to communicate its interest to political actors by such techniques as letter writing, personal contact, petitions, rallies, or political violence.

Provision of material resources. Political interest groups also can provide goods or services to political actors. Such a strategy assumes that provision of goods and services will influence decision makers to be more favorably disposed toward the interests of a group. Each political system develops its own rules about the methods and amounts of money or goods that can be given legitimately to political actors. The line between legal and illegal provision of money and goods varies dramatically across political cultures. In some political systems, all it takes to shock people is the revelation that an interest group has given a political actor a small gift, but in many political systems, it requires a multimillion-dollar kickback to a politician to upset the citizens and provoke action.

The United States is one of the countries where extraordinary amounts of money are now contributed to political actors by interest groups. In the 2002 elections, for example, political action committees (PACs) contributed nearly $1.25 billion to congressional candidates, and interest groups contributed an additional $.5 billion in "soft money" (Center for Responsive Politics 2003). Most of these contributions are legal, although some are not (e.g., in 1997 the Democratic Party returned more than $1 million to questionable donors, and President Clinton was widely criticized for "renting the Lincoln bedroom" for overnight visits in the White House by big contributors).

The ethics of a system in which political interest groups can make huge contributions is increasingly questioned. It is obvious that money is given in the expectations of influencing the making of public policies. Although cause-and-effect relationships are hard to establish, there are striking linkages between groups' campaign contributions and beneficial legislation. In the 1996 election in the United States, for example, tobacco companies contributed $11.3 million; soon after, legislation was passed directing a 15-cent-per-pack cigarette tax to a fund offsetting lawsuits, a benefit estimated at $50 billion. Oil, energy, and natural resource firms contributed $18.3 million and then gained $18 billion in benefits from exemptions from the passage of an alternative minimum tax law (O'Connor and Sabato 2004: figure 16.3). No one knows the amount of illegal resources that are distributed,

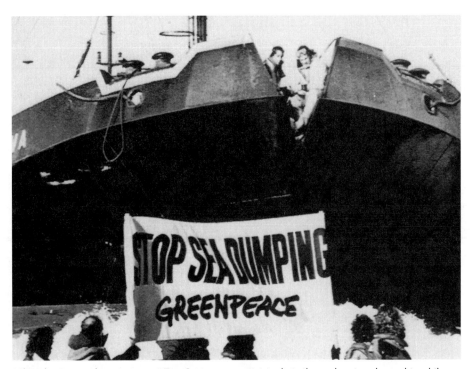

Political action can have an impact. Two Greenpeace activists chain themselves to a dump ship while other supporters demonstrate on a nearby boat. The group prevents the dump ship from loading industrial waste along the English coast, forcing it to return to port.

although in most countries, scandals regarding bribes and kickbacks seem to be reported with increasing frequency. In 1992, for example, the kingpin of Japan's dominant Liberal Democratic Party, Shin Kanemaru, was imprisoned for accepting more than $50 million in illegal contributions from construction companies. This is not a new phenomenon. In a wry comment on American politics, humorist Will Rogers once observed that "our Congress is the best that money can buy."

Exchange of information.   Another activity performed by some interest groups is to provide data and information to those within the political system. The interest group may have specialized information that the political system would find difficult or impossible to attain from other sources. These private groups have a vested interest in the public policies that emerge, and so most actively provide data that support their own interests. For example, in the early 1980s, the U.S. Congress began considering a law requiring mandatory air bags as a safety restraint in automobiles. In attempting to determine whether to pass such a law, legislators were particularly influenced by information provided by automobile manufacturers (whose data indicated that air bags were costly, would reduce fuel economy, and would not substantially reduce overall injury levels in automobile collisions). This critical information, from a highly interested party to the decision, was an important rationale behind the refusal of Congress to require air bags (Reppy 1984). Later in the decade, a barrage of counterinformation from another powerful interest group, the insurance industry, persuaded Congress and the public that air bags could save lives and lower insurance premiums. This resulted in laws requiring air bags.

In many countries, as the scale of government and the reach of public policy have expanded, many organizations in society need detailed, insider information about what the government is doing or intends to do that might affect their organization. Thus, Salisbury (1990; Salisbury et al. 1991) has concluded that American interest groups in Washington, D.C., now spend more time gathering information *from* the government that is relevant to their organizations' interests (e.g., changes in rules or laws) than they do providing information *to* the government that might influence its policies.

Cooperation.   Major interest groups can also exert influence through their compliance or noncompliance with the government policy process. In many countries, government actors understand that successful policy implementation is enhanced when they develop policies that are acceptable to the affected interest groups. There are many countries (especially industrial democracies such as France, Japan, South Korea, and Sweden) in which government cultivates a special relationship with the interest group representatives of major economic organizations, such as business, labor, and farmers. When such interest groups can help the government implement policy, they enjoy a privileged position. Governance based on close cooperation with major sectorial interest groups is termed "corporatism" (see Box 8.3). For example, the British ministry responsible for agriculture and food works closely with the interest group representing the food manufacturers so that the manufacturers, rather than the government bureaucracy, take most responsibility for inspecting and monitoring food hygiene (Wilson 1991). Obviously, an organization benefits greatly when its interest group persuades the government to allow the organization to regulate itself.

Constraints on a Group's Behavior

Each interest group must decide what mix of activities is most likely to serve its political agenda. This mix depends on many things, including the nature of the group's political resources, the objectives it pursues, and the political environment in which it operates.

Political resources.   A group's **political resources** are *those elements, controlled by the group, that can influence the decisions and actions of political actors.* The political resources that are most effective can differ according to the situation and the political system. The previous section emphasized the impact of financial resources and information, but certain other political resources can also be influential: control of factors of production, social status, legality, special knowledge or skills, ability to mobilize large numbers of people (who are the source of demands or supports), capacity for social disruption, and access to decision makers. Various groups will usually have dramatically different levels of such resources. An interest group's behavior will depend on the kinds of resources it has available and its calculation of the costs and benefits associated with using a particular mix of resources.

Objectives.   The *objectives* that interest groups pursue in the political world are as diverse as the different policy issues upon which the government might act. One group might want one specific thing, such as a subsidy for growing wheat, while another group might have very broad objectives, such as a set of policies to eliminate poverty. The groups' strategies and the probability that they will be successful are each related to the nature of the groups' political objectives. In general, an interest group is advantaged to the extent that its objective (1) is quite similar to existing policy and (2) is a value allocation that the political system has the capacity to make. For example, the Greenpeace groups in France and Germany are more likely to influence government policies on safer disposal of nuclear wastes than they are to stop the development of new nuclear power stations, and these groups have little capacity to achieve their goal of worldwide nuclear disarmament.

Political environment.   At the most basic level, the demands that groups can make and the actions in which they can engage depend on the boundaries of acceptable political action within the particular *political environment.* Every example of interest group action given thus far in this chapter has focused on a group operating in a democratic political system. An essential feature of democratic systems is that interest groups have quite extensive rights to make political demands and engage in political actions.

In democracies such as Great Britain, Italy, and Japan, professional representatives of interest groups (lobbyists) are as much a part of the accepted set of governmental actors as elected legislators and their staffs. In Japan, it is common for senior government officials to "descend from heaven" (*amakudari*) to a high-paying lobbyist's job for a major corporate interest. In the United States, more than 17,000 active, full-time professional lobbyists work in Washington, DC (Steele 1999), and one analyst contends that the total number of people engaged primarily in lobbying activities is more than 80,000 (that is, more than 140 professional lobbyists per member of Congress) (Birnbaum 1993).

In contrast, repressive political systems tolerate only a very narrow range of interest group activities that are in opposition to the leadership. Such groups, especially their leaders, usually face extensive harassment and punishment from the authorities. Nonetheless, groups periodically emerge to articulate demands for political, social, and economic changes. Occasionally, the state responds positively to these demands. Some interest groups are eventually granted a major role in the political process. This happened in South Africa to the African National Congress, which began in 1912 as an interest group to promote the human rights of black Africans, was later a government opposition movement, then an outlawed violent protest group (in 1961); finally it became the country's major political party whose leaders (Nelson Mandela and Thabo Mbeki) have been elected presidents of the country. Other groups have successfully engaged in a combination of political violence and mass mobilization to overthrow the existing regime, as did the Sandinistas in Nicaragua in 1979.

In general however, one of the key features of a repressive political system is its capacity to stifle or crush opposition interest groups. Such groups therefore operate on the margins of the political system, ranging from small revolutionary cells such as FARC in Columbia to mass movements such as the democracy demonstrations in China in 1989.

Types of Interest Groups

Gabriel Almond proposed a relatively simple and widely accepted taxonomy of four types of political groups (Almond et al. 2004): (1) associational, (2) institutional, (3) nonassociational, and (4) anomic.

Associational interest groups.   The first type, the **associational interest group**, is organized specifically to further the political objectives of its members. One example is the British Medical Association (see Box 3.1). Another example is Common Cause, an American interest group whose citizen-members pay a membership fee to support the lobbying activities of a central staff. The leadership of Common Cause identifies political issues of significance to the group's members and then attempts to mobilize political action (such as letter-writing campaigns and press releases) in support of a particular position on the issue. The group also provides decision makers with information and data and contributes funds to some political candidates.

Institutional interest groups.   This type of group has been formed to achieve goals other than affecting the political system but also acts to seek political objectives. Most occupational and organizational groups recognize that the decisions of the political system sometimes have major impacts on their own interests. Thus they have a formal or informal subunit whose primary purpose is to represent the group's interests to the political system. For example, the University of California is a large institution of higher education, but its interests are strongly affected by local, state, and national policies on educational funding, research funding, regulation of research, discrimination in admissions and hiring, tax law, patent law, collective bargaining, and many other policies. Consequently, the university has full-time professional and student lobbyists on each campus, in Sacramento (the state capital), and in Washington, DC.

BOX 3.1

The British Medical Association: An Effective Associational Interest Group

The British Medical Association (BMA), a professional organization for doctors in Great Britain, exists primarily to provide technical and professional information to member doctors and to protect the standards and practices of the medical profession on matters of education, training, qualifications to practice, and discipline in instances of malpractice.

The BMA is a good example of an effective associational interest group because, in protecting the professional and financial interest of its members, its professional staff and members take many actions to influence the policies of the British government regarding the health care system. Some of the policies of obvious interest to the member doctors are those concerning training of doctors, pay issues, client choice of doctors and hospitals, and the quality and quantity of medical facilities.

The BMA also is concerned about public policies regarding such issues as advertising by professionals, judicial rulings on liability, personal and business taxation policies, certification of health care paraprofessionals (e.g., chiropractors), support for medical research, and so on.

Given the wealth of its members, the BMA can contribute substantial amounts of money to influence policy makers directly or to finance public information campaigns. Its members command respect from political actors because of the doctors' high status and social standing. The BMA is also a source of vast information and expertise about health care issues for those public officials who must formulate and implement health care policy. But the BMA's greatest leverage on political actors is its capacity to cooperate or withhold cooperation, since it can powerfully influence the extent to which most doctors support the nationalized health care system in Britain. Thus the British Ministry of Health works extremely closely with the BMA, as the interest group representing most doctors, in all public policy decisions relevant to health care.

Nonassociational interest groups.   These groups are fluid aggregates of individuals who are not explicitly associated with a permanent organizational entity but who share some common interest regarding certain issues and become politically active on an issue. A loosely structured organization might temporarily emerge to plan and coordinate political activities, but the group will be temporary and relatively informal and, once the issue has lost its immediate salience, the group will disappear. If an interest group emerges in your community to stop a building development, or to recall a public official, or to promote a particular law, it can be categorized as a nonassociational interest group.

Anomic interest groups.   These groups are short-lived, spontaneous aggregations of people who share a political concern. What defines an anomic interest group is a group political action that emerges with little or no planning and then quickly stops after the action is completed. For Almond, a riot is the clearest example of this type of interest group—the participants tend to share a common set of political interests or grievances that they express through a generally disorganized outpouring of emotion, energy, and violence. A political demonstration is a somewhat more organized version of anomic interest group activity.

POLITICAL PARTIES

An interest group is transformed into a **political party** when *the group attempts to capture political power directly by placing its members in governmental office.* The political party is the broadest linkage institution in most political systems because most parties are overarching organizations that incorporate many different interests and groups. While countries can have thousands of political interest groups, most have only a handful of political parties.

Activities of Political Parties

There are six broad activities, or functions, fulfilled by political parties in most countries: They (1) serve as brokers of ideas, (2) serve as agents of political socialization, (3) link individuals to the system, (4) mobilize and recruit activists, (5) coordinate governmental activities, and (6) serve as organized sources of opposition to the governing group.

Serving as brokers of ideas.   The first, most central activity of political parties is to serve as major brokers of political ideas. Many individuals and political groups have interests and demands regarding the policies of government. A crucial function of political parties is to aggregate and simplify these many demands into a few packages of clear alternatives. To the extent that political parties are effective in this activity, they dramatically reduce the complexity and scale of the political process for the decision maker, who must perceive and respond to the individual and group demands, and for the voter, who must select political leaders whose overall policy preferences are closest to his own.

While all political parties are brokers of ideas, parties can be differentiated into two broad categories—ideological and pragmatic—on the basis of their intensity of commitment toward those ideas. *Ideological parties* hold major programmatic goals (e.g., egalitarianism, ethnic solidarity, Islamic fundamentalism) and are deeply committed to the implementation of these goals to achieve comprehensive changes in the sociopolitical order. Ideological parties are usually extreme within the context of their particular political culture. The Islamic Salvation Front in Algeria, the North Korean Communist Party, Sínn Fein in Northern Ireland, the American Libertarian Party, and the German Green Party (see Box 3.2) are examples of ideological parties.

In contrast, *pragmatic parties* hold more flexible goals and are oriented to moderate or incremental policy change. To achieve electoral success, pragmatic parties might shift their position or expand the range of viewpoints they encompass. Parties of the center are characteristically pragmatic parties. Examples include the Christian Democrats in Germany, the Congress-I Party in India, the Institutional Revolutionary Party (PRI) in Mexico, and the Democratic Party in the United States.

Facilitating political socialization.   A related activity of political parties is their socialization of people into the political culture (see Chapter 4). In many political systems, most people develop a clear "party identification." This means that a person trusts one political party to represent his political interests. The person's political beliefs and actions are influenced by information that a political party provides or by the person's perceptions of what the party supports. Even if a person does not have strong party identification, political parties can be an important source of his political knowledge.

 # BOX 3.2

Let's Party! The Rise of the Green Party in Germany

Few political interest groups transform into successful, modern political parties. The Green Party in Germany seems to have achieved this transformation. It began as a diverse set of loosely affiliated interest groups and declared itself a political party in 1980. Its electoral fortunes in the national legislature have gone up (27 seats in 1983, 42 seats in 1986) and down (zero seats in 1990) and then up again (49 seats in 1994, 47 seats in 1998, and 55 seats in 2002).

Where did the Green Party come from? Like all political groups, it began with people who wanted to influence politics. There were people in West Germany who were displeased by their government's policies in the late 1960s, especially the West German government's support of U.S. actions in Vietnam and Southeast Asia.

But some West Germans were also concerned about other political issues. For these people, their government, and the entire "establishment" in their society, had been corrupted in its quest for ever-expanding power and wealth. Some were angered by the huge inequalities in wealth and welfare within their society and between countries. Some disliked the discrimination against certain groups, such as women and ethnic minorities. Some were fearful that the huge buildup of nuclear weapons by the superpowers would result in war in Europe. And some felt that the quest for material well-being and the thoughtless use of new technologies were taking a huge toll on the quality of the environment.

In the late 1960s, these antiestablishment sentiments appeared in most industrial democracies. Often, as in Germany, "leftists" and students were most visible and active in expressing these political views. They demonstrated, they marched, they formed protest groups—they tried all forms of political action that might reduce the political failures they saw. In contrast to most other countries, however, the politically disaffected West Germans did not disappear from politics with the end of the Vietnam War period. Energized mainly by young, countercultural Germans, small citizen groups emerged in many German towns.

These citizen groups continued to press policy makers at all levels to respond to the major political issues noted above, and they criticized the existing political parties for their failure to deal effectively with the problems. By the late 1970s, these

BOX **3.2** (CONTINUED)

groups moved from protest politics to electoral politics and began to elect some of their members to local office, especially in larger cities. Some of the most dynamic people in these local groups developed a national network. They decided that the objectives shared by the local groups could be best promoted by the formation of a single, national political organization. After several conventions, representatives of more than 1,000 of the local groups agreed in 1980 to form a national political party, Die Grünen (the Greens). (This discussion is based on Mewes 1987.)

The common concern that holds together the many individuals in the Green Party is a commitment to preserving the environment. Thus most Germans initially viewed the new party as an environmental party, and it drew support from the right, center, and left of the traditional German political spectrum. Its electoral support in the national elections of 1982 and 1986 came particularly from younger voters and from the more educated, middle classes. In Europe the Greens are viewed as the first important party representing the "postmaterialist values" discussed in Chapter 2.

The Green Party is an ideological party, but it is now composed of people with quite diverse ideological concerns. The core activists in both the local groups and the national party tend to be radical in their politics. Thus the platform of the Green Party includes strong antiestablishment elements. The party ideology emphasizes the transformation of Germany from capitalism to a system in which workers own and control industry; from a militaristic, NATO-based country to one that becomes neutral, eliminates nuclear weapons, and stops preparing for war; and from a leading postindustrial society to one that uses only those technologies that do not damage the environment.

The Green Party had substantial impact on German politics in the 1980s but struggled for electoral support in the early 1990s. It then became a somewhat uneasy junior partner in a governing coalition with the large Social Democratic Party after both the 1998 and 2002 elections, currently with 55 of the 603 seats in the Bundestag. Despite its resurgence, the future of the Green Party at the national level remains uncertain. Will major parties, especially the Social Democratic Party, capture the Green's electoral base by effectively promoting moderate environmental protection policies? Can it avoid self-destruction caused by the strong ideological differences among its moderate and its more radical factions? Some analysts suggest that this party is too wild to last much longer.

Linking individual and system.   In its role as a linkage institution, a political party connects individuals and the political system. Most individuals rely on political groups to represent their interests within the political system. More than other groups, political parties function in a general manner to formulate, aggregate, and communicate a coherent package of demands and supports. And, if the party gains political power, it can attempt to implement those demands on behalf of the individuals whose interests it serves. Thus political parties greatly facilitate the individual's sense of integration into the political process.

Mobilizing and recruiting political activists.   The political party offers a well-organized and obvious structure within which a person can direct his political interests. It is a source of political information, of contact with other politically relevant individuals and groups, and of effective access to the political system. In many political systems, involvement with a political party is the primary mechanism through which individuals are drawn into roles as political foot soldiers and, ultimately, as political leaders. Often it is political parties that select the candidates for political positions or have the power to place people directly in positions within the political system. Whether one is considering a highly democratic polity such as Great Britain or an extremely nondemocratic one such as China, most or all individuals in key executive and legislative positions have achieved these positions through recruitment and selection by a political party.

Coordinating governmental operations.   The fifth major activity of political parties is to coordinate the actions of the government. The political party can encourage or require its members to work together to achieve shared policy goals. It can establish an internal hierarchy, with party leaders (e.g., in the U.S. Senate, majority and minority leaders, whips, committee chairs) controlling the actions of the party

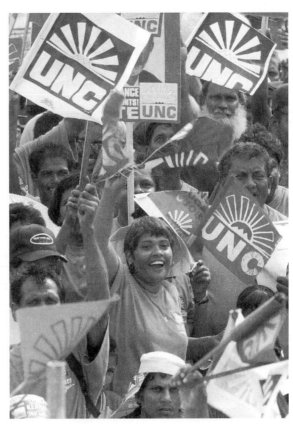

Mobilizing citizens into political action is one important function of political parties, as in this rally for the United National Congress Party in Trinidad.

members in the conduct of government. The parties can also provide mechanisms for facilitating cooperation and regulating conflict among different parties. Leaders of several parties might form a coalition in order to secure majority support for certain policies. Such coalitions are especially important in legislatures in which no single party commands a majority. Political parties can also establish forms of power sharing in the conduct of government business. For example, the parties can agree to formulate executive or legislative committees in a manner that reflects the political strength of the various parties.

Serving as sources of opposition.   Finally, where the political system has more than one party, the parties not participating in the governing group can serve as an explicit and organized source of opposition. The function is most fully institutionalized in Great Britain, where the major out-of-power party in Parliament is explicitly designated as "Her Majesty's Loyal Opposition." The party should oppose, but never obstruct, the actions of the governing party, since the opposition party remains loyal to crown and country. In Britain, the opposition party is guaranteed control of a specified amount of time during legislative sessions. The opposition leaders receive salaries to serve as a "shadow government," with a member of the opposition serving as the alternative, and potential future replacement, for each top official in the government. Hence there is a "shadow prime minister," a "shadow minister of defense," and so on, who articulate what they would do if they held ministerial positions as the governing party.

DOING POLITICS

Politics comes alive when people engage in political action. The participation in a protest march, the attempt to persuade a friend to share your political perspective, even the act of voting can be a moment of heightened experience. Acting alone or with others, the individual who takes political action can seek to serve his own most crass self-interest or the altruistic goal of global prosperity.

This analysis has indicated the diverse modes of political action as well as the rather modest levels of such actions reported by most people. Some people are shocked that so many citizens do not even bother to vote in a country such as the United States. Others are surprised that anyone really thinks that one person's involvement in politics, whatever the level of commitment, will make any difference in the grander scheme of things. Political participation is a crucial topic for analysis because people's actions are at the heart of the political process.

In this chapter, you have been introduced to the methods and findings of micropolitical analysis. Could you undertake such an analysis yourself? Yes! Before you conclude this chapter, Box 3.3 shows you how you might do it by studying your own peers.

To this point in the book, our treatment of micropolitics has focused mainly on description and taxonomy—on what people believe about politics and on what political actions people are prepared to undertake. For a richer analysis, however, we must at least attempt to answer the *why* questions: Why do people engage in a particular political action? Can we explain the apparent differences in people's political beliefs? Explaining political beliefs and actions is the essential issue in Chapter 4.

BOX 3.3

Measuring Students' Political Behavior: An Example of Micropolitical Analysis

Let us consider how you might study the political participation of American college students. Do you consider yourself an active participant in the political world? How many of the actions listed in Table 3.1 have you engaged in during the last three years? How might you assess whether most college students are politically active? Using the methods of survey research, you might begin to analyze your own or others' political activity level. Here are the key steps:

1. *Conceptualizing variables.* Our objective is to describe and explain college students' political participation. The first task of such an analysis is conceptualization. This entails developing a set of concepts that clarify and elaborate on the basic idea(s) that you wish to analyze. Table 3.1 provides one useful framework for conceptualizing various modes of political participation (e.g., voting, rioting, contacting officials).

2. *Operationalizing variables.* Once you have decided which modes of participation you will study, you need to specify them more carefully so that you can delimit those instances where the activities have actually occurred. This process is called the operationalization of variables. You indicate in detail how key concepts are identified and measured in actual research settings. Operationalization of variables must be done with care and often is more complicated than it initially seems. For example, in operationalizing the concept of voting, do you want to distinguish between voting in national elections and in local elections, as Verba and Nie (1975) did? Do you want to determine the proportion of elections in which the person voted? Do you want to distinguish between those who are and are not registered to vote? Notice that many such questions merit consideration when you attempt to operationalize a major political variable. You must make these decisions before you gather data, or you will not get all the information necessary for your analysis.

3. *Data collection.* Once you have defined your operational indicators, the next activity is to collect data. This step entails identifying the population (the set of subjects) you wish to study and developing a strategy to gather empirical data that measure your key variables for all or some sample of this population. Assume that the population for your study is the students at your college (notice that this is an extremely limited sample for generalizations about all college students).

Typically, it is not feasible to gather data for everyone in the group about whom the analyst wishes to generalize, and so a procedure is developed to sample a subset of the group. This can be done by gathering data for anyone who is willing to respond, by selecting people at random, or by devising a more sophisticated sampling strategy that ensures adequate representation of certain key characteristics among those studied (e.g., age, gender, ethnicity, socioeconomic class, region). This

BOX **3.3** (CONTINUED)

last strategy for sampling is normally used by professional public opinion pollsters and by political scientists. The idea is to gather data from a subset that reflects the most interesting characteristics of the larger population.

In your study, you might not have time to gather data for all the students at your college (and certainly not all college students in America), so you might randomly select 1 out of every 50 students in the student directory to serve as your sample. It would be simpler to study the students in your political science class, but consider why a study of your political science class is likely to be more biased than a study of the sample from the student directory.

The next problem is deciding how to collect data about each student's actual political behavior. Since you cannot observe the behavior of all students, you would probably have to settle for asking them to report their own political activity through some form of personal interview or questionnaire. To elicit accurate responses about the political actions you are interested in studying, you need an approach that encourages the respondent to answer honestly, with careful wording of the questions and precise recording of the responses.

4. *Data analysis: creating variables.* Once you have gathered the data, you must organize them in the forms that enable you to manipulate the data in various ways to answer your analytic questions. You can merely do analysis based on each student's response to each question. Often, however, the analyst wants to categorize or summarize the specific responses into broader variables.

For example, you might create a taxonomy of types of participants, based on the student's set of political activities or frequency of activities. You could use nine modes of action based on the nine actor types listed in Table 3.1, counting the number of different modes in which a person had done something (during a specified time period). By this technique, each student would have a "political action score" ranging from 0 to 8. But you might decide that such a scoring system provides too little differentiation because it gives equal value to types of political activity that are quite different in effort and political importance. A more sensitive measure might give a different *weight* to each political action, on the basis of its relative significance—for example, 10 points for protest behavior, 3 for partisan activity, 2 for voting, and so on. By summing such weighted scores for each subject of study, you could create an *index* that measures each subject's overall political activity more precisely.

Even more refinements could be added by the inclusion of additional data, such as the frequency with which each activity is undertaken. Most contemporary political analyses attempt to develop these more complex variables because such measures allow for rich findings and generalizations.

Notice that virtually all the decisions in the analysis, and especially those about measurement and variable creation, are made by you—the individual political analyst. There are no fixed rules regarding these decisions, although they are not arbitrary. The analyst must attempt to make decisions that are reasonable in terms of

(continued)

BOX **3.3** (CONTINUED)

the analytic issues being considered and that are defensible, since others might question these decisions in the spirit of the scientific method.

5. *Data analysis: description and explanation.* With your data and variables, you can now *describe* the political behavior of college students in your study. Some of the questions you might examine include the following:

> What are the most frequent political behaviors that the students undertake?
>
> How frequently do the students discuss politics?
>
> What percentage are politically apathetic?
>
> What percentage have participated in political rallies?

As you will find in Chapter 4, political analysts are rarely satisfied with answers to these kinds of descriptive questions. Whenever possible, they also attempt to generate more *explanatory* (correlational or causal) statements that search for general patterns among the behaviors or indicate the conditions that seem to cause certain types of political behavior to occur. To do this in your study, you might gather such additional data about your respondents as their personal traits, background experiences, and political beliefs. Then you might be able to offer tentative answers to such questions as these:

> Do students who discuss politics more frequently also have higher grade point averages?
>
> Are older students more politically active than younger students?
>
> Is political protest more common among social science majors than among science majors?
>
> Is partisan activism correlated with parents' income level?
>
> Is ethnicity associated with interest in politics?

As you can see, there are many fascinating questions that you can examine as you become a more insightful political analyst. For example, are college students different politically from young people who do not attend college? It would be even more interesting to examine these questions across different cultures: For example, what are the similarities and differences in the political behavior of students in China, France, Mexico, Kenya, Poland, and the United States? As political scientists gather more extensive databases and use more refined analytic techniques, they can begin to develop stronger generalizations about the nature and causes of political beliefs and actions.

KEY CONCEPTS

extremist-activists (pg 54)
foot soldiers (pg 54)
ideological party (pg 67)
interest group (four types) (pg. 65)
political activism

political environment
political participation (pg 52)
political party (pg. 67)
pragmatic party

FOR FURTHER CONSIDERATION

1. Why and how might the absence of a political action be viewed as an act of political participation?
2. Apart from voting, what political action do you think is most important?
3. Imagine that you could engage in a conversation with the political activist, contemporary or historical, who most fascinates you. Whom would you choose? Why? What would you ask him or her?
4. Should there be any limits on people's rights to join political groups and to act to influence political decision makers? What principles can you offer to justify any such limitations?
5. What is the most extensive political action in which you have engaged? If the same circumstances arose now, would you behave any differently? Why?

FOR FURTHER READING

Ackerman, Peter, and Jack DuVall. (2001). *A Force More Powerful: A Century of Non-Violent Conflict.* New York: Palgrave. A series of engaging case studies set in many countries (e.g., Chile, Denmark, Poland, Serbia) reveals how political activism grounded in strategies of nonviolence (e.g., strikes, protests, boycotts) has achieved major political change in the face of repressive regimes and dictatorial leaders.

Brown, Michael, and John May. (1989). *The Greenpeace Story.* Scarborough, Ontario: Prentice-Hall. The fascinating history of an international group committed to fighting governments and huge corporations in order to protect the environment, but even more, a revealing study of its activist leaders.

Florini, Ann, Ed. (2000). *The Third Force: The Rise of Transnational Civil Society.* Washington, D.C.: Carnegie Endowment for International Peace. Interesting studies of the impacts of global citizen activists—groups whose members and activities cross national boundaries as they strive to alter state policies on such important issues as nuclear nonproliferation, human rights, sustainable development, and corruption.

Genovese, Michael A., Ed. (1993). *Women as National Leaders.* Newbury Park, CA: Sage. Detailed and interesting case studies of recent female political leaders, such as Corazon Aquino, Benazir Bhutto, Violeta Chamorro, Indira Gandhi, and Margaret Thatcher, assessing their leadership styles and whether they seem to govern differently than men.

Hoffman, Abbie. (1989). *The Best of Abbie Hoffman.* New York: Four Walls, Eight Windows. A selection of the funny, irreverent writings on radicalism and revolution by one of the key leaders (now deceased) of the student radical movement of the late 1960s and a member of the "Chicago 7," tried for conspiracy after the riots at the 1968 Democratic Party convention in Chicago.

Lowi, Theodore. (1979). *The End of Liberalism: The Second Republic in the United States.* 2d ed. New York: Norton. An incisive critique of the shortcomings of politics dominated by interest groups.

Ma Bo. (1995). *Blood Red Sunset: A Memoir of the Chinese Cultural Revolution.* New York: Viking. A harsh, gripping autobiography of a young person drawn into the fervor of Mao Zedong's Cultural Revolution. A Red Guard working on a hopeless program to create farmland in Mongolia, Ma Bo is transformed from a true believer into an embittered man fighting to clear himself from charges that he is a reactionary.

Meyer, David S., and Sidney Tarrow, Eds. (1997). *The Social Movement Society: Contentious Politics for a New Century.* Lanham, MD: Rowman & Littlefield. A stimulating set of essays examining the increasing acceptance of "social movements"—organized group social protest activities that are typically focused on a single issue area. Based on analyses in Western and Eastern Europe, Latin America, and the United States, there is an assessment of whether such protest is becoming a routine part of political participation and whether it has implications for democratic society.

Rueschemeyer, Dietrich, Marilyn Rueschemeyer, and Bjorn Wittrock. (1998). *Participation and Democracy East and West: Comparisons and Interpretations.* Armonk, NY: M. E. Sharpe. The current patterns of participation and activism are compared and analyzed, grounded in studies of the Czech Republic, Germany, Hungary, Norway, Poland, Sweden, and the United States.

Stern, Jessica. (2003). *Terror in the Name of God: Why Religious Militants Kill.* New York: Harper Collins. Based on detailed interviews with many terrorists, the author offers an interesting and accessible analysis of the psychology of terrorists and the nature of terrorist organizations, focusing mainly on Muslims, but also discussing Christian and Jewish terrorists.

Volgy, Thomas J. (1999). *Politics in the Trenches: Citizens, Politicians and the Fate of Democracy.* Tucson, AZ: University of Arizona Press. A political science professor offers a brief, highly readable and revealing description of the challenges and actual experiences of political leaders in American local politics, based on his many years as a local government elected official and his interviews with more than 300 elected officials.

Wilson, Graham K. (1990). *Interest Groups.* Oxford, England: Basil Blackwell. An introduction to the comparative study of interest groups.

ON THE WEB

http://www.politics1.com/parties.htm
This site offers a directory and description of U.S. political parties.

http://www.ifex.org
The International Freedom of Expression Exchange represents more than fifty groups committed to human rights and civil liberties and describes current situations of concern.

http://www.greenpeace.org
Greenpeace's web site describes some of the key initiatives taken by this global, action-oriented interest group.

http://www.protest.net/

Protest.net provides a comprehensive calendar of upcoming protests and political rallies taking place around the world. The site lists upcoming protests by both geographic region and political issue.

http://www.internationalanswer.org/

This web site serves as the electronic home of International ANSWER, an antiwar coalition. This electronic portal provides a wealth of information in regards to antiwar movements taking place throughout the international community.

http://www.wsu.edu/~amerstu/smc/smcframe.html

This site, developed by Washington State University, provides a number of links and articles related to both American and global social movements.

http://www.amnesty.org/

Amnesty International has been dedicated to human rights causes for well over forty years. The site provides information on a variety of topics ranging from refugees to arms control.

North Korean schoolgirls sweep the memorial to Kim Il Sung (1912–1994) to reinforce their respect for the "Eternal Leader" of their country.

CHAPTER 4 Influences on Beliefs and Actions

A friend who is skeptical about political science confronts you with a challenge. She brings three adults into the room and announces that one is an elected public official, one has never voted in a single election, and one has participated in many violent political protests. You must decide who has done what. You can ask each person two questions that make neither a direct nor an indirect reference to the three kinds of political behavior. How would you try to solve the problem? What questions would you ask?

In Chapters 2 and 3, we *described* people's political beliefs and political actions. Some of the most interesting questions in political analysis concern the *why* questions: Why do individuals hold particular political beliefs and engage in certain political actions? Figure 4.1 indicates four broad types of explanatory factors that might account for individual political behavior: (1) the environment, (2) agents of political socialization, (3) personal characteristics, and (4) personality and human nature. This chapter considers these four types of influences on the political beliefs and actions of individuals, from the apathetics to the activists. Thus it provides ideas about the kinds of clues that might help you respond to your friend's challenge.

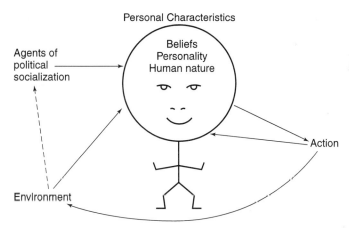

FIGURE 4.1   A framework for explaining individual political behavior

THE ENVIRONMENT

In a major election in Cuba in 2003, it was reported that 96 percent of the adults voted, whereas in the United States, only about 51 percent of the citizens voted in the 2000 national election. What best accounts for this difference? In Cuba, voting is an obligatory act, a required gesture of support for the current political leadership, rather than a genuine selection among candidates—indeed, there is no choice. Most Cubans vote because a comrade who does not vote risks unwanted scrutiny by Communist Party authorities. In the United States, voting has always been a voluntary act, and there are no sanctions for nonvoting. Thus the citizen decides whether her sense of civic responsibility or her desire to affect the outcome on ballot choices merits the effort of going to vote. Box 4.1 suggests why, from the perspective of rational choice theory, citizens might choose not to vote.

The example of voting in Cuba and the United States is suggestive of how a person's *environment*—the broad context in which an individual lives—can powerfully

 ## BOX 4.1

Are You Too Smart to Vote?

You know that you ought to vote in a democracy so that you can help determine policies and political leaders. However, a logical argument can be made that if you are truly rational, you will not vote.

Many formal theories in political science are grounded in the approach called "rational choice theory," or "public choice theory" (see the Appendix). This theory assumes that political actors are rational and calculating. They can establish the costs and benefits to themselves of each outcome, and they can select the most rational strategy to maximize the benefits relative to the costs. If you have studied microeconomics, you might recognize that this description is rather like the "economic man," another version of this rational actor.

From a rational choice perspective, you would be foolish to vote in a presidential election. The costs associated with voting are, at least, the time and energy you expend to register, to get to the polling place, to cast your ballot, and to get to the next place you want to go. You could also consider the time and energy spent trying to understand which candidates will establish certain policies and to calculate how you will benefit from each likely policy. Even if you cannot think of things you would rather do with all that time and energy, the benefits side of the calculation is more daunting. Assume that you are smart enough to decide which candidate will actually enact policies that benefit you. As a rational actor, you still must ask: What is the chance that my vote will make a difference? In U.S. national elections, about 100 million votes are cast for the presidency. The probability that there will be a tie so that one vote (yours or anybody else's) will determine the outcome is infinitesimally small—certainly less than one in a trillion. So what is the point of voting?

Since their theory assumes rational behavior, rational choice theorists need to explain why about 100 million folks are behaving irrationally. This is what such theorists call the "paradox of participation" (Riker and Ordeshook 1973). (Of course,

BOX **4.1** (CONTINUED)

they could point to the 100 million people who do not vote and suggest that about half of the population *is* rational.) Why do people vote?

One argument is that your vote matters as part of the set of votes from a larger group that shares your interests. If everyone in your group acted rationally, the loss of the total set of votes might be large enough to affect the outcome of the election.

A second argument is that the rationality of voting does increase somewhat in an election in which few votes are cast or in which you think the outcome will be close. This is occasionally true in local elections, where the margin between candidates can be rather small. Recent national elections in the United States have also been characterized by some very close races. In 1998, for example, Harry Reid, the victor for the Nevada senate seat, received only 459 votes more than John Ensign out of more than 415,000 votes cast. In 1994, a Connecticut seat in the House of Representatives was determined by less than 10 votes out of more than 158,000! And the Florida vote in 2000 revealed that the difference of only a few hundred votes *can* actually determine the American presidency.

A third kind of argument is that most people are not rational calculators. They make many decisions in their lives (e.g., whether to marry, whether to enroll in a class, whether to drive very fast) without any clear idea of the precise costs and benefits to them.

And a fourth argument is that voting is primarily an expression of citizenship, social solidarity, and political communication. In this view, you might vote because you love your country and its democratic tradition, or because you want to be a small part of a large voice saying yes or no to political leaders, or because you want approval from your peers.

In short, the decision to vote can be based on some elements of self-interest or civic commitment. But if you are very rational and very selfish, voting should probably be rather low on your agenda.

influence her political behavior. In its most comprehensive form, the environment includes literally everything outside the individual. It obviously includes political elements (e.g., governmental procedures, public policies, specific political events and actors), but it also includes elements of the social and cultural system (e.g., religious foundations, attitudes toward such characteristics as ethnicity, gender, and class), elements of the economic order (e.g., level of economic prosperity and development), and the physical features of the environment (e.g., topography, natural resources). For some analytic questions, it might also be important to distinguish between the environment as measured "objectively" by the analyst and the environment perceived "subjectively" by the individual who is attempting to understand and act in the political world.

For any particular political belief or action, there are various possible effects from an environmental stimulus. An element of the environment might activate, repress, transform, or amplify a person's political behavior. Most elements of the environment are likely to have little or no effect at any given moment, so the task of the political analyst is to identify those few environmental elements that do have especially significant effects on political belief or action and to explain how these effects occur.

Since the environmental context is, at least in theory, of enormous scope, it is helpful to consider different aspects of the way that the environment might affect political behavior: political, social, cultural, economic, and physical. First, here are two examples regarding the *political environment:*

1. *Effects on information about politics.* In Sierra Leone, information about politics is so limited that a villager might not be sure whether the most recent government coup has been successful and who the current political leaders are. In the United States, the politically interested citizen has access each day to hundreds of hours of television and radio and has available even more reading materials and Internet sites with information about worldwide political events.

2. *Effects on individuals' political party involvement.* From the late 1940s to the late 1980s, Romania had only one legal political party, the Communist Party. Party membership, open to only about 10 percent of the population, was essential for citizens who wanted to hold political office or gain many other advantages in the society, such as quality housing (see Chapter 15). Currently, dozens of political parties are active in Romania, and more than twenty-five hold seats in the Parliament. Party membership and opportunities to run for public office are now open to all citizens. However, party membership no longer affords the various advantages that existed during the Communist period, and thus the proportion of Romanian adults who are active party members of *any* party is actually lower now under multiparty democracy than it was during communism.

Second, the broader *social, cultural, economic, and physical environments* can have more indirect but no less powerful influences on a person's political behavior than the political environment. If the dominant religion in the cultural environment has traditionally relegated women to a secondary role, as in Saudi Arabia's adherence to the Shari'a laws of Islam, it is likely that most women's involvement in politics will be quite low. If the social environment has an undercurrent of racism, as in the United Kingdom, this will affect many aspects of the political behavior of both the majority and minority racial groups.

The impact of the environment on political behavior is sometimes hard to predict. If poverty is widespread in an economic system, will this influence the probability of political rebellion? On the one hand, such poverty might produce a frustrated population who will be responsive to a revolutionary movement promising future prosperity, and it might provoke a particular person to become the leader of such a movement. On the other hand, the people might be too concerned about basic survival to have the time or energy to engage in political action.

It should be evident from these examples that there are many aspects of the environment that might influence political beliefs and actions. The analyst must be sensitive to possible environmental effects when attempting to provide an adequate explanation for a particular political behavior.

AGENTS OF POLITICAL SOCIALIZATION

Each person has a complex blend of political beliefs—of cognitive, affective, and evaluative orientations regarding political phenomena. (These three kinds of orientations were defined in Chapter 2.) Even individuals who exist in the same environment can hold very different political beliefs. Political socialization research attempts to explain the sources of individuals' political beliefs.

Political socialization can be defined as *the processes through which individuals acquire their orientations toward the political world.* An understanding of how this process works is of obvious importance not only to political analysts but also to those, especially political leaders, who wish to influence people's political beliefs and actions. Plato (c. 428–347 B.C.E.) observed that society's most important function is civic training, the instruction of citizens regarding the nature of their social and political world and of their proper roles in that world. The appropriate content and style of such political socialization is subject to debate, since one person's vision of proper civic training might be viewed by another person as indoctrination and brainwashing.

Among political scientists, the emphasis in political socialization research has been on analysis of the *agents of political socialization*—the major sources of political training and indoctrination. The key concerns have been to identify these agents and to explain the processes through which they affect individuals' political orientations. There has been considerably less attention, and very limited empirical success, in linking the activities of specific agents of socialization to individuals' actual political actions. In this section, we discuss some of the most important agents of political socialization: the family, the schools, peer groups, the media and culture, and events.

The Family

The family is the first, and often the most powerful and lasting, agent of political socialization. The political orientations of most individuals are deeply influenced by behaviors and beliefs experienced in the family environment. Before individuals are capable of making judgments for themselves, they have absorbed perceptions about the political world from conversations overheard within the family. For example, most seven-year-old children in the United States already identify with one political party and have affective orientations toward both major parties (Jennings, Markus, and Niemi 1991).

Even the pattern of interactions between parents and children can have political implications. If the family is very hierarchical, with the father or mother ruling with an iron hand, preventing discussion and using strong sanctions for disobedience, the child might assume that this is the appropriate pattern of authority relations in the society. If the family tends to discuss issues before it determines rules or decisions, the child might feel more strongly that she has the right to participate actively in decisions, even in the political world.

Some leaders have viewed the family as a major obstacle to their political agendas. For example, Mao Zedong deeply opposed the traditional loyalties taught by Confucianism, which stressed obedience to the kinship group, to elders, and to males. When he came to power in China (1949–1976), he wanted every Chinese person to accept the equality of all individuals, regardless of age or gender. He also insisted that individuals should work cooperatively for the good of everyone in the society (the key slogan was "serve the people"). Mao identified the family as the major obstacle to these goals, called the family the "citadel of oppression" in society, and experimented with attempts to eliminate the nuclear family. When these attempts failed, Communist Party members put enormous pressure on families to "revolutionize" themselves by shedding their Confucian thinking and traditional behaviors. However, because Mao was pessimistic about the extent to which families would change themselves, he relied heavily on other agents of political socialization, especially the schools and peer groups, to counter the family's influence.

The Schools

From the perspective of the political authorities, the schools can be the state's most valuable agent for political socialization. Schools offer the opportunity for sustained and highly controlled contact with youth while they are at the extremely impressionable age when many political beliefs can still be molded. Apart from the family, the classroom is the most prevalent microcosm of society that most young people experience. The teacher is the authority figure, who rewards thinking and

"I GOT RICH, DAD. WHERE DID I GO WRONG?"
NATIONAL REVIEW

Frank Cotham

behavior that conform to what is deemed desirable by the society and who with-holds rewards from or sanctions those who fail to conform. In most societies, students are taught to accept the authority of the teacher, to suppress their own desires, to value the symbolic rewards offered by the education system, and to interact with their peers in the manner approved by the school system. Moreover, in every school system, there are rituals that support the political system. These might include songs, chants, or activities that express allegiance to political leaders or symbols.

Also important in shaping the student's understanding of the political world is the school curriculum. Educational authorities can control what subjects are taught, what textbooks contain, what content is tested, and even what teachers say and do. An extreme form of this central control over education was achieved during the French Fourth Republic (1946–1958). It was said that the minister of education in Paris could look at her watch and specify exactly what chapter in what textbook the children of a certain age were studying at that moment all over France.

Every textbook and every lesson in school is selective and thus contains biases regarding what is emphasized, what is ignored, and how meaning and value are established. Sometimes the level of indoctrination seems extreme, especially to those unsympathetic with the message. Here are four examples. As you read them, try to guess what subject is being taught and the country from which each example is taken.

1. Add *not* to the following sentence: "The Iranians are brave."
2. Our forefathers believed, and we still believe today, that God himself made the diversity of peoples on earth. . . . Interracial residence and intermarriage are not only a disgrace but also forbidden by law. It is, however, not only the skin of the Betas that differs from the Alphas. The Beta stands on a much higher plane of civilization and is more developed. Betas must so live, learn, and work that we shall not sink to the cultural level of the Alphas. Only thus can the government of our country remain in the hands of the Betas.
3. Imperialism knows no other type of relations between States except domination and subjugation, the oppression of the weak by the strong. It bases international relations on abuse and threat, on violence and arbitrariness. Between January 3 and June 10, 1961, Gamma military airplanes violated Delta airspace 3 times in the month of January, 15 in February, 17 in March, 9 in April, 8 in May, and 10 in June. What was the average monthly number of violations of Delta airspace by Gamma military airplanes?
4. Which of the following descriptions of America is incorrect?:
   a. The world's leading arms-exporting country.
   b. The world's most heavily nuclear-armed country.
   c. The world's leader in chemical weapons research.
   d. The world's most peace-loving country that never once was at war with other countries.

Were you able to identify likely settings for these educational offerings? The first one is from a 2002 sixth-grade Arabic language textbook in Iraq (Robinson 2003). The second one is an excerpt from a South African textbook on race relations during the era of apartheid (1948–1988, substitute "whites" for "Betas" and "non-whites" for "Alphas") (Thompson 1966: 100). The third one is mathematics as it is framed for Cuban children (substitute "Cuban" for "Delta" and "North American" for "Gamma") (Fagen 1964: 68). And the fourth is from a 2003 history test for South Korean eighth graders (Demick 2003).

These somewhat extreme examples reflect the manner in which the political authorities can influence the content of educational materials in order to buttress the view of the political world most aligned with their own interests. While subject matter in the schools of most countries is less openly political than these examples, school systems of *every* country present materials that are supportive of that country's politics and dominant cultural norms.

Have you noticed anything odd about the use of pronouns *he* and *she* in this book? To counter the male dominance in the language of many American textbooks, I alternate masculine and feminine pronouns in odd and even chapters. If you were conscious of the "strange" use of gender references in Chapter 2 and this chapter, your reaction may be indicative of the subtle way in which your cultural norms are reinforced by language and education.

Peer Groups

Although most people absorb a large proportion of their political socialization by the time they leave the educational system, learning never stops entirely (see Box 4.2). As the importance of parents diminishes and after formal schooling ends, peer groups become an increasingly significant influence on many people's political socialization. *Peer group* is a general term that includes friends, neighbors, and colleagues, at the workplace or in clubs and organizations.

The section on "'Everyone' as Authority" in Chapter 1 suggests the attraction of bringing one's views into closer conformity with those of relevant peer groups. In general, a person is more likely to be accepted by her peers if her beliefs and actions are consistent with those in the peer group. Also, it is possible that there is a subtle tendency for a person to be influenced by what "people like me" think. There is evidence that a person's social context (i.e., her peer groups) does modify political behavior (Agnew 2003; for contrary evidence, see Dunleavy and Husbands 1985).

In many cases, peers and others influence a person's political views via a *"two-step" communication flow* (Bennett 2003; Zaller 1992). People with greater interest and knowledge of politics absorb new information from various sources (step one). Then they relay what they have learned to others (step two), especially those in the mass public whose political beliefs are less salient and developed (recall Chapter 2). In general, direct communications from peers allow for a rich exchange of political information, since such political messages have the immediacy, credibility, and power of face-to-face interaction.

As noted earlier, under Mao Zedong, China used the peer group as a major mechanism for political socialization. Small groups on collective farms, in factories, and in other workplaces not only were required to discuss their political beliefs and actions but also were supposed to monitor the political behavior of everyone in the group. If a person's views or actions strayed from the "mass line," the group applied various types of pressure to help the person recognize and rectify her errors and return to the proper political position. If this pressure failed, more aggressive forms of peer pressure, including public ridicule (and ultimately, imprisonment), were employed to force the person to conform. In China, peer pressure reached an extreme form during the Cultural Revolution in the late 1960s. Groups of true believers in the views of Chairman Mao Zedong organized themselves as the "Red

BOX 4.2

Persistence versus Change in Political Socialization

The initial political socialization research emphasized the overwhelming importance of early socialization, from the family and from early educational experiences. According to this *lifelong persistence* interpretation, there is considerable stability in the political behavior of most people after adolescence. However, this view was challenged by evidence that political learning and attitude change do continue throughout adult life. This second interpretation emphasizes *lifelong openness* to further socialization, asserting that there is continual response to agents of socialization and only minimal lasting effects of early socialization. The idea that a person's political views can continue to change even during adult life is captured in the European saying that anyone who is not a communist at 20 has no heart and anyone who is still a communist at 40 has no head.

The current interpretation is essentially a compromise between these two extremes, the *life cycle* interpretation. In this view, persistence is the rule for political attitudes and behaviors that are learned early. However, political orientations can change as the result of the agents of political socialization, especially peer groups, and as the result of the individual's personal and social changes, especially at certain key points of development such as young adulthood (Jennings and Niemi 1981).

It is rare for people to undergo a dramatic transformation in their political thinking, but it does happen. A widely publicized instance of one person undergoing several political transformations involved 19-year-old American college student Patty Hearst. She had been raised in an extremely wealthy family, enjoying all the privileges of the upper class, and was a quiet, even dull, young woman. She had no apparent political views other than those common to her conservative, Republican background. All that changed one evening in February 1974. She was kidnapped by a radical group, locked in a closet for 55 days, and subjected to extensive physical and mental abuse and indoctrination.

In her next public appearance—robbing a bank—she had become Tania, revolutionary sister in the Symbionese Liberation Army. Tape recordings were circulated in which she denounced the "fascist ruling class" and "capitalist pigs," including her own parents, and called for a people's revolution. After a lengthy effort, law enforcement officials captured her, jailed her, and subjected her to another round of political indoctrination. Finally, she appeared in court in 1976, subdued and generally apolitical. She was convicted of bank robbery and served 23 months (of a 7-year sentence) in federal prison. President Carter commuted her sentence in February 1979. By this time, she had (again?) fallen in love with one of her jailers. She married him and now lives an apolitical life in suburbia, volunteering to social causes such as Alzheimer's disease and children with AIDS, and she published a mystery novel in 1996.

Many people were fascinated with this incredible tale of political transformations and argued about the "true story" and about which, if any, of Patty Hearst's

(continued)

BOX **4.2** (CONTINUED)

beliefs were authentic. Yet we can never fully know what another person really thinks, and in many instances, it is hard for us to be sure even of what we think ourselves. Most of us suspect what George Orwell (1949/1967) emphasized in his ominous novel *1984*—that under certain conditions of physical or psychological torture, we can be made to think we believe anything, even that we love Big Brother.

Patty Hearst as Tania

Guard" and engaged in widespread peer pressure, repression, and violence against any Chinese who did not conform to Mao's ideology (Wen 1995).

The Media and Culture

Very few of us directly experience the great majority of political phenomena about which we claim knowledge. For most adults, *the media*, especially television, radio, and the press, become the major source of political information. Dan Nimmo and James Combs (1990: xiii) argue: "Few people learn about politics through direct experience. For most persons, political realities are mediated through mass and group communication, a process that results as much in the creation, transmission, and adoption of political fantasies as it results in independently validated views of what happens." They claim that each of us creates a personal vision (a "fantasy") of political reality, based mainly on what is communicated to us by such information sources as other people, the mass media, and popular culture. Regardless of how fantastic our political visions are, it is important to understand that the media can be a crucial agent of political socialization for either stability or change.

These information sources really do *mediate* between the individual and most political reality. While most media content is not explicitly political, much of it does contain subtle information that influences how one thinks about politics and society. Exposure to television and radio is extensive in most countries. Thus the individual is bombarded with messages about values, lifestyles, and so on. While sweeping generalizations about the impacts of the media on people's political beliefs and actions are not possible, two broad observations can be offered.

First, the research generally concludes that few people absorb media information in a way that significantly changes most of their political attitudes or actions. Rather, people interpret and retain media information selectively to reinforce their existing attitudes. And many people, especially those with less sophisticated political belief systems and minimal political knowledge (Chapter 2), do not even pay much attention to the media that provide political information. The media-based information for such people often comes from a politically knowledgeable peer who, as described previously, seeks information from the media and then transmits such information to others.

Second, however, there is considerable evidence that the media are of growing importance in shaping many people's understanding of specific political phenomena. The mass media are especially significant in drawing people's attention to some political phenomena rather than to others—a situation termed *agenda setting*. Also, a person can absorb the overall tone and key themes in the media coverage of the issue, influencing her reactions to it (Iyengar 1994).

For most people, the media have their greatest impact during situations of political drama (e.g., war, major political crises, elections). Newspapers are still credited with the greatest effect on knowledge about politicians and issues among more educated people (Davis 1998; Graber 2001a). However, for the reasons suggested in Box 4.3, television is increasingly the mass medium with the most substantial political influence on the largest number of people. It is at least possible that for young people in high-tech countries, it will be the Internet, even more than television, that becomes a key source of political information (Center for Media Education 2001). Indeed, information and communications technologies are an increasingly rich set of media in most countries, although their political implications remain somewhat ambiguous (see Box 16.1; Bimber 2003; Becker and Slaton 2000).

As noted in Box 4.3, much of what you know about the political world from the media is contingent on what topics the media choose to expose you to and what content the media select to report. Like textbooks, the media are not neutral; someone has made selections regarding subjects and content. Of course, you are not completely passive in the process. In most countries, people can choose among alternative media sources and can attempt to evaluate the truth of what they read, hear, and see in the media.

However, in many countries, the major media are owned and controlled by the government or by members of the wealthy, dominant class in that society. The print

BOX 4.3

What You See Is What You Get

You probably have a hunch that television has become *the* most powerful form of communication now shaping peoples' political orientations. While the empirical evidence on this point is not conclusive, there are some very significant reasons why television might increasingly be such a significant force in political life.

1. *High exposure.* Citizens in both industrial countries and developing countries watch increasingly greater amounts of television each year. In the United States, for example, most adults spend as many hours with the mass media (predominantly television) as they do at work, and their children spend more hours watching television than attending school. Many other societies are also reaching these levels (Skidmore 1993). There is growing evidence that such a high level of exposure to television has an impact on a person's social and political values, even if little of the programming is explicitly political (Savage and Nimmo 1990).

2. *The power of the visual.* The biochemistry of the human brain affects the impact of television. Generally, the brain responds very strongly to visual cues, less to complex patterns of sound and imagery, and even less to written text. Moreover, visual input produces direct emotional arousal, which is the most potent neurochemical condition for learning and attitudinal change. Because the images on television are generally simple and can evoke strong emotional response, they generate visual information that is both easy to process and has a relatively high impact on learning and attitudes (Masters 1992).

3. *Agenda setting.* People's immediate views on politics are greatly influenced by what they believe to be important. Television, and especially television news, focuses on certain political issues, people, and events and not others. Most people tend to identify as significant those political topics that are "in the news," and think topics that receive little or no media coverage are not very important. Thus television increasingly sets the political agenda by establishing what issues are worthy of attention and public concern (Iyengar 1994).

4. *Priming and framing effects.* Television "primes" viewers about a political topic by providing them with information about how they should understand the topic, the kinds of information that are relevant, and the criteria that they should employ to evaluate it. Television "frames" the topic by providing viewers with a broader structure and context within which to consider it. Television generally simplifies complex issues by using specific and dramatic examples to explain a topic. For example, television news will typically examine an issue— say, poverty—by creating a visually engaging story involving specific poor people, not by emphasizing the basic societal dynamics that generate poverty. Thus television's treatment leads viewers to attribute responsibility for a political issue to the personal shortcomings of individual actors. It discourages viewers from recognizing underlying social, political, or economic forces that have created the problem and are appropriate targets for solutions (Iyengar 1994).

BOX **4.3** (CONTINUED)

Many people rely on television to provide them with information about the political world. As television directs our attention to the simple, the visual, the individual, and the evocative on only selected political topics, our ability to understand and evaluate politics in complex and subtle ways atrophies. Many researchers argue that these factors account for some of the most undesirable features of contemporary politics: the prevalence of simplistic political discourse based on sound bites, the decline of political parties, single-issue politics, negative political campaigns, and spin doctors who further distort the media's presentation of politics (Graber 2001a, 2001b; Kellner 1990; Neuman 1999). Interestingly, those currently reaching adulthood in developed countries increasingly view the Internet as the key source of information. Can you hypothesize how, if at all, this shift to the Internet will change people's political understandings?

And now we get to watch them govern

Source: TOLES © The Buffalo News. Reprinted with permission of UNIVERSAL PRESS SYNDICATE. All rights reserved.

and broadcast media are free of substantial government censorship in only about two-fifths (41 percent) of all countries, and these countries include only 20 percent of the world's population (Karlekar 2003: 12). Through its ability to control the media in the past, most governments had a significant resource for affecting people's political socialization, exposing them to "news" and information that reinforced their views of the political world. The recent explosion of telecommunications technologies (such as satellite television transmissions and the Internet) has made it increasingly difficult for a government to control all of the sources of information reaching its citizens. Consequently, most governments are becoming less effective in shaping people's political beliefs through the media, even as the media are an ever more important source of people's political "reality."

Culture offers an interesting alternative to the media and to other agents of political socialization. Culture, like the media, can be extensively controlled by the dominant political order in a society and can be used to reinforce the state's view of the political world. Cuba, like many of the communist states in the past, has generally insisted that culture must meet the standards of "socialist realism," which means that no art, theater, or cinema is to be produced that is abstract or, most importantly, that fails to celebrate the virtues of socialism, Cuban style.

Culture need not reinforce the dominant order, however. It can inform and criticize subtly, by means of metaphor and symbol, in ways less likely to be interpreted as a direct challenge to the established authorities. This is especially true in societies where there is considerable censorship of the media and state control of most sources of public information. During the 1980s, for example, an extensive body of fiction, cinema, poetry, theater, art, and music emerged with political content critical of the state's views in still-communist countries such as East Germany and Poland (Larkey 1990). Culture can also be openly subversive, directly attacking mainstream values or advocating opposing values. For example, Jamaican reggae music offers a revolutionary vision of an alternative social and political world for its people. While most contemporary Anglo-American music has little explicit political content, this kind of expression can be found in some rap music and in songs by such performers as Sting, U2, Public Enemy, and Bruce Springsteen (Coles 2003).

Events

The general effects of the environment on political beliefs and action have already been discussed. While the context of everyday life has slow, evolutionary effects on a person's political behavior, a particular event can act as a sudden and powerful agent of political socialization. For example, Sarah Brady shifted from "politician's wife" into a tireless activist on behalf of gun control legislation after her husband, James Brady, President Reagan's press secretary, was shot and paralyzed in a 1981 assassination attempt on the president. Another example of mobilization due to a dramatic event is the transformation of Micky Sadoff into a MADD activist (recall the example at the beginning of Chapter 3).

While an extraordinary event can transform a person's political behavior, it is also possible that the general flow of events during an entire period can influence political orientations, especially of individuals who "come of political age" during the period. For example, the combined impacts of such events as American military involvement in Vietnam and Southeast Asia, the hippie culture, and the Nixon presidency seem to have had strong effects on the political understanding of many Americans who were reaching adulthood during the late 1960s. And young people currently growing up in the West Bank and Gaza are deeply affected in their political beliefs and actions by the intense rhetoric and chaotic ultraviolence emanating from the Israeli government and military, the Palestinian Authority, and such groups as Hamas.

PERSONAL CHARACTERISTICS

As one part of your strategy for solving the challenge offered at the beginning of the chapter (to link the three people to specific political behavior), you might consider their physical appearance or *personal characteristics.* The research suggests that you can make some broad inferences about a person's political behavior on the basis of certain "objective" personal features. Sometimes called demographic characteristics, these include both visible characteristics, such as age, gender, and ethnicity, as well as less visible ones, such as education, income, social class, and occupation. What underlying dynamic might link personal characteristics with political behavior?

Personal characteristics can be thought of as filters that influence how the environment and the agents of political socialization affect an individual's political behavior. For example, the relevance of the environmental factor of Islamic fundamentalism will have very different effects on the political beliefs and behaviors of Saudi men and women. Similarly, the current impact of parents as agents of political socialization is likely to be far greater for their offspring of age 4 than of 64.

Much of the empirical research on political behavior attempts to establish and clarify the relationships between personal characteristics and specific political beliefs or actions. No single personal characteristic is a certain predictor of political behavior, but empirical research (based on relational analysis) in many countries indicates that some personal characteristics are associated with certain political beliefs and actions. And when key personal characteristics seem to reinforce each other, you might have greater confidence in a correct prediction about political behavior. Of particular interest to researchers (and to politicians) have been studies indicating who is more likely to vote and identifying factors that seem to explain the particular voting choice.

For example, can you think of any personal characteristics that might inform your prediction of whether a particular person voted for Bush, Gore, or Nader in the 2000 U.S. presidential election? Table 4.1 (like the example of correlational analysis in the Appendix) provides actual data for exploring those linkages. Do any personal characteristics seem associated with a tendency to vote for a candidate? In addition to comparing a particular category across candidates, another reasonable technique for assessing this question is to determine whether there are instances where the candidate's percentage for a category (e.g., high school graduates) is noticeably different from the candidate's percentage of the total vote.

While most of the differences are not dramatic, some demographic characteristics do seem to correlate with support for particular candidates. Notice, for example, that people's probability of voting for George W. Bush was substantially higher among those who had any of the following characteristics: Protestant religion, Caucasian ethnicity, and male gender (and particularly married men). People's probability of voting for Al Gore was especially high among: African-Americans, Chicano-Latinos, and Asian-Americans; women (particularly single women); those under 30 years old; those with low family income; and Jews. The people who voted for Nader were distributed somewhat more equally across most demographic categories than were those who voted for Bush or Gore, although Nader did have relatively stronger support among single men and younger voters and was relatively weak among Catholics and Jews and among all ethnicities except Caucasians.

TABLE 4.1
Voting Choices in the 2000 American Presidential Election, by Personal Characteristics

Total	% of All	Gore (49%)	Bush (48%)	Nader (3%)
Gender				
Male	48	43	54	3
Female	52	55	43	2
Gender and Marriage				
Married men	34	40	58	2
Single men	13	48	45	7
Married women	32	49	49	2
Single women	16	66	30	4
Ethnicity				
African-American	9	90	9	1
Asian-American	2	62	37	1
Caucasian	80	43	54	3
Chicano-Latino	7	61	38	1
Age				
18–29	15	54	41	5
30–44	34	46	51	3
45–64	37	51	47	2
65 and older	14	46	52	2
Education				
High school diploma or less	24	54	44	2
Some college	26	45	51	4
College degree or more	50	49	48	2
Religion				
Protestant	52	40	58	2
Roman Catholic	28	53	46	1
Jewish	4	77	22	1
Annual Family Income				
Under $20,000	10	63	33	4
$20,000–$39,999	25	51	45	4
$40,000–$59,999	23	47	51	2
$60,000–$74,999	15	48	49	3
$75,000 and over	27	46	52	2

Due to rounding, not all categories total 100%.
Source: Los Angeles Times exit poll (http://www.latimes.com/timespoll).

While there are clear associations between variables, we cannot conclude that any personal characteristic actually *caused* a person to vote for one of the three candidates (see the distinction between correlational and causal analysis in the Appendix). And when several personal characteristics are associated with voting choice, we also cannot determine which of them are the most powerful predictors of candidate choice without statistical analysis (such as regression analysis, a statistical technique that identifies how much variance in the dependent variable—vote choice, in this case—can be attributed to each subject's level on various independent variables). Nonetheless, Table 4.1 does provide reasonable support for our assumption that personal characteristics are sometimes associated with political behavior.

While generalizations are always difficult, there is some consistency in the empirical research on the personal characteristics of those who do *vote* (in political systems where there are genuine voting choices). In general, a higher probability of voting is correlated with such characteristics as membership in organizations that have explicit interests in politics (e.g., political parties, unions), higher education, higher income, higher social class, greater age, and male gender. Incidence of voting is also associated with the person's political beliefs, especially a strong identification with a party, a greater sense of personal capacity to influence the political world ("political efficacy"), and better understanding of the available political choices.

Research findings on *other modes of political behavior* are less extensive and less consistent. As in the taxonomies of participation, the crossnational studies by Verba and his colleagues (Verba and Nie 1972; Verba, Nie, and Kim 1978) remain among the most influential in identifying the individual characteristics correlated with each mode of political action. Participation in campaign activities is especially linked with higher education, higher income, and male gender. Socioeconomic characteristics are also most strongly correlated with the likelihood that a person engages in communal activities, and identification with a particular social group (religious, ethnic, or linguistic) can be extremely important if there are political cleavages associated with these group differences. Contacting government officials personally is least clearly related to personal characteristics, and some research suggests that the decision to engage in personal contacting depends more on whether the person has an effective private means to gain her objective or whether she must rely on contacting public officials to achieve this objective. Contacting officials might be the domain of political action that has increased most during the last several decades (Verba, Schlozman, and Brady 1995), and it is increasingly facilitated by e-mail and other digital communications innovations.

In studying *extremist-activists*, many analyses attempt to specify the personal characteristics that typify a particular type of activist, relative to the general population. For example, most rural extremist-activists, who are usually engaged in a struggle for control over land, tend to be male, poor, and of limited education. The urban activists who promote leftist ideologies (e.g., Marxism, environmentalism) are generally characterized as being well educated, middle class, mainly young, and only slightly more likely to be male than female. The right-wing urban activists are more varied. Those promoting an ethnic or racist position (e.g., neo-Nazism) tend to be young, male, working or lower class, and somewhat lower in education. But those promoting causes such as the antiabortion movement are more middle-aged, female, middle class, and relatively well educated (Dalton 2002: ch. 4; Meyer and Tarrow 1997).

Overall, what would you expect about the personal characteristics of *top political leaders* in a given society? Perhaps the broadest generalization is that leaders' personal characteristics tend to be quite consistent with those of the socially dominant groups within their society. Why do you think this occurs? Among the most common shared characteristics, across many societies, are high education, upper-middle-class or upper-class background, adherence to the society's dominant religion, and male gender.

Given our general fascination with extraordinary political actors such as presidents, charismatic leaders, and revolutionaries, it is interesting to assess whether particular environments, socialization experiences, and/or personal characteristics seem to account for the political behavior of these individuals. Box 4.4 briefly describes the environment, socialization, and personal characteristics of two remarkable political activists. Do these factors seem relatively comparable for the two men? Do these factors seem to produce similar political behavior?

BOX 4.4

You Go Your Way, I'll Go Mine

The two young men have some common roots. Both are born into societies ordered by traditional social systems of hierarchy and male domination and by strong, fundamentalist religion. Both are sons of prosperous professional fathers who are devout and emphasize the importance of orthodox religion in the home. Each young man displays high intelligence and receives an excellent education.

As young adults, each trains successfully for a professional career and enters that career. Each is shocked by his exposure to religious or racial discrimination and by his realization of the severe deprivation that characterizes the lives of the great majority of people in his society. Each becomes a deeply devout follower of his religion. These beliefs, along with family background, training, and experiences, cause each to develop a powerful commitment to the independence of his people from foreign powers, whom each believes are the source of oppression and injustice. Each decides to devote his life to political activism and to employ extreme political acts, as necessary, to achieve his vision of social justice. But each man follows a very different path.

The first man travels to another country to join the revolutionary struggle against a major colonial power. He is trained and supported in guerrilla warfare tactics (see Chapter 11) by the U.S. Central Intelligence Agency and becomes an effective leader. After successfully defeating the foreign power, he returns home to Saudi Arabia to work in the family business. However, he is deeply offended by the presence of and influence of foreigners in his religion's holiest lands. His open commitment to the expulsion of foreigners and the establishment of a pure, religious state results in conflict with the authoritarian regime in his homeland. He is harassed by the regime, his citizenship is revoked, and he is forced to leave the country. He moves to another country in the region, but powerful foreign governments force his expulsion from this country as well. He returns to the country where he had fought on behalf of the revolution and is given protection.

By this time, he is convinced that his righteous cause can be advanced only by extreme acts of violence. He uses his considerable personal wealth ($300 million) and his ideological vision to establish a loosely connected international network of small groups of extremist-activists. Eventually, he has loyal, highly trained opera-

BOX **4.4** (CONTINUED)

tives living in more than sixty countries. He calls upon all his followers to use whatever means are necessary to serve their cause: freeing their lands from foreign occupiers and influences. Members of his network are linked to numerous acts of international terrorism. These include the bombing of the World Trade Center in New York City in 1993; a massacre of tourists in Luxor, Egypt, in 1995; and the bombings of the U.S. embassies in Kenya and Tanzania in 1998. Many plots are unsuccessful, including an attempt to fly a hijacked airplane into the Eiffel Tower and assassination attempts on President Hosni Mubarak of Egypt, Jordanian Crown Prince (now King) Abdullah, and Pakistani Prime Minister Benazir Bhutto. He is identified as the mastermind behind the most brutal terrorist attack ever undertaken in the United States, with hijacked passenger airplanes crashing into two towers of the World Trade Center and another into the Pentagon on September 11, 2001. These attacks result in more than 3,000 deaths as well as worldwide fear and disruption of both travel and financial markets. The CIA labels his Al-Qaeda organization "the most dangerous terrorist organization in the world," a $25 million reward was offered for his capture, and he became the prime target in the "war on international terrorism" led by U.S. President George W. Bush.

In response to criticism that he targets "innocents" and supports terrorism, he comments:

> Each action will solicit a similar reaction. We must use such punishment to keep your evil away from Muslims, Muslim children and women. American history does not distinguish between civilians and military, and not even women and children. Americans are the ones who used the bombs against Nagasaki. Can these bombs distinguish between infants and military? America does not have a religion that will prevent it from destroying all people.

> Your situation with Muslims in Palestine is shameful, if there is any shame left in America. In the Sabra and Shatilla [Lebanon refugee camps] massacre, a cooperation between Zionist and Christian forces, houses were demolished over the heads of children. Also, by testimony of relief workers in Iraq, the American led sanctions resulted in the death of over 1 million Iraqi children. All of this was done in the name of American interests. We believe that the biggest thieves in the world and the terrorists are the Americans. The only way for us to fend off these assaults is to use similar means. We do not differentiate between those dressed in military uniforms and civilians; they are all targets in this fatwa [death decree]. (http://abcnews.go.com/sections/world/dailynews/terror_980609.html)

The second man witnesses racism against blacks while serving as a lawyer in South Africa. To resist such injustice, he develops a strategy of political activism. This strategy, inspired by an American, Henry David Thoreau, as well as by his own religious principles, emphasizes civil disobedience. His fundamental principle is *ahimsa*—nonviolence in thought as well as in action. He advises his followers: "Not to submit; to suffer." He is repeatedly jailed for his nonviolent resistance to laws that he believes are unjust. He assumes that the opposition will discredit itself by its repressive responses to nonviolent protest.

(continued)

BOX **4.4** (CONTINUED)

Returning to his native India, he begins to organize protests demanding independence from the British imperialists. His protest techniques continue to be based on nonviolence and *satyagraha*—soul force. In contrast to brute force, soul force provokes constructive change through positive action and reconciliation, not through harming and angering the enemy. He observes, "My experience has shown me that we win justice quickest by rendering justice to the other party." He becomes an extraordinarily powerful and inspirational leader through his theatrical acts of civil disobedience and through his personal sacrifices, including extended fasts, lengthy marches, and sexual abstinence. His nonviolent activism captures world attention, and his Indian followers expand into the tens of thousands. His supporters call him *"Mahatma"*—great soul. His tireless political activism, in deed and in word, contributes substantially to the developments that lead, three decades later, to the granting of independence to India by the British. His life of struggle is not a complete success. He fails to prevent the division of India into separate countries dominated by Hindus and Muslims, a struggle bloodied by 500,000 deaths. He fails to persuade Hindus to repudiate the divisive and unjust social caste system. And he is assassinated by a Hindu extremist within months of India's independence. (Discussion based on Broomfield 1982.)

Osama bin Laden (1957–) and Mohandas K. Gandhi (1869–1948), despite their early similarities, diverged onto nearly opposite pathways of political activism in the pursuit of their personal visions of social justice and human liberation.

Osama bin Laden

Mohandas Gandhi

POLITICAL "PERSONALITY"

The three types of explanatory factors discussed to this point either are outside the person (the environment and agents of political socialization) or are surface traits (e.g., age, ethnicity). However, some political analysts insist that an adequate explanation of political behavior requires explication of the *political personality*—the deeper psychological dynamics inside the individual that affect her response to political stimuli.

Personality

Personality can be broadly defined as *the propensities within an individual to act a certain way, given a particular context.* If someone is usually cheerful or aggressive or thoughtful under a variety of circumstances, this style of behaving could be termed a personality trait of that individual. The cluster of basic personality traits that dominates an individual's attitudes and behavior is what most people mean when they talk about someone's personality "type." It seems plausible that personality could influence the political beliefs and actions of any individual. Most of the empirical research examining political personality has focused on the beliefs and actions of political activists. Political personality analyses are found in biographies, in opinion pieces in the media, in our conversations about top political leaders, and even in leaders' own speeches and writings.

Normative approaches. People have always had strong opinions about the kind of personality that a political leader *ought* to have. What personality characteristics do you think are desirable in a political leader? Perhaps no one is better known for advice about the kind of personality a political leader needs than Niccolò Machiavelli (1469–1527), author of *The Prince* (1517/1977). Machiavelli believed that society tends toward disorder, in part because events are substantially dependent on "*fortuna*"—a combination of chance, fate, luck, and unpredictable circumstances. The political leader must act decisively to overcome *fortuna*. She must think strategically, suppress moral judgments, and act with fierce resolve.

"Everyone sees what you seem to be," Machiavelli (1517/1977: ch. 18) observed; "few know what you really are." Thus the leader must combine the qualities of the lion (aggression, bravery) and the fox (cleverness) and must make the citizens completely dependent on her every decision and action. In the pursuit of the good society, the leader must be single-minded and, if necessary, ruthless, in order to achieve desirable ends. Machiavelli insisted that the effective political leader will face many situations where the ends justify the political means, even if ethics must be sacrificed: "To preserve the state, he often has to do things against his word, against charity, against humanity, against religion. . . . [H]e should not depart from the good if he can hold to it, but he should be ready to enter on evil if he has to" (Machiavelli 1517/1977: ch. 18). Most politicians work hard to project certain personality traits that they think will appeal to their followers (e.g., honesty, responsiveness, compassion, thoughtfulness), and few contemporary politicians want to be characterized as "Machiavellian."

Empirical approaches. While some studies offer normative perspectives on political personality, most contemporary studies are empirical and aim to explain the behavior of top political leaders and activists. These studies attempt to identify their key personality traits (such as idealism, aggressiveness, decisiveness, and so on) and then to link those traits to specific political beliefs and actions. Some political personality approaches delve quite deeply, explaining the psychological needs, drives, or experiences embedded in the person's psyche that are the underlying forces resulting in her political behavior. In this perspective, activist political behavior is seen as a response to a person's psychological life history. For example, Harold Lasswell (1960), one of the intellectual founders of behavioral political science, argues that the activist political personality is motivated primarily by the drive to overcome a low sense of self-esteem.

A related example of political personality research is the classic study *The Authoritarian Personality,* by T. W. Adorno and his colleagues (1950). In the aftermath of the horrors of German Nazism and anti-Semitism during World War II, these scholars attempted to analyze people who become supporters of rigid, ideological political movements or who are deeply prejudiced. On the basis of many types of psychological testing of individuals, the researchers characterized a personality syndrome they termed **authoritarianism.** Initially, they defined the personality traits of those with this syndrome:

Authoritarians are extremely conventional in their attitudes and morality.

They are particularly hostile toward minorities or those with unorthodox lifestyles.

Their world is organized on the principle of hierarchy—they offer obedience to those of high status and they attempt to dominate those perceived to be below them in the sociopolitical order.

Adorno and his colleagues were particularly interested in moving beyond description to answer a crucial *why* question: Why does someone develop an authoritarian personality? While their answers are complex, their basic explanation, rather like Lasswell's, emphasizes "externalization." Adorno's group argues that the people who become authoritarians experienced aggressive impulses and strong sexual drives during childhood, like most of us; but these people had iron-handed parents who suppressed their children's opportunities to express these impulses and drives. As teenagers and adults, they projected (externalized) this pent-up hostility onto groups that they judged to be inferior to themselves, such as ethnic minorities and gays. At the same time, their love and fear of the authoritarian parent led them to venerate those who exercised great power in the society.

There have been many criticisms of the methods and findings of Adorno and his colleagues (1950). Some research has suggested that authoritarianism can be found among people who support extremist politics of either the right or the left (McClosky and Chong 1985; Rokeach 1960). Adolf Hitler seems to have believed this. He instructed Nazi Party officials to accept immediately into membership anyone who had previously been a Communist, the archenemies of the Nazis. Presumably, Hitler assumed that these people, who were called "Beefsteak Nazis" (brown on the outside, red on the inside), would redirect their vigorous political support from one ideological extreme to the other. But most studies have reinforced the basic notion in *The Authoritarian Personality* that the syndrome is fundamentally associated with a psychological and political conservatism.

Empirical, personality-based approaches have also been used to account for the behavior of other types of political activists, such as student radicals. As someone who has experience with other students, what do you hypothesize about the student radicals? Are student extremists different from other students in their intelligence or idealism or independence? Are student radicals of the left different from student radicals of the right?

While a few empirical studies identify some student radicals with substantial personality disorders, the research generally concludes that student radicals tend to be more intelligent, creative, idealistic, and independent than the nonradicals (Fendrich 1993). In studies of British and French students, the radical (leftist) activists exhibit "highly principled moral reasoning," in which their political behavior is justified in terms of a logical and consistent belief system and abstract notions about social justice (O'Connor 1978). Although these admirable characteristics are often attributed only to leftist radicals, there is evidence that they apply to all political radicals, whether their political orientation is left or right (Kerpelman 1972). Similarly, the most systematic empirical evidence about top political leaders suggests that, contrary to Lasswell's claim above, the majority actually rank higher on measures of self-esteem and psychological well-being than does the average adult (Sniderman 1975).

At a general level, it has been posited that the behavior of political leaders can be explained by their responsiveness to some combination of seven "incentives" that they connect powerfully with political action: (1) the urge to solve public problems; (2) the need to be accepted by others; (3) the search for fame and glory; (4) the desire to follow their conscience in serving society; (5) the pleasure derived from competition and manipulation of others; (6) the satisfaction from commitment to a transcendental mission; and (7) the desire for praise and adulation (Woshinsky 1995: ch. 11).

Some of the most detailed analytic work using the political personality approach develops an extensive *"psychobiography"* of the individual political activist. In essence, such analyses attempt to provide information about the political activists' personalities and to explain how such information helps us make better sense of how and especially why they act as they do. Erik Erikson (1958, 1969), among the most influential scholars in this tradition, adopts a Freudian framework to identify the crucial importance of child rearing and early socialization through adolescence in determining the activist's later political behavior. (See Erikson's psychobiographies of Martin Luther [1958] and Mohandas Gandhi [1969] and Lucian Pye's [1962] application of Erikson's approach to analyze an entire class of political leaders in postcolonial Burma/Myanmar.)

Human Nature

Some of those who offer a psychological explanation for political behavior do not focus on individual personality or even on a particular culture; rather, they emphasize a more generalized conception grounded in human nature—in innate motivation and invariant drives shared by all people. At some time, most of us have engaged in a discussion about the possibility of a utopian society. Typically, someone takes the position that a benign utopia is not possible because humans are imperfect—men and women are intrinsically greedy or self-serving or violent. The person making such an argument is linking the political behavior of individuals and groups with notions about innate (and possibly universal) human nature.

Certain political psychologists address this issue, asking whether there are innate human motivations that affect political behavior. Some assume that such human nature is prior to nurture (i.e., prior to the learned behavior emerging from socialization) and is only marginally altered by personal characteristics. Given the obvious difficulty of studying political behavior independent of socialization and personal characteristics, the applications of this perspective to political behavior have been modest and quite derivative. In most cases, general psychological theories have been only loosely related to politically relevant behavior.

The links between human nature and political behavior raise fascinating issues. Are there fundamental elements of human nature that cannot be significantly altered by socialization and institutions? On one side, some theorists claim that nearly all human behavior is based on essential biological/genetic foundations (see, e.g., the sociobiology approach of Edward Wilson 1978; Masters 2001). In dramatic contrast, a fundamental tenet of Marxist theory is that nothing is intrinsic about human nature (although this is not the view in some of Marx's own early writings, which do suggest basic human needs and patterns of development). From this second perspective, it is assumed that people's social values and behavior, if not their basic nature, can be shaped via proper socialization and enlightened institutions. Such shaping of people into a cooperative society is the theme of *Walden Two*, a novel by behavioral psychologist B. F. Skinner (1948). However, the power and danger of such pervasive socialization are a central theme in Aldous Huxley's (1932) classic novel *Brave New World*.

In general, one claim underpinning the human nature approach seems reasonable—we are not merely the product of our environment. But the crucial issue relevant to understanding politics concerns the extent to which individual personality and human nature *cause* political behavior. In the late-night debates in college dormitories about the possibility of a utopian society or the inevitability of conflict and war, the issues often boil down to one's view of the malleability of human nature. Are there innate characteristics of human nature so invariant that they are subject to only minor modifications from particular patterns of political socialization and from specific political environments? Empirical social science has yet to provide decisive answers to these questions about nature versus nurture in relation to politics.

CONCLUDING OBSERVATIONS

Our exploration of micropolitical analysis has continued with a consideration of primary explanations for individuals' political beliefs and political actions. The research and theories that attempt to answer the *why* questions regarding political behavior emphasize four types of explanatory factors: the environmental context, the agents of political socialization, personal characteristics, and political personality. The basic assumption is that some combination of these factors influences the kinds of political stimuli to which people are exposed, the manner in which they interpret these stimuli, and their responses to the stimuli.

The *environment* presents the individual with stimuli and opportunities as well as with obstacles to certain political beliefs and actions. While a person can ignore or misperceive these broad environmental constraints, they do constitute a framework that guides, and to some extent determines, political behavior. In most micropolitical research, the analyst can (and should) identify the major features of the environment that might affect the probability that an individual will manifest certain political beliefs or actions.

In a similar manner, an individual's *personal characteristics,* such as age, gender, social class, and education, can have a powerful cumulative influence in several ways. First, they can influence the kinds of political phenomena to which the person is exposed. Second, they can influence the expectations that others have regarding how the person ought to think and act politically. The empirical evidence is sometimes quite clear (as are the data on voting in the 2000 U.S. presidential election) that certain personal characteristics (in a given environmental context) are correlated significantly with particular political beliefs and actions. Thus personal characteristics, such as the environment, can be understood as a set of forces that influence the nature and intensity of, but do not determine, individual political behavior.

The inadequacy of either the environment or personal characteristics as a complete explanation for most individual political behavior is reflected in the fact that people with comparable personal characteristics or who operate in a similar environment do not necessarily manifest identical political beliefs or actions. For example, of two intelligent 19-year-old Chicanas at the same university, one might become an activist deeply involved in Democratic Party politics while the other might be politically inactive. Similarly, consider the quite divergent paths of political activism pursued by Mohandas Gandhi and Osama bin Laden, despite some notable similarities in their characteristics and environments. While the environment and personal characteristics might not provide a total explanation, a strong case can be made that these factors do tend to set the boundaries within which much political behavior occurs.

The attempt to build an empirically validated causal theory of the effects of *political socialization* on political behavior is intriguing. However, a major analytic shortcoming in most of the empirical political socialization research has been the difficulty in demonstrating empirically that there is a clear causal linkage among a specific agent of socialization, a particular belief, and then a politically relevant action. In most instances, researchers lack the methodologies and the data-gathering instruments to measure how the messages of various agents of political socialization are absorbed, interpreted, and responded to by people. Rather, the researchers must attempt to infer what socialization agents have been important by asking individuals to recall the major sources of their own political beliefs.

Despite these empirical difficulties, the study of political socialization has been quite useful in increasing our understanding of the major forces that influence how people learn about the political world and evaluate political phenomena. In their attempt to use the agents of political socialization, political regimes affirm their own belief that these socialization processes can either create and preserve popular support for the existing political order or create a new political consciousness. Research suggests that where the agents of political socialization are ineffective or provide contradictory messages, a person's political behavior will tend toward apathy or, in a few cases, toward total activism (producing the politically committed gladiator). While the precise linkages among agents of political socialization, political beliefs, and political behavior have yet to be empirically verified, this area of inquiry remains an important one for political scientists.

The explanation of micropolitical behavior by reference to *political personality* is perhaps the most intriguing of the four sets of factors. The political behavior of ordinary men and women is seldom analyzed using explicit, personality-based approaches. The studies that have been done have tended to be broad and overly simplified characterizations of "national character" or "modal personality," such as those described in Chapter 2. Most of the personality-based work has examined activists, such as authoritarian personalities, revolutionaries, and top leaders.

Personality-based approaches are the explanatory framework for political behavior that has been least fully explored by means of social scientific inquiry. These approaches use some of the same evidence as the other approaches. For example, this approach might explain political personality in terms of the relation of the child to the parents, as would an explanation based on the family as an agent of political socialization. Thus personality is difficult to isolate from other forces—the environment, personal characteristics, and political socialization and learning—that intervene between human nature and political behavior and that shape personality. To a large extent, the psychological perspective differs from the other approaches less in the evidence it examines than in the more subjective, psychoanalytic framework within which the evidence is interpreted.

We began this chapter by asking whether it is possible to explain political beliefs and actions. In general, analyses can rarely prove that any of the four types of explanatory factors we examined is almost always *the* basic causal factor accounting for a particular micropolitical behavior. Nonetheless, the evidence summarized in this chapter suggests that appropriate knowledge about each of these four sets of explanatory factors can provide significant insights regarding political behavior.

KEY CONCEPTS

agenda setting *(pg. 96)*

agents of political socialization *(pg. 95)*

human nature *(pg. 102)*

personal characteristics *(pg. 93)*

political environment *(pg. 103)*

political personality *(pg. 99)*

political socialization *(pg. 83)*

rational choice theory

FOR FURTHER CONSIDERATION

1. Which agent of political socialization has been most potent in influencing *your* key political beliefs? Which of your key beliefs have been least influenced by this agent? What accounts for the agent's minimal influence on these beliefs?

2. Under what conditions are personal characteristics likely to have particularly powerful effects on an individual's political beliefs or actions?

3. To what extent are people either a blank page upon which political beliefs can be written ("nurture") or genetically determined actors ("nature")? Do you think that this overall assessment is valid for you?

4. In a contemporary society, what are the conditions that cause the schools or the media to be the more powerful source of people's political orientations?

5. What is your assessment of Machiavelli's advice to the leader that ethics, the leader's word, and even "the good" must sometimes be sacrificed to achieve desirable ends?

FOR FURTHER READING

Bao, Ruo-Wang (Jean Pasqualini). (1976). *Prisoner of Mao.* New York: Penguin Books. A French citizen of Chinese origin recounts his imprisonment in China and his rigorous indoctrination into the communist (Maoist) vision of class thinking and personal behavior.

Erikson, Erik. (1969). *Gandhi's Truth.* New York: Norton. Applying his rich psychobiographical approach, Erikson explains the crucial points of development shaping the personality and political style of Mohandas Gandhi.

Esposito, John, and John Voll. (1996). *Islam and Democracy: Religion, Identity and Conflict Resolution in the Muslim World.* New York: Oxford University Press. By means of a sensitive analysis of both Arab and non-Arab Islamic countries, the authors conclude that the core elements of Islam, as a system of beliefs, can be compatible with certain forms of participatory government.

Gobodo-Madikizela, Pumla. (2003). *A Human Being Died that Night: A South African Story of Forgiveness.* Boston: Houghton-Mifflin. A psychologist who was a member of the Truth and Reconciliation Commission in South Africa explains the importance of this public acknowledgement process in creating a new peace and reducing the likelihood of future ethnic or racial atrocities.

Hayhoe, Ruth. (1992). *Education and Modernization: The Chinese Experience.* New York: Pergamon Press. An insightful analysis of the impacts of education on the political socialization process and on culture and modernization in China, from Confucianism to Marxism.

Huxley, Aldous. (1932). *Brave New World.* London: Chatto & Windus. A chilling vision of a society in which the state effectively uses socialization and material conditions to control the thoughts and actions of citizens.

Mandela, Nelson. (1995). *Long Walk to Freedom.* Boston: Little, Brown. In his autobiography, Nelson Mandela provides a compelling narrative of his extraordinary life of political activism against racial injustice and apartheid, culminating in his election as president of South Africa.

Masters, Roger. (1989). *The Nature of Politics.* New Haven, CT: Yale University Press. A fascinating exploration of the biological bases of people's political beliefs and actions.

Nixon, Richard M. (1962). *Six Crises.* New York: Doubleday. Richard Nixon, one of the most controversial American presidents, provides a revealing self-assessment of his reactions to six critical points in his early political career.

Sigel, Roberta, Ed. (1989). *Political Learning in Adulthood: A Sourcebook of Theory and Research.* Chicago: University of Chicago Press. Scholars of political socialization assess what we know about this phenomenon, particularly as it continues to occur for adults.

Skinner, B. F. (1948). *Walden Two.* New York: Macmillan. A renowned behavioral psychologist presents his conception of a setting in which socialization is used to create a benign and cooperative community. An intriguing counterpoint to Huxley's *Brave New World.*

Wills, Gary. (1970). *Nixon Agonistes: The Crises of a Self-Made Man.* Boston: Houghton Mifflin. A scathing psychobiography of Richard Nixon that is an interesting complement to Nixon's *Six Crises.*

Wolfenstein, E. Victor. (1967). *The Revolutionary Personality: Lenin, Trotsky, Gandhi.* Princeton, NJ: Princeton University Press. A classic study of three great revolutionary leaders from a psychoanalytic perspective.

ON THE WEB

http://www.americanrhetoric.com/informationindex.htm

The News and Information Index from American Rhetoric is an extremely rich set of links to newspapers from around the world, other online news sources, magazines, search engines, polling databases, and legal databases.

http://www.cddc.vt.edu/feminism/

The Feminist Theory Web Site, developed at the Center for Digital Discourse and Culture at Virginia Tech University, provides a large number of links to information on beliefs, as well as groups and movements, that are inspired by a feminist perspective on political and social issues in many countries.

http://www.cnn.com/WORLD

The site for CNN, the 24-hour, U.S.-based international news organization.

http://www.itn.co.uk

World news and British news from Independent Television News, based in London, are provided.

http://www.webdopresseweb.ch/

"Webdo" is a Swiss-based link that enables you to access current articles in a diverse set of newspapers from many countries and in a variety of languages.

http://www.nytimes.com

This is the site for key articles and information from one of the premier newspapers in the United States.

http://www.worldnews.com/

WorldNews provides an electronic news portal with international sites in multiple languages categorized by geographic region and subject.

http://news.bbc.co.uk/

The Internet home of the British Broadcasting Company, this site offers world political, business, scientific, and entertainment news from an English perspective.

http://news.google.com/

Using the same technology utilized in the Google Internet search engine, this site provides access to thousands of different news sources.

This land is *my* land! The Palestinian and the Israeli soldier are seated in a place (Hebron, in the West Bank of Israel) that each deeply believes belongs to his nation.

CHAPTER 5 **States and Nations**

"O, Canada! Our home and native land! True patriot love in all thy sons command. . . ." Voices fill Toronto's Skydome as the Blue Jays baseball game is preceded by the singing of the national anthem. But then as the vocalist intones, "O Canada! Terre de nos aieux, ton front est ceint de fleurons glorieux!" there are boos and catcalls. The national anthem continues to glorify the same native land of brave forefathers and heroic exploits. What has happened?

The lyrics are now a symbol of the conflict and disagreement within Canada. Canada is a single territorial space with one government that is attempting to rule a population in which "all thy sons" (and daughters) are deeply split into two groups that share neither culture nor identity. The English-speaking Canadians and the French-speaking Canadians are unable to establish peaceful coexistence within the same state. Many argue that the only solution is separation of Canada into two distinct countries.

The disjunction between state boundaries and peoples with shared identities, a central theme of this chapter, is a fundamental problem in many countries. It is arguably the greatest source of violence and death in the contemporary political world. While Chapters 2 through 4 primarily examined the political beliefs and actions of individuals, this chapter increases the scale of our subject unit considerably, focusing on large collectivities of people. Initially, this chapter examines and distinguishes two crucial concepts, *state* and *nation*. This is followed by discussion of the *political system*, a third major concept used to analyze these collectivities.

THE STATE

Anthropological evidence suggests that early social organization among humans was probably based on small living groups of family or kin. As suggested by humanistic psychologist Abraham Maslow (1954), human groupings formed to increase the capacity with which people's physiological, safety, love, and belonging needs could be met. As groupings became larger, tribes or bands were formed on the basis of more extensive kinship ties. It might be argued that the first "state" emerged when a multiplicity of such tribes combined under some leadership structure and some pattern of organization. By this definition, there have been states since ancient times, in the sense that a state exists when there are distinctive leadership roles, rules for social interaction, and a set of organizational arrangements to identify and serve collective needs (see Box 5.1).

A Legal Definition

The social scientific concept of the state, however, is a relatively modern one, based on the legal notion that the **state** is *"a territorially bound sovereign entity."* The idea of sovereignty emerged in the sixteenth and seventeenth centuries. In current interpretations, **sovereignty** is *the premise that each state has complete authority and is the ultimate source of law within its own boundaries.* Sovereignty is the key element in the legal concept of the state. It is a basic assumption of international politics and is reflected in a fundamental principle of the United Nations, the sovereign equality of all member states. This means that, before the law, Cambodia is equal to China, Jamaica is equal to Japan. While sovereignty has legal standing and moral force in international law, the reality of international politics is that a state's sovereign rights depend ultimately on whether the state has sufficient power to enforce its position. Thus it is not likely that, when major national interests are at stake, China will yield to Cambodia merely on the basis of Cambodia's sovereign rights.

 # BOX 5.1

The States of the "State"

"State" is among the most extensively used concepts in political science, and it has various meanings. A source of confusion for American students is that they are accustomed to thinking of a state as one of the 50 units of subnational government in the United States, such as Illinois or Alabama. This is one appropriate meaning of the concept. However, in the general language of political science, *state* usually refers to the set of organizational units and people that performs the political functions for a national territorial entity, such as France, Indonesia, or Nigeria. In this chapter, and in this book, the term "state" will usually denote this full array of governmental units and people within the society.

You should also be aware that the language of political science often treats the state as though it were a single actor. For example, consider the statement (page 111) in the discussion of sovereignty that "a state has the right to resist . . . any aggression. . . . " In reality, the state is composed of many people who behave as individuals but whose combined behaviors are characterized as if they were performed by a single actor. In this book, there are other collectivities (e.g., the group, the political party, the army, and the bureaucracy) that are complex aggregates of individuals but are discussed as though they operate as a single actor.

Associated with the idea of sovereignty is the doctrine of **territorial integrity.** This holds that *a state has the right to resist and reject any aggression, invasion, or intervention within its territorial boundaries.* As with the more general notion of sovereignty, a state's protection of its territorial integrity depends on the state's capacity and political power.

It might seem there are many relatively clear examples of a state's territorial integrity being violated, such as the Iraqi army's invasion of Kuwait in 1990, but there is often considerable disagreement over claimed violations of territorial integrity. First, territorial integrity is a fuzzy concept when there is a *dispute over boundaries.* For example, both Canada and the United States claim that certain fishing waters are within their territorial boundaries, and each state attempts to exclude the other's commercial fishing fleets from its territorial waters. In this case, the dispute has been settled by adjudication. But border disputes can also become a cause of violence between states, as when Iran and Iraq each claimed certain land along their mutual border, precipitating a war in 1980 (see Box 14.4).

Second, attempts to exercise sovereignty can be disputed when there is *disagreement about whom the legitimate rulers are.* Box 5.2 describes some of the puzzles about sovereignty during the devastating civil war that absorbed Angola for almost thirty years. Similar problems have arisen recently in Indonesia (East

BOX 5.2

Don't Tread on My Sovereignty!: Angola

Despite its centrality in international law, sovereignty does not ensure that the international community will support a country's claim that its territorial integrity has been violated. In Angola, the period since independence in 1975 has been one of constant turmoil between competing leadership groups claiming to be the country's rulers and of serious issues about sovereignty. At independence, the three major nationalist groups were unable to agree on who should have government power in this resource-rich country of 10.5 million people in southern Africa. When one group (MPLA) took control of the capital city, the other two groups (UNITA and FNLA) began a military campaign from the regions where they were strong. Two years later, the United Nations recognized MPLA as the country's legitimate government.

However, some countries, especially South Africa and the United States, preferred to see the UNITA–FNLA groups in power. Thus, South Africa provided these groups with military troops to fight MPLA, and both South Africa and the United States provided aid to UNITA and engaged in extensive covert activities within Angola to undermine MPLA. MPLA's leaders protested that such actions violated Angola's territorial integrity and hence its sovereignty. The United Nations did not actively support Angola's rights. MPLA then requested and received military aid from the Soviet Union and more than 20,000 troops from Cuba. The arrival of Cuban troops drew protests from the United States and South Africa, which increased their involvement.

(continued)

BOX **5.2** (CONTINUED)

With all this outside "assistance," Angola became mired in a lengthy civil war. With the end of the cold war and the dismantling of apartheid in South Africa in the early 1990s, major outside powers lost interest in Angola. The rival groups in Angola finally agreed to a national election in 1992, and foreign troops withdrew. The MPLA won a relatively fair election, but UNITA, led by Jonas Savimbi, refused to accept the results and continued to fight. When Savimbi was killed in a gun battle with government soldiers in 2002, a ceasefire was finally negotiated.

This protracted struggle has resulted in social and economic chaos in Angola. Inflation in the last years of the war averaged about 300 percent per year. The proportion of land under cultivation in this fertile agricultural country has declined to only 2 percent. Angola has among the lowest life expectancy levels and the highest infant mortality rates in the world. The toll from 27 years of struggle includes 4.5 million refugees, tens of thousands who lost limbs to millions of land mines, and the death of more than 1.5 million Angolans as a result of the fighting (Central Intelligence Agency 2003; Ramsey 1999: 143–144).

Given this history, consider the following questions:

- Before the 1992 election, was the MPLA leadership correct in protesting that Angola's sovereignty had been repeatedly violated by South Africa and the United States?
- Was it valid for states such as the United States to claim that the presence of Cuban troops violated Angola's sovereignty?
- Should the United Nations have done something to protect Angola's sovereignty? What?
- When there is a dispute over legitimate rulers, how should it be determined who can exercise sovereignty?

Clearly, answers to such questions depend on one's interpretation of how sovereign power is established and maintained. Similar claims regarding violation of sovereignty are made by almost every state experiencing substantial political violence generated by internal or external forces.

Timor), Cambodia (see Box 5.5), Congo, and Somalia. Leaders in post–Hussein Iraq objected strongly to the delays by the American-led military forces in returning sovereignty to the Iraqis. And third, the international community has become less sensitive to the protection of sovereignty when there is strong evidence that the government is committing *serious human rights violations* against its own citizens.

Controversies about whether sovereignty has been violated are becoming more frequent. One recent (1999) example is the aggressive intervention of NATO, the United Nations, and the United States in Kosovo, a region of Yugoslavia. The stated justification for violating Yugoslavia's sovereign rights over its internal affairs was concerns about the government's support for "ethnic cleansing" targeting non-Serbs (mainly Albanians). Another example is the U.S.-led "war on terrorism" waged against the Taliban regime in Afghanistan. A rationale for such interventions was offered by Secretary-General Kofi Annan, as he accepted the 2001 Nobel Peace Prize awarded to the United Nations: "The sovereignty of states must no longer be used as a shield for gross violations of human rights. When states undermine the rule of law and violate the rights of individual citizens, they become a menace not only to their people, but also to their neighbors, and indeed the world" (Holley 2001). However, others are concerned that the increased use of such justifications undermines weaker states, since sovereignty can be one of their best protections under international law from military intervention by outside powers (Sassen 1996).

A Structural-Functional Definition

As an alternative to defining the state in terms of its legal standing, the state can also be defined by the key organizational structures that operate as "the government" and the key functions that the state performs. In this structural-functional perspective, the **state** might be defined as *the organized institutional machinery for making and carrying out political decisions and for enforcing the laws and rules of the government.*

For Max Weber (1864–1920), the great political sociologist, the one function that distinguishes the state from all other organizations is its monopoly on the legitimate use of force and coercion in the society. That is, only the state has the right to use violence to enforce the society's laws and decisions.

The "state-centered" definitions of the state offer a more expansive conception of the state's essential functions—to maintain order and to compete with other actual or potential states (Skocpol 1979: 30). The state is an autonomous actor, composed of public officials making decisions. The state has goals, broadly understood as the "national interest," that it attempts to achieve against resistance from both domestic and international actors (Morgenthau 1993; Waltz 1995). The particular way in which a state's structures are configured has crucial effects—on the content of the public officials' policy preferences, on determining whose preferences will be adopted as those of the state, and on the state's effectiveness in implementing those policy preferences in the society.

A widely used approach emphasizing the structures and functions of the state is based on the work of Gabriel Almond and his colleagues (e.g., Almond et al. 2004). Their conceptual framework is based on two central questions:

1. What functions must be performed if the state is to persist?
2. What structures perform these necessary functions within a given state?

Chapter 10 provides a recent elaboration of this basic structural-functional approach called "capabilities analysis." In the classic version of this approach, Almond identifies eight *requisite functions*—that is, functions that must be performed in every state (Almond et al. 2004: ch. 2):

1. *Political socialization* is the processes through which individuals acquire their cognitive, affective, and evaluative orientations toward the political world.
2. *Political recruitment* is the processes through which people are drawn into roles as political activists.
3. *Political communication* is the mechanisms by which political information flows through society.

4. *Interest articulation* is the low-level communication, by individuals and groups, of what they need or want from the state.

5. *Interest aggregation* is the transformation of all these political needs and wants into a smaller number of coherent alternatives.

6. *Policy making* is the process by which the state establishes laws, policy decisions, and value allocations.

7. *Policy implementation* is the actual application of such laws and policy decisions.

8. *Policy adjudication* is the interpretation and resolution of disagreements regarding what the policies mean and how they should be implemented.

Given these functions, analyses using Almond's approach have primarily attempted to identify the particular structures within a state that are most significant in the performance of each function and to describe how the structures contribute to performing each function. While it might seem obvious at first glance that a certain structure always performs a particular function, more reflection (and later chapters) will suggest it is more complex than that. For example, it is not simply the case that Congress performs the policy-making function in the United States. Many policy decisions are made by the president, by the cabinet departments, by the bureaucracy, by the courts as they both interpret and reshape laws, by structures at the local levels of government, and by the citizens through electoral initiatives.

In most contemporary societies, virtually every political function is performed by a variety of structures. Many of these structures are part of the state, but others are nonstate actors, such as interest groups, religious organizations, media, social groups, private businesses, and international organizations. Thus the central questions in structural-functional research address the characteristic processes of each structure and the subtle interrelationships among structures as they contribute to a given function. These questions are especially germane in comparative research, where the analyst attempts to specify how the structure-function patterns vary between states.

The Domain of State Action

One other way of characterizing the state is to define its appropriate domain of action. When we examine "appropriate" rather than "actual" state action, the central question is normative rather than descriptive or analytic. A normative question asks how something should be rather than how it is (recall Chapter 1). Many of the most fascinating and fundamental issues in the political world have normative components. Political scientists attempt to distinguish the normative elements of their discussion from the descriptive-analytic elements, but, as Chapter 1 observed, there are always subtle normative judgments organizing the manner in which every political question is examined.

A fundamental, unresolved debate in everyday political discussion, as well as in political theory, concerns how extensive the state's role in society should be. Everyone agrees that the boundaries of state activity should be limited to *res publica,* a Latin phrase meaning "things of the people." But what "things" should be included? And how expansive should the state's involvement with these things be?

In contemporary political thought, certain broad views regarding the appropriate boundaries of *res publica* are associated with the three political ideologies (the major "isms") outlined in Chapter 2. In the *conservative* view of the state, an important domain of state action is military power, which functions to protect and promote the country's interests abroad and to defend against intervention by other states. Internally, the expectation is that the state will use its monopoly of force to maintain social order and to protect private property rights. State policy will also be used to preserve traditional values, especially regarding family life, religion, and culture.

As suggested in Chapter 2, a view of *res publica* based on *classical liberalism* would be more limited. Similar to the conservative view, the state must defend the country's sovereignty against external aggression or influence. However, there is great confidence in the dynamics of the free market to motivate and coordinate human behavior. Thus the state should be mainly a night watchman, a low-profile policeman who ensures the basic safety and freedom of every individual. Thomas Jefferson's slogan captures this perspective on *res publica:* "That state governs best which governs least." In its extreme form, the domain of appropriate state action is reduced to almost nothing, a perspective usually termed *libertarianism.*

There are several different interpretations of the domain of state action across the major variants of *socialism* described in Chapter 2. Democratic socialists believe that the state must constrain many powerful and self-interested groups whose behavior will harm the collective good of the society. Also, the state must intervene to provide assistance to the many groups in the society that are deeply disadvantaged by the workings of the system and must enact policies that ensure greater equality of condition. Marxist socialists believe that most non-Marxist states are expansive and repressive, serving mainly to preserve the interests of the dominant class in the society. In the words of V. I. Lenin (1870–1924), the Soviet revolutionary leader and theorist, such a state is "a body of armed men, weapons, and prisons." After a successful revolution, however, a more benign and positive state can be installed. Its domain of action is to implement any policies necessary to serve the fundamental goal of equality of political, economic, and social resources in the society. Some Marxist socialists assume the state will ultimately be eliminated (in Marx's words, the state will "wither away"), but even in this view, organizational structures would remain to administer policy. The extreme form of this view, in which there is no role for the state, is labeled *anarchism.* This does not mean a situation of chaos and disorder; rather it is a stateless society where individuals and groups organize spontaneously to create a society in which all people participate and all benefit from the goods and services that are produced.

While these three views of *res publica* are dominant in Western political thought, there are other conceptions that do not emphasize a unique, political "state." For example, in some societies dominated by all-encompassing religions, there is no political state that is independent of the religious order. In fundamentalist Islamic regimes, Shari'a law, the law of Islam, establishes a religious state that defines all aspects of social life, including such issues as the content of *res publica.* And in historical terms, many societies have no conception of a distinct political order. For instance, no specifically political structures existed in most precolonial African societies. Rather, the rules governing the society were based on tradition, as interpreted by community leaders (such as tribal elders or religious authorities).

THE NATION

The concept of the nation has a psychological and emotional basis rather than a legal or functional basis (as the state does). A **nation** is defined as *a set of people with a deeply shared fundamental identification.* Different factors might constitute the basis of such identification: shared descent (belief in a common kinship or history), shared culture, shared geographic space, shared religion, shared language, or shared economic order. The nation is a community of understanding, of communication, and of trust (Connor 1994).

Most people feel some identity with a variety of different reference groups or communities, such as a religion, local community, ethnic group, social club, and sports team. In the usage here, what distinguishes a nation from other reference groups is that the nation is a major group, beyond the family group, with whom a person identifies very powerfully. It is an essential division between "us" and "them." The strength of a person's primary national identity depends on the relative importance he places on various identities and the extent to which the most important identities reinforce this basic conception of "us" versus "them." Thus **nationalism** is *a powerful commitment to the advancement of the interests and welfare of an individual's own nation,* in contrast to minimal concern about the conditions of those outside the nation. The best situation for effective governance is a *nation-state,* which has a citizenry whose primary national identity is shared among a grouping of people who reside in an area that has the same territorial boundaries as a single state. Only a few modern states have the combination of common culture, history, ethnicity, religion, and language that result in a strong sense of shared nationality among nearly all the citizens governed by the state. Japan is an example of a relatively homogeneous nation-state.

Occasionally, one nation is split into two states, such as North and South Korea. In such cases, the citizens often dream of reunification, even when their governments and ideologies differ fundamentally. This occurred in Germany, which was split into communist East Germany and capitalist West Germany after World War II. In 1990, citizens of the single German nation were finally reunited in a single country after nearly half a century of antagonistic separation into two very different states.

The reality of the post–cold war world, however, is that most countries are *multinational states.* Such countries include groups whose fundamental identities are associated with different nations. Nationalism based on ethnicity and/or religion (also termed "ethnonationalism") has become a major problem within (and between) states in the contemporary political world (Connor 1994; Snyder 2000). It is particularly dangerous where it produces intense animosity and violence between groups with different nation-based identities. The example of the Indian subcontinent in Box 5.3 illustrates the kinds of differences that exist between states and nations and how these can generate instability and political violence.

The problems of ethnic and religious nationalism and of multiple nations within a single state are endemic in the contemporary world. For many of the states that gained independence after 1945, territorial boundaries were based on the arbitrary administrative decisions of colonial powers. Thus in most of Africa and Asia, states were formed with boundaries that were not sensitive to nationality differences in the area. Many of these states have experienced traumatic nationality conflicts, and few of these conflicts have been permanently resolved. There are reports every day of struggles such as those of the Armenians in Azerbaijan; the Tamils in Sri Lanka; and the Kurds in Turkey, Iran, and Iraq.

Even in some of the more established states, nation-based cleavages frequently explode (sometimes literally). When the Soviet Union, the world's most multinational

BOX 5.3

State and Nations: The Indian Subcontinent

The problem of discontinuities between nations and states is often most severe in states that have gained independence within the last sixty years. The Indian subcontinent exemplifies these problems. The vast Indian subcontinent was a feudal society divided into many small kingdoms ruled by kings (*maharajahs*). From the sixteenth century, the riches of India were pursued, and often exploited, by many traders, including the British, Dutch, French, and Arabs. The states from which these traders came began to struggle for dominance over the Indian trade, and the British finally gained hegemony in the eighteenth century after defeating the French. From that time until 1947, the Indian subcontinent was the major jewel in the British imperial crown, treated as a single territory under colonial rule.

After a lengthy and often violent campaign of political and social action by Indian nationalists, the British relented and granted the subcontinent independence in 1947. However, despite the desires of the British and the efforts of some Indian leaders such as Mohandas Gandhi (recall Box 4.4), the subcontinent was deeply split on the basis of religion between Hindus and Muslims. Since it seemed impossible to fashion a single state out of these two nations, two states were formed in 1947: India, which was predominantly (82 percent) Hindu; and Pakistan, which was predominantly (90 percent) Muslim.

The situation was further complicated by the concentration of Muslims in two geographically distinct areas in the northeast and northwest regions of the subcontinent. As a consequence, Pakistan was composed of two parts, separated by more than 1,500 miles of rival India's territory. Many Hindus in Pakistan and Muslims in India were forced to leave their homelands and migrate to the new state sharing their religion. The hostility and bloodshed associated with the partition resulted in 1 million deaths. There have been periodic violent boundary conflicts ever since. The testing of nuclear weapons by India and then Pakistan since 1998 accentuates the need to resolve the conflicts between the two states. Renewed efforts at peace began in 2001, with a summit meeting between the Indian prime minister and the Pakistani president.

While the major religious difference on the Indian subcontinent was generally resolved by this partition, many other nationality problems remained. For example, there has been continual disagreement between India and Pakistan since 1947

(continued)

BOX **5.3** (CONTINUED)

regarding which country should control the region of Jammu and Kashmir. At independence, India was given control of the region, although the majority of the population was and remains Muslim. Disputes over control of the region have resulted in more than a half-century of military conflicts and intermittent guerrilla war, despite persistent United Nations' involvement.

Within Pakistan, an even more substantial nationality dispute emerged between two major ethnic groups, the Punjabis and the Bengalis, after independence. When the Bengalis, dominant in East Pakistan, were victorious in a national election, the Punjabi-dominated West Pakistan attempted to reassert political power through its control of the military. When the Bengalis attempted to form their own independent nation-state (with some support from India), a terrible civil war resulted. After hundreds of thousands of deaths due to war and starvation, the Bengalis of East Pakistan were successful in the civil war and created a new sovereign state, Bangladesh, in 1971.

And while India is dominated by Hindus, major nation-based cleavages continue to plague the country, creating tremendous barriers to forging a single identity as a nation-state. There are 17 official languages in addition to the 2 "national" languages, Hindi and English, that are each understood by only about one-third of the population. In all, there are about 1,650 different dialects in India, most of which are mutually unintelligible.

Moreover, there are at least five major religious groupings in India: Hindu, Muslim, Sikh, Christian, and Buddhist. Hindu nationalism has increasingly been expressed through a political movement, resulting in the growing power at the regional and national levels of Hindu parties, particularly the Bharatiya Janata Party (BJP). The BJP became the dominant party in the national legislature in 1998, constituting the most serious threat to a secular Indian government since independence. With this increase in Hindu nationalism, the levels of violence against Christians and Muslims have risen significantly.

Most of the non-Hindu groups are regionally concentrated, enhancing their identity as religion-based nations. One major source of political unrest in India since 1980 has been the Sikhs, who are concentrated in the northwest part of India called the Punjab. The Sikhs have a very strong identity as a religious community and an ethnic group. Their sense of nationality is heightened by their belief that they are discriminated against politically by the Hindus. The Sikhs have been increasingly militant in demanding greater political autonomy, and since the early 1980s, some have insisted on full independence to create the state of Khalistan. The best known of a continuing series of violent confrontations between the Sikhs and the Hindu majority in India began when the Indian army stormed the Golden Temple, the Sikhs' holiest shrine, to drive out Sikh militants who had taken refuge there. In retaliation, Indian Prime Minister Indira Gandhi was assassinated in 1984 by two Sikhs among her private guard.

Rajiv Gandhi succeeded his mother as prime minister, only to be the victim of another nation-based dispute. The Indian army had also intervened on the neighboring island-country of Sri Lanka in an attempt to limit the extremely violent civil war between the Tamil and the Sinhalese ethnic groups. Southern India has a sub-

BOX **5.3** (CONTINUED)

stantial Tamil population that do not support the return of the Tamils from Sri Lanka. Sri Lankan Tamils have been angered by the lack of support from India and from the treatment they received from the Indian army. In 1991, Rajiv Gandhi was assassinated by a Tamil woman who had strapped a bomb to her body. In sum, the many deep cleavages in India, based on religion, ethnicity, culture, and region, have exposed the state to persistent instability, conflict, and nation-based carnage.

state, collapsed in 1991, it was replaced by 15 states that were generally organized on nationality grounds. However, the large nationality minorities in many of them (e.g., Chechnya in Russia) have produced extensive nation-based struggles. The bloodiest nationality violence in Central and Eastern Europe has been the devastating ethnic battles among the Bosnians, Croatians, Kosovars, Macedonians, Serbs, and others in the former Yugoslavia (see Box 15.3). Even this carnage is overshadowed by the horrendous ethnic conflict in Rwanda and Burundi between the Hutus and the Tutsis resulting in more than 1 million deaths since 1994.

Meanwhile, the agitation of the Quebequois in Canada, the Basques in Spain, and the Irish Catholics in Northern Ireland are testimony to the possibility that even centuries-old states might split apart. Some scholars predict that the current reorganization of states based on nationality identities will produce more than fifty new states in the next decade. In the interim, nation-based conflicts might remain the major cause of violence and instability in the post–cold war period (Barber 1995; Huntington 1996; but also see Sadowski 1998)

THE POLITICAL SYSTEM

While concepts such as state and nation are extremely useful, political scientists have sought an additional, more general and analytic concept to describe the structures and dynamics of organized politics at all levels. Many political scientists use some version of the concept of the political system developed in the work of David Easton (1953, 1965). Easton was searching for an analytic concept that would facilitate the development of a general theory of politics. He found the basis for such a concept in the notion of general systems theory used in biology.

Systems in General

The essential concept is the idea of a *system,* which is a group of components that exist in a characteristic relationship to each other and that interact on the basis of regular patterns. Because the components are interdependent, change in one component will have some effect on other components. Such change can cause minor or even major alterations in how the total system functions. In a mechanical analogy, an automobile engine can be viewed as a system, a set of components interacting in a regular way. If one spark plug is dirty, the performance of the automobile-as-system will be substantially altered; if the spark plug is removed, the system might not work at all.

The same interdependency of components is evident in human systems, such as families, sports teams, factories, or bureaucracies. The components of human systems—people in roles—are more likely to vary in the range of their actions than are the components of most mechanical systems, making their performance far more variable and less predictable than that of mechanical systems. Human systems function relatively smoothly as long as most of the components (the people) interact within a tolerable range of expected action. For high performance, some human systems, such as a symphony orchestra or a drill team, require far more rigid adherence to predictable roles than others, such as a jazz combo or a basketball team. Because of people's capacity to adapt and improvise, human systems can sometimes adapt effectively to unexpected circumstances. But human variability can also result in system performance that is disorganized, with negative or even disastrous effects.

The Political System Defined

For Easton (1953, 1965), the **political system** is a system of behavior, and it is defined by its distinctive activities, the *authoritative allocation of values for a society.* This definition is central to the idea of a political system as it is used in this book and in many political analyses. Thus it is appropriate to examine each aspect of the definition in greater detail.

"Values."   *Values* are those things that have significance and importance to people. We can discuss values in terms of the idealized abstractions that inspire or justify much political action: liberty, equality, freedom, justice. Values can also be defined more concretely: They can be material goods, such as a decent house or road system; they can be services, such as quality health care or protection from crime; they can be conditions, such as clean air or security from national enemies. Values can also be symbolic goods, such as status. In addition to positive values, there are negative values, such as coercion or imprisonment, polluted water, epidemic disease, and so on. (Notice that this social scientific concept of values is broader than the notion of values as moral judgments that people use to guide their actions.)

By definition, values tend to be scarce resources—either there is an insufficient amount of a given value to satisfy everyone, or the enjoyment of one value by some requires a loss of value to others. To use an example from the previous paragraph, there is no political system in which all citizens have housing they would consider adequate. There are people who would view their housing as too small, or too expensive, or in the wrong location, or lacking in sufficient luxuries. Even if a state could provide everyone with identical housing, some would be dissatisfied because they want better housing or because they object to the use of their taxes or work to subsidize the housing of others. A state's vast arsenal of nuclear weapons may make one person feel quite secure while making another person extremely insecure. One person might favor large state expenditures on missile systems while another would prefer to spend the resources on housing, and a third might prefer lower taxes to expenditure on either weapons or housing. Every value distribution entails trade-offs between different values as well as some inequality in the distribution of benefits and burdens. Thus there are always disagreements, competition, and even violent conflict over whose values will be served and whose will not. What are *your* top two values for your society?

"Allocation."   Pierre Mendes-France, a distinguished French premier (1954–1955), observed that "to govern is to make choices." *Allocation* refers to this choice making—to the process by which decisions and actions are taken to grant values to some and deny values to others. One useful definition of politics is that it is the processes through which competition and conflict over values are resolved by choice making. Value allocations occur at each moment when decisions are made to alter or even to sustain the existing distribution of values.

"Authoritative."   Value allocations are taken as *authoritative* when the decisions are accepted as binding by people affected by the decisions. One of the most fascinating questions in political analysis is: Why do people accept the authority of the political system to allocate values in a manner that is not to their direct advantage?

That is, why do people accept the imposition of taxes, policies, and laws that they judge to be undesirable to themselves? The discussion in Box 5.4 suggests some of the reasons why the authority of the state is accepted.

"For a society." The final element in Easton's definition of the political system is meant to solve the difficult analytic problem of defining the boundaries of the political world. Easton limits the domain of the political system to those areas where values are being allocated "for a society"—that is, to those values where the state must act to protect and serve the public's interests. Recall the notion of *res publica*—"things of the people." The political system, in establishing the range of value allocations included in *res publica,* also sets the boundaries of its own domain of action.

Every political system defines its boundaries of legitimate action differently. This crucial point is reflected in the contrasting views of the role of the state discussed earlier in this chapter. We shall see throughout this book, and especially in Part Five, that some political systems allocate values in virtually every aspect of their citizens' lives

BOX 5.4

Why Do People Accept Authority?

There are many answers to the question of why people accept the authority of the state. In the classic definitions, authority is voluntaristic. **Authority** is based on a subjective belief in the *legitimacy* of the state: *A person willingly accepts the decisions of the state to be binding because it is "the right thing to do."* The individual's judgment that the state's authority is legitimate might be grounded in one or more of the following phenomena (see Weber 1958a: 295–301):

1. *Law.* The individual believes that the laws of the state are rationally established, purposeful, and enacted with formal correctness by appropriate public actors, and thus compliance with those laws is proper behavior.

2. *Tradition.* The individual is influenced by a long-standing habit among most people in the society to accept patterns of authoritative action.

3. *Charisma.* The individual is persuaded by a dynamic leader whose personal qualities are so extraordinary that the leader wins the individual's trust and unquestioning support. (Among the examples of twentieth-century charismatic political leaders are Winston Churchill, Adolf Hitler, Nelson Mandela, and Mao Zedong.)

4. *Social contract.* Most broadly, classical political theorists such as Thomas Hobbes (1588–1679) and John Locke (1632–1704) suggest that acceptance of the state's authority is due to a "social contract" in which each individual sacrifices certain personal values to a state whose actions ensure that social order will replace the violent state of nature.

5. *Socialization.* The effective efforts of the agents of political socialization might convince (indoctrinate?) the individual that the state has authority to make decisions and that obedience is proper, without relying specifically on any of these other sources of authority.

BOX **5.4** (CONTINUED)

In many contemporary states, explanations of the acceptance of the state's authority by most citizens are often based on a more explicit assessment of material incentives or sanctions, as described by types 6 and 7:

6. *Individual utility.* The individual is satisfied with the array of values that the state provides specifically to him, or with the broad values provided to all citizens, such as economic growth or social stability, to which he attaches great importance.

7. *Fear of sanction.* The individual might fear the negative values, such as deprivation of valued benefits, coercion, imprisonment, or even death, that the state can inflict on him if he openly challenges the state's authority. With sanctions, the line between authority and power exercise might have been crossed.

The debate over the legitimacy of the state's authority is a perpetual one. A fascinating literary expression of the authority debate is the classic play *Antigone,* by the Greek dramatist Sophocles (496–406 B.C.E.). Antigone violates a rule promulgated by Creon, who is not only her uncle (and potential father-in-law) but also the king. In defense of social order, Creon argues, "He whom the State appoints must be obeyed to the smallest matter, be it right or wrong. . . . There is no more deadly peril than disobedience"(Sophocles 1967: 144). In a similar way, contemporary political analyst Samuel Huntington (1968: 7–8) observes: "The primary problem is not liberty but the creation of legitimate public order. Men may, of course have order without liberty, but they cannot have liberty without order."

Ultimately, Antigone decides to do what seems morally correct to her, and she breaks the law. Thus Antigone represents the other side of the debate, which is characterized by eloquent defenders of the individual's right and even the obligation to resist his state's authority, when he believes the state to be wrong. In "Civil Disobedience," American philosopher Henry David Thoreau (1817–1862) writes: "If [the law of the state] is of such a nature that it requires you to be the agent of injustice to another, then, I say, break the law. Let your life be a counter friction to stop the machine. What I have to do is to see, at any rate, that I do not lend myself to the wrong which I condemn" (Thoreau 1849/1981: 92).

In some cases, the objective of resistance to authority is social change. Mohandas Gandhi's essential strategy in resisting British rule in India was repeated episodes of (generally) nonviolent resistance to a system of laws and authority that Gandhi judged to be immoral. Civil disobedience also was used by Dr. Martin Luther King, Jr., and others in the civil rights movement in the United States during the 1960s to protest laws that failed to prevent discrimination on the basis of race. In other cases, the resistance to established authority is more aggressive, and the objective is establishment of a new political order. Marx and Engels, in the famous *Communist Manifesto* (1848/1978: 500), conclude: "In short, the Communists everywhere support every revolutionary movement against the existing social and political order of things. . . . They openly declare that their ends can be attained only by the forcible overthrow of all existing social conditions. Let the ruling

(continued)

BOX **5.4** (CONTINUED)

classes tremble at a Communist revolution. The proletarians have nothing to lose but their chains. They have a world to win. Working men of all countries, unite!"

Despite such stirring calls to question authority, most people do usually obey the commands of others who seem to be in authoritative positions. In a famous series of disturbing social psychology experiments, subjects were told by a researcher to administer increasingly high levels of electrical shock to another person (who was collaborating with the researcher to fool the subject). Despite the shrieks of pain and suffering from the person they were shocking, most subjects continued to increase and administer the electrical shocks when told to do so (Milgram 1974). At some point, almost everyone justifies the unjustifiable by relying on the "I was only following orders" defense most associated with Nazi war criminal Adolf Eichmann.

while other systems intervene minimally. One political system might provide a total health care delivery system to all citizens, with no direct charges for doctors, hospitals, or treatment, whereas another system might subsidize only hospitalization for the very poor. One political system might require daily religious instruction in school while another system might forbid even the general discussion of religious philosophies.

It should be noted that Easton's definition seems to cover only national political systems. The idea of a political system for an entire society serves the purposes of this book well, since the book focuses primarily on countries. But analytically, a political system could exist at any level, even one that does not have ultimate authority. This concept could certainly apply to subnational political systems (including such American examples as states, counties, and municipalities). It could also apply to a supranational system that encompasses more than one state (e.g., the European Union). Perhaps a more generalized definition of the political system might describe it in terms of "the authoritative allocation of values *for a collectivity*."

Conceptualization of the Political System

Easton's (1965) conceptualization of the political system, characterized in Figure 5.1, is based on the idea of an *input-output system* within a broader environment.

This means that, within an environment, the system receives certain phenomena as inputs, does some processing of those inputs ("conversion" in the figure), and then generates outputs back into the environment. Each of the elements in Figure 5.1 is specified more fully in the following sections.

Environment.   The *environment* is the name given to all those activities that are not included within the state's activity domain of *res publica*. Thus it encompasses all those physical and social domains where the authoritative allocation of values for the society is *not* the dominant activity. Do not think of the environment as a separate physical area; the political system often operates in the same physical environment as other subsystems such as the economic environment and the social environment. The activities in the "intrasocietal" environment are occurring in the same spatial area as are the activities being performed by the political system. The environment is vast, because it includes not only all the activities within the society but also an "extrasocietal" environment that includes virtually every activity in the world that is external to the territory of the state.

Clearly, only a few aspects of this enormous environment are considered in any particular analysis of a political system. What is important about the concept of the environment is the idea that any aspect of it might affect the political system. That is, the environment provides opportunities and obstacles, resources and constraints, that are relevant to the functioning of the political system.

For example, there might be a shortage of fossil fuels within the state (i.e., in the intrasocietal ecological system). This "input" might provoke the political system to take some action (policy decision) to ensure more fuel for its citizens and its economy. Among the various policies the political system might adopt are these:

1. Stimulate additional fuel production within the society through subsidies for exploration.
2. Reduce fuel consumption through a very high fuel-use tax.
3. Encourage innovative alternatives by supporting research and development of synfuels.

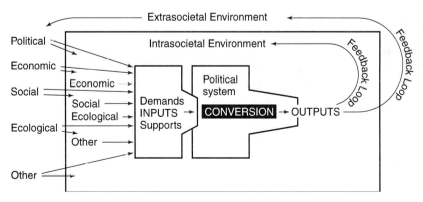

FIGURE 5.1   Conceptualization of the political system
Source: Based on Easton 1965: 31.

4. Obtain fuel resources from outside the state by using military force to capture some other state's fuel resources.

Can you think of other feasible policy responses to this problem in the political system's environment?

Demands and supports.   Among the inputs from the environment, the most direct are demands and supports. *Demands* are wants or desires for particular value allocations. Demands might come from individuals, groups, or systems either within or outside the society. When a citizen prefers lower taxes, or more expenditure on health care, or greater regulation of corporations, or a freeze on nuclear weapons construction, these preferences become demands to the political system when they are communicated directly by the citizen or by other actors such as spokespersons, interest groups, or political parties. (This process corresponds, in functional language, to interest articulation and political communication.)

Supports are actions by individuals or groups that indicate either favorable or unfavorable orientations toward the political system. These actions can be directed toward individual *actors* in the political system (e.g., Britain's Tony Blair, Cuba's Fidel Castro), toward elements of the *regime* (e.g., the prime minister, the supreme court, the municipal council), or toward a broad *political community* (e.g., the Sikhs, Francophones [all peoples speaking French], the Third World, dar al Islam [the World of Islam]). Support can be positive, as when a person pays taxes, serves in the state's military, salutes the flag, or votes. There can also be negative support, in the sense of actions that criticize or oppose the political system, such as a person refusing to pay taxes, avoiding military service, burning the flag, or defacing the ballot.

Conversion.   At the heart of the political system framework is *conversion*—the process by which political actors assess demands and supports within the context of the relevant environmental forces and then determine what values will be allocated to whom. In Easton's own discussions, the conversion process is treated a bit like a black box, in the sense that little detail is provided about how decisions are made.

Many analysts, however, have been especially interested in studying how the political system actually does make policy decisions and allocate resources. The most widely proposed general explanations of the decision process are the *class approach,* the *elite approach,* and the *group approach.* In each, certain groups in society (the dominant class, the small ruling elite, or a diversity of private groups) exercise their power and influence. The state's decision makers respond to these societal forces, implementing public policy decisions that are responsive to the interests of the most powerful groups. Each of these three approaches will be explained in detail in Chapter 9.

There are other analytic descriptions of the dynamics of the political decision-making system in addition to the class, group, and elite approaches. Here are brief sketches of several of these alternatives:

> In the *state-centered approach,* the major public decision makers act autonomously from the diversity of groups in the society. They define a national interest and then formulate and implement policies to achieve this national interest, regardless of contrary views from subunits in the government or from groups in the society (Krasner 1978).

In the *rational choice approach,* decision makers calculate the expected utility (the net benefits minus the net costs) for each alternative decision and then select the action with the most favorable benefit-cost calculus (Mueller 1993).

In the *incremental approach,* policy decisions are typically marginal changes from existing policies. Decision makers lack the cognitive capacity and the comprehensive information that would enable them to calculate expected utilities with precision. Moreover, the existing policy is usually a reasonable compromise—the result of a balance of political forces that has emerged over time. For these reasons, it is more sensible and more politically prudent to make periodic small changes that readjust policy toward the decision makers' current goals (Lindblom 1977).

The *bureaucratic politics approach* emphasizes that a decision maker's particular role in the organization greatly influences the way he structures the issue, the information he receives, and the choices he makes. Decision makers are loyal to their own subunit and its perspective rather than to the organization as a whole. Decisions are compromises based on bargains blending the agendas and values of the different subunits involved in the process (Allison 1999).

The *organizational process approach* assumes that an organization develops certain routine, standard operating procedures that determine the flows of information, the formulation of alternatives, the patterns of interaction, and the criteria for choice. Thus the established routines for making decisions are more important than the views of particular actors (Cyert and March 1963).

Outputs.   Once political decisions have been made, they become outputs of the political system. Some analysts find it useful to distinguish *outputs,* which are the decisions and the implementation process, from the *outcomes,* which are the impacts of those decisions. Some outputs are visible and obvious, as when the political system authorizes the development of a new missile system, spends the money to build the missiles, and points them toward its enemies. But it is sometimes quite difficult to identify decisions (outputs), since they might involve subtle actions, secret policies, or even "nondecisions" that perpetuate the existing value distribution or bury issues. For example, if some people demand government subsidies for small farmers and the government does nothing, there has been an allocation decision even though no visible policy action can be identified. A policy might also be implemented in a multiplicity of ways for different people, making it difficult to specify exactly what the policy output is. For example, the state might have a law that a person cannot kill another person, yet the state does not mete out identical punishment to all those who do kill.

Policy outcomes are another interesting subject for inquiry. Ultimately, it is the impacts of the political system's policy choices that really affect people's lives. The essential questions are: What difference did that policy choice (that value allocation) make? How does the implemented policy affect people's health, welfare, security, knowledge, and self-worth? How does it influence their life, liberty, and pursuit of happiness? Even more than in the analysis of outputs, it can be extremely difficult to identify with precision the overall effects of a policy and its effects on particular individuals and groups.

Feedback.   The final component in the systems approach is the "feedback loop." It is assumed that outputs might have impact on aspects of the environment and thus will affect the next round of demands and supports reaching the political system. *Feedback* is the term applied to the dynamics through which information about the changing nature of the political system and its environment are monitored by the system. Political actors are supposed to monitor this information because changes in the environment, inputs, and the political system might require the political actors to revise the value allocations they have previously made. In Figure 5.1, feedback is characterized as a loop to emphasize that there is continuous, evolving interdependency among components in the system.

System Persistence

For Easton (1965), the underlying question is: How does a political system persist in a world of change? The political system is embedded within a complex and changing environment. The political decision makers must maintain a delicate balance of forces: The environments must be prevented from constraining or overwhelming the political system and must be exploited for the resources and opportunities that they present; political actors must be sensitive and accurate in their perceptions of the effects of all other components in the system; demands must be managed so that they are not irreconcilable and so they do not overload the resources available; positive support must be nurtured and negative support discouraged or suppressed through some mix of value allocations that maintain the loyalty or acquiescence of the citizens. In short, the conversion process must operate with political skill and political will.

What happens if there is insufficient political skill or political will? The pressures on the decision makers might overwhelm their capacity to respond effectively. If the political system's performance is poor, there is likely to be a reduction in the quality of the citizens' lives, more problems from the internal and external environment, loss of support for the political system, and a rise in disorder.

At any point, it is possible that there will be changes in the political system: (1) The *authorities* who hold political positions might be replaced by election, by political pressure, or by violence; or (2) the *regime* might change through the implementation of new governing structures or procedures or through significant alterations in the pattern of value allocations. If these changes in the regime are massive and fundamental, it is even possible for a political system to "die." Easton and others have never fully specified the necessary conditions for the death of a political system. This would involve sudden and major transformations in the nature of the conversion process or the configuration of value allocations. The discussion of Cambodia in Box 5.5 describes a rapid series of major changes, some of which might be considered deaths of the political system.

For political systems, the 1990s was the most deadly decade in history. The obituary list is headed by the Soviet Union and most of the regimes of Central and Eastern Europe, including Czechoslovakia, East Germany, Poland, Hungary, and Yugoslavia (all between 1989 and 1991; see Chapter 15). In Africa, political systems such as Congo (1997), Rwanda (1994), Sierra Leone (1996), and Somalia (1991) collapsed, and others, including South Africa (1994) and Uganda (1996), experienced major political system transformations. One-party, authoritarian regimes were replaced by multiparty democracies in such countries as Nicaragua, Nigeria, and

Taiwan. Many political systems, while not "dying," made substantial transformations away from command political economies (see Chapter 8) and toward greater political democracy (see Chapter 7). Regimes can also be transformed by external actors, as in the fundamental changes in Iraq in 2003. Whether a particular political system actually dies can be a matter of debate, but the recent period has provided ample evidence that rapid and dramatic changes do sometimes occur within political systems. It is still unclear whether the first decade of the twenty-first century will be as deadly for political systems as was the last decade of the twentieth.

The Utility of the Political Systems Approach

Political scientists disagree about the utility of the political systems approach. For several reasons, some think it is a flawed conceptual framework for political analysis. Crucial concepts are defined in several different ways, and clear operational measures have never been developed for these concepts. Moreover, the theory linking the concepts is not specified with much greater precision than is indicated in Figure 5.1. And the approach has provided few predictions or hypotheses that are subject to rigorous empirical measurement and testing. Therefore, critics dismiss the political systems

---

BOX 5.5

"Death" of a Political System: Cambodia

One way to grasp the idea that a political system might die is to examine Cambodia, a state that has undergone several major transformations in a short time span.

The Cambodia of 1962 (*Cambodia I*) was a small, beautiful state in Indochina that had been granted its independence by France in 1953. It has been said that the most important activities in the lives of the Cambodians were to dance, make love, and watch the grass grow. They were ruled under a rather authoritarian political system by Prince Norodom Sihanouk, a hereditary leader who attempted to balance the forces of the left and the right within Cambodia and to maintain Cambodia on a course as a neutral state.

However, in the late 1960s, Norodom Sihanouk was unable to prevent Cambodia from being drawn into the increasingly widespread and intense war in neighboring Vietnam, especially because of the underlying power struggle in the area between the Soviet Union, the United States, and China. Some Vietcong (the guerrillas attempting to overthrow the South Vietnamese state) took sanctuary in Cambodia; but Sihanouk insisted that Cambodian sovereignty prevented the United States and South Vietnamese armies from invading Cambodia to attack these Vietcong. Sihanouk also attempted to direct international attention to the "secret bombing" raids in Cambodia conducted by the American military but denied by the American political leadership.

Because of Sihanouk's resistance to their military objectives, the Americans supported (and perhaps directed) a March 1970 coup in which the leaders in the Cambodian army overthrew Sihanouk and replaced him with General Lon Nol, a rightist

(continued)

BOX **5.5** (CONTINUED)

dictator who was generally viewed as a puppet of the United States. Under the Lon Nol government (*Cambodia II*), there were dramatic changes in the political structure and foreign policy of the country, and there were considerable changes in domestic policy. This political system was maintained by the United States from 1970 to 1975. In turn, the Cambodian government and military assisted the U.S. military in fighting the communist insurgents. There was escalation of the guerrilla war by Cambodian communists (the Khmer Rouge) against the Lon Nol government and extensive fighting in Cambodia by the military forces of the United States, South Vietnam, the Vietcong, Cambodia, and the Khmer Rouge.

With the collapse of the U.S. military effort in Southeast Asia, Lon Nol's government was among the casualties. Thus the Khmer Rouge came to power in April 1975 and created yet another political system, renaming the state Kampuchea. Under the communist regime of Pol Pot, Kampuchea (*Cambodia III*) experienced one of the most dramatic shifts in a political system during the twentieth century. The new government immediately relocated everyone from urban areas into the countryside, organized the entire population into collective farms that were really forced labor camps, and implemented a massive reeducation (indoctrination) program. In a brutal reign of terror, about one-third of the population of 7 million was either killed or died during a total restructuring of the society.

The Vietnamese exploited this time of disruption, invading and conquering the Cambodians, their centuries-old enemies. The Vietnamese army installed a puppet government under Prime Minister Hun Sen (a dissident Khmer Rouge) in January 1979. Thus *Cambodia IV* replaced Pol Pot's barbaric regime with a new political system that operated as a satellite to the Vietnamese communist government.

After years of guerrilla warfare by groups loyal to the Khmer Rouge and Norodom Sihanouk, a treaty in Paris led to United Nations–supervised elections for a national legislature in 1993. The election and subsequent constitution created *Cambodia V*, an odd combination bringing together many of the old adversaries. Norodom Sihanouk became king, a constitutional monarch with mainly symbolic power. His anticommunist son, Prince Ranariddh, as "first" prime minister, shared political power with communist Hun Sen, the "second" prime minister. The Khmer Rouge, who refused to participate in the election, continued a punishing guerrilla war and controlled large parts of the countryside.

This unstable system collapsed in 1997. After a brief civil war, Hun Sen's forces were victorious in a coup that deposed Prince Ranariddh, who was exiled. Key supporters of the prince's political party either fled the country or were executed. Meanwhile, rival forces within the Khmer Rouge captured Pol Pot, who was imprisoned and soon died. In a 1998 election, Hun Sen's party received about 40 percent of the vote and the prince's party received 30 percent. The prince returned and another uneasy coalition government was created. The government controls the military and the national administration, although most of the country still seems beyond the control of the central government. It remains uncertain whether any group can govern Cambodia effectively.

In summary, the political system of Cambodia has undergone numerous dramatic changes during a 40-year period. Minimally, four regimes failed to persist.

BOX **5.5** (CONTINUED)

And it seems reasonable to argue that there was at least one clear-cut "death" of a political system, with the replacement of Lon Nol by Pol Pot. The elimination of the Pol Pot government by the Vietnamese might also be classified as a death and rebirth of the political system, since much of the coercive, massive restructuring of Cambodian society was undone (although not the commitment to collectivism). A phrase in the Cambodian national anthem aptly describes the country's recent history: "The bright red blood . . . spilled over the towns and over the plain." The life expectancy of *Cambodia V* is quite uncertain.

This memorial to the victims of the Pol Pot regime is close to the capital city of Phnom Penh. The sign indicates that 129 mass graves were found and 86 of them were opened, yielding the remains of more than 8985 Cambodians executed in "reeducation camps."

approach as a nontheoretical and nonempirical abstraction that does little to advance a science of politics.

Few political scientists expect that the political systems approach will fulfill the early hope that it might become the basis of a "real science" of politics (recall pages 17–20 in Chapter 1). Still, the approach has been quite influential as a *metaphor*—a conceptual framework that describes how the political system operates and that suggests key variables and their linkages. It encourages the analyst to think of politics in terms of political actors, structures, and processes that constitute a system that is dynamic and adaptive as it constantly interacts with its environment(s). The political system is open, in the sense that the environment and inputs generate forces that affect the system and to which it must respond. And the political system is itself an active force, since its decisions and actions are aimed at modifying and shaping its environment and inputs by means of a constant flow of outputs. Many political scientists use this conceptualization of the political system, either consciously or subconsciously, when they attempt to explain the dynamic processes of politics.

THREE MAJOR CONCEPTS: A REPRISE

This chapter has focused on three major concepts that characterize large political entities. First, *state* is a concept that emphasizes the legal standing of these governmental entities, the necessary functions that they perform, and the organizational structures through which they take action. The discussion of three alternative views of the appropriate domain of state activities reveals the considerable range of differences in defining *res publica*, "things of the people."

Second, *nation* is a concept indicating a mental state characterized by a sense of shared identity among a set of people, distinguishing "us" from "them" in the sociopolitical world. The Indian subcontinent is an example of the widespread problem of disjunction between state and nation .

Third, the notion of the *political system* attempts to provide political scientists with the basic analytic concept for building a general theory of political entities. It specifies the crucial components in a dynamic and adaptive system whose essential function is the authoritative allocation of values for its society. The concept of political system is one abstraction that facilitates discussion and analysis of the major political units in the world. In Chapters 6 and 7, our discussion of these political units becomes more concrete as we examine the actual political institutions and structures prevalent in contemporary political systems.

KEY CONCEPTS

authority (pg. 122)

conservative view of the state

demands (pg. 126)

environment of the political system

ethnonationalism

inputs

liberal view of the state

multinational state (pg. 116)

nation (pg. 116)

nationalism (pg. 116)

nation-state (pg. 116)

outputs

political system (pg. 121)

political values

res publica (pg. 114)

sovereignty (pg. 110)

state (pg. 110)

supports (pg. 126)

territorial integrity (pg. 111)

FOR FURTHER CONSIDERATION

1. Do you think there are circumstances under which a country's sovereignty should be violated? What is the most serious problem with your position on this question?

2. Do you identify with more than one "nation"? Is there any conflict between these identities? Under what types of circumstances might a person's multiple nationality identities produce serious internal conflicts?

3. To what extent is it possible to align states and nations in the contemporary world? Would doing this be desirable?

4. Develop a dialogue between person A, who believes that the authority of the state must be obeyed under virtually all conditions, and person B, who believes that the authority of the state can be disputed in any situation in which B substantially disagrees with the state's decision.

5. Describe several situations in which the decision-making capacity of the most powerful actors in the political system is almost completely constrained by factors in the extrasocietal or in the intrasocietal environment.

FOR FURTHER READING

Barber, Benjamin R. (1995). *Jihad versus McWorld.* New York: Random House. An incisive analysis of the current world trends, in which there is a simultaneous globalization of culture and economics on the one hand and the breakdown of peoples into distinct and hostile nationality groups on the other.

Barnett, Michael N. (1998). *Dialogues in Arab Politics: Negotiations in Regional Order.* New York: Columbia University Press. Focusing especially on the views of key leaders of Middle Eastern Arab states and their attempts to create effective interstate relations, this study also offers insights about the struggle to define nation and state, given the complex identities based on Arabism, Islam, tribes, and countries.

Becker, Elizabeth. (1986). *When the War Was Over: The Voices of Cambodia's Revolution and Its People.* New York: Simon & Schuster. A gut-wrenching description of Kampuchea under the Pol Pot regime (see Box 5.3).

Connor, Walker. (1994). *Ethnonationalism: The Quest for Understanding.* Princeton, NJ: Princeton University Press. A detailed analysis of the nature of and the imperatives driving the strong identity with nation as opposed to state, enriched by many illuminating examples.

Deutsch, Karl W. (1981). *Nationalism and Social Communication.* 3d ed. Cambridge: Harvard University Press. A conceptual and empirical approach to defining the nation in terms of the intensity of patterns of human communication.

Evans, Peter B., Dietrich Rueschmayer, and Theda Skocpol, Eds. (1985). *Bringing the State Back In.* Cambridge: Cambridge University Press. Significant essays arguing that the state is a major institutional actor whose role was being ignored in many analyses that emphasized individuals and groups.

Huntington, Samuel P. (1996). *Clash of Civilizations and the Remaking of World Order.* New York: Simon & Schuster. The author elaborates his controversial thesis that very broad, nation-based conflicts have reshaped the patterns of world politics in the post–cold war era, with particularly powerful conflicts emerging between the nine cultural systems ("civilizations") that the author characterizes as Western, Islamic, Japanese, Latin American, African, Sinic (Chinese), Hindu, Buddhist, and Orthodox (Russian).

Kaufman, Stuart J. (2001). *Modern Hatreds: The Symbolic Politics of Ethnic War.* Ithaca, NY: Cornell University Press. The manipulation of ethnonationalist sentiments to serve the political goals of leaders is described in a set of intriguing case studies.

Kesey, Ken. (1962). *One Flew Over the Cuckoo's Nest.* New York: New American Library. A funny, gripping novel (made into a film) that, at its core, considers the virtues and costs of defying institutional authority.

Krasner, Stephen D., Ed. (2001). *Problematic Sovereignty: Contested Rules and Political Possibilities*. New York: Columbia University Press. An exploration of how changes in the global system are shaping and being shaped by the role of sovereignty, which is now a far more "contested" (i.e., debated) concept.

Marx, Anthony W. (2003). *Faith in Nation: Exclusionary Origins of Nationalism*. New York: Oxford University Press. This study emphasizes the way in which nation-based identity is created mainly by excluding groups, especially based on religious differences, as an intentional strategy to establish nationalism and consolidate governmental power.

Philpott, Daniel. (2001). *Revolutions in Sovereignty: How Ideas Shaped Modern International Relations*. Princeton, NJ: Princeton University Press. In tracing the evolution of the concept of sovereignty, during both the early period of state formation and the postcolonial period, the author reveals how political forces have altered the meaning and nature of sovereignty in the relations among actors in the international system.

Rashid, Ahmed. (2002). *Jihad: The Rise of Militant Islam in Central Asia*. New Haven, CT: Yale University Press. Author of the widely discussed *Taliban* (2000, Yale University Press), Rashid offers a rich account of the rapid emergence of religious nationalism in the "Stans" of Central Asia (e.g., Tajikistan, Kazakhstan). This dynamic has been particularly driven by poverty, corruption, and a reaction to the suppression of Islam under Soviet rule as well as the events in such neighbors as Afghanistan and Pakistan.

Snyder, Jack. (2000). *From Voting to Violence: Democratization and Nationalist Conflict*. New York: W.W. Norton. In exploring four different types of nationalism (civic, ethnic, revolutionary, and counterrevolutionary), the author explores the relationship between nationalism and other dynamic forces, especially democratization, political leadership, and political violence.

Sorensen, Georg. (2001). *Changes in Statehood: The Transformation of International Relations*. New York: Palgrave. A useful taxonomy of states (modern, postmodern and postcolonial) is the basis for an exploration of how states attempt to achieve their security goals as they respond to pressures from external and internal forces.

Taras, Raymond, and Rajat Ganguly. (2002). *Understanding Ethnic Conflict*. 2nd ed. New York: Longman. In addition to a helpful conceptualization of the nature of ethnic conflict, there are revealing case studies of the problems of nation and state in such settings as Canada, Eritrea and Ethiopia, Sri Lanka, and Yugoslavia.

Thoreau, Henry David. (1849/1981). *Walden and Other Writings*. Ed. J. W. Krutch. New York: Bantam. These essays, especially "On Disobedience," constitute one of the most influential arguments in English for resisting authority.

ON THE WEB

http://www.atlapedia.com/

Atlapedia provides diverse statistical information and various maps for each country as well as recent political history.

http://cwis.org

The web page of the Center for World Indigenous Studies, an independent, nonprofit organization emphasizing the distribution of knowledge about the issues and status of indigenous peoples (nations not coterminous with states) and promoting greater autonomy of power to such peoples.

http://www.ipl.org.ar

The Internet Public Library provides links to numerous reference books, newspapers, and magazines about various countries.

http://www.cia.gov/cia/publications/factbook/index.html

The web site of the U.S. Central Intelligence Agency includes the CIA World Factbook, a detailed and relatively up-to-date compilation of information about the political, economic, geographic, and demographic characteristics of every country.

http://www.state.gov/www/ind.html

Operated by the U.S. Department of State, there are country reports and information on international organizations, human rights, and numerous other topics related to foreign policy and international relations.

http://www.countryreports.org/

Country Reports provides comprehensive reports for most countries and also includes access to international news and reference maps.

http://www.un.org/Pubs/CyberSchoolBus/infonation/e_infonation.htm

Infonation, developed by the United Nations, provides the latest statistics for all UN member states.

http://www.economist.com/countries/

This site, produced by the publishers of *The Economist*, a respected British news-magazine, contains detailed country profiles and links to international news resources.

George Tooker, "Government Bureau," 1956.
The Metropolitan Museum of Art, George A. Hearn Fund, 1956 (56.78).

CHAPTER 6 Political Institutions I: Structures

In framing a government which is to be administered by men over men, the great difficulty is this: you must first enable the government to control the governed; and in the next place oblige it to control itself.

—James Madison

Along with the other American Founding Fathers, James Madison grappled with many questions regarding how to design a set of political structures and institutional arrangements that would result in an effective government. What responsibilities should be reserved for the political executive? How large should the legislature be? How should its leaders be selected? How powerful should the administration be? What should the relationship be between the courts and the other branches of the government? Should subnational governments be under the control of the national government? Like the Founding Fathers, leaders in every country establish and later modify these structures and arrangements in the attempt to create a government that can achieve valued goals.

These issues are the central topics of Chapters 6, 7, and 8. Chapter 7 will examine forms of institutional arrangements regarding such matters as executive–legislative relations, party system, and citizen democracy. Chapter 8 will analyze the alternative frameworks through which the political system and the economic system are linked. Chapter 6 provides an analysis of the four major structures that are basic components of most contemporary political systems: *legislatures, executives, administrative systems,* and *judiciaries.*

Chapter 5 made the analytic distinction between certain *functions* of governance, such as policy making and policy adjudication, and the institutional *structures* that might be involved in the performance of those functions. This distinction between functions and structures can be confusing because there is a tendency to identify a certain function with a certain structure. For example, one might assume that the national legislature is the structure that dominates the policy-making function. However, the distinction between function and structure is useful because, minimally, there might be structures other than the legislature that are significantly involved in policy making. For instance, in the United States, major policy-making activities are performed not only in the Congress but also by the chief executive (the president), the upper levels of the administration (the Cabinet departments), and the judiciary (particularly the Supreme Court). In China, the national legislature has almost no real power over the policy-making function, which is carried out by the Communist Party and the political executive.

This chapter emphasizes the primary functions that are typically performed by each of the four major institutional structures. As you read, remember that each major structure can perform a variety of functions in a particular political system and can be composed of many different substructures. For these reasons, the discussions emphasize broad patterns and generalizations, although there are always exceptions and variations across the many national political systems.

THE LEGISLATURE

Most states (about 90 percent) have a **legislature** as a part of their basic structures of governance (Derbyshire 2000). Among the names of legislatures (which can have one or two "houses") are the Senate and the House of Representatives (United States), the Senate and the Chamber of Deputies (Chile, Mexico, and Venezuela, among others), the Legislative Assembly (Costa Rica), the National People's Congress (China), the Majlis (Iran), the National Assembly (Egypt and Tanzania, among others), the Lok Sabha and the Rajya Sabha (India), the Knesset (Israel), the House of Representatives and the House of Councillors (Japan), and the House of Commons and House of Lords (United Kingdom).

Roles of the Legislature

Legislatures have always been structures in which policy issues are discussed and assessed. Indeed, the roots of the name of the first modern legislature, the British Parliament, suggest this crucial function—the French word *parler* means "to talk." Most early legislatures were initially created to provide advice to the political executive, typically a monarch, and to represent politically relevant groups. Many legislatures have also been responsible for a second major function—enacting public policies. The roots of the word *legislature* itself are the Latin words *legis,* meaning "law," and *latio,* "bringing or proposing." Some of the earliest legislatures, such as the Roman Senate (c. 500 B.C.E.–A.D. 100), had great power to discuss and enact laws.

Most legislatures are supposed to have three broad roles: (1) enacting legislation, (2) representing the citizenry, and (3) overseeing the executive. In the following discussion of these roles, be aware that it is difficult to generalize about the actual functions of the legislatures in all contemporary political systems for several reasons. First, these functions are often quite different from those specified in the state's normative rules, such as those in constitutions. Second, the functions of legislatures vary considerably from state to state. Third, they vary through time within a state. Fourth, even in one time period, the role of the legislature within a state can vary by issue and by the personalities of those involved.

Enactment of legislation.   It might seem obvious that legislatures draft, modify, and then ratify public policy in the form of legislation. In some political systems, many laws are initiated and written by the legislature. However, most contemporary legislatures do not have the dominant role in the policy-making function; rather, it has passed to the executive.

The essence of the legislature's power in the policy-making process is, in most political systems, a constitutional provision that a majority vote of the members of the legislature is required to authorize the passage of any law ("legislative enactment"). One of the most important responsibilities of the legislative majority is the power to enact laws that raise revenue and to authorize its expenditure on public policies ("the power of the purse"). In some systems, legislatures have special committees that thoroughly assess and can amend all proposed legislation under the committees' jurisdiction.

Representation of the citizenry.   A second major role of the legislature is to represent, within the governing process, the opinions and interests of the citizenry. Most legislators are elected by some set of the eligible voters, and it is assumed that a key responsibility of a legislator is both to reflect and to serve the interests of those voters.

However, the concept of representation is not straightforward because there are at least four different views of the "interests" that a legislator might attempt to represent: (1) the group that is most dominant in the legislator's constituency, possibly a social class, religious group, or ethnic group; (2) the political party to which the legislator owes loyalty; (3) the country as a whole, whose broad interests might transcend those of any group or party; or (4) the legislator's own conscience, which provides moral and intellectual judgment about appropriate political behavior (a position made famous in a brilliant justification by British parliamentarian Edmund Burke in his 1774 "Address to the Electors of Bristol" [1790/1955: 219–222]).

Is it possible for a legislator to represent all four voices simultaneously? Most contemporary legislators do not feel it is necessary to do so for the following reasons:

- Some legislators hold office in undemocratic systems where their actions are dictated by the political leadership, and thus they act as little more than "rubber stamps." This position characterizes the behavior of a legislator in Cuba or Libya, for example.

- Some legislators in both nondemocratic and democratic political systems are deeply committed to adhering to their political party's line or they must obey the party to survive politically. This is usually the situation for most members of the British House of Commons, for instance.

- Some legislators have such deep loyalty to a particular ideology or to certain societal norms that they rarely feel obligated to consider how they might represent other groups or policy positions. Certain members of committed religious parties, such as BJP in India or Shas in Israel, have this perspective, as do some members of extremely ideological parties.

In many political systems, legislators will occasionally trade votes and compromise their positions on some policy issues to ensure greater support for the issues about which they care most deeply. But in only a few political systems are many legislators sufficiently unconstrained that they often try to balance all four competing views of representation. Some members of the U.S. Congress can be characterized in this way. They attempt to balance legitimate but competing interests and group pressures that reflect different views on policy against pressures from their party, their assessment of the national interest, and the guidance provided by their own conscience.

Oversight of the executive.   The third major role of legislators concerns their interactions with the executive. In general, the legislature is responsible for overseeing the political executive's actions. The legislators in some systems have substantial capacity to influence what the executive does. The legislature might have the constitutional right to select the executive, to authorize major policy decisions by the executive, and to approve the chief executive's selection of key appointments. In some systems, such as in India, the president is actually chosen by the legislature (although it is the prime minister, not the president, who is the most powerful executive officer).

Many legislatures have the right to approve the executive's selection of major appointments. The Israeli legislature must approve the cabinet as a whole. The U.S. Senate has the right to "advise and consent" on such presidential appointments as cabinet members or Supreme Court justices. The Senate's 1987 rejection of Judge Robert Bork, President Reagan's nominee for the Supreme Court, is an example of a legislature asserting its power over appointments. In parliamentary systems, the cabinet and prime minister hold office only if they have the confidence of the majority of the members of the legislature, and the cabinet's policies are enacted only if they are approved by the legislative majority (see Chapter 7).

A second area of legislative oversight involves the right of the legislature to scrutinize executive performance. In many political systems, there are regular procedures by which the legislature can question and even investigate whether the executive has acted properly in its implementation of public policies. At minimum, the legislature serves as a discussion and debating chamber. Subjecting the political executive's plans and actions to public debate serves as a modest check on executive power. Many legislatures have a regular opportunity, during their legislative sessions, to question the specific plans and actions of particular members of the executive. In Britain, Italy, and Germany, for example, ministers in the executive cabinet must appear before the legislature and respond to legislators' questions or criticisms about any actions taken by their department.

Most legislatures also have formal investigatory powers on a continuing or a case-by-case basis. The 2003 Parliamentary investigation of Prime Minister Tony Blair (regarding his claims that Iraq had weapons of mass destruction and that this justified Britain's military intervention) is an example of such oversight. In addition, some legislatures have followed Sweden's innovative idea, setting up an *ombudsman*—an independent agency that investigates complaints regarding the actions of the executive branch and its administrative units. If legislative questioning, committees, or the ombudsman discover inappropriate behavior by the executive, they put significant political pressure on the executive to correct it. Of course, if the executive resists such pressure, the ultimate resolution of the dispute entails either legal adjudication or, in most cases, a power struggle between the executive and the legislature.

The most fundamental power of oversight held by some legislatures is their capacity to overturn the government. In a parliamentary system, the legislature can oblige or pressure the executive to resign from office by a vote of censure or of no confidence, or by defeating a major bill put forth by the executive (see Chapter 7). In Italy, for example, the legislature has forced the executive to resign about one time per year (on average, since the early 1950s). Even in presidential systems, the legislature has the power to overturn the executive by means of the extraordinary process of impeachment, though this is quite rare. In the United States, no president has been removed from office because of impeachment and conviction. However, in 1868 President Andrew Johnson was acquitted on the House of Representatives' impeachment charge by only one vote in the Senate, Richard Nixon avoided an impeachment trial in 1974 only by resignation, and Bill Clinton was acquitted by the Senate on two articles of impeachment brought by the House in 1998.

Structural Arrangements

Number of houses.   There is one very visible difference in the structural arrangements of various legislatures—the number of houses (often called *chambers*). There are *unicameral* (one-chamber) *legislatures* in 71 percent of the countries with legislatures (Derbyshire 2000). The presumed advantages of a unicameral system are that political responsibility is clearly located in one body and that risks of duplication or stalemate between parallel legislative bodies are eliminated. Nearly four-fifths of the countries with a strong central government (see Chapter 7 on these "unitary states") have unicameral legislatures. Such states include Algeria, Bulgaria, China, Costa Rica, Denmark, Finland, Greece, Hungary, Israel, Kenya, New Zealand, South Korea, Sweden, and Tanzania (see also Box 6.1).

In contrast, 80 percent of the countries that have two legislative chambers—*bicameral legislatures*—are federations (states that share power between a central government and regional governments). These federal states include Australia, Canada, Germany, India, Mexico, the United States, and Venezuela. There are bicameral systems in 22 percent of the unitary states, including France, Great Britain, Italy, and Japan (Derbyshire 2000).

Given the apparent advantages of a unicameral system, what is the justification for two chambers? There are two major arguments. The first argument is that two legislative houses ensure more careful deliberation on issues and laws. Second, the two houses can be based on two different and desirable principles of representation.

 # BOX 6.1

A Peripheral Puzzle: Nebraska

Nebraska is the only American state government with a unicameral legislature. Can you suggest why Nebraska's decision was a good one or a bad one?

In about two-fifths of the bicameral legislatures (e.g., Germany and the United States), one house represents the regional governments and the other house more directly represents the numerical and geographic distribution of citizens. Some upper houses also represent functional groups in the society, as in the Republic of Ireland, where members are appointed as representatives of such groups as agriculture, labor, industry, culture, and public services.

Over time, some bicameral systems have evolved toward unicameral systems, especially in cases where the need for extensive checks and balances within the legislative branch has not seemed compelling, where representation in the "people's" chamber has seemed adequate, and where the problems of overlap and stalemate between the two chambers have increased. Some political systems, such as those of Sweden and Costa Rica, have constitutionally abolished one chamber. In others, such as Norway and Britain, the powers of one chamber have been so reduced that it can delay, but cannot veto, the decisions of the more powerful chamber. In fact, the United States is now the only bicameral political system in which the regional upper chamber (the Senate) is more powerful than the popularly based lower chamber (the House of Representatives) (Derbyshire 2000).

Size of legislatures.   The number of members within legislatures varies enormously, with some houses having fewer than ten members and others having thousands of members (e.g., the National People's Congress in China has 2,979 members). The single house or the lower house typically represents "the people," with legislators elected proportionately to the population. In general, there is a positive correlation between a country's population and its number of legislators (a ratio defined mathematically as a "cube root law" by Taagepera and Shugart 1989: 174–179). However, among the more populous countries, there is no obvious principle for determining the optimal numbers of legislators. In the U.S. House of Representatives, 435 members are elected, a ratio of 1 member per 554,000 people. Of the 165 countries with a legislature, only India has a higher ratio of population to members than does the United States. The United Kingdom, with less than one-third the U.S. population, has 659 elected members in its House of Commons, a ratio of 1 member per 87,000 citizens. More than half of all countries have a ratio of fewer than 50,000 people per representative (Derbyshire 2000).

Can you think of an appropriate criterion for deciding the number of members in a country's legislature? For example, are there reasons why the upper house in the United States (the Senate) has two rather than three—or four or more—representatives for each state?

The Decline of Legislatures

Many observers claim that for more than one hundred years, there has been a general decline in the power of legislatures relative to executives and bureaucracies. Is this true, and if so, why? Actually, it is very difficult to provide a definitive answer to these questions about relative power using the techniques of crossnational empirical analysis. In large part, this is because the precise measurement of power continues to be a puzzle for which political science has no clear solution (see Box 6.2).

Given the difficulty of assessing political power with precision, is it possible to provide *any* answer to the question of measuring the decline of legislative power?

Developing an empirical test that could do so is quite challenging. It requires measuring and comparing the power not only of the legislature but also of the executive and the bureaucracy at several points in time and across several (many?) countries. Since no studies have provided a rigorous analysis of this issue, we might begin with a more modest question: Is there evidence that contemporary legislatures display

BOX 6.2

The Problem of Defining Power

Few discussions about politics can occur without direct or indirect reference to power. There is general agreement that **power** *is exercised when A (one actor) induces B (another actor) to behave in a manner in which B would not otherwise behave.* This emphasizes a causal relation between what A wants and what B does. The two actors could be two individuals or groups or even countries.

The key question, of course, is: How does A exercise this power over B? Many political scientists and other social scientists have grappled with this question. (For different views, see Bachrach and Baratz 1962; Boulding 1989; Dahl and Stinebrickner 2003; Lukes 1997; and Wrong 1995.) Kenneth Boulding (1993) suggests that there are three major varieties of power:

1. *Force* (coercive power). Here, A indicates to B that unless B does what A wants, A will cause something to occur that B does not want. The concept of "power politics" is usually understood as a situation involving force—typically based on coercion or at least the threat of coercion by A. The instruments of force available to A might involve direct bodily harm to B (e.g., guns, bombs, torture) or imposing undesirable conditions on B (e.g., imprisonment, discriminatory treatment). Of course, B might not yield to A's threat of force, responding, for example, with a counterthreat. Also, B might resist A's actual use of force with counterforce, resulting in a fight.

2. *Exchange* (economic power). A can have economic resources that alter B's behavior. This exercise of economic power could be coercive, in the sense that A might prevent B from enjoying certain economic benefits. For example, A might refuse to sell or give to B an important resource that B needs (e.g., oil, economic aid) unless B meets A's demands. Alternatively, A and B might engage in a more cooperative arrangement, where A promises a resource to B (e.g., a trade agreement, a bribe) if B does what A desires.

3. *Mutuality* (integrative power). Power can also be exercised if B perceives a shared commonality with A. In this case, B conforms to A's demand because B feels a bond of affection or loyalty to A. For example, B might decide that A has legitimacy—that B should obey A because A is worthy of exercising authority (recall Box 5.4). Thus B feels a moral or social obligation to yield to A. Integrative power is the least coercive and most subtle form of power exercise; it is probably most widespread in the world of political relationships. It is

(continued)

BOX **6.2** (CONTINUED)

a power relationship because it causes B to do something that A wants but that B would not otherwise do.

Notice that these three forms of power cover an enormous range of processes. Many situations involve a complex mix of these dynamic processes, and it is hard to specify which particular type of power has actually caused the observed behavior. These kinds of conceptual and empirical problems have led most political scientists to admit, often with embarrassment, that operationalization and measurement of one of the central concepts in political science remains elusive. However, because most people share a broad common understanding of the idea of power, it is reasonable to continue to refer to it. And it is worthwhile to attempt to analyze empirical questions regarding the relative power of legislatures, executives, and other political actors.

significant political weaknesses? Despite the absence of precise measures, there are a few types of circumstantial evidence that do suggest legislative weakness.

To begin with, the weakness of the legislature seems undeniable in about one in twenty contemporary political systems that have no working legislature whose power we might assess.

Moreover, in about one-fifth of the remaining states, the legislature is essentially a rubber stamp for the actions of a powerful political executive. Thus in about one in four contemporary political systems, the legislature need not be considered a major power structure.

Among the political systems in which there do seem to be real legislatures, several indirect indicators point to their relative weakness. First, most legislatures do not provide a coherent structure within which power can be concentrated and exercised effectively. Many legislatures have relatively slow and cumbersome procedures for the lawmaking function, especially where there are regular legislative committees that amend legislation. This complexity in the legislative process is even more evident in bicameral systems since there is often disagreement between the two chambers.

Second, most legislatures react to policy initiatives from the executive more than they create policy. The legislatures almost never have the level of support services that are available to the executive. Their budgets, facilities, staff sizes, and even the legislators' own salaries are significantly lower than those of top members of the executive and administrative structures. Similarly, the technical expertise and knowledge resources available to legislatures are far less than those of the executive and administrative structures, a major liability when legislators attempt to deal with the complex subjects facing governments in modern societies.

Some analysts have argued that a third, more social-psychological weakness of legislatures exists: most citizens desire clear, dynamic, and singular political leadership, but legislatures are typically composed of many people who most citizens feel are either indistinguishable or offer too many different identities. In the United States, for example, it is usually possible to answer this question: What does the president think about issue Y? But how does one answer the corresponding question: What does the legislature think about issue Y? In this case, there are not only two chambers and two parties but also a great diversity of different opinions among the individuals and factions within the legislature. In a sense, even though legislatures usually have spokespersons and leaders, no one can truly speak for the legislature. One might even conclude that the legislature in a domestic society tends to fulfill one of its roles *too* well—its members too accurately represent the diversity of political beliefs among the society's population, and thus they speak with many voices.

While the empirical evidence is sketchy rather than systematic, the reasons cited in the preceding discussion suggest why the power of legislatures might not have kept pace with that of other institutions, especially the executive and the administration. Clearly, not all legislatures are impotent or dying institutions. Certain national legislatures remain extremely powerful political structures, such as those in Italy, Japan, Sweden, and the United States. In most other relatively democratic political systems, legislatures have significant impacts on the authoritative allocation of values through their roles in enacting legislation, in representation, and in oversight. And in virtually all societies that have a legislature, its members can exercise political power in many subtle ways. At the least, legislative members have dramatically more political power than most other citizens.

EXECUTIVES

The historical evidence indicates that as long as there have been political systems, there have been individuals or small groups who assume top leadership roles. Such leaders have the responsibility to formulate and especially to implement public policy, and can be broadly called the *executive structure.* The word "executive" comes from the Latin *ex sequi,* meaning "to follow out" or "to carry out." Thus the particular role of the **executive** is *to carry out the political system's policies, laws, or directives.*

One might be tempted to generalize that a few individuals emerge as the leadership cadre in *every* political order. But there are some historical counterexamples, especially from Africa and Asia, of societies that are "acephalous," that is, "without a head." In such systems, many people in the community share power relatively equally as a collective leadership. Nonetheless, in most sociopolitical systems, a few people do assume the positions of executive power.

At the apex of the executive structure, there is usually an actor who can be termed the chief executive. In a national political system, this might be a single person with a title such as president, prime minister, chief, premier, supreme leader, or queen. Or the top executive leader can be a role fulfilled by two or more people. In this case, there might be a president and a prime minister (as in the French example described in Box 7.3 in Chapter 7) or a group exercising shared executive leadership (e.g., a junta).

A broader definition of the executive includes not only the chief executive but also the entire administrative system. Such a definition derives from the notion that the policy-implementation function (the "execution" of policy) is shared by the chief executive and the administration. The top executive group cannot survive without the continuing support of an extensive system of people who interpret, administer, and enforce its policy directives. However, we will examine the chief executive and the administration in separate sections of this chapter so that we can differentiate analytically among the major structures in most political systems.

Roles of Executives

Leadership roles.   In the contemporary political world, political leadership is virtually always identified with chief executives. The leadership role entails taking the initiative in formulating, articulating, and implementing goals of the political system. The effective chief executive becomes the spokesperson for the aspirations of the people, attempts to galvanize the people's support for these goals, and develops strategies that facilitate their accomplishment.

To a large extent, the chief executive takes the initiative in policy formation. Executive policy leadership is especially crucial during times of crisis because the executive structure has the potential for coherence and unanimity of action that are often lacking in the legislature. Moreover, in most political systems, the chief executive has the capacity to veto, either directly or indirectly, the legislation that is initiated by the legislature. Increasingly, even the drafting of legislation is a function dominated by the executive, since many major bills require the expertise and policy direction of the chief executive and its staff.

Symbolic and ceremonial roles. The actors in the executive role usually function as the unifying symbol of the entire society, becoming the ultimate mother/father figures for the people. This is especially true if the chief executive has a strong image, as do such leaders as Cuba's Fidel Castro, Libya's Muammar Qaddafi, and King Mswati III in Swaziland. The executive's presence becomes central to many of the society's rituals and ceremonies, whether it be the Japanese emperor's wedding, the Kenyan president's official send-off of the national team to the Olympic games, or the British queen's Christmas Day televised message to her subjects.

Supervision of the administration. In virtually all contemporary political systems, the executive has primary responsibility for implementing the policies and laws of the political order. At the apex of this administrative hierarchy, which might include millions of public employees in the state's departments, bureaus, and agencies, is the top group of the executive structure. Most systems have an executive cabinet, with each member directly and personally responsible for some major area of administration. Given the scale and complexity of the activities in each area, these top executive actors can neither know nor control all of the actions that occur within their domain. Nonetheless, they are supposed to set the broad guidelines for policy implementation, and in many political systems, they are accountable for any major failures that occur. In parliamentary systems, for example, the minister of a department will usually resign if there is a serious shortcoming or blunder in the area under her responsibility.

Supervision of the military and foreign affairs. Given the state's monopoly of the legitimate use of force, the top political executive usually has direct control over the military (including internal security forces). In such cases, the top executive is the commander in chief of the entire military system of the state, including personnel and other resources (aircraft, nuclear weapons, military intelligence, and so on). The chief executive must set policy and supervise the organization and utilization of the state's military capabilities, a task that can carry the most serious consequences for the security and well-being of the society.

Associated with control of the military is the executive's responsibility for foreign affairs—the state's relations with other states. As Chapter 12 will describe more fully, the relations between states involve complex patterns of cooperation and conflict, as each state attempts to accomplish its own goals in the international environment. The chief executive (or the chief executive's delegates) represents the state in its dealings with other countries. Particular significance is often attached to situations where the chief executives of different states meet directly, as in a state visit or a "summit conference." In fact, such meetings among heads of state typically are symbolic gestures of cooperation or occasions for ratifying agreements that have been reached by the chief executives' representatives. But the concentration of the states' political power in the chief executives is so great that such meetings can provide opportunities for major breakthroughs in the relations between the states.

Structural Arrangements

Fused versus dual executive. Many political systems have a **dual executive.** One actor, the head of state, performs the more ceremonial aspects of top leadership while another actor, the head of government, is responsible for the more political aspects. The essential virtue of the dual executive is that citizens can be angry or hostile toward the head of government while still remaining loyal to the nation and to the political system through their affection and support for the more ceremonial head of state.

Constitutional monarchies are obvious examples of political systems with a dual executive. In these systems there is a ruling king or queen (e.g., Queen Elizabeth II in Britain, Queen Margrethe II in Denmark, or Emperor Akihito in Japan) and also a prime minister or other head of government. The monarch has little or no power to make authoritative value allocations but serves mainly symbolic or ceremonial functions, as an embodiment of the nation and the people. Monarchs with limited powers also operate in some less democratic countries, such as King Norodom Sihanouk in Cambodia. Some countries have attempted to create a dual executive in the absence of a monarch, establishing a second executive office as head of state (such as the presidency in Germany, India, and Ireland) that is typically insulated from the daily struggles of politics and thus can be a symbol of national unity. In countries where the culture is deeply grounded in a religious belief system, the head of the religion can function like a head of state, as in Iran, where the president and legislature lead the political system, but the religious leader (the "Leader of the Islamic Republic and of the Nation"), Seyyed Ali Khamenei, also has formidable power over aspects of political life.

Most political systems have a *fused executive.* Here a single actor fulfills both the ceremonial roles associated with the head of state and the political functions associated with the head of the government. In such cases, it can be difficult or impossible to distinguish (dis)loyalty to a partisan political leader from (dis)loyalty to the nation. Clever chief executives use this fusion of roles to their advantage, "wrapping themselves in the flag." Such executives criticize or even punish their opponents by claiming that they are traitors to the political order (even though the opponents are usually only criticizing the political actions of the leader). For example, Zimbabwe's President Robert Mugabe has used this tactic very effectively against his rivals.

Some political systems have two actors who perform parts of the chief executive role but are not really dual executives in the sense described in the preceding paragraphs. For example, there are countries (e.g., France and Russia) where both a prime minister and a president perform essentially political functions, although one does usually have a stronger claim to the head-of-state role (see Box 7.3 in Chapter 7). In certain political systems, there is a political executive and there is a monarch, who in addition to serving as head of state is also a powerful political actor. Bhutan, Kuwait, Morocco, and Swaziland are examples where the monarch is the head of state but also has greater political power than the prime minister.

"The executive." While the term *chief executive* refers to the one person or small group at the apex of the executive structure, *the executive* is a broader term, including all the people and organizational machinery that are below the chief executive in the executive structure. Thus it encompasses upper- and middle-level decision makers in all the departments, agencies, or other administrative units that are in the chief executive's chain of command. As was noted earlier, a definition of the executive far broader than the one in this book might also include the entire administrative system.

The British Parliament opens yearly with Queen Elizabeth II, the head of state, delivering a speech written by the prime minister, the head of government. The speech outlines the legislation that the prime minister's government will introduce. The queen comes to the House of Lords, whose members surround the Law Lords (the highest judiciary group, wearing white wigs). By tradition, the prime minister and the members of the now-powerful House of Commons symbolically "demand" entry into the chamber and stand in the back of the House (they are not visible in the photo).

In theory, and usually in practice, this is a hierarchical system of political control, in the sense that the actors in the executive structure are supposed to follow the directives of the chief executive. But the chief executive's power over the rest of the executive is rarely absolute. Among the reasons why the chief executive's directives might not be carried out are these:

1. Units within the executive might be too disorganized to act effectively.
2. The executive might lack the resources to carry out policies in the manner desired by the chief executive.

3. Some units might be more involved in competing against other units than in coordinating their actions to meet the chief executive's policies.

4. Units might misunderstand, resist, or defy the chief executive.

Can you think of other reasons?

The Age of the Executive?

Although chief executives have nearly always been evident, and usually ascendant, in political systems, some analysts call the twentieth century the "age of the executive." This label reflects the apparent concentration of power in executives and the relative decline of legislatures' powers. What might account for this concentration of power? To some extent, this is a chicken-and-egg issue: The reduced capacity of many legislatures for coherent and decisive state action is linked to the emergence of coherent and decisive executives.

In comparison with legislatures, the executive structure tends to be more streamlined and less prone to stalemate and inaction. Also, the executive, centered in a single person or small group, can offer a unified focus for a mass public that either desires simplicity and clarity in an age of great complexity or wants a form of heroic leadership. The chief executive typically speaks with one voice and, when effective, can assure the people that political power will be exercised with certainty and efficiency to respond to the pressures and demands in the society and in the international environment. Even if a chief executive cannot deliver, she can at least promise decisive leadership in a manner that no other political structure can.

Can you specify conditions under which a state might be dominated by a structure *other* than the political executive?

THE ADMINISTRATION

While the chief executive is the top manager of the policy-implementation function, the administration consists of the thousands or even millions of public employees who do the ongoing business of interpreting and implementing the policies enacted by the state. These employees are divided into organizational units called by such names as departments, ministries, agencies, or bureaus. The state's military and police forces are often a particularly crucial component of the administration.

The administration is the machinery of government without which the political system could barely function. The units perform such important activities as maintaining order, collecting revenues, keeping records, providing public goods and services (e.g., roads, education, solid-waste disposal, health care, monetary aid for the needy), and regulating or controlling the factors of production (e.g., production of steel, provision of transportation, growth and distribution of food).

Bureaucracy as One Form of Administration

In most discussions, administration and bureaucracy are synonymous concepts; but in the attempt to clarify our language of political analysis, it is helpful to distinguish them. In this view, **administration** is the general term used to describe *the machinery and the processes through which rules and policies are applied and implemented.* **Bureaucracy** is a particular structure and set of processes through which the administration can operate. Its definitive description is by Max Weber, the great German sociologist we first encountered in Chapter 1. Structurally, bureaucracy is characterized by hierarchical organization and specialization by means of an elaborate division of labor. Weber also defined the concept of bureaucracy by a key process: Its members (1) apply specific rules of action to each case; therefore, the resulting treatment of each case is (2) rational, (3) nondiscretionary, (4) predictable, and (5) impersonal (Weber 1958a: 196–244).

Some readers may have regularly been treated by public administrators in ways that are consistent with these features because some countries have deeply incorporated this bureaucratic style. But there are also many contemporary political systems, and even more examples historically, where public administrators frequently treat people unpredictably and personally (see Box 6.3).

Among contemporary political systems, situations such as that in the imaginary country of Delta in Box 6.3 are widespread. Personal contacts and bribes (in various societies called *chai, baksheesh, mordida,* or *dash*) are often an essential element of success in dealing with the administration. Indeed, in some societies, people view a style such as that in Delta as normal and even appropriate because they assume individual treatment and personal favors are preferable to rigid application of the rules.

Is there a reasonable argument against a Weberian-style bureaucracy? In complex societies, terming an organization "bureaucratic" is not usually intended to be a compliment. Some criticisms of bureaucracy are really directed at all large administrative structures that exercise increasing control over people's lives and that expand their organizational domain (i.e., their turf) to a level where they are seen as too large and powerful. But at its heart, the negative use of the bureaucracy label has come to connote a system that is too inflexible and impersonal. The application of rules is so rigid that extenuating circumstances tend to be overlooked, and every individual is treated merely as a number. Bureaucrats themselves are seen to be relatively free of political accountability because they are protected by professional norms and hiring and firing rules that give them quasi-permanent tenure and insulate them from political pressure.

Despite criticisms of its occasional excesses in practice, most people in contemporary political systems conclude that the Weberian bureaucracy is the best administrative form because they prefer an administrative system that is overly rigid and impersonal to one that is based on corruption and personal favoritism. Many countries claim to be operating in terms of the ideals of Weberian bureaucracy, but there are enormous differences in the extent to which such ideals are consistently applied, especially in environments where they are contrary to traditional practice.

Administrative Functions and Power

The scale of activity of a state's administrative structure depends on that political system's definition of *res publica* (recall page 114). In political systems that penetrate a larger sphere of the society and economy, there is a corresponding need for

BOX 6.3

"Dealing" with the Administration in Gamma and Delta

An imaginary example might help illustrate the contrast between a classic bureaucracy and an administrative system that does not fulfill Max Weber's criteria. Two citizens, A and B, each intend to undertake an identical activity: to open and operate a small shop selling tea and pastries in the market district.

In the country of Gamma, both A and B apply to the Ministry of Business, where an employee requires each to complete a standard form and to pay a fixed application fee. An inspector from the Ministry of Health examines the premises to ensure that all health and sanitation regulations are met. When rat droppings are found in both premises, both A and B are obliged to hire an extermination service. Each receives the health certificate only after pest eradication and a second inspection. Both A and B open their shops.

In the country of Delta, citizens A and B make the same application. However, A is a member of the dominant ethnic group and B is not. When A applies to the Ministry of Business, she is given a form to complete by the clerk, also a member of her ethnic group, and the form is approved. When B applies, she is told that the maximum number of permits for the market district has already been issued. After lengthy discussion, B telephones her cousin, who is an important politician in the local government. The cousin contacts the undersecretary in the Ministry of Business on behalf of B, and the application form is now provided and permission is granted. When the inspector from the Ministry of Health examines A's shop, she finds rat droppings. She threatens to refuse the certificate, and so A offers her a substantial amount of money if she will ignore the problem. The inspector takes the money and then completes a report in which the shop passes the inspection. When the same inspector goes to B's shop, she again claims to find evidence of rats. When she can show B no evidence, B demands her certificate. The inspector shrugs, provides the name of the only extermination service she "guarantees," refuses the certificate to open the shop, and leaves.

The contrast between the two imaginary cases is clear. The administrators in Gamma behave in accordance with the bureaucratic ideal. Both A and B receive fair and identical treatment, and all rules of procedure are scrupulously followed. In Delta, however, the treatment of A and B is very different. Citizen A manages to succeed because she is a member of the favored ethnic group and because she is willing to bribe an inspector. Citizen B overcomes the hurdle of her unfavored ethnicity because she has an influential contact, but she fails to open her shop because she is not willing to accede to the extortion attempt by the inspector.

more extensive administrative structures, since the administration is the basic apparatus through which the state interprets, implements, and monitors its policies. There are at least five broad functions that the administrative structures in contemporary political systems perform, more or less extensively:

1. *Information management.* Administrators are responsible for the collection, storage, and analysis of huge amounts of information about the people and processes in the society. This information provides a crucial database—for recording activities and conditions in the society, for measuring the nature and impact of public policies, and for informing many ongoing decisions and actions related to the allocation of public values.

2. *Provision of knowledge.* Many administrators develop great expertise within their specialized areas. This knowledge can be of enormous utility for virtually every decision and action undertaken by the political system.

3. *Provision of public goods and services.* The essential work of the administrative structure is the implementation of policy. Administrators must constantly interpret and apply public policies that provide public goods and services to individuals and groups.

4. *Regulation and enforcement of public policies.* The administrators are also responsible for interpreting and applying many public policies that set guidelines for the behavior of individuals or groups. These can vary greatly, from monitoring collusion among corporations to enforcing traffic laws to protecting the civil rights of ethnic minorities.

5. *Extraction of resources.* In roles such as collector of revenues from citizens and businesses or operator of state-owned companies producing goods and services, the administrative structure is in charge of many tasks that generate resources for the political system.

This brief and general list of functions suggests the enormous breadth and depth of the administrative structure and its activities. Some observers argue that in the complex, extensive, and knowledge-based political systems of the early twenty-first century, the power of the bureaucracy is supreme. Although the administrators are, in theory, "servants" of their political masters and clients, it might be that in reality, these roles are reversed. Bureaucrats have such unmatched knowledge and experience in their specialized domains that generalist politicians rarely have sufficient expertise to question the bureaucrats' information, recommendations, or actions (Weber 1958a). Also, their power to grant or withhold benefits provides them with considerable leverage over clients. Career administrators have quasi-permanent tenure while politicians and clients come and go. The modern bureaucracy has such wide-ranging power and competence that it is typically credited with maintaining political systems when executives and legislatures are ineffective, as in the Third and Fourth Republics in France and in many modernizing states in Africa and Asia. Max Weber himself might have had the last word when he observed that "in the modern state, the actual ruler is necessarily and unavoidably the bureaucracy" (1958a: 211).

THE JUDICIARY

In a Hobbesian state of nature, disputes among people would normally be resolved by force or the threat of force. In such a setting, "might makes right." Thus a primary reason for the social contract is to authorize the state to intervene in the potential and actual disputes among individuals and groups by creating and enforcing rules regarding proper forms of interaction. Every society holds that those who violate its rules and laws (i.e., its policies) must be sanctioned. Because the rules in each society are deeply influenced by its unique culture, history, and politics, there are usually ambiguities regarding the rules:

What does the rule mean?

Has a rule been violated?

Who are the "guilty" actors?

How serious is the offense?

What sanctions are appropriate?

These kinds of ambiguities are resolved through the adjudication function in every political system. Many political systems have established judicial structures whose primary role is, or at least appears to be, adjudication.

Aspects of Adjudication

The **adjudication** function attempts to *interpret and apply the relevant rules or laws to a given situation.* When the issue involves civil law—the rules regarding the relations between private actors (individuals or groups)—the main objective of adjudication is to *settle the dispute.* Examples of such rules include divorce, contracts, and personal liability litigation.

When an individual or group behaves in a manner interpreted as an offense against the social order, adjudication can be an important mechanism of *social control.* Much of this is the area of criminal law, and examples of offenses are murder, substance abuse, theft, bribery, extortion, and environmental pollution. The state represents the public interest and protects the social contract, ensuring that the relations among actors are within the boundaries of "acceptable social behavior." In the same manner that the definition and scope of *res publica* differs greatly across political systems, the definition of acceptable social behavior varies dramatically. In some political systems, social control entails little more than regulation of the conditions under which people can do physical and economic violence to one another. In contrast, other political systems view mere public criticism of the political order or its leaders as a violation of acceptable social behavior punishable by imprisonment or death.

In some instances, adjudication can center on *arbitration regarding the behavior of the political system itself.* This is especially evident in cases involving constitutional, administrative, or statutory law—the rules concerning the rights and actions of the political system. The main issues for adjudication involve questions about the legitimate domain of action by a governmental actor in its relations with other governmental units or private actors. Such a dispute might concern a highly technical disagreement over the implementation of a specific policy (e.g., is a person with vision correctable to 20/400 qualified to receive state-subsidized services for the "visually impaired"?), or it might raise fundamental constitutional questions about the distribution of political power (e.g., can the chief executive order the military into a violent confrontation with another country if the majority of the legislature opposes the action?).

Judicial Structures

Most, but not all, political systems have specialized structures of the **judiciary**—the *system of courts and personnel that determine whether the rules of the society have been transgressed and, if so, whether sanctions ought to be imposed on the transgressor.* (Some broad definitions of judicial structures even include agencies of law enforcement, such as police and security forces, as well as agencies that apply sanctions against rule breakers, such as jails and prisons, although in this book, these are included among the administrative structures.)

In the United States, the adjudication function is closely linked with explicit judicial structures. The United States has one of the world's most complex systems of judicial structures, with its Supreme Court and extensive system of federal, state, and local courts, including judges, prosecuting attorneys, defense attorneys for the indigent, court clerks, and so on.

While there are significant crossnational variations, most political systems do have a hierarchical system of judicial structures, with appeal processes possible from lower- to higher-level courts. Most judicial systems also have subsystems that are

"I WAS IN JAPAN FOR A WHILE. VERY BORING. NOBODY SUES ANYBODY THERE."

Source: Sidney Harris

responsible for different aspects of adjudication. For example, the French judicial structure separates the criminal and civil law system from a second system that handles administrative law. In Ukraine, one major system handles criminal and civil law and a second major system is composed of special prosecutors who monitor actions in all types of cases and who can challenge, retry, or even withdraw cases from the regular courts. In Great Britain, one major judicial system is responsible for criminal law and a second handles civil law.

Among the contemporary countries that do not have judicial structures as part of the government are the Islamic countries that adhere to Shari'a law. Shari'a is the divine law, detailed in the Koran and further elaborated in the *hadith,* the teachings of Muhammad. It is Shari'a, not the laws of humans, that is the dominant judicial framework in such countries as Iran, Saudi Arabia, and Sudan. The Koran prescribes all aspects of social, spiritual, and moral life. As part of that prescription, the sections on law provide the details of what, in Western jurisprudence, includes criminal law, civil law, and administrative law. Shari'a is strictly applied by religious courts, and even the punishments for violations of the law are specified in the Koran.

The constitutions of many states, especially those that have been written in the last three decades, include provisions meant to create an "independent" judiciary. The notion that a judicial system can be independent is an interesting one. The legal system and the set of judicial structures in *every* political system are political. By its very nature, adjudication entails crucial decisions about the allocation of values and meanings for a society. Thus the only sense in which it is reasonable to speak of an independent judiciary is in assessing the extent to which the judicial structures make decisions and take actions that are at variance with other powerful political structures in the society, particularly the executive, legislative, and administrative structures. While there is no systematic research to clarify this question, the judicial structures in most states consistently support and rarely challenge the power and authority of the top leadership groups in their society. In general, the judicial structures are *dependent* on political power for their own power and survival.

However, there are some political systems where the judiciary is relatively independent. By exercising the power of **judicial review,** such *judicial structures can reinterpret or even revoke the policy decisions of the other political structures.* About one in ten states has a very strong system of judicial review. These include Canada, Colombia, Germany, India, Israel, Italy, Mexico, Norway, Switzerland, and the United States. Even in states where the judiciary is relatively independent, it is ultimately dependent upon other political structures, especially the executive and the administration, to enforce its decisions.

Even when the judicial structure does strive to maintain some political independence, it still might respond to political pressure. The conflict between President Franklin Roosevelt and the Supreme Court in the 1930s (see Box 6.4) is a visible example of a process that occurs continually in a subtler manner—the impact of external political power on judicial processes and decisions. In most systems, the people in top judicial positions are likely to share the values of the ruling groups, since they are appointed by chief executive leaders. And when judicial officials displease the dominant power group, they can be ignored, replaced, or even eliminated. In Argentina during the 1970s, for example, more than 150 high-level judges "disappeared," and it is speculated that the Argentinean government ordered their executions.

BOX 6.4

Packing the Supreme Court: FDR versus the Judicial Branch

There is a constant interplay of power between the judiciary and other structures. A classic example occurred in the United States during President Franklin Roosevelt's New Deal (1933–1940). Roosevelt drafted and pushed through Congress a series of sweeping laws meant to use national government policies to pull the country out of the Great Depression. However, the Supreme Court consistently ruled these laws unconstitutional since the New Deal legislation gave the central government a role far exceeding its constitutional powers as the Court interpreted them. After considerable grumbling and frustration, Roosevelt devised a different strategy for influencing the Court. Since there was nothing in the Constitution that limited the Court to nine justices, Roosevelt announced that he would significantly increase the number of members on the SupremeCourt.

Congress blocked President Roosevelt's initiative to expand the Supreme Court. But his appointment of two replacement justices and his threat to "pack" the court were followed shortly by a change of heart on the Court regarding the constitutionality of New Deal legislation. By 1937, the Court majority no longer objected to the central government's expanded activities. While it cannot be proven empirically that Roosevelt's threat changed the judicial reasoning of the justices, it was punned at the time that "a switch in time saved nine."

Actually, the most common pattern among contemporary states is for the judiciary to be little more than a loyal administrative arm of executive power. While the rituals of the judicial structures offer the appearance of protecting "justice," the reality is that the judicial structures serve the political elite. In short, while most judiciaries exercise some discretion in adjudication, the existence of a truly independent judiciary is a rarity.

CONCLUDING OBSERVATIONS

Traditional political science assumed that a description of political structures is the best means to explain how politics works. But empirical research reveals considerable diversity in the roles of particular political structures. There is no straightforward and necessary correspondence between a political structure and the political functions that seem logically associated with the structure. Thus precise, behaviorally oriented, and process-based analyses of politics now treat political structures more richly.

For a while, political structures seemed so fluid that they were treated as secondary elements, merely forming a context with which various political, economic, and social groups must deal as the groups' actions result in the allocation of values for the society. More recently, many scholars have reemphasized the importance of institutional arrangements. For these "new institutionalists," the particular configuration of political structures can powerfully shape political actions and outcomes (March and Olsen 1989). For the "neostatists," the structures of the state—its institutional arrangements, the actors who have major roles in its institutions, and its policy activities—are autonomous and have fundamental impacts on political, economic, and social life (Evans, Rueschmeyer, and Skocpol 1985; Nordlinger 1987).

A full understanding of the political world requires a clear grasp of the essential features of executive, legislative, administrative, and judicial structures. Institutional structures are the skeleton and organs of the body politic. As one could explain certain biological functions and processes of the body without explicit reference to skeleton and organs, so one could explain certain functions and processes of the political system without reference to structures. But such an abstract description of a biological organism would be incomplete without indicating the way in which the structures constrain and shape the functions. Similarly, attempts to describe or explain politics, especially in actual settings, are much richer and more complete if they include a characterization of how political institutions constrain and shape the political process. The next chapter will extend further the explanation of how the structures interact to produce different forms of the body politic.

KEY CONCEPTS

adjudication

administration

bicameral legislature

bureaucracy

executive

dual executive

fused executive

head of government

head of state

judicial review

judiciary

legislature

ombudsman

power

representation

unicameral legislature

FOR FURTHER CONSIDERATION

1. Who should a legislator represent on policy decisions? Develop an argument justifying your rank ordering of importance in representing the following: those groups who voted for the legislator, the constituency, the legislative coalition, the political party, the party leader, the nationality group, the country, and the legislator's own best judgment.

2. Evaluate whether, on balance, it would be desirable to have an administrative system that is relatively flexible and is sensitive to unique, individual circumstances in the handling of each case.
3. The discussion of the judiciary asserts that every set of judicial structures is political. Is the notion of an independent judiciary a sham?
4. What are the benefits and shortcomings of a political system that has a weak chief executive? A fused chief executive?

FOR FURTHER READING

Abraham, Henry J. (1998). *The Judicial Process: An Introductory Analysis of the Courts of the United States, England and France.* 7th ed. New York: Oxford University Press. A clear introduction to the theory and practice of judicial decision making in the three countries, as well as reflections on the judicial process in other countries.

Campbell, Colin. (1998). *The U.S. Presidency in Crisis: A Comparative Perspective.* New York: Oxford University Press. Informative studies of recent U.S. presidents are related to analyses of top leaders in Australia, Canada, and the United Kingdom. The author argues that these chief executives have become ineffective, particularly because increasingly, they are political outsiders who operate independent of the party and no longer work productively with their administrative structures and their staff.

Cappelletti, Mauro. (1989). *The Judicial Process in a Comparative Perspective.* New York: Oxford University Press. A summary of different approaches to jurisprudence and judicial decision making among developed countries.

Derbyshire, Denis with Ian Derbyshire. (2000). *Encyclopedia of World Political Systems.* New York: M.E. Sharpe. A thorough inventory and discussion of the forms and processes of contemporary political institutions.

Fenno, Richard. (1978). *Home Style.* Boston: Little, Brown. A revealing, descriptive study of how members of the U.S. House of Representatives actually behave, with particular emphasis on their efforts to serve constituents in order to enhance their electoral support.

Hess, Stephen. (1996). *Presidents and the Presidency.* Washington, DC: Brookings. A series of thoughtful essays on executive leadership and power spanning two decades by a leading scholar of the modern American presidency.

Morgenstern, Scott, and Benito Nacif, Eds. (2002). *Legislative Politics in Latin America.* Cambridge: Cambridge University Press. This lengthy book includes illuminating comparative studies of the different styles of legislatures and the alternative strategic behaviors of legislators in numerous Latin American countries.

Morris, Norval. (1992). *The Brothel Boy and Other Parables of the Law.* A distinguished legal theorist presents a set of fictional short stories, set in Burma/Myanmar, as a mechanism to explore some of the most controversial issues of the law and justice.

Osborne, David, and Ted Gaebler. (1993) *Reinventing Government.* New York: Penguin. An influential critique of large, bureaucratic government and a framework (using examples from the United States) of how to make government more responsive and entrepreneurial.

Peters, B. Guy. (1995). *The Politics of Bureaucracy: A Comparative Perspective.* 4th ed. New York: Longman. A rich, analytic comparison of the behavior and power of bureaucracies in many countries.

Pitkin, Hannah F. (1972). *The Concept of Representation.* Berkeley: University of California Press. A thorough descriptive and normative exploration of political representation.

Sparrow, Malcolm K. (2000). *The Regulatory Craft: Controlling Risks, Solving Problems and Managing Compliance.* Washington, DC: Brookings. Writing as much for those who work in the public service as for scholars, Sparrow offers a positive and persuasive argument in support of administrative regulation, detailing the role of regulators as important innovators and protectors of the public interest within the policy process.

Wilson, James Q. (1990). *Bureaucracy: What Government Agencies Do and Why They Do It.* New York: Basic Books. An interesting analysis of the performance of American national administration, identifying both the value and the flaws of the system.

ON THE WEB

http://www.gksoft.com/govt/en

Governments on the Web provides a comprehensive database of governmental institutions on the Internet. The site currently contains 17,000 entries from 220 different countries.

http://thomas.loc.gov/home/legbranch/cis.html

http://www.loc.gov/global/executive/fed.html

http://www.uscourts.gov/

These Library of Congress sites provide information about the legislative, executive, and judicial branches of the U.S. government.

http://www.fedworld.gov/

This site provides a huge central information network of the U.S. federal government, with searchable access to agencies and departments, documents, databases, and so on—a comprehensive site for searching for, locating, ordering, and acquiring government and business information.

http://www.thisnation.com/

This electronic textbook provides an in-depth look into American politics and also includes links to other American government-related Internet resources.

http://www.firstgov.gov/

The U.S. government's Official Web Portal provides a wealth of government-related material including access to the Internet sites of every major U.S. government agency.

http://lcweb.loc.gov/rr/news/extgovd.html

This site allows you to browse through the Library of Congress' electronic government resources.

It is an extraordinary moment in the presidential system. U.S. Supreme Court Chief Justice William Rehn-quist (seated at the top) reports to the members of the Senate that they have voted against conviction on both articles of impeachment against President Bill Clinton. Seated at the front tables are the "managers" of the House of Representatives, which authorized the impeachment trial.

CHAPTER 7 Political Institutions II: Institutional Arrangements

Democracy is:

a. *an agreeable, lawless . . . commonwealth, dealing with all alike on a footing of equality, whether they be really equal or not. —Plato, c. 427–347 B.C.E., Greek philosopher*

b. *the theory that the common people know what they want, and deserve to get it good and hard. —H. L. Mencken, 1880–1956, U.S. journalist*

c. *a system where no man is good enough to govern another man without that other's consent. —Abraham Lincoln, 1809–1865, U.S. president*

d. *the substitution of election by the incompetent many for appointment by the corrupt few. —George Bernard Shaw, 1856–1950, Anglo-Irish playwright*

e. *all of the above.*

f. *none of the above*

We know that all political systems are not democracies. But what constitutes a democracy? We know that all political systems are not identical. But are they all different? A basic task in political analysis is to determine whether there are some criteria by which political systems can be classified. This chapter considers various ways in which the structural elements of a political system can be arranged.

Consider the 21 countries listed here:

Some countries

United States	Iraq	El Salvador
Libya	Kenya	South Africa
Kuwait	Poland	Saudi Arabia
Japan	Italy	Laos
Cuba	Thailand	United Kingdom
Zimbabwe	Venezuela	Philippines
Singapore	Russia	China

Do you make any distinctions among these political systems? Does your distinction enable you to establish two or more categories and then place each of the 21 countries into one but no other categories? Would other people agree with your classification?

BROAD TAXONOMIES

As indicated in Chapter 6, the great majority of countries, including most of those in the preceding list, have executive, legislative, administrative, and judicial structures. You might attempt to classify countries based on similarities in the way these political structures relate to each other. Or you might emphasize other political institutions, such as the type of party system or the division of power among different levels of government. You might distinguish democracies from nondemocracies. Or you might use a nonpolitical criterion to categorize countries, such as their levels of economic development, or their regional location, or their predominant religious culture.

When you attempt to classify countries by some criteria, you are engaged in **taxonomic analysis** (as discussed in the Appendix). Developing a taxonomy is often the first stage in political analysis because it groups cases for comparative analysis and the effort to develop generalizations.

Are you satisfied with your initial attempt to classify the political systems in the preceding list? What criterion did you use? To the extent that you have distinguished the political systems by means of criteria that are *inclusive* (include all cases), *mutually exclusive* (each case fits in only one category), and *consistent* (others could apply the same criteria and make the same classifications), you have developed an adequate taxonomic scheme. Whether your classificatory system is useful is another matter, and this depends on whether it provides a meaningful ordering of the cases.

This chapter will suggest various ways in which political systems might be classified on the basis of their key *institutional arrangements*—that is, the way in which certain key political structures are organized. The discussion should be useful both in the sense that it provides *analytic information* about the taxonomies used in the study of political systems and, in the broader sense, that it provides *descriptive information* about the basic differences among actual political systems. No taxonomy is used in all political analyses, because each taxonomy emphasizes different aspects of the political world. The choice of a taxonomy depends on the interests of the political analyst. This discussion begins by considering the classification of political systems using the venerable concept of "democracy."

DEMOCRACIES AND NONDEMOCRACIES

One of the most common methods by which political systems are classified is to distinguish democracies from nondemocracies. From our education, as well as our other socialization and experiences, most of us have an intuitive sense about which countries are democracies and which are not. However, the concept can become slippery when we try to apply it. North Korea calls itself the *Democratic* People's Republic. Is it? Sri Lanka calls itself the *Democratic* Socialist Republic. Is it? El Salvador, France, Kenya, and Libya also consider themselves democracies. Are they?

"Democracy" is such a highly valued label that most states, except a few systems ruled by a hereditary monarch, claim that they are democratic. Is virtually every contemporary political system to be termed a democracy? If not, what general label do you give to countries that are not democratic? "Dictatorships"? "Communist systems"? "Totalitarian regimes"? "Authoritarian systems"?

While we work toward acceptable definitions and labels, let us use "dictatorship" as the opposite of democracy. To begin to clarify your thinking, use your current understanding of democracy and dictatorship to classify the seven political systems in the first column of the list of countries on page 163. If you have been raised in the United States or Western Europe, you probably view Japan, the United States, and possibly Kuwait and Singapore as democracies, and Cuba, Libya, and Zimbabwe as dictatorships.

The qualification in the previous sentence regarding the site of your upbringing is a crucial one—it alerts us to a fundamental problem with any such discussion. Chapter 4 attempted to persuade you that how one understands and uses political labels is dependent on one's own political socialization and political environment. Thus you should not assume that people from other cultures will necessarily agree with your labels.

It might be argued that this problem regarding interpersonal differences in assessments underscores the virtue of the scientific method. The scientific method requires the analyst to specify what a particular concept means with great precision and in an empirically measurable manner. This method might be the only way in which people with fundamentally different ideological views could agree on which of the states are democracies and which are dictatorships. The discussion in this chapter will proceed in the spirit of the scientific method, although the author acknowledges his own lifetime socialization, which is grounded in the political conceptions of the American and Western world.

How might individuals with dramatically different political worldviews attempt to agree on the accuracy of the classifications suggested earlier? For example, consider these issues:

Libya calls itself a *"jamahiriya"*—Arabic for a "state of the masses" in which the people rule through local councils and leader Muammar Qaddafi holds no official title. Assume that we are able to establish empirically that the majority of the Libyan population supports the Qaddafi government (this is arguably the case, although we do not know it empirically because there are no genuine elections or reliable public opinion surveys in Libya). Under such an assumption, is Libya a dictatorship?

The same issue might be raised regarding Cuba under Fidel Castro. By what criteria is Cuba a dictatorship when a far greater proportion of people vote in Cuban elections and the government provides far more extensive social benefits to all its citizens than in either the U.S. or Japanese democracies?

By what criteria is Zimbabwe not a democracy when there was an election in 2002 with competition between different parties?

By what criteria is Singapore a democracy when virtually all of the members of the national legislature have, since independence, been members of a single political party?

In asking and responding to such questions, you begin to establish the standards that must be applied when you attempt to distinguish between democracy and dictatorship. These kinds of questions also underscore the importance of defining with precision the concepts that we use in political analysis.

Defining Democracy

What are the necessary and sufficient conditions for democracy? In its classic sense, true **participatory democracy** is government of and by the people—there is *active, direct participation by all citizens in the authoritative allocation of values.* Realistically, there is no such political system; indeed, Jean-Jacques Rousseau (1712–1778) claimed that only a society of gods could be a true democracy. If our definition is less stringent, democracy might entail the relatively equal capacity of all citizens to influence the allocation of values. It would be difficult to make a persuasive case that this condition holds in *any* political system, including Japan or the United States. In *every* political system, some are more equal than others. In every political system, some make value allocation decisions and others observe.

You might use a notion of **representative democracy,** wherein the *citizens elect people to represent them in the political process and to allocate values on their behalf* for the society. Another general term used to describe representative democracy is a *republic.* In fact, the majority of the countries in the world, in their formal title, call themselves republics (examples, from the A's: Republic of Albania, Democratic and Popular Republic of Algeria, People's Republic of Angola, Argentine Republic, Republic of Armenia, Republic of Austria, Republic of Azerbaijan. You might think that some of these A "republics" are not particularly democratic).

Kuwait seems to meet this criterion for representative democracy, although few would classify it as a democracy since about 90 percent of its resident adult population (all women and most men who cannot trace their Kuwaiti ancestry to 1920) are not allowed to vote in legislative elections.

Thus the definition needs to be refined to specify that the elections for representatives must be held under conditions of *universal (adult) suffrage.* Cuba meets this condition, but few would consider it a democracy, because, among other reasons, there are very limited choices for governmental office—all candidates are members of the single (Communist) party.

Is the definition of democracy adequate if it further stipulates that the elections provide voters with alternative choices among representatives? Since Cuba actually does present alternative candidates (from the single party) for the legislature, it seems the definition must also specify that there must be genuine choices. Even with this clarification, there are cases such as Singapore, where more than 95 percent of legislators are elected from one party. Thus even the notion of genuine choices among alternative candidates can be ambiguous.

It also is important to establish the recurrent right of the people to select political leaders who do take office. This condition, called the *limited mandate,* means that the electorate grants the authority to govern (the mandate) for only a short, fixed (limited) period of time and that the electorate then has the opportunity to select representatives again.

These are the key conditions of an *"electoral democracy,"* in which citizens periodically select political leaders from among alternative contenders who accept this

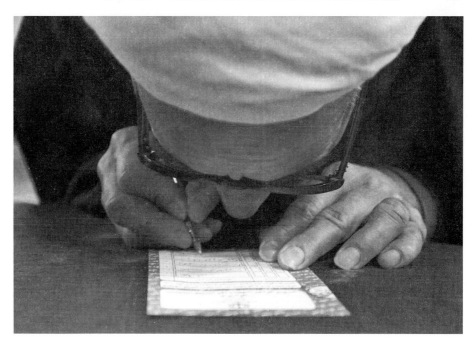

An Iranian cleric considers his vote in the 2004 election of the national legislature.

limited mandate. In Zimbabwe, there are multiparty elections with universal suffrage, most recently in 2002. Various parties put forth candidates for both the presidency and the legislature. In the recent elections, members of parties other than that of current President Robert Mugabe's own ZANU-PF party received almost half the votes and gained nearly half the seats in the legislature. Alternative candidates run for president against Mugabe in each election. However, Mugabe has used widespread intimidation and legal manipulations to prevent any serious electoral challenge to his presidency. Thus it might be concluded that Zimbabwe lacks a legitimate limited mandate and should not be classified as a democracy until Mugabe allows a genuine electoral process in which he is willing to surrender office peacefully at the end of his term.

More broadly, should a complete definition of democracy have more than electoral components? Perhaps a democracy must ensure not only voting rights and a limited mandate but also must allow the citizens and the media to exercise such freedoms as speech, assembly, and political opposition. We can classify a political system as a **"liberal democracy"** when *citizens enjoy not only electoral democracy but also these more extensive political rights and civil liberties regarding participation, personal freedoms, and opposition.* Some scholars include additional elements, such as an independent and neutral judiciary and civilian control of the military (Diamond 2000).

Even a liberal democracy is still less than the literal notion of full *"participatory democracy"*—understood as active rule by all the people. In a liberal democracy, the citizens have extensive rights, but there is still only "contestation" among competing elites, with most citizens exercising minimal or no direct control on policy decisions by the ruling leadership group (see Dahl 1971, 1991; Schumpeter 1950; Schattschneider 1960).

Perhaps we have now established one possible set of sufficient, as well as necessary, conditions for a **democracy:** *governance by leaders whose authority is based on a limited mandate from a universal electorate that selects among genuine alternatives and has some rights to political participation and opposition.*

This is a modest notion of democracy, since it guarantees the people little more than an occasional opportunity to select among the competing elites who govern them. Yet among the first seven political systems in the list on page 163, only Japan and the United States are clearly classified as democracies by this definition. Singapore is more problematic since the extent to which there is genuine contestation is unclear. While all seven systems encourage some forms of political participation and allow some political opposition, the authority of the political leadership in Cuba, Kuwait, Libya, and (probably) Zimbabwe is not based on its electoral selection, by universal suffrage, among genuine alternatives, for a fixed period of time.

A very expansive conception of democracy might emphasize not only the processes by which political authorities are selected but also the nature of *outputs* (value allocations) produced by those authorities. For example, Austin Ranney (2001: 111–118) defines democracy as a form of government in which power to make decisions or select public officials is granted to all adult citizens, based on majority rule, and in which "having ascertained the people's preferences, public officials must then put them into effect whether they approve or not" (Ranney 2001: 114). Notice that the first part of Ranney's definition refers to the processes of selecting political authorities and making value allocations, while the second part addresses the actual content of the value allocations, at least in the sense that those allocations must be consistent with what people want.

However, an analytic problem with this policy-output conception of democracy is deciding how to establish whether decision outputs do reflect the "people's preferences." Are they determined by yesterday's opinion polls? By the insights of the public officials? By an assumption that the voters in the previous election were approving the complete array of policies discussed during the campaign? None of these measures seems promising.

In fact, consideration of how the citizens' policy preferences are expressed raises associated questions about the **electoral system**—the *framework by which the citizens' votes select those candidates who receive a limited mandate to govern.* How are the electorate's votes converted into the selection of a particular set of representatives? Do you have a clear answer to how this should be done? In fact, in most countries, it is not merely a matter of counting votes. Box 7.1 suggests that choosing the best method for this conversion of votes to seats is not as straightforward as it might seem. Could a political system that meets all the other conditions for democracy be faulted because its conversion of votes to seats greatly disadvantages some voters?

Minimally, a process-and-output conception of democracy must incorporate a vision of the effects of the political system as well as the procedures by which value allocations are made. Thus it ensures the population of: (1) participatory rights to select and influence political decision makers empowered for a limited term of office, and (2) broader political and social rights such as freedom of speech, press, assembly, and religion. An extremely broad conception of the "output" aspects of democracy might also include provision of such value allocations as the right to employment, health care, housing, and other forms of social welfare.

This discussion might help you to identify the criteria that *you* think are necessary for an adequate definition of democracy. (It is certainly possible that your definition will differ from any of those suggested here. You should, however, be

---

 BOX 7.1

How Much Is Your Vote Worth? Converting Votes into Political Representation (via the Electoral System)

In Chapter 4 (Box 4.1) we considered how much casting a vote is worth to an individual—especially a rational person who evaluates all the personal costs and benefits connected with that action. At another level, every political system that allows its citizens to vote for elected officials must determine how those votes will be converted into a distribution of political representatives. How much is one vote worth to the political system?

When All Citizens Vote for a Single Office

When there is an election for a single office, such as a national president or a regional chief executive, the most obvious approach is to empower the individual who garners the largest number of votes. But some political systems complicate this straightforward approach by allowing preliminary elections in which some candidates are eliminated (e.g., primary elections in the United States) or in which candidates can volunteer to drop out after a first electoral round (e.g., the French elections for the legislature). Even more countries require that the winner receive a majority of the votes; if no candidate receives a majority in the first round, there is a runoff election between the two top vote-getters.

The United States is one of the few presidential democracies that does *not* allow its citizens to elect their chief executive directly. Even if they were previously unaware of the actual dynamics of electing their president, most Americans were confronted with some notable facts in the Bush–Gore 2000 election: *Fact:* Your vote for president can count for absolutely nothing because if your candidate does not gain the largest share of votes in your state, all the state's electoral college votes are cast for another candidate. *Fact:* One presidential candidate can garner the largest share of votes nationally and not be elected because the winner is the candidate who wins states that hold a majority of the electoral college votes. *Fact:* In 1824, 1876, and 2000, the presidential candidate with the largest popular vote was not elected. Does this seem right? *Fact:* If there is no majority in the electoral college, every state gets a single vote in the election of a president. Does it seem right that California, Wyoming, New York, and Rhode Island would all have equal impact on the selection of the president?

(continued)

BOX **7.1** (CONTINUED)

When All Citizens Vote for a Legislature

The conversion of votes into representatives in a legislature can require some interesting decisions.

First, how many representatives will be elected from each district? It is possible to elect one representative per district, as in the U.S. House of Representatives, but the districts in many political systems have more than one representative. The U.S. Senate has two legislative representatives per district, but many countries vary the number of representatives per district, depending on the population in the district, with as few as one and as many as thirty-nine representatives per district (Taagepera and Shugart 1989: table 12.1). At the extreme, some countries (e.g., the Netherlands, Israel) treat the entire country as one giant electoral district. Can you think of a sound argument for having all the legislators elected by everyone?

Second, how is the number of votes converted into the number of legislative seats? Table 7.1 presents a possible distribution of votes among candidates for four parties that are distributed ideologically from right (Party A) to left (Party D).

In a *plurality* system (column [a]), used in most countries with single-member districts, each voter casts a vote for a specific candidate, and the candidate with the largest number of votes wins. The virtue of this approach is that the representative is the candidate preferred by the largest number of voters in the constituency. In column (b) of Table 7.1, can you see a serious problem with this plurality victory for Candidate A?

In a system of *proportional representation (PR)*, which has typically been used with multimember districts, candidates from each party are elected in proportion to their party's share of the total district vote. For example, if there were twenty legislative seats in the district, the outcome would be that shown in column (c) of Table 7.1. Can you see how this distribution of seats was determined? The calculations

---

TABLE 7.1

Converting Votes into Elected Officials: Number of Representatives Elected per District in Each Electoral System

	(a) Percentage of Votes	(b) Plurality	(c) PR	(d) Preferential	(e) Approval
Party A	31%	1	6	0 (38%)	0 (46%)
Party B	15%	0	3	0 (0%)	1 (75%)
Party C	29%	0	6	1 (61%)	0 (69%)
Party D	25%	0	5	0 (0%)	0 (54%)

Note: Regarding this hypothetical example: In the proportional representation (PR) system, there are twenty seats distributed among competing parties in the district, whereas there is only one seat per district in the other three electoral systems. In preferential voting, it is assumed (in this example) that the votes for party B split evenly between A and C on the second count, and then all of D's votes go to C on the third count. In approval voting, it is assumed that each voter judges any candidate adjacent to his first choice to be acceptable. The percentages in parentheses (for the preferential and approval voting systems) reflect the ultimate percent of voters who support a particular party's candidate, given these assumptions.

BOX **7.1** (CONTINUED)

within PR systems can become very complicated if "leftover" votes are transferred into other districts or are pooled nationally for certain additional legislative seats.

An increasing number of countries have attempted to combine favorable aspects of both the PR and plurality approaches in a *mixed-member (MM)* system. Such systems were implemented in more than forty countries during the 1990s, including Italy, Japan, and Russia (Shugart and Wattenberg 2001). There are many variations. In some systems (e.g., Mexico), there is direct plurality voting for part of the legislature, and additional seats are distributed by proportional representation. In other MM systems, the particular representative who is elected is the person preferred by the largest number of voters in the district, but the party's total number of representatives in the legislature is proportional to its national electoral success.

Most political systems use one of the many variations of either plurality or PR voting, but other calculations are possible. A few political systems (e.g., Australia) employ *preferential voting*. Voters rank candidates in the order of preference, and then the votes for the candidate with the lowest total are redistributed to those voters' second choice, and so on until a majority candidate appears (see column [d] of the table). And some scholars have argued in favor of yet another voting scheme, called *"approval voting"* (see column [e]). In approval voting, voters can vote for all the candidates they find acceptable, and the winner is the candidate who is acceptable to the largest proportion of the electorate (Brams and Fishburn 1983).

Table 7.1 reveals that each of these alternative approaches can produce a different outcome! Which approach makes most sense to you? As you reflect on the virtues of these broad alternatives, you might notice that every system is flawed in some manner. There is no system that can perfectly mirror the voters' preferences in the composition of a representative legislature. Compared with plurality systems, PR systems and MM systems tend to enable more parties to gain seats in the legislature, which is good for representing citizens' preferences but might be less desirable for producing a coherent governing majority. Or it might also be argued that although the candidate of Party B is the first choice of the fewest citizens, he enjoys the broadest support and is the best "consensus candidate"—a virtue of approval voting.

So, how much is your vote worth? How much should it be worth? How should votes be converted into a fair distribution of representatives? These are intriguing political puzzles.

able to justify your criteria.) Can you now articulate a conceptual definition of democracy and use it to classify the political systems in the list on page 163? Do you think your friends will accept your definition and classification? Would a Cuban or Libyan student accept it? You might be surprised how difficult it is to develop a generally accepted definition of this most widely used political concept.

Defining Nondemocracies

How about nondemocracies? What concepts can be used to characterize those systems that are not democratic?

Dictatorship.   One conventional concept is dictatorship. Is dictatorship more easily defined than democracy? A stringent definition of a "dictator" might be a ruler with absolute power and authority (independent of any consideration of the process through which power was acquired). Can any one person or even a small group exercise "absolute" power? Would a system not be a dictatorship if the ruler is unable to exercise absolute power? Alternatively, **dictatorship** might be better defined by *the absence of a limited mandate*—a critical factor in our definition of democracy. That is, if the citizens have no regular and realistic opportunity to replace the political leadership, then the political system is a dictatorship. Clearly, an unpopular ruler or ruling group that has forced the population to accept its authority is dictatorial. However, even a political leadership that has popular support from the majority but does not provide opportunities for the population to renew the mandate in competition against alternative leaders could be defined as dictatorial. This definition seems to characterize the situation in Libya under Qadaffi, in Cuba under Castro, and in Zimbabwe under Mugabe.

Authoritarian regime.   In the current taxonomies of political scientists, the most common concept applied to nondemocratic systems is *authoritarian regime.* One critical element of authoritarianism, shared with a dictatorship, is the absence of a limited mandate. But **authoritarianism** adds another dimension—*the political actions and decisions of the ruler are not constrained, while the political rights and freedoms of the citizens are significantly limited.* In other words, under authoritarianism, the population has few, if any, political rights. An authoritarian regime places severe restrictions on the activities of individuals and groups who desire to influence the allocation of values by the political system. The great majority of the population is not allowed to participate in any political activities except those expressly encouraged by the regime. In most instances, this means that occasional public expressions of support for the system, such as mass rallies, are the only forms of political behavior that are acceptable (Linz 1993).

Citizens are not permitted to question the political institutions, procedures, or value allocations of an authoritarian regime. However, the nonpolitical aspects of people's lives, such as occupation, religion, and social life, are not generally under the direct control of the political system. In some countries, these other areas of life are still significantly controlled, but the control is by traditional societal values or by overriding religious values, not by the political system.

Totalitarian regime.   In a *totalitarian regime,* the definition of *res publica* becomes total. Thus under **totalitarianism,** *the political system's allocation of values and its control penetrate into virtually every aspect of its people's lives.* The totalitarian political system demands complete obedience to its extensive rules regarding culture, economics, religion, and morality. It prescribes and proscribes the behavior and even the thoughts of its population in virtually every domain of existence. Every political system intervenes occasionally in such domains, but the defining characteristic of the totalitarian regime is its constant and pervasive efforts at total control of its population's lives.

All organizations are subordinated to the totalitarian state. Every activity of the individual citizen is subject to scrutiny by the state in the name of the public interest. As an example of the penetration of the totalitarian state into all aspects of social life, the North Korean state defines the acceptability of films and plays, determines what and how much of each type of crop will be produced on every farm, discourages or prohibits the activities of organized churches, and decides which families will live in which housing units.

Totalitarian regimes, even more than authoritarian regimes, depend on the use of extensive coercion for their survival. The state employs its military, internal security forces, and other instruments of violence to suppress any citizen or group that challenges its authority. To sustain its pervasive control, the totalitarian regime also makes extensive use of the agents of political socialization, especially the media, the educational system, and cultural forms. Often, the totalitarian state is dominated by a single leader, venerated in a cult of personality and by a single political party. George Orwell's novel *1984* (1949/1967) is a literary vision of the totalitarian state, and recent examples include Afghanistan under the Taliban, Cambodia under Pol Pot (see Box 5.5 in Chapter 5), North Korea, and Sudan.

Some political systems are probably best classified on a continuum between totalitarianism and authoritarianism. These are authoritarian regimes whose political systems extend their control into important nonpolitical domains but do not exercise the totality of control associated with absolute totalitarianism. For example, Myanmar, Saudi Arabia under the Saud family, Uzbekistan, and Iran during the period under Ayatollah Khomeini (1979–1989) are not totalitarian regimes but do assert extensive control over culture, religious practice, and social life. Even further toward authoritarianism on the continuum are political systems dominated by a powerful military or bureaucracy that uses laws and coercion to constrain some aspects of the citizens' lives beyond politics. Examples of such authoritarian regimes are Zimbabwe, Indonesia under Suharto (1966–1998), Iraq under Saddam Hussein (1979–2003), and Congo (Zaire) under Mobuto Sese Seko (1965–1997) (see Box 12.2).

A Democracy–Nondemocracy Continuum

Consideration of several of the cases among the first seven countries named in our list, especially Singapore, Kuwait, and Zimbabwe, suggests that there are gradations of democracy among political systems. None of these cases is an example of totalitarianism, because significant areas of life are free from extensive political control. None of these countries is even fully authoritarian because citizens have some limited rights to criticize and oppose the leaders (although see Box 15.5 on behavioral controls in Singapore). In all three countries, the citizenry occasionally votes, which can result in turnover within the national legislature. The electoral process determines Singapore's top executive, whereas Zimbabwe's leader achieved power in a flawed election, and Kuwait's top leaders are hereditary.

Few, if any, actual political systems are perfect examples of democracy or its opposites. Do you think it is appropriate to think of democracy and dictatorship as two ends of a single continuum? Are democracy and authoritarianism two ends of a continuum? Or democracy and totalitarianism? Not all political analysts are consistent in how they employ these concepts. In this book, at least, dictatorship, authoritarianism, and totalitarianism will all be treated as modes of politics that contrast with democratic regimes. *Dictatorship* will especially emphasize the absence of a limited mandate for the political leaders. *Authoritarianism* will connote a more encompassing array of nondemocratic practices and significant controls over citizens' political behavior. And *totalitarianism* will be used to describe systems whose oppressive control goes far beyond the strictly political sphere into personal and social life as well.

Notice that the dictatorship dimension differs in an important respect from the authoritarian and totalitarian dimensions. Many authoritarian or totalitarian regimes are dictatorships. However, there are instances where people elect their leaders but the political system substantially limits the people's personal and political freedoms. Thus, as in Singapore, the Ukraine, and Iran, there can be an authoritarian regime with relatively nondictatorial leadership. Indeed, since the early 1990s, many countries that were previously nondemocratic, especially in Latin America, the former Soviet bloc, and Africa, have engaged in serious attempts to establish democratic political systems, although they might fall short of liberal democracies.

What proportion of national political systems are democratic? The precise number of countries in this "wave of democracy" (a key theme in Chapter 10 and in Part Five of this book) ebbs and flows yearly as some countries establish democratic systems while others retreat or revert to nondemocratic systems. Freedom House (2004) is an organization that uses the various conceptualizations of democracies and nondemocracies to analyze this question.

First, Freedom House identifies those countries that meet the minimal conditions for an electoral democracy. Second, those countries that do not meet these conditions can be classified as nondemocracies. Third, Freedom House analyzes the extent to which each country, whether an electoral democracy or not, grants its citizens the *political rights* (e.g., to form political parties promoting genuine alternatives, to allow contestation in elections) and *civil liberties* (e.g., religious and ethnic freedom, press freedom) that define a liberal democracy.

Freedom House has developed a widely cited 14-point scale, with a country scoring from 1–7 points on political rights and from 1–7 points on civil liberties. A country's combined score on the two measures can range from 2 points, the most extensive liberal democracy, to a worst score of 14 points in the world's most repressive regimes. Based on actual conditions, a country is classified as "free" (2–5 points), "partly free" (6–10), or "not free" (11–14) (Freedom House 2004; Karatnycky 2003). If a country is an electoral democracy but its citizens' political rights and civil liberties are assessed to be only partly free or not free, the country is also classified as an *"illiberal democracy"* (Zakaria 2003).

Table 7.2 indicates the classifications of selected countries by Freedom House, circa 2003, and Figure 7.1 provides a visual representation of the overlapping relationships among these related concepts. According to that analysis, 121 (63 percent) of the 192 countries are electoral democracies. However, 32 of these countries (17 percent of all countries) are "illiberal democracies," and thus only 89 (46 percent) of the countries in the world are "liberal democracies" (electoral democracies with full freedoms) (Karatnycky 2003).

To report these same data from the "underside," 37 percent of the countries are nondemocratic. More broadly, fully 56 percent of the world's population live in countries that do not provide the full political rights and civil liberties associated with democracy. Generally authoritarian regimes rule 21 percent of the world's population, who are "partly free," while 35 percent of the world's population are "not free" and live in conditions approaching totalitarianism (Freedom House 2003).

TABLE 7.2
Classification of Selected Countries by Level of Freedom and Regime Type, Circa 2004

Level of Freedom Country	(Score)[a]	Regime Type
Germany	Free (1,1)	Liberal democracy
Sweden	Free (1,1)	Liberal democracy
United States	Free (1,1)	Liberal democracy
Costa Rica	Free (1,2)	Liberal democracy
Hungary	Free (1,2)	Liberal democracy
Japan	Free (1,2)	Liberal democracy
Poland	Free (1,2)	Liberal democracy
South Africa	Free (1,2)	Liberal democracy
Mexico	Free (2,2)	Electoral democracy
South Korea	Free (2,2)	Liberal democracy
Brazil	Free (2,3)	Electoral democracy
India	Free (2,3)	Liberal democracy
Thailand	Free (2,3)	Liberal democracy
Yugoslavia (Serbia)	Free (3,2)	Electoral democracy
Argentina	Partly free (3,3)	Electoral democracy
Indonesia	Partly free (3,4)	Electoral democracy
Turkey	Partly free (3,4)	Electoral democracy
Nigeria	Partly free (4,5)	Electoral democracy
Singapore	Partly free (5,4)	Electoral democracy
Russia	Partly free (5,5)	Electoral democracy
Cambodia	Not free (6,5)	Nondemocracy
Swaziland	Not free (6,5)	Nondemocracy
Congo	Not free (6,6)	Nondemocracy
Egypt	Not free (6,6)	Nondemocracy
China	Not free (7,6)	Nondemocracy
Vietnam	Not free (7,6)	Nondemocracy
Myanmar	Not free (7,7)	Nondemocracy
Saudi Arabia	Not free (7,7)	Nondemocracy
Syria	Not free (7,7)	Nondemocracy

[a] *Scores:* The first score is for the level of political rights enjoyed by the population and the second score is for civil liberties. The highest level of rights and liberties is 1 on each score, and 7 is the lowest score.
Source: Freedom House 2004.

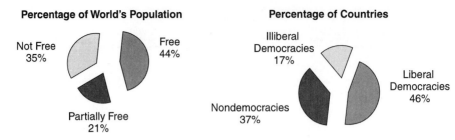

FIGURE 7.1   Distribution of countries and people regarding democratic regimes and practices

Sources: Freedom House 2003; Karatnycky 2003.

Note: Totals do not add up to 100 percent due to rounding.

Now that some of the complexities of defining political systems on a democracy–nondemocracy continuum have been explored, do you have a clearer notion of how you might define and operationalize democracy?

CONSTITUTIONAL AND NONCONSTITUTIONAL REGIMES

A related classification of political systems also emphasizes aspects of the relationship between the rulers and the ruled. In this schema, the key question is whether the political system abides by the provisions in the state's constitution or fundamental laws. A **constitutional regime** *operates in terms of the rule of law and ensures effective restraints on the power holders,* as defined within the constitution. In contrast, a **nonconstitutional regime** is characterized by *unchecked political power, and the structural arrangements of the constitution are not upheld.* In theory, at least, a state might scrupulously follow a deeply repressive and undemocratic constitution imposed by the political leadership and thus qualify as a constitutional regime. However, those who employ this distinction typically assume that the guarantees within the constitution provide for a generally democratic and humane political order.

Constitutions

At the heart of most political systems is a **constitution,** *a set of statements describing the fundamental rules of the political system.* Most constitutions are composed of a single, written document, in the manner of the U.S. Constitution. However, some political systems do not have such a document; their fundamental rules are embedded in major statutes, precedents, and legal decisions, as in Great Britain's "unwritten constitution" or in Israel's "basic laws."

Although the idea of a constitution has a certain timeless quality associated with it, the constitutions of political systems are always changeable. For example, in the 1970s, Belgium revised a 170-year-old constitution in an attempt to resolve conflicts between its Flemish and Walloon nations. And Sweden rewrote Europe's oldest constitution to alter the structure of the legislature and reduce the power of the king.

The constitutions of more than two-thirds of the contemporary countries have been enacted since 1945. (Box 7.2 discusses the interesting history of the 1947 Japanese constitution.) First, many of these constitutions are in states that achieved independence in the postcolonial period after 1945. Second, there has been a recent burst of constitution writing as more than two dozen states that had been part of the Soviet Union or its Central and East European allies have been drafting and revising constitutions in the attempt to establish new institutions and principles for their political lives.

And third, dozens of other countries have abandoned their existing constitutions and ratified new ones in an attempt to rejuvenate their political systems. For example, new constitutions have recently been adopted in Afghanistan (2004), Nigeria (1999), Poland (1997), Thailand (1997), and Venezuela (1999). The process does not always succeed. In the late 1980s, Israel abandoned its most recent effort to draft its first-ever constitution due to deep disagreements regarding issues of minority rights and religious practices.

 # BOX 7.2

Constitution by Fiat: Japan

One of the most extraordinary constitution-drafting episodes occurred in Japan. The Japanese operated under the Imperial Meiji Constitution from 1889 until they were defeated by the Allies at the end of World War II. After the war, Japan was under the control of the American occupation forces, led by General Douglas MacArthur. Concerned about possible communist influence in Japan, both MacArthur and officials in Washington, DC, insisted that the Japanese write a new, democratic constitution. A newspaper leak revealed that a Japanese commission charged with writing it was unwilling to propose major changes in the Meiji Constitution. Thus in February 1946, MacArthur took decisive action. He convened a

Source: Library of Congress

Entitled "The Real Japanese Diet," this racially antagonistic 1946 American cartoon suggests that the Japanese will be reformed by a "Diet" (the actual name of the Japanese legislature) imposed by the United States.

group of 17 American military officers stationed in Tokyo and told them that he wanted a constitution for Japan in one week. The group included four lawyers but

(continued)

BOX **7.2** (CONTINUED)

no one with constitutional specialization, no political scientists, and no one who was deeply knowledgeable about Japanese culture.

Using their knowledge of the American political system and their imperfect understanding of the British parliamentary system, the group completed the constitution in just eight days! The English version was translated into two forms of Japanese: formal bureaucratic language and common Japanese. Some of the Americans' perspectives were so alien to Japanese culture and political traditions that there were concepts in the new constitution, such as "civil rights," that were not even words in the Japanese language and required new ideographs. The constitution copied much of the preamble to the U.S. Constitution and referred to George Washington, President Roosevelt, and even Douglas MacArthur. The Japanese political leadership was shocked by and deeply opposed to the new constitution, but it was faced with a variety of even more undesirable threats (especially the possibility that the emperor would be tried as a war criminal). Consequently, the leadership capitulated and accepted the "MacArthur constitution." The Japanese cabinet presented the constitution to the Japanese public as its own. It was passed almost unanimously in the legislature, and it became binding in May 1947.

This constitution, written by inexpert foreigners, has been in force in Japan since 1946. It was not amended for nearly fifty years and it seems to have worked, in the sense that the Japanese maintained a stable and working political system in the subsequent decades. Can you explain this constitutional "success"? Perhaps the military officers developed a sound constitutional framework for the governance of contemporary Japan. Perhaps the constitution is primarily a symbolic document and its details are unimportant for the actual functioning of the political order. Or perhaps this was an early example of Japan's postwar skill: taking an American product, reflecting on how to improve upon it, and modifying it into a superior product.

While early constitutions tended to be relatively short and general, many recent constitutions are quite detailed. The Nigerian Constitution has 245 articles, and the Indian Constitution has 395 articles. The language of constitutions is also becoming increasingly similar because drafters liberally borrow ideas and even specific language from the constitutions of other countries. For example, more than three dozen countries have borrowed Abraham Lincoln's felicitous phrasing regarding government "of the people, by the people, and for the people."

Constitutional Regimes

The defining feature of a *constitutional regime* is that the state does attempt to fulfill the provisions of its constitution. The constitution declares the existence of the state, and it expresses the most important fundamental rules of the political system. Three sets of rules are crucial. First, the constitution allocates governmental activities, defining what actions are within the domain of *res publica* and what political structures will perform these various actions. Second, it establishes the formal power relationships among the political structures, indicating the conditions under which each is independent or dependent upon the actions of the others. Third, the constitution limits the power of the rulers and guarantees the rights of the ruled by defining the maximum extent of the state's authority over its citizens and by enumerating citizens' freedoms and benefits from the state.

This third set of rules is most important. A political system becomes more fully a constitutional regime to the extent that it abides by constitutional limits on the rulers' power and the guarantee of rights to the ruled. Even among constitutional regimes, the limits on the state and the rights of the citizens are not absolute and are not absolutely implemented. Some states justify suspension of major constitutional provisions as a "temporary" response to circumstances that threaten the stability of the society. Such a suspension can last for months or years. A regime becomes less constitutional when the disparity becomes larger between the provisions in the constitution and the actual politics of the society. In fact, the disjunction between promise and reality is frequent and extensive in many political systems.

Ultimately, the force of the constitution depends on the will of those with political power to enforce its provisions. The actual drafting of every constitution is either directly or indirectly controlled by those with political power in the society. Many groups in a society might offer interpretations of what the constitution means and how it ought to be applied to particular circumstances—governmental officials, courts, political parties, interest groups. But in the short run, at least, who has political power in the society establishes whose interpretation of the constitution will prevail and how the constitution's provisions will be implemented. In constitutional regimes, the interpretations are generally reasonable and judicious, and the implementation is fair (Sunstein 2001).

Few constitutions provide a precise description of how the political system actually works. Yet constitutions are significant. In the turbulent debate over the creation of Spain's new constitution in 1978, the distinguished historian Julian Marais insisted, "If the constitution does not inspire respect, admiration and enthusiasm, democracy is not assured." Even if the state makes major diversions from its constitution's provisions, the constitution remains a moral yardstick against which to measure actual performance and is a persistent reminder of the high ideals and goals that have been set for the political system.

Nonconstitutional Regimes

Almost every political system occasionally violates or ignores some principle in its constitution. But the political system can be termed a nonconstitutional regime when there is persistent nonenforcement of crucial limits on rulers or rights of the ruled. In this sense, most authoritarian or totalitarian regimes are nonconstitutional.

Several sets of conditions produce nonconstitutional regimes. First, some political systems (e.g., Bhutan, Saudi Arabia) simply do not have a constitution and are governed by hereditary rulers, religious principles, or traditions that guarantee no rights to the ruled and place few limits on the rulers. Second, in some countries (e.g., Myanmar, Sierra Leone, Somalia), the rule of law collapses because of the ruling group's complete disregard of the constitution or because of a disintegration of the social order through civil war. Third, there are instances where either the entire constitution or major constitutional rights are suspended "temporarily" because of a crisis in the society. In Israel, for example, this temporary suspension of constitutional rights (there is no written constitution) has persisted since independence in 1948.

AREAL DISTRIBUTION OF POWER

With the exception of small political systems serving only a few thousand citizens, most political systems have found it desirable or necessary to create governmental structures at several levels. The *areal distribution of power* describes the allocation of power and functions across these levels of government. National political systems, in particular, can be classified into three major forms (1) unitary states, (2) federations, and (3) confederations.

Unitary State

In a **unitary state,** there is *a central government that holds all legitimate power.* While the central government has indivisible sovereignty, it can delegate power or functional responsibilities to territorial units, which are given such names as departments, regions, or prefectures. These peripheral governments serve only at the convenience of the central government, which can revoke their power or functions at any time. More than 70 percent of the current countries are unitary states. Examples include China, France, Japan, the United Kingdom, and most Latin American and Asian political systems.

Why are most contemporary states unitary? Its major advantage is the presence of clear, hierarchical authority. While there might be a conflict between the central and the peripheral governments, the center's superior constitutional power is clear, and center-periphery stalemates are uncommon. In addition, because the loyalty of all citizens is focused on the governmental authority embodied in the national government, citizens tend to identify with the country as a whole, rather than with regional authorities.

Federation

A **federation** has *a constitutional division of power and functions between a central government and the set of regional governments,* which have such names as states, provinces, or cantons. In contrast to a unitary state, there is an explicit sharing of power among levels of government in a federation, and no level has legal power to dominate any other level in all policy domains. The essence of a federation is coordination, not hierarchy.

There are five major rationales for a federation:

1. *Large size.* Many states become federations to distribute governmental power where there is a huge area to be governed. Fewer than twenty-five states are federations today, but this group includes nearly one-half of the land area of the world. Most of the largest states are federations, including Brazil, Canada, India, Mexico, Nigeria, and the United States. During the constitutional debate in the United States, Thomas Jefferson observed, "Our country is too large to have all its affairs directed by a single government." The assumption here seems

to be that responsiveness is higher when government does not become too massive in scale.

2. *The prior existence of strong states.* A federation can be an acceptable compromise when strong peripheral governments create a central government. In the formation of the United States, for example, the already strong state governments were unwilling to give up the bulk of their power to a central government, as in a unitary state. Rather, they agreed to delegate certain functions to the new central government while retaining all other "residual" powers for themselves.

3. *The attempt to create unity or accommodate diversity.* Chapter 5 described the serious problems of conflict between states and nations, especially in the newer states. Federations appear to bond diverse nations into a unified state while still recognizing the different nations' diversity and desire for power. The peripheral governments represent major ethnic, linguistic, religious, or other nation-based characteristics of regions. India is a federation with 28 states, most of which are related to linguistic-ethnic dominance in the area and a few of which are related to religious dominance. The Indian Constitution defines a complex pattern of power distribution, with the center responsible for 97 governmental functions; 66 functions are reserved for the states, and 47 functions are shared between the 2 levels.

4. *The desire to concentrate power and resources.* In some instances, a federation is created to combine several states into a stronger political system. In the effort to create Arab unity and to expand the political and economic power of the state, Egypt has several times attempted to forge federations with its neighbors. Thus at various times Egypt has been part of federations with Syria, Yemen, Iraq, and Jordan. For similar reasons, Kenya, Tanzania, and Uganda formed the East African Federation. As in these examples, federations are often short-lived because the prior states are unwilling to sacrifice sufficient power and resources to a potent central government.

5. *The desire to disperse political power.* In contrast to the previous rationale, a federation can be established to prevent the overconcentration of power in the central government. After the trauma of Hitler, West Germans formed a federation to impede the emergence of another overly powerful central government. The bulk of legislative power was granted to the central government, but most power to administer and adjudicate the laws is held by the Länder (regional) governments.

Confederation

A **confederation** is *an association in which states delegate some power to a supranational central government but retain primary power.* It is a loose grouping of states in which each state's membership, participation, and compliance to the central government are conditional, depending on the state's perception of its own national interest. Confederations are usually created when states decide that the performance of certain functions is enhanced by structured cooperation with other states. To facilitate such cooperation, the states establish permanent supranational machinery. The United Arab Emirates is a confederation of ministates, and the

TABLE 7.3
Relative Strengths and Weaknesses of Areal Distributions of Power

Form of Areal Distribution	Strengths	Weaknesses
Unitary state	Clear authority	Hyperconcentration of power
	Decisive control	Weak representation of diversity and minorities
	No stalemates between center and periphery	
Federation	Diversity represented	Duplication and overlap of power
	Checks on center's power	Conflicts over ultimate power
	Unity created	Sluggishness; compromises
Confederation	Facilitation of cooperation	Conditional compliance
	Power retained by subunits	Instability
		Limited power

United Nations is a confederal structure containing more than one hundred and ninety member states. Confederations can emphasize economic cooperation, such as the European Union (EU), or military cooperation, such as the North Atlantic Treaty Organization (NATO).

Although confederations can serve many useful functions for member states, their activities and even their very survival are always contingent upon the members' continuing support. A member state will often refuse to comply with confederation policies that conflict directly with the state's definition of its own national interest. Disagreements among the members can necessitate negotiation and compromise, as in the periodic adjustments within the EU regarding such issues as farm subsidies to member states and a common monetary policy. A confederation can wither if the supragovernment is ineffective, as in the case of the Articles of Confederation in colonial America, or if members refuse to support its directives, as in the League of Nations after World War I.

Table 7.3 indicates some of the major advantages and shortcomings of each approach to the areal distribution of power. While each seems to have relative advantages under certain conditions, none is without considerable drawbacks, and none can ensure the effective functioning or even the survival of a political system. The general trend toward the centralization of political power within states has meant that the distinctions between unitary states and federations are less clear than in the past and that confederations have become particularly fragile.

FORMS OF EXECUTIVE–LEGISLATIVE RELATIONS

Another conventional method of classifying and especially of describing political systems is by defining the pattern of power and interaction between the legislative and

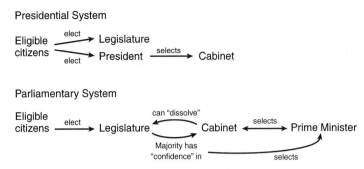

FIGURE 7.2   Presidential and parliamentary systems of government

executive structures. The taxonomy in this section emphasizes the two most common patterns through which the executive and the legislative structures interact to perform the functions of policy making and policy implementation: the presidential form and the parliamentary form of government. Three other types of executive–legislative arrangements are also examined: the hybrid, council, and assembly systems.

Presidential Government

The crucial feature of **presidential government** is the *separation of executive and legislative structures.* Figure 7.2 portrays the electoral chain of command that is supposed to order the relationships between citizens and major political structures. In separate electoral decisions, the citizens select the chief executive (usually called the president) and the members of the national legislature. This electoral process provides both the president and the legislature with independent mandates to represent the citizens in the governing process. The length of the term of each is predetermined, and thus the tenure in office of each is not dependent on the other (except in the rare case of impeachment of the chief executive).

The separation of executive and legislative powers is explicit and intentional, in order to ensure a system of checks and balances in the policy-making and policy-implementation processes. Primary responsibility for policy making (debating, modifying, and enacting policies as law) resides in the legislature. Although the chief executive can veto legislation, the legislature can override that veto. Primary responsibility for the implementation of policy is with the president, who has control of the government's administrative departments. The president also appoints a cabinet, whose members are responsible for overseeing policy in the government's administrative departments and are controlled directly by the president.

In practice, it is common to find considerable interdependence and blurring of functions between the executive and legislative structures, and especially for the president to have substantial involvement in the policy-making function. The United States is the model example of presidential government, and it is also found in many Latin American and some African and Asian states, including Colombia, the Ivory Coast, Kenya, Mexico, Sri Lanka, Venezuela, and the Philippines.

Parliamentary (Cabinet) Government

In contrast to the presidential system, the crucial element of **parliamentary government** is the *fusion of executive and legislative functions and structures.* As is indicated in Figure 7.2, the people elect the legislature (the parliament), whose majority empowers a cabinet, which then empowers one of its members to be the chief executive, typically called a prime minister or premier. The length of the legislature's mandate is often five years, but its term can be shorter under the circumstances described next. The complex relationships among cabinet, legislature, and prime minister merit further detail.

Cabinet and legislature.   The cabinet is a collective leadership group of 6 to 30 people who are, in most systems, also members of the legislature. The cabinet is responsible to the legislature. This means that the cabinet serves only as long as it can maintain the "confidence" of the majority of the members in the legislature. While serving, the cabinet has primary responsibility for both the policy-making and policy-implementation functions. Although policies must be voted into laws by the legislative majority, it is the cabinet that devises, drafts, and implements most policies.

In an intriguing manner, the cabinet and the legislature are at each other's mercy. At any time, the legislative majority can pressure the cabinet to resign, either by a negative vote on a major piece of legislation proposed by the cabinet or by a general motion of "no confidence" in the cabinet. Also at any time, the cabinet can "dissolve" the legislature, requiring immediate new elections. In the subsequent election, voters select a new legislature, whose majority then identifies a cabinet it will support, and the process begins anew. Thus the cabinet and the legislature, rather like two gunfighters standing gun-to-gun in a spaghetti Western, each has the power to eliminate the other but each might also be destroyed in the exchange. Since new elections put everyone's position in jeopardy, it is more common for the cabinet to resign or reconstitute itself than for the cabinet to dissolve the legislature.

Legislature and prime minister.   In the parliamentary system, the prime minister (or premier or chancellor or whatever the chief executive is called) is not directly elected by the citizens to be the top leader. The prime minister is the member of the legislature who is supported as chief executive by the majority of the legislature. This executive can be removed at any time by a no-confidence vote of the legislature and might also be obliged to resign if the legislature defeats a major legislative initiative of the prime minister. The prime minister directs the overall thrust of decision and action in the legislative process.

Cabinet and prime minister.   The balance of power between the cabinet and the prime minister can be subtle, although both depend on majority support of the legislature. Traditionally, a cabinet that had legislative support could select one of its members to serve as prime minister. The prime minister was *primus inter pares* in the cabinet—the first among equals. The prime minister exercised broad policy leadership within a collective decision-making body. If a cabinet majority no longer supported a prime minister, however, the prime minister either resigned or attempted to reconstitute a cabinet that supported him and was supported by the legislative majority.

In many contemporary parliamentary systems, however, there has been a substantial shift of power from the cabinet to the prime minister. In these systems, the electorate selects legislative candidates from a party committed to support a particular prime minister. If a legislative majority can be created, its leader becomes prime minister. The prime minister then appoints the members of the cabinet and clearly dominates the cabinet in the governmental process. In Figure 7.2, the two-headed arrow between cabinet and prime minister indicates these alternative patterns of power.

Thus the parliamentary system is characterized by the fusion of executive and legislative functions because the cabinet and prime minister formulate policies, guide their passage through the legislature, and administer policy through the administrative departments. However, the actual policy process in a parliamentary system depends on whether there is a coherent majority group in the legislature.

There are both "stable" and "unstable" parliamentary systems. In a stable parliamentary system, there is a clear majority in the legislature (such a majority may be composed of either one party or a coalition). This majority provides the cabinet and prime minister with sufficient legislative support to enact their policy program, without the problems of stalemate and confusion of accountability that can result from the separation of powers in the presidential system. Australia, Canada, Denmark, Great Britain, and Japan are examples of parliamentary government systems that are usually stable.

In contrast, an unstable parliamentary system often emerges when there is no coherent legislative majority. Instead, policy making requires agreement within a coalition composed of multiple parties that tend to disagree on some important policy issues. If the legislature votes no confidence in the cabinet or defeats it on a major bill, the cabinet usually resigns. Then the media report that a parliamentary government has "fallen" or that there are efforts to form a "new government" (a new cabinet, actually). The new cabinet might have almost all the same people as members, or it might have a quite different set of people, drawing its majority support from different groups within the legislature. In general, prime ministers in unstable parliamentary systems are weaker than those in stable parliamentary systems.

Unstable parliamentary systems have been prevalent in contemporary legislatures in which stronger ideological differences and multiple political parties have emerged. Italy has had an average of one cabinet (new government) per year since 1945. During the French Fourth Republic, the parliamentary system was so volatile that the average cabinet served for only 11 months; one cabinet lasted less than six hours!

Hybrid Systems

An increasing number of political systems attempt to blend desirable aspects of both the presidential and parliamentary systems. These **hybrid systems** *have a prime minister and an elected legislature that can both enact and implement policies, but they also have a president* (elected for a fixed term and having some independent executive powers) who, as a single individual, can act with decisiveness (Elgie 1999; Shugart and Carey 1992).

Some hybrid systems function more like parliamentary systems: The president has limited power, and the prime minister and cabinet exercise most of the control.

In India, for example, the president is elected by the legislature for a five-year term and has notable responsibilities, including the appointment of state governors and the right to take over governance of the states during emergencies. However, the prime minister is the dominant political power in the system, with the president performing mainly ceremonial roles, such as appearances on national holidays. Germany, Austria, and Ireland are other examples of this style of the hybrid.

In other hybrid systems, there is a more balanced sharing of power between the president and the parliament. In Finland, for example, the presidential executive controls the administration and has oversight powers. Although the president does attend meetings on major legislation and both the president and the prime minister must sign a law before it is enacted, the cabinet and legislature undertake most of the legislation. In these more balanced hybrids, the relative power of the president and of the prime minister/cabinet vary, depending on the constitutional rules, the personality of the officeholders, and the political situation in the society (see Box 7.3 on the French hybrid system).

Hybrid systems have been implemented in virtually all of the countries that emerged from the Soviet Union and in the post-communist countries of Central and Eastern Europe. In nearly all of these countries, the position of president is the

BOX 7.3

A Hybrid System in Action: France

Many recent constitutions establish a hybrid model in which both a president and a prime minister have significant political power. A central issue is whether two independent executives can share power effectively. An early example of this complicated system is the French Fifth Republic, based on the "de Gaulle Constitution" of 1962. France created this hybrid to overcome the highly unstable parliamentary government system of the Fourth Republic. The premier (prime minister) and cabinet are responsible for the day-to-day functioning of the government, as in a parliamentary system, but the president (an office Charles de Gaulle fashioned for himself as a condition for his return to government) has extensive power and the freedom to exercise it. The president is elected popularly for a fixed five-year term and then selects a premier, who selects a cabinet. The cabinet controls the budget and legislative agenda as in a normal parliamentary system; however, the president can dissolve the legislature while retaining the cabinet. And Article 16 in the constitution provides that the sweeping powers of the presidency may be exercised whenever the president *alone* deems the political situation to be dangerous for the country.

De Gaulle served as the first president of the Fifth Republic from 1958 to 1969. He was an extraordinarily powerful man, and he demanded extraordinary power. He established a precedent that the president can act far more extensively than the constitution allows. He dominated every premier who served during his presidency. The presidents after de Gaulle (Pompidou, Giscard d'Estaing, Mitterrand, and Chirac) continued to follow the de Gaulle precedent, exercising considerable power. This approach was reasonably workable during this period because the majority in

BOX **7.3** (CONTINUED)

the legislature, and thus the cabinet and premier, usually shared the ideological orientation of the president.

Many people felt that the French "dyarchy" (dual rule) would lead to a constitutional crisis as soon as a premier and cabinet challenged the president's extensive power. The first strong test of the French hybrid finally occurred between 1986 and 1988, when Socialist President François Mitterrand was faced with a legislative majority dominated by conservatives. But Mitterrand accepted the situation, appointing the conservatives' leader, Jacques Chirac, as premier. Despite strong ideological differences between the president and the premier-cabinet-legislative majority, there was a reasonable sharing of power and authority, which the French call "cohabitation." President Mitterrand continued to be very active in foreign policy but allowed the premier to control the domestic policy agenda. From 1993 to 1995, a conservative legislative majority produced a second period of cohabitation. A weakened Mitterrand acknowledged that "it is not the task of the president of the Republic to govern" (Safran 2003: 169–172). In 2000, the French altered a 127-year pattern, voting to shorten the presidential term to 5 years, ostensibly to increase the political accountability of the president. In 2002, cohabitation ended because both the president and prime minister were from the coalition of conservative parties. After these varied periods of cohabitation, the powers of the president in the French hybrid seem to be sufficiently limited and institutionalized to survive the conflict inherent in a dyarchy. Through constitutional safeguards and precedents, the hybrid system in every country must establish an effective power balance between its two executives.

one of greater power, and includes the right to dismiss the prime minister. However, the prime minister is responsible to the elected legislature and has direct control of the government. In most of these countries, the president does periodically exercise his right to dismiss the prime minister, an act that can relieve temporarily the citizens' dissatisfaction with the failures of the political system. But many of these states face huge governability problems (see Chapter 14), which suggests that the more ambiguous power relationships of the hybrid structure are not desirable.

Council Systems

In **council systems,** *a small group shares collective leadership and is responsible for both executive and legislative functions.* Although one member of the group might be deemed the leader for symbolic reasons, all members of the council are equal in constitutional terms, and they make decisions and actions based on the will of the council majority or, ideally, on council consensus. In American local government, the weak-mayor–council system and the boards of commissioners/ supervisors (prevalent in many counties, school districts, and special districts) are council systems. Also, many tribal societies in Africa were traditionally ruled by a council of elders who collectively made decisions that were binding on the members of the tribe.

In many situations in which a small collective group forcefully removes the top leader, the group initially shares power. When the group that has taken power is from the military, this council-type group is called a *junta.* There have been many such juntas in Latin America and Africa (e.g., in Algeria since 1992; in Argentina from 1976 to 1983). In most cases, council rule evolves into more dictatorial rule as a single political leader increasingly dominates the others.

Assembly Systems

In **assembly systems,** *collective leadership is exercised by a large group, usually constituted as a legislature.* There might be an executive officer, but the legislature is clearly dominant. Switzerland has an assembly system in which the legislature dominates the collective seven-member executive council that it elects. Most confederations, such as the United Nations and the European Parliament (the elected legislative wing of the EU), are assembly systems in which legislatures delegate administrative power to an appointed executive. The New England town meeting in American local government is an extreme version of the assembly system because all citizens directly participate in key decisions and oversee the administration of policy.

In theory, most communist states are assembly systems because the constitution grants most power for policy making to the legislative body. In reality, however, the legislatures in such states have traditionally been rubber stamps that authorize the policies and administration of a single leader or a small collective leadership group, as in China and North Korea. In fact, there are few if any national political systems that operate as true assembly systems, since power for policy making and policy implementation rarely remains dispersed among a large group of relatively equal rulers.

Which Form Is Optimal?

Which form of executive–legislative relations is best? If there were agreement on this question, we might reasonably expect most states to have adopted the same form of government. In fact, however, each form has its strengths and weaknesses.

The parliamentary form offers the advantages of a clear and decisive authority structure for the allocation of public values from the initial formulation of policy through its administration. But it can be argued that there are too few checks on a coherent legislative majority that can bulldoze its policies through the system. Conversely, there might be too little capacity for decisive action in a parliamentary system when there is no stable majority. The presidential system offers checks and balances, but it does not ensure consistency between legislation and execution. Also, a presidential system can so balance power between the legislature and the executive that there are damaging stalemates and confusion of accountability.

Because hybrid systems attempt to fuse the strengths of the parliamentary and the presidential forms of government, an increasing number of states are adopting some version of them. However, a significant risk with these hybrids is the increased potential for major power struggles, especially between the cabinet and prime minister on one side, and the president on the other side. A council system has the virtue of distributing power among a manageable number of people, but there is a strong tendency for collective leadership to result in persistent internal power struggles as one or a few members attempt to assert their dominance. Finally, assembly systems are the best approximation of a genuine representative democracy, but they lack the clear and decisive executive leadership that people in most contemporary states seem to want.

POLITICAL PARTY SYSTEMS

Another taxonomy for political systems is based on political parties. Party systems are generally classified according to the number of political parties and the interactions among the parties in the governing process. In the comparative study of political parties, there are usually four types of party systems: (1) two-party systems, (2) multiparty systems, (3) dominant-party systems, and (4) one-party systems. The distinguishing features of each type are described in this section, and representative examples are identified in Figure 7.3.

Two-Party Systems

A *two-party system* is characterized by two major political parties alternating in governmental power. Each party has a realistic possibility of forming a governing majority, although the electoral success of each party varies over time. Significant third parties can exist in two-party systems, but the third party has limited power unless a major party needs its support. Great Britain is an example of a two-party system in which the major parties (Labour and Conservative) have distinct ideologies. However, there can be a substantial ideological overlap between the two parties. In Honduras, for example, the two major parties (the Liberal and National parties) often present similar political orientations and objectives (Figuere 7.3).

Multiparty Systems

As you might expect, a *multiparty system* has more than two parties whose participation can be essential in the formation and activities of government. In parliamentary systems, this means that the creation of a legislative majority (a government) might require a coalition of two or more parties.

Working multiparty systems.   In a "working" multiparty system, there is a relatively clear split between sets of parties capable of forming a governing majority. For example, one or several cooperating center- and right-oriented parties might form one group, with a social democratic or socialist left party constituting another. This is the case with France and Norway, as well as in Sweden, where the government majority is usually dominated by the Swedish Social Democratic Party (see Figure 7.3; also see Box 13.1). It is also possible to have a working multiparty system in which various parties are willing to cooperate in a long-standing governing coalition. A notable example of this situation is Switzerland, where four major parties that range across the ideological spectrum typically share governing power, and it is viewed as undesirable for any one of the parties to govern independently.

Unstable multiparty systems.   Multiparty systems are often unstable. In these cases, the parties that form the government (the majority coalition) have underlying ideological disagreements, as in Israel, where the conservative Likud Party leads

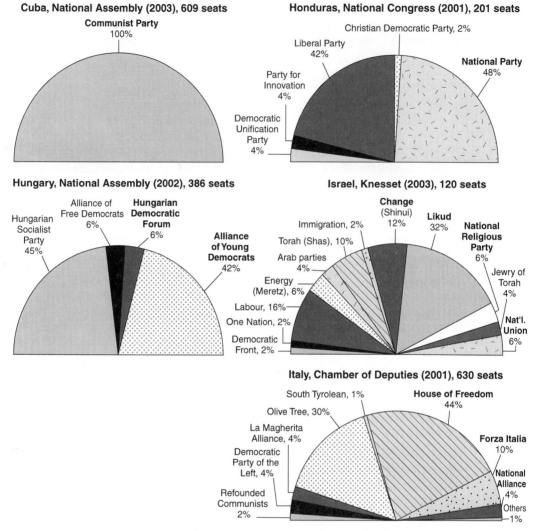

FIGURE 7.3   Examples of party systems, with governing parties in **bold**.

a complicated, changing multiparty coalition (that has varied between four and ten parties). At some point the government's policy on some issue induces a coalition partner to withdraw its support, causing a crisis for the government. In parliamentary systems, such a crisis often leads to the resignation of the government or the dissolution of the legislature. In presidential or assembly systems, this situation tends to produce paralysis in the legislature. Clearly, the difficulty of forming a governing majority among multiple parties increases as different parties are more firmly committed to their unique ideological orientations.

Instability is a particular problem where extreme parties (of the left or right) refuse to participate in any coalition. This was generally the case in Italy from World

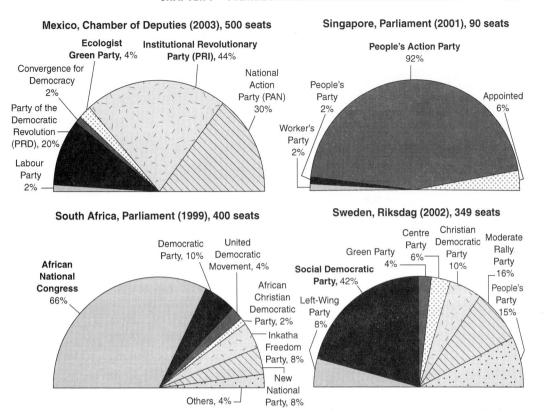

War II until 1994. Typically, the centrist Christian Democratic Party formed the heart of a coalition government, often a minority government, because neither left nor right extreme parties would be part of the government coalition. The system was unstable, with governments resigning, on average, more than once per year. Then in 1994, the parties of the right swamped the Popular Party (the renamed Christian Democrats) to form a different, but no more stable, majority coalition. While several center-right governments fell during the next two years, a new electoral system was implemented. This system was designed to reduce the number of parties by encouraging the formation of party coalitions, which would compete for 475 seats, with only the remaining 155 seats being allocated by the traditional proportional representation (PR) method (recall Box 7.1). Ironically, fully 251 parties put forth candidates in the 1996 election, no coalition gained a majority of seats in the legislature, and a left-center minority alliance governed. However, in 2001, the House of Freedom alliance, led by three right-center core parties, formed a majority government (Figure 7.3). It is actually possible that, if these alliances become more stable and effective, Italy's multiparty system will begin to operate like a two-party system.

In the initial years of democratic politics in the post-communist states of Central and Eastern Europe, an extreme form of multipartism existed. Many groups

Moir, CARTOONISTS & WRITERS SYNDICATE/cartoonweb.com

formed fledgling political parties, and as many as two hundred parties competed for political power. Even in 1999, for example, Russia still had 40 parties running for seats in the national legislature, and 14 parties won seats. When many parties win representation, it has been extraordinarily difficult to form the stable coalitions necessary for coherent policy making. There has been a significant reduction of effective parties in most of the post-communist states. In Hungary, for example, the party system now has only four major parties, two of whom form a stable governing coalition, and Hungary might become a two-party system.

Dominant-Party Systems

In a *dominant-party system,* the same party repeatedly captures enough votes and seats to form the government, although other parties are free to compete. Among the examples in Figure 7.3, Singapore provides the most clear-cut case of a dominant party. The People's Action Party wins nearly all the seats in the legislature, although candidates who are not members of the party are allowed to run. In South Africa, the African National Congress (ANC) has emerged as a dominant party in the initial post-apartheid period, with 12 other parties holding seats, and the capacity of the ANC to remain a dominant party will be tested.

A dominant party can eventually lose support and become a competitor in a multiparty system. This happened to the Congress Party in India, which lost its legislative majority in the late 1970s after nearly thirty years in power and is now one of nearly forty parties holding seats. Similarly, the Institutional Revolutionary Party (PRI) dominated Mexico's national political system, winning the presidency and a majority in both houses of the legislature in every election from 1929 to 1994. However, PRI lost its majority in the Chamber of Deputies in 1997, and in 2000, it also lost the presidency with the election of Vicente Fox from the PAN (National Action Party). In 2003, PRI and its ally regained the legislative dominance, but now as a party in a competitive multiparty system. A similar decline might be occurring for the Liberal Democratic Party (LDP), which was a dominant party in Japan for more than forty years after the ratification of the MacArthur constitution in 1947 (recall Box 7.2). But scandals involving party leaders and changing attitudes among the Japanese electorate are among the reasons that a non-LDP coalition government was formed after the 1993 election. Disagreements in that coalition resulted in the return to power of a less-dominant LDP, with a minority government after the 1996 election and the major party in a coalition in 2000.

One-Party Systems

In a *one-party system*, the single party of the governing group is the only legal political party. The clearest examples of one-party systems are in states dominated by the Communist Party, such as China, Cuba, and North Korea. In its effort to control all aspects of public life, the state accepts no institutional opposition to its rule, and a second political party would be the most direct and objectionable form of such opposition. Similarly, many authoritarian regimes do not tolerate the existence of any political parties other than the one that represents the state and its vision of political order, as in Myanmar and Sudan.

In some states, multiparty systems have ultimately been reduced to one-party systems, particularly in states that have not institutionalized the electoral mandate. The party entrenched in power is reluctant to relinquish that power to another group. Moreover, if the acceptance of political opposition is not strong, the governing group tends to view any party that expresses opposition to its rule as disloyal or even seditious (which means that the party is stirring up resistance or rebellion against the government), rather than as a "loyal opposition." The eventual result can be the abolition of any party other than the single "party of the state/government/society." There are currently few one-party systems in a technical sense, given the high ideological premium associated with the appearance of democratic processes. Thus most countries now inject some form of party competition. For example, Tanzania has shifted from a strictly one-party system (its system had alternative candidates from the single party for each of the 200 seats), and it now does allow other parties to run in certain seats, although few are elected. And in Syria, all parties are government controlled, and the ruling group is guaranteed the great majority of legislative seats. Thus most one-party systems are currently best understood as dominant-party systems.

No-Party Systems

Although it is not a party system in the normal sense, the taxonomy should have a category for those political systems that have no political parties. Historically, there were many political systems that had no organized parties. In addition, a few contemporary political systems do not allow political parties. Such countries as Oman and Swaziland have banned political parties, either because the rulers do not want organized bases of opposition to their authority or on the grounds that parties divide people's loyalty to the society. The latter argument is a primary justification given for the nonpartisanship (lack of political party affiliations or organization) of candidates for public office in many American local governments.

CLASSIFICATION AND CLARITY

Most theorizing about political systems begins with some classificatory scheme. Classifying political systems into a taxonomy can be straightforward, especially when the categories are based on clear institutional characteristics (e.g., federations, confederations, and unitary states). But many of the most interesting classifications (e.g., democracies and dictatorships) are challenging because political systems tend to be complex mixtures of characteristics that do not fit tidily into any category. In addition, any classification is time-specific because evolutionary and revolutionary processes can change the nature of a political system.

There are at least three important reasons for classifying political systems. First, such classification can provide us with useful descriptive information about political systems. Most people have a vague sense that other political systems are different from their own, and by describing how various political systems are organized between central and peripheral units or between executives and legislatures, we expand our grasp of alternative forms of governmental structures.

Second, the classification of political systems helps us to undertake political analysis—to identify patterns of similarities and differences among the political systems of the world. Rather than positing that every political system is unique, the development of a taxonomy assumes that some generalizations can emerge from an analysis of these systems. Sets of political systems that share important characteristics can be compared with each other, or compared with sets that do not share those characteristics. Such taxonomies provide us with a basis for thinking more clearly about the kinds of generalizations that we can articulate. Comparative analysis can then increase our confidence regarding what we know about the political world.

Third, the taxonomies in this chapter might encourage us to specify with greater precision what we mean by value-laden terms such as "democracy" and "dictatorship." In this manner, the analytic study of political institutions improves our understanding of how these terms are most appropriately used as thoughtful descriptors rather than as mere rhetorical labels.

Ultimately, the development of greater precision in our use of key political concepts and the increase in our knowledge about the political world can do more than clarify our thinking. They can also enhance our ability to evaluate the nature and desirability of the political structures in our own nation and in other countries, and to decide whether there is a "best" form of government.

Would you argue that one form of areal division of power and one form of executive–legislative relations and the same constitution are best for *all* states? Or might the best institutional arrangements be contingent upon the major goals and key characteristics of the particular political society? As a closing puzzle, if your country were to convene a constitutional convention now, would you argue in favor of retaining all the same governmental forms that exist in your political system? Why, or why not?

KEY CONCEPTS

assembly government	liberal democracy
authoritarian regime	limited mandate
authoritarianism	nondemocracy
confederation	parliamentary (cabinet) government
constitution	participatory democracy
constitutional regime	party system
council government	presidential government
democracy	representative democracy
dictatorship	taxonomic theory
electoral democracy	totalitarian regime
electoral system	totalitarianism
federation	unitary state
illiberal democracy	

FOR FURTHER CONSIDERATION

1. What is your definition of a democratic political system? What are the minimal conditions necessary for a country to be classified as a democracy? If you opt for the definition used in this chapter, explain which elements of the definition are the most essential and the least essential for democracy.

2. In the late eighteenth century, the United States opted for a federal, presidential, two-party system with plurality elections. Given the situation at the beginning of the twenty-first century, what are the major shortcomings of each of these decisions? Speculate what politics in the United States might be like if the country became a unitary state with a parliamentary government or a multiparty system based on proportional representation.

3. Some analysts argue that democracy is not possible unless there are at least two political parties. Provide a critical evaluation of this viewpoint. In theory, might we expect any relationship between the number of parties and the extent to which the political system is democratic?

FOR FURTHER READING

Arendt, Hannah. (1973). *The Origins of Totalitarianism.* New York: Harcourt. The classic study of the forces underlying totalitarian regimes.

Barber, Benjamin. (1984). *Strong Democracy: Participatory Politics for a New Age.* Berkeley: University of California Press. A persuasive argument that democracy can and should be based on active and extensive participation by the citizenry.

Bratton, Michael, and Nicolas van de Walle. (1997). *Democratic Experiments in Africa: Regime Transitions in Comparative Perspective.* New York: Cambridge University Press. Numerous examples are provided of the attempts to establish and sustain liberal democracy in sub-Saharan Africa, which, due to its history, informal institutions, and elite behavior, has been less successful in this transition than any other region.

Elgie, Robert, Ed. (1999). *Semi-Presidentialism in Europe.* New York: Oxford University Press. An exploration of how similar forms of executive–legislative structures (hybrids with a directly elected president and a prime minister responsible to the legislature) can result in different patterns of politics and power.

Fulbright, William J. (1989). *The Price of Empire.* New York: Pantheon. The highly respected former chair of the Senate Foreign Relations Committee argues that the United States could reduce government gridlock by changing to a parliamentary system.

Hesse, Joachim Jens, and Vincent Wright, Eds. (1996). *Federalizing Europe?: The Costs, Benefits and Preconditions of Federal Political Systems.* New York: Oxford University Press. From the perspective of developments within the European Union and its member states, the problems and prospects of federal forms of governance are debated.

Lijphart, Arend, Ed. (1992). *Parliamentary versus Presidential Government.* New York: Oxford University Press. A wide-ranging set of readings examining the advantages and disadvantages of the two major forms of executive–legislative relations as well as hybrids.

Peterson, Paul E. (1995). *The Price of Federalism.* Washington, DC: Brookings. In the context of a detailed consideration of federalism in the United States, the author analyzes the strengths and problems associated with this form of areal distribution of power.

Stepan, Alfred, and Juan J. Linz. (1996). *Problems of Democratic Transition and Consolidation: Southern Europe, South America and Post-Communist Europe.* Baltimore, MD: Johns Hopkins University Press. Based on illuminating examples from two continents, the authors explore the difficulties associated with the shift from authoritarian or communist regimes to democratic ones.

Wheare, K. C. (1966). *Modern Constitutions.* London: Home University Library. Although first written in 1951, this description of the content and impacts of constitutions is arguably still the best.

ON THE WEB

http://www.constitution.org/cons/natlcons.htm

The constitutions of many countries are provided, often in English, by the Constitution Society, which also offers commentary (usually rather conservative) about the country.

http://freedomhouse.org

The site of Freedom House, which includes current ratings for every country, along with topical discussions, regarding those countries' levels of political rights and civil rights as well as press freedom and religious freedom.

http://magnet.undp.org/docs/parliaments/

This site covers governing systems and executive-legislative relations within presidential, parliamentary, and hybrid systems along with information about political parties.

http://www.politicalresources.net/

This is a very useful and accessible site with information on many countries, including current data on party systems and the web sites of most parties from each country.

http://temple.edu/federalism/

The site of the Center for the Study of Federalism at Temple University (Philadelphia), with links to other sources and written work that focuses on issues of federalism.

http://www.odci.gov/cia/publications/chiefs/

The Central Intelligence Agency manages this database that lists the chiefs of state and cabinet members of all foreign governments.

http://wc.wustl.edu/parliaments.html

The Weidenbaum Center at Washington University in St. Louis provides a listing of the web sites of most national parliaments.

CHAPTER 8 **Political Economy**

In all the political systems of the world, much of politics is economics and most of economics is also politics. . . . For many good reasons, politics and economics have to be held together in the analysis of basic social mechanisms and systems.

—Charles E. Lindblom, *Politics and Markets* (1977: 8)

This book is about the *political* world. But if Lindblom is correct, understanding contemporary politics requires an understanding of its linkages with economics. This combination of politics and economics is called **political economy**. This chapter explains this concept. First, it describes the connections between the economic system and the political system. Then it characterizes the three different types of political economies: (1) the *market economy,* (2) the *command economy,* and (3) the *mixed economy.* Finally, it examines how these political economies are related to major "isms" in the political world, especially capitalism, socialism, and communism.

POLITICS AND ECONOMICS

Many of the decisions by the political system can have significant impacts on the economy. Can you think of how the following state policies might affect the economy?

No state involvement in the construction or repair of highways and roads.

State ownership of all factories producing cars.

Very high state taxes on the profits of businesses.

State financing of all education for all citizens, from preschool through post-doctoral training.

Absolutely no state restrictions on the right of foreigners to enter and work in the country.

State regulation of the price of all basic foods.

Similarly, the actions of major economic actors and the performance of the economic system can have a major impact on the political system. The political order depends on the economic system to generate goods and services for the survival and prosperity of its citizens. For example, what policy responses might you predict from the U.S. government to the following economic factors?

> A lengthy nationwide strike by air traffic controllers.
>
> The proposed sale of the country's major computer company to a Japanese company.
>
> The discovery that there are fewer than five years' worth of underground oil reserves within the country's boundaries.
>
> A disastrous harvest that reduces the nation's grain output by 50 percent.

The more one reflects on modern political systems, the clearer it becomes that the political system and the economic system are inextricably entwined.

Understanding political economy requires a grasp of some basic economic concepts. This chapter describes a framework for the economic system that is similar in spirit to Easton's framework for a political system (see Chapter 5). The framework deals only with some core ideas that have been simplified considerably. (If you want the full treatment, read an introductory economics book such as Heyne [2003] or take an introductory economics course.) However, the discussion does involve some complicated abstractions, so hang in there!

A POLITICAL-ECONOMIC FRAMEWORK

The abstract models presented in Figure 8.1 are our starting point for understanding the idea of a political economy. The figure offers an extremely simple characterization of the way in which extraordinarily complex systems of production and exchange operate (see Baumol 2003: ch. 8; Ruffin and Gregory 2000: ch. 6).

Factors, Firms, and Households/Consumers

In the beginning (according to this model), there are three kinds of important productive resources—the three major *factors of production* (A) (see part A of Figure 8.1). *Land* means the ground plus any raw materials (such as coal ore and bananas) on or in the ground. *Labor* is human productive input (our common understanding of "work"). *Capital* is the nonhuman productive input from other resources (especially financial resources, machinery, and technology). Each factor of production is controlled by an owner who, in the language of economics, is referred to as a *household* (B).

Some actor called a *firm* (C) (in this book, the terms "firm" and "producer" are used interchangeably) attempts to acquire a combination of these productive resources (factors of production) in order to produce a *good* (D1). A good can be a product (e.g., a pencil, a nuclear missile) or a service (e.g., a massage, transportation on an airplane).

A firm might be a single person who produces a good from her own resources. For example, a masseuse (massage giver) provides a massage through her own labor skills. Or a firm might be a large organization that uses many productive resources (of land and commodities, workers and capital). For example, a firm that produces

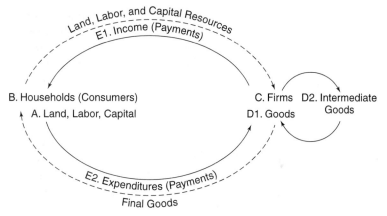

Part A. An Economic Framework: The Income-Expenditures Model

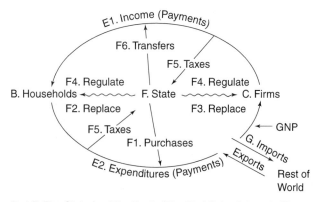

Part B. The State (and the Rest of the World) Are Integrated into the Income-Expenditures Model

FIGURE 8.1   A Political Economy framework

(part A): An Economic Framework: The Income and Expenditures Model

(part B): The State Is Integrated into the Income-Expenditures Model, with the State Having Six Possible Roles:

F1. It can be a consumer, purchasing any good from a firm.

F2. It can replace (that is, be) a household, in the sense that it controls some or all factors of production.

F3. It can replace (that is, be) a firm, producing any good.

F4. It can regulate the manner in which either households or firms operate by enacting policies that encourage or prevent certain behaviors by those other economic actors.

F5. It can tax (extract resources from) the payments to any actor.

F6. It can transfer payments to any actor.

Note: The gross national product (GNP) is the sum of household expenditures (including investment via the financial system), government purchases, and exports minus imports.

something as simple as a pencil needs such productive resources as wood, graphite, rubber, machines, and workers. The firm transforms these factors of production into the final good—here, a pencil. Often some goods are acquired in order to make more complicated goods; these goods used in the firm's production process are called *intermediate goods* (D2). The pencil firm, for example, has probably acquired such intermediate goods as graphite (which it acquires from another firm that has mined and refined this chemical element) and wood (which has come from a firm that owns, cuts, and mills trees).

A household has a second role, as a *consumer,* when it wants to acquire a final good. A consumer offers something of value to the firm in exchange for the good that the consumer wants. What emerges between the household/consumer and the firm is a system of *payments* (E1 and E2 in the figure). A firm must pay something to those households that control the relevant productive resource(s) necessary for the firm to produce goods. And a household, in its role as a consumer, must pay something to the firm in order to get the final goods that it wants. Notice that any individual or group can act as either a consumer or a firm, depending on whether the individual or group is transforming productive resources into goods or is acquiring a final good.

The size of a payment (the price) is established when there is an agreement between one actor, who is willing to exchange (give up) something to get the good, and another actor, who is willing to give up the good for what the first actor offers. In the language of economics, each actor increases her *"utility"* (her overall happiness) in such an exchange because each has higher utility after the exchange than before it. So, for example, the actor who has grown a dozen tomatoes might have a higher utility when she exchanges them with someone, say the masseuse, who will give her whatever else she values highly enough to give up the tomatoes.

In every system, there are some good-for-good exchanges, called barter trading (e.g., the dozen tomatoes are traded for a massage). But most economies are dominated by exchanges where some form of currency (money) becomes the medium for the exchange. In good-for-money exchanges, the consumer gives the producer some amount of money in exchange for the final good (e.g., four tomatoes might be exchanged for $1, or a massage might be offered for $12).

If firms want to sell more massages than customers want to buy, the price of a massage is likely to come down. This is how *supply and demand* operate: If demand is low relative to supply, the price comes down; and if demand is high relative to supply, the price goes up. In theory, with enough producers and consumers making exchanges, the price of a good reaches a perfect balance point between supply and demand, known as the "equilibrium point" (see Figure 8.2).

The payment by a consumer to a firm (E2) might be different from the payments by the firm for the productive resources necessary to produce that good (E1) (see Figure 8.1). A firm is successful if it can sell the good for more than it paid to produce the good. This return to the firm in excess of its payments is called *profit.* If the firm must sell the good for less than the cost of producing it, the firm suffers a "loss." Obviously, firms normally try to increase their profit and to avoid loss.

Getting and Spending

In this way, the system of exchanges goes around and around. The households expend their resources on goods, and the firms provide the households with income

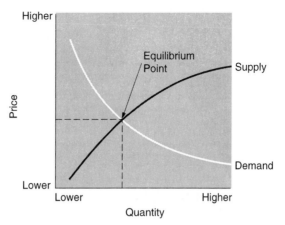

FIGURE 8.2 The relationship between the supply of a good and the demand for the good

as they pay for productive resources. Ideally, everyone is exchanging things of value for other things that they value even more. As the system becomes more complex, many actors are involved in the production and distribution of goods. In addition to offering goods for money and exchanging money for desired goods, some actors can operate as brokers, organizing complicated or large-scale exchanges.

As the cycle continues, more and more goods are produced, bought, sold, and consumed by all the actors in the economic system. The complexity of the actual exchanges in most economic systems is beyond comprehension. As an example, see how long a list you can quickly develop of the number of different people who contributed some fraction of the value (the one dollar) that you pay for a tomato at the supermarket. (Think about the actors involved in the production and distribution of that tomato to you.) With sufficient time, you could probably identify hundreds of people who share in the resource that you have sacrificed (i.e., the payment you have provided in exchange for the tomato).

To the extent that others are willing to offer substantial payments in exchange for the factors of production or the goods that you control, you have more resource power. You have many choices regarding the use of your own resources. If you have 12 tomatoes, you could (1) eat them all; (2) eat 6 and sell/trade 6 for as much money or goods as you can get; (3) eat 2 and sell/trade the rest for a loaf of bread and a book of verse; (4) eat 2, sell/trade 2 for a loaf of bread, and use the remaining 8 to make 16 tomato sandwiches that you sell/trade (for as much as you can get); (5) give all the tomatoes to hungry people; or. . . . The possibilities are extensive. And if you chose approach 2, 3, or 4, you would now have further choices to make with your new bundle of resources.

Presumably, you attempt to pursue a strategy that maximizes your utility (i.e., that results in your most-preferred mixture of goods and resources) and hence enhances your life. Individuals (and groups) can have very different sets of preferences. One person might want to hoard money or food or precious metals; another might want to spend everything on consumption for personal pleasure. One person might actively seek the resources to own a mansion and a Mercedes-Benz, while another person might be happiest with no possessions other than the bare necessities

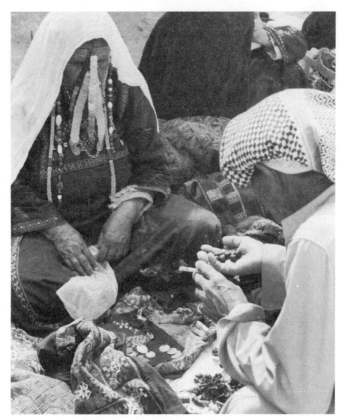

The richest merchant in a Bedouin market in Egypt displays the goods she will sell, proudly wearing the chains of gold coins that attest to her entrepreneurial skills as a "firm" in a market economy.

she carries in a backpack. One person might work obsessively to increase her total package of resources, while another person might join a meditation society, giving up all possessions in favor of the contemplative life.

Of course, it is a tough world, and so all people are not equally capable of maximizing their value preferences. A person's success in getting her preferred mix of goods and resources can be affected by such things as the kinds and amounts of resources she already controls, her skills in producing desired goods, the constraints in her environment, the actions of others, and even luck. Over time, there are likely to be huge differences in the mix of goods and resources controlled by different individuals and groups.

The State (and the World) Join In

We now have our first approximation of an abstract model of the economic system. The cyclical exchange of payments for factors of production and payments for final goods becomes a perpetual motion machine. This model is extremely simplistic. One crucial omission is the absence of the political system. The state (F) is added in part B of Figure 8.1, and the interaction between the economy and the state results in the dynamic processes we term the *political economy.* The state can powerfully affect the economic system in the six general ways labeled F1 through F6 in part B of Figure 8.1. Notice that the state can regulate any economic activity, can replace either a consumer of goods (a household) or a producer of goods (a firm), can tax any actor, and can transfer goods or money to any actor. It will become evident in the next section that the state's actions regarding the six dimensions of behavior distinguish different types of political economies (remember that the state, like other aggregate actors, is really a complex organizational structure composed of many individuals whose combined decisions and actions constitute the behavior attributed to "the" state).

Part B of Figure 8.1 also recognizes that there are boundaries that affect the behavior of economic actors. Producers can sell goods outside of the state's boundaries to some consumer in the rest of the world (these are *exports*). Or consumers can purchase goods from producers outside the state's boundaries (these are *imports*). Thus there is a net flow of income into or out of the economic system, based on the levels of imports and exports (G). In addition, a state (the actor's own state or another state) can implement policies that either restrict freedom (e.g., tariff barriers) or facilitate freedom (e.g., conquest of one state by another). The frameworks in this chapter generally ignore the role of political economies in the rest of the world. However, in the global economy, in most countries, the actions of those outside the state's borders are as significant as those inside the borders. The significant role of such external actors will be emphasized in Chapters 13 through 16. As Figure 8.1 indicates, the total productive effort of the economy is called the *gross national product (GNP)* or *gross domestic product (GDP)* (also see Box 8.1).

Other key elements of a fully specified model of an economic system are missing from this simple model. For example, part B of Figure 8.1 does not explicitly identify the role of certain financial actors that would be shown in a fuller model. A household can save some of its income rather than spend it all. These savings are put into the financial system. Its investors pay households to use these resources as capital, which the investors offer to firms in exchange for payment.

Also, although the actors are presented as independent individuals in our model, an economic actor, like a political actor, might be an individual or a collectivity. In an actual economy, some actors will combine their resources with those of others in order to enhance their relative advantages in the processes of production and

BOX 8.1

A Gross Product

The total level of production in an economy is usually measured by one of two monetary figures that summarizes "gross product"—the total value of all the final goods produced by a state's economic actors during a certain time period. The *gross national product (GNP)* includes the production of all citizens of the state, whether they are inside the state's boundaries or not. *Gross domestic product (GDP)* is the

(continued)

BOX **8.1** (CONTINUED)

total value of all final goods produced by all people within a state's boundaries, whether or not they are citizens. Although GNP is still the measure referred to most frequently in the United States, most international economic actors now opt for GDP as a more accurate indicator of a country's economic vitality, given the large numbers of noncitizens who produce goods within many countries.

Since these gross products are greatly influenced by the size of the country, attempts to compare the relative prosperity of the people in different countries have typically divided the productive total by the number of citizens (as "per capita"). As measures of a country's prosperity, both GDP per capita and GNP per capita have at least three important flaws:

1. They do not measure how the prosperity is distributed among the country's economic actors, and thus many citizens have an individual level of prosperity that is sharply different from their country's average production per capita.

2. Only the goods that actually enter the society's monetary sector are measured, while many other valued goods are ignored. These unmeasured goods include household work and goods in the "underground economy," particularly trade in illegal goods, barter trade, and the black market. In some countries, GDP and GNP are particularly misleading because such unmeasured goods are a very significant proportion of total economic activity.

3. GDP and GNP are often used to compare the prosperity of one country versus another. However, there are huge between-country disparities in the exchange value of money. In comparing two countries, the same amount of money (converting local currencies into an international exchange currency, usually dollars) can buy much more or much less of the same specific goods (e.g., a loaf of bread, a bus ride, a book, a computer).

Due to these disparities, there is increasing use of a third prosperity measure that attempts to establish equivalent value, an index based on *"purchasing power parity" (PPP)*—that is, correcting monetary levels to reflect the amount of local currency required to buy certain standard goods in that country.

Using PPP indexing, the World Bank (2004: table 1.1) reports that while India's GDP per capita is only $494 per year, this equates to $2,571 per capita in "purchasing power." The purchasing power of Japan's $44,108 is actually $25,650. In purchasing power dollars, the economic gap between the wealthier countries and the poorer countries usually decreases. Indeed, for many of the poorer countries, the purchasing power dollars are five to eight times greater than GDP per capita. However, it is important to note that when a country attempts to participate in the global economy, and especially when it attempts to import goods, the purchasing power of its currency is directly tied to international exchange rates, not to the price of bread at home (or PPP dollars), and its relative wealth or poverty remains.

Table 8.1 compares how GDP per capita and the same measure adjusted for PPP differ for each of 24 countries. For most countries, wealth relative to other countries changes less than 20 ranks out of 210 economies. However, there are a few instances, such as China, where the relative position between gross product per

BOX **8.1** (CONTINUED)

capita and the correction for PPP are rather large. What might explain a disparity like that in China?

More broadly, which of the measures do you think is the best means of measuring general prosperity? Is there another measure you think would be better than any of these? Why?

TABLE 8.1
Alternative Measures of Economic Prosperity

Country	GDP/capita in PPP [a]	GDP/capita [b]
United States	35,158	31,977
Canada	28,699	23,590
Germany	26,324	32,807
Japan	25,650	44,108
Sweden	25,315	32,117
Singapore	23,393	27,254
South Korea	16,465	14,280
Czech Republic	15,148	5,691
Poland	10,187	3,762
Mexico	8,707	3,713
Costa Rica	8,470	3,927
Russia	7,926	2,734
Brazil	7,516	4,644
WORLD Average	5,654	7,648
Iran	6,339	1,787
Turkey	6,176	2,942
China	4,475	942
Egypt	3,701	1,250
Syria	3,385	801
India	2,571	494
Angola	2,053	598
Ghana	2,050	432
Kenya	992	325
Nigeria	851	248
Congo	606	87

[a] PPP = purchasing power parity, in current international dollars
[b] in constant US 1995 dollars
Source: World Bank (2004).

exchange. They might develop cooperative arrangements, forming groups and institutions that attempt to control the use of a resource. Such cooperation might emerge among individual owners of labor, such as a farming collective or a labor union; among those owning a commodity, such as a cartel; or among those controlling capital, such as a syndicate or a diversified corporation.

Two Ideal-Type Political Economies

Based on this framework, we can distinguish two ideal-type political economies: *market economy* and *command economy*. An *ideal type* is a description of what a certain phenomenon might be like in its pure form, but it does not necessarily correspond exactly to any real-world example.

In distinguishing the market economy from the command economy, it's useful to consider five fundamental questions:

1. Who controls the factors of production?
2. Who determines what goods are produced?
3. Who establishes the value attached to different resources and goods?
4. Who decides how resources and goods will be distributed?
5. What is the role of the state?

Table 8.2 provides brief responses to each of these key questions. The table also provides answers for a "mixed" economy, which is less an ideal type than a real-world compromise between the two. (For other approaches that explain political economy, see, e.g., Heyne [2003] and Lindblom [1977]). The next two sections consider these questions in detail for each type of economy.

The Market Economy: Total Private Control

1. **Who controls the factors of production?** In the ideal-type **market economy,** there is total private control. Every actor has direct, personal control over all her own factors of production (although she cannot control the value attached to those factors). The worker decides who, if anyone, she will offer her work to and the type and amount of resources she will accept in exchange for that work. The owner of land or capital similarly decides the conditions under which she will allow her productive resources to be employed in the productive system. And the firm determines what productive resources it will acquire.

In general, every household and every firm are motivated to maximize the value associated with the resources and goods they control. As an actor operates in this economic order, she continually attempts to expand the total package of resources that she controls. Thus she aims to take actions such that every exchange will increase her accumulated value. To the extent that she can exchange some resources(s) and receive an even greater amount of resources in return, she has increased her total resource base. Of course, it is also possible that she can make bad decisions about what to control and thus reduce her total resource base.

2. **Who determines what goods are produced?** As all the actors make their own separate decisions in an attempt to maximize their own utilities and resources,

TABLE 8.2
Comparing Command, Market, and Mixed Political Economies

	Command	Market	Mixed
Who controls the factors of production?	• The state owns all significant factors (land, labor, and capital).	• Every private actor (household) controls her own factors.	• The state and private actors each control some factors.
Who determines what goods are produced?	• The state devises a detailed economic plan that specifies what level of each good will be produced. • The system is supply oriented.	• All actors (firms) make their own separate decisions about production in an attempt to maximize their own utilities. • The system is demand oriented.	• Some firms are under direct state control, but most make decisions in the market. • The state regulates some actions of many firms and households. • The system is mainly demand oriented.
Who establishes the value attached to different resources?	• The state sets the value (price) in all exchanges.	• The market (via the "invisible hand"), based on the equilibrium of supply and demand.	• The market. • The state regulates some prices to serve national priorities.
Who decides how resources and goods will be distributed?	• The state's plan indicates who will receive which goods and in what amounts.	• Distribution is based on a summation of the actions of all consumers and producers in the market.	• Mainly the market. • The state intervenes in some cases to ensure that certain actors have access to particular goods.
What is the role of the state?	• Dominant, controlling virtually all aspects of the political economy.	• Minimal role in the political economy. • The state does enforce the "social contract," protecting all from violence or law-breakers.	• The state attempts to strike a balance between: • Competition and state control • Private profit and a sharing of societal resources

a pattern emerges regarding what goods are produced. In particular, every firm acts to maximize its profits through the process in which it pays to acquire productive resources and then produces goods that are sold to consumers. The firm's decisions about what goods to produce are based on its assessment of how it can achieve maximum profit. In the phrase of the famous Scottish economist Adam Smith (1723–1790), production is guided by the "invisible hand" of the market. This invisible hand is the summation of the actions of every household and every firm regarding the uses of the factors of production.

If one thinks of an economy in terms of the supply and demand for goods, this system is demand oriented. The most important consideration for a firm that is deciding what to produce is this: What good can I offer that others will demand and for which others will offer the highest payments, in comparison with my costs of production? Thus the firm attempts to assess the demand for various goods in the market and then to transform the factors of production it controls in order to provide whatever good it thinks will maximize its own profit.

3. **Who establishes the value attached to different resources and goods?** Similarly, the invisible hand of the market establishes value. Each factor of production and the goods that are produced through transformation of these factors are valued at their opportunity cost—the value (e.g., money, good, factor of production) that is sacrificed by someone in the market in exchange for them. Hence nothing has value except to the extent that some other actor will exchange resources to obtain it.

In most circumstances, many actors offer similar resources and goods. The result is vigorous competition among private actors, as each one tries to gain the maximum payment from others in exchange for her own resources and goods. Ultimately, the value of every resource and good is subject to this competition, based on both its supply and the existing demand for it (recall Figure 8.2). Sometimes production is controlled almost completely by one firm (a monopoly) or a few firms (an oligopoly) that can manipulate the supply and value of goods.

Competition is particularly intense where supply and demand are quite unequal. For example, if five workers will drill holes in metal (supply) and one firm needs two workers with this resource (demand), the firm can bid down the resources it must pay for the work (this is usually a wage rate, but it can also include other resources, such as work conditions, benefits such as housing or health care, or shares of the firm's profits) by inducing the five workers to undercut each other's wage claim. Conversely, if there are only two workers available with this skill and the firm needs five, the workers can bid up the resources that they will be offered.

A basic economic assumption in a market economy is the continual adjustment of supply and demand toward an equilibrium point. For example, some workers might move to a different place or offer a different labor skill if the wages for drilling holes get too low or there are too few jobs. And a firm might find a substitute for the labor it needs if hole-drilling labor is too expensive or too scarce to enable the firm to make a profit (e.g., technology, outsourcing). (Can you think of other supply-demand adjustments that the workers or the firm might make?)

4. **Who decides how resources and goods will be distributed?** Again, it is the invisible hand of the market, rather than anyone in particular, that determines the distribution of resources and goods in the market economy. As each person pursues her own private utility, economic actors accumulate dramatically different bundles of resources and goods, depending on their preferences, the resources they control, and their skill and luck in exchanging and transforming resources in the market.

5. **What is the role of the state?** State intervention is minimal. The state is passive in the productive system, allowing private actors to operate in a relatively unconstrained manner. The state is obliged, under the social contract, to prevent private actors from doing violence to each other. Also, the state protects its citizens from the external environment, preventing or resisting the violation of its sover-

eignty or its citizens' rights by other states. In meeting these responsibilities, the state might purchase some resources, might levy minimal taxes, and might affect firms' import and export activities. But the general principle in the ideal-type market economy is that the state does not have a significant role in the economy.

The Command Economy: Total State Control

1. **Who controls the factors of production?** In the ideal-type **command economy,** the state assumes total control of virtually all the significant factors of production. The state replaces or eliminates the role of private owners of labor, land, and capital whose activities are so crucial in the market economy. The state owns the land, the natural resources, the factories, the machines, and so on. The state even owns labor, in the sense that the state decides the conditions and purposes for which all individuals must offer their labor. Thus it is the state that determines how every factor of production will be used.

2. **Who determines what goods are produced?** In terms of part B of Figure 8.1, the state is the firm that produces virtually all major goods in the system. The state devises a detailed *economic plan* that specifies what levels of each good will be produced from what combination of resources. A political ideal guides this plan for production: the commitment to provide every citizen in the society with the goods that enable each citizen to enjoy a life of material well-being. Thus the state's plan sets production decisions that are supply oriented (in contrast to the demand orientation of the market economy). The state/firm attempts to use productive resources optimally to maximize the supply of appropriate goods available for consumers. Centralized planning guided by a broad vision of social needs, rather than independent decisions by many profit-seeking actors, guides the complex actions resulting in the production of a particular mix of goods.

3. **Who establishes the value attached to different resources and goods?** Since the state controls all the factors of production and is the firm producing all goods, it also can set the values (i.e., establish the payments) for all exchanges within its boundaries. Competition is eliminated since the state, rather than the market, establishes the payments for every factor of production and every good in the society. Thus the state tells a group of farmers to produce a million tomatoes and then sets the exchange value of those tomatoes. Similarly, the state decides which individuals will have jobs drilling holes, and it establishes the wages and benefits they receive for their work. The state is not completely free to set payments—for example, the scarcity of a productive resource can influence its cost—but given availability, value is set primarily by the state's decisions.

4. **Who decides how resources and goods will be distributed?** The state is equally active in the decisions on the distribution of goods to the population. The state's plan indicates who will receive which goods in what amounts. The plan will specify, for example, that automobile-producing factory X will receive 46 tons of steel each month, and that a town will receive three tomatoes per family per week. The plan can also indicate precisely where these goods will come from (i.e., steel from factory Y and tomatoes from farm Z).

In the real world, most near-total command economies base their plan on the objective of distributing necessary goods (especially food, shelter, education, health care) to every person on a relatively equal basis. As an ideal type, however, a command economy need not be committed to such egalitarianism. The state could decide that one particular group will receive a very large share of the goods and that other, less favored groups will receive very little. The crucial decisions about distribution of goods are made by those with power in the political system.

5. **What is the role of the state?** Clearly, the state has a dominant, even an overwhelming role in this type of political economy. The state controls virtually all of the important factors of production, plans the manner in which they will be utilized in the production of goods, establishes the official value of all resources and goods, and decides how the resources of the society will be distributed among individuals. In the command economy, surplus value ("profit") is accumulated by the state, not by individuals. The state then determines how this surplus value will be used to serve its objectives and to provide goods to certain actors.

KEY PROBLEMS FOR EACH IDEAL-TYPE POLITICAL ECONOMY

There are potential shortcomings in the actual operation of either the market economy or the command economy that are important to consider. These, along with the benefits, are summarized in Table 8.3.

Market Economy

Resource inequality.   One problem with the market economy is that substantial resource inequalities tend to emerge. Competition is everywhere, and it tends to become ruthless. As every actor strives to maximize resources and control over the factors of production, some are extremely successful and others are total failures. Most importantly, the market system is indifferent to the problems of those who do not succeed. Over time, the rich tend to get richer (especially if they cooperate a bit) while those with few resources tend increasingly to lose economic power in the market.

Neither the successful actors nor the state intervene to protect those who fail to capture many resources. Thus some people, and perhaps even large numbers of people, lack the resources to enable them to consume the goods they need for a secure and comfortable life. As inequalities of wealth, power, and status increase, there is greater likelihood of alienation among the less successful and of conflict between the rich and the poor.

Production for profit, not need.   A second problem is that a demand-oriented system of production does not necessarily produce goods that meet human needs. Rather, production decisions are dominated by actors who produce only those goods that they believe will maximize their own resources. Thus there can be a proliferation of extravagant or marginal goods that are profitable, while more essential goods are produced in insufficient amounts because they are less profitable. For example, there might be an abundant supply of plastic surgeons to serve the rich, while large numbers of poor people lack adequate basic health care because private

TABLE 8.3
Benefits and Problems of Market and Command Economies

Market Economy	Benefits	Problems
Competition	Energetic and efficient production	Ruthless interactions; huge inequalities in wealth and resources
Demand orientation	Goods' cost and quality responsive to consumers' desires	Creation of demand for and proliferation of goods that have limited social value
No central plan	Local decision and "invisible hand" stimulate innovation, facilitate freedom	Economic cycles of boom and bust, inflation and recession
Command Economy		
No competition	Work for common good; relative equality of wealth and income	Little initiative; shoddy products; low productivity
Supply orientation	Production and distribution for social and individual needs	Oversupply and shortages; lack of coordination
Central plan	Rational use of societal resources	Overcentralized control; limited innovation and lack of responsiveness to changing circumstances

producers see too little profit in treating them and the state is passive in the production and regulation of health care.

There also might be wasteful competition, as many variations of a good are offered. Considerable resources can be spent manipulating demand for these goods through such techniques as advertising. For example, there might be literally hundreds of different breakfast cereals available. A cereal's cost might be less associated with its nutritional value or the cost of the factor payments to produce it and more associated with the expense of advertising and packaging (to create demand for that particular brand) and with the profit margin (to the producer and the supplier).

Severe economic cycles. A third problem is that a market economy can experience major economic cycles. There is no guarantee that the very large number of private decisions about production and consumption (the "invisible hand") will mesh in a manner that ensures steady growth and prosperity for the economic system as a whole. The economy is prone to large swings in the direction of either hyperactivity (causing inflation and scarcity) or serious economic decline (causing recession or depression), and the state does not intervene to counteract these swings. Fluctuations between boom and bust, even if infrequent, can be deeply disruptive

THE WORLD ACCORDING TO NIKE

Drawing by Jeff Danziger © Tribune Media Services, Inc. All Rights Reserved. Reprinted with permission.

to the productive system and especially to those actors whose limited resources make them vulnerable to bad times.

Command Economy

Limited incentives for efficiency. The absence of competition in the command political economy can result in problems as serious as those from excessive competition. First, if there is no competitive market of alternative goods, there is minimal incentive to produce goods of high quality. People are obliged to accept goods that are unexciting or poorly made. Second, if payments are standardized by the state and there are no major economic incentives for individual initiative and hard work, managers and workers tend to become passive and even lazy.

Unresponsive production. The state's emphasis on a supply orientation means that production decisions are not directly responsive to consumer demand. The supply-oriented political economy is guided by the central planners' ideas of what people should want, not what consumers actually do want and will purchase. Thus the plan typically results in substantial oversupply of some goods and severe shortages of others.

Overcentralization and inflexibility. Command economies are usually so centralized that they lose touch with the differences and complexities of individual firms and consumers. The central planners usually do not receive and react effectively to information regarding miscalculations and mistakes in either the development or the implementation of the state's overall plan. Such rigidity and unresponsiveness make the efficient use of productive resources unlikely. In short, the political economy that combines minimal competition, a weak demand mechanism, and inflexibility is prone to low productivity, inferior goods, and inefficient use of resources.

The Mixed Economy

Given the potential shortcomings of the ideal-type market and command political economies, is there an alternative? The **mixed economy** can be understood as an attempt to combine the strengths of these two ideal-type economies while also minimizing their shortcomings. As a hybrid, the mixed economy is not a "pure" ideal type. It compromises on each of the five major issues considered earlier (see Table 8.2).

1. **Who controls the factors of production?** Control of the means of production is shared between the state and private actors. The state owns or directly controls some of the major factors of production, such as those relating to key commodities (e.g., coal, oil, steel), key infrastructure systems (e.g., transportation, telecommunications), and key financial resources (e.g., the banks). However, private actors (households) control a substantial share of the factors of production.

2. **Who determines what goods are produced?** Production decisions are primarily demand oriented, driven by the market mechanism. Most public (state) sector firms are under direct state control, as in a command economy, but they usually must interact and even compete with many private firms when acquiring productive resources and when selling goods to consumers. However, firms and households can be constrained by the state in the mixed economy. The state can regulate the behavior of private actors, and it can implement an economic plan that specifies broad guidelines for all actors in the system.

3. **Who establishes the value attached to different resources and goods?** The value of a good is established in a manner more akin to that of the market system. Value is generally determined through the market processes of supply and demand, which interact to determine the opportunity costs, and thus the price, of most goods. But the state does intervene to ensure that national priorities are protected. For example, the state might establish the value of certain factors of production, including wages; it might set guidelines to control the market prices of key goods; it might regulate the manner in which households and firms collaborate and compete; and it might employ taxing and expenditure (purchases [F1] in part B of Figure 8.1) to influence the productive system.

4. **Who decides how resources and goods will be distributed?** Decisions on the distribution of values are the most complicated element of the mixed economy. Private actors are allowed to make decisions and take actions that maximize their profits and their share of the resources. The state then intervenes through a variety of taxation mechanisms (F5 in Figure 8.1), recapturing some of the payments received by every private actor. In turn, the state uses these taxes to purchase goods (F1) or as transfer payments (F6), both of which the state redistributes to certain actors in the social order. The state undertakes only a partial redistribution of resources (unlike the case in the command economy), leaving private actors with considerable resources and freedom to make their own decisions about production and consumption.

5. **What is the role of the state?** In sum, the mixed economy is a middle way between the market and the command political economies. The state's rules, actions, and direct involvement in the productive system moderate and limit the market of private households and firms. The state attempts to blend a demand orientation and a supply orientation, to facilitate some competition but to mitigate the effects of ruthless competition, and to allow private actors to benefit from their skillful use of resources while ensuring a certain level of necessary goods for the less success-ful actors. The great challenges for the state in a mixed economy concern the diffi-culties of striking a proper balance between competition and control, between a free market and a planned economy, and between private profit and a sharing of soci-ety's resources. Real-world economies are so immensely complex and dynamic that the search for such a balance is continual and in some cases impossible.

POLITICS PLUS POLITICAL ECONOMY: THE OTHER "ISMS"

The Three "Isms"

One set of great "isms" in political analysis includes the ideologies of conservatism, classical liberalism, and socialism (see Chapter 2). Another set explicitly links pol-itics to political economy: capitalism, communism, and socialism. In twentieth-cen-tury politics, these were extremely emotive labels, endowed with powerful ideological content. In their most straightforward form, capitalism, communism, and socialism correspond loosely to market economy, command economy, and mixed economy, respectively.

Capitalism is a system in which private economic actors are quite free from state constraints, and the state engages in only the most limited efforts to shift resources among private actors. It is founded on the philosophy of laissez-faire eco-nomics celebrated by Adam Smith, and it imposes the severe limitations on gov-ernment activity that are associated with classical liberalism. While the freedom of economic actors from government intervention is critical, there is no assumption that capitalism requires any particular form of political processes to function effi-ciently (Thurow 1997).

Communism has as its centerpiece the socialization of resources—the notion that the state must control society's land, labor, and capital. The state must guide the utilization of all these major means of production by means of a central plan, so that the production and distribution of goods serve the best interests of the entire population. Although it is primarily an economic system linked to the command economy, communism emphasizes an ideological commitment to economic and social equality among all its citizens. It also typically posits that government and politics, like the economic system, must be guided powerfully by a unified leader-ship. Communism is generally associated with the theories of Karl Marx and with the economic systems that were developed in such countries as China (1949 to about 1990), Cuba (since 1959), North Korea (since the early 1950s) and the former Soviet Union (1917–1991).

Socialism is in the middle of the three "isms" and thus it is not precisely differen-tiated from the other two. It attempts a complex balance between state involvement and private control, in common with the mixed political economy. Some major productive resources are owned or controlled by the state, and the state actively intervenes in the economy, but most production decisions are private, and value is established primarily by supply and demand. While the policies in a socialist state attempt to reduce inequalities significantly, they do not aim for total economic equality. Sweden and Denmark are typical examples of what are known as democratic socialist systems (or "social market" systems, see Box 13.1) because they blend socialist economics with democratic politics. Some nondemocratic countries, such as China and Libya, also define themselves as socialist regimes because they claim that "the people" control society's major productive resources but the political economy incorporates significant elements of the private market system. Socialism is a confusing term, in part because certain "communist" countries, such as Cuba and North Korea, are sometimes called socialist regimes, based on the manner in which Karl Marx and Marxists use the concepts of socialism and communism (recall Chapter 2, and see Box 8.2).

Communism is distinguishable from socialism in an analytic sense because the communist state (on behalf of "the people") attempts to control virtually all important factors of production in the society and has a fundamental commitment to total economic and social equality among all citizens. (Notice that such egalitarianism is not

BOX 8.2

Communism versus Socialism in Marxist Theory

It is worth noting that Marx and Marxist theorists use the terms "socialism" and "communism" in a different manner from either the political economy approach of this book or contemporary Western media and politicians. In Marxist theory, communism is a higher stage of political economy that follows socialism. In a *socialist system*, the state strives to achieve social control of resources (of the means of production) by eliminating private property. As private property is eliminated, there will be a reduction in the presence of the different strata (classes) of citizens that are separated by substantial variations in the amount of private property that each controls. (A detailed description of the class approach to explaining politics is provided in Chapter 9.)

In Marxist theory, *communism* emerges only when all classes (and the inevitable conflict between those classes) cease to exist. Thus most Marxists acknowledge that no "socialist" state (e.g., Cuba) has yet completely eliminated classes and the class struggle; in this sense, communism remains a goal. In the classless society, everyone will work for the good of all, not to gain private value. Under socialism, everyone provides resources (work) according to ability and receives resources according to that work, while under communism, everyone provides according to ability and receives according to need.

This book employs the common Western usage: Communism exists if a state has nearly total control over the major factors of production. Given the recent shift away from communism (see Chapter 15), only a few contemporary states (e.g., North Korea) meet this criterion.

a necessary condition of the ideal-type command economy.) A socialist system, in comparison with capitalism, tends to use public policy to redistribute societal resources toward those citizens who are less advantaged economically, and the socialist state is substantially more involved in economic planning, regulation, and even ownership of productive means than a state under capitalism (Przeworski 1985).

The Real World

It is possible to make several conclusions about the political economies of contemporary countries. First, no country has a political economy that corresponds exactly to either the market economy or the command economy. Since these are ideal types, this fact is not surprising. While it is possible to locate countries generally along a continuum from a "pure" market economy to a "pure" command economy, all actual political economies are mixed. However, this does not mean that all political economies are basically the same—the mix of elements varies a great deal from country to country.

Second, regardless of how different states describe themselves, the concepts of communism, socialism, and capitalism might be best understood as broader, somewhat ideological labels that signify considerably more than the way in which each country's political economy is organized. For some countries, these labels also connote *sociopolitical* orders. Communism is viewed as a system that denies individual freedoms in noneconomic spheres and in which government does not depend on the consent of the governed. Capitalism signifies a system of self-interested individualism that denies the need for collective action to nurture society as a whole, to promote social values and culture, or to protect the ecology (Heilbroner 1994).

Third, every state engages in some regulation of some economic actors and some redistribution of resources. Politics and values play a powerful role in establishing exactly what kinds of interventions the state will undertake and what values and interests the state will serve. Thus understanding the mixed nature of actual political economies entails more than simply comparing the proportion of the GDP controlled by private actors versus the state.

In theory, at least, two countries might have the same overall levels of market freedom and state intervention in the economy (as well as the same level of taxation and the same share of GNP in the public sector) and yet be guided by very different philosophies. In one country, the state's role could be to limit the power of large firms, to ensure labor's participation in national economic policy making, and to facilitate domestic consumption. In another country, the state might be no less interventionist, but its involvement might be based on policies that support the growth of large firms, that suppress labor unions, and that channel citizens' resources into savings.

The latter profile is consistent with the political economies of some of the most successful industrializing countries of Asia, such as Singapore and South Korea, whereas countries such as Spain and Uruguay generally fit the first profile. These issues will be examined in more detail later in the book (in the study of economic development in Chapter 10, and in the comparative analyses of strategies for achieving prosperity in Chapters 13–15). The four examples that follow here suggest some of the features of actual political economies relative to ideal types.

Generally market and capitalist: Switzerland.   The wealthiest major country in the world (measured as GNP per capita in purchasing power parity [PPP]), Switzerland, has a relatively weak central government. This decentralization of political power is linked to a political economy that strongly emphasizes private control and limited government involvement. Switzerland is ranked seventh among 123 countries on a measure of freedom of the economy from state regulation (Gwartney and Lawson 2003). Nearly all factors of production are privately owned, and most decisions and actions regarding the use of those resources are in private hands. On the expenditure side, central government spending is less than 15 percent of GNP. Apart from defense expenditures and education, relatively few resources are allocated to the provision of public goods, given the wealth of the society. Although still low, welfare spending rose substantially in the 1990s, generating a national debate about limitations on public expenditure on social programs.

Generally mixed and capitalist: South Korea.   In South Korea, the state has little commitment to use the political economy for direct improvement of its citizens' quality of life. Apart from education, the state does not provide many welfare goods and services to its citizens. Central government expenditure is only about 16 percent of GNP. It is not a purely capitalist system, however, because the state is extremely interventionist in promoting economic development. The state bureaucracy works very closely with firms to implement a comprehensive, collaborative strategy for economic growth. This strategy has particularly favored the development of a few major Korean companies. Government loans, tax credits, and other subsidies are channeled to these companies, which are expected to operate and diversify in directions suggested by the government. In turn, the government has assured the companies of high profits and of a labor force that is well educated, disciplined, and unable to organize effectively for high wages. The state has also employed many hidden subsidies and import restrictions to provide competitive advantages in the international market to its export-oriented firms. (This "developmental-state" approach is discussed further in Chapter 10.)

Generally mixed and socialist: Denmark.   Denmark is among the top ten major countries in terms of GDP per capita. The great majority of productive resources in Denmark are privately owned, and the state allows entrepreneurs considerable freedom of action. However, the state is an active and visible force in the Danish political economy. First, it enforces strong policies that regulate private economic actors, especially "corporatist" policies that control working conditions and environmental quality (see Box 8.3 on corporatism). Second, the state provides an extensive array of welfare services to the population, including income supplement programs, a comprehensive free health care system, state-subsidized housing for the elderly and for low-income groups, free child care and education from infancy through university, and an extensive public transportation system. And third, to finance these programs, the government collects various forms of taxes equal to more than 50 percent of the GDP.

Generally command and communist: Cuba.   In response to the global movement toward more market-oriented systems, Cuba has reduced the level of centralized state control over the economy. However, the state still owns and controls the major means of production, and there is a detailed central economic plan. Thus Cuba is among the 11 countries (of 178) with the highest level of state regulation of the economy

BOX 8.3

From the "Ism" File II: Corporatism

Recently many scholars have referred to the political economy of some states by another "ism," corporatism. *Corporatism* is characterized by extensive economic cooperation between an activist state and large organizations representing major economic actors. The corporatist state identifies a few groups that control major productive resources. These "peak associations" (organizations that represent these big groups) usually include large industries, organized labor, farmers, and major financial institutions. The organizational leaders of the peak associations are given great influence in working with the state to determine answers to key political economy questions regarding production decisions and the distribution of resources.

    The idea is that there will be consultation, cooperation, and coordination among the state, big capital, big owners, and big labor, rather than conflict and competition. The peak associations have some autonomy from the state, but they are supposed to work together for common national interests. In short, corporatism blends features of capitalism (e.g., private ownership, private profit) and socialism (e.g., extensive state economic planning, coordination of major factors of production with the state's conception of the national interest).

    Italy under Benito Mussolini created the first modern corporate state—one with a strong fascist bent—between 1922 and 1943. Twenty-two corporations were established, including ones for chemical trades, textiles, lumber and wood, credit and insurance, and inland communications. Each corporation had owner, employee, and managerial representatives who met with state officials to develop economic policy (Macridis and Burg 1997: 220–226). France, Japan, Portugal, and Spain are among the contemporary states with strong corporatist tendencies (see Royo 2002; Schmitter 1993; Wiarda 1997).

(Freedom House 2001). Agriculture and manufacturing operations remain collectivized. The state promises work for all (although there is unemployment) and it controls workers' wages. Consistent with the ideals of communism, the state retains a fundamental commitment to egalitarianism through its control and allocation of societal resources. Many state policies are guided by the quest for economic and social egalitarianism. There has been a strong emphasis on state spending on education and health care and on policies to equalize the distribution of land and income in order to increase equality between races, between genders, and between urban and rural citizens.

CONCLUDING OBSERVATIONS

This chapter has introduced you to an approach that classifies and characterizes political systems in terms of their political economies. These concepts are abstract and require the fusion of political science and economics. They are important concepts because the linkages between the political system and the economic system are fundamental and pervasive in the contemporary political world. Indeed, the two systems have become so interrelated in most states that it is difficult to separate them, except in an analytic sense. There is substantial variation in the extent to which the political system intervenes in the system of production and distribution of resources. At one extreme, the state can leave every activity to private actors, while at the other extreme, virtually all economic activity is planned and controlled by the state.

In considering a system such as communism or capitalism, you might find it difficult to avoid strong normative judgments due both to your political socialization and to your tendency to identify an "ism" with particular states for which you have definite positive or negative feelings. For example, your evaluative orientations of communism might be negative because you associate it with the governments of North Korea or the former Soviet Union, states that you might have been socialized to distrust. It is certainly reasonable that you will make both analytical *and* normative judgments about the virtues and shortcomings of every form of political economy and every "ism."

Indeed, assessing the appropriateness of a country's political economy might be the most crucial issue in understanding its effectiveness in the contemporary political world. In recent years, the support for communism and the command political economy has substantially declined among the leaders and citizens in many countries. However, as you will see in Part Five, that decline has not necessarily led countries to adopt a full implementation of a market economy. It has not even meant that most political leaderships and most citizens have abandoned their support for all of the principles associated with a more command-oriented political economy or with communism.

Despite your own political socialization, you might reflect on a fundamental question: Is *every* state, regardless of its current economic and political development, best served by exactly the same political economy? If you allow for variations in the most appropriate form of political economy for countries in the current global system, you leave open many challenging and important questions about political choices, questions that will be considered from a variety of perspectives in the remainder of this book. This exploration begins in Part Four, with chapters that examine crucial issues associated with political decision making; political, social, and economic change; and political violence.

KEY CONCEPTS

capitalism	gross national product (GNP)
command economy	household (consumer)
communism	market economy
corporatism	mixed economy
factors of production	political economy
fascism	socialism
firm (producer)	supply and demand
goods	surplus value (profit)
gross domestic product (GDP)	utility

FOR FURTHER CONSIDERATION

1. The economic productivity of command political economies has always been inferior to that of market political economies in comparable countries. What, then, might have been the attraction of this approach to many groups and to many countries between the 1950s and the 1970s?
2. What would be the greatest benefit to individuals if the state played virtually no role in its political economy? What would be the most serious problem with such a system?
3. Are there measures other than the growth in GDP per capita that might indicate the success of a political economy? Why are leaders in most states so worried if there is no growth in GDP per capita?
4. Do you agree with those who contend that capitalism is so individualistic that it fails to protect the collective good?

FOR FURTHER READING

Courtois, Stephane, Nicholas Werth, Jean-Louis Panne, Adrzej Paczkowski, Karel Bartooek, and Jean-Louis Margolin. (1999). *The Black Book of Communism: Crimes, Terror, Repression.* Trans. by Jonathan Murphy and Mark Cramer. Cambridge, MA: Harvard University Press. A detailed and profoundly critical analysis of the history of communism in the twentieth century. Its core argument is that a series of regimes and ruthless dictators, ranging from Lenin and Stalin in the Soviet Union to Mao Zedong in China to Pol Pot in Cambodia to Kim Il Sung in North Korea, have led communist regimes that engaged in brutal "class genocide" in their societies, resulting in as many as one hundred million deaths. There are powerful chapter-length analyses of communist regimes on every continent.

Friedman, Milton. (1981). *Capitalism and Freedom.* Chicago: University of Chicago Press. The major contemporary explication of the classical liberal preference for a strong market economy with only limited state intervention.

Garson, Barbara. (2003). *Money Makes the World Go Around.* New York: Penguin. The controversial social critic offers a wonderfully readable exploration of the global economy by tracking the money in two small investments and revealing how that money has various effects on people around the world.

Heilbroner, Robert. (1994). *Twenty-First Century Capitalism.* New York: W.W. Norton. An economist and social critic outlines the challenges facing capitalism and the continuing need for the state to guide the market economy and serve the social good.

Johnson, Chalmers. (1985). *MITI and the Japanese Miracle.* Stanford, CA: Stanford University Press. Characterizes the innovative manner in which Japan created a highly successful blending of a market political economy with an interventionist and supportive state furthering a well-defined national economic development policy.

Kristol, Irving. (1978). *Two Cheers for Capitalism.* New York: Basic Books. A leading American neoconservative argues that capitalism is superior to alternative forms of political economy.

Lindblom, Charles E. (1977). *Politics and Markets: The World's Political-Economic Systems.* New York: Basic Books. A rich comparative analysis of the relative merits of the political economies of modern socialism and capitalism.

Royo, Sebastian. (2002). *"A New Century of Corporatism?": Corporatism in Southern Europe—Spain and Portugal in a Comparative Perspective.* Westport, CT: Praeger Publishers. Detailed case studies of the last three decades in Spain and Portugal are the basis of an exploration of how technological and postindustrial changes have created the conditions for a resurgence of corporatism (Box 8.3) in European settings.

Thurow, Lester. (1997). *The Future of Capitalism.* New York: Viking-Penguin. A leading economist critically assesses the strengths and weaknesses of capitalism as a political economy and as a system that must deliver prosperity to most of its citizens.

Westoby, Adam. (1989). *The Evolution of Communism.* New York: Free Press. A thorough and illuminating history of the development of communist thought and practice.

Yergin, Daniel, and Joseph Stanislaw (1999). *The Commanding Heights: The Battle Between Government & the Marketplace That Is Remaking the Modern World.* New York: Simon & Schuster. A sweeping, readable account of how major countries in Europe, Latin America, Asia, and North America embraced extensive state intervention in their political economies in the period after World War II and then shifted away from the mixed economy toward a stronger form of market economics in the last several decades.

ON THE WEB

http://imf.org/

The key documents and agreements among all states and for particular members of the International Monetary Fund (IMF), an organization that includes more than one hundred and eighty countries who cooperate to sustain a smoothly functioning system of interstate trade and to provide loans and other financial assistance to countries.

http://freetheworld.com

A site containing reports and data from the Economic Freedom Network, a congery of researchers "committed to bringing economic freedom and growth to all the countries of the world."

http://worldbank.org

The official site of the World Bank, an international consortium of banks and other major financial institutions, includes extensive economic data regarding the structure and performance of the economies of more than one hundred and eighty countries.

http://www.wto.org/

The World Trade Organization (WTO) (see Box 11.2 in Chapter 11), which coordinates trade policy for more than one hundred and forty countries, offers this web site to provide key documents and agreements as well as sections that articulate/justify the WTO philosophy of open trade relations among countries.

http://www.freetrade.org/

From the Cato Institute, this site offers evidence for the benefits of free trade and the costs of protectionism, including various on-line studies and articles.

http://www.weforum.org/

The site of the World Economic Forum, an organization designed to allow world leaders to address global issues, contains a substantial amount of information on a variety of international economic issues (e.g., sustainable development, globalization).

http://secretariat.efta.int/

The official site of the European Free Trade Association (EFTA) provides access to EFTA bulletins, conference information, and official documents.

http://www.economist.com/

The electronic home of *The Economist*, a leading British weekly, provides access to selected articles examining issues of political economy and world finance.

"You asked us to build a computer which could replace the government."

CHAPTER 9 Politics as a Value Allocation Process

How does politics actually work? Here is one answer:

You may very appropriately want to ask me how we are going to resolve the ever-accelerating dangerous impasse of world-opposed politicians and ideological dogmas. I answer, it will be resolved by the computer. Man has ever-increasing confidence in the computer; witness his unconcerned landings as air transport passengers coming in for a landing in the combined invisibility of fog and night. While no politician or political system can ever afford to yield understandably and enthusiastically to their adversaries and opposers, all politicians can and will yield enthusiastically to the computer's safe flight-controlling capabilities in bringing all of humanity in for a safe landing.

—R. Buckminster Fuller,
Operating Manual for Spaceship Earth (1970: 46) [emphasis added]

It is likely that R. Buckminster Fuller's description does not match your idea of how most political decisions are currently made. You probably think that self-interest, pressure from interest groups and parties, ideology, and even irrationality are embedded in many of the actual value allocations by a political system. (It is worth noting that Fuller is a futurist offering a normative vision of how he thinks politics *ought* to work, not an analytic political scientist attempting to describe and explain things as they are.)

One of the most obvious yet most fascinating questions in political science is: How does politics work? How does a political system handle the incredibly difficult and complicated value allocations that are the stuff of politics? If someone from another country asked you how major policy decisions are made in your country, what would you say? What are the key points you would emphasize?

Earlier chapters have introduced you to many of the major actors and significant structures in the political world and have indicated how these actors and structures operate. This chapter details three extremely "political" analytic explanations of the value allocation process: (1) the elite approach, (2) the class approach, and (3) the group approach.

Each approach provides a different explanation of how politics works, how influence is exercised, and what political forces seem to shape political decisions. No country or political system is likely to operate exactly like any of these three analytic approaches. Rather, each approach is a rich illustration of a pattern of power and decision making that is prevalent in some systems at a given point in time. The approaches also share two important analytic features:

1. They are constitutive approaches (as a type of functional analysis; see the Appendix) in the sense that they attempt to define *the* fundamental unit of analysis that explains politics.

2. They explain politics in terms of the interactions among aggregations of individuals who use the political system to pursue their own particular interests.

Our discussion begins with the elite approach.

THE ELITE APPROACH

Key Concepts

Two key concepts are central to the **elite approach.** First, politics is defined as *the struggle for power.* Second, the *political world* is characterized by *political stratification*—that is, the population is segmented into separate groups that are in layers (or "strata") with higher or lower amounts of power. In the elite approach, there are only two major strata. The stratum that does more of what there is to do (in the policy process) and that gets more of what there is to get (in the allocation of values) is called the **political elite.** The stratum that does less and gets less is called *the mass.*

Elite theory can be visually represented by a power pyramid, as shown in Figure 9.1. Such a depiction emphasizes that the elite is composed of a relatively small number of individuals who are in a dominant position on top of the large mass. Notice that there is a third stratum between the elite and the mass. This is *the understructure,* composed of political officials and state administrators who carry out the elite's policy directives.

Major Theorists

The elite approach has been particularly grounded in the writings of European political theorists of the late nineteenth century, especially the Italians Roberto Michels, Wilfredo Pareto, and Gaetano Mosca. In *The Ruling Class* (1896/1939), Mosca analyzes the political histories of a variety of political systems and concludes that they all have two strata, the political class (the elite) and the nonpolitical class (the mass). The political class controls all political functions, holds virtually all political power, and dominates the allocation of values. The basis of elite power has varied across time and location, but Mosca identifies broad historical stages during which the primary basis of elite domination has been military power, then religious control, then economic power, and most recently, technical knowledge. According to Mosca, the major role of the political system is as an instrument of the political class, serving the elite's interests in the allocation of values.

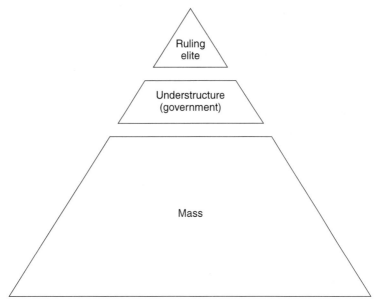

FIGURE 9.1 Characterization of an elite system

A well-known American application of the elite approach is *The Power Elite* (1956) by C. Wright Mills. Mills concludes that the power elite in American society is composed of those who control society's most powerful institutions: (1) the "warlords" in the military establishment; (2) the "corporation chieftains" in the economic sector; and (3) the "political directorate" at the top positions in the political system. Mills observes that the members of the elite share crucial values about how society in general, and the political system in particular, ought to operate. The members of the elite tend to come from similar social and educational backgrounds, to circulate among major positions in each of the three key institutional structures, and to have long-standing personal relationships with each other. Like other elite theorists, Mills does not claim the elite is a conspiracy that continually plots to retain control. But some of its active members do meet periodically to discuss common interests, and most of its members will act in concert during times of crisis (see also Domhoff 2002).

Most elite theorists focus on the elite itself—the identity and socialization of elite members, and how the elite maintains its domination through a variety of techniques, such as the manipulation of symbols, the strategic distribution of resources, control of the state, and the use of force. There is a normative element in the discussions of many elite theorists, indicating their disapproval of a system in which there is such a high concentration of political power serving only a small minority within society. But others respond that elite theory merely reveals the inevitable tendency for a few people to take control and to dominate the political order, while those in the mass willingly subordinate themselves to the few who are capable of giving coherence to political society.

The Value Allocation Process

The value allocation process is explained primarily in terms of the elite's actions. Some members of the elite decide that a particular public policy decision is in the elite's interest. They then discuss whether this policy should be enacted and how it should be implemented. When there is general consensus among those members of the elite who are concerned about the decision, representatives of the elite instruct the relevant members of the understructure to perform the policy-making and policy-implementation activities that serve the elite's interests.

In the elite explanation of the policy process, the active elites are subject to little direct influence from the mass or even from the understructure of governmental officials. The mass is politically apathetic and impotent, and policy is imposed on this large proportion of the population. The understructure follows the elite's directives because its members depend on the elite's power and resources as the basis of their own political positions and authority.

The Prevalence of Elite-Based Political Systems

How many countries have elitist political systems? As noted in Chapter 7, about two-fifths of contemporary countries (containing more than half the world's population) are nondemocratic systems. It seems reasonable to infer that most of these systems are dominated by an elite in the manner described by the elite approach.

However, the issue might be more complicated. Is it true that all the key conditions of elitism are met in every nondemocratic country? This empirical question could be examined in specific political systems (e.g., Congo, El Salvador, Saudi Arabia, or Singapore) by assessing these kinds of analytic questions:

1. Does the political leadership act with unanimity on all major issues?

2. Is there active and effective political participation by nonelite groups?

3. Are some major political decisions responsive to nonelite demands, even when the decisions are contrary to the elite's interests?

4. Is there dramatic inequality in the distribution of resources between the elite and the mass?

While definitive answers to these issues are very difficult, our knowledge of political systems suggests that many contemporary states are generally characterized by elite rule. (Consider the brief description of Swaziland in Box 9.1.) The power to make crucial political decisions and the benefits from those decisions do seem predominantly concentrated in the hands of a small elite.

The issue can also be considered in a different way. Is it possible that a country classified as a democracy is actually run by an elite? That is, even if a political system meets such basic criteria of democracy as a limited mandate and freedom to criticize and oppose the leadership (recall Chapter 7), does this necessarily mean that the system is not elitist?

This question underlies a fierce debate among analysts regarding whether the elite approach best describes politics, even in many "democratic" political systems. Some, such as C. Wright Mills (1956), provide arguments and evidence that there is elite rule even in most democracies. In this view, a small proportion of the population

BOX 9.1

Elite Politics in Swaziland

One of the many contemporary examples of elite politics is Swaziland, a small African country between Mozambique and South Africa. While Swaziland was a British colonial protectorate (1902–1968), a local king (Sobuza II) became a hero of his people by leading the movement for independence (from 1921). After independence in 1968, Sobuza became the ruling monarch of the new country. A British-style parliament with competing parties was installed. Parties competed in three parliamentary elections, although the king's party dominated in each election.

In 1973 the king banned all opposition groups and declared that European government forms were "un-Swazi." Since then, political parties have been banned, and the nonpartisan parliament essentially affirms the king's decisions. The king actually appoints two-thirds of the members of the Senate and one-fourth of the members in the House. Indeed, according to

A day after being called back from high school in England and being crowned as the ruler of Swaziland, King Mswati III attends a party in the palace. The 18-year-old king moved quickly to establish rule under his personal control.

Swaziland's official publications, even the method for selecting the next king is "a secret," except it is stipulated that he must be a young, unmarried prince. When Sobuza II died in 1982, the ensuing private power struggle among members of the royal family and the king's council resulted in the selection of King Mswati III.

In fact, everyone in Swaziland has always understood that real political power is concentrated in the king and his small group of advisers, known as the National Council. Young King Mswati III quickly dissolved the council, removed many of his rivals from positions of authority, and elevated his own set of trusted advisers to positions of decision-making power. Under King Mswati III, as under King Sobuza, both policy making and the major sectors of the economy (the mines and most farmlands) are directly controlled by a king's council. Thus one key criterion of elite politics is clearly met: Virtually all major political decisions are made by a small group, and the mass of people in Swaziland have little direct impact on the policies or politics of the state.

(continued)

BOX **9.1** (CONTINUED)

    Moreover, most of the benefits of policy are enjoyed by this elite, a second key criterion of an elite system. A clear indicator of this is the substantial inequality in the distribution of resources between the few rich and the many poor. Swaziland currently has the highest inequality in the distribution of income (with a Gini index score of 60.9) among all 111 countries for which there are data. Similarly, two-fifths of the population live in absolute poverty, and the richest 10 percent of the Swazi population have the highest share of total income (50.2 percent) in the society of all 111 countries (UNDP 2003: table 12).

dominates most significant political decisions and enjoys a hugely disproportionate share of the benefits from the value allocations made by the government. Box 9.2, on the local political system in Oakland, California, suggests that a powerful few can dominate a city's development decisions.

    Such empirical assessments of the elite approach, whether of a single city or an entire country, are highly controversial and ideologically charged, since they represent a direct attack on the existence of democracy. Moreover, a definite proof of the elite approach in most political systems would be a massive undertaking, requiring the documentation of systematic elite dominance on a large number of key decisions across a variety of issue areas.

THE CLASS APPROACH

    The **class approach** shares certain fundamental concepts with the elite approach, but it offers a very different explanation of the continuing dynamic processes of politics. The most important shared concept is the notion of *stratification,* the basic fact of *structured inequality* in the distribution of values in society.

    The strata identified in the class approach are called classes, the second key concept. *Class* denotes a large group of individuals who are similar in their possession of or control over some fundamental value. The most fundamental value that distinguishes classes differs for different class theorists. Karl Marx (1818–1883), the best-known class theorist, differentiates classes primarily on the basis of a group's relationship to the major factors of production in the economic system (Marx 1867/1981: ch. 52). At the simplest level, Marx divides society into two classes: (1) the *capitalist class,* which includes those who own significant amounts of the major factors of production (especially financial resources, raw materials, and capital—the physical facilities to manufacture goods); and (2) the *proletariat class,* which includes those who own little more than their own labor.

    Analysts suggest various modifications that refine Marx's distinctions between classes in most contemporary societies. First, most class theorists identify more than two major class strata, with each class characterized by its particular levels of social,

BOX 9.2

Elite Domination of Development in Oakland, California

When the Oakland, California, Planning Commission reported that large areas of the downtown and adjacent districts were blighted and required redevelopment, the residents and property owners in the area were threatened and outraged. (This discussion relies on Hayes 1972.) The Oakland City Council even passed a resolution declaring that there was no blight in Oakland. But Oakland's economic elite could see that its members would realize great benefits from redevelopment. Thus the members of this elite initiated a strategy to ensure that their redevelopment plan would be implemented.

First, the city's real estate board hired costly outside consultants to advise the city's business leaders on how to accomplish their objectives. Then the elite persuaded the newly elected mayor to appoint a committee to lay the groundwork for redevelopment. This committee (called OCCUR, the Oakland Citizens' Committee for Urban Renewal) was led by a top manager from a major local industry, the executive vice president of the home builders association, the past and current presidents of the real estate board, a corporate attorney, and the manager of a large department store.

OCCUR raised, refined, and promoted redevelopment proposals and coordinated the public and private activities necessary for their enactment and implementation. The committee soon offered a comprehensive plan for redevelopment and conservation in all areas of the city. When the city council initially rejected the plan, OCCUR mounted an extensive campaign to ensure support for the plan from the council and other local groups. The national association of large real estate developers sent its president to assist the process. The local chamber of commerce prepared a promotional film on redevelopment that was shown to scores of local groups. Oakland's major newspaper ran countless articles and editorials in support of redevelopment. The city council was even provided with a chartered airplane trip to successful urban renewal projects in cities around the United States. By this point, the city council reversed its original stance and initiated the first of several large redevelopment projects proposed by the business elite.

Overall, these projects displaced the poor, increased the tax burden on the middle class, provided subsidized new facilities for major local and national business corporations, and generated huge profits for the local building, real estate, and banking elites. This apparently democratic process of policy making can be described in terms of elite theory. The economic elite dominated the formulation of policies, guided their passage, and reaped a very large share of the benefits from those decisions. The political understructure implemented the policies formulated by the elite, and the mass of citizens—politically ineffective and relatively passive—benefited little from the outcome.

political, and economic power. Second, some argue that it is *control* (rather than ownership) of the means of production that is most important. Third, others observe that in certain social systems, the key elements that distinguish different class strata are status, kinship, ethnicity, religion, or tradition-based authority (rather than ownership of the means of production). And fourth, still others posit that possession of information resources and knowledge has become the crucial resource distinguishing classes in postindustrial, high-tech societies (Castells 2000). In general, these analysts assert that there is strong empirical evidence for the continuing prevalence of class politics, even in developed countries (see, e.g., Dahrendorf 1959; Esping-Andersen 1990; Poulantzas 1973).

Figure 9.2 provides three models of class systems. Each reveals a different conception of the size of classes, the number of classes, the extent of differentiation between classes, and the extent of hierarchy among the classes. While part A shows a characterization similar to the elite approach in its hierarchical and pyramidal form, it also emphasizes a clear separation between multiple classes. Part B highlights the overlapping nature of the classes. Here the boundaries between classes are permeable rather than distinct, and some members of "lower" classes have as much or even more political power than those in the class above them (see Lenski 1966: 284). The interactive and even reciprocal nature of power in interclass relations is emphasized in part C. Although there is still substantial inequality in this system and the higher classes clearly dominate the lower classes, there is more interdependence among classes, and the lower classes do affect the actions and domination of the higher classes by means of a variety of constraints and obligations.

The third crucial concept of the class approach is *class conflict.* It is assumed that classes lower in the class system can increase their share of key values only at the expense of the classes above them. Given the fundamental inequalities in the distribution of values, struggle between classes is inevitable. The higher classes employ various strategies, and ultimately coercion, in order to prevent a significant loss of values (and of relative advantage) to the classes below them. Lower classes find that only violence enables their class to increase its relative share of values. Thus class conflict is systematic and ubiquitous, although its most visible and violent manifestations (such as strikes, riots, and rebellion) might be suppressed for periods of time if the higher classes are effective in their distribution of benefits and use of coercion.

Most class analysts do not explain in detail how policy decisions are actually made. Like elite theorists, they assume that the common interests shared by members of a class will result in general consensus on what public policy decisions should be enacted. Class analysts also view the political system as a set of structures that are subordinate to the dominant class. Thus the policies and actions of the state serve the preferences of that class and preserve the existing distribution of values.

The class approach centers on the examination of the tactics of class domination and the dynamics of the class struggle. Not every value allocation by the state is coercive or of direct benefit only to the dominant class. The state might implement policies to shorten the length of the working day or to increase health care benefits to the middle classes. Such policies either ameliorate the worst conditions that might provoke violence or provide certain classes with advantages over classes below them. In such uses of public policy, benefits are provided to some classes in

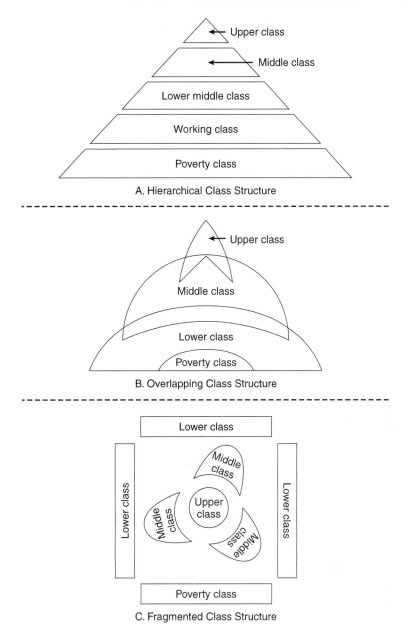

FIGURE 9.2   Three different characterizations of class structures
Source: Based on Bill and Hardgrave 1981: 181.

an effort to buy their support or their acquiescence, or at least to dampen their propensity for conflict.

Despite such strategies, the systematic inequalities in fundamental values generate continuing conflict between classes in the society. Periodically, this conflict explodes into class violence. Ultimately, in an episode of the class war, a lower class

succeeds in overthrowing the highest class. At this point, a new class gains dominance in the system, including control over the political system and superiority in
the distribution of values. In the view of Marx and many other class theorists, major
class conflict can end only when the elimination of dominant classes reduces the
system to a single class, and hence society becomes classless. In the absence of class
inequalities, the state serves all groups, and there is no cause for further conflict
among groups.

THE GROUP APPROACH

The **group approach** offers a very different account of the political process. This
approach is grounded in the concept of the *group,* which is defined as any aggregate
of individuals who interact to pursue a common interest. A political group, as an
analytic concept, exists whenever individuals have a shared interest regarding some
allocation of values by the political system.

The explanation of politics as a complex web of group interactions has many
historical roots, but this approach is particularly identified with American social
scientists, especially *The Process of Government,* by American political scientist
Arthur Bentley (1908/1967); David Truman (1951); and Robert Dahl (1961, 1967,
1971), who is the modern political scientist most strongly associated with the development and defense of the group approach.

The group approach begins with the assumption that an individual's group
memberships are multiple and nonreinforcing. That is, any particular individual can
belong to many different groups. Individuals are not stratified into large, permanent groups as described by the elite and class approaches because the aggregation
of people who share common identity on one political interest is not the same as
the people who are part of groups regarding other political interests. Table 9.1 shows

TABLE 9.1
Group Memberships of Six Hypothetical Individuals in the United States

Groups	Individuals					
	Person 1	*Person 2*	*Person 3*	*Person 4*	*Person 5*	*Person 6*
Democratic Party	✓				✓	
Republican Party		✓				
AFL-CIO union	✓					
Christian Coalition			✓			✓
Mothers Against Drunk Driving		✓			✓	✓
National Abortion Rights Action League	✓					
National Rifle Association	✓		✓			
Parent–Teacher Association	✓	✓				

Note: Each checkmark (✓) indicates a group with which the individual is affiliated. This distribution supports the concept of non-overlapping
(nonreinforcing) group memberships. An individual shares group membership with different people across various groups.

six hypothetical people whose group memberships overlap in different ways, depending on the issue. The second important assumption is that *many different political resources* might influence those who make value allocations for the political system. As discussed in Chapter 3, the kinds of resources that might be used to influence political decisions include money, numbers of supporters/voters, monopoly of expertise, political skill, access to information, and status. It is also assumed that every individual (and hence every political group) has some political resources with which he can attempt to influence policy decisions.

In the group approach, *politics* can be understood as *the interaction among groups that are pursuing their political interests.* The role of the government is to manage the interactions within this giant system of interacting groups. Thus *public policy* is defined as *the balance point of the competition among groups on an issue at the time when government makes a policy decision.*

Figure 9.3 provides a visual model of how a policy decision is made according to the group approach, using health care policy in a country such as the United States as the example. There is a continuum of possible policy decisions, ranging from free state provision of all health care to all citizens at one extreme to total private provision based on fee-for-service at the other extreme. The analytic framework of the group approach can be summarized in five major steps:

1. Identify the key groups that you think would have an active interest in decisions in this policy area.

2. On a continuum of possible policy outcomes, locate the preferred policy decision of each group.

3. Estimate the level of political resources each group is likely to employ to influence the decision regarding this policy (represented as a "weight" on the continuum,

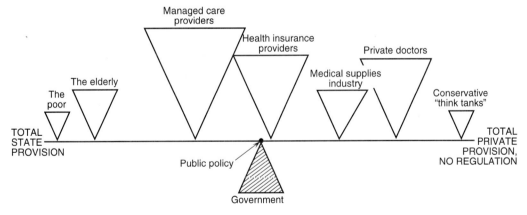

Symbols:

— = Continuum of possible public policies regarding health care policy

▽ = Interest group mobilized on this issue, with volume of triangle representing the group's political resources applied to the issue

△ = Government, which determines the equilibrium point and ratifies that point as public policy

● = Public policy position, which is the equilibrium point in the competition among groups, given each group's political resources

FIGURE 9.3   A group approach model of the policy process: a hypothetical policy decision based on both the political resources that the group has and the level of its actual use of those resources).

4. "The government" establishes the equilibrium point that balances the "weights" of the political resources mobilized by all groups.

5. This equilibrium point is described in terms of a public policy decision that corresponds to this position on the policy continuum. The decision corresponding to this point will be the political system's "authoritative allocation of values" (recall Chapter 5).

In this model, the particular functions of the government are: (1) to establish rules of the game for the group struggle; (2) to determine the interests of competing groups and the levels of political resources mobilized by those groups; (3) to find a public policy that approximately balances the positions of all active groups in terms of their interests and resources; (4) to enact these balance points as public policy decisions; and (5) to implement the resulting value allocations. Government, as an analytic construct in the group approach, is best understood as a neutral arbiter in the competition among groups.

However, in a more realistic interpretation, government is not merely an automated weighing machine that totals the value of each group's influence resources. The government might have an ideological position and thus place greater emphasis on some objectives than others. For example, the government might enforce rules that help or hinder some groups in using their political resources, it might value some political resources more substantially than others, it might allow certain groups

Individuals and groups *can* influence the policy-making process in some political systems, as in this New England town meeting.

BOX 9.3

Group Politics in New Haven, Connecticut

The two Lebov brothers, wealthy local businessmen in New Haven, Connecticut, acquired 65 prefabricated metal houses from military surplus. They received permission from the city's building department to erect these houses on a site that was zoned for industry in a working-class neighborhood called The Hill. Their proposal also had the support of the mayor and the city's lawyer.

But the (mainly) Italian-American residents of the neighborhood were outraged. They viewed the metal houses as an "instant slum" that would threaten the property values of their modest but well-kept houses and would bring African-American residents to The Hill. Miss Mary Grava emerged as the improbable leader of the residents' opposition to the project. An elderly spinster, she had never been involved in politics before this. She was tireless in contacting people who might influence the city's decision. She mobilized the residents to telephone members of the city council and others in city government and played Republican politicians against Democratic politicians in order to gain support from both groups for the neighborhood's opposition to the metal houses.

Under severe pressure from the neighborhood, the council drafted legislation to stop construction of the metal houses. But the Lebov brothers began building anyway, with added support from the local newspaper, which saw the houses as affordable housing for needy low-income families. The city's lawyer ruled that the council had no legal power to stop construction. The council nonetheless voted to stop the project. The mayor vetoed the council's legislation. In response, The Hill residents organized a neighborhood association led by Mary Grava's brother, who happened also to be the mayor's godfather. This local association widened its base, gaining support from the middle-class League of Women Voters (which wanted to expand its membership among ethnic working-class groups), from the current mayor's chief Republican rival on the council, and from the Democratic candidate for mayor. The council overrode the mayor's veto. After an arson fire destroyed one of the metal houses, the fire inspector withdrew his support for the project. Ultimately, the metal houses were never placed in the neighborhood.

In Robert Dahl's view (1961), this is a compelling example of how people can organize into a political group when they care deeply about an issue and can combine their limited political resources to influence policy on the issue. In this case, "just plain folks" formed a group that fought city hall and beat the rich developers, the mayor, and the city's lawyer. (This section is based on Robert Dahl's seminal advocacy of the group politics approach, *Who Governs?* [1961: 192–199].)

greater access to important information, or it might be more or less willing to find the financial resources necessary to implement a certain policy. In addition, certain elected and career governmental actors have their own personal and institutional interests (e.g., for political support, for growth of their unit's power, for personal wealth). When such interests are relevant, these actors can become active as groups that participate in the decision process (with obvious advantages because they are inside "the system").

Like all models, Figure 9.3 substantially simplifies reality. But it should help you to understand the logic of the group approach. A policy decision can change at any time if a different distribution of group interests is mobilized and the issue is taken up by policy makers. The group approach explicitly rejects the notion that a small elite or a single class dominates the resource allocation process. Rather, many different groups become active in the political process on a narrow range of issues relevant to their interests. Mobilized groups use their political resources to affect the decision. While a group might not always win, its participation can affect the policy decisions made in the area. Box 9.3 provides a case study from Robert Dahl's important book *Who Governs?* (1961), which reveals how a group can form and use its resources to influence public policy.

Critics of the group approach argue that the government/state, far from being neutral, is guided by a strong ideology and is especially responsive to powerful interests in the society. Thus, some groups *are* likely to win almost every time they play the game of politics because they have a huge advantage in their political resources, such as wealth, access to decision makers, and political skill. Even though "the little people" might occasionally win a particular episode, the powerful groups in the system are persistent winners and big winners, and the system perpetuates very substantial inequalities in the distribution of benefits (Bachrach and Baratz 1962; Parenti 2002). Indeed, even in the metal houses case discussed in Box 9.3, the biggest losers are probably the poor families in New Haven for whom this housing would have been a substantial improvement over their existing conditions.

THE THREE APPROACHES COMPARED

Which Approach Is Correct?

The three approaches offer powerful answers to the basic political questions of who gets what, why, when, and how. Which of these three approaches is correct? Is one the most accurate explanation of politics for all political systems? For most political systems at a given historical moment? Do different approaches account for the politics of particular systems? For particular kinds of issues?

Advocates of each position offer both theoretical and empirical evidence to show that the politics of actual systems correspond to the description provided in their approach. As an indirect method of providing support for their approach, advocates also provide considerable evidence indicating the inaccuracies and contradictions of the other approaches. As you might suspect, the debate has been most acrimonious between, on the one hand, supporters of the group approach and, on the other, supporters of the elite and class approaches, which both assume persistent stratification and deep inequality. Some scholars contend that virtually all political systems, even "democratic" ones, are elitist, in the sense that the policy process is guided by and generally supports the interests of a dominant elite (Domhoff

By permission of Mike Luckovich and Creators Syndicate, Inc.

2002). In the United States, the debate has been most intensive among those who study power at the local level, prompted by the dispute five decades ago between such "elitists" as sociologist Floyd Hunter (1953) and such "pluralists" (supporters of the group approach) as political scientist Robert Dahl (1961).

Political scientists and other social scientists have yet to establish a critical test that reveals which of the approaches best describes or explains politics. After hundreds of studies in various political systems at the local, regional, and national levels, the disagreements among the advocates of the three approaches remain as deep as ever. In order to decide which approach provides the greatest insight into the politics of a particular political system, you might consider numerous conceptual and empirical questions, a few of which follow:

> For the *elite approach*, look for evidence of actual collaboration among the elite in the formulation of public policy, the frequency with which the elite seems to lose on policy decisions of significance to its members, or whether there is a mass of citizens who are uninformed, inactive, and impotent regarding policy choices.

> For the *class approach*, analyze whether the state almost always operates to serve the interests of a dominant class group, whether most people's interests and behaviors can be defined in class terms, or whether most significant social changes are directly attributable to violence.

> And for the *group approach*, analyze whether there are persistent winners and persistent losers on policy decisions, whether the state applies rules and policies fairly and equally to all groups, or whether competition among groups

can be fair if there are huge inequalities in the levels of political resources available to different individuals and groups.

Essential Similarities and Differences

In attempting to explain the value allocation process, the elite, class, and group approaches all focus on the interactions among aggregates of individuals. The elite and class approaches share certain crucial premises. For both approaches, the fundamental feature of society is stratification—the unequal distribution of values across distinct groups. Also in both approaches, the government is one of the key mechanisms controlled by the dominant group, and the government's policy decisions are intended to maintain that group's domination. Thus in the elite and class approaches, the political system and the value allocation process operate of, by, and for the dominant group.

But the elite and class approach differ in their conceptions of the nature of the groups and their interactions. For the elite approach, there are two broad groups, the elite and the mass. For the class approach, there can be more than two distinct class groups. Most discussion by elite theorists focuses on the elite—its membership, the basis of elite domination, and the strategies employed by the elite to maintain its control. The mass is assumed to be inactive politically and is rarely subjected to detailed analysis.

In contrast, most class theorists emphasize the dynamic interactions among the classes. There is substantial political energy inherent in the lower classes, and they are the active agents of major political change. The class approach attempts to explain why class conflict is inevitable, how it manifests itself, and how it produces transformations in the sociopolitical system. In short, the elite approach tends to provide a top-down perspective in a two-group system, whereas the class approach often takes a bottom-up perspective that emphasizes the dynamic processes of conflict and change among multiple groups.

The group approach differs fundamentally from both the elite and class approaches, beginning with its rejection of the notion of social stratification. It conceptualizes a sociopolitical world composed of many groups, with individuals belonging to multiple (and nonoverlapping) groups. Different groups emerge on each particular political issue, and each group has an array of resources that can be organized in order to influence decisions on that issue.

For the group approach, the government is a relatively neutral referee in the process by which various groups compete to influence public policy decisions, rather than the instrument of only one particular group or class. The state ensures that the policy competition among groups is fair and that all participants accept the outcome of any given competition. There is a dispersion of power, of resources, and of benefits from policy decisions, rather than a pattern of "structured inequality." Overall, different people, as members of many different groups, prevail on particular issues. Everyone wins some and loses some, but the losers can always win on the next issue.

Vigorous and often hostile debate has persisted among the advocates of these three conceptions of how politics works. This debate is deep and serious, for it reflects fundamental disagreements about the very nature of society and politics. The elite and class approaches are based on a *coercive view of society.* Conflict and change are ubiquitous features of the relations among groups. Social coherence is maintained by means of power and constraint, of domination by the most powerful class and its agent, the state. In contrast, the group approach reflects an *integrative view of society.* Society is essentially stable and harmonious, in the sense that there is a moving equilibrium maintained by a "fair" competitive game, refereed by the state and played by many groups who accept the rules and the outcomes. Social coherence is grounded in cooperation and consensus (see Dahrendorf 1959).

KEY CONCEPTS

class	nonoverlapping group memberships
class approach	political elite
class conflict	political resources
elite approach	political stratification
group approach	political understructure
mass	politics

FOR FURTHER CONSIDERATION

1. What do you think is the single most important flaw in the assumptions or knowledge claims of the elite approach? The class approach? The group approach?

2. How might a class approach theorist challenge the basic assumptions of the group approach and actual case of group politics presented in Box 9.3? How might a group theorist account for the cases in Boxes 9.1 and 9.2?

3. In a sense, all political systems are elitist, since a few govern and many are governed. Does this observation seem accurate? Is it a persuasive basis for confirming the validity of the elite approach?

4. Are you and your peers characterized by nonoverlapping group memberships in the manner claimed by the group approach?

5. List six groups that have a political agenda and with which you have a membership or a strong identity. Ask a variety of friends to provide you with a similar list. How much overlap is there in your group affiliations? Does this seem to support the group approach tenet of nonoverlapping memberships? (To undertake a fuller test, you would need to survey many individuals from a variety of backgrounds.)

FOR FURTHER READING

Balulis, Joseph, and Vickie Sullivan, Eds. (1996). *Shakespeare's Political Pageant: Essays in Politics and Literature.* Lanham, MD: Rowman & Littlefield. These articles offer a rich exploration of how the interplay of politics, power, and human nature is illuminated in the extraordinary plays of William Shakespeare.

Burki, Shahid J. (1991). *Pakistan under the Military: Eleven Years of Zia ul-Haq.* Boulder, CO: Westview Press. A detailed description of elite rule in Pakistan under an authoritarian regime.

Curtis, Gerald L. (1999). *The Logic of Japanese Politics: Leaders, Institutions, and the Limits of Change.* New York: Columbia University Press. A fascinating account of how contemporary Japanese politics works, emphasizing competition among individuals and groups rather than consensus building, which is the more widely accepted explanatory framework for Japan.

Dahl, Robert. (1961). *Who Governs? Democracy in an American City.* New Haven: Yale University Press. This remains the classic theoretical and empirical statement of the group approach to explaining politics.

Domhoff, G. William. (2002). *Who Rules in America? Power and Politics.* 4th ed. Boston: McGraw Hill. The author updates Mills's *The Power Elite,* using more data and an elaborated theoretical base and reaching similar conclusions confirming that an elite governs the United States.

Evans, Geoffrey, Ed. (1999). *The End of Class Politics?: Class Voting in Comparative Context.* Oxford: Oxford University Press. In a series of revealing country-based studies, the contributors to this volume present a data-based case, grounded particularly in analyses of elections, that class politics continues to be a powerful force in certain developed countries and post-communist developed countries.

Ibsen, Henrik. (1882/1964). *Enemy of the People.* In *Six Plays by Ibsen.* Trans. by Eva Le Gallienne. New York: Random House. A classic Norwegian play revealing the political processes by which self-interest and greed overwhelm the efforts of a good citizen to prevent his town from making a policy decision that will result in grave environmental damage and a risk to public health.

Mills, C. Wright. (1956). *The Power Elite.* New York: Oxford University Press. A widely cited study that identifies the elite system underlying American national politics.

Rubin, Barry. (1987). *Third World Coup Makers, Dictators, Strongmen, and Populist Tyrants.* New York: McGraw-Hill. Portraits of political leaders and the elitist regimes that they have dominated.

Tuohy, Carolyn Hughes. (1999). *Accidental Logics: The Dynamics of Change in the Health Care Arena in the United States, Britain and Canada.* New York: Oxford University Press. An interesting description of group politics in the policy process in one important area—health care.

Yang, Benjamin. (1997). *Deng: A Political Biography.* Armonk, NY: M.E. Sharpe. A compelling characterization of Deng Xiaoping, the shrewd leader who followed Mao Zedong to power in China. This book also provides an intriguing and illuminating account of an elite political system in action.

ON THE WEB

http://www.trinity.edu/mkearl/strat.html

This site provides a comprehensive look at the study of social inequality and contains a wealth of information on related topics such as gender stratification and homelessness.

http://www.washingtonpost.com/wp-dyn/politics/fedpage/columns/specialinterests/

The Washington Post Special Interests page contains a weekly column on lobbying and the influence of interest groups on government.

http://www.marxist.com/marxisttheory.asp

"In Defense of Marxism" is a comprehensive site that argues for the relevance of class theory and Marxism in the contemporary world, with essays and research on many political topics.

http://www.angelfire.com/or/sociologyshop/CWM.html

This site offers a variety of links that explore the works and theories of elite theorist C. Wright Mills.

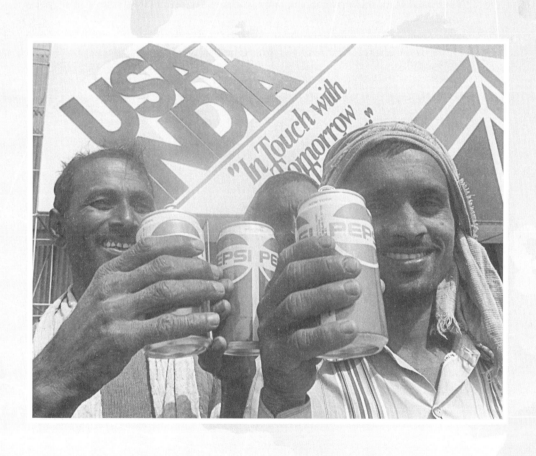

CHAPTER 10 **Change and Political Development**

Oman is a medium-sized country of 2.8 million people east of Saudi Arabia at a strategic point on the Persian Gulf. Although Oman has a long history of trading with other countries, its rulers attempted to maintain an extremely traditional society, even in the late twentieth century. The sultan who ruled between 1932 and 1970, Said ibn Taimur, faced an especially strong challenge after 1964, when vast oil deposits were discovered in Oman. Fearful that this huge wealth would corrupt his people, the sultan took extraordinary steps to prevent modernization. He declared a moratorium on the building of roads, schools, houses, even hospitals. All ten Omani doctors were forced to practice abroad because the sultan distrusted modern medicine. Many objects of modernity were prohibited, including sunglasses, flashlights, and European shoes. One could be imprisoned for traveling after dark with any light other than a kerosene lantern. The gates of the capital were locked after sunset, and no one was allowed to enter or leave. The sultan even confined his son, Prince Qabus, to a house far from the capital because he feared the ideas that his son had brought back from his education in England.

But there was a group of Omani citizens who had some experience of Western culture through education, travel, or working with foreigners. These people increasingly chafed under the sultan's "backward" rule. Encouraged by the influential British elite in Oman, this group took action in 1970, overthrowing the sultan and replacing him with Prince Qabus. The (now) Sultan Qabus and his advisers moved swiftly to bring improvements in the areas that his father had blocked. There has been a massive school building program (from 16 to 490 schools), and Sultan Qabus University opened in 1986. Hospitals and many health clinics are operating, and an extensive road system has been built. Females are now being educated, and Omani citizens purchase many Western consumer goods. Indeed, among 143 countries, only the United States has more television sets per capita than Oman (WABF 1997). With a GDP per capita (PPP) of $8,300, Oman ranks eighty-eighth (out of 231 countries and territories). On a comprehensive measure of quality of life (the "human development index" described in Chapter 13), Oman ranks

*seventy-ninth out of 175 countries, placing it above average in the
"medium" level on the index (UNDP 2003: table 1). Many Omanis now
have a lifestyle that attempts to balance the behaviors and morals of traditional Islamic culture and the material possessions of a wealthy, highly
modernized society. (This discussion is based on Spencer 2000.)*

CHANGE

The recent history of Oman indicates the virtual impossibility of preventing change
in any contemporary society. This chapter examines the concept of change and
focuses on the nature and processes of development in a society and within its political system.

A few cultures have generally avoided the processes of change and modernization. For example, the Masai of the Serengeti Plain in East Africa live in a manner
that has changed little from the ways of their ancestors of fifty generations ago. They
continue to raise their cattle ignoring the Kenya–Tanzania border and resisting the
attempts of the Kenyan government to alter their long-standing cultural patterns of
family and tribal life. But even the Masai have been affected by the modernization
surrounding them. It has brought health care and disease, money from tourists and
reduced land for grazing herds, education and cultural confusion.

There seems nowhere to hide from the forces of change. The Greek philosopher Heraclitus articulated this view in the fifth century B.C.E. His famous dictum,
"You can never step in the same river twice," is an extreme version of the viewpoint
that everything is in constant flux, that change is inevitable. It is presumed that just
as individuals undergo a developmental sequence of birth, growth, maturity, decay,
and death, social organisms (groups, organizations, societies) also have some form
of evolutionary development.

On the opposite side of the debate about the inevitability of change is the wry
French observation, *plus ça change, plus c'est la même chose.* This translates loosely
as "The more things change, the more they remain the same." Do you believe this?
Is this a wise commentary about the human condition? An erroneous cliché?

There are disagreements about the desirability of change as well as its inevitability. One normative position, most aligned with modern rationalism, is that change
is generally a positive force in human society. Change is the mechanism of growth,
development, and progress, all of which are assumed to increase knowledge, extend
control over the environment, and thus improve the human condition. This view is
reflected in the ideas of Sir Isaac Newton (1642–1727), Immanuel Kant (1724–1804),
and Charles Darwin (1809–1882). In the contemporary world, it is especially prevalent among those who believe in the benefits of science and technology.

A contrasting position is that change and development have significant negative effects, perhaps so many that change is undesirable. Plato (c. 428–347 B.C.E.),
Jean-Jacques Rousseau (1712–1778), and Sigmund Freud (1856–1939) are among
those who argue that knowledge, civilization, and excessive control over the environment result in a loss of innocence, goodness, and happiness, and create the capacity for great harm and destruction. Material progress has been achieved at the cost
of moral and spiritual decline. In this view, our capacity to increase our supply of
food and material goods cannot be separated from our development of repressive

and destructive forms of human interaction and technologies (e.g., weapons, chemicals) that degrade the environment and eliminate certain species of life, including, possibly, human beings. Most people now recognize the paradox that change and development simultaneously increase *and* reduce the quality of life. And most accept the serious problems and dangers associated with progress in order to enjoy the material benefits.

DEVELOPMENT

Characteristics of "More Developed" Social Systems

Contemporary changes of social, economic, and political systems are usually discussed in terms of *development* or *modernization.* While both of these concepts can be slippery, social scientific research usually employs the concept of development because modernization is particularly fuzzy (see Box 10.1). A social system is considered more developed (or more modern) when it displays certain key characteristics at relatively high levels. The concept of development can also refer to the processes through which these characteristics become more pronounced.

The more developed social systems exhibit several packages of characteristics that tap social, cultural, economic, political, and personal dimensions. These dimensions can be classified in various ways, such as the three that follow (Bill and Hardgrave 1981: 63):

1. The *organizational* dimension: behaviors and actions by groups, institutions, and societies that are based on specialization, interdependency, and differentiation of roles and functions.

2. The *technological* dimension: the use of increasingly complex and sophisticated artifacts to produce goods and services and to control the environment.

3. The *attitudinal* dimension: cognitive, affective, and evaluative orientations that are dominated by scientific knowledge, rationality, secular values, and individualism.

BOX 10.1

What Makes Millie Thoroughly Modern?

Suppose you were asked whether you like "modern music." What does that mean? What kind of music does it bring to mind? Atonal? Rock? Electronic? Hip-hop? It is extremely difficult to determine what is "modern." It depends very much on the particular historical moment and on the values and culture of the analyst. What seemed modern in the United States 30 years ago does not seem so modern now, given a world of rapid social and technological change. For example, the United States in 1975 was a world virtually without personal computers, DVDs, satellite television, AIDS, the Internet, or the global economy.

Virtually every state attaches high importance to economic development—the core of the *technological* dimension. The expansion of available goods and services in the society offers the promise of a life that, for at least some of the citizens, is more secure and more comfortable. Thus most states attempt to identify and implement strategies that facilitate economic development, which is usually measured as the national economic product (described in Box 8.1 as gross national product or gross domestic product, economic product per capita, or the rate of growth in economic product).

Most states also assume that there are societal benefits associated with advances on the *organizational* and *attitudinal* dimensions. These are reflected by such social indicators as greater urbanization, expanded communications, more extensive social networks, improved efficiency, increased education levels, higher literacy rates, and greater social mobility. While most analysts view these as measures of beneficial changes, there is less consensus about whether these aspects of development are always desirable. The example of Oman reflects the concerns of some individuals in every developing society: that many of the social changes associated with development can have negative effects on deeply revered social and cultural values. In some countries, these negative changes are referred to as "Westernization" and are evident in attitudinal changes that shift toward greater secularism, individualism, and materialism. Groups that are strongly committed to sustaining tradition and religious values, such as those of Islam or Hinduism, are usually very concerned by these types of attitudinal changes within their countries. In this and later chapters, we shall consider examples of cultures where there is deep disagreement about the benefits of change in the attitudinal dimension.

Indeed, even economic development is questioned by those alarmed about the negative effects of unrestricted economic growth on the environment. Concerns for the environment center on both the *depletion of the earth's resources* (e.g., the destruction of the rain forests, shortages of water, and the overcultivation of the land to increase agricultural production) and the *degradation of the environment* (e.g., severe air and water pollution associated with industrial processes and consumerism).

Can we define with precision what constitutes a "developed country"? No. There are no agreed upon measures for distinguishing sharply between systems that are developed/modern and those that are not. Currently, there is a broad distinction between the "developed countries" and the "developing countries," often based on a single measure of *economic* development (GDP per capita— recall Box 8.1). In Chapter 13 (e.g., Figure 13.1), this book offers a broader set of criteria for categorizing levels of development, combining economic development with the three dimensions of social development discussed above. For the discussion in this chapter, the more developed countries are those that are relatively high on productive output, urbanization, literacy, complexity, specialization, and secularization.

The Process of Development

Stage typologies. Many scholars have attempted to define the process(es) through which development and modernization occur. One approach is to define a series of stages or phases that each society passes through. Best known are the simple typologies, many of which have only two or three stages, such as *traditional* and *modern*,

By permission of Mike Luckovich and Creators Syndicate, Inc.

mechanical and *organic, folk* and *urban, less developed* and *more developed.* These labels are so broad that they do not provide much conceptual clarity.

Karl Marx proposed a more complex typology in which most societies pass through six stages of development. A society's particular stage of development depends on the existing distribution of control over the major productive resources in the society. Marx posited an initial stage of *primitive communism,* in which all individuals share control jointly over any available productive resources. The development process then continues through a series of stages in which there are increasingly subtle forms of domination by some classes over others: *slavery,* then *feudalism,* and then *capitalism.* Eventually, capitalist systems are transformed into *socialist* and finally to *communist* systems, an ultimate stage in which differentiated social classes and inequality in control of resources are eliminated (recall Chapters 2 and 8).

Response to key challenges.   Most explanations of the process of development do not incorporate Marx's conviction that history or logic reveals a single, inevitable sequence of stages. Rather, analysts identify a series of key challenges in the developmental process. Different processes are possible depending on the sequence in which the challenges occur, how the society responds to the challenges, and crucial features of the society and its environment. These challenges include the tension between traditional ideas and values and modern ones; the transition from a rural, agrarian society to an urban, industrial society; the transfer of social and political power from traditional elites to modernizing ones; and the fit among geographical territory, national identities, and state boundaries. Barrington Moore (1966), whose approach is discussed in Box 10.2, explains modernization in terms of the pattern of responses to key challenges facing the society; other theorists with similar approaches include Black (1966) and Rustow (1967).

 # BOX 10.2

Barrington Moore's Explanation of Development

Barrington Moore's *The Social Origins of Dictatorship and Democracy* (1966) illustrates one approach to the study of societal development. A social historian, Moore analyzes the changing patterns of relations among key groups in a society. He places particular attention on the actions of the landed aristocracy and peasants in the rural areas. He also examines the role of the bourgeoisie (those who operate factories, shops, and commercial establishments) and of governmental bureaucracies. He details eight historical case studies—China, England, France, Germany, India, Japan, Russia, and the United States—and concludes with analytic generalizations.

Moore's key questions about development concern the shift from agrarian society to modern industrial society. Does the landed aristocracy take the lead in the commercialization of agriculture? Are the peasants cohesive, and do they support or resist state authority? Is the urban bourgeoisie strong and effective in economic development? Whose interests do the governmental bureaucracies represent?

Moore distinguishes three different modes of modernization, depending on the dominant actions and evolving relationships among the key groups. There are *bourgeois revolutions,* which are driven by the modernizing efforts of the urban bourgeoisie who dominate the urban workers and gain control of the rural sector, as in England, France, and the United States. There are *revolutions from above,* in which development is effected by a coalition of the landed aristocracy and strong governmental bureaucracies, as in Germany and Japan. There are *peasant revolutions,* in which the peasants are more cohesive than the upper classes or the bourgeoisie, resist the powerful state apparatus, and eventually overthrow the old regime, as in Russia and China. And finally there are some societies where no groups have been able to lead a modernizing revolution, as in India.

Moore's most powerful assertion is his conclusion that all forms of development and modernization are essentially revolutions from above, that the great majority of the population does not want these changes, and that the changes are implemented by a ruthless minority at great cost to the large majority. But Moore also argues that, despite the widespread suffering generated during the developmental process, the costs (in terms of cumulative hardship to the population) of going without a modernizing revolution are even more severe for the people of a state in the contemporary world.

Individual-level change.   Most analyses of development, whether emphasizing stages, sequences, or international political economy, focus on the macro-level structural dynamics—that is, on the nature of the organizational and technological dimensions of social systems. But attention to the attitudinal dimension shifts the analysis to micro-level dynamics. This perspective emphasizes the social-psychological factors of the individual that might account for variations in rates and patterns of development (Inkeles and Smith 1999; Inkeles et al. 1985; Inkeles 1997; McClelland 1961). Such analyses are similar to the political behavior studies described in Chapters 2 through 4 (e.g., the political culture analyses, pages 31–35), although the focus here is on a broader array of beliefs (not just political beliefs).

In the attempt to establish the attitudinal traits associated with modernity, the work of Alex Inkeles and his colleagues (Inkeles and Smith 1999; Inkeles et al. 1985) is noteworthy. This group gathered extensive survey data from more than five thousand, five hundred men in six developing countries (Argentina, Bangladesh, Chile, India, the "Oriental" Jews of Israel, and Nigeria). Statistical analyses have produced a set of seven qualities that the researchers believe constitute a "syndrome of modernity"—that is, the general attitudinal traits of a modern person in a developing society:

1. Openness to new experiences regarding both people and behaviors.
2. A shift in allegiance from those individuals in traditional authority structures (e.g., parents, religious leaders) to those representing modern institutions (e.g., government leaders).
3. Confidence in modern technologies (e.g., science, medicine) and a less fatalistic attitude about life.
4. Desire for social mobility for oneself and one's children.
5. Belief in the value of planning and punctuality.
6. Interest in local politics and community affairs.
7. Interest in news, especially national and international affairs.

Inkeles and his colleagues conclude that there is remarkable similarity in these clusters of beliefs among the modern men in all six societies they studied. On this basis, they claim that there is a "unity of mankind, in terms of psychic structure" (Inkeles et al. 1985: 102); in other words, that the same traits are present in modern individuals in virtually all cultures. Some believe that this uniformity of ideas is one part of a broader set of forces that are homogenizing everyone into a global economy, a global culture, and a global information network (Barber 1995). Karl Deutsch (1961: 497) terms these individual-level changes as *social mobilization,* defined as "the process in which major clusters of old social, economic, and psychological commitments are eroded or broken and people become available for new patterns of socialization and behavior." In general, such social mobilization does seem to be associated with elements of broader social development, including increased education, exposure to modern media, and work within modern industrial or bureaucratic organizations (Inkeles et al. 1985).

In the large literature on the traditional and modern personality, many issues are unresolved. For example, most studies have not established the existence of a single syndrome of modernity that exists across all cultures. Also, it is unclear whether the rate of economic or political development is associated with the presence of modern attitudes among a certain proportion of the population. Indeed, in some cases of Islamic fundamentalism, it seems that leaders who display the activist and outward-oriented psychological traits associated with the syndrome of modernity are actually working to return the society to its traditional pattern of attitudes and actions (Banuazizi 1987).

In most developing societies, some people and groups enthusiastically embrace the new beliefs and new behaviors while others cling tenaciously to the old ones. Box 10.3 summarizes a powerful literary account of the trauma some individuals experienced when tradition and modernity collide. You probably think it is obvious that development and modernization involve an interplay among emerging modern individual-level behavior (both beliefs and actions), group behavior, and societal development. Virtually all the researchers agree with you. But there are still many interesting and generally unanswered questions: Why do old patterns erode?

BOX 10.3

How Ideas Undermine Culture: Things Fall Apart in Nigeria

You might be able to understand individual-level change intuitively if you think about what happens to a society when it is infused with major threats to existing values via education, new religions, television, and travel. As a popular post–World War I song asked about the returning soldiers, "How are you going to keep 'em down on the farm, after they've seen Paree?" The erosion of traditional values and behaviors can be rapid or slow. But as the Oman case suggested, it is difficult to prevent change in the face of major unsettling forces. The Islamic religion explicitly recognizes the importance of personal values in shaping society. As one Koranic verse observes, "Lo! Allah changeth not the condition of a people until they first change what is in their hearts."

A rich illustration of these change processes is Chinua Achebe's 1959 novel, *Things Fall Apart,* which describes the dramatic and traumatic changes experienced by the Ibo people of Nigeria at the turn of the twentieth century. The key theme is the conflict between the binding power of the Ibo's traditional views of life and religion and the disruptive ideas introduced into the culture by the Christian missionaries and British colonial administrators. The story centers on the members of one Ibo village who are increasingly divided between those who continue to be guided by traditional patterns of behavior and religion and those who no longer accept those traditions.

The major character, Okonkwo, is a great farmer and a strong leader. He follows the traditional patterns very rigidly, even participating in the murder, decreed by tribal law, of a boy he has treated like a son for years. This murder so alienates Okonkwo's own son that the son becomes one of the first in the village to be persuaded by the missionaries to convert to Christianity. Okonkwo continues to follow the traditions of his tribe, and this results in a series of major setbacks, including being banished for seven years and losing his land and his possessions. Eventually,

BOX **10.3** (CONTINUED)

Okonkwo's anger and frustration at the collapse of Ibo village life leads him to murder a colonial administrator's messenger. Rather than be executed by the white men, he finally does violate a basic Ibo law by committing suicide.

Before Okonkwo dies, his friend Obierika articulates how these external ideas have caused the collapse of the village (and of Ibo) society. In a key passage, he says:

> Our own men and our sons have joined the ranks of the stranger. They have joined his religion and they help to uphold his government.
>
> If we should try to drive out the white men in Umuofia we should find it easy. There are only two of them. But what of our own people who are following their way and have been given power? They would go to Umuru and bring the soldiers. . . . [The white man] says our customs are bad; and our own brothers who have taken up his religion also say that our customs are bad. How do you think we can fight when our own brothers have turned against us? The white man is very clever. He came quietly and peaceably with his religion. We were amused at his foolishness and allowed him to stay. Now he has won our brothers and our clan can no longer act like one. He has put a knife on the things that held us together and we have fallen apart. (Achebe 1959: 161–162)

Which kinds of people are most inclined to accept new patterns? Are there certain sectors or a certain proportion of the population whose social mobilization is necessary before macro-level change occurs? What macro-level conditions seem particularly conducive to individual-level change? And most broadly, what are the causal linkages between psychological modernity and societal development?

Civil society.   The attitudinal changes in individuals are especially important when they create new patterns of interaction at the group or societal level. Thus one key consideration in assessing the nature of development is the extent to which a "civil society" has emerged. Certain attitudes are centrally associated with the existence of civil society, including tolerance of differences in opinions and behaviors, willingness to cooperate with others, propensity to negotiate in order to approach consensus and to avoid violence in the resolution of differences, and a sense of shared identity with others. Some analysts conclude that, while a society could certainly be "developed" without being a civil society, the prevalence of these values of civility is crucial for sustaining effective community and democracy (Diamond et al. 1997; Stepan and Linz 1996; Putnam 1993).

Culture and change.   Some studies of development have emphasized the importance of culture in the processes of change. Since Max Weber's classic study (1958a) of the linkage between the culture of Protestant religions and the rise of capitalist political economies, there have been continuing efforts to clarify the relationship between broad cultural systems and economic development. Some, like Weber, have argued that Protestantism has motivated people to make substantial, even irrational, sacrifices of material consumption and the pleasures of life in order to work extraordinarily hard and accumulate wealth rather than spend it. Similarly, it is contended that in developing European societies these religions promoted an acceptance of hardships, another feature associated with transformation to a modern society and economy (Davis 1987: 223–234).

Weber (1951, 1958b) also applied an analysis of culture and religion to India and China in explain the absence of development there. But since the 1980s, there has been a dramatic surge of economic development among the Asian newly industrializing economies (to be discussed later in this chapter). These Asian countries have had substantially higher levels of development than in other countries attempting to employ similar development strategies. Consequently, recent explanations have emphasized how Asian culture has *facilitated* development (Davis 1987; Huntington 1987: 21–28, 1991; Pye 1985; and see Chapter 15, especially Box 15.4).

The Dynamics of Economic Development

The actual economic development of a country is the product of a complex set of actions by both major players (e.g., the government, large corporations, international banks) and small players (e.g., individuals as consumers and workers, small businesses) that is staggering in scale and incomprehensible in nature.

In the abstract, however, the discussion of political economy in Chapter 8 (look again at Figure 8.1) provides the key to understanding what is happening. Economic development occurs as more and more households and firms are engaged in ever-higher levels of production and consumption. More goods (and, ideally, more diverse and complex goods) are produced, more income and expenditures are exchanged, and thus the GDP gets larger relative to the number of people sharing in the carnival of production and consumption. Given the presence of the rest of the world (Figure 8.1B), a political economy is normally healthier and more vibrant if it not only is growing but also is bringing in more income via exports than it sends out to pay for imports. Chapter 8 explored some of the general challenges facing every political economy in the quest for economic development. For every state, the underlying puzzle is: What should the political system do in order to facilitate economic development? In the latter part of the twentieth century, two competing visions guided the answer to this question in many political economies: statism and neoliberalism.

Statism.   Between the 1950s and the 1980s, many developing countries (e.g., Brazil, Mexico, India, Tanzania) implemented versions of **statism.** This approach emphasizes the importance of strong actions by the state to support the system of production and distribution of goods. The state extensively regulates the market and the actions of firms and households, and it protects firms from external competition. Many important areas of production are publicly owned and are operated as state enterprises (e.g., transportation, power, banking). The state also controls the prices of certain basic goods (e.g., foods, fuel), and it distributes many free or subsidized goods and services (e.g., shelter, health care), especially to less advantaged groups. The political economies of many communist countries (e.g., Bulgaria, China, Cuba) were extreme forms of the statist approach.

Neoliberalism. Alternatively, many countries have applied variations of **neoliberalism.** Grounded in the market political economy model (see Chapter 8), the guiding principle of the neoliberal approach is to maximize the economic freedom of individuals, households, and firms. Thus there is an attempt to limit severely the state's economic actions, which are seen to undermine and distort the efficiency of the free market. Public expenditure is minimal, there is little government regulation of the economy, and direct foreign investment and free trade across state boundaries are encouraged. The state is mainly concerned with maintaining fiscal and monetary discipline (not spending much, keeping currencies stable) and facilitating the dynamics of the local, national, and global marketplaces. Beginning in the mid-1970s, an increasing number of countries adopted variations of the neoliberal approach. This includes many regimes, such as Brazil, Kenya, and Mexico, which reformed their political economies in the direction of neoliberalism in reaction to the disappointing levels of economic growth they achieved with the statist approach and due to pressure from the international banking community (Stepan and Linz 1996). It also includes many countries that abandoned the strong statism associated with a command political economy (e.g., Poland, Zimbabwe).

The "developmental-state" approach. Some countries adopted a hybrid development strategy, combining elements of both the statist and the neoliberal approaches. Based on the Japanese model in the post–World War II period, this *"developmental-state" approach* has been quite effective in achieving a high level of economic growth in some countries. It is grounded in three broad strategies:

1. *State-supported, export-oriented capitalism.* Aggressive capitalism is favored, and there are minimal governmental constraints on firms, as in neoliberalism. However, the state is very interventionist, providing strong support for firms by insulating the political economy from "politics," shaping the labor force via education, and employing taxing and spending policies to facilitate investment, promote the export of goods, and discourage high levels of domestic consumption.

2. *Targeting market niches.* Firms and the state work cooperatively to produce particular goods that can be successfully sold in the international marketplace. Initially, modest-quality goods are sold at or below cost in order to capture a share of the market and gain consumer support. Gradually, prices and quality are increased. The balance of production shifts slowly from simpler, more labor-intensive goods such as textiles, shoes, and toys to more complex goods requiring sophisticated production technologies such as shipbuilding, electronics, and automobiles. The state's policies (e.g., tariffs) protect producers against imported goods, although investment of foreign capital is usually encouraged.

3. *Agrarian support.* Government policy strongly encourages efficient domestic food production, even if self-sufficiency in food is not attainable. This element can include redistribution of land to small private farmers, price support subsidies on domestic food production, and tariffs on imported foods (Johnson 1985; Simone 2001).

As Chapter 14 will discuss in more detail, very few developing countries utilizing the statist approach achieved high levels of economic growth in the last three decades. Some developing countries employing neoliberalism have enjoyed periods of solid growth, but only a few have experienced the sustained growth and the distribution of prosperity that would be associated with developmental success. In general, those developing countries that have managed solid and sustained economic growth during this period have pursued some variant of the developmental-state approach. Most of these success stories have been in Asia, particularly Singapore, South Korea, Taiwan, and to a lesser extent Malaysia and Indonesia (see Chapter 15 for additional discussion of the newly industrializing countries—the NICs). Other developing countries that have attempted variations of the developmental-state strategy have had mixed success, with some achieving relatively high levels of multiyear economic growth (e.g., Argentina, Chile, China—see Box 10.4) but others failing to sustain such growth (e.g., Brazil, India, Mexico).

BOX 10.4

Big NIC?: China

As the world's most populous country, China has always drawn attention. However, in the current global system, China's growing economic power has become one of the most widely discussed issues. While still generally classified as a developing country, China increasingly has the characteristics of a NIC. Between 1980 and 1995, China's economic output and average income per capita quadrupled as it has sustained a remarkably high rate of economic growth. It has rapidly created a substantial manufacturing sector and exports more goods than any other country. China is now the second largest economy in the world and is predicted by some to become the largest by 2015 (passing the United States).

Once the world's greatest civilization, China had been a leader in science and the arts for many centuries. But for most of the nineteenth and twentieth centuries, China seemed an unlikely economic powerhouse, weakened greatly by many difficulties, including internal conflicts, devastating famines, pervasive corruption, and foreign intervention. Then, in 1949, the Communist forces under Mao Zedong gained power in China after a lengthy civil war. Since that point, China has undergone a remarkable transformation. What accounts for the turnaround?

Despite the open opposition to China by most other countries, especially the United States, "Chairman Mao" established an institutionalized political system between 1949 and his death in 1976. There were strict, totalitarian controls over the political life of the people under the guardianship of the oppressive Communist Party. There was an attempt to implement an extensive command political economy, with state ownership of virtually all productive means. Although considerable chaos characterized China under Mao, the period also laid the foundations for economic development. Among the many important changes were: the establishment of an effective central government; land reform; weakening of the rigid Confucian hierarchy of gender, age, and class; great improvements in health and education; and the transformation from an agrarian to an industrial nation.

BOX **10.4** (CONTINUED)

Deng Xiaoping, Mao's successor (and China's most powerful leader from 1978 to the late 1990s), followed a variant of the NIC strategy, given the constraints of China's size, stage of development, and Communist rhetoric. The political system has remained oppressive and authoritarian, firmly under the control of the Party. Citizens enjoy few political or civil rights. However, the economic system was rapidly opened up to market forces, a hybrid Deng termed the "socialist market economy." Under Deng, the share of industrial output under state ownership dropped from 78 percent to 26 percent, and virtually the entire agricultural system shifted from state communes to control by households. China's total GDP and foreign trade each rose more than twelvefold, and both rural and urban income per capita increased more than tenfold.

Deng was pragmatic. When challenged about abandoning communism for capitalism, he replied that he did not care whether the cat was red or white, as long as it caught mice. Deng integrated China into the global economy, aggressively shaping the domestic economy to produce for export. There has been a rapid shift to manufacturing, and the product mix is steadily moving to more sophisticated goods. Profit has become not only an acceptable motivation but also a highly desirable one (Deng's famous comment is: "to get rich is glorious"). The entrepreneur, not the people-serving, hard working employee, is the new hero of the society. A greater proportion of Chinese enjoy a high standard of material living than at any point in the history of the country. Yet many millions of Chinese still live in relative poverty, especially in rural areas, and increasing inequalities in the distribution of wealth are creating substantial tension. There is also growing pressure for some loosening of the tight control of the Communist Party over political life. The direction of the "big NIC's" development is arguably the most significant factor in the evolution of the world's economy in the near future. (This discussion is based on Meisner 1999.)

In the late 1990s, things seemed to go awry even in the more successful Asian NICs. Beginning in July 1997 with Thailand's currency problems, the booming economies of Asia suddenly and unexpectedly fell into a severe decline that was evident in negative GDP growth, high unemployment levels, and a huge decrease in the value of such assets as property and stocks (more details are provided in Chapter 15). Although some countries with rapid economic growth seemed to avoid severe problems (e.g., China, Singapore), the economic "crisis" in Asia was soon followed by similar problems in other rapidly developing countries in Latin America (Mahon 1999).

The breadth and depth of these negative economic conditions, even in Japan, resulted in widespread reconsideration of the flaws as well as the potential benefits of the developmental-state model. There was recognition of a variety of problems, such as overprotection of favored firms by the state, inadequate regulation of the banking system and currency flows, and unrestrained speculation in land and stock. Some of these economies have regained their economic momentum, but others are still struggling to recover. The economic turbulence has produced renewed uncertainty in many developing countries about whether the developmental-state approach is the best way to maximize broad economic growth and economic stability.

Dependency within the international political economy. With the exception of a few of the NICs, most developing countries have enjoyed only modest success in sustaining high economic growth during the postcolonial period (since about 1960). Why is this? Some analysts conclude that the difficulties facing the developing countries are due to their vulnerability to, and perhaps their dependency on, the countries that are highly developed. This view is most explicit in an explanation known generally as the dependency approach or as world-systems theory.

The **dependency approach,** which has both ideological and descriptive elements, argues that the "late developers" cannot follow the same processes that produced strong economic growth in the now-developed countries. The world system within which they are attempting to develop is quite different from the one that faced the now-developed countries (Isbister 2004).

According to the *ideological* element, the key problem is a long history of exploitation by the more developed "capitalist/imperialist" states. These states have manipulated and controlled the political economies of the developing countries for decades or even centuries by means of their economic, military, and political domination of the global system. Indeed, one of the main reasons the capitalist states have sustained their prosperity since the mid-twentieth century is that they are still able to exploit the political economies of developing countries, especially through their overall control of capital, markets and prices, and technology. Thus they continue to reap huge profits at the expense of the less developed countries. In this view, the activities of the developed countries have not merely retarded the progress of the late developers, they have actually "deformed" (distorted and ruined) the efforts of the developing countries.

The *descriptive* element of the dependency approach provides a similar analysis but without heaping blame exclusively on all the capitalist states. Rather, it posits an economic hierarchy in which many economic actors take advantage of those below them in the global economic system. At the top of the heap is a **core,** composed of the states, firms (especially multinational firms such as Siemens, Matsushita, and General Motors), and financial institutions of the most developed countries (e.g., Germany, Japan, the United States). At the bottom of the heap are the villages of the developing countries at the edge of the *periphery.* Many actors engage in exploitation. The resources of the villages are exploited by local and regional economic actors, who are in turn exploited by national economic actors, who are also exploited by the powerful core actors. There is also a middle group of states (a *semiperiphery* including such countries as Brazil, Mexico, South Africa, and Taiwan) whose national economic actors are able to take advantage of the periphery and to limit the level of exploitation by the core states.

Within most developing countries, certain modern sectors and some prosperous actors do emerge because these sectors and actors cooperate with the international capitalists. But development in such countries is extremely uneven. Organizational and technological development is evident mainly within the state (especially in its bureaucracy and repressive military) and within a few limited sectors of the economy. A large proportion of the population, however, remains trapped in conditions of underdevelopment and poverty (Heredia 1997). For example, in Evans's (1979) analysis of development in Brazil, there is an alliance composed of three key sets of actors: (1) the multinational corporations, (2) the Brazilian capitalist class, and (3) the Brazilian state apparatus. Only the groups in the alliance, and especially the multinationals, gain most of the benefits from Brazil's rich resources, whereas the great majority of the Brazilian population remains poor and backward. Brazilian cartoonist Ziraldo offers his view of the rules of this game.

In general, the states of the periphery remain suppliers of raw materials and providers of cheap labor for core states. The economic choices and options available to these developing states are severely constrained by other actors in the international environment. Small movements up the chain of exploitation are possible; but dependency and low economic development are continuing conditions for most in the periphery (Isbister 2004; So 1990; Wallerstein 1974, 1980, 1991; Wilber and Jameson 1996).

Look again at the photograph at the beginning of this chapter. Why are these men smiling? Probably because they got free Pepsis. But the bigger story is that a

Ziraldo/CARTOONISTS & WRITERS SYNDICATE/cartoonweb.com

major U.S.-based multinational corporation has just won a fierce political battle against Indian politicians and local cola manufacturers. Pepsi was granted franchising licenses in the huge Indian market, despite arguments from locals that a major, multinational soft drink company would squash local producers and extract massive profits from the country.

Continuing dependency?   It is clear that the process of development is substantially affected by the current global economy. However, the four following arguments are offered by many analysts who dispute the validity of the dependency approach. First, some argue that in the current global system, the developed capitalist countries behave no differently than other states (Weatherby 2003). Second, some note that the rapid economic development of the NICs seems to contradict key contentions of the dependency approach. In this view, the success of some Asian developing countries, relative to those in Africa and Latin America, may mean that cultural factors might be more crucial to development than is the level of dependence on foreign capital or foreign companies (Fallows 1995; Huntington 1987, 1991). Third, many observe that serious internal problems, especially extensive corruption and conflicts between nationality groups, are major limitations on development in many developing countries (Isbister 2004). And fourth, the low- and middle-income countries of the developing world, measured either as a group or by region, actually had higher average annual rates of economic (GDP) growth during the 1990s than the developed countries (World Bank 2003: table 11).

In response to such arguments, dependency theorists observe that economic actors from the core have become more active in exploiting cheap labor in the periphery as well as its natural resources. They note that this can generate a higher growth rate for a few years but that rate is unlikely to be sustained for very long, as revealed by the economic declines in many growth economies in the late 1990s. Moreover, growth is extremely uneven—many developing countries experienced only minimal growth, and even in the developing countries with high growth rates, most of the actual benefits are enjoyed by elites, not by the great majority of the population. More than half the people in the developing world (56 percent) live on less than $2 per day, and one in four average only $1 per day (World Bank 2003). Worldwide, the disparity in income between the top 20 percent and the bottom 20 percent of the population has doubled in the last three decades, to a ratio of 60 : 1 (World Bank 1999; UNDP 1999).

Dependency theorists claim that, at best, the patterns of dependency and the deep inequalities within the world system became more complicated in the past decade. The dependency approach continues to raise controversial and significant questions about the obstacles to economic development and about the level and distribution of benefits to a developing country when advanced industrial countries and their corporations are extensively involved in its political economy. The flow of foreign investment capital into the developing countries has been growing rapidly and is now more than $200 billion per year. But if the developing countries become more reliant on international capital, who will benefit most? Will the gap between the rich countries and the poor countries be reduced? Will the patterns of dependency merely take a new form? These questions are part of the contemporary debate about economic development.

POLITICAL DEVELOPMENT

To this point, the discussion has broadly considered development in all spheres of human activity, and particularly in the economic sphere. Let us now turn our attention to the specifically *political* aspects of development. **Political development** refers to the emergence of more extensive capabilities in the political system, especially in the sense that political structures and processes become more specialized and more effective in managing internal operations and responding to the environment.

Characteristics of Political Development

Like development more generally, political development is typically measured by the extent to which a political system exhibits higher levels on the following four dimensions:

1. *Concentration of power in the state.* Most power and authority are increasingly centralized in a single state-level governmental system, and traditional sources of political authority weaken. The citizens agree that the state has the right to allocate public values and recognize their own responsibility to accept those allocations as authoritative. The formal-legal aspects of government (e.g., constitutions, laws) are well established.

2. *Specialized political structures.* Most key political functions are fulfilled by complex, organized political institutions such as legislatures, executives, political parties, and political interest groups. The actions of these institutions are generally guided by such bureaucratic principles as rationality and efficiency.

3. *"Modern" forms of political behavior.* Individuals develop a strong identity with the political system and the state, which become the entities, beyond familial groups, that receive individuals' primary loyalty and support. Active political roles become widespread as individuals become participants in the processes of politics, as voters, communicators, and so on (recall Table 3.1).

4. *Extensive capabilities of the political system.* The political system becomes better able to generate support, to respond to demands from its population, and to control the environment. Overall, its organization is more stable and coherent, its structures are more efficient, and its actions more effectively serve its goals and objectives.

A "capabilities analysis" of the political system (item 4) arguably provides the best set of indicators for assessing the level of political development. The late Gabriel Almond and his colleagues (2004) posit that a political system achieves a higher level of political development when it improves in any of five key capabilities:

1. *Extractive:* using human and material resources from the environment.

2. *Regulative:* controlling individual and group actions.

3. *Distributive:* allocating values through institutionalized structures and procedures.

4. *Responsive:* making decisions and policies that react to demands for value allocations.

5. *Symbolic:* manipulating images and meanings, and distributing nonmaterial rewards and values.

The Process of Political Development

The process through which political development occurs is a topic of great interest to those attempting to shape their society as well as to those attempting to analyze the political world. From one perspective, increases in important elements of modernization, such as greater economic development, urbanization, and social mobilization, create the need for a more developed political system, which in turn provides the infrastructure for complex economic activities and serves the needs of a modern citizenry.

This is the causal framework characterized in Model A of Figure 10.1. Political development is essentially a *dependent variable*. (The **dependent variable** is the phenomenon that changes in response to the impacts on it of other significant forces; these forces that can cause change are called the **independent variables.** See Appendix.) Thus the elements of modernization (the independent variables) provide the material and human resources that make a developed political system possible. Greater economic capability produces goods that the political system can distribute. An urban population with increasingly modern beliefs is more willing to accept the authority of government and to participate meaningfully in politics. In short, the political system develops more complex and specialized structures as a response to changes that are occurring in the society and the economy.

Conceptualizing political development as primarily a response to economic and social change is based on historical analyses of political systems that developed in the eighteenth and nineteenth centuries. However, the power and impact of the political system itself, as a causal force for change, is more evident when one analyzes the societies that have undergone substantial development during the last fifty

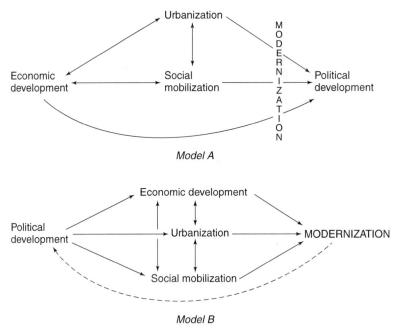

FIGURE 10.1 Models of development

years. This leads to a second perspective in which the political system is the crucial force (the independent variable) that causes development of the social and economic systems.

Model B of Figure 10.1 emphasizes the central importance of the political system as an agent of change in relation to other societal characteristics. As Kwame Nkrumah (1909–1972), the first president of Ghana, observed: "Seek ye first the political kingdom, and all else shall be added unto you." This widely quoted, nearly religious invocation asserts that if the political system is developed first, it can then serve as the instrument through which social and economic development are achieved. Value allocation decisions by the political leadership can guide or even determine the direction of changes in individual and group behavior, the political economy, and the society.

According to Model B, when a new political elite takes control, the area over which the elite has the most direct control is the political system. Thus an assertive political leadership (group or individual) can initially take explicit policy decisions and actions to create specialized political structures and encourage modern forms of political behavior. The leadership can, for example, enact policies that establish new governmental structures, reduce the power of traditional authority sources, empower governmental bureaucracies to perform new functions and allocate new resources, create political parties, mobilize certain groups into the political process, or assert state control over human and natural resources.

The political leadership can then deploy these more developed political structures, processes, and public policies to modernize other domains of social and economic life, such as the political economy, the educational system, the culture, national identity, the media, and religious practices. The efforts of a strong political leader have often been crucial in shaping developmental change: Chairman Mao in China and Pol Pot in Cambodia are examples from earlier chapters of a leader's explicit use of the political system as a powerful instrument to change many aspects of the society. Another example of leader-based change is Kemal Atatürk's efforts to modernize Turkey, described in Box 10.5.

Obviously, change and development in the political, social, economic, and other domains are interdependent—that is, they affect each other. But Model B emphasizes the central role of political choice and politics as drivers for development. In this conception, development is shaped by the ideology, will, and actions of political leaders rather than driven by economic growth.

Political Development as Democratization

In contrast to the capabilities analysis described above, some scholars (e.g., Cutright 1963) define political development as the establishment of the rule of law, legitimate elections, and representative institutions. Others object that this conception of a "developed" political system is extremely biased. Can you see why? What concept do such characteristics seem to measure?

You might answer that the characteristics in the previous paragraph describe a *democratic* political system (recall Chapter 7). However, if you agree that the essence of political development is the capabilities of the political system to handle basic functions, it is possible to have a political system that is developed but

BOX 10.5

Political Development and Modernization in Turkey

The modernization effort in Turkey is an example of "seeking the political kingdom first." Historically, the area of the Turkish nation was part of the large Ottoman Empire ruled by a sultan. After World War I, an army commander named Mustafa Kemal led a fierce military struggle for national independence. Victory resulted in the creation of the sovereign state of Turkey in 1922. Mustafa Kemal, who seized political power in the new republic, was committed to rapid modernization. At the time, Turkey had very traditional political, economic, and social systems, with Islamic law dominating the actions of the 98 percent Muslim population. The new leader decided that the key to modernization was to reduce the hold of Islam on the people.

In a stroke of symbolic politics, he began his modernization drive at the personal level. He changed his name to Mustafa Kemal Atatürk, the addition meaning "father of the Turks." (Kemal was also a fortunate name, since it means "perfect one.") Atatürk initially focused on political development, establishing a new state based on the principles of independence and democracy. A constitution was approved in 1924, executive power was granted to a president, the sultan was exiled, a legislature was elected, and a single political party was established. Atatürk thus created a political system with modern structures of governance and modern forms of political participation. This political system then became the instrument for Atatürk's broader efforts to reform Turkey.

From 1925 until his death in 1938, Atatürk employed his great political power to implement three major sets of public policies that were meant to modernize Turkey and to separate it from the traditional Muslim world. First, he promulgated laws that prohibited the wearing of religious garments in everyday life, abolished religious schools, and closed religious tombs as places of worship. Second, he encouraged the emergence and empowerment of a nationalist elite by such steps as creating a new Turkish language and banning the public use of other languages, replacing the Ottoman script with the Latin alphabet, and establishing Turkish literacy programs, especially in urban areas. Third, he established a new civil code (copied from Switzerland) to govern the legal relations between individuals and collectivities, relegating Shari'a law and the Koran to peripheral status in guiding public life. For example, he reduced the subordinate role of women, encouraging them to work, providing them with rights of divorce and inheritance, allowing them to vote and hold public office, and banning polygamy.

Many of Atatürk's changes are evident in Turkey. While 70 percent of the population lived in villages in 1964, Turkey is now 71 percent urban. The economy, 75 percent agrarian in 1978, has become predominantly industrial and service-based. Turkey's 68 million people remain 99 percent Muslim, but the country now has the most educated and modern women in the Muslim world. From 1993 to 1996, Tansu Çiller was Turkey's first female prime minister. While gender inequality remains, about one-fourth of Turkish professionals are women, and the proportion of female doctors in Turkey is higher than in the United States.

BOX **10.5** (CONTINUED)

Politically, the attempt to create an effective multiparty democracy in Turkey remains unfinished. There have been periods of serious social instability and governmental corruption, and three periods of military rule since 1960, although the military returned governmental reins to civilians in each case, once order was restored. For the first time since Atatürk, an Islamist party (the Welfare Party) came to power in 1996. When the government began to promote numerous policy changes based on Islamic principles and practices, the military responded with warnings and then forced the party from office in a "soft coup" that revealed the continuing power of the military in what is perhaps best characterized as an illiberal democracy (Chapter 7). A reformulated Islamist party (Justice and Development) again took govern-

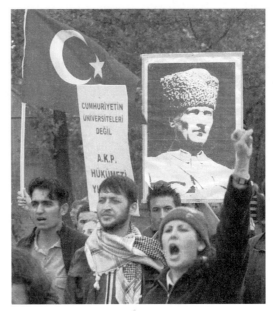

30,000 Turkish students march to the mausoleum of Atatürk (photo on poster) to protest the anti-secular education policies of the Islamist government. The banner reads: "The government will be overthrown, not the universities of the republic.

mental power with a large majority in the election of 2002. Despite its leader's continual attempts to reassure the military of his support for Atatürk's secular society, the military is extremely wary of this combination of political power and religious ideology, and the political situation is unstable.

Thus Atatürk's strong policies have not totally transformed Turkey. However, his legacy is an illuminating example of how a committed political leadership can reform the political system and then use political power to achieve considerable social and economic development within a society, consistent with Model B.

nondemocratic (e.g., Cuba, China, Syria). However, it is certainly valid to conclude that a highly desirable outcome of political development is a system that is democratic. At present, many national and international actors, including the United Nations, the World Bank, and the United States, actively promote democratic practices in the countries with which they deal.

Samuel Huntington (1991) suggests that there have been three long waves of democratization among modern states. The first occurred between the 1820s and 1926, when about thirty states established liberal democracies. Some of these then "reversed" (democracy was abandoned), until a second wave produced 36 democratic governments between 1945 and 1962. After another period of reversal, the third wave began in 1974. There are currently more electoral democracies (121) than at any time in history (Freedom House 2003). Of course, the total number of states has also expanded dramatically during this period, but the proportions of states that are electoral democracies has increased from 40 percent in 1987 to 63 percent in 2003 (recall Figure 7.1). Since 1990, the push toward democratization has been strong in many of the post-communist states that emerged from the former Soviet Union and in Central and Eastern Europe and in some previously military regimes in Latin America, Asia, and Africa (e.g., Chile, Panama, South Korea, Taiwan, Uruguay).

What might account for the recent expansion of democracies? Consider the following five explanations (Huntington 1991).

First, the pressure of *external actors* has been an important force in the shift toward democracy. As noted above, the World Bank and others have been increasingly insistent that countries introduce democratic reforms as a condition for economic assistance (Maxfield 1997). Also, the Catholic Church reduced its doctrinal emphasis on obedience to governmental authority, which led to a decline in citizen acquiescence to authoritarian regimes in such Catholic countries as Argentina and Brazil. And by the late 1980s, the Soviet Union under Mikhail Gorbachev was no longer willing to intervene in support of unpopular totalitarian leadership in East European states such as Hungary and Poland.

Second, the *breakdown of authoritarian and totalitarian regimes* has provided a window of opportunity for democratization. In such cases, nondemocratic political systems have lost their capabilities to suppress the pressure for change. This seems to have been a particularly important factor in the states of the former Soviet Union and Central and Eastern Europe as well as in such countries as Algeria, Argentina, Benin, Chile, and Jordan (Stepan and Linz 1996).

Third, the level of *economic development* can also be crucial. Many scholars conclude that democracy is most viable in relatively wealthy countries or, conversely, that poverty is a serious obstacle to sustaining democratic government (Diamond et al. 1997). Greater wealth might reassure both citizens and leaders that the increased participation and demands associated with democratization can now be handled with less risk of instability because sufficient resources are available to meet those demands. In this way, the trend toward democracy has been facilitated in increasingly prosperous states such as South Korea and Taiwan.

Fourth, the expansion of democracy might be enhanced by a *contagion effect:* When the perception grows that many other countries are making the transition to democracy, citizens conclude that they should also adopt this desired form of government in their own countries. Thus they become more insistent that their leaders implement democratic reforms.

Fifth, a key factor in the transition to democracy is often the presence of *political leadership* committed to democracy. In many countries, new leaders gain broad popular support and attain power based on their commitment to pursue democratization as a central goal of the political system (as with Vincente Fox in Mexico, South Africa's Nelson Mandela, Iran's Mohammed Khatami, and Indonesia's Megwati Sukarnoputri). Indeed, there is so much ideological value attached to democratization in the contemporary world that nearly every political leader must at least declare her allegiance to expanding and protecting democratic processes in order to maintain her popular support. Thus it is possible that opinion leaders in the country and also leaders from other countries and from international institutions are all pressing and reinforcing the leader's actions to implement and deepen democratic practices (Diamond et al. 1997; Sorensen 1998).

Political Institutionalization and Political Decay

Samuel Huntington (1968, 1987) offers incisive commentary regarding the illusion of political development. He describes many political systems that seem developed politically but then experience a substantial deterioration of political structures, processes, and roles. For Huntington, political development is a function of higher levels of **political institutionalization,** which he defines as *political organizations and procedures that have acquired value in the eyes of the population and the stability to withstand significant pressure.* Political institutionalization is measured in terms similar to the capabilities analysis described earlier in the chapter: the political system's capacity to regulate its citizens, respond flexibly to citizen demands, extract and distribute resources efficiently, and adapt to changing circumstances.

Huntington contrasts political institutionalization with a situation he terms **political decay**—*a significant decline in the capabilities of the political system, and especially in its capacity to maintain order.* Political decay can have multiple causes, but it is more likely when there are excessive demands on the political system, low levels of citizen support, or negative impacts from the environment. Moreover, the likelihood of political decay is also associated with aspects of the modernization process, such as social mobilization, economic growth, urbanization, education, and so on, which are inherently destabilizing. Social mobilization can undermine the traditional values and beliefs that sustained social order; economic growth produces new resources over which there is competition; urbanization concentrates heterogeneous groups into large, densely packed masses; and increases in education and communications make these masses aware of the many resources and values that they do not currently enjoy.

Many political systems are confronted with challenging combinations of these causes of political decay. If a political system cannot generate the resources to respond effectively to these challenges, its level of political institutionalization can be tested. And if the political system lacks the authority to persuade the citizens to accept its actions and value allocations, rising social, political, and economic frustrations can erupt into demonstrations and protests, and even riots and rebellion. In response to these forms of political decay, several scenarios can evolve:

- The political leadership reasserts control or is replaced by other leaders committed to order maintenance.
- The political system cracks down on disorder, limiting the rights of protest groups, opposition parties, the free press, and so on, and deploying its security forces (e.g., the police, the military) against any antiregime activities.
- A charismatic leader emerges. The leader gains the support and obedience of the people but only by personalizing power and thus weakening the overall processes through which power and political structures are institutionalized.

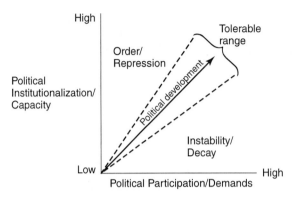

FIGURE 10.2 Political institutionalization and political decay
Source: Based on Huntington 1968.

- The military—the one organization in most societies that *is* institutionalized—forcibly takes over political power under the justification of restoring order.
- In cases where no individuals or institutions have the capacity to reestablish social peace, disorder and violence become widespread and can result in civil war or revolution.

From Huntington's (1968) viewpoint (see Figure 10.2), political decay must be prevented. As characterized in Figure 10.2, there is a tolerable range for the ratio between the level of demands placed on the political system and its capabilities, given pressures from the environment, social mobilization, economic development, and extensive demands. Huntington posits that the political leadership must balance participation and demands, on the one hand, against political institutionalization and system capabilities, on the other. If the political system acts in ways that move it substantially in the direction of institutionalization, it achieves what Huntington terms greater *political order;* if demands and participation become extensive relative to the system's capabilities to maintain order, there is *political decay.*

From this very choice of terms (*order* rather than *repression, decay* rather than *activism*), it should be evident which overemphasis Huntington prefers. He recommends such state actions as reducing citizen participation, limiting the activities of political parties and opposition groups, censoring the communications media, and controlling the content of the educational system. Recall Huntington's insistence (quoted in Box 5.4) on the primacy of order over liberty. What do you think of Huntington's preferences and assumptions here? If stability is preferred so absolutely, what kinds of objectionable actions by the state might be justified?

ACHIEVING POLITICAL DEVELOPMENT

Ultimately, all political systems aim to increase their capabilities and thus to increase their level of political development. There is general consensus that a more developed political system should enable the political actors to accomplish their objectives more fully. But there is considerable disagreement about the specific shape that political development should take.

In general, most people assume that political development in other countries should result in political systems and political economies that resemble those in their own country. It is debatable, however, whether all states should or even can follow the same developmental path. Some, perhaps most, newly developing countries might have basic value systems, cultures, histories, economies, or social systems that are not compatible with the patterns of development or the political structures and processes that "worked" in other countries, especially those that emerged in earlier eras.

The leaders in most countries try to assess whether the prior experiences and strategies of some other state provide a model for their own change and development. Even if leaders of developing countries do select a model that seems compatible with their own goals and unique characteristics, achieving political development and attaining political institutionalization are extremely difficult in the contemporary world. The remainder of this book will continue to illustrate the extent to which the choices and actions of states are influenced and sometimes controlled by other states in the global system and by limits on their own resources. This is a particular problem for states with low capabilities and minimal stability—that is, in states that lack political institutionalization.

Huntington is certainly correct that the challenges to political development are great. There have been periods of major political instability even in some European and Latin American countries—and these countries had the advantage of a long period in which the structures of a modern state could evolve into more complex and effective forms and in which the citizens could come to accept and value their political system.

In contrast to those countries, most states in the contemporary political world began creating their own modern political systems after 1945. While these systems have the appearance of modernity—complex, specialized political structures, widespread political participation, and so on—many lack the stability and value that come with a long evolutionary development. The fundamental dilemma for the political elites in these states is how to allocate public values effectively while maintaining political order, expanding political participation, and strengthening the political economy.

How much political participation and opposition should be allowed? How large should the domain of *res publica* be? To what extent and by what policies should the state control the political economy? What levels of which values should the state allocate to particular groups? All states continually deal with these challenging issues. But in the absence of strong political institutionalization, it can be particularly difficult to determine and implement effective responses to these issues.

WORLD OF CHANGES

Notice that both political development and democratization are more narrow concepts than political change. Only those changes that *increase* capabilities are typically defined as political development. And only those changes that *deepen* democratic processes are termed democratizing. The concept of political decay calls attention to the possibility that a political system can decline in capabilities and lose its capacity to allocate values effectively. And, if the theory that democratization occurs in waves continues to be accurate, the current number of democracies will also crest and then recede. Many of the states that are being swept up in the current wave might lack the capabilities and the level of economic development necessary to sustain viable

This Samburu herdsman in a remote area of Kenya seems to balance tradition and modernity with ease.

democracy. Some democracies will reverse into illiberal democracies. There is evidence that the current wave is already receding among the developing countries, especially in "frail democracies," and that there is a reversion to authoritarian regimes in some countries even as other countries institutionalize democratic practices (Diamond 2000).

Recently, researchers have been particularly interested in refining theories that specify the necessary and sufficient conditions for enhancing the strength of democratic political institutions. Such strengthening is often referred to as the "consolidation" of democracy. There is a related focus on democratic "breakdown" and, more broadly, on political decay (Diamond et al. 1997; Linz and Stepan 1996; Schedler 1998).

In fact, most political systems, like the global environment in which they function, are constantly engaged in political change. Most political change is modest, resulting from the effects of: (1) new policy decisions, (2) alterations in the way existing policy is implemented, or (3) variations in the inputs from the internal or external environment of the political system (recall the Easton model in Chapter 5). In some political systems, we could probably identify thousands of small changes in a single week. Although substantial political change can result from the gradual accumulation of small shifts, it is more noticeable when there is a rapid shift. For example, there could be a change from: a dominant party to a multiparty system, authoritarianism to electoral democracy; a period of war to a period without military hostilities; a statist political economy to a neoliberal one; male-only to gender-neutral political rights; and an elected leader to a military dictatorship.

Even more fundamental change in the nature of the political system or the political economy can be termed a *"system transformation."* The death and rebirth of political systems in Cambodia (Box 5.5), the emergence of a secular regime in Turkey under Atatürk (Box 10.4), and the abandonment of state socialism in Russia (Box 15.1) are examples of system transformation. One characteristic feature of the political world in the last two decades has been the substantial number of such transformations.

In this and earlier chapters, we have discussed two sets of recent changes that have received substantial attention. First, many countries have shifted from authoritarianism to electoral democracies, and some have become liberal democracies. Second, many political economies have promoted free-market capitalism and more openness to the global economy while generally abandoning planned economies and state socialism. Chapter 15 will focus on political systems in which political and economic transformation have been particularly extensive in recent years: in Central and Eastern Europe and in the newly industrializing countries. In addition, two major transformations seem to be occurring at the international level: (1) from the bipolar, cold war world to a multipolar, "post–cold war" period; and (2) a complex of changes generally called "globalization." A central objective of political scientists is to describe this world of political changes, to explain the conditions under which change occurs, and to evaluate such changes. These issues will be recurrent themes in the remainder of this book.

KEY CONCEPTS

change
civil society
core states
dependency approach
development
developmental-state strategy
economic development
modernization
neoliberalism

newly industrializing countries
    (NICs)
political decay
political development
political institutionalization
social mobilization
statism (statist strategies)
Westernization

FOR FURTHER CONSIDERATION

1. Most people in Western societies have been socialized to believe that change is associated with progress and is generally a good thing. However, the ideology of conservatism (as outlined in Chapter 2) does not make this assumption. What are the conservative's views about change? More broadly, can you specify types of change that would not necessarily be positive for a given political system?

2. The success or failure of the developmental-state strategy in certain developing countries is sometimes attributed to elements of culture. What factors other than culture might affect a country's capacity for rapid development? How important do you think a society's culture might be? Why?

3. Many countries have recently established democratic political processes. Is political decay inevitable in most of these countries? Why or why not? What strategies, general and specific, seem most promising in the attempt to avoid serious political decay?

4. Write a dialogue between two analysts: One contends that the dependency approach offers the best explanation for the failure of many countries to achieve development, while the second analyst argues that other factors best explain why some countries have limited development.

FOR FURTHER READING

Achebe, Chinua. (1969). *Arrow of God.* New York: Doubleday. In themes similar to those in Achebe's highly acclaimed *Things Fall Apart* (1959) (see Box 10.3), this novel describes how West African villagers' beliefs in their local gods are undermined by a Christian missionary, leading to the disintegration of their cultural traditions.

Bales, Kevin. (1999). *Disposable People: New Slavery in the Global Economy.* Berkeley, CA: University of California Press. A powerful description of the emergence of new forms of human slavery, particularly among females and child laborers, in exploited work forces in such countries on the periphery of the global economy as Brazil, India, Pakistan, and Thailand.

Bornstein, David. (1996). *The Price of a Dream: The Story of the Grameen Bank, the Banking Program that Is Changing the Lives of the Poor.* New York: Simon & Schuster. As suggested by the subtitle, the Grameen Bank has gained international acclaim for its program of small loans that transform poor people into entrepreneurs. This book describes the philosophy of the Grameen Bank and provides examples of its development activities in Bangladesh. Box 14.2 describes the bank's "microcredit" program.

Diamond, Larry, Marc Plattner, Yun-han Chu, and Mung-mao Tien, Eds. (1997). *Consolidating the Third Wave Democracies.* Baltimore, MD: Johns Hopkins University Press. In two volumes (*Themes and Perspectives; Regional Challenges*), a diverse set of top scholars thoughtfully and comprehensively assess the issues and empirical realities associated with efforts to "consolidate" (institutionalize) liberal democracy in countries in every region of the world.

Harrison, Neil E. (2000). *Constructing Sustainable Development.* Albany, NY: State University of New York Press. This brief, useful exploration of the various meanings attached to the concept of "sustainable development" concludes that the core values associated with the concept are inconsistent but argues nonetheless that there are policy actions that could advance sustainable development.

Huntington, Samuel P. (1991). *The Third Wave: Democratization in the Late Twentieth Century.* Norman: University of Oklahoma Press. The wide-ranging assessment of contemporary transitions to democracy by one of the major scholars of comparative development. The general argument about political institutionalization and political decay discussed in this chapter is fully elaborated in his earlier sweeping study, *Political Order in Changing Societies* (New Haven, CT: Yale University Press, 1968).

Johnson, Chalmers. (1996). *Japan: Who Governs? The Rise of the Developmental State.* New York: W.W. Norton. An elaboration of his important earlier analyses of the Japanese development strategy (Johnson 1985), this book provides a broader framework characterizing the government-industry cooperation that produced the "Japanese miracle" and has become the basis of the development approach taken by other Asian NICs.

Judd, Ellen, and Marilyn Porter, Eds. (1999). *Feminists Doing Development: A Practical Critique*. Useful articles and case studies examine development theory from a feminist perspective, with both approaches emphasizing the crucial roles of women in development.

Lipset, Seymour Martin. (1988). *Revolution and Counterrevolution: Change and Persistence in Social Structures*. Rev. ed. Rutgers, NJ: Transaction Books. Provocative essays on the processes of change and development, with a particular emphasis on the effects of culture.

Roberts, J. Timmons, and Amy White, Eds. (2000). *From Modernization to Globalization*. Malden, MA: Blackwell. A readable set of articles explaining most of the key theories of development (e.g., traditional modernization, dependency, world system) including those based on contemporary globalization theory.

Sorensen, Georg. (1998). *Democracy and Democratization: Processes and Prospects in a Changing World*. 2d ed. Boulder, CO: Westview Press. A wide-ranging discussion of the spread of democratic processes in many countries, defining the patterns and conditions under which democracy is viable and the likely evolution of various democratic systems.

Weiner, Myron, and Samuel P. Huntington. (1987). *Understanding Political Development*. Boston: Little, Brown. A series of important essays on such aspects of political development as participation, culture, dependency theory, ethnonationalism, and the role of the state.

ON THE WEB

http://www.undp.org/hdro/

This is the site for the United Nations' Development Programme office, the source of the yearly Human Development Report.

http://worldbank.org

At the official site of the World Bank, an international consortium of banks and other major financial institutions, there are extensive economic data available, including selections from the annual World Development Report as well as information on issues of development and trade.

http://iisd1.iisd.ca/

The web site of the International Institute for Sustainable Development offers information and essays on this topic, ranging from policy statements and economic data to book-length studies.

http://w3.acdi-cida.gc.ca/Virtual.nsf/

This site from the Canadian International Development Agency provides links to many sources of information about development issues, such as aid, economic growth, environmental impacts, human rights issues, and so on.

http://www.un.org/esa/sustdev/

The homepage of the United Nations Division for Sustainable Development, this site provides access to a wide variety of relevant UN resolutions and publications.

http://www.ulb.ac.be/ceese/meta/sustvl.html

The World Wide Web Virtual Library contains an extensive listing of Internet resources related to sustainable development and political change.

http://www.intl-crisis-group.org/

This is the International Crisis Group's "Crisis Web," which details the current crises within countries with serious levels of political decay and offers policy suggestions for conflict management and a return to political order.

CHAPTER 11 **Politics Across Borders**

Imagine an island state, Buena, blessed with temperate climate and rich natural resources that provide sufficient food and other necessities for the population. A few hundred miles to the south is a similar island, Malo; but Malo is cold and windy and has few resources to support its population. Each island is located about fifty miles off a large landmass composed of several states.

If you knew nothing more about either state, could you make any educated guesses about the political and economic relations these states have with each other and with the states on the large landmass?

In considering the relations between these states, the following issues could emerge: Is either island state more needful of trading relations with outsiders? Does either state have strong reasons to protect itself from intervention by outsiders? How could such protection be accomplished? If either state establishes a military, what kind of forces would make most sense? What kind of political alliance would each state be most likely to forge (with states on the landmass or with each other)?

One traditional method of thinking analytically about states is based on precisely these kinds of assessments. This method of **geopolitics** assumes that the geography of a state—that is, its physical characteristics (e.g., location, topography) and its natural and human resources (e.g., population size, fossil fuel resources, arable land, water)—might significantly affect the politics of the state (Parker 2000).

While only a few argue that "geography is destiny," it does seem reasonable to assume that a state's geography can be the source of both opportunities and constraints on its actions. Consider, for example, the effects on a state of conditions such as insufficient domestic food production, abundant fossil fuel resources, a small population relative to land area, the absence of any natural barriers separating the state from surrounding states, being snowbound eight months per year, enormous variation in yearly rainfall, or strategic location in a major international shipping lane.

It should also be obvious that other important features within a state's boundaries, such as its political culture, the style of its major political leaders, and the nature of its political structures, might powerfully affect the state's behavior toward other political systems.

The poet John Donne wrote, "No man is an island, entire of itself, every man is a piece of a continent." In the contemporary political world, it is clear that not even an island is insulated from the global society and economy. Indeed, our imaginary Buena and Malo (or actual islands such as Cuba, the Falklands, Great Britain, Japan, or Sri Lanka) will find that their politics are heavily dependent on what other state and non-state actors are doing. In the model of the political system in Chapter 5, this point is made explicitly in the concept of the extrasocietal environment. The behavior of every political system is affected not only by its own characteristics but also by the actions of external actors in its environment. These external actors might include other states, "transborder" actors (actors whose political activities cross state borders, such as international organizations, multinational corporations, and nongovernmental organizations), and other external systems (such as economic, cultural, demographic, and social systems in other states or in the international system as a whole).

As globalization has dramatically increased the penetration of states by outside forces, many states expend much, and in some cases most, of their political energy on their relations with other states and with external actors. The individual state's decisions and actions relative to other states and external actors are termed *foreign policy*. The *interactions* among two or more states and external actors are termed *international relations*.

This chapter examines the politics across borders involving states. First, it details major goals pursued by all states. Second, it discusses the means by which states and transborder actors attempt to facilitate cooperation and resolve conflict. Third, it examines key forms of interstate competition, such as balance of power and colonial domination. The causes and use of force and violence across state borders will be considered in Chapter 12.

THE GOALS OF STATES

Realist and Idealist Perspectives on the State's "Motives"

To understand how states behave in relation to other actors in the global system, it is helpful to identify what motivates them. From this perspective, states can be analyzed, almost like individuals, as having motives and values that they attempt to pursue in the international environment. However, the context within which the states exist is different from that for individuals because most analysts assume that the politics between states occurs in an international system that is *anarchic*. This does not mean that the system is chaotic, but does mean that there is no overarching authority that can impose order and "good behavior" on all the states in their relations with each other and with other actors. Scholars attempt to explain how and why states interact in the ways that they do in the absence of such an authority. Two perspectives have especially influenced international relations theory: political realism and political idealism.

Political realism assumes that people are naturally disposed to behave selfishly. This same selfishness extends to the behavior of the states that people form. In the international system, there is no supreme authority that protects the states from predatory behavior by other states. Thus all states experience permanent insecurity ("the security dilemma"), and the fundamental goal of each state is to ensure its own security and survival. Its security increases to the extent it maximizes its own power (e.g., economic power, knowledge power, and especially military power) relative to the power of every other state. States are in constant competition for power, especially because power is a "zero-sum" commodity—an increase in power for one actor results in an equivalent decrease for another. There is no expectation that another state can be trusted, will avoid violence, or will act ethically. A state makes treaties or breaks them, makes war or cooperates with other countries for only one reason: to maximize its security goals.

In contrast, the crucial assumption of **political idealism** (also termed "political liberalism") is that human nature *is* basically good. People, and the states they construct, can be altruistic and cooperative. States have many goals, and aggressive, power-maximizing behavior is not inevitable. If a state's actions reduce the welfare of people in any country or increase interstate conflict and war, it is usually because of poorly designed institutions (e.g., governments, economic systems, legal systems), not because people are evil or selfish. For the political idealist, it is possible to establish an international system in which well-designed institutions can facilitate cooperative behavior among states and create a situation that is "positive sum"—everyone is better off.

It is obvious that realism and idealism (and their recent elaborations, neorealism and neoliberalism, respectively) lead to very different explanations of a state's behavior toward other states (Kegley and Wittkopf 2004; Keohane and Nye 2001; Mearshimer 2001). They also provide contrasting prescriptions about how a state ought to respond to the actions of another state. Are you strongly oriented toward the realist or toward the idealist perspective? Consider how the assumptions of realism or idealism alter someone's interpretations of the topics in this chapter.

Major Goals

What major goals might a state pursue? The political system of each state attributes different levels of relative importance to a wide variety of goals. However, most can be subsumed under three overarching goals: *security, stability,* and *prosperity.* Each of these three goals includes component goals that the political system might act to serve. The significance of each component goal and the capacity of the political system to achieve each goal depend on many factors, such as the state's relative tendency toward a realist or idealist orientation, geopolitical situation, history, culture, leaders, political structures, and interactions with other states. Notice that some of these factors depend primarily on dynamics internal to the state and others are substantially affected by the actions of other global actors. Figure 11.1 illustrates this framework of basic goals. In the lists that follow, major components of each overarching goal are presented in the general order of their priority for most states.

Security

1. *Survival* is the fundamental element of security. It entails the very existence of the state, such that other states do not conquer it and absorb it.

2. *Autonomy* refers to the capacity of the state to act within its own boundaries without intervention into or control of its affairs by external actors.

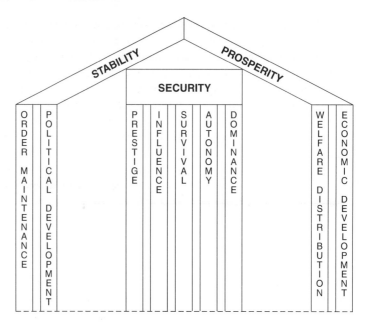

FIGURE 11.1   Basic goals of states

3. *Influence* involves the state's ability to alter the actions of external actors in desired ways by means of persuasion or the use of inducements.

4. *Prestige* is the desirable situation wherein external actors admire and respect the state.

5. *Dominance* is the use of power or violence to enable the state to impose direct control over external actors.

Stability

1. *Order maintenance* is the capacity of the state to ensure social peace for its citizens through the prevention of individual and group violation of societal norms, especially those involving violence.

2. *Political development* refers to the concentration of political authority in a state that has strong capabilities to make and enforce effective policies and to gain support from its citizens (recall Samuel Huntington's conception of institutionalization in Chapter 10).

Prosperity

1. *Economic development* refers both to (a) the increasing scale, complexity, and specialization of the productive system and of the goods produced, and (b) the capacity of the political economy to obtain, manage, and transform resources into valued goods.

2. *Welfare distribution* refers to the private or public allocation of adequate and increasing levels of valued goods to enhance the quality of life of the citizenry.

Few, if any, states can fully achieve their desired level on even one of these nine major goals, and they must make difficult trade-offs when pursuing multiple goals. For example, when a state makes a costly increase in the amount of welfare goods and services allocated to its citizens, it uses resources that it might otherwise have reinvested in the state's economic system to facilitate economic development. This trade-off is often referred to as the fundamental policy choice of "growth versus welfare." In another example, resources that the state allocates to the military for major security goals are not available for either welfare or the production of consumer goods. This policy trade-off is characterized by the phrase "guns versus butter."

Notice that Figure 11.1 gives particular priority to security goals. While survival is a fundamental goal of every country, this priority on all security goals reflects the realist view. In some states, prosperity goals or stability goals are probably more important than some of the security goals, such as dominance. Of the nine major goals listed in Figure 11.1, which ones do you think are most complementary? Most competitive?

Usually, the politics across state borders are characterized by cooperation or competition. The rest of this chapter explores these two dominant patterns in international relations. In most instances, a state realizes more benefits and fewer costs if it pursues its goals without using force against other states. However, the competition between states can escalate into conflict. The final section in Chapter 12 will examine those crucial situations where conflict resolution fails and the result is interstate violence and war.

MECHANISMS OF COOPERATION BETWEEN STATES

Diplomacy and Interstate Agreements

Do you agree with the proposition that, under most circumstances, a state is likely to accomplish more of its goals at lower costs if it can develop mutually advantageous cooperative arrangements with other states? From the neoliberal (contemporary idealist) perspective, a state will have an inherent preference to establish arrangements through which such cooperation can be nurtured. Realists are likely to be more cynical about such cooperation, viewing such arrangements as strategic ones to be made or broken as they serve the state's national interest.

States formalize and coordinate their interactions through many mechanisms, the most widespread being *diplomacy*. Diplomatic practices developed so that a state's own skilled representatives could engage in regular discussion and negotiation with the representatives of other states. Thus most states maintain an array of actors (e.g., ambassadors, cultural attachés) and institutions (e.g., embassies, trade delegations) whose objectives are to further interests shared with other states and to resolve potential problems by means of "normal diplomatic channels" and informal communications.

The essence of traditional diplomacy is sensitive and strategic face-to-face discussions between diplomats on behalf of their countries. However, modern communications technologies (e.g., videoconferencing) have provided new modes of interactions between leaders as well as diplomats, allowing them to deal with each other directly, even if not in person. An interesting example of these new hybrids is "teleplomacy"—the use of broadcast television as a means for high-level communications between states. For example, during the Gulf War (1990), Libya's leader, Muammar Qaddafi, telephoned Cable News Network (CNN) and requested that he be allowed to propose a peace settlement on television. CNN staff hung up on Qaddafi several times because they assumed that this was a crank call. Finally, the Libyan ambassador contacted CNN to verify that it was Qaddafi on the telephone. Now CNN recognized its opportunity for a scoop. Soon Qaddafi was explaining his plan to the world on live television from his tent in Tripoli. In another example, during the "war on terrorism" begun in late 2001, United States President George W. Bush, on one side, and Afghanistan's Taliban leaders and Al-Qaeda leader Osama bin Laden, on the other, communicated with each other via television speeches as they also used these broadcasts to persuade others to support their actions.

More explicit cooperation among states is usually established by bilateral (between two states) or multilateral (among three or more states) agreements. Distinctions are sometimes made between three forms of these agreements: alliances, treaties, and regimes. *Alliances* are informal or formal agreements between states that they will cooperate or assist each other militarily, economically, or politically. During World War II (1939–1945), for example, both the Allied Powers (Britain and France) and the Axis Powers (Germany, Italy, and Japan) established alliances about cooperation and coordination if there was a war. **Treaties** are also interstate agreements that deal with the same areas but tend to be more formal and legalistic, and there is a stronger expectation of compliance. These agreements can range from a straightforward arrangement for a cultural exchange between two friendly nations to a complex nuclear-arms reduction pact between many hostile states. Most alliances and treaties involve a limited set of countries. For example, the North American Free Trade Agreement (NAFTA) is a treaty between three neighboring states to cooperate on a complex set of trade arrangements. And the European Union, described in Box 11.1, is an example of a multistate, multipurpose confederation based on treaties for economic, political, cultural, and military cooperation among 25 European nations with a combined population of more than four hundred twenty five million. Examples of security pacts are the North Atlantic Treaty Organization (NATO) and the Strategic Arms Reduction Treaties (START II, 1993, between the United States and Russia).

Some of the agreements are also called **international regimes** to signify *a set of norms, rules, and procedures accepted by many countries that guide their behavior regarding a particular issue* area, such as international trade (e.g., the World Trade Organization [WTO]), or arms control (e.g., the Nuclear Nonproliferation Treaty, 1968, now including 187 countries), or environmental protection (e.g., the 1997 Kyoto Protocol on greenhouse gas emissions). Many international regimes establish a permanent organization through which the member states can enact, modify, and implement the agreements.

The direct, day-to-day interactions among most states are substantially governed by alliances, treaties, and regimes. Like other forms of international cooperation, such agreements are binding only as long as the participating states are willing to abide by the conditions of the agreement or are willing to submit disputes to some form of resolution. But such agreements can collapse for various reasons.

1. Some participants might find their national goals are not well served, so they ignore or violate the agreement. Thus, for example, the needs of particular Organization of Petroleum Exporting Countries (OPEC) member states for

BOX 11.1

The More We Are Together: The European Union

According to some observers, the Soviet Union is dead and the United States is in long-term decline, but there is a new giant emerging in the world. It was born in the 1950s, when West European countries battered by World War II developed three cooperative communities regarding interstate trade, atomic energy, and coal and steel production. The underlying objectives were mutual self-help in economic redevelopment and military defense. It has evolved from a loose alliance into a powerful confederation that is the largest and wealthiest single consumer market in the world.

The original "Six" (Belgium, France, Germany, Italy, Luxembourg, and the Netherlands) added six more countries during the 1970s and 1980s (Denmark, Greece, Ireland, Portugal, Spain, and the United Kingdom) and three more during the 1990s (Austria, Finland, and Sweden). The "15" then added 10 more in May 2004 (Cyprus, the Czech Republic, Estonia, Hungary, Latvia, Lithuania, Malta, Poland, Slovakia, and Slovenia). This European Union (EU) now includes more than four hundred twenty-five million people and a combined GNP of more than $7 trillion per year, greater in both population and economic product than its nearest rival, the NAFTA (North American Free Trade Agreement) group of Canada, Mexico, and the United States. With only 6 percent of the world's population, the EU is the source of more than 40 percent of international trade (The Economist 1999).

In the vision of its strongest proponents, the EU is becoming a true *supranational organization*—an international organization with autonomous policy-making and policy-implementation powers over national states that have ceded considerable sovereignty and have agreed to abide by its collective decisions, even when those decisions are not in the states' own national interests. The scope of EU decisions will cover a vast array of policies that would normally be controlled by national political systems. In economic terms, this means that the EU is a single economic market in which people, money, and goods flow freely without regard to national borders. In military terms, there will be a common foreign policy and joint armed forces under a single command. And in political terms, the goal is a "United States of Europe," with an elected European Parliament that passes legislation binding on all citizens, a Council of Ministers operating as a collective executive under a president, a Court of Justice serving as the interpreter and enforcer of laws that supersede the laws of individual countries, and a large administrative branch of "Eurocrats" applying the laws.

All of the key elements of the EU are now in place, including the elected European Parliament of more than six hundred delegates and all the other institutions previously described. As examples of the shared policies, there is now a common European passport and a common currency, the euro. Every country has been obliged to convert to the metric system. And labor and capital move freely between countries. However, some member countries are not prepared to concede a substantial share of their sovereignty to the EU, resisting compliance on key issues that they perceive to affect their national interest. There have been continuing problems

(continued)

BOX **11.1** (CONTINUED)

with fiscal policy, tax structure, and agricultural policy, and some still do not use the euro. Disagreements on foreign policy have also been evident, especially regarding the level of military involvement in the Gulf War and in the conflicts between Serbia and both Bosnia and the ethnic Albanians of Kosovo. In 1999, the EU countries agreed that they would create their own autonomous military force and a common policy on security and defense.

After its indecisive response to the Gulf War, Belgium's Foreign Minister Mark Eyskens observed that Europe "is an economic giant, a political dwarf, and a military worm" (Kegley and Wittkopf 1995: 165). The EU's role as an economic giant is somewhat tempered by the ongoing squabbles among member states unwilling to sacrifice sovereignty to it. If it does achieve political and military unanimity of action as well, the EU will be the undisputed superpower in the world.

Despite its failure to achieve complete union and unanimity of action in all cases, it is clear that the EU is now a formidable player in international politics (see Box 13.2 on the relative power of the EU, Japan, and the United States). Ironically, as more European countries achieve membership, the power of the EU might be diluted rather than enhanced because it will be more difficult to achieve consensus on major issues. The evolution of cooperative arrangements within the EU is one of the most fascinating and important developments for international relations in the early-twenty-first century world. (Discussion based on Nugent 2003; Kegley and Wittkopf 2004.)

additional revenue have resulted in their violations of OPEC's interstate agreements on production and pricing.

2. Participants can disagree on what actions are acceptable. After the Persian Gulf War, the United States (usually backed by the United Nations) repeatedly accused Iraq of violating elements of the peace treaty relating to the dismantling of its chemical and nuclear weapons capabilities, while Iraq insisted that it was complying with the agreements and that the United States was violating Iraq's sovereignty. This disagreement was the crucial justification that the United States presented for attacking Iraq in 2003.

3. Fulfillment of the key objectives in an agreement might be impossible. For example, the Treaty of Locarno (1925) between Britain and Italy failed in its attempt to deter Germany from violating the borders of France and Belgium because Britain and Italy were not strong enough to counteract the reemergence and assertion of Germany's military power, and Italy's government eventually concluded that Italy's interests were better served by becoming more pro-German.

International Law

The broadest attempt to formalize and constrain the interactions among states is **international law.** In 1625 Hugo Grotius, the "father" of international law, published *De jure belli et pacis* (*On the Laws of War and Peace*) (Grotius 1625/1957). This document emphasized **natural law**—sensible forms of behavior that ought to guide the relations among states and restrain hostile or destructive interactions.

Unfortunately, states often define "sensible" action according to their own political interests rather than shared abstract moral rules. Thus, by the nineteenth century, natural law had been supplanted by **positivist law**—*explicit written agreements that define both appropriate and unacceptable behaviors between states,* in the form of international treaties or conventions. Positivist laws have attempted to adjudicate geographic boundaries (e.g., the three-mile limit on the waters around states), to regulate states' use of environmental resources (e.g., laws limiting whale hunting in international waters), and to establish states' rights and limits over non-national resources (e.g., the law of outer space).

The treaties and conventions of positivist law even attempt to distinguish acceptable from unacceptable behavior during conflicts between states. For example, the Helsinki Agreement binds the combatants to use no glass-filled projectiles or other forms of violence that produce "unnecessary suffering." The Geneva Convention on "fair" war prohibits the use of poison gases and insists that captured soldiers be treated with dignity, although it does not preclude most of the terrible forms of suffering or death that a soldier can experience *before* he becomes a prisoner.

While positivist law has the great advantage of being formulated in explicit written agreements, the effectiveness of such agreements ultimately depends on the willingness of states to comply with them. Even if states sign a particular agreement, they sometimes openly violate the agreement, and states typically deny accusations that they have violated such agreements. The International Court of Justice (the World Court) at The Hague was established in 1946 to adjudicate violations of positivist international law, serving as the highest judicial body in the world.

The court, part of the United Nations Organization, has occasionally provided a valuable mechanism for conflict resolution between states. However, the court has jurisdiction and binding decision authority only if both parties to the dispute accept its ruling. In fact, juridical resolution between states is more likely to be found in the domestic court system of one of the disputants than in an international court. Less than one-third of the member-states of the United Nations have agreed to accept automatically the court's jurisdiction in matters affecting them; most of these states have added qualifications to their acceptance. When the political or economic stakes are high or even when emotional elements of the disagreement are intense, states have often refused to accept the court's jurisdiction or to be bound by its judgments. The United States is among the majority of states that rejects the court's jurisdiction, as it did in a 1984 case brought by the Nicaraguan government, which objected to covert U.S. actions against it (such as mining Nicaraguan harbors).

Thus, prior to the 1990s, the International Court of Justice was not particularly active. Between 1946 and 1991, it considered only 64 cases, gave advisory opinions in 19 cases, and handled very few cases that actually concerned violent conflicts between states. However, there has been a substantial increase in court activity in the last ten years. The court heard 24 cases between 1992 and 1995, has averaged fourteen cases per year since the mid–1990s, and is now issuing numerous advisory opinions (Kegley and Wittkopf 2004: 585–586).

Another important recent development is the expanded use of international law to arrest and prosecute political leaders and others who are accused of extensive human rights violations. A permanent International Criminal Court now convenes at The Hague to prosecute those accused of being responsible for crimes against large numbers of people, especially "crimes against humanity" and genocide. Some cases target those leaders who have directed establishment violence against their own population, as in Cambodia (Pol Pot's Khmer Rouge regime, Box 5.5) and Chile (former President Augusto Pinochet). Most cases involve prosecution for the deaths of large numbers of people from other nationality groups, such as the actions taken against the leaders of the Serbs (President Slobodan Milosevic, Radovan Karadzic, and others), the Hutus (responsible for the killing of Tutsis and Hutus in Rwanda), and the Kurdish rebels (Abdullah Ocalan) (Gutman and Rieff 1999). There is currently a debate about whether to extend the jurisdiction of these courts, to hold national leaders directly responsible for war crimes in cases of particularly violent actions by their soldiers (e.g., both Saddam Hussein and former U.S. President George Bush in the Gulf War, former British Prime Minister Margaret Thatcher in the Falklands War).

The increased activities of these international courts reflect a strong commitment to use international law more aggressively, not only to adjudicate disputes between states but also to hold individuals accountable for the ultra-violence perpetrated by their states. Do you think political leaders should be legally responsible for the actions of their soldiers? More broadly, is it acceptable for a state to refuse the court's jurisdiction? What do you think would happen to international politics if all states automatically accepted the jurisdiction of the International Court of Justice?

International Organizations

"International organizations" is a broad term for many of the transnational institutional mechanisms whose objectives are to influence the behavior and policies of states. Some attempt to prevent or resolve conflict among states, although most focus on a specific issue area within the full range of economic, social, environmental, cultural, and political concerns that have global significance. There are two primary types of international organizations, intergovernmental organizations (IGOs) and international nongovernmental organizations (NGOs). A third type is multinational corporations (MNCs).

IGOs.   Members of **intergovernmental organizations** are states, not private groups or individuals. Although there are currently less than three hundred permanent IGOs, they have vast potential to shape the politics across borders. States jointly establish these IGOs for a variety of different purposes: to provide a forum of communication between states; to implement policies that respond to political, social, or economic problems transcending national boundaries; to enact international laws and treaties; and to intervene in disputes between states. Most IGOs are regional, such as NATO, the Association of Southeast Asian States (ASEAN), the Arab League, and the EU. Others have a global membership and focus, such as the World Health Organization (WHO), the International Monetary Fund (IMF), and the WTO, arguably the most controversial IGO in the current global system (see Box 11.2).

BOX 11.2

The WTO: Nasty Business?

There is no IGO that is subject to more hostility and more intense political protest than the World Trade Organization. To its detractors, the WTO is "one of the most powerful, secretive and antidemocratic bodies on Earth" and the main results of its actions are to "preside over the greatest transfer in history, of real economic and political power away from nation-states to global corporations" and to "run roughshod over the rights of people and nations, causing all manner of environmental and social harms" (Mander 1999). Why are people saying such nasty things about the WTO?

In characterizing its own work, the WTO states that its main goal is "to ensure that trade flows as smoothly, predictably and freely as possible" among all countries, and that the primary result of its actions is "a more prosperous, peaceful and accountable economic world" (WTO 2004). Established in 1995, the WTO emerged from an international trading regime that had evolved over the prior fifty years. It has 146 member countries, and most other countries are attempting to join. Located in Geneva, Switzerland, the WTO is run by a permanent staff of about six hundred. It holds periodic meetings with representatives of all member countries (e.g., Seattle in 1999, Cancun, Mexico, in 2003), and these meetings provoke extensive, violent protests.

The WTO is committed to establishing policies that eliminate all barriers to global free trade (e.g., tariffs on imports, subsidies to producers, "dumping" strategies [selling goods abroad at below cost to cripple competitors]). WTO representatives and staff negotiate trade agreements that are then ratified by the governments of the member countries. The WTO enforces these agreements, sets penalties for countries that violate any agreement, and settles trade disputes between countries.

Critics assert that, as elite theory posits (recall Chapter 9), WTO rules and agreements primarily serve the interests of financial elites and multinational corporations that dominate the trade policy process and reap the greatest benefits from the decisions. The WTO can prevent a government from implementing any policy that constrains global free trade, even if the government judges that the policy is in its national interest or will benefit its citizens. In this view, the free trade agreements implemented by the WTO increase the profits of MNCs but reduce the power of workers, are indifferent to violations of human rights, fail to protect the environment, and even undermine the sovereignty of national governments. Opponents provide many graphic examples of these effects. For example, in its single-minded enforcement of free trade, the WTO has prevented governments from banning the sale of such imported products as: foods that have been genetically modified, fish caught in dolphin-killing nets, clothing made by child forced labor, and manufactured goods whose production releases toxic byproducts into the environment. Moreover, although the WTO claims its actions are associated with the increase in global prosperity, critics respond that inequalities across countries and

(continued)

BOX **11.2** (CONTINUED)

within countries have both risen significantly since the WTO regime began (Global Exchange 2003; Wallach and Woodall 2004).

The many individuals negatively affected by the sweeping changes associated with globalization (discussed later in this chapter) have increasingly focused on the WTO as the most visible source of their pain and as the prime target for their wrath. Yet many people in both the developed and developing countries enjoy the profusion of less expensive and/or higher quality imported products that WTO agreements make available for their consumption. Governments are locked in a love–hate embrace with the WTO: they appreciate the beneficial economic effects of global free trade when it opens new markets to their firms and when it improves the options of their citizen-consumers, but they resist WTO agreements and rulings that limit their freedom of action on either trade policy or economic policies that advantage their firms and citizens. Only global corporations seem to find little about the WTO that they don't like.

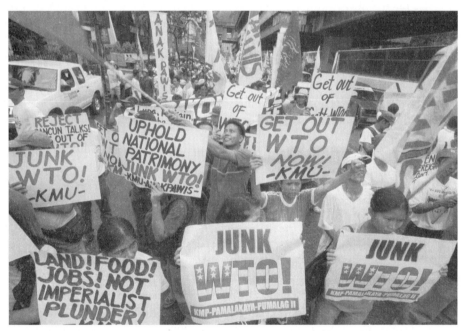

Filipinos participate in one of many worldwide protests of the WTO meeting in Cancun, Mexico.

The most powerful and wide-ranging IGOs in the twentieth century were two major international organizations—the League of Nations and the United Nations (UN). The League of Nations was formed in 1921 as a mechanism for collective security against aggression. But Italian aggression in Ethiopia and Japanese aggression in Manchuria in the 1930s revealed that the League lacked the diplomatic, political, or military power to achieve its goal.

After World War II, the UN was created in 1946 as another attempt at international organization. While the UN has a mixed record of success and failure in its central objective of keeping the peace, it *has* improved the international political climate. At the least, the UN has been a highly effective setting within which rivals can engage in continuing diplomacy. UN officials and representatives from various countries can attempt to mediate conflicts and prevent escalation to war. The UN can also pass resolutions that might constrain certain countries from acting in opposition to the moral force of international public opinion.

Most directly, a *United Nations peacekeeping force* can intervene between combatants. This is an impartial multinational military and civilian force authorized by the UN Security Council with the consent of the disputing parties. The peacekeeping force literally stands between the combatants in the attempt to ease tensions, and it uses force only in defense. During the cold war, the United States and the Soviet Union used their veto power in the Security Council to block many peacekeeping initiatives that the UN might have undertaken. Nonetheless, more than a dozen UN peacekeeping operations were deployed between 1948 and 1988, including forces between India and Pakistan in 1949 and again since 1965, in the Congo in 1960, between the Greeks and the Turks in Cyprus since 1964, and on the border between Israel and Lebanon since 1978. In such cases, the UN troops patrol a cease-fire line while the states attempt to negotiate a peace agreement. Ironically, while the presence of the UN usually prevents the escalation of political violence, it also lowers the incentives for the opponents to reach a workable peace agreement. For example, the UN forces have been trying to keep the peace between India and Pakistan in the border region of Kashmir for more than fifty years.

By its various actions, the United Nations has also contributed to what former UN Secretary-General Dag Hammarskjold (1953–1961) termed "preventive diplomacy"—limiting the extensive political and military involvement of major powers during conflicts between other countries. In 1988 the UN peacekeeping operations were awarded the Nobel Peace Prize.

During the post–cold war period (beginning in the late 1980s), the UN's role has expanded. The source of one global police force, the Soviet Union, has disintegrated. The other, the United States, has sometimes promoted a "new world order" in which collective military action by many countries is supposed to enforce the global peace. The UN is the obvious choice to organize and implement such collective military action. Thus 39 major UN peacekeeping operations have been deployed since 1990, compared with only 18 in the preceding 42 years (United Nations Peacekeeping 2003).

Significantly, most of the post–cold war operations differ from the previous ones in that their central objective is to maintain *internal* peace among factions within a country. Of 15 peacekeeping missions active in 2003, for example, the primary objective in 10 (including East Timor, the Democratic Republic of Congo [Box 11.4], Kosovo [Box 15.3], Lebanon, and Sierra Leone) was to prevent political violence among groups within the country. It has been difficult for the UN forces to end the violence in these internal conflicts where both borders and the identity of combatants are ambiguous. However, a study of 124 UN peacekeeping operations in internal conflicts concludes that they have generally been successful in ending the violence and increasing the likelihood of greater democratization (Doyle and Sambanis 2000).

The UN also provides many nonmilitary services that enhance states' security, stability, and prosperity. In a quiet manner, its committees, agencies, and commissions, such as the WHO; the United Nations Educational, Scientific, and Cultural Organization (UNESCO), and the United Nations Conference on Trade and Development (UNCTAD), attempt to mitigate global problems and enhance the quality of human life in such areas as human rights, agricultural development, environmental protection, refugees, children's health, and disaster relief. These efforts are one important way to reduce human suffering and thus limit the conditions that might cause political violence.

The continuing level of political violence in the international system underscores the fact that the UN lacks the power to prevent all interstate conflict. Many states withdraw their support (financial and political) when UN actions are at variance with the states' perceptions of their national interest. However, through its agencies, its debates and resolutions, its continuous open forum for formal and informal communications between states, and its peacekeeping operations, the UN does contribute to greater cooperation and reduced conflict among states. These contributions were recognized in 2001 when the United Nations and Secretary-General Kofi Annan were awarded the Nobel Peace Prize.

NGOs.   The second type of international organizations is transnational **nongovernmental organizations.** NGOs are composed of nonstate actors (private individuals and groups) who work actively in a particular issue area to provide information, promote public policies, and even to provide services that might otherwise be provided by government. NGOs work with each other, with governments, and with IGOs to address the full array of problems that cross state borders. Between 1960 and 2000, the number of NGOs active in at least three countries rose from 1,000 to more than thirty thousand. This includes about five thousand major NGOs that are very

The United Nations contributes to world betterment in various ways, such as humanitarian aid programs (here, providing food at a refugee camp in Pakistan) and peacekeeping forces (here, in Lebanon).

active in a large number of countries (Weiss 1996). Transnational NGOs, which enjoy higher public trust than either governments or business, are using new strategies of engagement with business and have a growing economic base (more than $1 trillion). They are "increasingly important in shaping national and international politics, governance processes and markets" and are "amongst the most influential institutions of the twenty-first century" (Elkington and Beloe 2003).

The members of NGOs are committed to furthering political and social issues with transnational dimensions. Although their issues tend to be regional or global, the actions and effectiveness of these NGOs can be analyzed in the same framework applied to the analysis of national interest groups (in Chapter 3). These groups encourage concerned individuals, groups, and even the governments of other states to write letters; organize demonstrations or boycotts; or engage in other political actions to pressure a government or transnational actor to change its practices (Keck and Sikkink 1998).

For example, you might be aware, from media, mailings, or other information sources, of the environmental protection actions of Greenpeace, the animal preservation goals of the World Wildlife Federation, or the lobbying to control destructive technologies by the Union of Concerned Scientists. Amnesty International, another well-known NGO, is concerned with protection of human rights and is engaged in campaigns to focus attention and pressure on governments that are violating the rights of their citizens. It is one of the leading NGOs among an expanding group of transborder organizations that promote protection of human rights. Often, local movements of human rights activists coalesce with others outside their state's boundaries to promote this issue.

The actions of some NGOs extend far beyond lobbying as they generate resources and actually deliver goods and services, such as the humanitarian medical services provided by Doctors without Borders. With the globalization of communications and greater mobility, there are many other groups, advocacy networks, and social movements that are able to engage in a mix of persuasion and action, although most operate in only a limited set of countries. And while many transnational actors are admired for their pursuit of noble goals, some engage in illegal or violent activities that are relevant to states, such as the al-Queda terrorist network or international drug cartels.

MNCs.   It is also clear that the actions of many MNCs (also referred to as TNCs—transnational corporations) have significant impacts on the politics within and between states. From a political economy perspective, MNCs are powerful firms, such as General Motors, Exxon, British Petroleum, Samsung, or Sumitomo, that produce and sell a diversity of goods in many states in pursuit of private profit. (Box 11.3 describes a moderate-sized MNC.) In terms of comparative economic power (measured as gross economic product in 2001), only 49 of the top 100 economic units in the world are countries, and 51 are multinational corporations (Kegley and Wittkopf 2004: table 5.2). While a MNC can have substantial consequences for a country's political system, it operates without significant, direct participation in or control by any government, and it can avoid many of the laws and taxes of any state (Keohane and Nye 2001; Russett, Starr, and Kinsella 2003; United Nations Commission on Transnational Corporations 1991).

COMPETITION AMONG STATES

Balance of Power

When the competing interests between states are stronger than their mutual inter-ests, the states are unlikely to agree on a cooperative strategy. From the realist per-spective in particular, states should expect this pattern to be the most crucial feature of the international system. In such situations, direct conflict can be avoided if a **balance of power** emerges. This occurs when there *is a rough equality in the power resources (political, economic, and especially military) that can be exercised by sets of competing states.* An actor is prevented from taking advantage of others because of the power that other actors have to retaliate.

The term "balance of power" is widely used and has many meanings. A few key elements in the classic notion of balance of power, listed below, are especially asso-ciated with the political realist perspective (described earlier in this chapter; see also Kaplan 1957; Morgenthau 1993).

1. It is an attempt to maintain a general stability in the relations among states and to preserve the status quo.

2. It assumes that peace can be ensured only by a balancing of contending states because potential aggressors will be deterred only by overwhelming opposing power.

 # BOX 11.3

Here, There, and Everywhere: Portrait of an MNC

In 1926, four large British companies involved in chemicals (e.g., explosives, dyes) combined to form Imperial Chemical Industries (ICI). During the next seven decades, the company evolved into a major MNC, dramatically extending its global reach and expanding its product array. Its total annual sales of more than $23 bil-lion placed it among the top 100 economic entities in the world, with an annual product higher than the GNP of more than two-thirds of the world's countries (Kegley and Wittkopf 1993: table 6.1).

One crucial feature of major MNCs is their *globalization.* Operating in many countries enables an MNC to move its activities in order to exploit opportunities and avoid problems in any host country and even in the home country. For exam-ple, until the mid-1970s, ICI had about two-thirds of its work force and its capital in Britain (the home country). But a weakening British economy and costly labor due to problems with Britain's powerful unions caused ICI to spread its operations around the globe.

Within ten years, ICI had dramatically increased its active involvement in the political economies of many countries. It shifted its emphasis in production and sales to countries promising the highest profits and best growth potential. It now has factories in more than forty countries and selling companies in more than sixty, including virtually every West and East European country, the United States,

BOX **11.3** (CONTINUED)

Canada, six major Latin American countries, 12 Asian and Middle Eastern countries, 13 countries in sub-Saharan Africa, and extensive operations in Australia and New Zealand. Thus by the 1980s, ICI had been dubbed "International" Chemical Industries.

A second feature of most MNCs is *product diversification,* which also reduces their dependence on any single country or good. ICI produces and sells goods in ten major product areas: agriculture, fibers, general chemicals, organic chemicals, industrial explosives, oil, paints, petrochemicals, pharmaceuticals, and plastics. No product area constitutes more than 17 percent of the overall sales, a reflection of the balanced diversification of this huge corporation.

When the 1973–1974 oil crisis occurred (raising the cost of petroleum), ICI's profits in several petroleum-based product areas (e.g., petrochemicals, plastics) collapsed. ICI immediately cut back dramatically on its operations in these areas, resuming production only when profit ratios were favorable again. It quickly redirected its efforts, investing heavily in the development of its own oil division, which became a high-profit area within only a few years.

MNCs such as ICI have the capacity and willingness to shift their production activities from country to country and to alter the complex mix of goods they produce in order to serve their profit drive. The indictment of MNCs includes the criticisms that they monopolize the production and distribution of important goods in the world marketplace, widen the gap between rich and poor nations, and challenge the sovereignty and autonomy of the state. From the perspective of national governments, labor, and consumers, such MNCs can seem to be everywhere and nowhere and can seem uncontrollable. Thus "the MNC remains one of the most controversial actors in the international political economy" (Jenkins 1993: 606). (Discussion based on Clarke 1985.)

3. There are typically a few (usually four to six) major power states that are decisive in ensuring that the balance is sustained.

4. These states, and others, constantly create shifting alliances based only on self-interest and system equilibrium, never on friendship or ideology.

5. To prevent actions that seem to threaten the overall balance of the system, one or more power states must intervene in the affairs of a single state or the relations between states.

6. There will be periodic political violence and war, because states must use force to preserve themselves and because the system is not always in such balance that all conflict between states is deterred.

Since the emergence of modern states in the seventeenth century, there have usually been only a few states that, at any point in time, had both the desire and the power to project their interests over many other states. Some scholars characterize the international relations dominated by European states during most of the period from the Peace of Westphalia in 1648 to the beginning of World War I in 1914 as a period of classic balance-of-power politics. Great Britain often played a major role as the "balancer." As Winston Churchill (1948) observed, "For 400 years the foreign policy of England has been to oppose the strongest, most aggressive, most dominating power on the continent, in joining the weaker states."

However, by the late nineteenth century, there were changes in the international system that made balance-of-power politics less possible. The growing importance of both ideology and nationalism were especially significant because these factors hindered the ease with which alliances between states were made and broken. This was most clear in the deep antipathy that developed between France and Germany, who would inevitably be on opposite sides of any conflict.

After World War II, the classic balance-of-power system was replaced by a *bipolar* balance-of-power system in which the United States and its allies were generally balanced against the Soviet Union and its allies. The groups associated with each superpower were rigid in their ideological antipathy to the other bloc and were inflexible in their alliance formation. Thus, the old pattern of flexible, nonideological balancing between a handful of independent states had broken down. In addition, the arena of between-state power struggles expanded from its narrow European base to a worldwide one. But the two blocs did prevent each other from achieving *hegemony* (i.e., clear domination of the international system). And the military power on each side deterred them from fighting each other directly during a 40-year "cold" war (see page 371).

From the early 1970s until the breakup of the Soviet Union in 1991, the international system became increasingly *multipolar*. During these two decades, there was a decline in the coherence of the U.S. bloc and the Soviet bloc, as powerful actors such as China, Japan, Western Europe, and groupings of "nonaligned" states began to act with greater independence. Although multipolar, this was not a classic balance-of-power system, since alliance formation remained inflexible and guided by ideology. At the same time, the United States and the Soviet Union continued to be the preeminent global powers and to engage in a massive buildup of military capability and nuclear weapons.

In the "post–cold war era" (since 1991), the state system remains somewhat transitional. The system continues to have multipolar elements, although the military and economic dominance of the United States suggests some characteristics of a *unipolar* period in which the international system is generally controlled by a single "hegemon." U.S efforts to utilize the United Nations in peacekeeping roles have been described earlier in this chapter, but the United States has also often taken the lead in establishing collective military action through the United Nations (e.g., in the 1990 Gulf War) or through NATO (e.g., the 1999 actions against the Serbs in Kosovo). In some cases, the United States has operated somewhat unilaterally (e.g., the military campaign against Afghanistan beginning in late 2001 and the war against Iraq in 2003).

Balance of Terror

The enormous destructive capacity of modern military technologies was a key element that undermined traditional balance-of-power politics. War became far less controllable as an instrument of foreign policy between major states when each had the capacity to wreak massive devastation on the other and to risk equal destruction at home.

The problem with this strategy of nuclear deterrence is that each state fears vulnerability: Does the rival have a numerical superiority in weapons or firepower? Does the rival have a technically superior system for attack or defense? Could a rival's first strike destroy one's own capacity for second-strike retaliation?

To overcome such uncertainties about mutual deterrence, a state expands its destructive capacity, numbers of weapons, and technical sophistication to a point where it has great confidence that under any conditions of conflict, it can inflict catastrophic and unacceptable damage on a rival. Thus the balance of power evolved into a balance of terror, a system of *mutually assured destruction (MAD)*. Even at this point, the fear of technological breakthroughs by rivals and the inherent desire for superiority induce each state to expand its military capability to an extraordinary, and excessive, magnitude. In the 1970s and 1980s, this continued expansion of military power and destructive capacity resulted in an arms race that produced nuclear arsenals capable of massive, even total, annihilation of humankind. In short, balance-of-power politics became a dangerous and possibly irrational mechanism for regulating the relations among powerful states in the nuclear age.

Since 1990, the United States and Russia (the country that inherited most Soviet nuclear power) have negotiated significant reductions in nuclear weapons. Although the likelihood of a nuclear war between these two cold warriors has shrunk, U.S. President George W. Bush has indicated that the United States will no longer be constrained by earlier nuclear weapons reductions agreements and intends to develop new antimissile systems. Moreover, the stockpiles of operational nuclear weapons in key countries remain far in excess of MAD: Russia (8,600); the United States (8,000); China (400); France (350); the United Kingdom (200); Israel (200); and less than one hundred each in India and Pakistan (Bulletin of Atomic Scientists 2002). Indeed, of these eight countries, only France is not currently engaged in violent conflict. And it is clear that other actors (e.g., Iran, North Korea), including states that support international terrorism and even some terrorist groups, will soon (or already) have access to nuclear weapons. For all these reasons, new forms of instability in the balance of terror are emerging (Cimbala 2000).

Domination and Dependence

While all states enjoy sovereign equality, it is obvious that some states are far more powerful than others. This section discusses the situation in which one state exercises very substantial power over another. The capacity of one state to alter the actions of another state can be based on different forms of leverage, the primary three of which are listed below:

1. *Economic* leverage is based on the advantageous trade, financial interactions, or economic aid that the state can provide (or withhold from) another state.

2. *Military* leverage can be applied either negatively, via the use or threat of military action against a state, or positively, via military assistance in the form of protection, provision of military resources, or training.

3. *Political* leverage is derived from the ability of a state to affect the actions of another state by the application of its political resources, such as its negotiating skills, its effective political institutions, or its influence in interstate relations.

Colonialism/Imperialism.   Since the early twentieth century, particular attention has focused on **colonialism** or *imperialism,* which is characterized by one state having extensive dominance over another state. A state might have a variety of reasons for attaining mastery over another state. First, the subordinate state can provide resources, both human and physical, for the dominant state. Second, the subordinate state can be a controlled market for the products of the dominant state. Third, the subordinate state can serve important strategic functions, either as a buffer between the dominant state and its rivals or as a staging area for the dominant state's political or military objectives. Fourth, a state with a missionary zeal might dominate another state to ensure that its values (usually political or religious) guide the subordinate state. Fifth, a state might want to dominate another state to gain international prestige.

While all forms of colonial domination entail a mix of economic, military, and political control, dominant states have employed different styles, listed below.

1. In the *segregationist* style of colonialism, the exploitation by the dominant state is explicit. There is little or no attempt to improve the economic, political, or social systems in the subordinate state. This style generally characterized the relations of Belgium, Germany, and Portugal with their African and Asian colonial territories.

2. In the *assimilationist* style, the dominant state makes some attempt to transform the subordinate state into an external extension of itself. While the subordinate state is still being exploited, the institutions, knowledge, and culture of the dominant state are introduced to the elite of the subordinate state and become a basis for political, economic, and cultural development. This style is particularly associated with French colonialism in Africa and Asia and with Soviet colonialism.

3. In the style of *indirect rule,* the dominant state uses the traditional leaders and institutions of governance and culture in the subordinate state as intermediaries in its control, but it also introduces the modern forms of the dominant state that will eventually supplant traditional forms. The British approach to its vast empire (prior to the independence movement after 1945) is the classic example of indirect rule, and this mode of colonialism also seems to correspond to the style used by the United States in some Latin American and Pacific Rim states.

Neocolonialism.   In the half-century since World War II, most states have, willingly or reluctantly, granted independence to their colonial holdings. But political independence has not necessarily ended these states' subordination to strong states. The label **neocolonialism** is given to new forms of domination and dependence that are nearly as powerful as those under colonialism. These new forms were described in Chapter 10's discussion of dependency approaches, which explained the lack of development in many of the states gaining political independence in the postcolonial era (i.e., after 1945).

Although the dominant state has officially withdrawn, especially its direct political and military presence, it has maintained domination, primarily by economic leverage. Through foreign aid, loans, technology transfer, military support, and economic intervention, the dominant state can continue to control many of the actions of a supposedly independent state. The dominant state's actions become relatively invisible, and its interests are served by a subtle alliance of a small internal elite, transnational corporations, and other transnational actors, such as the IMF (Maxfield 1997; So 1990). The recent history of the Democratic Republic of Congo (Box 11.4) exemplifies the impacts of colonialism and neocolonialism on vulnerable Third World states.

BOX 11.4

The Faces of Colonialism: Congo/Zaire/Congo

The Congo is a large, resource-rich state (one-fourth the size of the United States) located in the center of the African continent. It encompasses more than thirty million people and two hundred and fifty ethnic groups. King Leopold of Belgium sponsored expeditions down the Congo River and in 1879 claimed the area as his own private kingdom. Leopold's companies extracted the natural resources ruthlessly and treated the people with brutality. In 1908 the area was placed under Belgian colonial administration as the "Belgian Congo." Military forces were used to "pacify" the population, and local men were forced into virtual slavery as workers in the mines and on the plantations. The colonial regime provided only minimal education to the population and encouraged Catholic missionaries to teach the population the great virtue of obedience to authority.

The Belgians continued to exploit the resources of the Congo until internal unrest and the general liberation of African colonies made it clear that the time of Belgian colonial rule in the Congo was over. Within about one year after substantial resistance to Belgian rule emerged, Belgium granted the Congo its independence on June 30, 1960. Belgium withdrew its military and administrative personnel and most of its financial and technical support.

Unprepared for self-rule, and without the Belgians' order-maintaining institutions, the Congolese elite broke into competing factions, and the country collapsed into civil war when the wealthy province of Katanga attempted to secede. The remaining Belgians fled, leaving the country in chaos. The United Nations sent in a peacekeeping force, and the Soviet Union also began to provide support for some groups in the Congo. With assistance from Western countries (and the apparent assistance of the U.S. Central Intelligence Agency [CIA]), an army leader, Joseph

(continued)

BOX **11.4** (CONTINUED)

Mobutu, led the army of the central government to victory over Katanga and assassinated the prime minister.

In 1965 Mobutu, now army chief of staff, led a coup that overthrew the civilian government and installed himself as the leader in a one-party, authoritarian system that ruled for more than three decades. Mobutu "Africanized" his society, changing his own name to Mobutu Sese Seko ("all powerful one") and the country's name to Zaire. Another insurrection in Shaba (previously Katanga) was defeated in 1977. Despite Mobutu's repressive rule, the clear evidence of widespread corruption, and the persistent failure of the economy, his staunch anticommunism won him substantial economic and military support from the United States.

After "independence," Mobutu's victories over Katanga/Shaba and his long tenure in office depended on foreign aid, loans, technology transfer, and military support from Western countries, especially the United States. Zaire relied heavily on foreign corporations to build and maintain its mines, factories, and infrastructure facilities. But volatility in the world prices of key export commodities and the massive diversion of funds to Mobutu and his cronies from state-owned mines (e.g., copper, cobalt, diamonds) resulted in huge state deficits.

The IMF (the consortium of Western banking institutions) loaned Zaire enormous amounts and repeatedly restructured Zaire's debt of more than $4 billion (the largest in Africa). But the IMF has demanded "conditionality"—the requirement that Zaire accept crucial economic policies, including devaluation of the currency, cutting real wages, and drastically reducing social welfare programs. There were extended periods when Zaire was obliged to allow its national banking system to be run by a six-person group of Europeans sent in by the IMF.

The combination of internal corruption and exploitation by foreign economic interests left little for the people. The level of education continued to decline, the country could no longer feed itself, and the infrastructure system (e.g., roads, water supply, telecommunications) was in shambles. The real wages of urban workers had fallen to less than one-tenth of what they were at independence. Surrounded by the appalling poverty of most of the population, Mobutu was rumored to be the wealthiest person in sub-Saharan Africa, with holdings of more than $10 billion.

With the cold war over, even the United States found Mobutu an embarrassment and tried to pressure him into democratic reforms. Mobutu responded with a promise in 1990 to begin a transition from single-party rule to democracy. He finally allowed elections in 1993, but when his own candidate for prime minister was defeated, he ordered the armed forces to prevent the winning candidates from taking office. Instead, he installed a puppet government and sustained Zaire's "kleptocracy" (rule by thieves). The multinational corporations, however, still found much in Zaire to appreciate and they maintained their business dealings with Mobutu.

After years of deepening political decay, Mobutu's end came suddenly. A low-level guerrilla war that had been waged against Mobutu for many years was substantially expanded after more than 1.2 million Hutus fled from the ethnic chaos in two neighboring (Tutsi-controlled) countries, Burundi and Rwanda. When the

BOX **11.4** (CONTINUED)

Hutus settled in refugee camps in eastern Zaire, they were attacked by the Zairean guerrillas, who were mainly Tutsis, and large numbers of additional Zairean Tutsis joined in the political violence. When the Hutus had been expelled, the enlarged rebel army focused on the civil war.

By early 1997, neither the alienated citizenry nor the army, demoralized and undisciplined after years of low pay in a corrupt society, were willing to risk their lives for Mobutu. The United Nations, the United States, and the multinationals also abandoned Mobutu. Facing little opposition, the rebels advanced rapidly to the west, reaching the capital city of Kinshasa by May 1997. As Mobutu fled the country, the rebel leader, Laurent Kabila, declared himself president and renamed the country the Republic of Congo. However, other Congolese groups refused to accept Kabila's rule and engaged in a widespread and destructive civil war to topple him. The conflict soon became regionalized with the involvement of troops and military aid from six other African countries, including Rwanda, Uganda, and Zimbabwe. When Kabila was assassinated in 2001, his son, Joseph Kabila, seized power. Although most regular military forces accepted a cease-fire under a 2001 truce, many groups have continued the violent struggle, and more than 2.5 million have died in the recent civil war.

Despite these changes of leaders and even country name, the Congo's economic and political systems remain deeply dependent on Western capital. After 90 years under a brutal and exploitative colonial system, 40 years of "independence" have brought no blossoming of democratic politics, no sharing of the society's abundant resources among its people, no economic development. Rather, contemporary Congo is a tragic product of colonialism and neocolonialism as well as its own internal failings, a state characterized by poverty, corruption, oppression, economic chaos, and dependence on foreign states and foreign economic actors.

Some analysts such as Immanuel Wallerstein (1980, 1991) take this perspective a step further, arguing that individual dominant states have been replaced by a *world system* of domination and dependence. As noted in Chapter 10, a handful of powerful "core" states have the capacity to manipulate the international political economy to their enormous advantage. These core states (especially the United States, the members of the European Union, and Japan) can use their superior technology, financial resources, diversified economy, and skilled labor to control the production and sale of most modern goods and services in the international market. States on the "periphery" (especially many developing countries) mainly provide labor, raw materials, and simple goods for export and are subject to systematic exploitation by and subordination to the core states.

One of the most ideologically charged issues in international politics is the extent to which a few states do reap enormous benefits through their domination of many less developed countries. The dependency approach provides both an explanation for underdevelopment (Chapter 10) and an ideological rationale for demands that the prosperous states redistribute their resources to those states that have been exploited. It also posits that the patterns of dominance and dependence that were established under colonialism have become global and systemic.

Globalization?

"A new international system has now clearly replaced the Cold War: globalization. That's right, globalization—the integration of markets, finance and technologies in a way that is shrinking the world from a size medium to a size small and enabling each of us to reach around the world farther, faster and cheaper than ever" (Friedman 1999: 110). Like many other commentators, Thomas Friedman, author of the widely discussed *The Lexus and the Olive Tree* (1999), asserts that the forces of globalization are reshaping everything, from international politics and economics to our individual values. In the past decade, the discussions of globalization and its implications for the international system, economies, states, and individuals have proliferated.

What is globalization? As a working definition, **globalization** can be viewed as the increasing integration of diverse economic, sociocultural, military, and environmental phenomena by means of dense networks of action and information that rapidly span vast distances around the world. This definition is guided by the sug-

GADO
DAILY NATION
Nairobi
KENYA

Gado/CARTOONISTS & WRITERS SYNDICATE/cartoonweb.com

gestion of Keohane and Nye (2000: 105) that we first define "globalism" as "a state of the world involving networks of interdependence at multicontinental distances." There are two defining characteristics of a linkage that affects globalism: (1) networks of connections that are increasingly dense, and (2) extremely rapid transmission of phenomena across substantial, multicontinental distances. These networks allow the movement of people, goods, ideas, information, financial capital, and even biological substances. "Globalization," Keohane and Nye suggest, refers to an increase in the level of globalism.

What aspects of human existence are affected by globalization? It is particularly associated with economic factors: an international market political economy with private economic actors minimally constrained by states or borders, open capital markets, vigorous competition, and a reduction of state control over the economy (Brawley 2003). However, the linkages associated with globalization can affect many important aspects of our world. Thus Keohane and Nye (2000: 106–107) suggest four major domains of globalism: (1) *economic globalism:* the long-distance flows of goods, services, capital, and information that shape market exchanges (e.g., less costly imports, instantaneous transfers of financial capital); (2) *social and cultural globalism:* the movement of ideas, people, information, and images, which then influence the individuals, societies, and cultures into which they flow (e.g., MTV, international tourism); (3) *military globalism:* the long-distance networks of interdependence in which the threat or exercise of force is employed (e.g., mutually assured destruction; international terrorist networks); and (4) *environmental globalism:* the long-distance transport of materials and biological substances via natural movement (e.g., ozone depletion) or via human agency (e.g., the intercontinental spread of SARS and AIDS).

Are there benefits from globalization? For its advocates, globalization replaces the walls and divisions among peoples with networks and integration. This facilitates many things. There is a more effective global sharing of technology and knowledge, promoting innovation and the diffusion of best practices. There is more efficient production and distribution of goods in an open, global market, resulting in widespread economic growth, lower prices, and improved products. Financial capital flows quickly to the places where it will produce the highest return on investment. There is greater crossnational communication, enhancing understanding across cultures. Individuals who are geographically spread but have shared interests can join together so they can engage in effective political or social participation and thus be empowered (Friedman 1999; Rodrik 1997).

Are there drawbacks from globalization? Its many critics assert that globalization dramatically increases the disparities in wealth and power between the privileged haves and the vast numbers of have-nots in the world. In a "race to the bottom," profit-driven companies, many of which are multinational corporations, rapidly move production, capital, and jobs in search of the countries with the cheapest labor, least restrictive environmental and labor laws, lowest taxes, and least political control over their operations. Most of the cultural elements that spread worldwide are of low quality, undermining the special and unique elements of national cultures and identities under the weight of mediocre, global homogeneity. Globalization has rapidly accelerated environmental degradation, from global warming to the transcontinental spread of pathogens and diseases (Galbraith 1999; Ramonet 1999; Lyman 2000).

As is often the case, there is considerable truth as well as substantial hyperbole associated with the assertions of both the advocates and the foes of globalization. It is clear that the extraordinary increases in the speed, distance, and density of networking have altered the global economic and sociocultural systems, facilitating capitalism and markets and richly connecting some peoples and groups. Yet most of the world's population continues to live, work, and experience life on the margins of those systems. There are powerful and contradictory forces at work. Some forces create enhanced interactions and shared identities across vast spatial and political boundaries, while other forces, in reaction against globalization, intensify the importance of local activities and particularistic identities.

Even as states are increasingly penetrated by outside forces, the states remain formidable actors in the international system. Thus it is possible that globalization could be substantially limited by the policy actions of the most powerful states. This might occur if those states conclude that their national interest (especially their prosperity and stability) is being undermined by globalization and if there is strong pressure to resist from powerful, well-organized internal groups harmed by globalization. Alternatively, states might cooperate with each other to coordinate their national policies in ways that limit the most negative effects of globalization. In this case, the calculus of the states would be, as in other forms of interstate cooperation, that collaborative approaches are the best means to serve their major goals. However, most analysts conclude that intentional state policies will not stop current globalizing trends. They emphasize that states have less and less capacity to control their participation in or insulation from the globalizing international system. Borders become more permeable to goods, people, capital, and ideas. There is also considerable skepticism that states could sustain sufficient cooperation in the brutally competitive system. Indeed, virtually all analysts assume that the forces of globalization are transforming the international system in ways that are probably not controllable and are certainly not understood (Barber 1995; Brawley 2003; Rodrik 1997; Rosenau 1997; Waltz 2000).

Competition in the Globalized, Post–Cold War World

The disintegration of the Soviet Union (1991) is regarded as the crucial event ending the cold war era. The international system that is evolving in the new conditions of the post–cold war period is premised on the disappearance of the bipolar balance-of-power system dominated by a conflict between the U.S. bloc and the Soviet bloc and the shifts toward globalization outlined above. Four major trends are likely to be important in this evolution in the international system.

First, *military power* remains a significant factor in the relations among states. While the lessening of cold war tensions has resulted in a reduction in worldwide military expenditure, more than $850 billion per year is still being spent on defense (SIPRI 2003). Despite the presence of multilateral military forces and multistate alliances, most military power remains under the control of individual states. If powerful and politically effective groups are increasingly threatened by globalization, it is possible that they will pressure their governments to be more active in protecting their citizens, their economies, and even their cultures. And leaders might become more assertive in response to the breakdown of borders and challenges to state sovereignty. This might produce protectionist and isolationist policies toward other states and the use of the state's military to protect and project the state's interests. It is quite likely that conflicts will be more frequent in a diffuse, multipolar world in which globalization and ethnonationalism are rampant. As was discussed earlier in the chapter, it is not obvious that the UN or any other actors have the will and capacity to prevent such conflicts.

Second, intense *economic competition* will split the developed countries that were allies during the cold war. In fact, competition among the major powers will pivot more on economic issues than on military or ideological issues. In the global economy, regional groupings have formed as states coordinate their policies with similar states ("harmonization") in order to protect the set of states from outside pressures. The EU might become this type of coordinating mechanism for its member states. The major economic competition might be among three groups: North America under leadership from the United States, the European Union, and an East Asian group under Japanese or Chinese leadership. Other regional economic groups have formed in South America and among the Muslim states of Central Asia.

Third, the state-centered system is evolving toward one in which *transnational entities* are extraordinarily important. The dynamics of globalization seem to be generally beyond state control, as does the extensive and growing power of the MNCs, described above. States might actually be willing accomplices of these transborder actors, since the most powerful elites controlling these states could reap substantial benefits from the globalized international order. IGOs such as the IMF and the WTO become the tools to facilitate further globalization.

Alternatively, states might continue to lose power to transborder, global actors and, as a consequence, lose their central role in structuring the international system. State borders have little significance for transnational actors. IGOs and NGOs pursue international agendas that are not shaped by the goals of individual states or negated by state sovereignty. A MNC can shift its resources and its operations from country to country in a single-minded pursuit of profit maximization within the global economy. Although located in a home country, MNCs have operations in other host countries as well. The MNC's loyalty to the prosperity and security goals of its home country can be limited or nonexistent. Such a system of weakened states might become more multipolar and anarchic, or the system might be dominated by a core set of nonstate, transnational actors who cooperate for mutual advantage.

Fourth, due to these trends and other factors, a *more complex international system* has emerged. As noted above, the United States has become such a dominant military power that the system has some unipolar (hegemonic) characteristics. Currently, 43 percent of the world's total military spending is by the Unites States alone (SIPRI 2003). However, the EU and other key countries, including China, Japan, and Russia, constitute potential poles in this new system, which is based on both military and economic power. As this diverse set of states and other actors jockey for position in a more fluid set of alliances and interstate relationships, a complicated multipolar system might be emerging. There is disagreement among scholars regarding the extent to which this multipolar system will result and also whether it would be characterized by more international conflict than a bipolar system or hegemonic system. However, empirical research suggests that in the twentieth century, unlike the nineteenth century, aggressive competition and military conflict were more likely as the international system became highly diffuse and multipolar—rather like the system that seems to be emerging (Brecher and Wilkenfeld 1997; Kegley and Wittkopf 2001: ch. 12, 14; Russett, Starr, and Kinsella 2000).

Some analysts conclude that the emerging international order will soon be dominated by "imperial corporations" whose globalized systems of production and distribution of goods, finance, technologies, and communications enable them to transcend sovereign states and shape the global system (Barnet and Cavanagh 1994; Falk 1993). For these reasons, some predict that a key conflict in the early twenty-first century will be between the MNCs or between MNCs and states (Heilbroner 1993; United Nations Commission on Transnational Corporations 1991). Do you think it would be desirable to have an international system dominated by transnational actors rather than by states? Would the relentless pursuit of profit produce a more peaceful or a more just world than the relentless pursuit of national interest and state power? Is global security characterized by an increase in international political violence? This last question is among those addressed in Chapter 12.

KEY CONCEPTS

balance of power	international regime
colonialism	international relations
diplomacy	multinational corporation (MNC)
foreign policy	mutually assured destruction (MAD)
geopolitics	neocolonialism
globalization	peacekeeping force
intergovernmental organizations (IGOs)	political idealism
	political realism
international law	transnationalism
international nongovernmental organizations (NGOs)	world system

FOR FURTHER CONSIDERATION

1. In the post–cold war period, the bipolar international system dominated by the equilibrium between the United States and the Soviet Union has ended. A new pattern must structure the relations among states. What is the most desirable pattern? What is the least desirable? What seems most likely for the international system in the first decades of the twenty-first century?

2. Can the United Nations, or *any* multinational body, be so effective in imposing an international order that major conflict between states becomes highly unlikely?

3. Who, if anyone, can judge whether there are appropriate conditions under which a country's sovereignty can be violated? What might such conditions be?

4. What is the most effective strategy to produce increased cooperation among key actors in the international system?

5. Is globalization likely to change the distribution of power among states and other transnational actors in significant ways? Who is likely to benefit most from globalization?

FOR FURTHER READING

Barnet, Richard J., and John Cavanagh. (1994). *Global Dreams: Imperial Corporations and the New World Order.* New York: Simon & Schuster. A rich, insightful, and often scathing analysis of the enormous power and impacts of the MNCs on the international system and the lives of citizens in many countries.

Claude, Inis L. (1984). *Swords into Plowshares: The Problems and Progress of International Organization.* 4th ed. New York: McGraw-Hill. A classic study of the development and roles of the United Nations.

Dougherty, James E., and Robert L. Pfaltzgraff. (1990). *Contending Theories of International Relations.* 3d ed. New York: Harper & Row. A readable and comprehensible explanation and assessment of the major theories of international relations.

Gruber, Lloyd. (2000). *Ruling the World: Power Politics and the Rise of Supranational Institutions.* Princeton, NJ: Princeton University Press. The author argues that although countries decide voluntarily to transfer power to such supranational institutions as the EU and NAFTA, many of the countries, and perhaps the international system itself, do not benefit from the increasing power of these supranationals.

Nugent, Neill. (1999). *The Government and Politics of the European Union.* 4th ed. Durham, NC: Duke University Press. A thorough description of the most significant regional alliance in the global system (and the subject of Box 11.1).

Parker, Geoffrey. (1998). *Geopolitics: Past, Present and Future.* New York: Continuum Publishers. The emergence, development, and explanatory power of geopolitical thinking is explained, with particular emphasis on relevant themes of contemporary interstate relations, including ethnonationalism, globalization, inequality, and environmental degradation.

Pastor, Robert A., Ed. (1999). *A Century's Journey: How the Great Powers Shape the World.* New York: Basic Books. Noted scholars explore the foreign policy behavior and resulting international impacts during the twentieth century of each of seven major powers— China, France, Germany, Great Britain, Japan, Russia, and the United States. The authors illuminate the pervasive influence of these powers on the relations between states, the international political economy, and the international system.

Stearns, Jill. (1998). *Gender and International Relations: An Introduction.* New Brunswick, NJ: Rutgers University Press. A comprehensible and thoughtful explanation of feminist perspectives on international relations theory, an approach that particularly challenges the key assumptions and interpretations of realist theory on such core topics as interstate relations, violence and militarism, and international political economy.

ON THE WEB

http://www.unsystem.org

The official web site for the United Nations Organization, including detailed information about many of its major agencies and programs.

http://europa.eu.int/index.htm

The official web site of the European Union, with extensive information about workings of the EU and its major institutional elements.

http://www.people.virginia.edu/~rjb3v/rjb.html

This wide-ranging web site provides many links regarding matters of international relations, international law, and foreign policy.

http://www.aseansec.org/index.asp

On the official web site of the Association of South East Asian Nations, there are information and documents relevant to ASEAN and news about countries in the region as well as somewhat self-serving web pages constructed by each member state.

http://www.nato.int/

This web site focuses on military, strategic, and policy issues of importance to the North Atlantic Treaty Organization, a collective security association of 19 partner countries dominated by the United States and West European powers.

http://www.g7.utoronto.ca/

The G8 Information Centre, developed by the University of Toronto, provides a wealth of G8-related (a cooperative institution with representatives from the major developed countries—the "G-7" plus Russia = G-8) information ranging from academic journal articles to recent summit information.

http://osce.org

The official web site of the Organization for Security and Co-operation in Europe (OSCE), the largest regional security organization in the world with 55 participating states from Europe, Central Asia, and North America, active in conflict prevention, crisis management, and postconflict rehabilitation.

http://www.apecsec.org.sg/

The electronic home of the Asia-Pacific Economic Cooperation (APEC), an organization focusing on economic growth, cooperation, trade, and investment among 21 governments in the Asia-Pacific region, including Canada, China, Japan, Russia, and the United States.

http://www.oas.org/

The homepage of the Organization of American States provides a comprehensive database of information regarding the group's activities and policies.

http://www.unhcr.ch/

The United Nations High Commissioner on Refugees is the agency that attempts to document the scale and details of the movement of populations across borders and to suggest appropriate policy responses to deal with the challenges of coping with the large numbers of dislocated people.

Bosnian civilians run for cover in the capital as Serbian troops shell the town.

CHAPTER 12 **Political Violence**

Yesterday in the political world:

An ethnically based militia used machetes to kill 65 men, women, and children in a village in northeastern Democratic Republic of Congo.

In Colombia, two of four mayors who were meeting with leftist rebels were shot dead by the rebels, and two escaped into the jungle.

Eight Algerian soldiers were killed in a bomb ambush by Islamic militants south of Algiers.

Tamil Tiger rebels in Sri Lanka abducted 23 children from a school to force them into serving as child soldiers.

Three protesters were killed by police during antigovernment demonstrations in Port au Prince, Haiti.

Three U.S. soldiers died in two roadside bomb attacks near Baghdad, Iraq.

A female suicide bomber killed 19 patrons in a restaurant in Haifa, Israel.

The Israeli military immediately retaliated for the Haifa attack by bombing six villages in Syria suspected of being Islamic Jihad training sites.

Four army soldiers were killed in an attack by rebels in northeastern Liberia, despite the ceasefire in place.

A leading Sunni militant, his driver, and three bodyguards were killed when his vehicle was attacked by gunmen, possibly government paramilitary forces, in Lahore, Pakistan.

Two UN peacekeepers from Canada died when a landmine destroyed their vehicle on a road near Kabul, Afghanistan.

The struggle for local political power was blamed for the grenade attack on a mosque in Mindanao, Philippines, killing 3 and wounding 20.

Police in Caracas used rubber bullets and tear gas to disperse a large group protesting the government's shutdown of a TV news channel that had been critical of the Venezuelan president.

*North Korea announced it was "ready and able" to produce nuclear
bombs, raising regional tensions.*

*Five police officers in Bahrain were seriously wounded in a bomb attack
of their vehicle.*

Such incidents of violence are often at the center of our awareness of the political
world. On a given day, the media rarely report that the great majority of countries
and billions of people experienced no bombings, kidnappings, riots, or revolutionary acts that had an explicit or implicit political motivation. Rather, the media are
likely to report on the few settings that do experience armed conflict, riots, assassinations, terrorist incidents, and so on. In part, this selective reporting reflects our
general fascination with the horror of violence. And in part, it indicates our underlying sense that such political violence is extraordinary, or even an aberration, from
politics-as-usual.

Violence is excluded from some definitions of politics, such as the group approach,
since violence is viewed as a breakdown of politics, which is understood as consensus
building and conflict resolution. Indeed, politics has been defined as "bloodless conflict" (Donovan, Morgan, Potholm, and Weigle 1994). However, other definitions,
including the class approach, treat conflict and violence as one possible, and perhaps
even inevitable, form of politics. Indeed, some approaches argue that political violence
can be a positive force, producing necessary change and constructive outcomes. This
chapter discusses the nature and dynamics of political violence.

VIOLENCE

Before the discussion can unfold, we need to consider briefly the concept of violence itself. The most common notion is that *violence* entails the use of physical
force, usually with the purpose of injuring or damaging the target of the violence.
In the political world, the tools of such violence can range from flying fists and feet
to clubs and bullets to nerve gas and nuclear missiles.

But notice that some analysts take a much broader view of violence. First, the
threat of violence might be understood as a form of violence, even if the violent act
is not committed. If someone points a gun in your face and you give him your
money, you will probably view this interaction as a violent one, even if the person
never fires the gun. In parallel, then, if a state points many nuclear missiles at the
state across its border but does not launch any, would you classify this as an act of
violence? Is it a violent act if an interest group threatens to blow up a public building unless its demands are met? Is it a violent act if a group shouts down a speaker
at a public rally? Do you think that such acts of intimidation and threat of force
have a violent element, even if there is no actual physical injury or damage?

Second, an even broader view of violence includes various forms of subjugation and manipulation that do not involve even the threat of direct physical harm.
For example, consider a group that is an "underclass" within a society. The group
is subjected to discrimination in education, in health care, in jobs, in housing. This
intentional pattern of systematic deprivation continues over time. The group is not
targeted for any specific physical violence, but the economic and cultural systems

provide the group with minimal opportunities to gain a significant share of the values in the society. Some would classify such oppression as a form of violence by the dominant group(s) against the fundamental rights of this group as it pursues the goals of life, liberty, and happiness. The extensive use of propaganda techniques might be considered an even subtler form of violence against those people.

Political violence is defined as *the use of actual physical violence or very serious threats of such violence to achieve political goals.* As you assess the role of violence in politics, however, consider the other ways in which the world of politics generates actions and impacts that "do violence" to many people. Although resorting to physical force is quite evident in politics, the more subtle forms of coercion and manipulation are more extensive, if less visible.

POLITICAL SOCIETY

For Thomas Hobbes (1588–1679), the formation of political society is an attempt to overcome the frequent reliance on force and violence in human interaction. He describes life in the state of nature as "solitary, poor, nasty, brutish, and short." To overcome this pervasive interpersonal violence, individuals submit to the social contract in an attempt to submit force to reason—to ensure that force becomes the *ultima ratio* (final resort), not the *prima ratio* (first resort) in human interactions. In essence, individuals cede to the state a monopoly over the legitimate use of violence, sacrificing their own right to do violence in exchange for a similar sacrifice from others.

Some individuals and groups argue that the existing political society and its social contract have no authority over their actions and that they are therefore not morally bound to refrain from engaging in "justifiable" violence. Indeed, those who commit political violence virtually always offer a justification for their actions, such as the preservation of values, the restoration of order, self-defense, or retribution. Broadly, they make such justifications based on claims that they have never accepted the right of a particular government to command their obedience or that the political system has failed to act properly (it has gone too far or it has not gone far enough in its value allocations).

TYPES OF POLITICAL VIOLENCE

A simple taxonomy of political violence can be based on specifying the *source* of the violence and the *target* of that violence. Either party may be a state or an individual/group. Figure 12.1 categorizes the four resulting types of political violence. Although these categories help organize and clarify our discussion, this taxonomy is imperfect and the boundaries between categories are imprecise because the states, groups, or individuals who engage in political violence can operate in fluid groupings, are usually motivated by multiple objectives, employ complex strategies, and focus on several targets.

State Violence against Individuals or Groups

Given the state's monopoly of the legitimate use of violence, there are many instances where the state's application of political violence seems justifiable. The

	Target	
Source	**Individual/Group**	**State**
Individual/Group	Crime Terrorism Nation-based conflict Class conflict	Riots/Rebellion Separatist violence Coup Revolution
State	Order maintenance Establishment violence	War

FIGURE 12.1   Types of political violence

state typically characterizes its own use of violence as an *order-maintenance* activity. The state often acts as police officer, judge, and executor of punishment when individuals or groups seem to have violated the society's legal system. The state's agents might arrest, try, and punish an actor who breaks a criminal law, such as by robbery, or a civil law, such as by tax fraud. In such cases, most citizens are likely to support the state's efforts to create and maintain public order.

But some uses of violence by the state are more problematic. Recall Lenin's definition of the state as "a body of armed men, weapons, and prisons" (in Chapter 5). Because the state has the capacity to define the nature and severity of all "crimes," it is possible for it to be highly repressive and discriminatory in its use of state violence. Thus excessive reliance on force and oppressive laws can be viewed as *establishment violence* rather than as the state's legitimate use of violence to maintain public order.

The boundary between a crime against society and a crime against the existing political order can blur. In some countries, a "political crime" is no more than opposition to the actions of the current political leadership. Thus political opponents become "enemies of the people," and are subject to constraints on freedom of action, deprivation of resources, imprisonment, and death. The state can also institute systematic policies of violence against certain groups who are not overt opponents of the regime but are blamed for problems faced by the state and thus are made scapegoats.

A key instrument of state power against its enemies is its security forces, which include official groups such as the regular military and the secret police as well as unofficial armed groups (e.g., Columbian paramilitary forces) or civilian vigilante groups (e.g., the Iranian Revolutionary Guards). Another form of state power is judicial systems and prison systems, which punish those whose behaviors displease the state. According to Amnesty International (2004), an NGO that monitors violations of individual civil rights by agents of the state, political prisoners are being subjected to establishment violence in the majority of contemporary states. In addition, the state can cause great suffering or even death to individuals through its power to withhold access to such rewards as good jobs, shelter, and welfare services.

TABLE 12.1
Death by Government in the Twentieth Century

	Total Deaths (Millions)			Percentage of Total Deaths
	Domestic	*Foreign*	*All*	
Establishment Violence	129.9	39.3	169.2	83.3%
By communist governments	101.9	8.3	110.2	54.2
By other totalitarian governments	2.1	26.1	28.2	14.0
By authoritarian governments	25.7	3.0	28.7	14.1
By democratic governments	0.2	1.9	2.1	1.0
War	4.8	29.2	34.2	16.7
TOTAL	134.7	68.5	203.2	100.0%

Source: Adapted from Rummel 2004: table 1.6.

In the contemporary world, there is extensive attention to certain forms of political violence, especially violence between states (war) and individual/group violence (such as terrorism). This attention is understandable because such violence is dramatic and terrifying. But, according to an extensive analysis by political scientist R. J. Rummel (2004) of "death by government," the death toll from establishment violence far outweighs the deaths from war during the twentieth century. These data are summarized in Table 12.1.

According to Rummel, the deaths of more than two hundred million people in the twentieth century are directly attributable to government violence and war. The most staggering aspect of these data is that fully 83 percent of these deaths are establishment violence. While about 34 million people were killed in wars, it is (conservatively) estimated that governments killed almost 170 million of their own citizens—the people they are supposed to serve. Rummel reports that almost all of these deaths through establishment violence have been the work of nondemocratic governments. Nearly two-thirds of the deaths (65.1 percent) are attributable to communist regimes, about 17 percent are the responsibility of other totalitarian governments, and 17 percent are by authoritarian governments (Rummel 2004: table 1.2, table 1.6, figure 1.4).

Rummel particularly emphasizes the massive death totals attributable to the twentieth century's "bloodiest dictators": Joseph Stalin (whose Soviet regime killed 42.6 million between 1929 and 1953), Mao Zedong in China (37.8 million from 1923 to 1976), the elimination of more than 20.9 million by Hitler and the German Nazi regime (1933–1945, recall Box 2.2), and the deaths by execution and starvation of 2.4 million Cambodians under Pol Pot's regime (recall Box 5.5). If you need evidence regarding the fundamental importance of the state in determining the quality of citizens' lives, the 170 million deaths attributable to the citizens' own governments should be compelling.

Individual Violence against an Individual

When an individual is the source of violence and another individual is the target, the violence is usually not explicitly political. Most such violence (e.g., murder, robbery, rape, assault, and certain crimes against property, such as burglary and arson) is best characterized as *ordinary crime.* Since only the state (and its agents) have a legitimate right to use violence (Chapter 5), an individual who does violence independent of the state is normally in violation of the law. This type of violence is therefore implicitly political in the sense that the state is usually involved in determining what behavior is criminal and then in apprehending violators, judging them, and punishing them.

Analyzing individuals' motivation in violent ordinary crimes is complicated by the fact that in most societies, members of deprived or subordinate groups tend to engage in these crimes far more frequently than members of the more advantaged classes. Can you think of ways in which this pattern might suggest that the commission of some violent crimes has, at least in part, a subtle political origin?

Occasionally one individual commits violence against another individual in a situation where the motivation is personal as well as political. In such cases, neither the source nor the target is acting primarily as the representative of some larger political group. In a famous example from 1804, U.S. Vice President Aaron Burr shot and killed Alexander Hamilton in a duel that had its origins in a personal and political disagreement between the two men (see Box 12.1). In another example, in 2001, King Birendra of Nepal, the queen, and six other members of the royal family were shot to death by the king's son, the crown prince, who had reputedly quarreled with his mother over his choice of a bride. Two American presidents (James A. Garfield in 1881 and William McKinley in 1901) were assassinated by individuals who seemed to be acting primarily on political motives.

Group Violence against an Individual

Most situations in which a person is targeted for political violence, including assassinations, are usually committed on behalf of a group, even if the act is performed by a single individual. Box 5.3 described the assassinations of two Indian prime ministers, Indira Gandhi and her son Rajiv Gandhi, seven years later. Although Indira Gandhi was killed by two guards and Rajiv Gandhi by one woman, in each case the assassins believed that they were acting on behalf of the political interests of their nation (the Sikhs and the Sri Lankan Tamils, respectively). Similarly, Israeli Prime Minister Yitzhak Rabin was assassinated in 1995 by an individual who belonged to Kach, an extreme right-wing Jewish religious group, in an attempt to undermine the "land-for-peace" agreement between Israel and the Palestinians. President Abraham Lincoln was assassinated in 1865 as part of a broader group attack on the American political leadership, and some believe that John F. Kennedy's death in 1963 can be attributed to more than one person. The Armenian prime minister was among six members of government shot to death by five anti-Armenian gunmen who invaded the parliament building in 1999. And the Israeli military has assassinated numerous leaders of resistance organizations such as Hamas.

BOX 12.1

Politics Will Be the Death of Me

After a long and extraordinary career in politics, Alexander Hamilton (1757–1804) took up the life of a country gentleman in 1800. But the seminal Founding Father, cowriter of the *Federalist Papers,* and first U.S. Secretary of the Treasury was unable to withdraw from the political world. He was alarmed by the growing dominance of the Jeffersonian Republicans over his own Federalist Party. In Hamilton's view, the Republicans were undermining values in which he believed deeply—a powerful and independent judiciary, a strong national government and military, and an evolution away from slavery in the United States.

Hamilton was increasingly displeased with the Federalist policy responses. He toyed with the idea of reentering politics to establish a new political party, the Christian Constitutional Society, which would appeal to people's religious sensibilities and their concern for collective good rather than their selfish, individual interests. He was dismayed when the Federalists in his home state of New York decided for strategic reasons to support Jefferson's vice president, Aaron Burr, in the election for governor of New York. Hamilton had never liked Burr, either for his political views or for his personal style. Hamilton was vocal in his opposition to Burr, who failed to win the governorship.

Shortly after the election, Burr sent a note to Hamilton demanding an explanation for negative remarks that Burr believed Hamilton had made about him. Burr cited comments overheard by others in which Hamilton is purported to have said that he "looked upon Mr. Burr to be a dangerous man, and one who ought not to be trusted with the reins of government" and other, unquoted opinions that Burr claimed were "even more despicable" (McDonald 1979: 359–360).

At that time, the *code duello* required that a gentleman was obliged to explain or apologize for remarks that caused affront to another gentleman. The code further allowed the aggrieved party to challenge the other man to a duel in order to obtain "satisfaction." In such cases, men of honor would normally duel with pistols, intentionally miss each other, shake hands, and consider the disagreement resolved.

Hamilton did not deny his disdain for Burr or Burr's politics, but he refused to explain or apologize on the grounds that the charges against him were too vague. When negotiations between their representatives broke down, Burr challenged Hamilton to a duel. As a gentleman, Hamilton could not decline. On the early morning of July 11, 1804, Burr and Hamilton met in the woods. After Hamilton shot in the air, Burr shot Hamilton through the liver. Carried back to his home, Hamilton forgave Burr, repented his sins, and died after 36 hours in great pain (based on McDonald 1979).

Usually, the politics of death are impersonal. The killer and the killed know each other only as types. But there are a considerable number of instances where

(continued)

BOX **12.1** (CONTINUED)

personal animosities and grudges, with political undertones or overtones, are resolved violently. Murders of political rivals, such as assassinations of leaders, are among the most dramatic moments in the political life of a country. A deadly conflict such as that between Hamilton and Burr might seem odd to you—today, people are more civilized than these "gentlemen." When individuals (especially boys and men) have personal–political differences, they now resolve them through discussion and compromise, not with weapons and violence. Don't they?

Alexander Hamilton is mortally wounded in his 1804 duel with Aaron Burr, the ultimate resolution of their political dispute.

Terrorism.　When the target of premeditated violence serving an underlying political objective is an "innocent," the act is usually termed **terrorism**. Bombs can be planted in public places such as pubs or airplanes, civilians can be kidnapped or murdered, harmful chemicals can be placed in food, water, or air. Many terrorist acts are committed by residents of the country in which the terrorism occurs. For example, Timothy McVeigh bombed the U.S. federal government building in Oklahoma City in 1995, killing 168 adults and children. In 2002, Indonesian militants bombed two nightclubs in Bali, killing 202 clubbers.

Particular attention often focuses on "international terrorism"—incidents where the terrorism is committed by individuals from another country. Since the early 1980s, there have been about three hundred to four hundred international terrorist acts per year. Recent years have been characterized by fewer acts of terrorism but higher numbers of deaths. Deaths peaked in 2001 when 3,547 were killed in 346 terrorist acts (U.S. Department of State 2004). Almost 90 percent of those deaths

People flee from the site where the two towers of the World Trade Center in New York are collapsing after a terrorist attack on September 11, 2001. The attack killed more than 2,500 people.

occurred on September 11, 2001, when the United States was the target of what is arguably the most massive international terrorist attack in modern history. A well-organized group, composed mainly of Saudi Arabians, hijacked four transcontinental passenger airplanes departing from Boston, Newark, and Washington, D.C. Two of the planes flew directly into the tallest towers of the World Trade Center in New York, one crashed into the Pentagon in Washington, D.C., and the fourth plane crashed in an uninhabited area after passengers struggled with the hijackers. The carnage was staggering, with more than three thousand deaths, and the direct and indirect costs of the attack have been more than $100 billion. These attacks caused many countries to make sweeping changes in their approaches to security from international terrorism in the high-tech age.

For some, the central question regarding those who engage in terrorism is: Why harm innocents? The motives of political terrorists vary, but several rationales guide most such acts. First, the terrorist act can be a means to gain international publicity for the group's cause. Unlike those committing ordinary crimes, terrorists typically claim credit for their violent actions and hope for extensive media coverage. A second motive is to secure financial resources for the group's political activities or to demand the release of imprisoned members. Many of the acts of violence entailing hostages and ransom demands are of this type. Third, the terrorists attempt to punish an existing state even when innocents are the direct target of their actions.

From the terrorist's perspective, no citizens of that state are viewed as innocent of their state's misdeeds. (Recall the perspective of Osama bin Laden in Box 4.4.) And a fourth objective of terrorist violence can be to promote revolution—a strategy discussed later in this chapter.

Since the late 1990s, it has become evident that terrorism is undergoing ominous changes. First and most importantly, terrorists have increased capacity to inflict massive damage and disruption. The terrorists' ability to move people, information, weapons, and so on is enhanced in the global society, where national borders are permeable and cross-border travel is extensive. And the rapid expansion of technology benefits terrorists, providing them with a far greater ability to obtain and use technological artifacts ranging from computers (cyberterrorism) to chemical and biological weapons (bioterrorism) to weapons of mass destruction (WMD).

A second change is that an increasing proportion of terrorist acts are committed by those who neither claim responsibility nor make specific demands. The risk of revealing one's identity is now far greater, as law enforcement agencies have become more effective in tracing and apprehending terrorists. Also, more acts are being classified as "rage terrorism"—violence provoked by a diffuse anger against a world that seems too threatening and complex and that is seething with interpersonal and intergroup hostility. In either case, the terrorist can gain satisfaction from the profound public anxiety associated with what seems an act of random, senseless violence (Marquand 1996).

There are ambiguities in the assessment of terrorism. One problem is that in many acts labeled "terrorism," the targets are not truly "innocents"; they are agents of the enemy state. For example, a Palestinian group bombed and killed 241 U.S. Marines in their barracks in Beirut, Lebanon in 1984, a bomb killed 17 U.S. Navy personnel on the *U.S.S. Cole* while it was docked in Yemen in October 2000, and hundreds of U.S. soldiers have been killed in Iraq since the end of the war in 2003. U.S. spokespersons term these attacks "terrorism"; yet Marines, sailors on a battleship, and the soldiers of the invading military can hardly be construed as innocents. Another common target of terrorists are police officers or judges who are accused of having done violence to individuals associated with the terrorist group or those sympathetic to its cause. These are terrible acts of political violence, but you must decide whether group violence against agents of the state is appropriately defined as terrorism.

Ironically, some groups labeled terrorists are actually employees of a political system that uses them as "death squads" to eliminate opponents and to keep the citizens in line. And some terrorist groups are mercenaries who are subsidized by one state to perform violent acts against a rival state. In such cases, the actor actually causing the political violence is best understood as a state, not a group, making such acts *state-sponsored terrorism.* In 2004, the United States government designated six national governments as the primary sponsors of international terrorism: Cuba, Iran, Libya, North Korea, Sudan, and Syria. These governments are accused of either engaging in terrorist activities themselves or providing arms, training, safe haven, financial backing, and so on for international terrorists.

With the proliferation of groups employing terrorist tactics, it is wryly observed that "one person's terrorist is another person's freedom fighter." The root problem with using terrorism as an analytic concept is that it has become a powerful and negative label in the manipulative language of politics. It is sometimes used regardless of the innocence of the victim, the identity of the actual sponsor of the violence, or the justifiability of the ends. The label communicates a disgust for extreme political violence against innocent individuals, but it can also be used to discredit any group that uses violent means to achieve its political ends or to condemn a group whose political ends, as much as its means, are unacceptable. Ultimately, the issue centers in moral and political values: Are there *any* circumstances in which group political violence against individuals is justifiable? If so, what kinds of violence are acceptable under what circumstances?

Group Violence against a Group

Nation-based violence.   When one group engages in political violence against another group, it is usually motivated by a deep animosity toward some element of the other group's identity, such as ethnic or religious differences. Such nation-based violence is the source of most of the political violence occurring in the post–cold war period. Nearly all of the major military conflicts during this period have been within, not between, countries (SIPRI 2003: chapter 1). Nationality groups are increasingly mobilized to demand political autonomy, a process that is termed **ethnonationalism** (Connor 1994; Gurr 2000). Many of the groups are prepared to use political violence against other groups with whom they share territorial boundaries, generating an ethnic conflict that can be termed a "war of identity."

In some cases, one or more groups attempt to establish their own sovereign state based on national identity, a situation discussed later in the chapter as separatist violence. However, in many instances, the nation-based groups are struggling against each other for political and cultural domination rather than for separation. The continuing violence between Hindus and Muslims in India (Box 5.3) is a revealing example of how the antipathy between nationality groups can poison the relations between them as they attempt to share a country or even a remote village. Box 5.2 described the prolonged civil war (1975–2002) in the southern African country of Angola. More than 1.5 million Angolans died in the violence among three rival groups, each representing a different linguistic/ethnic region, that struggled for control the entire country. In a strikingly similar pattern, the central African country of Chad has experienced a continuing nation-based internal war, with an estimated four hundred thousand deaths since independence in 1960. And the toll from a civil war in Sudan since 1983 between the Islamic north and the mainly Christian and animist south is more than 1.5 million people—at least one in five southern Sudanese.

When group political violence entails the murder of many members of one ethnic group by its rival, it can be called *genocide*. The political system is often a partner in such situations, since its machinery of violence is employed by the dominant group. When the state organizes the campaign against an ethnic group, such genocide can be classified as establishment violence (see Figure 12.1). Twentieth-century examples of genocide include the killing of Armenians by the Turks (in 1915), of six million Jews by Hitler's Germany (1933–1945), of the Tutsis by the Hutus in Rwanda (1963–1964), and of the Hutus by the Tutsis in neighboring Burundi (1988). In the 1990s, the killing of nearly one million Tutsis in Rwanda and the Serbs' brutal destruction of civilian populations of Bosnians and of ethnic Albanians (in

TABLE 12.2
Deaths and Refugees Resulting from Recent Major Ethnic Conflicts

Country	Number Killed	Displaced Refugees
Sudan	1,500,000	4,300,000+
Afghanistan	1,050,000	6,200,000+
Rwanda	800,000	3,500,000+
Myanmar	500,000	1,000,000+
Colombia	250,000	1,000,000+
Iraq	250,000	1,500,000+
Algeria	100,000	105,000+
Sri Lanka	70,000	900,000+
Kashmir (India/Pakistan)	50,000	213,000+

Source: Wright 1999: A15.

Kosovo), which they called "ethnic cleansing," have renewed international concern about the prevention of genocide and the punishment of those who are responsible for it. Table 12.2 shows the massive toll in death and displaced refugees caused by some of the major ethnic conflicts during the last decade.

Class conflict.   In some cases, intergroup violence might be attributable to an underlying *class conflict* (Chapter 9), which is often linked to an ethnic or religious cleavage. In Lebanon, Northern Ireland, and Sri Lanka, for example, one of the groups in the conflict has dominant social, economic, and political power over the others. Thus class theorists argue that the "real" conflict in many settings is not actually due to religion or language or ethnicity, but is the inevitable class struggle that emerges from stratification and inequality. Of course, class conflict can occur between any strata, such as the peasant class against the landlord class or the capitalist class against the worker class, independent of any nation-based cleavage that might reinforce the class distinctions. The group-based political violence in some Latin American countries, such as Colombia, Guatemala, and Mexico, seems best interpreted as a struggle between deeply unequal classes.

Individual or Group Violence against the State

Individual or group political violence directed against the political system can stem from several bases. At one extreme, such violence might be a person or group's spontaneous outburst of frustration with their life conditions. At the other extreme, the individual or group might have such deep-seated hostility against the existing political system that they undertake a lengthy series of violent actions in order to overthrow it.

Riot and rebellion.   When people feel their political, social, or economic conditions are intolerable, their frustration can escalate into demonstrations and civil disobedience and then into riots.

Citizens' frustrations with the policies of the state can trigger public demonstrations that lead to violent confrontations, as in this street battle between South Korean students and workers and the state's riot police.

Riots are usually spontaneous and relatively disorganized. They can involve group violence against property, agents of the political system, perceived opponents in the society, or random targets. Riots are often triggered by a specific incident, such as the police shooting someone, or with an economic problem, such as a sudden large increase in the price of basic foodstuffs. Once riots start, they can spread as others are motivated to demonstrate their dissatisfaction with the political system or social conditions.

Riots are expressions of frustration in which there is an implicit or explicit demand for redress of grievances. The basic grievances might involve opposition to or support for certain public policies or political leaders. Black South Africans engaged in many riots in the ultimately successful opposition to apartheid during the 1980s. Similarly, widespread rioting by Indonesians in 1998 led to the fall of Suharto, ruler for more than thirty years.

Such political violence turns into *rebellion* when riots become more frequent, premeditated, and widespread and involve more people. At this point, many of those engaged in violence have lost faith in the likelihood that the system will respond to their problems. This deterioration of citizen support and escalation of political action into more intense political violence is at the heart of Samuel Huntington's description of political decay (in Chapter 10).

The Palestinian Intifada ("uprising") is an example of a rebellion. Some leaders of the Palestinian movement decided that a rebellion would be an effective intermediate strategy, since neither negotiations nor terrorism had resulted in their gaining an independent state on lands held by Israel. When the Intifada began in 1987, people of all ages were encouraged to participate in limited political violence, mainly throwing rocks but not using firearms. The leaders hoped that world opinion would be sympathetic to the underdog rock throwers when the powerful Israeli military responded violently. Some scholars conclude that the Intifada is a key reason why Israel agreed to negotiate a home rule settlement with the Palestinians (Khalidi 1993). Palestinian groups became increasingly dissatisfied when they decided the autonomy that Israel granted to the Palestine National Authority was inadequate and when Israel continued to expand its control over Palestinian territory. Consequently, the Intifada was resurrected in 2000. This second Intifada became a more complex combination of a rock-throwing popular uprising and bloody terrorist actions, and the Israeli response has also been more violent, resulting in high levels of death and destruction.

Separatist violence.   At the heart of most nation-based violence is the nationality group's struggle for the right to control its own political and cultural destiny—for autonomy. In the post–cold war world, when the desire for autonomy is strong and the existing political system seems unresponsive, groups increasingly engage in *separatist violence* to achieve their goal. If the separatist group is small and lacks political resources, it usually turns to acts of terrorism or attacks against specific individuals or structures within the political system. This characterizes the actions of the Irish Republican Army (IRA) throughout much of the twentieth century as it attempted to separate Northern Ireland from the United Kingdom and establish a united Republic of Ireland. Targets of the IRA's bombs and murders have usually been the British "occupying army" and members of the Protestant paramilitary groups in Northern Ireland. Separatist violence characterized recent activities by the Kurds against Turkey and Iraq, by those in Aceh province against Indonesia, by Chechens against Russia, by Sudan's southern Christians and animists against the Islamic rulers in the north, and by both Sikhs and Kashmiris against India.

Violent uprisings against colonial power have usually been one element in the native people's political struggle for independence. In some cases, organization of the separatist violence has been weak or nonexistent. But in others, the separatist violence has been coordinated by an organized group, such as the Mau Mau versus the British in Kenya (1950s), the Muslim League versus the British and Hindus in the Indian subcontinent (late 1940s), and the Vietminh/Vietcong versus the French and then the Americans in Vietnam (1940s–1970s). The violent resistance (after 2003) to the U.S. military and its allies in post-war Iraq is also characterized by some as native opposition to foreign occupation.

A **civil war** results when *a significant proportion of the population in a region actively supports a separatist movement and political violence emerges on a large scale.* In the United States in the early 1860s, the political leaders of the slaveholding Southern states decided that they no longer wished to maintain their participation in the American federation, and they announced that their states were seceding (withdrawing formal membership) from the federation. The central government rejected their request to secede, forcing 11 Southern states to declare their independence, create a confederation, and initiate a military struggle against the central government. In the bloody Civil War (1861–1865), the Union forces of the central government ultimately defeated the army of the Confederacy and forced the Southern states to remain in the federation.

A similar civil war occurred in Nigeria (1967–1970). The Ibo tribe, differing from other major tribes in religion, language, and political traditions, attempted to secede from the Nigerian federation and create a separate state called Biafra. After four years of civil war and nearly one million deaths, the central government's army was victorious, and Biafra was stillborn as a state. In contrast, the Bengalis were successful in their separatist civil war against the central government of Pakistan (recall Box 5.3), and thus the new nation-state of Bangladesh was created (in 1971).

The devastating struggle among the Serbs, Bosnians, Croatians, Macedonians, and other nationality groups after the breakup of Yugoslavia in 1991 is a graphic example of separatist violence. These groups' differences in ethnicity, history, language, and religion all reinforced their separate national identities (see Box 15.3). The widespread separatist violence resulted from the groups' antipathy toward each other and their efforts to determine precisely what states would emerge and where the boundaries between the states would be.

Coup. A **coup** occurs when *the top leader or part of the leadership group is replaced by violent means or the explicit threat of violence.* Those performing the coup have no intention of overthrowing the entire political-economic order, although their opposition to the existing leadership can be based on differences in policy as well as on personal rivalry. Coups are a common form of leadership turnover in political systems that have no institutionalized procedures for leadership succession. Political violence against the top leadership group is typically organized by other members of the political leadership, by a rival political group, or by the military. In the postcolonial period, coups have been especially common in Latin American and African states. An extreme example is Bolivia, where 190 coups occurred over a 156-year period. Despite the enthusiasm with which many countries are democratizing their political systems in the post–cold war period, coups continue, ousting the leaders of Algeria, Afghanistan, Argentina, Bolivia, Burundi, Comoros, Congo (Brazzaville), Democratic Republic of Congo, Ecuador, Ethiopia, Fiji, Gambia, Guinea-Bissau, Liberia, Mali, Niger, Pakistan, Sierra Leone, Somalia, Tajikistan, and Thailand, among others.

Revolution. As Lennon (John, of the Beatles, that is) observed, "You say you want a revolution, well you know, we all want to change the world." In a **revolution,** there is *a rapid and fundamental transformation of the state organization and the class structure* (Skocpol 1979). In contrast to the other forms of political violence against the state, the explicit object of revolution is to destroy the existing political system and establish a new one with a fundamentally different distribution of value allocations. However, it is difficult to specify the extent of transformation that must occur to achieve "revolutionary" changes in the state organization, class structure, or distribution of values (for reasons similar to those discussed in Chapter 5 for determining whether a political system has "died").

In many instances, new leadership takes power claiming that it will serve a new ideology and will allocate power and resources to new/different groups. When Colonel Muammar Qaddafi overthrew the hereditary king and installed a new revolutionary council committed to total egalitarianism (in 1969), it was clear that there had been a revolutionary change in the Libyan political system. But there are many instances where it is not clear whether the essential features of the political system have dramatically changed. This situation can occur either because the attempt to transform the political system is a charade or because it falls far short of its objectives. This issue will be considered further at the end of this section in discussing the outcomes of the revolution. First, consider four broad strategies that can be employed to achieve a revolution.

Strategy 1: Terrorism. The dynamics of terrorism were described previously. As a revolutionary strategy, *terrorism* involves selective acts of violence, usually by small organized cells of political activists that lack sufficient membership and resources to sustain a direct struggle against the existing state. While an "innocent" might be the apparent target of this political violence, the state is the actual target.

Terrorists use violence to disrupt public life, by such means as bombings in public places, interrupting basic services such as electricity and food distribution, and disabling key political actors within the regime. Terrorists believe that these tactics might further their revolutionary objectives in two ways. First, the acts of terrorism might provoke harsh and repressive order-maintenance actions by the state, such as large-scale detention of citizens and crackdowns on opposition groups and opposition media. In this situation, terrorists assume, many citizens will become alienated as they see the "true" repressive nature of the political system. Second, terrorist acts might prevent the political system from effective allocation of such values as distribution of food, provision of transportation, and, most fundamentally, maintenance of public order. It is assumed that either repressive or ineffective state behavior will undermine citizen support for the system and decrease resistance to (and possibly even increase support for) revolutionary change.

The anticolonial resistance in Algeria is a clear example of the successful use of terrorism. A mixture of random public bombings, disruptions of infrastructure services, and violence against the agents of the colonial French led to a dramatic decline in the quality of life and provoked repressive responses from the French political and military authorities. As conditions deteriorated, France decided to abandon the ungovernable country, and the anticolonial/terrorist leadership, under Ben Bella, formed a new political system. (Pontecorvo's powerful film, *The Battle of Algiers,* documents this period.) Many Palestinian groups, such as Hamas, have utilized this strategy against the Israelis.

Obviously, terrorism, like other revolutionary strategies, does not always produce the expected results. Often the terrorists are crushed without achieving any of their objectives, as was the case with terrorist groups in the United States in the 1960s, including the Weathermen and the Symbionese Liberation Army. And sometimes the repression evoked by terrorism merely makes things worse. The leftist terrorists in Iran were successful in destabilizing Shah Reza Pahlavi's regime, but it was the Islamic fundamentalists supporting the Ayatollah Khomeini who succeeded in grasping political power and forming a new fundamentalist political system even more unappealing to the leftists than the shah's. The situation in Uruguay (see Box 12.2) is another example of revolutionary terrorism that backfired. Nonetheless, terrorism continues to be the preferred strategy for certain revolutionary groups without widespread popular support, such as the Sendero Luminoso in Peru and FARC in Colombia.

BOX 12.2

Terrorism Makes It Worse: Uruguay

Between 1903 and the early 1960s, Uruguay became widely respected as the exemplary Latin American democracy (this discussion is based on Goodwin 2003). It had a stable two-party system that was the basis of a liberal democratic government that facilitated increasing social welfare and economic prosperity. But political decay emerged in the 1960s, grounded in economic decline, high inflation, and governmental incompetence and corruption. These failures spawned the Tupamaros, an urban guerrilla group that engaged in widespread violence and terrorism to overthrow the state and establish a more just political order. This terrorism completely undermined the citizens' confidence that the political system could maintain order. The civilian government was overthrown, not by the Tupamaros but by the conservative military in a 1973 coup.

The Uruguayan military dictatorship then launched a massive campaign to suppress not only the Tupamaros but all civilian opposition. During this period, Uruguay became known as "the torture chamber of Latin America," with widespread human and civil rights abuses. By 1979, more than one in one hundred of all Uruguayans were political prisoners, estimated to be the highest proportion in the world. And one-sixth of the population (a half-million people) were in exile. The economic crisis worsened under the military regime, with inflation of more than 60 percent and unemployment higher than 30 percent. When the military promoted a referendum on a new constitution in 1980, 60 percent of the population rejected it.

Eventually the military allowed elections, returning governmental power to civilian rule in March 1985. In a second election in 1989, the opposition political party regained power, and the transfer of authority was smooth. Soon, political interest groups became active, press freedom was reestablished, and the independence of the judiciary was assured. Even the Tupamaros reemerged, not as a terrorist movement but as a political party championing the interests of the poor.

There is considerable optimism that Uruguay has returned to its earlier, democratic ways. It has been classified as a "free," liberal democracy by Freedom House (2003) since 1985 and now is in the very top group with scores equal to such countries as the United States and Canada. Its population of 3.3 million enjoy nearly universal literacy and good health care, and the society and economy have opened substantially as a consequence of Uruguay's membership in the regional free trade association (Mercosur). However, the military remains in the background, watching quietly for signs of disorder. The military vetoed the candidacy of the most popular presidential candidate in the 1994 election. And its security service continues extensive surveillance of key political and labor leaders as well as the media. The impacts of terrorism on democratic practice are still evident after nearly three decades.

Strategy 2: Revolution from above. The swift overthrow of the elite is the essence of the *revolution from above,* which has three key characteristics (Johnson 1983). First, activity is centered primarily on the urban capital. Second, some members of the existing political elite are usually supportive of the revolution and thus the existing political structures have been infiltrated by those who intend to create a new political system. Third, it enjoys toleration or support by the armed forces.

In this form of revolution, the old regime is eliminated in a few minutes or a few days. The revolutionaries might storm the leader's residence and capture or execute key figures of the old regime. Sometimes the revolutionary group takes control while the leader is away from the capital on business or pleasure. In either case, the new leadership uses the media to declare the elimination of the old leadership and the creation of a new political order, and then it proceeds to create new political institutions. Finally, the new political system slowly penetrates into the hinterlands outside the capital city.

Historically, many revolutions most closely resemble the revolution from above. The Russian Revolution is an example, although the armed forces did not acquiesce to the change. This led to Trotsky's observation that if the forces of coercion are split, there will be civil war rather than a decisive revolutionary victory. Other twentieth-century examples include Gamal Abdel Nasser's replacement of King Farouk in Egypt (1952), Muammar Qaddafi's victory over King Idris in Libya (1969), the execution of communist Premier Nicholae Ceauçescu in Romania (1989), and the flight of socialist leaders Mengistu Mariam in Ethiopia and Said Barre in Somalia (1991).

Strategy 3: Guerrilla war. The strategy of revolutionary guerrilla warfare has been highly refined in the twentieth century, especially during the Chinese Revolution (victory in 1949). Guerrilla war contrasts with the revolution-from-above strategy in four crucial ways. First and most important, the essence of **guerrilla war** is *a long, protracted campaign of political violence against the state from rural bases,* although the fighting can be in both rural and urban areas. Second, it is a direct struggle against the military. The strategy, rather like that followed by the boxer Muhammad Ali in his youth, is to "float like a butterfly and sting like a bee." The guerrilla's forces persistently harass the regime's army by fighting in a hit-and-run style, suddenly attacking an exposed point and then literally disappearing into the population and the countryside.

Third, there is an extensive and continuing effort to win the support of the peasants, mixing two techniques: (1) propaganda—promises of land reform and exhortations for resistance against domestic traitors and foreign invaders, and (2) terror—disrupting the village stability, eliminating local leaders loyal to the government, demanding food and shelter, and dragooning locals into the guerrilla army. China's Mao Zedong observed that if he had ten points to give for success in the revolution, he would award three points to the urban dwellers and the military and seven to the peasants, for "without the poor peasants, there can be no revolution."

Fourth, guerrilla warfare creates new political institutions *prior* to the collapse of the old regime. Ultimately, the guerrilla army defeats the regime's military and marches victoriously into the capital city, the previous leadership having fled or been killed. The leadership and political institutions developed in the countryside are empowered in the urban capital.

Many of the successful Third World revolutions in the last fifty years have employed guerrilla warfare, including Cuba under Fidel Castro (1959), Vietnam under Ho Chi Minh and his successors (1975), Zimbabwe (formerly Rhodesia) under Robert Mugabe (1980), and Nicaragua under the Sandinistas (1979). It is evident in recent struggles in Afghanistan, Algeria, Colombia, and Congo. Guerrilla war directly contradicts two key principles of the Marxist-Leninist-Trotskyist conception of revolution. First, it undermines the principle that revolution emanates from the urban proletariat. Second, it rejects the view that revolution cannot be made against the elite's armed forces.

Strategy 4: "Democratic" revolution. There is also a strategy for *democratic revolutionary change.* In this case, legal, nonviolent political action is effectively mounted to achieve a fundamental transformation of the political system. In one form, the population uses the democratic electoral process to select a new leadership elite, which then dismantles the existing political system and creates a new one. This form describes the rise of Hitler and the establishment of the Third Reich in Germany (1933), the election of Salvador Allende's Marxist government in Chile (1970), and the election of the anti-Sandinista coalition in Nicaragua (1990).

In a second form of democratic revolution, widespread but generally nonviolent resistance to a regime forces the elite to resign. The new leadership, although not initially elected, implements fundamental transformations in the political system. This occurred in such Soviet bloc states as Czechoslovakia, East Germany, and Poland in the late 1980s. When Soviet leader Gorbachev indicated that the Soviet Union would no longer support unpopular leaderships, citizens in these states participated in mass demonstrations against the existing communist governments. With a minimum of violence, the regimes rapidly collapsed, and the repressive, one-party communist states were replaced by more democratic, multiparty systems. (The revolutions in Central and Eastern Europe are discussed further in Chapter 15.)

The conditions for revolution. The conditions under which political revolution occurs is an issue that has fascinated many people, especially those who want to analyze revolution and those who want to lead a successful revolution. The most widely cited studies of major historical revolutions include those by Hannah Arendt (1963), Crane Brinton (1957), Chalmers Johnson (1983), Barrington Moore (1966), and Theda Skocpol (1979). The revolutions in postcolonial states are analyzed in works by Joel Migdahl (1974) and Eric Wolf (1969).

One long-standing explanation of revolution is the "theory of rising expectations," associated with Alexis de Tocqueville (1835/1945), James Davies (1971), and others. In this view, the key cause of revolution is a sudden growth in the disparity between the values that the population expects to enjoy from the government and the actual value distribution the population receives. Contemporary research calls this the "J-curve" theory because, as is indicated in Figure 12.2, the disparity resembles an inverted J. At the point where this gap between expected and actual values becomes substantial, political violence emerges and can escalate into rebellion and then revolution. Although this explanation is intuitively appealing, most scholars find the empirical research testing the J-curve to be unconvincing. In particular, it has been difficult to establish the size of the gap that provokes revolutionary violence, and the approach does not specify which or how economic, social, and political conditions are crucial.

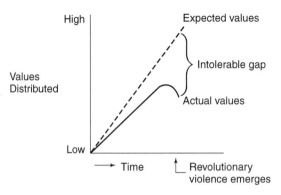

FIGURE 12.2   "J-curve" description of revolution
Source: Derived from Davies 1971.

Although the various theories of revolution present evident differences in the specific causes and dynamic process, most theories of contemporary revolutions share certain commonalities (Hagopian 1984: ch. 6). First, the state has experienced *broad, destabilizing forces* that have affected the culture, the economy, or the political system. These might include the decline of traditional social and religious values, the emergence of a modern state, a transformation of the economic system, social mobilization (recall Chapter 10), or the global expansion of capitalism into a world economic system. Second, there are more *direct and immediate forces of disruption,* such as violent conflict with another state, major economic decline, serious financial problems for the state, or incompetence or division within the ruling elite.

The outcome of revolution.   Since the ultimate objective of revolution is a fundamental transformation in the political system, an assessment of the outcomes of revolutions is at least as important as an analysis of causes and processes. Many scholars still distinguish the three postrevolutionary phases identified by Crane Brinton (1957), based on his extraordinary study of the French Revolution of 1789:

1. *Rule of the moderates.* After the revolution, the leadership group that comes to power attempts to fashion a new political order but not to use governmental power to transform drastically the social and economic system. Often the moderates are committed to increasing the democratic nature of politics in the society.

2. *Rule of the radicals.* The moderates are displaced by more ideological and aggressive political groups. These radical groups want to use political power to implement a far more extensive transformation of society, including greater centralization of political and economic power in the state. The radicals also direct substantial and continuing political violence against any groups who are viewed as obstacles to this transformation.

3. *Reaction and moderation.* At some point, a new set of moderates regains control from the radical groups. There are various reasons why the radicals might lose control: They might destroy each other through internal struggles over power or

ideology; the revolutionary violence might become so extreme that there is insufficient popular support to sustain the radicals; or the new entrenched elite might begin to enjoy the privileges associated with power and lose its revolutionary fervor. At this point, the "old regime" is dead, but the resulting political system is far less extreme than that during the rule of the radicals.

Brinton's three-phase model does not fit most revolutions in the post–World War II world. First, in many recent revolutions, initial rule by moderates is either fleeting or nonexistent. The groups who seize power after many of the revolutionary guerrilla wars in peasant societies are committed to move quickly into a phase that resembles the rule by radicals. This was certainly true in such postrevolutionary states as Cambodia, China, Cuba, and Vietnam. Extremist groups have also taken immediate control in many countries where religious fundamentalist groups seized power, as in Afghanistan, Libya, and the Sudan.

Second, in many states, the third-phase shift to moderation either is limited or emerges only very gradually. Rather, the new society forged during the radical phase is institutionalized, at least for as long as the revolutionary leadership remains in power. Sometimes there is an alternation between periods of significant revisionism and renewed radicalism. Fidel Castro reveals the persistent commitment to radicalism of most such leaders with his 1992 comment: "The revolution is like a bicycle; it has brakes but no reverse." However, once the initial radical leadership dies or is replaced, moderate leadership does seem to emerge in many post–cold war states, as occurred in China, Iran, Mozambique, and Vietnam. In an era of expanding democratization, the key question is whether a transformation to more democratic and moderate politics will follow phase three.

Use of Force between States

The final box in Figure 12.1 includes those cases where both the source and target of violence are states. While this form is primarily referred to as a war (discussed in the next section), in some situations the use of violence between states is more limited (Gochman and Maoz 1984):

In a *blockade*, the military (e.g., ships, troops, munitions) of one state is used to seal off territory (e.g., border crossings, harbors), preventing entry or exit by the rival state.

In *state-sponsored terrorism*, the state provides financial or material support to groups committing occasional acts of political violence within the rival state.

A state can engage in a brief, *single use of force*, such as a bombing raid, firing of munitions into the enemy state, or rapid invasion for a specific purpose (e.g., the sabotage of a facility).

In a *clash*, there is a brief engagement between the armed forces of two states, as in a border skirmish.

In a *low-intensity conflict (LIC)*, a group uses conventional weapons in a rival's territory in a sporadic and prolonged manner that does not involve full-scale military conflict, with the goal of inflicting maximum harm while suffering few or no casualties (Klare 1988). This concept is also applied to situations in which a government or a powerful external state directs persistent uses of violent force against groups resisting the government, such as ethnonationalists or guerrillas. The source of violence can be regular military units, paramilitary groups, or mercenaries. Despite the label, the violence associated with low-intensity conflict *is* intense for those involved, especially the targets.

War

War is *interstate violence that is sustained and organized* and (usually) involves hostilities *between the regular military forces of the states*. Such violence is the ultimate mechanism for resolving conflict between states. For those who define politics as conflict resolution, war represents the utter failure of politics. But many probably agree with Karl von Clausewitz's (1833/1967: 87) famous dictum, "War is regarded as nothing but a continuation of political activity by other means." Thus war is the use of violence by one state to achieve its political goals at the expense of another state.

Robert Ardrey (1966: 27), a well-known ethologist (a person who studies animal behavior to better understand human behavior), wryly observed that "human war has been the most successful of all our cultural traditions." Indeed, the study of world history is usually dominated by wars and recurrent episodes of organized violence among nations and states.

The elimination of war is not among the accomplishments of the modern world. The comprehensive analysis of major interstate wars between 1816 and 1980 found

With his machine gun and teddy bear backpack, this Liberian preteen is among the world's rapidly growing number of child soldiers.

good news: Wars are less frequent, are considerably shorter, and involve fewer states. But the bad news is that the number of wars "in progress" at any given time has increased substantially since 1900, and the total number of war deaths has risen astronomically (Singer 1991; Sivard 1996). Moreover, the post–cold war context has not significantly reduced the number of major armed conflicts. Since 1990, more than half of the world's countries have suffered the enormous costs of a major armed conflict (SIPRI 2003: Appendix 1A; Smith 1997).

Few of the major recent conflicts are *conventional wars*—that is, wars that entail the direct, sustained confrontation of the military forces of two or more states within a defined space, usually occurring on the soil of one of the combatants. Conflicts that do fit the definition of a conventional war include the Argentina–United Kingdom War (Falklands War, 1982), the Iran–Iraq War (1980–1988), the Iraq–Kuwait War (Persian Gulf War, 1990), the Ecuador–Peru War (1995), the Ethiopia–Eritrea War (1998–2000), and the Iraq–U.S.(-led coalition) War of 2003.

Many contemporary conflicts are more complicated mixes of internal regional and transborder combatants. Africa's first "world war" in Congo (Box 11.3) seems a prototype of the contemporary unconventional war. At one level, it is an internal, civil war between the military forces loyal to President Kabila and several large, paramilitary groups who reject his authority to rule. Some of the cleavages underlying the conflict are regional, some are ethnonationalist, and some are merely based on personal animosity and ambition in a situation where no one has a legitimate mandate to rule. But the conflict increasingly includes many non-Congolese combatants—ethnically based paramilitaries from Rwanda and Burundi; regular military forces from Angola, Namibia, Rwanda, Uganda, and Zimbabwe; and the United Nations peacekeeping forces. Another striking example of these complex "wars" is the bloody conflict in Israel and Palestine, where all forms of political violence collide (see Box 12.3).

BOX 12.3

Ultra-Violence among the Children of Abraham: Israelis and Palestinians

Both groups share a common understanding of their beginnings, yet they split into two nations whose recent history is marked by ultra-violence. Perhaps more than anywhere in the world, virtually every type of political violence in Figure 12.1 occurs with depressing regularity. Helicopter gunships fire missiles at cars to assassinate leaders, suicide bombers kill and maim scores of innocents, bulldozers destroy neighborhoods of homes, bloody wars wreak havoc in several countries. How did things get so bad?

According to legend, the patriarch Abraham settled in and was eventually buried in the land of Canaan, near what is now Hebron, Israel, in about 2000 B.C.E. Abraham developed the foundational principles of a new religion, Judaism. Of his

(continued)

BOX **12.3** (CONTINUED)

two wives, the offspring of one line of descendents (son Isaac and grandson Israel) followed this new religion. The line descending from Abraham's other wife continued to live in the area and did not embrace Judaism. The teachings of Mohammed (born in Mecca in 570 C.E.) attracted most of this line to another new religion, Islam. Arab military conquests in the seventh to tenth centuries added to the near-total religious domination of Islam in the region.

Although "the Children of Israel" (the Jews) did live in the Canaan area from about 1300 to 700 B.C.E., before that date and after that date until the twentieth century, most of the Jews migrated to many countries. Almost everywhere, the Jews felt themselves to be a target of discrimination, and described themselves as part of a wandering and dispersed ("diaspora") nation with no homeland. Thus in 1897, European Jewish leaders founded the World Zionist Movement, whose central goal was to realize the ancient dream of a Jewish homeland and a sanctuary from anti-Semitism. After a debate in which various locations in Europe, Africa, Latin America, and the Near East were considered, the Zionists concluded that their target for a homeland was the Promised Land of Abraham's birth—now called Palestine. They began purchasing land and establishing colonies of Jewish settlers in Palestine. By the outbreak of World War I (1914), they owned 100,000 acres and 70,000 Jews had migrated to Palestine, living alongside more than eight hundred thousand Arab Muslims (Table 12.3).

After the war, the United Kingdom was given a mandate to govern Palestine. Under pressure from European Jews, the British government agreed that it would assist the Jews in establishing a Jewish "home" in Palestine. As discrimination against the Jews in Europe reached horrendous levels with the rise of Nazism, the flow of Jewish immigrants to Palestine became a flood. By the outbreak of World War II, the number of Jews had increased almost sixfold.

The Muslim Arabs in the Palestine area were increasingly distressed by this massive invasion of Jewish "foreigners." This hostility provoked violence, terrorism, and guerrilla war between extreme groups of Arabs and Jews, as well as against the British occupying army. The recently founded United Nations proposed a plan to split Palestine into two states, maintaining Jerusalem as a shared city under UN trusteeship. While the Jews accepted this plan in 1947, the Arabs rejected it, angry that the invaders, who constituted only one-third of the population, would receive the majority (55 percent) of the land. Two hours before the British mandate in Palestine was to end in 1947, the Jewish leaders declared the founding of a new sovereign state, Israel. The next day, the armies of all the surrounding Arab states, Egypt, Transjordan, Syria, and Lebanon, declared war on Israel. The defeat of these armies by the Israeli Army resulted in 800,000 homeless Palestinians, many of whom fled to the neighboring lands.

Full-scale war erupted three more times between Israel and its Arab neighbors (1956, 1967, and 1973). In each case, Israel defeated the Arab armies and conquered more land, the "Occupied Territories" (especially the West Bank and Gaza Strip). By the late 1960s, these territories were inhabited by 1.2 million Palestinians, who were now an unwelcome nation subjugated within the Israeli state. More than one million additional Palestinians were exiles living in Jordan and other Arab states.

BOX **12.3** (CONTINUED)

Moreover, there was continual expansion of Jewish settlements, new outposts of Jewish control over the best land in the Occupied Territories.

Frustrated Palestinians formed many active resistance groups, most notably the Palestine Liberation Organization (1964) and Hamas (1987). These groups were convinced that only political violence and the destruction of the state of Israel would allow them to regain control of their lands. The combination of civil disobedience, armed resistance, and terrorist acts by Palestinian groups on the one hand, and the strong and often brutal responses by the Israeli military and Jewish militant groups on the other hand, have resulted in an endless cycle of violence and retaliation. The more militant groups on each side assume that there are no innocents in the struggle and are willing to engage in "whatever means necessary" to protect their land.

The United States, the United Nations, and others have attempted to find an approach that produces stability and peace in the region, but all agreements have collapsed. The UN is committed to a sovereign Palestinian state that will coexist with Israel, some Palestinian groups have renounced terrorism and accept the continued existence of Israel, and some Israelis agree that there should be Palestinian self-rule in a fixed territory; but there is continuing, horrific violence, due to the fundamental distrust and antagonism between some Israelis and Palestinians.

Beneath this basic story-line there are extraordinarily complex subplots. There are factional struggles within each nation, disagreements about the level of acceptable compromise, and the complicated agendas of external actors (e.g., other Arab states, the U.S., MNCs) regarding Islam, oil, international terrorism, and so on. The land of Abraham has become the cauldron in which this volatile stew of violence boils furiously.

TABLE 12.3
Population in Palestine/Israel at Key Dates

Date	Arabs	Israelis
1914	800,000	70,000
1937	900,000	400,000
1947	1,200,000	570,000
1993*	2,825,000	3,960,000
2004*	4,025,000	5,275,000

*Includes the West Bank and Gaza Strip

The changing nature of many contemporary wars is most evident in the enormous increase in the proportion of civilian deaths. Whereas in World War I there was only one civilian death for every eight military deaths, in World War II there were two civilian deaths for every military death. In the 1990s, nine out of every ten war deaths were *civilians,* and the wars going on since 1990 have been killing more than half a million civilians each year (Sivard 1996: 7, 17). Even more distressing is the huge increase in the total number of deaths in war. Ruth Leger Sivard (1991: 20) notes: "The twentieth century in particular has been a stand-out in the history of warfare. Wars now are shockingly more destructive and deadly. So far, in the 90 years of this century, there have been over four times as many war deaths as in the 400 years preceding."

Worldwide, the more than $850 billion per year that states spend to support their security objectives could, if redirected to their prosperity goals, greatly enhance their citizens' quality of life (SIPRI 2003). The problem, of course, is that the policy makers believe that security goals have highest priority and that security is the *sine qua non* for fulfilling prosperity goals. And in an era of high-tech warfare, virtually no one feels truly secure. This insecurity leads every state to push itself and its rivals into an accelerating, unending, and potentially devastating expansion of the capacity for massive political violence (recall the discussion of balance of power in Chapter 11).

What Causes War?

Are there fundamental causes of war? Studies have attempted to determine whether some states or their populations have particular attributes that result in a greater propensity to engage in war. These attributes include the state's size, its economic system, its political system, its cultural features, its geographic position, its wealth, its religion, and its rate of modernization. Although studies have attempted to isolate the key characteristics of more "warlike" states, the findings of such analyses are inconclusive, and there are always unique contingencies associated with particular wars. However, empirical research does suggest seven state characteristics that are generally correlated with the likelihood of war (Kegley and Wittkopf 2004: 411–418):

1. *Newer nations* are more likely to initiate war than are mature states.
2. War is more likely in states that have effectively *socialized their citizens to accept the government's actions* on national security.
3. The most warlike states have *rising prosperity* yet are *relatively poor,* though they are not the very poorest states.
4. Countries with *desirable geopolitical features* (i.e., resources and location—recall Chapter 11) have higher probablility of warfare.
5. Countries *less well linked to the global economy* are more likely to engage in war.
6. States that are most *highly militarized,* and especially those that are rapidly expanding their military power, are more warlike.
7. Countries whose political culture reflects a high degree of *nationalism* are more warlike.

- Countries with market economies are as likely to participate in war as those with command economies.
- Democracies are as likely as nondemocracies to be involved in war.

The contemporary global system has created conditions that make many analysts (particularly those with the political idealist perspective described in Chapter 11) particularly optimistic that war between the most powerful countries is highly unlikely. They emphasize two major forces that limit the likelihood of such wars: (1) democracy has spread to many major countries, and democracies rarely fight each other (the "democratic peace"), and (2) globalization has increased countries' economic interdependence and the importance of transnational organizations, both of which cause countries to recognize their shared interests and create strong inducements for cooperation (Jervis 2002; Russett and Oneal 2001). However, realists point to the many significant interstate conflicts that continue, and they postulate that the dominance of a single great power (the United States) will ultimately unravel, resulting in major conflict between it and rising powers (Mearshimer 2001).

Another way in which various states' propensity for war is examined empirically is to compute the number of times that a state has engaged in such conflicts. Do you think some states have a more extensive history of interstate conflict than others? Box 12.4 challenges you to answer this question and then provides relevant data.

 # BOX 12.4

Top Ten List: States That Are Bad!

Some people seem especially prone to getting into fights while others seem able to avoid conflict completely. There seem to be similar differences among states. What states do you think have been most likely, over a long period of their history, to get into violent disputes with other states? Before you look at the list below, make some informed guesses about which states are in the "top ten."

One study by Gochman and Maoz (1984) analyzed the frequency with which countries engaged in interstate conflict between 1816 and 1976. Their analysis focused on 14 types of "militarized interstate disputes" including the threats of force, displays of force, and uses of force described earlier in this chapter. A state is considered to be in a dispute whether it is the initiator or the target of the conflict. Since some countries have considerably longer histories as states, the analysis measured disputes per year of the state's existence.

So who are the most dispute-prone states? Rated from highest to lowest, the top ten are:

1. Israel (1.55 disputes per year)
2. United Kingdom (1.12)
3. India (1.07)
4. United States (.99)
5. Pakistan (.90)
6. Germany (.82)
7. Russia/Soviet Union (.82)
8. France (.80)
9. China (.60)
10. Italy (.50)

Are you surprised by the composition of the top ten? Do you notice any pattern or commonalities among these states? Many inferences have been made from

(continued)

BOX **12.4** (CONTINUED)

analyses of such data. First, a limited number of states engage in most of the disputes. Of more than a hundred states in the analyses, 30 initiated more than 70 percent of all disputes and were the primary targets of more than 60 percent of the disputes. Second, major powers in the international system are, in general, far more dispute prone than minor states. However, the postcolonial, middle-power states of Israel, India, and Pakistan also have very high levels of disputes. Third, among these ten most dispute-prone states, nine (except Pakistan) are more frequently initiators of disputes than the targets of a dispute. And fourth, the states that most often initiate disputes are also the ones most likely to join ongoing disputes involving other countries.

In short, it is evident that some states are fighters and are far more likely than other states to be involved in interstate violence.

At the "ultimate" level, there are three broad alternative explanations for the causes of war:

1. War can be attributed to scarcity in *nature.* Because the consumption goals of states are greater than the natural resources available, states undertake war to protect or capture resources from other states. Thus states struggle with each other for the control of such resources as people, food, minerals, and strategic locations.

2. War can be attributed to the inadequacy of *institutions.* In this view, neither the existing sociopolitical structure nor the rules governing the conduct among states are adequate to prevent states from using force to achieve their objectives. Thus states are guided by self-interest, and there are no conflict resolution mechanisms that prevent the occasional explosion of large-scale interstate violence.

3. War can be explained by *human nature.* From this perspective, humans are innately aggressive as a biological species. Humans are virtually the only species that engages in widespread killing of its own kind. And humans, it is claimed, are acquisitive, competitive, and selfish by nature rather than by nurture. Thus war becomes a predictable group-level manifestation of these inherent qualities. A variation on this explanation emphasizes the critical importance of an aggressive leader who draws his country into war (Stoessinger 2005).

The first and second explanations are clearly associated with the idealist perspective outlined in Chapter 11. And the third reflects the essence of political realism. Each of the three explanations of war also suggests possible "solutions" that might eliminate war:

1. If the problem is scarcity of natural resources, one might look to *technological solutions,* as states develop new techniques for more efficient exploitation of natural resources and for the development of substitutes for scarce resources.

2. If the problem is inadequate institutions, the need is for *social engineering*—for the creation of organizational arrangements that more effectively structure the relations among individuals and states. In the political domain, this might ultimately entail the creation of a viable world government.

3. If the problem is human nature, the solution is found in *human engineering* by means of comprehensive political socialization or perhaps even genetic manipulation to create a population with the "proper" qualities.

There is some evidence in support of each of these three general explanations of the causes of war. But there is also sufficient counterevidence so that none of the three positions is compelling as a complete explanation. Neither abundance of natural resources nor advanced technology has ensured the absence of intergroup violence. And while there are societies whose members have not been driven by human nature into warlike behavior against their neighbors, no set of human institutions has been shown inevitably to generate war or perpetuate peace between states.

While the complete elimination of war might be impossible, it does seem that a combination of material abundance, effective institutions, and thorough socialization might reduce the incidence of war. This leads to more questions: Can this combination be identified and implemented by political actors? Might the solution not produce human conditions nearly as unpalatable as occasional wars?

EVALUATING POLITICAL VIOLENCE: MEANS AND ENDS

Political violence must be understood as a failure of institutionalized political action. A strong and persuasive normative perspective contends that political violence is unacceptable, deviant behavior. Conservative ideology provides the most explicit condemnation of such violence, concluding that the only legacy of violence is to undermine order in the society. Moreover, the resort to violence is part of an erroneous belief that radical social change can lead to lasting improvements. As Englishman Edmund Burke (1729–1797) observed: "Time is required to produce that union of minds which alone can produce all the good we aim at. Our patience will achieve more than our force" (Burke 1790/1955: 197).

A contrary perspective argues that political violence is often the best or even the only mechanism for liberation from oppression and tyranny. This view contends that most societies are controlled by dominant elites who manipulate the state to serve their interests, not the collective good. If a government and its leaders refuse to be constrained by a limited mandate and are not responsive to the citizens, then the people have the right to overthrow them by any available means. Although this perspective is mainly associated with class theorists and Marxist ideology, the counterpoint to Burke is provided by another English political thinker, classical liberal John Locke (1632–1704), who argued that citizens create government to protect their rights to life, liberty, and property. If the existing government does not serve these purposes well, argued Locke, the people can and must revolt in order to replace tyranny and create a new and better government (Locke 1690/1963: 466).

Political violence can be either a source of progress or a source of nearly universal suffering and chaos. Clearly, there are fundamental issues about means and ends tied up with any assessment of political violence. On the one hand, if the maintenance of public order and political institutionalization are valued goals, you must consider whether the resort to political violence undermines longer-term prospects for peaceful, orderly governance. Many cynics would share Italian novelist Ignazio Silone's (1937) assessment: "Every revolution begins as a movement of liberation but ends as tyranny." On the other hand, if you value social and political justice, it is important to consider whether the processes of political violence can be a legitimate means of last resort to ensure such justice. Those who justify some forms of political violence might sympathize with African-American Eldridge Cleaver's claim that "a slave who dies of natural causes will not balance two dead flies on the scale of eternity."

There are no tidy answers to the question of whether or when political violence is justifiable. Perhaps one way to organize your own assessment of political violence is to reflect on three basic questions:

1. Are the means of political violence unacceptable under *every* possible circumstance?

2. If you answered no, could an outcome emerge from the use of political violence that is so preferable to the existing situation that establishing the precedent of using political violence is justifiable?

3. If you answered yes to question 2, what specific circumstances would be necessary to justify the resort to political violence?

These issues about the conditions under which political violence might be legitimate are germane on an even larger scale regarding the justification of war. Despite the massive human and financial costs of war, few would support the proposition that there are absolutely no conditions under which war is justified. But what are the circumstances that justify war?

A classic justification is the doctrine of *self-defense,* a position associated with St. Augustine (354–430 C.E.). A victim of an unprovoked attack has the right to use violence as a means of protection. Apart from total pacifists, there are few who would reject the principle of self-defense as a legitimate rationale for violence. But the application of this principle might be subject to considerable disagreement, especially in the relations among states. Here are some examples: Might state A engage in nonviolent actions that are so provocative that state B is justified in responding with violence? What if the initial violence against state B is by an actor from state A who does not have the sanction or the explicit support of state A? What if the violence by state A was unintentional? What if the initial violence is within the territory of state A but is perceived as directly harmful to citizens or interests of state B? What if state B uses violence to prevent state A from the (expected) use of far more substantial violence? What if the violent response of state B is of far greater magnitude than the violence by state A? Wars sometimes develop because there are such patterns of misperception, accident, preemption, and incremental escalation (Schelling 1960).

Frequently, however, war is justified on the more ambiguous rationale, associated with St. Ambrose (339–397 C.E.), as the *defense of universal principles.* In this view, "man has a moral duty to employ force to resist active wickedness, for to refrain from hindering evil when possible is tantamount to promoting it." In the contemporary world, however, it is difficult to identify truly universal principles in whose defense war is always justifiable. Even the interpretations of "active wickedness" and "evil" are not shared across all cultures. For example, many citizens in most countries were persuaded that Iraq's Saddam Hussein was an evil ruler. However, most did not find this an adequate justification for U.S. President Bush's insistence on a "pre-emptive" war, especially in the absence of compelling evidence that Iraq endangered other countries with weapons of mass destruction that could not be eliminated except by war.

In most cases of international political violence, a justification based on universal principles is invoked. State power is used against other states in the name of many principles, such as freedom, social justice, human rights, self-determination, territorial integrity, egalitarianism, religious freedom, religious orthodoxy, anticommunism, communism, and so on. But all states do not accept a single vision of natural law that provides universal principles to govern international relations. Moreover, the international system itself has not implemented powerful and effective institutional mechanisms that eliminate conflict. Thus occasional outbreaks of interstate conflict and war are inevitable.

The crucial point is that the context of international politics is essentially *amoral*. Recognition of this fact is the key to understanding most behavior in international relations, whether diplomatic activities, alliances, or war. In some instances, a state's actions in the international environment are constrained by *its* views of morality and universal principles. But in other instances, a state's decision makers might decide that virtually any action is acceptable if the action seems to further the state's achievement of its security, stability, and prosperity goals. If either view is correct, what are the chances that contemporary states will ever meet the requirement of the UN Charter that the states "settle their international disputes by peaceful means in such a manner that international peace and security, and justice, are not endangered"?

In the current technological era, the mechanisms for committing violence are more efficient, powerful, and horrifying than at any time in human history. The implications of this fact are especially evident in the relations between states. But even subnational political groups can now inflict massive and destructive political violence. Thus, questions about the use of force and the balance between liberation and destruction are more pressing now than at any time in human history.

KEY CONCEPTS

civil war
class conflict
coup
democratic revolution
establishment violence
ethnonationalism
genocide
guerrilla war
J-curve theory
low-intensity conflict
nation-based violence

political society
political violence
rebellion
revolution
riot
separatist violence
state-sponsored terrorism
terrorism
violence
war

FOR FURTHER CONSIDERATION

1. Is the state more to be feared than its enemies? Assess the implications of the predominance during the twentieth century of "death by government" in which the state is the actor and the state's citizens are its target.

2. Summarize the key elements of a three-way debate between an absolute pacifist, a committed revolutionary, and yourself regarding the conditions under which political violence is justifiable.

3. It is suggested that much of the contemporary political violence is nation based. Analyze the nation-based conflicts about which you have some awareness. Is most of the violence caused by fundamental antipathy between two nationality groups due to differences in ethnicity, religion, language, and so on? Or is the violence primarily motivated by other issues, such as inequality and class conflict, quest for power, geopolitics, or some other cause?

4. Must every revolution end in tyranny (á la Ignazio Silone)? Can you identify a revolution that, by the criteria you establish, can be viewed as a success?

5. Which of Kegley and Wittkopf's (2004) seven characteristics of warlike states is most surprising to you? Why? What characteristic did you expect but is not among those listed?

FOR FURTHER READING

Aguila, Juan D. del. (1988). *Cuba: Dilemmas of a Revolution.* Boulder, CO: Westview Press. Pessimistic observations of a famous revolution by a former minister of the Castro government, now an exile.

Brecher, Michael, and Jonathan Wilkenfeld. (1997). *A Study of Crisis.* Ann Arbor: University of Michigan Press. A comprehensive, usable database from the International Crisis Behavior project provides valuable information on 412 crises between 1929 and 1992, following the authors' thoughtful analyses of and generalizations about the patterns of interstate crises.

Cimbala, Stephen. (2000). *Nuclear Strategy in the Twenty-first Century.* Westport, CT: Praeger. A provocative analysis of the implications of nuclear proliferation and high technology warfare on the relations among states. Among other arguments, Cimbala explains why the danger of nuclear war is increasing and why weaker states and marginal groups are gaining greater advantage from nuclear weapons than the major powers in the nuclear club.

Cinema of War. Film has often been a compelling visual and visceral medium for evoking the heroism and absurdity of war. Among the films that are especially effective are: John Agar, *The Sands of Iwo Jima* (1949); Francis Ford Coppola, *Apocalypse Now* (1979; reissued in 2001 as *Apocalypse Now Redux*); Samuel Fuller, *The Big Red One* (1980); David Lean, *In Which We Serve* (1942); Lewis Milestone, *All Quiet on the Western Front* (1930) and *Pork Chop Hill* (1959); Jean Renoir, *The Grand Illusion* (1937); and Oliver Stone, *Platoon* (1986).

Freedman, Lawrence, Ed. (1994). *War.* New York: Oxford University Press. A splendid collection of readings, ranging from the greatest classical treatments of the reasons for and the nature of war to significant contemporary analyses.

Goldstein, Joshua S. (2001). *War and Gender: How Gender Shapes the War System and Vice Versa.* Cambridge, U.K.: Cambridge University Press. This widely discussed book explores why warfare is dominated by males, concluding generally that it is primarily due to culturally constructed male domination and "militarized masculine stereotypes" rather than genetic differences.

Goldstone, Jack A., Ed. (1994). *Revolutions: Theoretical, Comparative and Historical Studies.* 2d ed. San Diego, CA: Harcourt Brace. A readable set of articles that includes both detailed case studies of revolutions and more analytic work that attempts to develop generalizations about revolutionary violence.

Gourevitch, Philip. (1998). *We Wish to Inform You That Tomorrow We Will Be Killed with Our Families: Stories from Rwanda.* New York: Farrar & Giroux. A gripping exploration of the manner in which ethnonationalist rhetoric was used to mobilize the Hutu people to massacre almost one million Tutsis and Hutu moderates in Rwanda in the mid-1990s, while the international community was unwilling to intervene to prevent the genocide.

Gurr, Ted Robert. (2000). *Peoples Versus States: Minorities at Risk in the New Century.* Washington, D.C.: United States Institute of Peace Press. Based on the valuable Minorities at Risk Project database, the book is an exceptionally rich blend of data-based analyses and case studies of ethnopolitical conflict.

Gutman, Roy, and David Rieff, Eds. (1999). *Crimes of War: What the Public Should Know.* New York: W. W. Norton. Authorities on the laws of war and experienced members of the media offer diverse and enlightening discussions on the legal and ethical issues regarding war crimes and international humanitarian law, with powerful commentaries on such cases as Cambodia, Chechnya, and Rwanda, and dramatic illustrations by photojournalists.

Hoffman, Bruce. (1998). *Inside Terrorism.* New York: Columbia University Press. A broad-ranging and troubling exploration of terrorism, with particular attention to the recent evolution of strategies and goals of terrorists.

Jenkins, Philip. (2003). *Images of War: What We Can and Can't Know About Terrorism.* New York: Aldine de Gruyter. A fascinating array of examples is provided to examine how stories about terrorism are transformed in public discussion, especially by the media.

Klare, Michael. (2001). *Resource Wars.* New York: Henry Holt. A persuasive argument regarding the "new geography of conflict" between states in the early twenty-first century. Grounded in specifics from such areas as the Persian Gulf and the Nile Basin, Klare argues that wars will increasingly be driven primarily by geopolitical struggles over scarce natural resources, such as water, oil, gas, minerals, and timbers.

O'Brien, Tim. (1990). *The Things They Carried.* New York: Doubleday Broadway Books. In 22 fictional short stories about an American military platoon in the Vietnam War, the author powerfully conveys more universal themes regarding the horror of war from the perspective of the individual soldier.

Sassoon, Siegfried. (1968). *Collected Poems: 1908–1956.* London: Faber & Faber. The deeply moving poems about war by a young British intellectual who suffered the horrific experiences of European trench warfare during World War I.

SIPRI. Stockholm International Peace Research Institute. http://www.sipri.se. A revealing yearly discussion and assessment providing comparative data, for most states in the world, reflecting the current aspects of military expenditure, war, and arms control.

Small, Melvin, and J. David Singer. (1982). *Resort to Arms: International and Civil Wars, 1816–1980.* Beverly Hills, CA: Sage. Analyses of political violence based on the largest available data set on interstate conflict between 1816 and 1980, generated by a research group at the University of Michigan. See also J. David Singer and Melvin Small, *Wages of War, 1816–1965* (New York: Wiley, 1972).

Stoessinger, John G. (2005). *Why Nations Go to War.* 9th ed. Boston, MA: Bedford Press. A readable set of descriptive case studies of modern wars, particularly emphasizing individual behavior and motives, including World War I, Korea, Vietnam, India–Pakistan, Israel–Arabs, Iran–Iraq, and Yugoslavia.

Walter, Barbara F., and Jack Snyder, Eds. (1999). *Civil Wars, Insecurity, and Intervention.* New York: Columbia University Press. Centering on thoughtful case studies of the recent civil wars in Bosnia, Cambodia, Somalia, and Rwanda, important scholars analyze why the international community has not been particularly effective in either preventing the outbreak or achieving the resolution of civil wars.

Walzer, Michael. (1992). *Just and Unjust War.* 2d ed. New York: Basic Books. A political philosopher presents a careful argument about the morality of war, grounded in the context of numerous actual wars.

Weiss, Peter. (1965). *Marat-Sade: The Persecution and Assassination of Jean-Paul Marat as Performed by the Inmates of the Asylum at Charenton under the Direction of the Marquis de Sade.* New York: Atheneum. A brilliant play (and a dazzling film with the same title directed by Peter Brooks) offering a debate about revolution between Jean-Paul Marat, a leader of the French Revolution who attempts to retain his idealism about revolutionary change despite having become a victim of the "rule of radicals," and the Marquis de Sade, the ultimate cynic. Their debate occurs as a play-within-a-play in an asylum where both have been committed.

ON THE WEB

http://web.amnesty.org/report2003

Amnesty International is the world's leading NGO monitoring establishment violence and human rights abuses and attempting to mobilize citizen support to pressure governments to end such actions by governments.

http://nsi.org/Terrorism.html

The web site of the National Security Institute provides links regarding terrorism, including data and details of terrorist acts and policy and legislation regarding terrorism.

http://www.cfcsc.dnd.ca/links/wars/index.html

A clickable map and linked database from the Information Resource Centre of the Canadian Forces College provides links to numerous sites detailing every current major international conflict.

http://www.sipri.se

The site of the Stockholm International Peace Research Institute, which conducts research on questions of conflict and cooperation relevant to international peace and security, includes rich databases and significant articles on topics of peace and violence.

http://www.terrorism.com/

The site of the Terrorism Research Center, Inc., which describes itself as an independent institute dedicated to the research of terrorism, information warfare and security, critical infrastructure protection, homeland security, and other issues of low-intensity political violence.

http://usinfo.state.gov/topical/pol/terror/

The U.S. Department of State's Terrorism page provides a substantial amount of information regarding U.S. policies and programs related to political violence and terrorism.

http://www.un.org/terrorism/

On the official site of the United Nations, one can access both Security Council and General Assembly resolutions related to political violence.

http://www.hrw.org/

The electronic home of Human Rights Watch provides access to an extensive database regarding human rights violations taking place throughout the international community.

http://www.sfcg.org/

The site of Search for Common Ground, the world's largest NGO working on conflict resolution, is an excellent source for material on this topic.

http://www.historyguy.com/new_and_recent_conflicts.html

The electronic home of the "History Guy" provides a number of links to articles and news reports related to recent political conflicts.

http://www.pcr.uu.sc

The Conflict Data Project at Uppsala University (Sweden) maintains a rich and current database on armed conflicts in the world.

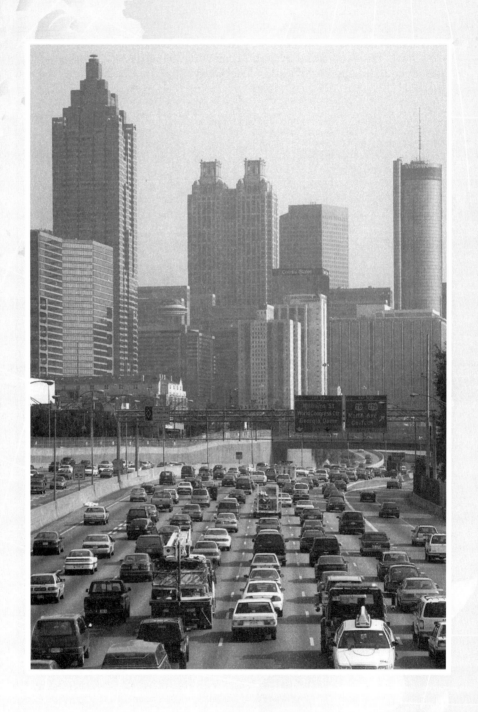

CHAPTER 13 The Developed Countries

AN INTRODUCTION TO THE NEXT THREE CHAPTERS: GROUPING THE STATES IN THE CONTEMPORARY WORLD

Chapters 13 through 15 aim at the near impossible: to characterize the key features of politics, both within and between the more than one hundred ninety countries in the contemporary political world. As you discovered in Part 1, a central goal of political analysis is to develop general descriptions and explanations of political phenomena. To generalize about all these countries, it is necessary to use a taxonomic system that allows discussion of a few groups that include most states.

Given the complexity and variations among states, however, no taxonomy is fully satisfactory. The situation is further complicated by the extensive and rapid transformations occurring in many states in the post–cold war world. In particular, the former Soviet Union and its East European allies have made dramatic efforts to alter fundamentally their economic and political systems. Certain other newly industrializing countries, especially in Asia and Latin America, are also undergoing especially rapid change.

Chapters 13 through 15 use a taxonomy that groups countries according to their level of development. One dimension of development is economic. But the broader issues of development discussed in Chapter 10 suggest a second dimension for the classification, based on a country's level of social development.

1. **Economic development.** The most conventional indicator of economic development measures the value of goods produced in a country, divided by the population of the country. Chapter 10 defined the two most widely used indicators, GDP per capita and GNP per capita. On the basis of GNP per capita, the World Bank (2004) distinguishes 29 major states (and 12 ministates) as "high-income countries," with GNP per capita greater than $9,076 per year; 88 "middle-income countries" (the MICs), with GNP per capita between $9,075 and $736; and 64 "low-income countries" (the LICs), with GNP per capita below $735. Figure 13.1 indicates that this book utilizes GDP/capita in purchasing power parity to measure relative levels of economic development.

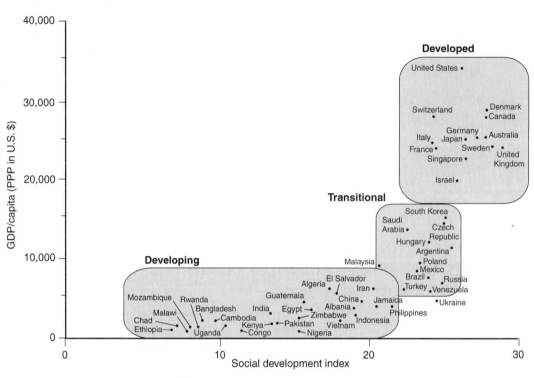

FIGURE 13.1   Classification of selected countries based on economic and social development

2. **Social development.** To enrich the classificatory scheme, this book employs a second dimension. It is grounded in the more subjective and less quantifiable dimensions of a country's level of development. Here the criteria are the extent to which the country is characterized by the types of organizational, technological, and attitudinal development discussed in Chapter 10. Every country is a mix of complex and simple organizational structures, high and low technologies, modern and traditional attitudes. But in relative terms, there are very substantial crossnational differences in countries' general levels on these social components of development, and it is these differences that constitute the second dimension of the taxonomy. The specific indicators in this index, which is scored from 0 to 30, measure the country's level of adult literacy, extent of urbanization, and average number of televisions per household. In the aggregate, these measures reflect some key underlying aspects of relative level of social development, as reflected in the pervasiveness of knowledge, urban lifestyles, and modern communications in the environment of the population. Figure 13.1 locates a selection of countries on the two dimensions and suggests labels for clusters of countries

The Developed Countries

The countries in the upper-right part of Figure 13.1 are among those usually referred to as the *developed countries;* they are also called the *"Global North"* and the *"First*

World." The developed countries group includes most of the countries with the highest levels of GDP per capita in the world, and these states are also relatively high on the social dimensions of development. They are generally urbanized and secularized countries, with highly specialized and institutionalized organizational systems. Their technological infrastructure is advanced, and most people are frequently and directly involved with advanced technologies of communications, transportation, and information. These developed countries are also sometimes referred to as (1) the *industrialized countries,* because of their large manufacturing sectors, or (2) the *postindustrial societies,* because of the growing dominance of the knowledge-based and service-based sectors of their economies.

The Developing Countries

Social scientists, political actors, and the media frequently refer to a large group of countries as the *developing countries*, a term used in this book to designate a set of more than one hundred and fifty countries. As you would expect, these countries have lower levels of economic development and are relatively less developed on the technological, organizational, and attitudinal dimensions than the developed countries. Thus in Figure 13.1, the developing countries are located on the lower half of the figure and are especially clustered in the lower-left quadrant.

In the late 1950s, many of these developing countries were also called the "*Third World.*" Initially, this term was applied in the context of the cold war to those states that, by their own definition, were "nonaligned": The country's leaders claimed their country was not under the domination of either the United States and its allies (the "First World") or the Soviet Union and its allies (the "Second World"). Others have used the term Third World even more broadly to refer to almost all countries other than the developed countries, those in the Soviet bloc, and a few newly industrializing countries. Currently, many commentators still refer to a large and loosely defined set of countries as the Third World; however, other analysts conclude that the concept is no longer a useful term in the post–cold war environment (Lewis 1999). Thus some scholars now refer to this group of countries as the "*Global South,*" because nearly all of them are located geographically south of the developed countries (in the "Global North"). The large cluster of countries explored in Chapter 14 as "the developing countries" is a diverse group and the states in this category, however defined, vary substantially. Chapter 14 will focus on this group and suggest other criteria by which it can be further categorized into subsets.

The Transitional Developed Countries

The developed countries and the developing countries are standard categories in analyses by governmental agencies and social scientists. But there are countries in Figure 13.1 that are along the boundaries between these two broad groupings and thus are particularly difficult to classify. At this time, the levels of economic and/or social development in these countries put them "in the middle." In this book, these countries-in-the-middle of Figure 13.1 are called *transitional countries* to reflect their middle range, and sometimes their high rate of change, on one or both dimensions of development.

While all the countries in the world are always in transition, Chapter 15 distinguishes and examines in detail the two subsets of transitional countries identified in Figure 13.1. Each of these subsets is made up of countries with some important commonalities regarding their economic situation and/or their political culture. These countries also face interesting challenges, and their approaches to achieving their goals are worth studying.

One subset is composed of most of the countries that emerged after the breakup of the Soviet Union as well as its former Eastern and Central European allies in the Warsaw Pact. This group of *post-communist developed countries (PCDCs)* includes such states as Belarus, Bulgaria, Estonia, Georgia, Hungary, Poland, Russia, the Slovak Republic, and the Ukraine. These states are high on most dimensions of social development, especially in the attitudinal and organizational domains, and most have moderately high (by world standards) levels of economic development. Most are engaged in attempts to transform their economic systems from command-oriented to market-based and their political systems toward democratization. The World Bank refers to them as the "transitional economies" (World Bank 2003).

The second group of transitional countries examined in Chapter 15 is termed the *newly industrializing countries,* because of the capacity of the economic systems. NICs have established strong, export-centered economies in which substantial value is added to goods during the production process. Most NICs are included in one of two subgroups with distinctive regional and political-cultural differences—East Asia (e.g., Malaysia, South Korea) and Latin America (e.g., Argentina, Brazil, Mexico). On the economic dimension and increasingly on the social dimension, the NICs are reaching levels of development that approach those of some of the developed countries. The successful development strategy of the leading Asian NICs has become a model for many developing countries (Chapter 10).

Thus Chapters 13 through 15 examine the developed countries, the developing countries, and the transitional countries. Each chapter describes critical issues for countries in these groups as they attempt to achieve the key goals of prosperity, stability, and security. General patterns and similarities within each group are emphasized; but you should recognize that:

- There are substantial differences among states within each group, especially among the large number of states lumped together as the developing countries.

- Each state has unique features that will be lost in such generalized discussion.

- In some instances, a trait is more similar among certain states across groups than among all the states within one group.

As these qualifications suggest, this method of grouping countries for analysis and generalizations is not perfect. Like any taxonomy (see the Appendix), there is an attempt to create groups that can be distinguished analytically, are based on some specifiable criteria, and seem to make sense. However, it is inevitable that not every country will fit neatly into a category. Classification can be especially difficult at the "edges" between groups. The categories proposed here are acceptable if their use provides clarification and insight and, ideally, if they facilitate the development of generalizations and theory. As a political analyst, it is appropriate for *you* to assess the utility of this taxonomy, relative to alternative ways of grouping countries for analysis. The remainder of Chapter 13 focuses explicitly on the developed countries.

IMAGES OF THE DEVELOPED COUNTRIES

When you think of countries in the developed world, what images come to mind?

Anyone reading this book has probably lived in at least one of the developed countries listed in Table 13.1. Among other things, you might envision large cities with tall buildings, extensive use of high technologies such as computers and cell phones, liberal democracies, an ethic of individualism, a generally high standard of living, quality medical care, rock and roll, and. . . .

What traits do *you* think best characterize life in the developed countries? As you come up with your own list, you might become aware of how difficult it is to capture complex reality with straightforward descriptors. The life of a poor farmer in rural Mississippi is different from that of a wealthy banker in Zurich, a housewife in a suburb of Yokohama, an unemployed factory worker in Milan, or a teenager in the Australian outback. This is a further reminder that the generalizations offered in these

TABLE 13.1
Classification of Countries

Classification	Countries		
Developed Countries	Australia	Iceland	New Zealand
	Austria	Ireland	Norway
	Belgium	Israel	Portugal
	Canada	Italy	Singapore[d]
	Denmark	Japan	Spain
	Finland	Liechtenstein	Sweden
	France	Luxembourg	Switzerland
	Germany	Monaco	United Kingdom
	Greece	Netherlands	United States
Post-Communist	Belarus	Hungary	Russia
Developed Countries	Bulgaria	Kazakhstan	Serbia/Yugoslavia
(PCDCs)	Croatia	Latvia	Slovak Republic
	Czech Republic	Lithuania	Slovenia
	Estonia	Poland	Ukraine[a]
	Georgia[a]	Romania	Uzbekistan[a]
Newly Industrializing	Argentina	Mauritius	Thailand[a]
Countries (NICs)	Brazil	Mexico	Turkey[a]
	Chile	South Africa	Uruguay
	Malaysia[a]	South Korea	Venezuela
	Malta	Taiwan	

(continued)

TABLE 13.1 (Continued)

Classification	Countries		
Developing Countries: "Third World"/"Global South"	Albania[b]	Ghana	Peru
	Algeria	Grenada	Philippines[d]
	Angola	Guatemala	Qatar[c]
	Antigua and Barbuda	Guyana	Saint Christopher-
	Armenia[b]	Honduras	Nevis
	Azerbaijan[b]	India[d]	Saint Lucia
	Bahamas	Indonesia[d]	Saint Vincent and the
	Bahrain[c]	Iran	Grenadines
	Barbados	Iraq	Saudi Arabia[c]
	Belize	Ivory Coast	Seychelles
	Bolivia	Jamaica	Sierra Leone
	Bosnia and Herzegovina[b]	Jordan	Solomon Islands
	Brunei	Kenya	Sri Lanka
	Cameroon	Kuwait[c]	Sudan
	China	Kyrgyzstan[b]	Suriname
	Colombia	Lebanon	Swaziland
	Congo Rep.	Libya[c]	Syria
	Costa Rica[d]	Marshall Islands	Tajikistan[d]
	Cuba	Micronesia	Trinidad and Tobago
	Cyprus	Moldova[d]	Tunisia
	Dominica	Morocco	Turkmenistan[d]
	Dominican Republic	Nicaragua	United Arab
	Ecuador	Nigeria	Emirates[c]
	Egypt	North Korea	Vietnam
	El Salvador	Oman[c]	Yemen
	Fiji	Pakistan	Zimbabwe
	Gabon	Panama	
Developing Countries: Fourth World[e]	Afghanistan	Dijibouti	Malawi
	Bangladesh	Equatorial Guinea	Maldives
	Benin	Eritrea	Mali
	Bhutan	Ethiopia	Mauritania
	Botswana	Gambia	Mongolia
	Burkina Faso	Guinea	Mozambique
	Burundi	Guinea-Bissau	Myanmar
	Cambodia	Haiti	Nepal
	Cape Verde	Kiribati	Niger
	Central African Republic	Laos	Rwanda
	Chad	Lesotho	Samoa
	Comoros	Liberia	São Tomé and
	Congo (Zaire)	Malagasy Republic	Principe

TABLE 13.1 (Continued)

Classification	Countries		
Developing Countries:	Senegal	Togo	Yemen
Fourth World[e](continued)	Sudan	Tuvalu	Zambia
	Somalia	Uganda	
	Tanzania	Vanuatu	

[a]This country is sometimes classified among the developing countries.
[b]This country is sometimes classified among the post-communist developed countries.
[c]This country has high wealth per capita.
[d]This country is sometimes classified among the NICs (newly industrializing countries).
[e]All of these countries could also be classified as Developing Country: Third World/Global South or Least Developed Countries.

chapters will, at best, capture broad tendencies that oversimplify the diversity of political situations. We begin with a brief discussion of political culture in the developed countries.

POLITICAL CULTURE

Each of the developed countries contains a variety of political (sub)cultures. While the political cultures vary across country and time, they can be characterized broadly in terms of the tension and balance between elements of the three ideologies outlined in Chapter 2: classical liberalism, conservatism, and democratic socialism.

Classical liberal ideology is the basis of the assertion by some individuals and groups in the developed countries that their governments have grown far too large and too interventionist. To promote greater individual and economic freedom, they believe their governments should reduce regulation of both the economy and of behavior in private life and should facilitate globalization.

Conservatism shares with classical liberalism an antagonism toward the extensive use of government taxing and spending policies to redistribute wealth in the direction of greater equality. But those influenced by conservatism do advocate a strong role for government in preserving the global preeminence of the developed countries through military strength and an assertive foreign policy, in supporting economic entrepreneurship, and in maintaining order within societies that seem increasingly disorderly. Conservatives also urge that government policies support the traditional family, religious, and moral values that they believe are being undermined by modern culture. For these reasons, conservatives are more uneasy with many of the impacts of globalization.

In contrast, those influenced by democratic socialism advocate an activist state that ensures that the substantial societal wealth of the developed country enhances the quality of life for all the citizens. Government policies should serve the goal that all citizens receive adequate education, health care, shelter, and security against economic hardship. And state policies should mitigate other negative effects of the developed countries' market-oriented political economies by taking the lead in providing social goods, such as environmental protection, and infrastructure needs, such as transportation systems. Democratic socialists are also concerned about preventing certain problematic impacts of globalization, particularly the declining economic standing of many classes of workers and the degradation of the environment, globally as well as in their own country.

Given the relatively free political expression allowed in the developed countries, there are strong and articulate advocates of each of these three ideologies as well as for an array of other ideologies such as environmentalism, fascism, feminism, and religious fundamentalism. The belief systems of most individuals and the collective political culture of each developed country are influenced by these ideologies, especially the three primary ones. As every developed country pursues the major political goals of prosperity, stability, and security, its policy decisions are influenced by the current ideological balance within its political leadership and its political culture as well as by such factors as its history, culture, economic situation, and distribution of political power. In most of the developed countries, the period from 1945 to the mid-1970s was characterized by relatively greater support for policies associated with democratic socialism; since then, the balance has shifted back and forth, but generally toward more conservative and classical liberal values.

By the late 1990s, some leaders, especially British Prime Minister Tony Blair and German Chancellor Gerhard Schroeder, were advocating a *third way*. This is an ideological blend of both classical liberalism and democratic socialism, and it advocates a reduced level of state intervention in the political economy, allowing

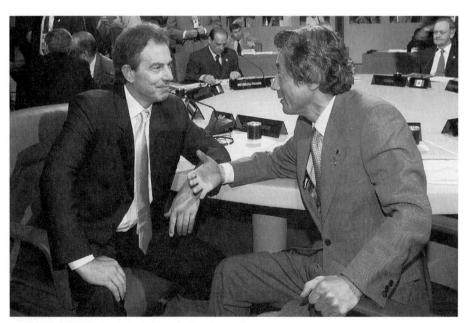

Talking heads: The Prime Ministers of the United Kingdom (Tony Blair) and Japan (Junichiro Koizumi) engage in personal diplomacy.

the market to dominate the system of production and distribution of goods. There is little enthusiasm for extensive social welfare programs by the government. Yet there is also a willingness to use public policy to prevent any groups from being marginalized in the society, to provide quality education and health care to all, to protect the environment, and to support humanitarian values internationally (Dahrendorf 1999).

GOAL: PROSPERITY

The developed countries pursue the goal of prosperity (and its components of economic development and welfare distribution) with great energy. The emphasis is on sustaining a high level of economic development under the assumption that this will generate an expanding economic base that directly provides more material benefits to the population and enables government to distribute greater welfare to the citizens.

Mixed Economy

To achieve prosperity, these countries have relied on a mixed political economy. There is considerable private ownership and control of productive resources (land, labor, and capital) and substantial freedom in their use. Private actors are encouraged to use their resources aggressively in order to acquire desired goods and resources, to produce goods, and to maximize their profit. Chapter 8 characterized the state's key roles in the mixed political economy: regulating the free market, providing guidance and incentives for production decisions, and redistributing some money and goods to the less advantaged individuals in the society.

A central policy debate in most of the developed countries is the appropriate level of state activity in the political economy. Should the state reduce the taxes and state regulation imposed on private actors under the assumption that the market economy is most likely to stimulate greater production and higher economic growth, benefiting all? Or should the state capture more of the surplus and then redistribute it as welfare to the poor and the underclass, who suffer most in an economic downturn? This choice is sometimes posed as "growth versus welfare."

There is considerable variation in the extent to which the free market dominates in the political economy of particular developed countries. One broad comparative measure of the public-private mix is the percentage of productive capacity (measured as GDP) that is in the public sector. Table 13.2 indicates that this varies substantially, from more than 50 percent in Sweden, Denmark, and Austria to only about 30 percent in the United States. The mixed political economy designation seems especially appropriate for countries in which public expenditure is about 40 percent or more of total GDP, including 10 of the 16 states in the table.

Mixed systems are evident in the Scandinavian states, the "Benelux" states (Belgium, the Netherlands, and Luxembourg), and many major West European countries. When political power is held by those oriented to social democratic ideology, taxation is more aggressive, and more revenue is reallocated either as transfer payments or as subsidized goods and services (e.g., health care, housing, educational and cultural opportunities) to the citizens. The state is also more active in protecting individuals and groups against firms whose actions are contrary to the public

TABLE 13.2
General Government Total Outlays Per Cent of Nominal GDP
in Selected Developed Countries

Country	Percentage of Nominal GDP (2001)
Sweden	52.2 %
Denmark	50.6
Austria	50.1
France	48.8
Italy	46.4
Germany	45.7
Finland	44.3
Greece	42.9
Netherlands	42.0
Norway	41.2
United Kingdom	38.3
Canada	38.0
Spain	37.5
Japan	36.7
Australia	32.7
United States	31.2

Source: Organization for Economic Cooperation and Development, *Economic Outlook No. 73* (June 2003): annex table 26.

interest (e.g., price fixing, unsafe working conditions, environmental degradation). In some of these social democracies, the public sector retains control or ownership of some major productive resources (e.g., energy, transportation) that have strategic importance for the political economy and the society. In the international marketplace, domestic producers and workers are protected from aggressive or "unfair" foreign competition by means of tariffs and quotas on imports and subsidies for domestic production and consumption. These mixed economies are sometimes called **social market systems** because the state encourages the operation of an extensive free-market economy but is also committed to social welfare distribution and income redistribution. The example of Sweden is presented in Box 13.1.

When the political elite is more committed to conservatism or classical liberalism, market incentives are extended to encourage efficient production for private profit, and the state shifts toward leaner, more limited government with lower taxes, less regulation of the economy, and reduced provision of goods by the state. The developed countries in which a larger proportion of economic activity remains in

BOX 13.1

The Social Market System: Sweden

Sweden is an example of the more progressive form of the social market system. A culturally homogeneous country of 8.9 million, the state is committed to capitalism, with more than 90 percent of the economy in private hands. Economic policy facilitates increasing distribution of Swedish goods in the world market. Sweden's prosperous economy ranks among the top fifteen in the world on GDP per capita (World Bank 2004).

At the same time, Sweden has one of the most expansive welfare states among the developed countries. About one-third of the national economic output is spent on social programs. Among the universal benefits available to citizens at little or no direct cost are health care, education, day care, maternity/paternity leave, job training, and public transportation. Those suffering economic hardship receive substantial income supplements and support for amenities such as housing. As one example of Sweden's social welfarism, the state provides complete nursing home care to any elderly citizen for less than 5 percent of the actual costs. The regulatory policies of the state are also expansive in both economic and social life (e.g., environmental protection, working conditions). The state has even banned parental spanking to protect children against physical abuse.

Many celebrate Sweden as the model social democracy. A vigorous, multiparty parliamentary system operates under a constitutional monarchy, and there is high citizen involvement in the political process. Citizens are satisfied with the quality of life in their country. Sweden has one of the most equal distributions of wealth and income in the world. And it has the second highest quality-of-life score in the world on the human development index (Table 13.3).

One cost of social welfare has been high taxes. Total taxes paid by citizens and firms are about 57 percent of GDP, in comparison with about 38 percent in Germany and 30 percent in the United States. This tax burden reduces Swedes' disposable income and, along with regulatory policies, has made Swedish goods less competitive in the international market. In 1991, the Swedes followed many other electorates in the developed countries that had turned to governments of retrenchment. The Social Democrats, the governing party in Parliament for 53 of the previous 59 years, were replaced by a minority governing coalition of center and right parties that has lowered taxes and reduced the public sector. But by 1994, the Swedes had returned the Social Democrats to power. And again in 1998 and 2002, despite troubling levels of budget deficits and unemployment, the Social Democrats retained their control of both the prime minister's position and the legislature (as the largest party, with support from another, more leftist socialist party). Thus Sweden's government and citizens continue to support one of the most social of the social market states.

the private sector, usually designated as **market economies,** include Australia, Japan, Switzerland, the United Kingdom, and the United States. Social welfare services are reduced toward a basic "safety net" with which the state protects individuals only from the harshest consequences of poverty. Government also reduces its constraints on economic activity (e.g., fewer antitrust actions, less protection of unions, industry deregulation). Private ownership and control of the productive system are extended, particularly by **privatization** (i.e., the selling off of state-owned firms and the use of private firms to provide public goods and services). Most states also reduce tariffs or quotas on imported goods and cut subsidies on domestic production in order to encourage companies to be strong and competitive in the global market.

The extent of final goods that are provided by the public sector also varies among these states. Certain domains, such as education, public safety, utilities, and national defense, are primarily the responsibility of the public sector in all the states. In the mixed political economies that are more committed to the social market, the state also tends to be very active in the provision of health care, housing, transportation, and income support. Influenced by the strength of classical liberal and third-way ideas, most developed countries have reduced the direct participation of the state in the political economy, and most percentages in Table 13.2 are considerably lower than they were ten years ago.

Performance

The developed countries assess their prosperity primarily in terms of economic activity, usually measured as GDP or GNP per capita, and there is particular interest in the rate of change in GDP per capita over time. Former U.S. Secretary of State George Schultz reflected a widely shared view among leaders in the developed countries when he stated: "The immediate international imperative is . . . adequate growth. Without that, no one's objectives are achievable." But some accuse the developed countries of "growthmania," claiming that quality of life and citizen satisfaction are better measures of performance than an increasing GDP.

Table 13.3 provides comparative data on GDP per capita (adjusted for purchasing power parity) for most developed countries. If one accepts the idea that the value of a society's total production of goods (relative to population size) is a reasonable indicator of its prosperity, these countries do enjoy considerable prosperity. In a rank ordering of GDP per capita (PPP) among 133 major countries in the world, the top 3 are Norway, the United States, and Denmark. Nineteen of the top 20 states are developed countries. The only other state in the top 20 is the oil-rich ministate, the United Arab Emirates.

A *human development index* (HDI) is the second measure of prosperity in Table 13.3. This measure is computed by the United Nations Development Programme (2003) to reflect the quality of life enjoyed by citizens in a country. It is a composite index that gives equal weight to three indicators: "a long and healthy life, as measured by life expectancy at birth; knowledge, as measured by the adult literacy rate . . . and school enrollment levels; and a decent standard of living, as measured by GDP per capita (PPP US$)" (UNDP 2001: 240). The HDI scores range from 100 to 0.0, and a score of 100 would indicate that all the country's citizens have attained the most desirable levels of health, education, and living stan-

TABLE 13.3
Prosperity Measures for Selected Developed Countries

State	GDP/Capita (PPP $U.S. 2002)	Human Development Index
Norway	$ 36,047	94.4
United States	35,158	93.7
Denmark	29,975	93.0
Canada	28,699	93.7
Switzerland	28,359	93.2
Australia	27,756	93.9
Netherlands	27,275	93.8
Germany	26,324	92.1
France	26,151	92.5
United Kingdom	25,672	93.0
Japan	25,650	93.2
Italy	25,570	91.6
Sweden	25,315	94.1
Singapore	23,393	88.4
Spain	20,697	91.8
Israel	19,790	90.5
Greece	18,184	89.2
Portugal	17,808	89.6

Source: World Bank 2004; United Nations Development Program 2003: table 1.

dards. Broadly, a score of 80 or above currently represents a high level of human development (48 countries), scores in the 79–50 range are attributed "medium" levels of human development (78 countries), and a score below 50 indicates a relatively low level (36 countries) (UNDP 2003: table 1). A more comprehensive quality-of-life index might include many other indicators in addition to the three employed by the United Nations (see, e.g., Estes 1988). If you were attempting to create a comparative measure of the quality of life across many countries, what indicators would *you* include?

The developed countries in Table 13.3 have very high scores on the human development index. Every country scores above 89.0, with almost all scoring greater than 90.0, and thus all achieve "high" scores. Norway currently has the highest score in the world (94.4), followed by Sweden (94.1) and Australia (93.9). Singapore (87.6) and Greece (89.2) have the lowest scores among the developed countries. Thus on both a basic measure of economic production and on a quality-of-life index that adds measures of literacy and health, the developed countries seem relatively successful in achieving their overall prosperity goals.

Challenges

Erratic economic growth. Despite the clear accomplishments of most of the developed countries, there are problems evident in the quest for prosperity. Most of these states have periods of solid economic growth (about 4 percent or more per year), and they averaged 2.3 percent annual growth in GDP/capita between 1990 and 2001 (World Bank 2003). However, there are also extended periods, such as in the early 1980s, the early 1990s, and again in the early 2000s, when many of the states have not sustained the high levels of economic growth that are essential to their own definition of prosperity. Either there is low growth or, more seriously, there are periods of recession (a negative change in a key economic growth measure). Certain underlying problems seem to be associated with periods of low growth.

First, *productivity* increases can decline, shrinking the level of profit. Several explanations for this have been proposed. Some suggest that government regulations and taxes on firms stifle the firms' incentives for expansion and reduce their profit margins. Some emphasize the firms' failure to develop and fully exploit new technologies. Still others claim that the state-controlled areas of the economy are the problem because they lack the drive for profit that vitalizes the private market sectors.

Second, a country can experience a period of significant *inflation,* which occurs when there is high demand for productive resources or goods. While high demand might seem good for the economy, high inflation undermines economic stability, planning, and development. Also, domestically produced goods can become more costly, and thus less competitive in the world market. And if high demand for goods is financed by extensive borrowing, the higher levels of private and government debt can also undermine the value of the currency.

Third, and most importantly, the economies of the developed countries can suffer from the increasingly *competitive international economic system.* Economic actors have less direct control of resources and markets than they did when their states were colonial powers (Chapter 11). These firms also face increasing competition from the newly industrializing economies, from the post–communist developed countries, and from developing countries that have substantially lower production costs. Moreover, there is growing competition *among* the developed countries, as their firms attempt to sell goods in one another's markets and to other countries. Box 13.2 suggests the comparative strengths of Japan, the European Union, and the United States in this economic competition among the developed countries, which might be the crucial issue for these countries in the current global system.

A combination of low productivity, inflation, and international competition can result in a reduction of income in the national economy, lower levels of production, higher levels of unemployment, trade deficits and balance of payments problems with other states, and other factors that slow the national economic machine. In recent years, even such prosperous countries as Germany and Japan have had problems sustaining economic growth in the competitive international economic marketplace.

Inequality of prosperity. Another problem in some developed countries is the unequal distribution of their prosperity. Economic inequalities can be measured in various ways. One widely used measure, the "Gini index" of wealth distribution, computes a score in which a perfectly equal distribution of wealth in the population would

BOX 13.2

When This Battle Is Over, Who Will Wear the Crown?

With the end of the cold war against the Soviet Union, the developed countries have turned their attention from military domination to economic domination. This is a new game, with new stakes and different rules. Ironically, the major players were teammates in the military game: Japan, Western Europe, and the United States. Many analysts have attempted to determine which player will prevail in this global battle for economic hegemony. Which one do you think will win? Why? Political economist Lester Thurow provides a comprehensive handicapping of this competition in *Head to Head: Coming Economic Battles among Japan, Europe and America* (Thurow 2003). In his analysis, each competitor has impressive assets and serious shortcomings.

Japan

The positives: The strategic leader in global economic competition, Japan has the world's largest trade surplus. Among its greatest strengths is a superb educational system, which is particularly distinguished for the fine education provided to the less able half of its population. Japan's cohesive national culture facilitates cooperation and purposeful shared action to achieve its collective goals. The state and industry collaborate very effectively, employing the developmental-state model (Chapter 10) to target investment and resources for maximum economic return.

The problems: Japan must reduce the protectionist trade policies that have been central in its drive to create the ultimate export-driven economy. This is necessary to prevent a serious backlash in which it is shut out of its important markets in Europe and North America. This might also deal with the "rich Japan, poor Japanese" problem by relieving the frustration of its own citizens with policies that stifle domestic consumption and limit their enjoyment of Japan's prosperity. For more effective overseas expansion, Japan must overcome its cultural insularity, developing better strategies for cooperating and compromising with governments and workers in other cultures. And it must revise both its educational system and its research and development policies to encourage greater innovation and inventiveness. The growing economic power of Japan's neighbors, the NICs and China, might provide opportunities for Japan's continued economic expansion but is more likely to constitute dangers.

Europe

The positives: With its combination of many cultures and skills, Europe is the excellent all-rounder. It can draw on such strengths as German technological and scientific expertise, British economic and financial acumen, and Italian aesthetics. Its population is well educated, generally prosperous, and comfortable with its institutionalized, highly pluralist political order. Its citizens are confident that their governments' social market systems will protect their welfare and ensure them of a

(continued)

BOX **13.2** (CONTINUED)

secure life. The EU is now the world's largest single market, with an annual GNP of more than $7 billion, making Europe the richest economic actor in the global system (recall Box 11.1 in Chapter 11).

The problems: The EU is a source of strength, but the move to complete integration is an unresolved challenge. Some member states continue to guard their sovereignty jealously and are unwilling to sacrifice national interest for collective good. There have been persistent policy disagreements, especially between the larger and smaller countries and between the more and less prosperous countries. There are also long-standing nation-based animosities between some countries. The attempts by the EU to establish fully its stated goals of complete economic, military, and political unification have become a source of continuing tension and even major conflict between the countries of Europe.

The United States

The positives: The United States has the largest national political economy, with vast resources and a big internal market. The NAFTA trade agreement with Canada and Mexico further expands its regional economic options. The United States remains the world leader in the development and use of high technology, which partly accounts for its continued capacity for productivity gains. Its extensive commitment to higher education has produced a very large pool of what is arguably the world's best-trained and most-skilled knowledge workers. Its political system is deeply institutionalized, and its public policies allow freedom and profit incentives to economic actors.

The problems: Its role as the world's only military superpower provides it with considerable leverage in international relations. But the United States spent $4 trillion to win the cold war, and its continuing high level of global military involvement results in massive expenditures that limit the resources available for economic competition. Although about half the population receives an excellent college education, nearly half of the adults end their schooling with a mediocre education that prevents most of them from contributing importantly to a postindustrial economy. NAFTA and global trade might create explosive policy problems as the United States deals with the large number of Americans who are not knowledge workers and whose skills will make them noncompetitive with the low-wage workers of Mexico. And compared with their rivals, Americans are big spenders and poor savers. The mix of high consumption, low investment, and a willingness to mortgage the future have produced the world's largest debtor nation, with a cumulative debt of more than $6.9 trillion.

And the winner is:
After his detailed analysis, Thurow concludes that the winner will be "the House of Europe," whose overall balance and more limited problems provide it with the winning edge. However, much has changed in the years since Thurow's initial (1993) analysis. Japan's economy has suffered serious decline through the entire period. The confidence of the United States has been shaken by the effects of international terrorist attacks, the costly intervention in Iraq, and the global shift of not only pro-

BOX **13.2** (CONTINUED)

duction work but also knowledge work outside the United States. Europe has struggled with the challenges of implementing political and economic integration in the face of continuing resistance among its members and with the great complexity of dealing with ten diverse new members from Central and Eastern Europe. Japan, the EU, and the United States are all attempting to adapt to the rapidly evolving global economy. At this point, no one is certain who will win this economic battle. (Based on Thurow 2003.)

equal 0.00 and a completely unequal distribution would score 1.00. As the Gini index increases, and especially as it is higher than about .40, the distribution is very unequal. A second measure is the ratio of the country's personal income that is held by the top 20 percent of the population relative to the lowest 20 percent.

Table 13.4 provides these data on economic inequality for the populations in the developed countries. In global comparisons (as you will see in Table 14.4), the developed countries have relatively less wealth inequality than most countries in the contemporary world. The ratio of income inequality between richest and poorest households is more than 5 : 1 in nearly all of the developed countries. The poorest 40 percent of households in these countries get only 18 percent of the total income. This suggests that the wealth differences between those in the top and bottom fifths of the income distribution are substantial but not huge.

Among developed countries, prosperity seems to be distributed most equally in the social market systems, including Denmark, Sweden, and Belgium, countries that have among the most equal distributions of income in the world. To a significant degree, this level of equality is attributable to the effects of sustained public policies that, as in Sweden's social market system, redistribute wealth to provide a diversity of state-supported services and subsidies. The political cultures in these states also tend to be more accepting of governmental actions that attempt to ensure a better quality of life for all citizens.

Not everyone in the developed countries enjoys a life of material well-being. About one hundred thirty million people in these countries live below the poverty line, and 100 million are homeless (UNDP 2001: 9). There are higher proportions of the relatively poor in certain developed countries, especially those where the values of classical liberalism and conservatism are dominant in the policy-making process. Such states tend to have less focus on reducing inequalities and distribute relatively less welfare through the provision of human services. The United States, Germany, Italy, and the United Kingdom, for example, rank among the bottom half of the world's countries on measures of equal wealth distribution. In the United States, the poorest 20 percent of households (which also tend to have more members) have only about one-ninth as much disposable income as the wealthiest 20 percent of households. About one in eight U.S. citizens is "in poverty," according to the government's own statistics, and one in five children is born poor. Such substantial and persistent inequality can produce a permanent *underclass* of citizens

TABLE 13.4
Income Inequality in Selected Developed Countries

State	Gini Index of Income Inequality	Ratio of Household Income, Highest to Lowest 20 Percent of Households
United States	40.8	9.0 to 1
Germany	38.2	7.9 to 1
Italy	36.0	7.1 to 1
United Kingdom	36.0	7.1 to 1
Israel	35.5	6.4 to 1
Australia	35.2	7.0 to 1
Switzerland	33.1	5.8 to 1
France	32.7	5.6 to 1
Netherlands	32.6	5.5 to 1
Spain	32.5	5.4 to 1
Canada	31.5	5.4 to 1
Belgium	25.0	4.5 to 1
Sweden	25.0	3.8 to 1
Japan	24.9	3.4 to 1
Denmark	24.7	4.3 to 1

Sources: United Nations Development Programme 2003: table 13.

who are also disadvantaged in education, job skills, housing, health care, and, most broadly, quality of life (Wilson 1987, 1996).

No developed country has permanently resolved the issues related to sustaining economic growth and distributing prosperity. These issues remain at the heart of the political debate in virtually all of these countries. Nevertheless, the developed countries have a better overall record than any other set of countries in the world in delivering higher absolute levels of prosperity to most citizens.

GOAL: STABILITY

The developed countries have been generally successful in achieving their stability goals of political institutionalization and order maintenance. Within a framework of representative democracy, the politics of these states is characterized by the group approach, with multiple competing elites and groups. There are substantial pressures on some of the governments where existing economic and social problems are exacerbated by vigorous group politics. But overall these states enjoy relatively high levels of social and political stability while allowing widespread participation in the political process.

The developed countries have the highest levels of economic prosperity in the world, but some also have substantial inequality in the distribution of that prosperity, with significant numbers of very poor people such as this homeless man.

Chapters 6 and 7 described the variation in the political structures of different developed countries. Most have parliamentary governments based on coalitions formed from a multiparty system. Some are very stable, with alternating left then right governments (Great Britain) or coalitions (Canada, Denmark, and Germany). Others experience substantial instability due to the fragmented nature of the party system (Greece, Israel, and Italy). While there are some hybrids, with an elected president in addition to the cabinet and prime minister (France), the United States is an exception as a presidential government with a two-party system, and Switzerland is an exception as a council system. Many countries have dual executives, often with a constitutional monarch.

Political power is distributed rather than being concentrated in a single governmental structure. Most are unitary states, although there are several federations (e.g., Canada, the United States, Germany). Even in the unitary states, policy implementation for many human and welfare services is the responsibility of local governments. The national legislatures are important actors in the policy process, with most being unicameral or having one dominant chamber. These countries have large, efficient bureaucracies and relatively independent judiciaries. Chapter 3 indicated that the developed countries allow a diversity of modes of political participation by their citizens and that most countries have considerable political involvement, at least in terms of elections and interest in politics.

Political Institutionalization

The developed countries have high levels of political institutionalization—that is, substantial value and stability are attached to political structures and processes. They are all constitutional democracies, and thus leaders and policies are constrained by the rule of law, and the rights of the ruled are guaranteed by law and tradition. Individuals and groups have substantial freedom to criticize and oppose the government and to engage in a wide variety of nonviolent political actions to change leaders and policies. Leaders operate with a limited mandate, leadership succession is regularized, and the selection of many public officials is based on citizen elections and genuine alternatives. While many countries have had relatively strong leftist or socialist parties and some have well-supported parties of the far right, even these parties are generally committed to working within the democratic parliamentary system.

The governments in some of the developed countries have evolved over centuries by means of gradual and generally nonviolent mechanisms of political change. This pattern applies to such states as Belgium, Canada, Denmark, Great Britain, Sweden, Switzerland, and the United States. The distribution and uses of political power have changed as new groups gain admission to and influence in the political system, extending participation steadily until mass representative democracy is created. This "politics of inclusion" has drawn important groups into the political process and built their support for the political system, reducing their need to use extraconstitutional mechanisms such as violence to capture political power (see Box 13.3). While this emphasis on the relative absence of violence is accurate, it is useful to recall Barrington Moore's observation, discussed in Box 10.2, that development in virtually all societies has involved a considerable amount of violence against some groups.

Some developed countries have substantially restructured their political system in the last sixty years. Many created new constitutional systems after World War II had undermined the legitimacy of their previous political regimes, as in Austria, France, Italy, Japan, and Germany. At this point, democratic political processes appear to be firmly established.

Order Maintenance

The developed countries have had varying levels of success in meeting the stability goal of order maintenance. This goal can be interpreted as the *absence of disorder* in the political, social, and personal domains. As discussed in Chapters 3 and 12, explicitly political violence includes illegal demonstrations, riots, rebellions, coups, and revolutions. Failure to maintain public order is also reflected in social disorder, such as murder, rape, robbery, white-collar crime, and organized crime as well as in personal disorders, such as suicide and substance abuse (alcohol, drugs).

BOX 13.3

Building Political Institutionalization by Political Inclusion: The British Case

Great Britain is an excellent example of the evolutionary approach to building political institutionalization. Britain has the longest-lived modern political system in the world. During a period of nearly eight hundred years (after 1215) the powers of the hereditary monarch (the king or queen) were established, then constrained, and finally limited markedly. Now, in the twenty-first century, the monarch exercises some formal political functions but has virtually no direct political power. The monarch still dissolves Parliament for new elections, summons an individual to form a government and become prime minister, and delivers the opening speech in Parliament that sets the year's legislative agenda. But by convention, these activities are done in a politically neutral manner, with the monarch serving a symbolic role, merely implementing the decisions of the real executive power base, the prime minister and the cabinet.

In parallel, the political power of the legislative bodies, the House of Lords and the House of Commons, was gradually extended after 1215. The elective Commons, which began as a weak second house, slowly gained equality and then clear dominance over the Lords, whose membership has been mainly by heredity. The Commons, which directly represents the population, has emerged as the powerful house that selects the executive leaders (cabinet and prime minister) and authorizes legislation, an indication of the increasing influence of the citizens over the political process. In 1999, the Commons ended the hereditary aspect of the House of Lords, limiting its members to "life peers"—individuals appointed for life on the basis of merit (not heredity), in a set of appointments technically made by the monarch but actually controlled by the Commons.

Over the same period, the electorate expanded steadily, with new classes of citizens being enfranchised as wealth, gender, and age barriers to political participation were dropped. The Reform Act in 1832 increased the electorate from 500,000 to 813,000. Another Reform Act in 1867 increased it 82 percent, from 1,358,000 to 2,477,000 adult males. Legislation in 1884 reduced property requirements for voting so that virtually every working man could vote for members of the House of Commons as well as for the local council. In 1918 all adult men were allowed to vote as well as women over thirty (if married or property owning!). In 1928 voting rights were extended to all adult women, and the voting age for men and women was reduced to 18 in 1969 (Norton 2001).

The political parties also changed, becoming more representative of and responsive to the major groups in the society. As new groups entered the electorate, each party altered its program to include policies meant to attract the groups' support. Most important, the Labour Party, which explicitly represented the interests of the working class and the trade unions, emerged after 1906 and soon became one of the two major parties. The Labour government of 1945–1951 enacted an extensive set

(continued)

BOX **13.3** (CONTINUED)

of policy decisions, which implemented the British welfare state and greatly bene-fited the working class and lower class.

The great majority of the British population believes that the governmental bureaucracy serving it is honest and efficient and that the politicians have been rela-tively responsive to citizen needs and interests. (Recall the data on the British political culture in Chapter 2.) The period since 1945 has been difficult for Britain, as it has declined from a major world power to a marginal actor in international politics with a struggling economy. Thus there have been periods of substantial political unrest and recurrent outbreaks of internal violence by groups (especially by Britain's various eth-nic groups and also by workers in declining industries) who are frustrated by the fail-ure of the political system to serve their interests. There has also been a sharp decline in support for the monarchy, which has traditionally been a unifying force. Still, the British political system is highly institutionalized, with strong support from its popu-lation, stability, and effective performance of its functions.

While a few of these countries have exceptionally high levels of order mainte-nance, such as Switzerland and Singapore (see Box 13.4), most are neither the most orderly nor the most disorderly in the political world. Overall, most citizens in most developed countries enjoy secure lives. The differences among the states can be very substantial, and it is difficult to generalize. The Netherlands, Norway, and Japan, for example, have relatively low levels of social disorder such as violent crime. Yet Japan has one of the highest suicide rates in the world, alcohol abuse is high in Nor-way, and drug abuse is high in the Netherlands. The United States and France, in contrast, are relatively high on most measures of social and personal disorder and are among the increasing number of developed countries with substantial problems related to substance abuse and drug-related crime.

While the homicide rate in the United States is not dramatically higher than the rate in a few of the other developed countries (e.g., Canada), its murder-by-handgun rate is "exceptional": 11,000 handgun murders per year, a part of the 37,000 deaths per year caused by gunfire. In contrast, fewer than one hundred people per year are mur-dered with handguns in virtually every other developed country. Continuing prob-lems with violent nationalist groups (as in Britain and Israel) or with extremist political groups (as in Germany) result in higher levels of political disorder in some countries. What explanation(s) do you think best accounts for the fact that some of the devel-oped countries seem to have such high levels of social and personal disorder?

Challenges to Stability

Value conflicts and disputes.   Since the developed countries allow open group politics, the active disagreements about specific policies and even about fundamen-tal values can produce instability. Some enduring value conflicts center on disputes regarding the circumstances in which the *state regulation of individual behavior* is legitimate. Such regulation might be justified to preserve social peace, to promote

BOX 13.4

Welcome to the Brave New World: Singapore

Singapore has used government policy expansively to achieve order maintenance. A small island of 3 million people located off Malaysia, Singapore gained independence from Britain in 1963 and became a republic in 1965. Prime Minister Lee Kuan Yew exercised singular power for 31 years (until 1990) and guided the country to remarkable economic success. Its annual economic growth rate has averaged 8.3 percent since 1965. Its GDP per capita has risen to rank in the world's top 20, placing it among the leading developed countries in terms of its overall prosperity.

Singapore is also notable for the remarkable set of social-control policies first instituted by Prime Minister Lee and the parliament he dominated for three decades. For example, to deal with traffic congestion, the government maintains a strict quota on the number of cars imported. An individual who purchases a new car must pay import duties and registration taxes that triple the car's market price. To reduce the massive yearly auto-registration fee, the driver can save $10,000 per year by purchasing a special red license that allows only nighttime and weekend driving. The high toll-road charges and other auto fees are used to subsidize an effective system of mass transit.

To promote financial responsibility and personal savings by its citizens, the government places 34 percent of each worker's wages in a special fund, and the worker can use these forced savings only to buy government stocks, to purchase a house, or for retirement.

The state uses the media and the schools to support extensive campaigns to discourage certain behaviors, such as spitting in public, long hair on men, and littering. The stiff penalties imposed to enforce its social-control policies received worldwide attention in 1994 with the "flogging" of American teenager Michael Faye for spraying graffiti on automobiles. For many offenses, there are heavy on-the-spot fines: in U.S. dollar equivalents, $124 for driving without a seat belt, $250 for littering, $310 for eating on a subway, $310 for smoking in a restaurant. To prevent speeding, all taxicabs are equipped with a bell that begins to ring loudly as soon as the taxi exceeds the legal speed limit, and trucks have a yellow light on top that flashes when the driver goes too fast. Technological surveillance includes computerized camera systems that record the license plates of cars that violate traffic laws, and odor-activated videocameras in elevators that record anyone who urinates in the elevator (the person is also locked in). There is even a law against failing to flush after use of a public urinal.

Singapore also instituted a set of not-so-subtle eugenics/population-control policies. Women of less than high school education are given a government-subsidized home mortgage, but they lose the subsidy if they have a third child. To increase the low population "productivity" of college graduates, the government's Social Development Unit offers a computer-matching service for educated singles. One program, eventually discontinued, offered these smart singles a government-funded vacation at a romantic seaside holiday camp.

(continued)

BOX **13.4** (CONTINUED)

Because of such extensive policies of social control, Singapore has been subjected to jokes and serious criticism about its limitations on civil liberties. But no one denies that the country is exceptionally orderly, clean, and efficient. (This discussion is based on Sesser 1992.)

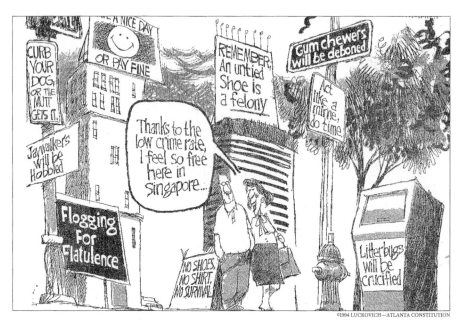

By permission of Mike Luckovich and Creators Syndicate, Inc.

the collective good, to protect the rights and freedom of others, or to protect the individual from himself and others.

In the United States, for example, state constraints on private behavior generate particular controversy between conservatives and others in such areas as the following:

Abortion

Development and use of private land

Discrimination/preferences (based on age, gender, ethnicity, sexuality)

Educational curriculum (religious instruction, sex education, evolution versus creationism)

Free speech (in the media, on the Internet)

Ownership and use of firearms

Sexual conduct

Substance abuse (alcohol, drugs).

Another source of instability in many developed countries is the conflict among *nationality groups.* Some countries have a long tradition of containing several nations, such as Canada's English-speaking and French-speaking populations or the Walloons and Flemish in Belgium. But many have struggled with the substantial increase in their cultural diversity in recent decades, either because of immigration from their former colonial states (as in Britain and France) or because of the immigration of large numbers of foreign workers (as in Germany, Switzerland, and the United States). A few states, such as Israel, suffer from a deeply entrenched antipathy between their largest nationality groups (recall Box 12.4).

For both cultural and economic reasons, the value conflicts between nationality groups have been intensifying in the developed countries. Most of the discrimination and violence is directed against the minority groups and especially noncitizens (e.g., physical violence against foreign guest workers and political asylum seekers in Germany). "Antiforeigner" policies have become a powerful issue in some countries (e.g., the French decision to ban the wearing of head scarves and other "religious symbols" in schools). This has generated counterdemands for policies supporting multiculturalism and protection/promotion of minority rights (e.g., bilingualism and the movement to partition Canada, affirmative action in the United States). Thus the rights and restrictions on noncitizens are volatile policy issues in many developed countries.

As previously described, there is also intense political debate regarding the degree to which the state should have an active role in the *political economy* and should distribute generous welfare benefits to various groups in the society. Many groups have strong ideological concerns or vested interests associated with government policies on taxing, public spending, and regulation of the economy. Thus there is active and sometimes rancorous conflict over these issues among a diversity of interest groups who demand that public policy be shaped to serve their particular agenda.

Hyperpluralism and political polarization. Resolving such value conflicts among competing groups and making difficult policy decisions are among the defining characteristics of politics. The political elites and the governments are generally committed to working within the framework of representative democracy and group politics. They are generally successful in establishing compromises on issues that might become highly politicized.

However, where value conflicts are intense and many groups are mobilized, efforts to maintain political order are particularly difficult. Chapter 9 suggested that group politics processes are not well suited to situations in which there are many mobilized groups with strong and irreconcilable preferences. The risk is **hyperpluralism,** a situation in which many effective groups are able to pressure the government to respond to their particular policy demands. As the government attempts to satisfy all these different group demands, public policy can become contradictory or muddled. Even worse, the government might find itself trying to accommodate so many interests that it becomes somewhat paralyzed, unable to respond to all the competing demands (Edwards, Wattenberg, and Lineberry 2004: 326–328). If key groups become very dissatisfied with government unresponsiveness and paralysis, they can make increasingly strident political demands, engage in aggressive political actions in support of their respective policy preferences, and produce high levels of political instability.

The risks of instability are especially great when there is substantial political polarization within the society. In such cases, center parties and centrist policies are only weakly supported by the citizens, and politics becomes a battleground between large, mobilized groups of the right and the left. The political system has an extremely difficult time making policy and providing any conflict resolution, since it is often impossible to satisfy both sides. This type of polarization and instability occurs periodically in countries such as Britain, France, Italy, and Japan.

A few states have concluded that the threats to stability are so great that they must restrain democratic processes. For example, Israel, faced with an extensive, combative political resistance from its minority Arab population (e.g., the Intifada, 1987–1992, 2000–), has reacted aggressively to maintain order. However, the governments of most developed countries tolerate hyperpluralism and political disorder rather than become too repressive in the pursuit of stability goals. Thus Britain, France, Italy, the United States, and other states have periodically experienced high levels of civil disorder during the past fifty years. Other states, such as the Netherlands, Norway, and Switzerland, have reduced the incidence of serious disorder by nurturing a cultural style of social tolerance or by developing political institutions that accommodate competing groups (Eckstein 1966; Lijphart 1978, 1984). Most analysts conclude that these factors are not a fundamental risk to political stability because political institutionalization is strong in the developed countries.

Domination and control.   Some analysts offer a far more critical description of how order maintenance is achieved in many developed countries. They describe societies in which the state controls its citizens by coercion rather than consensus, combin-

Reprinted with special Permission of King Features Syndicate ing limited welfare distribution, extensive political socialization, and effective restraints on public life by the state's agents (e.g., the police, the bureaucracy, the judicial system). Some class and elite theorists also argue that most developed countries are each controlled by a "hegemonic elite"—an extraordinarily powerful group that sustains its domination over a long period of time (Domhoff 2002; Esping-Andersen 1990; Poulantzas 1973). These theorists insist that politics in the developed countries is not a fair competition among groups, that the state is not a neutral referee, and that most public policies enable certain groups to maintain their advantaged position in society (Chapter 9).

It is clear that the developed countries do have powerful and effective institutions that can shape the political process, control groups, and contain the level of instability. Even the group politics explanation acknowledges that there are huge inequalities in political resources available to different groups (Dahl 1961; Parenti 2002). There is no doubt that certain institutions and individuals (such as media baron Rupert Murdoch, described in Box 13.5) have extraordinary powers to shape

BOX 13.5

Media Mogul Murdoch

Information is one of the critical resources that can shape politics in any society. If the control and dissemination of information is concentrated into the hands of a few major actors, the possibility of elite domination increases. Rupert Murdoch, an Australian (and naturalized American), stands tall among a small group of media moguls who are shifting global media power toward private actors (Hachten and Scotton 2003). Some other very influential members of this group include Jean Azcarraga of Mexico (Televisa) and Silvio Berlusconi of Italy (Mediaset TV).

Murdoch started with the ownership of two Australian newspapers. He then began a 40-year process of leveraging his holdings to acquire additional media resources in other parts of the world. He purchased control of the *Sun,* a London tabloid that he pushed to top ratings with a strong dose of sensationalism and sex. His next moves were to acquire a major London publishing house and the prestigious *London Times* newspaper. He pursued the same strategy with the United States media, even acquiring U.S. citizenship so that he could legally own an American television station. He purchased newspapers, including the *Boston Herald* and the *Star* tabloid, Fox broadcasting (Fox television and Twentieth-Century Fox films), *TV Guide,* the HarperCollins publishing house, and the Barnes and Noble bookstore chain.

Murdoch's next major step was the founding of BSkyB, a multichannel satellite network initially serving only Great Britain with news, sports, and entertainment. In 1993, he acquired Star TV, the major Asian satellite system broadcasting in Mandarin Chinese, Hindi, and English to 38 countries. He is now the world's largest distributor of videocassettes and owns television stations reaching 40 percent of American families and more than 2 billion people in Asia. He is also

(continued)

box **13.5** (continued)

gaining more leverage in other areas of popular culture, such as the control of professional sports teams (e.g., the Los Angeles Dodgers until 2004, the Manchester City Football Club).

Murdoch's dream of a communications empire with global reach is close to realization as he works to link these major systems and add satellite news service to southern Africa and cable television service to Latin America. His current net personal income of more than $200 million per year is derived from the profit of his $28 billion communications conglomerate.

Does Murdoch have any personal values that influence the content of the messages transmitted by his media? Murdoch himself has commented: "For better or for worse, our company (News Corp) is a reflection of my thinking, my character, my values." A staunch political conservative, his newspapers and television networks are openly supportive of conservative candidates and policies and antagonistic to most of those on the left, and particular targets have been the British trade unions and the Kennedy family politicians in America. In 1992, Murdoch purchased the story of Gennifer Flowers, who claimed that she had engaged in a 12-year affair with Bill Clinton, then candidate for U.S. president, and Murdoch's vast array of media relentlessly circulated the story. His Fox News Network was so vehemently pro-United States in its extensive reporting on the war in Iraq (2003) that many criticized the network for its biases and lack of objectivity.

After helping Murdoch gain a waiver allowing him to own the *New York Post* newspaper as well as a New York television station, then-Governor Mario Cuomo observed that while other newspapers might provide a politician with one editorial, "With Murdoch, he gives you the whole paper, page 1 to page 96, every day for six months—for you or against you." Although most of the content of Murdoch's media is not explicitly political, there can be little doubt that his information and "infotainment" empire help shape the ideas and views of millions of people on every continent. (Discussion based on Barber 1995; Shawcross 1991.)

political life in the developed countries. Yet most analysts and most citizens see no compelling evidence that these political systems are dominated by self-serving, nondemocratic elites. In response, radical (Marxist) theorists interpret such citizen views as tragic evidence that the state *can* fool most of the people all of the time. One of the great (and perhaps impossible) challenges for political scientists is to develop an indisputable empirical analysis of how political power is exercised, how values are allocated, and how order is maintained in the developed countries.

GOAL: SECURITY

The first half of the twentieth century was marked by two massive multistate wars among the developed countries. While most of the states survived intact (there are notable exceptions, including Austria-Hungary after World War I and Germany after World War II), many states were devastated in human, material, and political terms by these wars. However, since the end of Word War II in 1945, the developed countries have generally enjoyed success in the pursuit of their basic security goals, especially survival and freedom. Arguably, the greatest security victory of the developed countries during the recent period is the collapse in 1990 of the communist state in the Soviet Union, their major adversary. In the early twenty-first century, these countries are still establishing new arrangements for security in the altered, post–cold war international system.

The Era of Colonialism

Some developed countries have been extremely successful at extending their influence or control over other states in order to enhance their own security goals. Belgium, France, Germany, Japan, Portugal, Spain, and the United States dominated vast colonial territories until the mid-twentieth century. In 1945, Great Britain was the leading colonial power, controlling more than one-fourth of the world's population. Colonialism was a means by which many of these countries furthered virtually all of their security goals. While their colonial holdings are now independent states, the developed countries' dominance often continues through neocolonialism, as Chapter 11 described. From the perspective of many developing countries, the developed countries have very much "had it their own way" in promoting their security interests and projecting their will in the international political arena.

The Cold War Period

From World War II until the late 1980s, the security-oriented actions of virtually all of the developed countries were powerfully influenced by the international struggle between the United States and the Soviet Union, generally called *the cold war.*

During the cold war period, U.S. policy was based on the assumption that the main threat to the security of the developed countries was the Soviet Union, its allies, and the worldwide expansion of communism. In this view, the freedom, influence, and even survival of the developed countries depended on strong military power to balance the Soviet bloc. As the leading advocate of this bipolar balance-of-power perspective, the United States had a foreign policy based on at least two core elements

First, the United States used military power in an attempt to deter Soviet military activity outside of the Soviet Union and its European satellites. The United States was the key actor in NATO, a mutual security pact among the developed countries, and it was prepared to undertake military actions anywhere in the world where Soviet activities threatened its conception of international stability. The United States also developed a massive capacity for nuclear war. The nuclear arsenals of the United States and the Soviet Union created a balance of terror (MAD) in which neither side was willing to initiate direct military hostilities against the other (Chapter 12).

Second, the United States applied its considerable military, economic, and political power to affect the actions of many developing countries. It provided support to pro-American, anticommunist regimes (e.g., Congo/Zaire, El Salvador, South Korea) and to many nonaligned Third World states, and it attempted to destabilize leftist or pro-Soviet regimes (e.g., Cuba, Grenada, North Korea). This policy was generally successful, but the United States suffered its most catastrophic setback in its direct military involvement and ultimate defeat in Vietnam (1964–1975).

Not all political elites in the developed countries shared the United States' perception of a clear bipolar struggle between the forces of good and evil. Some states (e.g., Austria, Finland, Switzerland) maintained a position of neutrality. Others (e.g., Denmark, France, Greece, Italy, New Zealand, Sweden) emphasized a more conciliatory policy of détente ("relaxation" of tensions) with the Soviet bloc, based on the view that both blocs had common interests in maintaining their superior position internationally and preventing a global nuclear war. This latter view became more widespread by the late 1980s, due to Soviet leader Mikhail Gorbachev's effective peace initiatives.

Challenges to Security in the Post–Cold War Period

By 1990, with a speed that stunned the world, the Soviet bloc countries and even the Soviet Union were transformed (see Chapter 15). These countries moved away from communism and in the direction of democratic politics and market political economies. They sought economic cooperation rather than military conflict with the United States and Western Europe. The cold war seemed to end with the unification of East and West Germany (1990) and particularly with the breakup of the Soviet Union (1991) into 15 countries.

The global military power of the United States is now unmatched. But the costs of maintaining such massive military power for 50 years have taken a toll on the economic strength of the United States and on its willingness to serve as the world's "police." Although the United States projects its military power extensively in some cases, as against Iraq in 2003, most developed countries emphasize alternative security arrangements, such as collective security through the United Nations or NATO, and regional security agreements. As the developed countries reformulate their approaches to security, they are influenced by at least four major security challenges, described below.

Disorder in the developing countries.   During the cold war period, most major political violence occurred in developing countries, and it has become more extensive, given the growing ethnonationalism and increasing economic and political expectations associated with globalization in most developing countries. In each situation, governments of the developed countries must weigh the security benefits from stabilizing a distant part of the international system against the substantial costs of intervening and the difficulty (impossibility?) of maintaining stability in many of those countries. From Afghanistan to Columbia to Iraq to Zimbabwe, complex patterns of disorder have persisted, despite various strategies of intervention by the developed countries and international organizations. Thus the developed countries are grappling with complex decisions on when, how, and for what purposes to intervene (Falk 1999).

Proliferation of weapons. Significant reductions in the heavy armaments of Russia and the United States have occurred during the post–cold war period (e.g., START II). However, this period is also characterized by the expansion of military power in many states, the ease with which chemical and biological weapons can be acquired, and the sale of weapons of mass destruction to all who can pay for them. Equally serious, because they are the cause of most casualties from political violence, is the widespread distribution of "light weapons" (e.g., guns, shoulder-fired missiles, land mines) to large numbers of irregular forces in countries everywhere (Klare 1997). Although the number of suppliers is expanding, firms from the developed countries still lead the world in production and sales of military hardware. And the developed countries have failed as leaders in developing effective strategies to prevent the further proliferation of all these kinds of weapons.

The globalization of terrorism. Closely associated with the proliferation of weapons has been the spread of terrorist activities. While most terrorist acts are committed in developing countries, many affect the developed countries. Some developed countries are among the top terrorist targets, especially Israel. Also, an increasing proportion of the acts is directed against the citizens of developed countries, even when they occur in developing countries. The 2002 bombings at the Bali nightclubs that killed mostly tourists and the political violence in Iraq against Western corporate employees, journalists, and even aid workers are examples. Moreover, the extensive movements of peoples has placed cells of terrorists from developing countries in all countries in the Global North. The groups that committed the airplane attacks on the World Trade Center and Pentagon in the United States on 9/11/01 are one of numerous such examples. The developed countries have never been more vulnerable to terrorist attacks by individuals from the Global South.

International economic relations. In the absence of a common military enemy, economic competition becomes a source of more conflict. As noted earlier, the most powerful actors at the center of this global economic competition are the developed countries themselves (Box 13.2) as well as multinational corporations (Chapter 11). But the newly industrializing economies (see Chapter 15) and even the developing countries also intensify this competition. Fierce economic competition between states, regions, and multinational corporations could be the greatest source of insecurity for the developed countries in the era of globalization (Box 12.4; Brawley 2003; Thurow 2003).

THE DEVELOPED COUNTRIES OVERALL

In terms of pursuit of the broad goals of prosperity, stability, and security, the developed countries generally have the highest levels of "success" in the world. These states have the most developed systems of economic production, especially when measured by gross domestic product per capita. In the last five decades, these states have evolved political economies that effectively mix capitalism and democratic socialism. The majority of productive resources remain under private control, but in most developed countries, the state has established a substantial program of welfare distribution to the citizenry. Most of their citizens enjoy a higher standard of living than available to the majority of people in any other part of the world.

By exercising their considerable economic, military, and political power in the global system, the developed countries have also met their security goals. They have a strong record of survival, influence, and even control over other political systems. For many of the assertive developed countries, the approach to international balance-of-power politics was most extreme during the period of colonialism. The leading developed countries still exercise their power quite energetically to maintain their advantages in the international system.

In the pursuit of security goals, the greatest recent success of the developed countries is their "victory" in the cold war against the Soviet Union and its global promotion of communism. But security issues have actually become more complex since the end of the cold war era. The Soviet threat, which encouraged cooperation among the developed countries and shaped the international system after 1945, disappeared by the early 1990s. It has been replaced by more diverse and complicated threats, including increasingly violent regional instabilities in the Global South and the transitional developed countries, the insecurities associated with the current forms of international terrorism, and the complex impacts of globalization. The developed countries must now create strategies that respond to interstate and intrastate conflicts based on a different array of economic, political, and ideological issues. If they are ineffective, the risks include both a preoccupation with responding to global challenges to the detriment of meeting domestic needs and a return to the intensive conflicts among the developed countries that caused two devastating world wars in the twentieth century.

The success of the developed countries in achieving prosperity and security is not unqualified. While most citizens enjoy a high material standard of living, others live in relative poverty and despair, and such inequalities might be the Achilles' heel of their prosperity. Also, critics, especially in developing countries, argue that the developed countries have maintained their prosperity by exploitation—historically, of the poor within their own societies, and more recently and more systematically, of the populations and resources of other states, by means of neocolonialism and military intervention (see Chapter 14). They have not reached the top by being passive or generous.

The developed countries, perhaps because of their prosperity and security, have maintained a relatively open, fair, and stable group politics. Democracy and political equality do not prevent enormous inequalities in political influence and political power. And there are tensions between the commitment to individual freedom and limited government, on the one hand, and state intervention to increase equality of outcomes, on the other. While pluralism has occasionally been severely strained, there is tolerance of a wide range of political beliefs and actions. Many individuals and groups are able to mobilize their political resources to influence the processes of government and decision making, and citizens do have the right to select among leadership elites at regular intervals. In comparison with other countries during the past fifty years, the developed countries receive high marks for their maintenance of constitutional, participatory politics.

KEY CONCEPTS

cold war	newly industrializing countries
developed countries	political polarization
developing countries	post–cold war period
First World	privatization
Global North	social development
Global South	social market system
human development index	social welfarism
hyperpluralism	"third-way" politics
inflation	Third World

FOR FURTHER CONSIDERATION

1. How would you further classify the developed countries into two or more subsets? What criteria would you employ?
2. In the current period, what is the greatest threat to the stability of the developed countries? What is the most appropriate strategy to reduce that threat?
3. Consider the issue of hyperpluralism. Do you think that a country can be *too* democratic? What are several of the strongest arguments on each side of this question?
4. Write a script or role-play (with others) a situation in which a classical liberal, a conservative, and a democratic socialist discuss the virtues and failings of a particular developed country.
5. If you were to create a "quality-of-life" index, what measures would you include? Rank in order the importance you would attach to the various measures and explain why you have given those rankings.
6. How should the desirable level of distribution of prosperity among citizens in a society be determined? Should the state do anything to ensure that prosperity is distributed more equally among its citizens? What actions by the state are appropriate and might be effective?

FOR FURTHER READING

Allison, Graham. (1999). *The Essence of Decision: Explaining the Cuban Missile Crisis.* Boston: Little, Brown. Applies three important analytic frameworks to explain how democratic governments make decisions—in this case, the U.S. decision regarding a response to the placement of Soviet missiles in Cuba in 1962.

Almond, Gabriel, G. Bingham Powell, Kaare Strom, and Russell J. Dalton, Eds. (2004). *Comparative Politics Today: A World View.* 8th ed. New York: Addison Wesley Longman. Solid case-by-case studies of selected developed countries (England, France, Germany, Japan, and the United States) as well as Brazil, China, Egypt, India, Mexico, Nigeria, and Russia, employing Almond's structural-functional concepts (recall Chapter 5).

Bastow, Steve, and James Martin. (2003). *Third Way Discourse: The Crisis of European Ideologies in the Twentieth Century*. Edinburgh: Edinburgh University Press. An exploration of both the roots and the current forms of alternative "Third Way" ideologies, including Italian socialism, British New Labour, ecologism, and neo-fascism.

Burgess, Anthony. (1970). *A Clockwork Orange*. Harmondsworth, UK: Penguin. A dystopian novel describing a near-future Britain in which youth gangs rule the mean streets of a divided and amoral society. Stanley Kubrick's chilling film was based on this book.

Castles, Francis G. (1999). *Comparative Public Policy: Patterns of Post-War Transformation*. Northampton, MA: Edward Elgar Publishing Company. A rich, comparative characterization of how the governments of 21 developed countries have attempted to create effective policies to deal with the challenges of the last half of the twentieth century, with particular attention to issues of both the distribution of welfare and the control of the political economy.

Dinnerstein, Leonard, and David Reimers. (1999). *Ethnic Americans: A History of Immigration*. 4th ed. New York: Columbia University Press. The complex dynamics and processes of the American governmental and popular responses to waves of immigrants, with particular attention to the waves during the last two decades, are thoughtfully explored.

Freeman, Richard. (2000). *The Politics of Health in Europe*. Manchester, UK: Manchester University Press. The contemporary health care systems, as well as the policy debates regarding those systems, are effectively described for major European countries (France, Germany, Italy, Sweden, and the United Kingdom), which range from social market to more neoliberal orientations regarding the state role in health care.

Huber, Evelyne, and John D. Stephens. (2001). *Development and Crisis of the Welfare State: Parties and Policies in Global Markets*. Chicago: University of Chicago Press. A revealing explanation of the expansion of the welfare state and state policies of welfare redistribution in the developed countries from 1950–1980, and then the substantial reduction of those welfare programs since that time.

Kennedy, Paul. (1987). *The Rise and Fall of the Great Powers*. New York: Random House. A sweeping analysis of how countries such as the United Kingdom and the United States become the strongest in the world, and then decline.

Pharr, Susan J., and Robert D. Putnam, Eds. (2000). *Disaffected Democracies: What's Troubling the Trilateral Countries*. Princeton, NJ: Princeton University Press. A strong and diverse set of essays exploring the extent to which citizens in the advanced democracies have lost confidence and trust in their political leaders and political institutions, and even in democratic processes.

Pinder, John. (1999). *The Building of the European Union*. 3d ed. New York: Oxford University Press. A sound exploration of the institutions, processes, and challenges of the European Union as it attempts to extend its roles, power, and effectiveness in the complex post–cold war world.

Thurow, Lester C. (1992). *Head to Head: Coming Economic Battles among Japan, Europe and America*. New York: William Morrow. A rich study of the post–cold war shift in which the key conflicts will be economic ones among the developed countries (Box 13.2).

Wolferen, Karel van. (1989). *The Enigma of Japanese Power: People and Politics in a Stateless Nation*. New York: Knopf. A fascinating characterization of the linkages between culture and politics in contemporary Japan. The author's argument that Japan's politics are different from those in other democratic states, despite similar political structures, evoked very strong negative reactions from the Japanese.

ON THE WEB

http://europa.eu.int/index.htm

The official web site of the European Union, it provides detailed information about each EU member state.

http://www.oecd.org/oecd/pages/home/displaygeneral/

The Organization for Economic Co-operation and Development is a cooperative association that includes 30 member countries, primarily the developed countries plus a few of the most economically advanced countries in East Europe and Asia. The OECD site provides information about its activities as well as data on member states.

http://www.coldwar.org/resources.html

The homepage of the Cold War Museum contains a number of fascinating online exhibits and an online discussion forum regarding this important period.

http://www.weu.int/

The electronic home of the Western European Union provides extensive information regarding the organization's activities and policies.

http://firstgov.gov

The official web portal for the United States government, the site offers many links to the agencies and information associated with the various governmental institutions in the United States.

http://www.canada.gc.ca/

The official web site of the Canadian government, with links to the agencies of the central and provincial governments.

http://www.cnn.com/SPECIALS/cold.war/

An educational and entertaining introduction to the cold war is provided by CNN, with historical documents, details of the arms race, clips of key actors, and more.

http://ukonline.direct.gov.uk

The web site for the government of the United Kingdom, with multiple links to government agencies, services, and information.

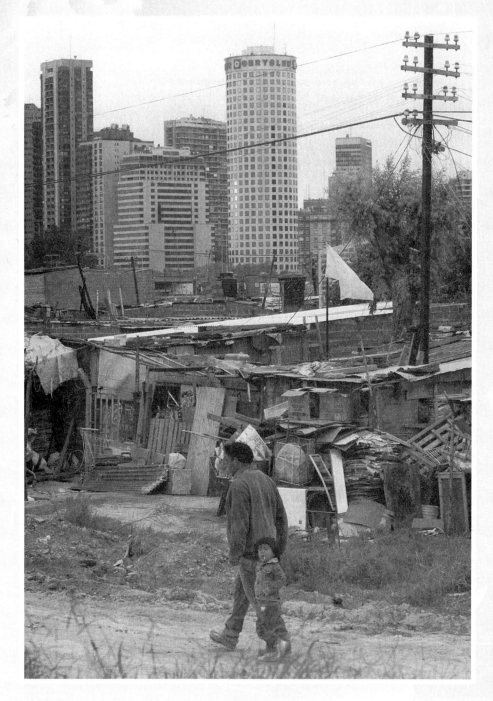

A shantytown grows on the edge of Buenos Aires, Argentina.

CHAPTER 14

The Developing Countries

IMAGES OF THE DEVELOPING WORLD

What is your image of *developing countries*? It might be of dusty villages where poor and uneducated people scrape out a subsistence diet from their small farms. It might be of large cities where some live and work in modern, technologically advanced settings but are surrounded by a huge, dense population living in abject poverty and squalor. It might be of a huge state attempting to govern 1 billion people or of a small island state with a population of fewer than fifty thousand. It might be of a country successfully adapting European political forms of representative democracy, popular participation, and freedom of opposition, or of a despotism where the small governing clique ruthlessly eliminates all opposition and change in leadership occurs only by political violence.

Developmental Classification

Somewhere in the 150 developing countries, with their combined population of more than 5.2 billion people, all of these disparate images are accurate. There are even a variety of ways that particular countries can be defined as "developing." The primary classification approach is based on a strictly economic definition, such as GNP per capita, which is the way the World Bank designates two subgroups of developing countries (middle income and low income): GNP per capita ranging from $80 per year to about $9,205 per year (see Chapter 13). This book also uses a second approach to classification that considers a state's overall level of social development, as discussed in Chapter 13.

Figure 13.1 displayed graphically the large and diverse cluster of developing countries considered in the present chapter. The post-communist developed countries and the NICs of Asia and Latin America will be explored more fully in Chapter 15. However, those transitional developed countries that are most comparable to the developing countries are occasionally included in the discussions in this chapter.

As Chapter 13 noted, there are several other labels applied to the developing countries. They are sometimes referred to as the *Global South*, which contrasts them with the Global North, the geographical location of the great majority of the developed countries, and the label *Third World*, still widely used, was originally devised during the cold war to refer to a large group of states that were at the margins of an international system dominated by two powerful blocs, led by the United States and Soviet Union. Soon, many commentators considered every country outside the two superpower blocs, or even every developing country, to be part of the Third World. Currently, some analysts reject the term on the grounds that it has become too vague, analytically and politically (Lewis 1999).

The United Nations, among others, sometimes refers to the four dozen least developed states in the Global South as a "Fourth World." (UNDP 2003). These states, which include more than half a billion people, show the fewest signs of progress toward overcoming the development gap with other countries. In the least developed countries, most people live close to subsistence and are hard-pressed to provide themselves with the basic essentials of food, clothing, and shelter.

The labels "developing country," "Global South," "Third World," and "Fourth World" are a useful shorthand for common traits attributed to states that, relative to the developed countries and even most of the transitional countries discussed in Chapter 15, are less economically developed, are less modern, and have a lower overall standard of living. Most also have high birthrates (sometimes higher than economic growth rates) and youthful populations (in more than forty developing countries, at least 45 percent of the population is below the age of fifteen).

This chapter attempts to specify dominant patterns and general trends among the developing countries, although generalizations oversimplify political reality and are subject to qualifications. These states differ in developmental styles and approaches to politics. Also, they encompass many different histories, traditions, religions, and political ideologies, and do not share a single political culture.

As you read this chapter, and especially as you formulate your own understanding about the developing countries, be sensitive to the variation *across* these states and, in many cases, *within* each state. Just as the most developed countries have some people living in abject poverty and primitive conditions, even the poorest developing countries have advanced technology, and some citizens enjoy enormous wealth and an exceptionally high standard of living.

Regional Classification

Although this chapter generalizes across all developing countries, Table 14.1 suggests a region-based clustering based on economic development levels. Excluding the world's ministates, most developing countries in sub-Saharan Africa and Asia are low-income countries, and most countries in Latin America and in the Islamic Middle East and North Africa are middle-income countries. For comparative purposes, the table also indicates the economic development levels of the transitional countries that will be assessed in Chapter 15. Some broad regional differences among the developing countries are summarized in the following sections.

Latin America. The countries in this subset tend to be relatively advanced in both economic and social development, with a modern, technological sector. Direct colonial control of these states was early, and most were granted independence before the mid-nineteenth century. In most, there is a strong national identity that corresponds to the country's geographic boundaries, and the state has considerable political institutionalization. There are also other well-institutionalized structures in the society, particularly the armed forces and the church, and many have a long-standing

TABLE 14.1
Distribution of Developing and Transitional Developed Countries,
by Economic Development Level (GNP per Capita) and Region

Sub-Saharan Africa	Asia	Latin America	North Africa and Middle East	Other
Low-Income Countries (below $755)				
Rwanda				
Mozambique				
Ethiopia				
Tanzania				
Burundi				
Sierra Leone				
Congo (Zaire)				
Malawi				
Liberia				
Chad				
Uganda	Nepal			
Madagascar	Bangladesh	Haiti		
Niger				
Kenya	Afghanistan			
Mali	Mongolia			
Nigeria	India		Yemen	
Burkina Faso	Laos			
Sudan				
Togo				
Somalia				
Gambia		Nicaragua		
Zambia				Tajikistan
Benin				
Cent. Afr. Rep.				
Ghana	Pakistan			
				Guinea
		Honduras		
Senegal				Azerbaijan
Ivory Coast				
Congo Rep.				Moldova
Angola				
Cameroon				Kyrgyz Rep.
Lesotho				Armenia
Middle-Income Countries (Lower: $756–2,995)				
		Bolivia		Macedonia
Zimbabwe	China			
	Indonesia		Egypt	Albania

(continued)

TABLE 14.1 (Continued)

Sub-Saharan Africa	Asia	Latin America	North Africa and Middle East	Other
	Middle-Income Countries (Lower: $756–2,995) continued			
	Sri Lanka			
	Philippines		Syria	
			Morocco	Uzbekistan
	Papua New Guinea	Guatemala		Kazakhstan
		Ecuador		Bulgaria
		Cuba		Romania
		Dominican Rep.	Jordan	Lithuania
		El Salvador		
		Jamaica	Iraq	
		Paraguay	Algeria	
		Colombia	Tunisia	
Namibia	North Korea			Ukraine
		Peru		Belarus
				Latvia
	Thailand	Costa Rica		
				Croatia
				Russian Fed.
			Iran	Estonia
	Middle-Income Countries (Upper: $2,996–9,265)			
		Panama		Slovak Rep.
		Venezuela		Poland
South Africa	Mauritius	Brazil	Lebanon	Czech Rep.
	Malaysia	Chile	Libya	Hungary
		Puerto Rico	Turkey	
		Mexico		
		Uruguay	Oman	
			Saudi Arabia	
		Argentina		
	High-Income Countries ($9,266+)			
			Kuwait	Slovenia
	South Korea		United Arab Emirates	
	Taiwan			

Note: Countries are listed in their relative positions on GNP/capita, from lowest to highest, allowing comparisons within and across regions.
Source: World Bank 2003.

upper-class elite. Most of these states are highly urbanized, and it is estimated that more than 80 percent of the population in Latin America now live in cities.

There are two distinctive sub-subsets in Latin America. One is composed of the Caribbean states. These hundreds of islands are extremely diverse in culture and geography. In comparison with the rest of the Latin American region, these island states tend to have longer colonial legacies, to be less developed and less urban, and to have an ethnic-cultural heritage that is African and Asian (and, secondarily, English and French) more than Indian and Hispanic (the heritages that predominate in the rest of Latin America). The second sub-subset comprises the half-dozen states that have achieved sufficient overall development to be classified as NICs: Argentina, Chile, and Uruguay and perhaps Brazil, Mexico, and Venezuela (Chapter 15).

Asia.   A second regional group consists of most of the states in Asia. This vast region covers one-third of the world's land and contains about two-thirds of the world's people. The area is characterized by great ethnic, cultural, and geographic diversity and is dominated in human and historical-cultural terms by China (with 1.29 billion people) and India (with 1.03 billion). The group of low-income countries includes India and several other populous South Asian states (e.g., Bangladesh and Pakistan) as well as some smaller East Asian countries, most of which have a recent history of communist political regimes (e.g., Cambodia, Vietnam). China and the Philippines are among the Asian countries with somewhat greater economic development, placing them among the middle-income countries. The world's leading NICs (e.g., South Korea, Taiwan) emerged in Asia, as have other countries on the transitional edge between developing countries and NICs (e.g., Malaysia, Thailand) (Chapter 15).

Asian developing countries are predominantly rural and agrarian, and a significant gap exists between the traditional society and the smaller modernized and technologically advanced sectors in the major cities. India and most of South Asia have experienced considerable and direct European colonial influence since the seventeenth century. Colonialism occurred later for much of East Asia, an area that has also been affected by the looming presence of China. Most contemporary Asian states reveal substantial nationality differences based on diverse ethnic, religious, and linguistic traditions. Political structures and the political economy also vary substantially from state to state.

North Africa and the Middle East.   This region includes the dozen states and ministates of southwest Asia (e.g., Afghanistan, Iran, Saudi Arabia) as well as the five North African states that are on the Mediterranean Sea and are dominated by the Sahara Desert (Algeria, Egypt, Libya, Morocco, and Tunisia). Most of the peoples of North Africa and the Middle East are Islamic in religion and culture and mainly Arabic in ethnicity and language (although not Iran). The area has major geopolitical importance because of its petroleum resources as well as its strategic location, including its waterways. Much of the region was controlled by the Ottoman Empire between 1453 and 1918. In the nineteenth and twentieth centuries, European colonial power was exercised mainly through indirect economic and military involvement. Despite some brief periods of direct colonial rule, European values and structures did not penetrate most of these states, and many remain socially conservative and somewhat tribal-feudal. Economically, most of these countries are in the middle-income group, although some of the oil states are more prosperous (e.g., Kuwait, United Arab Emirates).

Sub-Saharan Africa. Despite its substantial natural resources, sub-Saharan Africa (the African continent excluding the states of North Africa listed in the previous section) is the poorest and least economically developed region in the world. About two-thirds of the world's poorest countries (as measured by GDP per capita) are in this region. After the abolition of the slave trade, the experiences with colonialism in most of these states were late, occurring between the 1880s and the 1950s, and were extremely intensive and exploitative. Currently, these countries are generally in a neocolonial situation, with limited control over their own resources and a dependency on foreign financial and technological assistance. Few have a strong sense of national unity because colonial powers created states that arbitrarily merged many nationality groups that had no historical commonality. More than two-thirds of the population in these countries is rural, although the numbers of people migrating to cities are increasing. In many countries, the authority of the central, modern state is weak, and central political, social, and economic structures lack institutionalization.

GOAL: PROSPERITY

All developing countries strive for the benefits of prosperity associated with economic development and welfare distribution. While the developing countries employ the same economic strategies as the more developed countries, many of them have had only limited success in achieving prosperity. Table 14.2 presents two prosperity measures for selected developing countries.

Although GDP per capita can be difficult to determine in the many developing countries with less extensive cash-based economies, it is still the common measure of prosperity. A striking aspect of the table is the low GDP/capita levels in many countries, especially in comparison with the developed countries (recall Table 13.3). Most developing countries with a relatively high GDP/capita are either oil-rich states or countries now defined as NICs (South Africa and Costa Rica are arguably not yet NICs). A very low GDP per capita suggests limited production of goods within the society, but it does not reveal the additional factor that these goods are often very unequally distributed and that even the most basic goods are minimally available to many people. For example, 1.2 billion people live on less than $1 per day, and 2.8 billion live on less than $2 per day, conditions of severe poverty (World Bank 2003: 3). More than eight hundred and forty million experience chronic hunger, eating less than the daily subsistence level of calories, and one-third of children are malnourished and underweight. More than eight hundred and fifty million adults are illiterate, 1.5 billion lack basic health care, and nearly one billion are without access to clean water (UNDP 2001: 9).

Can you place these stark statistics in a human context? They are graphic illustrations of the life conditions that are also represented by the low human development index scores many developing countries have (Table 14.2), with the very lowest scores predominantly in Africa and Asia. The emerging NICs in Latin America (e.g., Argentina, Chile, Uruguay) tend to have the highest current HDI scores among developing countries, along with some of the oil-states (e.g., Brunei, Bahrain, Kuwait).

TABLE 14.2
Prosperity Measures for Selected Developing Countries and Nelwy Industrialized Countries (NICs)

State	GDP/Capita (PPP $U.S. 2002)	Human Development Index
Taiwan*	18,000	N/A
Saudi Arabia	13,330	76.9
Uruguay*	12,118	83.4
Oman	12,040	75.5
Argentina*	10,594	84.9
South Africa	10,132	68.4
Malaysia*	8,922	79.0
Mexico*	8,707	80.0
Costa Rica	8,470	83.2
Brazil*	7,516	77.7
Thailand*	6,788	76.8
Iran	6,339	71.9
Turkey	6,176	73.4
Colombia	6,068	77.9
Algeria	5,536	70.4
El Salvador	4,675	71.9
China	4,475	72.1
Jordan	4,106	74.3
Philippines	4,021	75.1
Morocco	3,767	60.6
Egypt	3,701	64.8
Indonesia	3,138	68.2
India	2,571	59.0
Zimbabwe	2,280	49.6
Vietnam	2,240	68.8
Angola	2,053	37.7
Ghana	2,050	56.7
Pakistan	2,014	49.9
Bangladesh	1,736	50.2
Cameroon	1,712	49.9
Laos	1,678	52.5

(continued)

TABLE 14.2 *(Continued)*

State	GDP/Capita (PPP $U.S. 2002)	Human Development Index
Cambodia	1,649	55.2
Ivory Coast	1,500	39.6
Kenya	992	48.9
Nigeria	851	46.3
Ethiopia	724	35.9
Congo	606	36.3
Tanzania	557	40.0

* = classified as a Newly Industrializing Country in this book.
Sources: World Bank 2004; United Nations Development Program 2003: table 1.

The 66 low-income developing countries have an average GDP/capita of only $482 per year (measured in GDP/capita in PPP as $2,082) (World Bank 2004). There is a broad correlation between GDP per capita (in PPP) and quality-of-life scores in Table 14.2, but the relationship is far from perfect. For example, Oman and the Philippines have nearly identical HDI scores (75), although the Philippines' GDP per capita is less than one-third as high. And while Vietnam and Angola have virtually the same GDP per capita, Vietnam's HDI score is nearly twice as high (68.8 versus 37.7). Assessing such variations, the United Nations concludes: "So, with the right policies, countries can advance faster in human development than in economic growth. And if they ensure that growth favors the poor, they can do much more with that growth to promote human development" (UNDP 2001: 13). It is clear that political choices (such as decisions regarding the education of women, the distribution of prosperity, and the response to ethnic differences) *can* have a powerful impact on the quality of citizens' lives.

These data suggest that a few developing countries are on a positive path toward high levels of economic development. But for many developing countries, prosperity is an elusive (impossible?) dream as much as it is a goal on which steady improvements can be assumed. These states attempt to prosper in a competitive global economy in which they face substantial disadvantages. Before assessing their strategies for development, certain key obstacles to prosperity must be considered.

Obstacles to Prosperity

High birthrates.   On average, each woman in the developing world has more than three children. Since death rates have dropped faster than birthrates, the population of the developing countries continues to grow at about 1.4 percent per year (see Box 14.1). Currently, more than 40 percent of the women in the developing countries, the source of 95 percent of the world's children, do not have easy access to family planning. If, from this moment, every female has only two children who reach adulthood, the world's population will not stabilize until it reaches about 8 billion. Even the goal of stability at 8 billion by 2050 requires an aggressive global approach to population control, based on programs costing more than $20 billion per year, substantially more than current spending. The UN recently estimated that global population could grow to about 8.9 billion (and in a less optimistic estimate, to as much as 10.6 billion) by the mid–twenty-first century (Kegley and Wittkopf 2004: 356–360; Mitchell 1998; UNPD 2003).

As noted previously, prosperity is typically measured as GDP/GNP *per capita* or as income *per capita* to indicate the average levels of goods and income that are

BOX 14.1

Can the Population Bomb Be Disarmed?

Before we hit 2000, we reached 6 billion. . . . The world population reached 6 billion in late 1999, and there are nearly eighty million babies born per year. The population of the developing countries has expanded from fewer than 2 billion in 1950 to 5.2 billion in 2003. Among these are 3 billion females under age 25 who are ready to enter their prime childbearing years. Although birthrates in almost all countries have

Kal/CARTOONISTS & WRITERS SYNDICATE/cartoonweb.com

(continued)

BOX **14.1** (CONTINUED)

declined in the last few years, the developing world is still projected to be home to 6 billion in 2015 and 8 billion by 2054. Of the nearly 4 billion births between 2000 and 2050 worldwide, 19 out of 20 births and virtually all population growth will occur in the developing countries. Already, China and India *each* has a larger population than the combined populations of all the developed countries (World Bank 2004).

Some analysts regard the large and growing population in most developing countries as the major cause of many problems—economic stagnation, famine, nationality conflicts, global warming, and desertification. This rapid increase has a variety of consequences, including the need for more than 1.2 billion new jobs, hundreds of millions of new schools and houses, and a major increase in food production. An underlying concern is that the sheer number of people is becoming so large that the regenerating capacity of the earth will be overwhelmed by the depletion of resources and degradation of the environment (e.g., cutting down the rain forests, polluting the water and the air, depleting fossil fuels). Thus some observers term this situation a *"population bomb"* that can wreak havoc on humanity as extensive as nuclear bombs could (Ehrlich and Ehrlich 1990).

Governments in developing countries offer extraordinarily different policy responses to overpopulation. Some countries have essentially taken a *Darwinian* approach to population control. Lacking either the will or the capacity to attack the problem, they allow the natural forces of famine and disease to cull their populations. They provide neither effective birth-control programs nor adequate prenatal and postnatal care; health care provision is meager, and there are few successful policies to boost agricultural productivity. Recurrent images of shocking levels of famine, disease, and death appear from Bangladesh, Ethiopia, Somalia, and other countries. Overall, more than two hundred million people have died in the past twenty years from hunger-related diseases.

The most common policy response to overpopulation is to offer *mild incentives* for birth control. The Mexican government, for example, implemented an extensive public relations campaign on television, radio, billboards, and print media, attempting to persuade its largely Catholic population that "small families live better." India is among the developing countries that distribute free birth-control devices; however, since more than two-thirds of the village women in India are illiterate, many do not use the oral contraceptives properly.

A few countries implement *aggressive public policies* to limit population. China is best known for its combination of rewards and sanctions. The government authorizes each couple to have only one child. If a couple has a second child, that child is not qualified to receive most of the free welfare benefits, such as health care. If the couple has a third child, the couple also loses welfare benefits for the first child. Since many Chinese have a strong culturally based bias toward male children, special cash "rewards" are given to families that have a single female child. The government offers abortions to any women who request them. It also authorizes certain women to monitor the menstruation of all women in their workplace, farm, or village to ensure that there are no pregnancies among women who do not have approval to have a baby. A woman with an unapproved pregnancy is subjected to substantial peer pressure to get an abortion, since the baby will be the financial

BOX **14.1** (CONTINUED)

responsibility of the entire work group, and the parents will receive no additional compensation from the state.

In the last decade, the birthrates in many developing countries have dropped significantly. And some analysts argue that technological innovations have outpaced and will continue to outpace the problems of an expanding population or that it is morally wrong to limit people's right to bear children (see, e.g., Simon 1998). Nonetheless, most analysts agree that the population increases in the developing countries continue to pose serious global threats to the environment and that the failure of governments to deal with the population problem is undermining their pursuit of prosperity, stability, and security.

available to each person in the society. Unless production increases more rapidly than population, more food must be produced, more schools and housing built, more health care provided just to maintain the existing, quite low standard of living. Until governments in many developing countries take decisive action to limit population, they will have few or no surplus resources for economic expansion and an increased level of welfare distribution.

Inefficiency and corruption.   The search for prosperity is also thwarted by high levels of inefficiency, corruption, or both (see, e.g., Isbister 2004). One source of organizational inefficiency is the limited availability and ineffective use of modern technologies. Many developing countries have been unable to maintain efficient economic infrastructure systems, such as those for transportation, communications, or information. Another major source of productive inefficiency is the absence of Weberian bureaucracies (as defined in Chapter 6) in most of these states. The functioning of the political economy is complicated or disrupted because citizens cannot assume that those who work in public and private organizations will behave predictably or follow rules.

An even more serious obstacle to prosperity is corruption. Chapter 6 noted that *baksheesh* ("something given"), *chai* ("tea"), and *mordida* ("the bite") are among the words describing the private payoffs that organizational personnel (from high-ranking leaders to low-level functionaries) expect to receive before they will grant the approval citizens need to fulfill their objectives. Widespread corruption demoralizes the population and drains productive energy from the political economy. Corruption exists in every society—major scandals involving government officials and businesspeople seem to occur with increasing frequency in many developed countries as well. Yet corruption seems especially pervasive in public and private organizations in the developing countries. According to Transparency International, an NGO that measures levels of corruption in more than one hundred countries, 22 of the 30 most corrupt countries are in the Global South, with the other 8 being countries that emerged from the former Soviet Union. Only 2 of the world's 30 least corrupt countries are in the Global South (the southern African countries of Botswana and Namibia) (Transparency International 2003).

Dependence on primary commodities for export.   During the colonial period, most developing countries relied on the export of a few primary commodities (raw materials such as oil or minerals and agricultural products such as coffee or bananas) to generate foreign exchange capital. In turn, they imported most manufactured goods and advanced services from the more developed countries. This reliance systematically disadvantaged virtually all developing countries, since the prices for primary goods have fluctuated greatly and decreased in value relative to manufactured goods over time. Most countries in the Global South have substantially diversified their mix of exports in the last several decades—the percentage of manufactured products increased from 24 percent in 1970 to 58 percent by 1990 (Kegley and Wittkopf 1995: table 8.1). But some countries, especially in sub-Saharan Africa and the Caribbean, still depend heavily on the export of primary commodities as their major source of foreign exchange capital.

Neocolonialism.   The discussions of the dependency approach in Chapter 10 and of colonialism and neocolonialism in Chapter 11 (including the example in Box 11.2 of Congo/Zaire) reveal that a developing country's political independence does not necessarily end its subordination. Rather, economic, cultural, and military domination by the developed countries' governments and institutions can continue as *neocolonialism*—a more informal and indirect, but no less extensive, control of the resources, economic systems, and markets of developing countries (Wallerstein 1980; Weatherby 2003: 36–42).

These patterns have become even stronger with globalization. The developed countries are the major source of the financial capital, advanced technologies, and product distribution systems that many firms in developing countries need in order to compete in the international marketplace. Thus these firms establish economic arrangements (described in the next section) with more developed countries, international financial institutions, and multinational corporations. It is debatable whether developing countries have much choice about whether to enter these dependency arrangements, given their history of resource exploitation and current economic underdevelopment (Rodrik 1999).

The Quest for Prosperity: Strategic Choices

Developing countries must deal with the challenges and obstacles noted above, which leave them less in control of their own prosperity, and with political economies that are especially vulnerable to the behaviors of the leading developed countries as well as the global corporations and institutions that are associated with the developed countries. There are at least five key strategic choices that a developing country must make in its broad approach to economic development in the global system: (1) The balance between state control and the market; (2) the balance between import substitution and export promotion; (3) the mix of manufacturing products, services, and commodities; (4) the role of agriculture; and (5) the extent of collaboration with foreign capital. While developed countries also face these choices, they are especially crucial in the developing countries.

Statism versus Neoliberalism.   A basic policy decision for a developing country is whether to foster economic growth by means of greater state control of the political economy or through a more market-oriented approach (Chapter 8). After independence, many developing countries opted for a *statist approach*—more extensive state control of the political economy—assuming that economic dependency and underdevelopment could best be overcome by a strong centralized effort to plan and control the production and distribution of goods in the society. In this approach, the state's role is expansive—it owns major industries and natural resources (nationalization), controls production decisions, regulates prices and wages, protects domestic producers from foreign competition, and encourages import substitution.

By the late 1980s, many developing countries had rejected this approach in favor of a strategy of *market-oriented development* (described as *neoliberalism* in Chapter 10). This strategy of neoliberalism has four key features:

- First, government regulation of both industry and agriculture is dramatically reduced, and many government-owned industries are privatized (sold to private entrepreneurs).

- Second, there is an emphasis on export promotion, combined with the elimination of trade controls (e.g., tariffs, quotas) in favor of globalized free trade.

- Third, the economy is opened to direct foreign investment and active participation by multinational corporations.

- Fourth, a combination of tax cuts and substantial reductions in public spending, especially on welfare services, further limits the government's role.

Producing for domestic consumption or export? As described in Chapter 9, every political economy produces some goods and services for its own population and some for export to other countries. And some products will be imported from other countries because the country cannot produce them or because of cost and quality considerations. In principle, a developing country will aim to export goods with greater value than the goods it imports. If the value of imported products is greater than the value of products exported, a country typically experiences such negative impacts on its economy as a "balance of payments" deficit and an increase in national debt.

Thus a second key strategic decision for a developing country is whether to use public policy to influence its mix of imports and exports. One policy option is *import substitution*—actions that decrease the share of goods that are imported by producing more of those goods internally. The government can exhort the citizens to buy internally produced products (e.g., "buy Nigerian!"). It can provide subsidies—directly to internal firms or to consumers—in order to lower the prices that are charged for internally produced goods and services. A more common tactic is trade protectionism—the use of tariffs and other procedures to discourage imports or make imports more costly than domestically produced goods. In the current globalized economic system, there is great pressure from powerful economic actors (e.g., the WTO, the IMF) forcing countries, especially the developing countries, to eliminate such protectionism and allow free trade.

A second policy option is *export promotion*—the use of public policy to encourage firms to produce goods and services that can be exported and sold at a profit. This option is viewed as more ideologically acceptable and also as more likely to be successful in the global economy. The governments of developing countries might use policy to provide firms with an advantage over global competitors in the total costs of production. Such policies might result in cheaper labor, lower rents, less restrictive environmental policies, less expensive raw materials and intermediate goods, less costly regulations on business practices, lower taxes on firms, and so on. In recent decades, virtually all developing countries have attempted to introduce policies that facilitate export promotion. This strategy has been used very effectively by the Asian NICs and, more recently, by countries such as China and India.

The mix of manufacturing products, services and commodities.   Every political economy also seeks diversification, which means the effective production of a wide variety of goods and services. Particularly in situations of colonialism and neo-colonialism, developing countries have been excellent sources of cheap raw materials (primary commodities) and intermediate (minimally transformed) goods. While some developing countries still sometimes reap substantial profits from the export of such commodities as oil, coffee, and diamonds, the prices of most exportable commodities are highly unpredictable, subject to sharp drops, and rise more slowly than the prices of manufactured goods.

Thus most developing countries are attempting to achieve growth by stimulating manufacturing (industrialization) and/or the provision of services for both export and internal consumption. Certain developing countries enjoy some competitive advantages over the developed countries in these areas, particularly due to their lower overall costs of production (e.g., lower wages, fewer regulations regarding worker safety and environmental protection, lower taxes, access to cheaper commodities). This draws both national companies and multinational countries to locate economic activities in those countries.

Industrialization is a classic strategy for increasing economic development and hence prosperity. The aim is to use labor and capital to transform commodities into intermediate goods (e.g., cotton to cloth, trees to lumber, ore to steel, water to electricity) and then into more refined and valuable goods (e.g., clothing, furniture, televisions, trucks). Thus developing countries such as Bangladesh and Indonesia produce an increasing share of the shoes and clothing that are exported to and purchased in developed countries. More electronic equipment, furniture, cars, and other relatively sophisticated goods in the global marketplace are now being manufactured in countries such as China, Brazil, and the Philippines.

In the post-industrial period, there is increasing emphasis on producing *services* (e.g., data entry, tourism) and knowledge-based goods (e.g., banking, computer software) instead of producing traditional "hard" goods. India, for example, has utilized some of its large population of well-educated, English-speaking technical workers so it has become an international center for such activities as the writing of computer software and staffing technical help desks.

The role of agriculture   Food is a crucial commodity in all economies. Many people in the least developed economies expend most of their labor producing enough food for survival (subsistence farming). The transition from subsistence farming to commercial agriculture can be an alternative or complement to other development strategies. *Commercial agriculture* means that people produce a surplus of food that can be sold or exchanged in a market. Ideally, production exceeds the needs of the rural-sector population, thereby providing extra food to support a growing urban population. Equally important is the production of food for export, since this generates capital that can be reinvested in either rural or urban economic development. The successful transition to commercial agriculture requires several elements: (1) stable and attractive prices within a reliable market, (2) an efficient system of distribution, and (3) techniques that increase crop yields and overcome such natural hardships as drought and pestilence. This third element has centered in replacing traditional approaches to agriculture with *new technologies* such as mechanization, better irrigation systems, and particularly (since the 1960s) the "green revolution," using chemical fertilizers, pesticides, and hybrid grains that provide higher yields.

As with industrial development, the political regimes of some developing countries established statist control over agriculture. They organized farmland into large state farms and developed a plan for production and distribution based on shared labor and technology. This approach was most fully implemented in command economies, such as Cambodia, China, Cuba, and Tanzania. It has had limited success, however, because most rural people resisted social restructuring and are not motivated to work as hard for the general welfare as for their own profit. Consequently nearly all developing countries now encourage market-based production of cash crops by private farmers or local collectives (Isbister 2004). Small, privately owned farms are common in some areas of the developing world where large landholdings were never widespread (e.g., Nigeria) or where land-reform policies have given local people the farmland that was previously controlled either by the state (e.g., China) or by large landholders (e.g., Kenya, Peru, Zimbabwe). However, most of the best productive land in many developing countries is privately owned by members of the national elite or by multinational corporations.

In agriculture, as in other areas of production, the developing countries generally suffer from substantial competitive disadvantages relative to the developed countries. The governments of the Global North pay their own farmers agricultural subsidies (e.g., on sugar, rice, and cotton) that result in a loss of $24 billion per year by the countries in the Global South. This is because the subsidies enable Global North farmers to make a profit even when selling (below cost) at prices lower than those of crops imported from the Global South. In addition, the developed countries employ protectionist trade policies which prevent developing countries from selling them agriculture exports that would generate an additional $40 billion per year (International Food Policy Research Institute 2003).

Collaboration with foreign capital.   Whatever a country's balance of manufactured goods, services, agricultural products, and other commodities, the production of higher quality, more diverse, and more desirable goods over time generates economic growth. This requires a stable political and economic environment, which in turn can provide purposeful control of resources, a trained and disciplined urban work force, effective use of technologies, an efficient infrastructure for distributing goods, and the infusion of financial capital. Most developing countries are challenged on all these dimensions and especially suffer from the absence of sufficient capital.

Thus an underlying issue developing countries face is whether to embrace the foreign devils—to make explicit deals allowing powerful actors from the international political economy to have direct access to their resources and markets. Developing countries need capital (particularly financial resources) to invest in the production system, to purchase imports, and to distribute welfare benefits to a needy population. Since their level of economic growth is often too low to serve all these needs, developing countries typically look to the developed countries (and their major national and multinational corporations and financial institutions) for financial capital as well as knowledge and technology. This capital can be derived from foreign aid, direct foreign investment, or loans.

Foreign aid. Foreign aid can take many forms, but most aid from the developed countries to the developing countries has been in the forms of shared technology, unconditional grants, loans with no expectation of full repayment, and debt forgiveness on existing loans. Many developing countries argue that the developed world "owes" them such aid as compensation for decades or even centuries of colonial and neocolonial exploitation that greatly benefited the developed countries and left the developing countries with depleted resources and severe underdevelopment. The developed countries have little enthusiasm for providing these kinds of aid since it might shift significant wealth *away* from their countries. Increasingly, they offer aid with strings attached that serve their own self-interest: economic (to obtain resources, to open markets for their own goods and services); political (to establish alliances or a political sphere of influence, to exclude ideological rivals); or military (to deploy strategic military power).

Direct foreign investment. The developed countries' current emphasis, consistent with the ideology of market-oriented development described above, is to promote direct foreign investment, not to provide aid. That is, external actors invest in the developing country's firms and are allowed to set up their own firms within the country. Most developing countries now take a pragmatic approach and attempt to negotiate the most favorable terms possible for obtaining capital and technology from these external economic actors (i.e., more developed countries, multinational corporations, and transnational institutions such as the World Bank). They accept substantial foreign involvement in their economy on the assumption that capital, jobs, and other

Gable/CARTOONISTS & WRITERS SYNDICATE/cartoonweb.com

economic benefits will "trickle down" to their population or that their country can insist on a significant share of the foreigners' profits (Maxfield 1997).

Loans and debt. Another approach to acquiring financial resources is to borrow funds from the international financial community, composed primarily of major banks and coordinated by the International Monetary Fund and the World Bank. Loans offer an enticing short-run solution for financing economic growth and distributing welfare benefits to the population.

Microcredit. Recently, an innovative approach to investment has emerged in many developing countries. This strategy recognizes that effective entrepreneurial activities often begin with the establishment of small, local firms. A key problem, however, is that billions of people in developing countries have virtually no capital with which to start their own small enterprises. Therefore, energetic but poor individuals are provided with tiny loans to enable them to launch such ventures. Women, who perform the substantial majority of all work in the developing countries, have been the recipients of much of this financial assistance. The emergence of this *microcredit approach* (it is also called "microfinance") is often associated with the Grameen Bank of Bangladesh, described in Box 14.2. Microcredit approaches have now been implemented in more than half of all developing countries, where they operate on the margins of the countries' neoliberal economic policies. Many countries and NGOs are actively expanding their efforts to provide such small-scale, local financial support, due to the success of this strategy. Of course, this modest level of internal capital does not substitute for the continuing need for large-scale infusion of capital from the international community.

BOX 14.2

Poor Women as a Major Source of Development: Microcredit and the Grameen Bank

Virtually every economic development project requires financial capital. Such funds are typically provided by national or global banking institutions to companies and other major economic actors who have a record of business success. However, a very different approach was crafted by some innovative thinkers in the Third World. Professor Muhammad Yunus and his colleagues in Bangladesh began with a bold and visionary assumption: that "millions of small people with their millions of small pursuits can add up to create the biggest development wonder." Yunus built on the novel concept of "microcredit." That is, he assumed that if motivated individuals in humble circumstances were given access to a small amount of financial capital, they would use their creativity and energy to establish successful small firms.

In 1976, Yunus and his associates established the Grameen Bank in order to test their faith in the untapped entrepreneurial abilities of ordinary women and men. The bank makes small loans to those Bangladeshis who present promising ideas and show willingness to work hard to implement them. These small loans, averaging $160, are extended to people without land or assets—people too poor to qualify for traditional bank loans. Before microcredit, most of these people had no option for borrowing

(continued)

BOX **14.2** (CONTINUED)

except from intermediaries who charged extremely high interest rates, worsening their economic situation. In contrast, the Grameen Bank offers these small loans at a reasonable interest rate and allows an extended period for repayment.

A notable feature of the Grameen Bank's microcredit program is that fully 94 percent of the 2.3 million borrowers are women. Prior to receiving a loan from the bank, the typical female borrower had never controlled much money. Most of the women have used the funds effectively, establishing a diversity of small businesses in their communities: such enterprises as paddy husking and lime making; such services as storage, marketing, and transport; and such manufacturing activities as pottery making, weaving, and garment sewing.

Overall, the women have been reliable borrowers and prudent entrepreneurs. Kept on track by peer pressure and peer support, the women repay their loans in tiny weekly payments and use their businesses to move themselves and their families out of poverty. Surprising virtually everyone in the global financial community, more than 95 percent of the borrowers have fully repaid their loans from the Grameen Bank. Eventually, many of the women reapply for larger loans as they expand their business enterprises. These loans have provided a rich base of small businesses and economic growth for the country. And, according to the bank, microcredit has "enabled women to raise their status, lessen their dependency on their husbands, and improve their homes and the nutritional standards of their children."

Microcredit (also termed micro-capital) has now spread to over half the villages in Bangladesh. More than $4 billion has been lent, and more than 10 percent of the Bangladeshi population has benefited directly from microcredit. At least fifty-eight other developing countries have replicated the methods of the Grameen Bank, and these loans have assisted more than fifty million families worldwide. The Grameen Bank remains a remarkable and inspiring model of the capacity of poor women and microcredit to be a powerful source of economic development. (Discussion based on http://www.grameen-info.org.)

Current Outcomes

Each developing country has established its own mix of strategies for gaining prosperity based on its economic history, its resources, its political leadership, and many other factors. Given the realities and pressures of globalization, most developing countries are currently pursuing some version of market-oriented and export-oriented development. Government and economic leaders have generally opened their countries' economies to international competition and to collaboration with global capital. Virtually all countries have attempted to diversify their production mix between commodities, manufacturing, and services, depending on national strengths and needs.

Both individual cases and aggregate statistics provide useful information about the recent performance of developing countries in the overall pursuit of prosperity. Table 14.3 reveals the varied success of developing countries during

TABLE 14.3
Economic Indicators for Selected Developing Countries and Newly
Industrializing Countries

State	GDP/Capita, Average Annual Growth Rate, 1990–2001	Inflation, Average Annual Rate, 1990–2001	Debt Service as Percentage of Exports, 2001
China	8.8	7.6	4.2
Chile*	4.7	8.3	5.2
South Korea*	4.7	4.9	7.1
India	4.0	8.7	12.6
Malaysia*	3.9	3.4	3.6
Bangladesh	3.1	5.1	9.0
Costa Rica	2.8	15.1	8.2
Egypt	2.5	8.1	8.8
Peru	2.4	23.8	20.8
Argentina*	2.3	7.4	48.6
Indonesia	2.3	13.9	13.8
Ghana	1.9	28.1	8.9
Turkey	1.7	77.9	24.6
Mexico*	1.5	18.6	14.1
Brazil*	1.4	161.6	28.6
Pakistan	1.2	9.1	21.3
Philippines	1.0	8	13.3
Morocco	0.7	3.5	21.9
Algeria	0.1	15.5	19.5
Nicaragua	−0.1	35.1	22.2
Zimbabwe	−0.2	31.8	3.4
Nigeria	−0.3	30.0	11.5
Kenya	−0.6	14.5	11.4
Saudi Arabia	−1.1	0.8	N/A
Armenia	−1.3	55.8	8.1
Rwanda	1.3	14.7	7.6
Congo	−7.7	813.4	(.)

* = country classified as a Newly Industrializing Country in this book.
Sources: World Bank 2003: tables 12, 16.

the recent period. Although each country has its own unique configuration, certain broad patterns are evident:

- A few states, such as China, Chile, and India, have enjoyed strong economic growth with only moderate inflation and little reliance on borrowing.
- A second pattern, reflected by such states as Argentina and Peru, is a solid level of economic growth tempered by inflation and major loan obligations.
- Another group, ranging from Ghana to Morocco in the table, have very low economic growth, despite substantial inflation, debt burden, or both.
- Some developing countries, such as Kenya and Saudi Arabia, have actually suffered from negative growth since 1990 —that is, their productive capacity per capita has declined.

Aggregate data provide a broader perspective. Since population growth has been outstripping economic growth in some developing countries, the annual GDP-per-capita growth rate between 1990 and 2002 is actually *negative* in sub-Saharan Africa (−0.2 percent), and is only slightly positive in the Middle East and North Africa (1.2 percent) and Latin America and the Caribbean (1.2 percent). Only eastern Asia and the Pacific (6.2 percent) and southern Asia (3.3 percent) achieved substantial real economic growth during the period (World Bank 2004).

These differences between countries and regions are one aspect of "uneven development." The distribution of prosperity at the *individual* level is also substantially uneven. In many developing countries, both the decisions of the political system regarding the allocation of values and the effects of pressures and demands from the international financial community have resulted in an array of policies that have generally shifted resources *away* from the most disadvantaged sectors of the population, especially the poor. Table 14.4 reports the level of inequality in the distribution of wealth in selected countries, based on the two measures described in Chapter 13, the Gini index of income inequality and the ratio of income held by the top 20 percent of the households relative to the lowest 20 percent. Most of the countries with huge inequalities in the distribution of prosperity are developing countries. Twenty-four of the thirty countries with the world's most unequal distributions of wealth are developing countries. And the other six are newly industrializing countries (the NICs are discussed more fully in Chapter 15). These thirty countries have extremely high Gini index scores, ranging from 70.7 in Namibia to 47.4 in the Dominican Republic. The pattern is similar on the measure of income ratios, where developing countries again are a highly disproportionate share of the countries with the greatest inequality in the distribution of wealth. The richest 20 percent often control ten to thirty times as much wealth as the poorest 20 percent of the population. It should be noted that a small proportion of the quartile of the world's countries with the most *equal* distributions of wealth are developing countries. This set includes Egypt, Bangladesh, Sri Lanka, Ivory Coast, and Indonesia.

This inequality in wealth is evident in many developing countries that have experienced limited or negative economic growth and have implemented cuts in government spending on education, health, and welfare. The result is that more than 1 billion people in the developing countries have experienced a substantial *decline* in their standard of living since the late 1980s. In Latin America, for example, the average income per person in 2002 was lower than in 1980 and fully 36 percent of the population was in poverty (measured as less that $2/day) by 1998. Similarly,

TABLE 14.4
Income Inequality in Selected Countries

Country	Gini Index of Inequality in Income Distribution	Ratio of Income, Top/Bottom 20%
Swaziland	60.9	23.8 to 1
Brazil*	60.7	29.7 to 1
South Africa	59.3	33.6 to 1
Chile*	57.5	19.3 to 1
Colombia	57.1	20.3 to 1
Mexico*	51.9	17.0 to 1
Nigeria	50.6	12.8 to 1
Malaysia*	49.2	12.4 to 1
Costa Rica	45.9	11.5 to 1
Russia	45.6	10.5 to 1
Kenya	44.5	9.1 to 1
Thailand*	43.2	8.3 to 1
United States	40.8	9.0 to 1
China	40.3	8.0 to 1
Ghana	39.6	8.4 to 1
Morocco	39.5	7.2 to 1
Germany	38.2	7.9 to 1
India	37.8	5.7 to 1
United Kingdom	36.0	7.1 to 1
Israel	35.5	6.4 to 1
Egypt	34.4	5.1 to 1
Switzerland	33.1	5.8 to 1
Poland	31.6	5.1 to 1
Canada	31.5	5.4 to 1
Austria	30.5	5.5 to 1
Belarus	30.4	4.6 to 1
Indonesia	30.3	5.2 to 1
Norway	25.8	3.7 to 1
Slovakia	25.8	4.0 to 1
Finland	25.6	3.5 to 1
Czech Republic	25.4	3.5 to 1
Belgium	25.0	4.5 to 1
Sweden	25.0	3.8 to 1
Denmark	24.7	4.3 to 1
Hungary	24.4	3.5 to 1

On the Gini index, perfect equality among all individuals in the distribution of income would have a score of 0.0, whereas total inequality in the distribution would have a score of 100.0. The data are for 111 countries, while approximately 80 other countries are not analyzed by the World Bank. Among those countries not analyzed, but given attention in this book are: Argentina, Cambodia, Congo, Cuba, Iran, Iraq, Japan, Myanmar, Oman, Singapore, Swaziland, Taiwan, Turkey, and Uruguay.
* = country classified as Newly Industrialized Country in this book.
Source: United Nations Development Program 2003: table 13.

more than 75 percent of the population is in poverty in sub-Saharan Africa, and population growth resulted in a 34 percent increase in the total number of poor (World Bank). Minimally, developing countries need to feed their own populations. Yet one in four people suffer chronic hunger, and the level of deaths from the effects of hunger is tragic: about forty-two deaths per minute, two thousand five hundred per hour, sixty thousand per day, and twenty-two million per year (Evans and Long 2000: 63).

While the five key strategies described above have significantly benefited some developing countries and some individuals in every developing country, it is clear that most of these countries are still relatively low in economic development. The strategies have not enabled these countries to overcome the obstacles described earlier in this chapter.

The example of agriculture shows how many developed countries have stumbled on these obstacles. Many large commercial farms are now relatively efficient, with production directed primarily to the export market. But in many cases, the political elite and national or foreign economic elites collude so that they capture the profits from commercial agriculture and do not use them for national economic development or welfare (e.g., in Chile, Congo, El Salvador, and the Philippines). Small farms still produce half of the food grown in developing countries. But in most developing countries with a large rural population and low market prices (e.g., Bangladesh, Ghana, Indonesia, Kenya), most farms produce little more than is necessary for family subsistence. Ironically, some of the most successful small farmers are those producing lucrative but illegal cash crops such as coca and opium rather than those producing legal crops, whose international prices tend to fluctuate greatly.

Moreover, some states have been so committed to producing agricultural goods for export that they do not produce enough for domestic needs, and the country must import basic foods for its own population. Many subsistence farmers now have access to only the most marginal land. The pressures to provide food and fuel for a growing population have caused many rural people to engage in extensive deforestation, overgrazing, and aggressive farming techniques that exhaust the soil, destroy forests, and harm ecologically sensitive areas. These actions, in a vicious cycle with serious droughts and flooding in some regions, have resulted in a substantial reduction in the amount of productive farmland. The environmental consequences are frightening. It is estimated that during the 1990s, mainly in the developing countries, 6.25 million square miles of timberland disappeared, 250 billion tons of arable topsoil vanished from croplands, and deserts claimed 5.3 million square miles (an area about one and one-half the size of the United States) (Population Institute 1992; Worldwatch 2003).

The green revolution doubled average yields for rice, corn, and wheat between 1960 and 1996. However, the costs of its components, especially fertilizers and pesticides, have risen dramatically. Moreover, unanticipated negative consequences from high-tech farming emerged. The example of Indonesia (Box 14.3) is indicative of the problems associated with overreliance on hybrid grains and chemicals. Increasingly, farmers are attempting to balance the use of modern technology with more traditional methods to stabilize agricultural productivity. The key puzzle regarding agricultural development seems to be how to encourage high levels of productivity in a manner that preserves the environment, feeds the domestic population, and produces surplus for export. An approach that achieves all three of these objectives would enable a developing country to support its own population

BOX 14.3

Something Can Be Done! Appropriate Technology and Agricultural Self-Help

Many developing countries are now engaged in agricultural self-help programs based on the use of natural farming techniques and "appropriate technologies." In Indonesia, for example, the green revolution using hybrid rice breeds and chemicals had dramatically increased rice yields in the 1970s. By the early 1980s, however, these new farming technologies caused huge areas to be devastated by insect infestation. First, eliminating traditional methods of crop rotation allowed the insect population, especially brown hoppers, to explode. Second, the new rice breeds were far less resistant to infestation. And third, the increasing use of pesticides actually increased the ratio of pests to "good" insects.

In 1986, Indonesia's President Suharto implemented aggressive policies that reversed the high-tech strategies of the green revolution. Laws prohibited the use of 57 pesticides and allowed the remaining 8 to be used only in very limited amounts. Government workers instructed the farmers to return to crop-rotation strategies, to use biological sprays that protect the good insects, and to limit severely the use of chemical fertilizers in favor of natural fertilizers such as dung and clover. By the mid-1990s, pesticide use was down nearly 80 percent and Indonesia's crop yields had rebounded.

Many developing countries have implemented small-scale projects that have improved their agricultural productivity with environmental sensitivity. A tree-planting program in place since 1990 in Niger (sponsored by CARE [Cooperative for American Relief to Everywhere]) has produced more than four hundred miles of trees in rows that now protect the soil from wind and erosion. As the trees mature, crop yields have increased more than 20 percent. Small farmers in neighboring Burkina Faso have been taught to use a simple level (provided by Oxfam [Oxford Committee for Famine Relief]) in order to survey their flat croplands. Groups of farmers then build low rock walls and dams that direct rainwater into areas where it moistens land for planting and then replenishes groundwater and wells, both of which irrigate crops and provide well water for year-round vegetable gardens.

while also creating a financial surplus for economic growth and welfare distribution. In most developing countries, this puzzle remains unsolved.

While direct foreign investment is helpful, most (70 percent) is actually between developed countries. More than 20 percent of direct foreign investment goes to eight developing countries, and less than 10 percent of these funds is shared among more than one hundred poor countries (Scott 2001). The majority of Global South countries therefore have to rely on loans as a source of funds, and unfortunately, loans require repayment. Many developing countries are now deeply indebted to financial institutions in developed countries. Their total external debt increased twentyfold during the 1970s and then tripled from 1980 to 1993. The Global South now has a staggering outstanding debt of more than $2 trillion.

Repayment of such debt is a debilitating additional burden for a state trying to generate economic surplus to finance current welfare and future growth. Currently, developing countries must expend an average of 22.3 percent of their export earnings merely to service their debts, and many countries spend much higher proportions than this (see Table 14.3), especially those in Latin America (where the region's average is 41.6 percent) (UNDP 2001: table 15).

Even worse, some governments resort to printing huge amounts of money to cover their expenses. But in the absence of a strong economy to back the money, it becomes worth less and less both internationally and at home, producing a serious inflationary spiral. Inflation rates in some developing countries have been quite high and occasionally staggering. The annual inflation rate throughout Latin America from 1980 to 1992 was about 230 percent per year, with some much higher. For example, from 1985–1995, Brazil's annual inflation rate was 900 percent, and in Peru, it was 492 percent (World Bank 1996: table 2). Obviously, maintenance of a coherent plan of national economic development is impossible in the face of such hyperinflation. However, there is now evidence of stabilization in the region, with average annual inflation in Latin America falling from 196 percent in 1991 to less than 20 percent at the end of the decade (World Bank 1999).

Because of a combination of debt repayment, the flight of capital, and the growing role of multinational corporations in their economies, the developing countries sent $150 billion more to the developed countries than they received from them through export earnings, new loans, and private investment between 1985 and 1990 (Raymond 1991). When developing countries request extensions on loan repayment or additional loans, the financial institutions in the developed countries have insisted on "structural adjustment programs." These programs (described more fully in the discussion on economic security later in this chapter) require developing country governments to open their economy to even greater direct foreign investment and to cut state spending dramatically.

In many developing countries, becoming more integrated into the global economy means a decrease in real wages, rising unemployment, and greater income inequality. Given such problematical results, some leaders, particularly in Latin America (e.g., Vincente Fox in Mexico), are attempting to formulate a new policy approach. Similar to the "third-way" ideas used in the developed countries (recall Chapter 13), this "fourth-way" approach does encourage the country to have greater participation in the global economy through expansion of the free market; but it also emphasizes the government's implementation of public policies that aim to improve the quality of life of all groups in the society, especially through the provision of substantially more welfare distribution, social services, and jobs for the poor and others most disadvantaged by the market approach (Conger 1998).

The balance sheet.   The pursuit of prosperity has produced extremely uneven results across the developing countries. There are some clear positives. First, economic diversification and growth have occurred in many countries, especially in those that successfully implemented market-oriented approaches to industrialization and agricultural development in recent years. Some countries that have sustained high levels of economic development, such as the NICs and China, offer inspiration and possible models for other developing countries. Second, the overall economic growth rates per capita for developing countries (1990–2001) averaged more than 2.9 percent per year, compared with a rate of only 1.7 percent in the developed. Indeed, the developing countries had higher average annual growth in GDP per capita (2.3 percent) than high-income countries (2.1 percent) for the period 1975–2001 (UNDP 2003: table 12). And third, the "average person in the developing world" is living longer (on average, 8 years longer than 30 years ago), is healthier and better educated, and has a higher real income (it has doubled in the past thirty years) and more material possessions than at any prior time (UNDP 2001: 10).

However, there are also clear negatives. First, the financial, industrial, and commercial-agricultural sectors in most developing countries continue to be characterized by high levels of dependency on the developed countries and multinational corporations. While almost two-thirds of developing countries' total exports are now manufactured goods (excluding oil-exporting countries), most countries still must borrow money to pay for imports, to support limited welfare distribution, and to repay their foreign loans. They remain net importers of capital, technology, manufactured goods, oil, and even food. Second, the gap in the level of general prosperity in the developing countries, relative to the more developed countries, continues to broaden. Per capita GNP is less than one-twentieth as large, life expectancy is about fourteen years shorter, and life is far less comfortable for the average person

School days in Cairo. Education is a top priority in many countries that are attempting to achieve both social and economic development.

(Sivard 1996: table III). Slightly higher growth rates in developing countries do not close these huge absolute differences.

Third, economic growth is very uneven across developing countries. It is noted above that growth is particularly concentrated in East Asia and somewhat in South Asia, while other areas of the developing world have languished on the overall growth indicators. The 66 low-income countries have the lowest average annual growth rates in the world, both since 1975 and since 1990. Moreover, inflation between 1980 and 2000 has been high enough in many developing countries to eliminate most or all of the apparent growth in GNP per capita when the real value of currency is considered (World Bank 1999). Thus a focus on growth rates alone can deflect attention from a broader notion that the essence of prosperity is economic and social betterment for most of the population. Growth statistics can merely reflect increased total output without creating any necessary changes that result in an enhanced life for most citizens. There are serious shortcomings in the pursuit of prosperity during a period when, despite apparent global economic growth, 1 billion people in the developing world experience a *deterioration* in their standard of living.

Prognosis

Many developing countries are rich in human and natural resources. Yet most have not been able to sustain a solid level of economic development or to distribute a modest level of welfare to most of the population, let alone do both. This seems unlikely to change in a period characterized by turbulence in the global economy, an increase in direct foreign economic involvement, and pressure to reduce government spending on citizens' welfare. Most countries in the Global South continue to vary their mix of development strategies as they search for an approach best suited to their particular political and economic situation. In the immediate future, the general pattern in most countries will remain economic underdevelopment and minimal welfare for the majority of people. The perplexing question for most leaders is how to convert their resources into prosperity, given underdevelopment, a disadvantaged position in a harshly competitive international environment, and the substantial challenges to their security and stability described in the next sections.

GOAL: SECURITY

The developing countries search for security in the face of pervasive insecurity. Their problems are grounded in low levels of political and economic development, which reduce their capacity to control their own population and resources and make them vulnerable to intervention by other states. Paradoxically, this relative weakness can also lead a state to be more aggressive in its interstate relations, both as a defensive reaction to perceived threats and as a means to divert its citizens' attention from internal problems.

Interstate Violence

At any given time, most developing countries are *not* involved in violent interstate disputes. However, most wars since 1950 and most instances of interstate violence are in the Global South, often between neighboring states (Cruikshanks 2000; SIPRI Yearbook 2003). The following list offers explanations of why interstate violence between *adjacent* developing countries is so frequent.

- Many of the *geographic boundaries* between current states do not correspond to the boundaries of historically established nations, so conflict develops in an attempt to realign national borders.
- Differences in the *cultures* of two states, especially those grounded in nationality, political ideology, or religious belief, can produce animosities so deep that violence erupts.
- States often look covetously at valuable *resources* in neighboring states and sometimes attempt to gain control of those resources by force.
- States with severe *internal problems* can use other states as scapegoats, redirecting internal frustration into violence against those states.
- Conflict is encouraged by the *actions of other states* that are attempting to serve their own national interests.

Most interstate conflicts between adjoining developing countries entail a combination of these reasons. The Iran–Iraq War, described in Box 14.4, is a revealing

---

BOX 14.4

The Third World War

The brutal war between Iran and Iraq, which raged from 1980 to the 1988 cease-fire, is characteristic of the complex causes of interstate violence between neighboring countries in the developing world, even among states that share a common culture—in this case, Islam. Iraq's effort to regain total control of the Shatt al Arab was the manifest reason for the war, which began officially when Iraq invaded Iran in September 1980. The Shatt al Arab, a narrow strait between the two countries, has strategic value as a trade outlet to the Persian Gulf. In addition, these five factors are partial causes of the long-standing hostilities that resulted in war:

1. There is historical, nation-based hostility between the Iranians, whose ethnicity is Persian, and the Iraqis, who are predominantly Arabic.
2. There have been periodic disputes along the Iran–Iraq border, which was established after World War I, because of the attempts by the Kurdish nationality (whose region, Kurdistan, is along the border) to establish autonomy from the Iraqis, and also because of Iranian support for separatist political violence by the Kurds.
3. The Kurdistan area has valuable oil resources that both Iraq and Iran want to control.
4. The Iranian revolution (January 1979) brought to power a fundamentalist Shia Muslim regime under the Ayatollah Khomeini. The Shia Muslims are deeply

(continued)

BOX **14.4** (CONTINUED)

antagonistic to the religion of the Sunni Muslim minority, who rule a Shia majority in Iraq. There was also a history of personal animosity between Khomeini and Iraq's President Saddam Hussein.

5. Internal political difficulties in each country, and especially major economic problems in Iran after the revolution, provoked each state to redirect the frustrations of its population against the enemy across the border.

Moreover, the actions and intentions of many other states were also significant factors. For example, Egypt and other Arab states supported Iraq's war effort because of their desire to prevent Islamic fundamentalism from spreading to their states. Syria, an Arab country that had long been in conflict with Iraq, was a primary supporter of non-Arabic Iran. When Shah Reza Pahlavi's pro-American Iranian government was replaced by a strongly anti-American Iran under Khomeini, who was deeply resentful of U.S. support for the shah, the United States began to aid Iraq. The U.S. shift toward Iraq caused the Soviet Union to limit its long-standing support for Iraq. And some arms-producing states, such as Brazil and France, sold large quantities of weapons to both countries.

The war was devastating to the human and economic resources of both Iran and Iraq, causing more than one million casualties. After the cease-fire in August 1988 stopped the fighting, Iran withdrew from international military struggle and focused on pursuing its prosperity and stability goals. It slowly normalized its relations with other states and achieved slight economic growth. However, the cease-fire provided no solution to the complex regional conflicts. Disputes regarding borders, resources, and religion were again among the reasons that Iraq invaded Kuwait in 1990. This time, the United States organized a major multinational military response against Iraq, which suffered another massive toll, with high casualties (estimates range greatly, between 10,000 and 500,000) and extensive destruction of its infrastructure. However, Iraq, under its defiant and dictatorial leader, Saddam Hussein, continued to provoke military reaction. This resulted in a 2003 war against Iraq led by the United States and Britain. The Hussein regime was quickly driven from power, although the country and the Iraqi people were again devastated by the combination of the war, the postwar occupation, and the resistance to the "invaders."

example of the interrelated themes of nationality, resources, ideology, internal problems, and external influences that are often at the core of such violence. As was noted in Chapter 11, these conflicts only occasionally expand into a war (e.g., Cambodia–Vietnam, Chad–Libya, China–India, Eritrea–Ethiopia, India–Pakistan). It is more common for the conflict to take the form of a militarized dispute (short of war) (e.g., Argentina–Chile, Bolivia–Paraguay, Cambodia–Thailand, Ecuador–Peru, India–Pakistan, Rwanda–Uganda) (Gochman and Maoz 1984).

Some interstate conflicts occur between a developing country and a developed country on its border. The most frequent have been the five wars and many militarized disputes since 1948 between Israel and the neighboring Arab states, especially Syria, Egypt, and Jordan. Developed countries can also intervene militarily in a neighboring developing country under the rationale of stabilizing its regime, as in the Soviet Union's involvement in Afghanistan (1979–1987).

When a developing country has been involved in interstate conflict with a *nonadjoining* state during the postcolonial period, the other combatant is usually a more developed country. A developed country might intervene with force to protect its strategic, economic, or ideological interests in an internal war, as the United States did in Haiti in 1994 and France did in the Central African Republic in 1996. Often, the developed country engages in low-intensity conflict (see Chapter 12) to support or undermine one side in a civil war or revolutionary war. Occasionally, the conflict escalates into a conventional war (e.g., between the United States and North Vietnam in the 1960s, between the United Kingdom and Argentina in 1982, and between the U.S.-led military forces and Iraq in 2003).

From the perspective of many developing countries, the entire period of colonialism and neocolonialism has involved developed countries' sustained use of military, economic, and psychological violence against them. Thus Third World people sometimes directed violence against the agents of the developed countries during the colonial period, especially during wars of liberation. And in the postcolonial period, developing countries have occasionally used political violence against a developed country that they perceive to be a source of oppression, claiming that they are doing so in self-defense—as exemplified by Libya's and Syria's apparent state sponsorship of terrorist activities against Europeans and Americans in the 1980s.

A striking feature of the post–cold war period has been the increasing use of the United Nations peacekeeping forces to provide security (see Chapter 12). In 2004, for example, twelve of the fourteen active UN peacekeeping operations were in developing countries (United Nations Peacekeeping 2004). Unlike most of the earlier UN operations, these recent ones are often attempts to maintain *internal* stability within a developing country rather than to intervene in an interstate dispute. In East Timor and Liberia, the UN forces' objective was to protect and implement peace agreements already signed by the belligerent internal groups. Despite differences in outward forms, most UN peacekeeping missions are explicit efforts, primarily organized and funded by the developed countries, to ensure the stability of "zones of turmoil" in the developing world. An emerging form of intervention is the use of external force on humanitarian grounds—to protect an ethnic minority that is the target of widespread, violent treatment by the state (Falk 1999)—but this is problematic because it seems to violate a state's sovereignty.

The search for security is often extremely costly. Many developing countries devote a substantial amount of their limited resources to military expenditure: They spend $70 million per day on arms, ammunition, and other military hardware. Since 1960, developing countries' total military spending has increased sixfold in constant dollars, and the number of people in their armed forces has nearly doubled. In 2002 alone, they spent more than $255 billion on their militaries. In the last decade, military spending has been increasing in every region of the Global South, particularly in North Africa (44 percent), South Asia (44 percent) and the Middle East (38 percent) (Kegley and Wittkopf 2001: 462–464; SIPRI Yearbook 2003; Sivard 1996: 44). Obviously, these huge military expenditures can enhance security and stability. But empirical analyses suggest that greater military might is actually associated with a *higher* probability that a state will be involved in interstate conflict (Bremer 1980). Moreover, expenditures on the military represent resources that are not available for economic development and social welfare.

Economic Security

The fact that many developing countries have such fragile economic systems is also a crucial element in their quest for security because a *state's goal of autonomy*—of controlling its own destiny—depends in part on its *capacity to resist external manipulation of its political economy*. When the developed countries and multinational corporations provide economic and technological assistance, they expect to have substantial influence and to receive generous benefits, such as advantageous terms for establishing firms, favorable trade relations, and rights to undertake strategic military activities within the state. When developing countries owe more than $2 trillion to the financial institutions of the developed world, it is inevitable that the international financial community will intervene and attempt to control their affairs.

This economic intervention has come most explicitly from the International Monetary Fund, a consortium of financial institutions that sets economic policy and monitors the behavior of lenders and debtors. To grant additional loans or to reschedule payments on existing loans, the IMF requires "conditionality"—the debtor state must fulfill specific conditions that the IMF sets. The IMF's conditions often include requirements that the state implement a *structural adjustment program* (SAP), which accelerates the debtor state's transition from a statist political economy to a free-market system and opens the country to the global economy. SAPs typically require that the state make an overall reduction in public spending, with particularly severe reductions in the distribution of welfare services to its population as well as currency devaluation, cuts in wages, and privatization of state-owned firms. The country must also facilitate direct foreign investment and freer trade by lowering its barriers to the entry of capital and goods.

The political and financial elites in nearly all developing countries seem to believe that their interests are best served by cooperation with the developed countries and the international financial community, and that loss of some control over their political economy and even over their policy process is an acceptable cost. However, many of the leading developing countries have recently become more resolute in their opposition to key elements of economic globalization, especially to the economic and trade policies of the Global North. The "Group of 21," including the largest developing countries, has organized a more coordinated resistance, demanding global economic and trade policies (implemented through the WTO) that do not put them in such severe disadvantage in relation to the developed countries. In addition, some developing countries are now attempting to organize their own regional free-trade zones to increase their autonomy from the developed countries. Such trade zones have emerged among states representing half of Latin America's population ("Mercosur"), including Argentina, Brazil, Paraguay, and Uruguay, and among a set of Islamic states with 300 million people, including Iran, Kazakhstan, Pakistan, and Turkey. For the foreseeable future, however, virtually every developing country will need some economic aid, goods, markets, and technology from the developed world.

This continuing need for support from the developed countries is captured in a paradoxical comment by Kenya's former President Daniel Arap Moi: "No country can maintain its independence without assistance from outside." In the contemporary political world, no state can survive as an independent entity. But the developing countries are particularly dependent upon outside assistance in many forms, especially economic and technological. Because they are susceptible to influence, manipulation, or even control by other states, few of them can escape this economic component of their insecurity.

GOAL: STABILITY

Many countries in the Global South find that achieving stability is as elusive as achieving prosperity and security. They have not been able to establish structures that maintain social order and ensure stable functioning of the political system through time.

Challenges to Political System Effectiveness

Recall (from Chapter 10) Kwame Nkrumah's credo: "Seek ye first the political kingdom and all else shall be added unto you." This perspective places primary importance on the political system as the crucial instrument for achieving the developing country's goals. It is assumed that the leaders will effectively use the state's policies and structures to create the conditions needed to increase the country's prosperity, security, and stability.

However, in many developing countries, the political system is a flawed instrument for achieving these goals because the state's effectiveness and stability are limited by a variety of factors. Some are the same factors that threaten prosperity and security:

1. The citizens of many developing countries have *little shared culture* or purpose. Rather, historical nationality cleavages grounded in ethnicity, religion, and language become the basis for intensive competition and conflict over value allocations (Barber 1995; Huntington 1996).

2. *Other actors in the international environment,* particularly states and major economic institutions (such as multinational corporations), often use the developing country to achieve their own goals. Typically, their actions reduce the state's political capabilities (Chapter 10) and its capacity to sustain economic development and internal security (Isbister 2004).

3. Most developing countries provide an *inadequate level of material well-being* to satisfy the majority of their populations. The problem is grounded in the country's lack of economic capacity to produce sufficient goods that, in turn, would provide a decent standard of living and support welfare distribution by the state. But Table 14.4 revealed that the problem is even worse: In general, these states have the world's most unequal distributions of wealth. As the examples in the table indicated, the disparity between rich and poor can be huge. The economic elite, and often the political elite, enjoy a very high standard of living, an island of luxury in a sea of desperately poor people. Insufficient prosperity is always a

potential source of political frustration, conflict, and instability, and severe inequality in the distribution of the existing resources makes the situation even more volatile.

Other obstacles to the search for stability, such as the two listed below, are more direct consequences of the political situation within the country:

1. Most of these states *lack a tradition of limited mandate*—an institutionalized, nonviolent procedure for the periodic transfer of power from one government leader to another. Despite recent trends toward democratization (described below), the top political leader in many developing countries has been replaced more often by political violence, such as a coup or an assassination, than by a genuine election. In one of the most extreme examples, Bolivia experienced 190 coups in the 156 years ending in 1982. And during the 1980s, only 3 of 170 leaders in sub-Saharan Africa left power voluntarily.

2. These countries *lack political institutionalization*—the infusion of value into political structures and roles rather than into personalized bases of power (Chapter 10). The political institutions in most developing countries (South American states are the general exception) have existed for fewer than sixty years. They have established modern political forms that are usually either a copy of the institutions of the former colonial master state or a hybrid between the colonial power's institutions and the traditional governing forms in the soci-

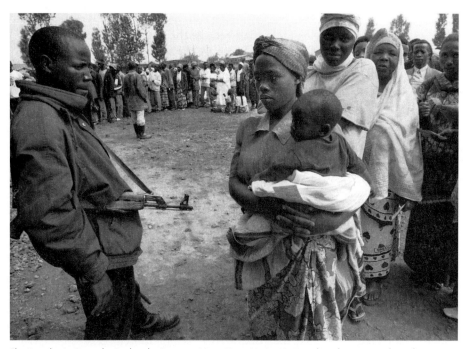

Election day in Rwanda. As developing countries attempt to institutionalize democracy, the military must achieve the delicate balance of maintaining order and protecting democratic practices without taking control of the government during the inevitable periods of instability.

ety. When subjected to the (inevitable) internal and external pressures, these political institutions function ineffectively or break down in political decay (Aguero and Stark 1998; Bratton and van de Walle 1997; Sorensen 1998; Stepan and Linz 1996).

The Decline of Political Order

Political decay.   Samuel Huntington's (1968) model of political decay, described in detail in Chapter 10, is based on the problems of instability in developing countries. The postcolonial history of Ghana (see Box 14.5), like the case studies of Cambodia, Congo, India, and Uruguay described in other boxes in this book, includes episodes of serious political decay. In such states, the combined effects of national independence, some modernization, some economic development, increasing social mobilization, and political leaders' rhetoric cause the population to have high expectations about obtaining increased prosperity and a higher standard of living.

BOX 14.5

A Case of Political Decay: Ghana

Historically, the Gold Coast of West Africa was dominated by the Kingdom of the Asante tribes and had trade linkages with many European powers. The British conquered the area only in 1901, gaining colonial control of the region. As the new state of Ghana, it was the first colonial territory in sub-Saharan Africa to gain its independence, in 1957. Its early leader, Kwame Nkrumah, became an articulate spokesman for African freedom and independence in the postcolonial era.

In the decade before independence, an active multiparty system was created and democratic elections were held. Nkrumah and his Convention Peoples Party (CPP) won the first postindependence election. But significant problems arose immediately, including economic shortfalls associated with world cocoa prices and widespread corruption and inefficiency within the CPP and the government bureaucracy.

Unfortunately, everyone lacked experience with the parliamentary style of government-versus-opposition. Other parties and groups vehemently criticized the failures of the CPP ("a party of incompetents") and the extensive powers exercised by Nkrumah ("a dictator"). These criticisms embarrassed, threatened, and angered Nkrumah and the CPP, and so they passed laws restricting opposition activities. Opponents protested verbally and then violently. The government responded with even more repressive measures, arguing that any opposition was unpatriotic.

The government became more and more autocratic. An election in 1960 was obviously rigged, and a referendum of support for the government in 1964 was a farce. By the 1965 election, legal opposition was virtually eliminated, and all CPP candidates were declared elected. Both the economy and social order were in collapse, and Nkrumah was behaving like a dictator. In 1966 the army intervened, overthrowing Nkrumah and installing a "temporary" military junta.

(continued)

BOX **14.5** (CONTINUED)

Since 1966 Ghana has alternated between civilian governments and military coups. In 1972, 1978, 1979, and 1981, military officers took control of the government in the face of civilian incompetence and corruption. A young air force officer, Flight Lieutenant Jerry Rawlings, led the last two coups. By 1981 Rawlings had become convinced that his leadership and solutions were superior to those of civilian governments. Despite several assassination and coup attempts, he ruled continuously from 1981 until 2000.

Whereas Nkrumah attempted to install a command economy, Rawlings used political power with equal purposefulness to shift to a market economy. He collaborated with the International Monetary Fund to secure loans, implement a structural adjustment program, denationalize most public corporations, and radically cut public services. Ghana's economic performance somewhat improved in the last decade, in the sense that GDP per capita has been growing slightly, at an average of about 1.9 percent per year, and inflation is being "held down" to an average of about 30 percent (see Table 14.3).

Under international pressure, Rawlings allowed a free and fair presidential and parliamentary election in 2000, and an opposition party became the leading force in the political system. Based on this election, Freedom House classified Ghana as a "free" electoral democracy. To this point, however, it is not evident that there is a permanent change in Ghana's persistent political motifs: high inflation and unemployment, corruption and mismanagement, dependency on external political and economic power, curfews, detention without trial, closed borders, and authoritarianism. Ghana, the state that was going to be a model for postindependence Africa, has instead provided a depressing model of economic stagnation and recurrent political decay. The next few years will offer an important test of whether the emergence of an electoral democracy and the recent economic growth will have staying power and will redeem the positive model.

Since the political economy is usually unable to deliver sufficient goods (e.g., jobs, housing, health care, food) to meet these expectations or even to sustain a reasonable level of economic development, there is a decline of citizen support for the political leadership and institutions. The leaders attempt different strategies: (1) some request trust and patience, promising that the system will eventually provide the desired goods; (2) some attempt to substitute symbolic rewards such as greater political participation, which generates some support if the citizens feel they are given a genuine role in their state's political destiny; and (3) some impose repressive policies and use force against any groups or media that criticize the political system.

In most developing countries, a major casualty of these strategies is democratic processes (Bratton and van de Walle 1997; Sorensen 1998). The people lose patience with promises, and the politically active groups are frustrated when their demands are not met. In many cases, the leadership does reassert order through increasingly authoritarian practices. If the state's repressive policies are ineffective, political violence spreads—resulting in strikes, riots, terrorism, and rebellion. In some cases, as political decay increases, social order can collapse into nation-based violence, separatist violence, or revolution. In other cases, external intervention (e.g., the UN, another country) reestablishes democratic practices. But most frequently, a new, even more "forceful" leadership elite emerges (Huntington 1968; Onwumechili 1999; Stepan and Linz 1996).

Military regimes.   Until the last decade, the new political leadership in many developing countries often came from the military. There are three reasons why the military emerges in the attempt to restore order under conditions of actual or potential political decay. First, a key norm within the military is a *commitment to order* and an abhorrence of social disorder. This norm induces the military to act when civilian (or even other military) leadership has failed to maintain order because of a major crisis, a breakdown in the transfer of political power, or evidence of serious political decay. Second, the military has the capacity to *exercise power effectively* since it is the most highly institutionalized and disciplined organizational structure in a developing country. Third, the military has the *capacity to subdue disorder* since it usually controls the greatest concentration of force and violence in the society (Macridis and Burg 1997: 133–135).

As in the example of Ghana (Box 14.5, and recall Box 5.5 on Cambodia and Box 12.2 on Congo), the emergence of strong military leadership is a recurrent pattern in the countries in the Global South. At one point in the early 1980s, military regimes were in power in 15 of the 22 major Latin American states and in 20 of the 26 major sub-Saharan African states. By the mid-1990s, the military in most developing countries had accepted the norm that it should support the civilian regime and prevent nondemocratic practices but that it should not seize power. Thus a substantial number of developing countries are now "protected democracies" in which a strong military protects the political leadership and democratic processes in exchange for public policies that the military supports, such as social stability and maintaining the military's privileged status in society (Colburn 2002; Loveman 1994). However, members of the military are still inclined to take political power in some countries when they perceive political decay, especially in sub-Saharan Africa and South Asia (e.g., Nigeria in 1998; Pakistan in 1999, Ivory Coast in 2000, Guinea-Bissau in 2003). When members of the military do take political power, they typically claim that they are restoring democracy, but they usually establish an authoritarian regime.

Internal war.   When political decay becomes so extensive that no groups, not even the military, can maintain order, a country is likely to become embroiled in internal war—either civil or revolutionary. Given the economic and political conditions outlined earlier, it is understandable why some populations are susceptible to ideologies that promise a dramatic improvement in the distribution of values. In some countries (e.g., Cambodia, Peru, the Philippines), variations of Marxism continue to appeal to frustrated groups who are persuaded their situation fits Marx's revolutionary call that the people have nothing to lose but their chains.

While the appeal of Marxist ideology has diminished in most developing countries, fundamental power struggles and deep inequalities among groups remain.

Conflict is fueled by some combination of ethnonationalist, class, and regional cleavages. In the past decade, rival groups competing for power and control of resources reduced Afghanistan, Burundi, Congo, Haiti, Ivory Coast, Liberia, Sierra Leone, and Somalia to anarchy. In a particularly volatile combination, four decades of conflict among government forces, leftist guerrillas, and drug traffickers has resulted in 35,000 deaths in Colombia as well as 22,000 deaths in Peru during the 1980s.

Major internal violence in developing countries is almost always supported by other states, which pursue their own national interests while providing financial or military assistance to combatants. Thus virtually every civil or revolutionary war in the developing world mobilizes overt and covert support from other states: Syria and Israel invade Lebanon; Uganda, Rwanda, and Burundi intervene in Congo; Libya, France, and the United States assist factions in the civil war in Chad; the United Nations intervenes in Congo, East Timor (Indonesia), Lebanon, and Sierra Leone. Indeed, a key element in the pervasive insecurity *and* instability of developing countries is the ease with which other states can pursue their own policy goals within the context of internal violence in these states.

Democratization

The trend toward democratization analyzed in Chapter 10 is evident in the Global South. Most developing countries are under considerable pressure to shift away from authoritarian and military regimes toward regimes with an elected leadership, a multiparty system, and open, pluralist politics. Two key sources of this pressure are citizen groups demanding political rights and the governments and financial institutions of the Global North.

Figure 14.1 summarizes the level of freedom in Global South countries, according to Freedom House (2003). A "free" country allows its citizens extensive political rights (e.g., to form political parties that represent a significant range of voter choice and to engage in vigorous, open political opposition to the leaders) and civil liberties (e.g., protection of religious, ethnic, economic, linguistic, and other rights). A country that is "not free" substantially limits these rights and liberties. "Partly free" means that there are significant political restrictions and violations of civil liberties, even though the country might be an electoral democracy (recall pages 174–176).

The spread of democratization is most extensive in *Latin America.* In 2004, every country in the Western Hemisphere had an electoral democracy, except Cuba and Haiti, the only "not free" countries in the region. During the 1990s, some, such as Brazil and Peru, weathered serious episodes of political decay that earlier would almost certainly have resulted in a military coup. Others, including Argentina, Haiti, and Venezuela, defeated coup attempts. Freedom House (2003) classifies almost two-thirds of the Latin American countries as fully free democracies (including Brazil, Chile, Costa Rica, Mexico, and Uruguay) (Figure 14.1). "Partly free" countries include Colombia, Guatemala, Nicaragua and Venezuela.

In *Asia,* the spread of democratization is mixed. China emphatically reversed its movement toward democracy in the violent crushing of pro-democracy protestors at Tiananmen Square in 1989. Cambodia, Myanmar, North Korea, Pakistan, and Vietnam are also among eleven Asian developing countries that are classified as "not free." Ten more (including Bangladesh, Indonesia, and Malaysia) are only

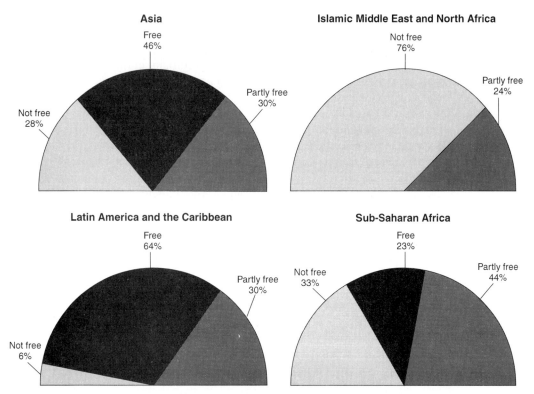

FIGURE 14.1   Level of freedom in the developing countries, by region, circa 2003

Source: Karatnycky (2003)

"partly free." The eighteen "free" countries include the Philippines, South Korea, Thailand, and India, still the world's largest democracy, although it has been battered by political decay, including parliamentary deadlock, assassination, and extensive violence among Hindus, Muslims, and Sikhs. Electoral democracies are functioning in 59 percent of the Asian countries, although some are fragile and under persistent pressure from dissatisfied groups.

Although less than two-fifths of the countries in *sub-Saharan Africa* are electoral democracies, this is the region's highest level of democratization since independence. Freedom House classifies eleven of the forthy-eight countries as "free," led by South Africa and Botswana, while twenty-one are "partly free" (e.g., Kenya, Nigeria), and sixteen are "not free" (e.g., Angola, Congo, Zimbabwe) (Karatnycky 2003). One analyst concludes that the prospects for further democratization are positive in nearly half of the countries in the region (Barkan 2002).

Even many of the developing countries of the *Islamic Middle East* and *North Africa* have introduced elements of democratic politics. Most countries now elect their political leadership (e.g., Egypt, Iran, Morocco), while others at least have a democratically elected legislature (e.g., Jordan). However, these countries do not have well institutionalized democratic structures, and Freedom House classifies only Turkey as an electoral democracy (Karatnycky 2003). When democratic processes threaten the elites, the elites usually reverse them, as occurred in Algeria and Syria. Not one country in the region is "free," and less than one-fourth (Jordan, Kuwait, Morocco, and Turkey) are "partly free."

Overall, democratization has expanded substantially in the Global South during the last two decades. Most regimes have granted some political rights to individuals and groups and have raised the level of elite accountability through elections. While the old elites have retained power in some elections, there are also many countries, especially in Latin America and Asia, where power has passed democratically to former opposition groups.

Nonetheless, the current wave of democracy (discussed in Chapter 10) might already be ebbing in every region of the Global South. Many elections lack legitimacy. For example, when Zimbabwe conducted a "democratic" election in 1996, Robert Mugabe, the president since independence in 1960, had significant advantages besides incumbency. His government controlled all media and all campaign funds, and both candidates opposing him withdrew before the vote (one was arrested). Not surprisingly, Mugabe won easily, and his party won 147 of the 150 legislative seats. He "won" an even more corrupted election in 2003.

Even in Latin America, there are numerous instances of both the breakdown of democracy and also a resurgence of popular support for strong, authoritarian leadership. For example, the Ecuadorian military overthrew its president in a 2001 coup. Peruvian President Alberto Fujimori, backed by the majority of his citizens, suspended the Constitution and seized power from the legislature in a creative political action in 1992 called a *self-coup* (autogolpe). Venezuelan President Hugo Chavez launched a more limited takeover of power in 1999 and faced violent protests in 2004 when he blocked constitutional efforts to remove him from office. Fujimori, like the elected leaders in Argentina, Bolivia, Haiti, and Paraguay, has recently been forced from power by popular uprisings.

Thus the positive developments that have facilitated the expansion of democratization in the Global South are balanced against three negative factors. First, these societies face the major destabilizing forces discussed in this chapter. Second, many elites do not have a genuine commitment to democratic practices. And third, these democratic regimes often have limited political institutionalization. Most will have periods of retreat from democratic governance and will struggle with economic decline, political decay, corruption, military intervention, and authoritarianism. "Hero" by well-known Egyptian cartoonist Toughan reflects the demoralizing obstacles to political and economic development facing citizens in many developing countries (page 417).

Political Approaches

For those who do first "seek the political kingdom" as the primary instrument for achieving political and economic goals, the fundamental question is: What approach will increase the likelihood of prosperity, security, and stability? Developing countries pursue these goals within various political frameworks. One method for categorizing these frameworks is to consider the political approach taken regarding two basic issues: resource equality and democratic participation.

Toughan/© Cartoon News

Resource equality concerns the extent to which the political system attempts to produce an equal distribution of key economic and social values (e.g., wealth, income, status, housing, health care, education, jobs). The state's authoritative allocation of these values can result in either greater equality or greater inequality. While a command political economy can most directly use public policy to distribute economic values, any type of political economy can implement policies aimed at increasing or decreasing equality. And many public policy decisions shape the broader level of egalitarianism in the society.

Democratic participation concerns the extent to which the people are mobilized into active and meaningful involvement in the political process. As was discussed in Chapter 7, a political system is more democratic when there is greater citizen participation in the selection of political leaders from among genuine alternatives and when individuals have a greater capacity to discuss and influence issues in the public domain. At one theoretical extreme, one person has all the political power in a country and all others are prevented from any political action. At the opposite extreme, every citizen has an equal role in political decisions and actions.

Obviously, there is no actual political system located on either end of the continuum for either resource equality or democratic participation. Figure 14.2 indicates four ideal-type political approaches that have different orientations toward the desired mix of equality and democracy: (1) conservative authoritarianism, (2) modernizing authoritarianism, (3) revolutionary socialism, and (4) constitutional democracy. The next sections describe features of each.

Conservative authoritarianism.   Conservative authoritarian regimes have little or no commitment to resource equality. There is an effort to preserve the traditional socioeconomic order and culture. Certain groups, defined by lineage, ethnicity, class, religion, or some other trait, enjoy great advantages in the distribution of economic and social power. This socioeconomic elite, with support from the government apparatus, exercises substantial control over the political economy and might also exercise great political power. In fact, many of these regimes are dominated by an elite drawn from the military or religious leaders. Most people are allowed little or no role in the political process. Political repression of the mass can be based on traditional practices, especially those associated with religion, or on state actions, especially those implemented by such agents of the state as the police and the military. In fact, many of these regimes are dominated by an elite drawn from the military or religious leaders.

Greater political stability tends to occur in conservative authoritarian states that have limited economic resources to distribute, that have no ideology of egalitarianism, and where those groups engaged in order maintenance are well organized and loyal to the elite. As these conditions become less strong, there is more chance the state will become unstable. Contemporary examples of such political systems are Haiti, Nepal, Saudi Arabia, Somalia, and Tajikistan.

Modernizing authoritarianism.   Modernizing authoritarian regimes differ from conservative authoritarianism primarily in the way their elites are willing to recognize that development is inevitable and perhaps even desirable. These states can have

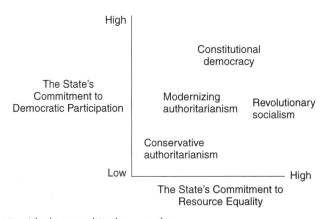

FIGURE 14.2   Ideal-type political approaches

well-institutionalized organizational structures in the public sector, and technocratic elites within the bureaucracy can be a key group within the ruling coalition. Typically, most of the political economy is under private control, although the state works cooperatively with economic actors.

Substantial economic and social inequalities remain, and the elites make no major attempt to reduce them. Rather, they seem to act under the assumption that economic development will have an indirect, trickle-down effect and will eventually raise the absolute level of economic and social power of the less advantaged. Many of these states claim to be evolving slowly toward democracy, as another effect of development. Minimal levels of popular political participation are allowed, but state policies regulate political behavior and restrain opposition. State leaders put a strong emphasis on stability and allocate considerable state resources to create strong capabilities for order maintenance. As in conservative authoritarian states, military leaders are often a prominent part of the political elite. Modernizing authoritarianism characterizes such regimes as China, Egypt, Indonesia, Kenya, Morocco, Nigeria, and Syria.

Revolutionary socialism.   Revolutionary socialist regimes have a strong commitment to economic and social equality but provide a very limited political role for the large majority of the population. The leadership contends that a small political elite is essential, since leaders must be decisive and unconstrained if they are to reduce the massive inequalities in the society. Thus the leadership acts on behalf of the population, asserting totalitarian control over the political economy and the society.

Revolutionary socialism emphasizes the political mobilization of the population, which is expected to support the policies of the elite. Leaders institute an extensive program of political socialization through the educational system, social and occupational groups, culture, and the media. The people are indoctrinated to recognize the political implications of virtually every action. The objective is to create citizens who want to "serve the people" rather than pursue self-interest and who serve collective interests as a matter of value preference rather than because they fear sanctions. In practice, these states do employ repression and sanctions on their citizens as well as positive socialization and peer pressure to induce desirable behavior.

China under Mao Zedong is a clear example of revolutionary socialism. Few current regimes follow this approach, although Cuba, Libya, and North Korea utilize some aspects. The military regimes in Myanmar and in Peru (between 1968 and 1976) are examples of revolutionary socialism in a non-communist system. Laos and Cambodia under the Pol Pot regime (described in Box 5.5) emphasized sanctions and repression of the masses.

Constitutional democracy.   Constitutional democracies emphasize an open politics in which citizens are allowed considerable freedom to undertake many modes of political participation. Political actors and political decisions are constrained by the rule of law, which guarantees the rights of the ruled and limits the powers of the rulers. And as a democratic regime, the leaders are directly accountable to the citizens and receive a limited mandate by means of an electoral system with genuine alternatives. Open political opposition is allowed, the media are relatively free to assess political actions, and public involvement in the political process is facilitated.

The political leadership is not committed to using public policy to achieve economic equality. A state-regulated but relatively free economic order is viewed as the best means to generate resources for the benefit of all. Thus the political system facilitates the operation of a mixed political economy, a substantial part of which is privately controlled. The state engages in some welfare distribution, particularly to those in greatest need, and there might be public policies to encourage modest increases in social equality.

Botswana, India, Jamaica, Malta, and Costa Rica (see Box 14.6) are states that have generally maintained constitutional democracies in the last thirty years. As

BOX 14.6

A Third World Democracy That Works: Costa Rica

Costa Rica is one of the few developing countries that has sustained a constitutional democracy for decades. This Central American country of 3.9 million has a small (57-member) unicameral legislature and a president elected for a single four-year term. There is an efficient (if large) public bureaucracy, a relatively independent judiciary, and a stable party system dominated by two parties that are generally pragmatic rather than ideological. For most of the twentieth century, the state and the society enjoyed high levels of political and social order. Currently, there is freedom of expression, a free press, and active political opposition. For those promoting constitutional democracy in the developing countries, the obvious question is: How has Costa Rica done it?

Costa Rica has had a few intrinsic advantages. The great majority of the population shares ethnicity and language, and there is no large subservient class of nonwhite laborers. Still, Costa Rica shares many features with other Latin American states that have not been able to sustain democratic politics:

It is small and hence a manageable size (but this factor has not helped neighbors Panama, Nicaragua, and El Salvador).

It has only limited natural resources, and its export economy has relied on a few commodities such as coffee, bananas, and sugar.

It was part of the Spanish colonial empire, then was under the general hemispheric dominance of the United States after its independence in 1821.

It has a small, wealthy upper class that controls the large plantations, a substantial middle class, and a significant number of poor and unskilled people who live primarily in rural areas.

Catholicism is the state religion.

Its population is about half urban and half rural (only highly urban Mexico is an exception to this pattern in Central America).

The success of Costa Rica as a constitutional democracy is based less on fortuitous conditions than on sensible policies and continuing commitment to democratic processes. The norms and the procedures of the political system encourage efforts to achieve political consensus within a framework of participatory govern-

BOX **14.6** (CONTINUED)

ment. The constitution prohibits the president from serving a second term, balances the power of the executive and legislative branches, and encourages cooperation within a legislature that often does not have a single-party majority.

Consistent with the ideal-type constitutional democracy in Figure 14.1, the Costa Rican state does not have a strong commitment to use public policy to equalize resources. The political economy is oriented toward the market system. The government has balanced some controls on the private sector and protection of workers' rights with policies that encourage and subsidize private farmers and business entrepreneurs. Economic and social inequalities remain.

However, a tradition of reformist policies has gradually expanded social welfare and reduced inequalities. Costa Rica has the fourth highest human development index score (83.2) among all countries in Central and South America. Public expenditure is allocated to subsidize extensive health services, public education, and financial support for the elderly (e.g., pensions, social security). Since the late 1880s, the state has provided free and compulsory education to all children. And after a brief civil war in 1948, Costa Rica replaced its military with a small national police, spending only 1.6 percent of central government expenditure on military support (CIA 2003).

Costa Ricans enjoy the highest standard of living in Central America, and the country is second among 22 major Latin American countries on per-capita GDP (World Bank 2003: table 1.1). Economic growth has been solid, although it is burdened by inflation and a large level of domestic and foreign debt. In the 1990s, Costa Rica had to cope with spillovers from the instability and natural disasters in neighboring Panama and Nicaragua and the in-migration of substantial numbers of refugees. Yet its generous social programs and accommodating political culture have helped generate strong support for the legitimacy of its political system from all major groups within the society. Costa Rica continues to provide hope, if not a model that can be duplicated, for other developing countries that aspire to political democracy. (This discussion relies on Goodwin 2003).

previously noted, many developing countries evolved toward more complete constitutional democracy during the 1990s. These countries still face substantial pressure when they undergo the inevitable problems achieving prosperity, security, or stability. Operating within democratic processes, the political system must attempt to satisfy groups on the left, which demand greater egalitarianism, and groups on the right, which demand greater economic freedom and a stronger government role in maintaining political and social order.

Which route?   Every state attempts to attain prosperity, security, and stability. But in terms of the dimensions depicted in Figure 14.2, leaders must make fundamental choices about the approach by which to pursue these goals. The rhetoric of political leaders in most developing countries (but not in conservative authoritarian regimes) includes a vision in which their society ultimately achieves both high levels of political democracy and considerable social and economic equality—the upper-right corner in Figure 14.2. The key question is: What is the most effective route to reach that "ideal location"?

The route the state takes will be influenced by many factors that its leaders cannot control in the short run: a country's relations with other states, its political culture, its geopolitical situation, its nationality composition, its history of political institutions and leaders, and so on. Within these constraints, political choices can be made regarding the route. One set of major choices concerns the structure of the political economy, especially the level and nature of state involvement in the economic system. Figure 14.2 reflects two other key choices. Modernizing authoritarianism, revolutionary socialism, and constitutional democracy place different emphases on the balance between attaining political democracy and achieving social and economic equality.

The most explicit trade-off between the two sets of objectives is evident between constitutional democracy and revolutionary socialism—between on the one hand, a state that allows greater individual and political freedom, and on the other hand, a strong interventionist state that promotes egalitarianism of social and material conditions rather than personal freedom. Modernizing authoritarian regimes tend to move slowly (sometimes very slowly, and sometimes backward) in both directions and in most cases do not promote either democracy or egalitarianism.

Leaders in developing countries have few models of states that have successfully reached the upper-right corner in Figure 14.2. An "enlightened" leader who would like to achieve the ideal (and who has a pragmatic grasp of the recent histories of most developing countries) might assess the options like this:

> Revolutionary socialism is best justified if our economic conditions are desperate. The strong interventionist state can try to "bootstrap" development by organizing the population and by installing a command economy that limits external economic control and makes best use of societal resources. Despite extensive efforts at political mobilization and socialization, maintaining stability in this system requires stringent restrictions on personal freedom and repressive social policies. And the economic performance of command economies has been mediocre, leading to an equality of poverty. Few populations have sustained enthusiasm and support for this approach. Indeed, most governments seem to have abandoned it.

> Constitutional democracies have the desirable features of allowing greater personal freedom and stimulating more economic initiative. The market-oriented political economy is vibrant but becomes dependent on the direct involvement of the multinational corporations and the developed countries, which enjoy many of the economic benefits from this neocolonial situation. It also tends to produce very uneven economic development across regions, economic sectors, and population groups, causing an increase in inequality between rich and poor, advantaged and disadvantaged. These conditions, in conjunction with a commitment to democratic political processes, tend to pro-

duce considerable political and social instability. A government committed to democratic processes will have trouble delivering prosperity, which could result in a loss of electoral support, so it might not be able to prevent political decay. At the least, I will be removed from office; at worst, there is a worrisome probability that my government will face a military coup, civil war, internal revolutionary political violence, and/or direct foreign intervention.

Modernizing authoritarianism is a compromise with the fewest risks and the lowest potential gains regarding either goal. Material conditions improve marginally for most of the population, but there has been minimal reduction in social and economic inequality. The Asian NICs have used a version of this approach to achieve prosperity and stability, although political democracy follows, only at a slow pace. The most problematic factor, however, is that many other developing countries in other regions have attempted a version of modernizing authoritarianism without duplicating even the economic growth of the Asian NICs. In other cultures, this approach seems to produce short-run stability but little significant progress toward democracy or social and economic equality. And even the Asian NICs had serious economic problems in the late 1990s. In the early years of the twenty-first century, the economies of most modernizing authoritarian states still seem dependent on the developed countries, international finance, and the multinational corporations. And the politics of many of these regimes seems to rely on repression as an antidote for the recurrent political decay.

What should my country do? And, more fundamentally, what can we do? The problems we face are not just management problems of choosing and implementing a strategy. We are not free and unconstrained. My country has substantial problems created by diversity and conflict. And the problems caused by globalization and external actors, especially those from certain developed countries and some hostile states in this region, are enormous and sometimes overwhelming.

CONCLUDING OBSERVATIONS: IT'S GETTING BETTER ALL THE TIME(?)

In political forms, as in goals, there are no fundamental differences between those of the developing countries of the Global South and those of the developed countries. Any developing country's selection of a particular political approach or political economy is dependent on many factors, especially historical patterns, geopolitical conditions, and current circumstances. While there are a few command economies and some total market economies, most implement some form of a mixed market system. Some countries are constitutional democracies and some are totalitarian dictatorships. *Economic* underdevelopment is obviously the main factor distinguishing the developing countries from the developed countries. But *political* underdevelopment is the pivotal problem if the political system is to be used as the crucial instrument for social and economic change.

Regardless of their political approach, virtually all developing countries face difficult challenges as they attempt to use the political system to achieve prosperity and security. Most have valuable natural resources and a population that is willing to apply its energies to achieve these goals. However, their underdevelopment places them at an enormous disadvantage in the contemporary world, with its globalized political, military, and economic patterns and where states are even more single-minded in the pursuit of national self-interest.

For many of these states, especially the low-income developing countries, it is possible that *no* political approach and *no* form of political economy can simultaneously achieve all these major goals. The leaders of any developing country must make very difficult decisions about how to gain partial success on some of their goals. Some objectives will have to be sacrificed in the quest for others, and there is no assurance that *any* objective can be accomplished. In the contemporary political world, the obstacles are formidable, and determining the best strategy is baffling. At every turn, the underlying political choices are fundamental: freedom versus security, economic development versus welfare, political equality versus economic equality, democracy versus efficiency, aid versus independence, market economy versus command economy, guns versus butter. Yet there are grounds for some optimism. Since 1990, the low-income countries have achieved some notable improvements: Life expectancy has increased by 2 years (to 59), adult illiteracy has declined from 45 percent to 37 percent, debt service has reduced from 23 percent to 11 percent of exports, and the number of "free" countries increased. Perhaps it is getting better, even if not in every developing country and not all the time. . . .

KEY CONCEPTS

conservative authoritarianism
democratization
direct foreign investment
export promotion
"fourth-way" approach
Fourth World
Global South
green revolution
hyperinflation
import substitution

industrialization
International Monetary Fund
market-oriented development
microcredit
modernizing authoritarianism
neocolonialism
revolutionary socialism
structural adjustment programs
Third World

FOR FURTHER CONSIDERATION

1. Assess the claim that the label "Third World" has no meaning, either analytical or political, in the globalized, post–cold war world.
2. Are the problems in achieving economic development in the developing countries attributable primarily to the actions of the developed countries, or are they best explained by domestic circumstances in these countries?

3. Specify the conditions in a real (or imaginary) developing country. In that context, provide a response to the comments of the "enlightened" developing country leader presented near the end of this chapter. Given your country's conditions, what political and economic arrangements make the most sense for progressing on the key development goals you emphasize?
4. Is political violence in the developing countries likely to be greater or less during the next ten years compared with the past ten years? Why?
5. In addition to greater economic prosperity, what conditions seem most likely to sustain the shift to democratization in many developing countries? In particular, what forms or arrangements of political structures are most important?

FOR FURTHER READING

Bill, James A., and Robert Springborg. (2000). *Politics in the Middle East.* 5th ed. New York: Addison Wesley. A sound comparative introduction to political systems in the area.

Ehrlich, Paul R., and Anne H. Ehrlich. (1990). *The Population Explosion.* New York: Simon & Schuster. Updating the earlier arguments in *The Population Bomb,* the Ehrlichs mount a powerful case that overpopulation in the developing world will lead to actions that result in catastrophic deterioration of the planet's resources.

Esposito, John L., and John O. Voll. (1996). *Islam and Democracy.* New York: Oxford University Press. Interesting case studies, including Algeria, Egypt, and Iran, are employed to develop a sensitive analysis of the ways in which Islamic countries adapt to democratic principles and to the forces of secularism.

Isbister, John. (2004). *Promises Not Kept: Poverty and Betrayal of Third World Development.* 6th ed. Bloomfield, CT: Kumarian Press. A sensible and balanced analysis of the difficulties that have prevented most developing countries from achieving sustained development, exploring both the external and the internal obstacles to prosperity.

Krasner, Stephen D. (1985). *Structural Conflict: The Third World against Global Liberalism.* Berkeley: University of California Press. A challenging critique of the political and economic domination of the developing countries by the more developed countries.

Li, Cheng. (1997). *Rediscovering China: Dynamics and Dilemmas of Reform.* Lanham, MD: Rowman & Littlefield. An insightful description of the powerful changes sweeping China at both the individual and the institutional level, based on Li's personal observations and interviews.

Mehta, Ved. (1993). *A Portrait of India.* New Haven, CT: Yale University Press. A sensitive characterization of one of the most complex and intriguing developing countries.

O'Donnell, Guillermo, Philippe Schmitter, and Laurence Whitehead, Eds. (1986). *Transitions from Authoritarian Rule.* Baltimore, MD: Johns Hopkins University Press. Important case studies regarding the development and decline of rule by the military and technocrats, especially in Latin American countries.

Onwumechili, Chuka. (1999). *African Democratization and Military Coups.* Westport, CT: Praeger. A sobering and occasionally encouraging characterization of 40 years of struggle to establish democracy in African countries and to limit the tendency toward violent takeovers and authoritarian rule by the military.

Simon, Julian. (1996). *The Ultimate Resource 2.* Princeton, NJ: Princeton University Press. A powerful critique of those, like the Ehrlichs, who predict disaster due to overpopulation and environmental degradation. It argues that the ultimate resource (people producing knowledge and then applying it as technology) will outstrip problems.

Skidmore, Thomas, and Peter Smith. (2001). *Modern Latin America.* 5th ed. New York: Oxford University Press. A helpful comparative introduction to society and politics in Latin America.

Weatherby, Joseph N., et al., Eds. (2003). *The Other World: Issues and Politics of the Developing World.* 5th ed. New York: Longman. Thoughtful general chapters on colonialism, women and development, and political economy precede informative chapters focusing on each region of developing countries.

World Bank. (Yearly). *World Development Report.* New York: Oxford University Press. Systematic yearly statistics on the economic, financial, and demographic aspects of development for more than 180 states. Each annual issue also emphasizes a key theme (e.g., 1990 on poverty, 1991 on environment, 1997 on the role of the state, 1998 on knowledge for development), with a strong emphasis on the developing countries.

ON THE WEB

http://www.africanews.org/

This site includes key stories from more than forty African newspapers and newsmagazines as well as other information about each country and links to important documents.

http://allafrica.com

Focusing on Africa, this site posts more than eight hundred stories daily in English and French and lists more than six hundred thousand articles in a searchable archive.

http://www.arab.net

Rich information on such aspects as the government, culture, business, and geography of every country in the Middle East and North Africa is provided as well as coverage of current news and issues.

http://menic.utexas.edu/menic/

The Middle East Network Information Center, hosted by the University of Texas, Austin, provides a vast number of sites with information regarding such areas as the politics, culture, and economic development of countries in the Middle East.

http://lanic.utexas.edu/index.html

The Latin American Network Information Center, hosted at the University of Texas, Austin, provides a vast number of Internet-based information sources about all countries in Latin America.

http://home.tampabay.rr.com/latinoconnect/

The Latino Connection provides numerous links to political, cultural, and societal information about each country in Central and South America.

http://www.undp.org

The web site for United Nations Development Programme, a key unit of the UN that specializes in issues of economic and political development.

http://www.aseansec.org/

On the official web site of the Association of South East Asian Nations are information and documents relevant to ASEAN, news about countries in the region, and somewhat self-serving web pages constructed by each member state.

http://www.unctad.org/en/subsites/ldcs/ldc11.htm

This part of the home page of the United Nations' Conference on Trade and Development focuses on issues regarding the world's least developed countries.

http://un.org/womenwatch/

This French-based bilingual site provides links to various research, documents, organizations, and activities that concern the role of women in the development process.

http://www.twnside.org.sg/

Based in Malaysia, the Third World Network links a variety of individuals and organizations that are concerned with the full range of issues facing developing countries.

A whole new world! A Russian veteran casts his vote, selecting from more than fifty political parties, under the disapproving gaze of V. I. Lenin, who had established one-party rule by the Communist Party of the Soviet Union.

CHAPTER 15 The Transitional Developed Countries

Even in a dynamic world, the forces of change seem especially powerful in certain countries, including the two groups of *transitional developed countries* whose characteristics were defined in Chapter 13: (1) the post-communist developed countries of the former Soviet bloc, and (2) the newly industrializing countries The specific countries in each group are listed in Table 15.1. They can be distinguished from most developing countries in the Global South (in Chapter 14) because they have relatively higher economic and/or the social dimensions of development, but they have not reached the levels of the developed countries (discussed in Chapter 13).

As noted in Chapter 13, the criteria for including or excluding a country from one of these development groups are imprecise and subject to interpretation. The countries in Table 15.1 are singled out for examination in this chapter because they are in particularly notable periods of transition. It is possible that the changes these countries are undergoing will ultimately result in levels of economic and social development comparable to that in the most developed countries. But they face significant obstacles that might prevent their achievement of such high levels in the near future, and some of these countries are most likely to remain at levels similar to those of other developing countries. Thus they are revealing case studies of "countries-in-the-middle" within our framework of analysis. This chapter explores the broad patterns of changes and the obstacles facing each group.

THE POST-COMMUNIST DEVELOPED COUNTRIES

The post-communist developed countries is a category that includes many of the states that emerged after the breakup of the Soviet Union in 1991 (e.g., Estonia, Georgia, Latvia, Russia, Ukraine) and the states that evolved from the Soviet Union's previous allies in Central and Eastern Europe (e.g., the Czech Republic, Hungary, Poland, Slovenia). The 19 states in this analytic category have a population of about four hundred million. The discussion in this chapter generally excludes the 8 (of 27) countries from this region that are classified as low-income countries by the World Bank (e.g., Azerbaijan, Moldova, Tajikistan). Although these 8 countries seem to fit the criteria for developing countries, some major NGOs still treat this evolving set of 27 countries as a single group. Freedom House (2003) clusters all 27 countries as "Central and Eastern Europe and the former Soviet Union," and

TABLE 15.1
Transitional Developed Countries

Country	Population	Former State
Post-Communist Developed Countries		
Belarus	10,000,000	Soviet Union
Bulgaria	7,900,000	
Croatia	4,400,000	Yugoslavia
Czech Republic	10,200,000	Czechoslovakia
Estonia	1,400,000	Soviet Union
Georgia	5,200,000	Soviet Union
Hungary	10,200,000	
Kazakhstan	14,900,000	Soviet Union
Latvia	2,400,000	Soviet Union
Lithuania	3,500,000	Soviet Union
Poland	38,600,000	
Romania	22,400,000	
Russia	144,800,000	Soviet Union
Slovak Republic	5,400,000	Czechoslovakia
Slovenia	2,000,000	Yugoslavia
Ukraine	49,100,000	Soviet Union
Uzbekistan	25,100,000	Soviet Union
Yugoslavia	10,700,000	Yugoslavia (parts)
Post-Communist Less Developed Countries		
Albania	3,200,000	
Armenia	3,100,000	Soviet Union
Azerbaijan	8,100,000	Soviet Union
Bosnia and Herzogovina	4,100,000	Yugoslavia
Kyrgyzstan	5,000,000	Soviet Union
Moldova	4,300,000	Soviet Union
Tajikistan	6,200,000	Soviet Union
Turkmenistan	4,500,000	Soviet Union
Newly Industrializing Countries: Asia		
Malaysia	23,800,000	
South Korea	47,300,000	
Taiwan	22,600,000	
Thailand	61,200,000	
Newly Industrializing Countries: Latin America		
Argentina	37,500,000	
Brazil	172,400,000	
Chile	15,400,000	
Mexico	99,400,000	
Uruguay	3,400,000	
Venezuela	24,600,000	

Source: CIA World Factbook (2004).

the World Bank (2003) refers to the entire group as "Europe and Central Asia" (it treats Western Europe as part of another group of "high income OECD countries").

The PCDCs are currently engaged in a process of substantial economic and political transformation. From the late 1940s to the late 1980s, they were communist states and were trying to achieve prosperity, stability, and security under the structure of a command political economy and totalitarianism. Beginning in the late 1980s, these states abandoned their communist ideologies and attempted to transform themselves into more market-oriented political economies and to implement democratic politics. These sweeping changes were the watershed events in the shift in the international system to the post–cold war period (described in Chapter 12).

Figure 13.1 in Chapter 13 reflects that these countries are relatively advanced on the social development dimension. Their populations are well educated and mainly urban, and they are incorporating high tech systems into their economies and their private lives. The states have adopted democratic political processes but are institutionalizing them in varied degrees. Their economic development is more difficult to assess by the standard GDP per capita measure because the performance of their political economies was significantly depressed during much of the 1990s, a period of fundamental change. While some citizens in these countries support the shift to a market economy, others are dissatisfied with the effects of this change on themselves and on their society. In their quest for prosperity, stability, and security, the PCDCs are attempting to find a reasonable balance between these newer forms of politics and economics and the "traditional" communist approaches. The next sections briefly describe key elements of the communist approaches that shaped these political systems for between forty and eighty years (and ended about 1990) and then characterize the current systems.

POLITICAL CULTURE

The peoples of the PCDCs have a rich and complicated history shaped by many political cultures. Most of the former Soviet Union was ruled autocratically by the Russian czars for three centuries before the Russian Revolution of 1917. The rest of the region was controlled for much of the same period by great empires, including the Ottoman Turkish Empire in Eastern Europe (e.g., Bulgaria, Macedonia, Romania) and the Austrian (Hapsburg) Empire in Central Europe (e.g., the Czech Republic, Hungary, Poland). Only in the late nineteenth century did independent states emerge in Central and Eastern Europe. The political cultures of these states are strongly influenced by their history of oppressive rule and by the multiple nationalities that live within the boundaries of most of these states.

Under Communism

The dominant influence on political culture in these states from 1945 to 1985 was *Marxist-Leninist socialism* (Chapter 2). This political philosophy began with Karl Marx (1818–1883) and evolved after the Russian Revolution through the decisions of such Soviet leaders as V. I. Lenin (in power 1917–1924), Joseph Stalin (1927–1953), and Mikhail Gorbachev (1985–1991). Marxism-Leninism is supposed to be a "scientific" description of reality, but it also provides a normative perspective (i.e., a prescription of how things *should* be).

This political culture has four central concepts. First, consistent with the class approach (described in Chapter 9), individual societies and the international system have historically been subject to patterns of *stratification and class struggle.* Over time, lower classes overthrow the oppressive class above them, and the political economy is then transformed.

Second, a political economy must be employed to achieve the ultimate goal: producing *equality* in the control of and benefits from societal resources, regardless of a person's status, role, age, gender, ethnicity, or any other such factor.

Third, until equality produces a classless society, politics must be *guided by an ideological elite.* This elite, the Communist Party, controls the state and the economy, makes all policy decisions, and monitors the behavior of everyone to ensure that all serve the core goals of the Party. Lenin called this phase "the dictatorship of the proletariat."

Fourth, when the transformation to communism is complete, the coercive state is no longer necessary and a true *people's democracy* is established. The state will, in the language of Engels, "wither away," to be replaced by "the administration of things" and by widespread democratic participation in politics at the local level.

Post-Communism

Opposition to Marxist-Leninist political culture always existed in these countries, although it was generally repressed by the state and the Communist Party until the 1980s. This alternative political culture grew more visible as the regimes lost tight control. The post-communist political culture rejects the monopoly of power by the Communist Party in favor of a system based on democracy and group politics. It also insists that the political economy must abandon extensive state control and state ownership, shifting toward a market political economy, private ownership, and greater freedom of action for firms and individuals.

Most people, especially younger people and those in the most successful PCDCs, now accept this new political culture. However, for many in the older generations and for those disadvantaged by the new system, key elements of Marxist-Leninist political culture continue to have a strong hold. The problems associated with the post-communist system have been so severe in Russia, for example, that in 2003, the Communist Party was still identified as the party that best represents the interests of "all Russian people" by 40 percent of the adults, a larger proportion than for any other party (Murphy 2003). Both the tensions between these viewpoints and also people's actual experiences under the communist and post-communist periods substantially affect their current beliefs about the best means to pursue the basic goals of prosperity, stability, and security. The next three sections characterize these countries' strategies for obtaining these goals and their performance during both periods.

GOAL: PROSPERITY

Under Communism

These states claimed that the main purpose of communist economic development was to allow for the equal distribution of abundant goods and material welfare to the entire population. The principal strategy for achieving prosperity was the *command econ-*

omy, as described in Chapter 8. The state and the Communist Party, guided by a comprehensive plan, attempted to control the use of society's valued resources so that the economy benefited all "the people," not just the rich and privileged.

Performance.   Under communism, these countries had relatively high scores on most quality-of-life measures (such as the human development index) that correspond more closely to the Marxist-Leninist political culture's own definition of prosperity than does GDP per capita. At the individual level, virtually every citizen had access to inexpensive or free health care, education, food, and shelter, and most had economic security against such problems as illness and old age. However, these countries' economic performance (as GDP per capita) was disappointing, relative to the developed countries (with which they compared themselves). Most did rank in the upper one-third of the world's states, between fifteenth (the former East Germany) and forty-ninth (the former Yugoslavia).

Problems.   Although basic goods were distributed to most people, the overall quality of goods was poor and there were persistent shortages of many goods and services. Three inherent problems with command political economies seemed particularly important (recall Chapter 8):

1. *Inadequate incentives.* Contrary to the Marxist ideal, workers were less inclined to work hard for the good of all the people than they were to work for their own private benefit. Since there were few wage incentives, many workers had minimal motivation to work efficiently. And managers were cautious, because the penalties for not following the economic plan were greater than the rewards for successful innovation.

2. *Overcentralization.* The states' large central planning bureaucracies were rigid and unable to foresee the precise needs of producers and consumers. Thus economic activities based on these plans were not responsive either to short-term opportunities and problems or to particular local circumstances.

3. *Inadequate capital investment.* Because the states emphasized development of heavy industry and military equipment, they did not make sufficient capital investment in machinery and modern technologies (e.g., computers) to stimulate productivity gains in agriculture, light industry, and consumer goods (Blasi, Kroumova, and Kruse 1997).

Post-Communism

Many countries (e.g., Hungary, Poland, Yugoslavia) had begun economic innovations in the 1980s, introducing elements of a market and encouraging some profit seeking by firms. Soviet leader Mikhail Gorbachev accelerated these changes with his support for economic *perestroika* ("restructuring") (Goldman 1992; Medvedev 2000).

Most of the PCDC leaders who came to power in the early 1990s have attempted to achieve a rapid transition to a market political economy. Central planning was abandoned. Private firms are allowed to produce goods for profit, and the prices of most goods are determined by supply and demand. Most state-owned enterprises have been sold to private actors ("privatized") or shut down. Firms must survive in the competitive global economy.

Performance. Governments varied considerably in the speed and depth with which they implemented these changes. Some countries (e.g., the Czech Republic, Poland, Romania) opted for radical market reforms (sometimes termed *"shock therapy"*), attempting to introduce the market political economy quickly and extensively. Other countries (e.g., Hungary, Russia, Slovenia) chose a more gradual (*"reformist"*) approach based on slower changes in the political economy (Rutland 1999). Regardless of approach, during the early 1990s most PCDCs experienced a substantial decline in GDP, high unemployment, hyperinflation (inflation averaging higher than 100 percent per year occurred in all but two of the PCDCs), and widespread personal economic hardship (World Bank 1996: table A3). Table 15.2 indicates that in 2001, about half of the countries still had not recovered to their 1990 levels, and some had lost enormous prosperity, as much as two-thirds of GDP per capita. But the other half of the PCDCs did achieve substantial economic growth levels by the mid-1990s, and their average annual growth for the entire period was positive, led by Poland's 3.2 percent average annual increase in GDP per capita.

At the individual level, the real income of most people has dropped substantially, cuts in welfare services have been deep, and unemployment has soared. Ten of the 13 PCDCs in the table have lower scores on the Human Development Index in 2001 than in 1990. As Table 15.3 indicates, the number of people in absolute poverty increased enormously in less than a decade—from 14 million people just prior to the "fall of communism" in 1988 (4 percent of the population) to 147 mil-

TABLE 15.2

Economic Growth and Decline in Selected Post-Communist Developed Countries, 1990–2001

Country	Average Annual Growth/Decline in Gross Domestic Product per Capita 1990–2001	Percentage Change in Human Development Index 1993–2001
Poland	3.2 %	1.2
Czech Republic	2.6	−3.5
Hungary	1.0	−5.6
Slovak Republic	0.3	−6.3
Estonia	0	−4.5
Belarus	−0.3	−6.6
Bulgaria	−0.9	−6.9
Romania	−1.2	9.0
Uzbekistan	−1.3	4.9
Kazakhstan	−1.5	−4.6
Russia	−2.8	−9.6
Ukraine	−5.7	−9.2
Georgia	−6.75	−10.0

Sources: World Bank 2003, Table 10; United Nations Development Program 1993: table 1.1; United Nations Development Program 2003: table 1.

TABLE 15.3

Level of Poverty in Selected Post-Communist Developed Countries, 1988 and 1995

Country	Percent of Population in Poverty		Total Number of Poor (millions)	
	1988	1995	1988	1995
Moldova	4%	66%	0.2	2.9
Ukraine	2	63	1.0	32.7
Central Asian States	15	53	6.5	25.0
Russia	2	44	2.2	66.1
Romania	6	39	1.3	8.9
The Baltic States	1	29	0.1	2.3
Poland	6	14	2.1	5.3
Hungary	1	2	0.1	0.2
Czech Republic	0	0	0.0	0.0
All PCDCs	4	40	13.6	147.1

Source: World Bank 1999: table 1c.

lion in 1996 (fully 40 percent of the population). By 2001, it had dropped, but one in four citizens in the PCDCs was still in absolute poverty, and the incidence was very high in some countries.

The problems in Russia were substantial, and its failure to achieve a more positive transition to a market economy, described in Box 15.1, dominates the situation in the region and is characteristic of those PCDCs that are still struggling. In contrast, several countries (especially Slovenia, the Czech Republic, and Hungary) are now approaching the economic levels of some developed countries. Nearly all PCDCs have economic performance levels higher than those of the countries in the Global South during the recent period (Table 15.5).

Although there is no simple explanation for the different levels of economic decline and then of growth among the PCDCs during this post-communist period, several factors seem important. First, these countries began the transition to market economies at varying points of economic development, and the less developed economies have generally been less successful in adapting. Second, the countries that undertook radical change have been more effective in shrinking the role of inefficient state enterprises and in expanding private sector activity. Third, an unanticipated problem with the gradualist approach has been "crony capitalism"—the tendency for the old Communist Party elite to use their connections in order to reemerge as the new economic elite. These insiders gained control of many of the most lucrative state assets when they were privatized, often at bargain prices, and then exploited those assets for personal gain (Goldman 2003; McFaul 2001; Rupnik 1999).

Challenges. Since their political economies now function like all other market systems in the global economy, the post-communist developed countries face all the formidable challenges to sustaining prosperity that confront the developed countries, as detailed in Chapter 13. However, these challenges are compounded in the PCDCs because many people and organizations in these states are still influenced by more than two generations of experience under the nearly antithetical framework of the command political economy and the political culture of Marxism-Leninism. States must meet several challenges for a more successful transition.

First, the state and key economic actors must *institutionalize free-market mechanisms* (e.g., capital markets, business contracts, business law), which did not exist under the command economy. Some countries have been reluctant to shrink the state sector too rapidly because the closure of state enterprises eliminates many jobs and the subsidized goods (e.g., food, electricity) that they produce. The states have also been slow to eliminate the extensive regulatory and bureaucratic obstacles to the formation of private firms. At present, many of these economic systems are also hampered by extremely ineffective systems of taxation (e.g., tax evasion is widespread) and considerable illegal economic behavior (e.g., extensive black markets) (Kramer 1998).

Second, these states must *determine an appropriate level of welfare distribution* for various groups in society. The state has drastically reduced its deep subsidies for food, shelter, health care, education, transportation, and other benefits, and has also eliminated its extensive transfer payments to the financially disadvantaged. These cutbacks have occurred during a period when the material living conditions of many people have declined significantly. At the same time, the prosperity of some individuals and groups has risen dramatically, creating highly visible inequalities. For those people socialized to believe in the virtue of egalitarianism and accustomed to

BOX 15.1

Russian Roulette: Economic Transformation with All Chambers Loaded

Russia's transition to a market economy has received the greatest international attention, not because its transition is typical of that in most other PCDCs but because Russia is the most prominent country in the region, given its size and international significance. Although the leaders did not opt for shock therapy, the Russian economy underwent a steady process of privatization in the 1990s. By 1996, 72 percent of large and midsized enterprises and nearly 90 percent of small shops and retail stores were under private ownership.

However, the political leadership was unwilling or unable to implement fundamental economic reform. About two-thirds of the private ownership of enterprises moved into the hands of insiders from the old regime (dominated by powerful entrepreneurs called "oligarchs"), whose agenda was to acquire the society's economic assets at bargain prices and then exploit those assets ruthlessly in get-rich-quick schemes (a system termed "crony capitalism"). The state did not privatize

BOX **15.1** (CONTINUED)

some of the most inefficient enterprises, which the state continued to operate at significant losses. Domestic production shrunk steadily. Corruption pervaded every aspect of economic life. Overall, the state was ineffective in guiding the economy, controlling public spending, or extracting taxes.

Table 15.4 provides some data reflecting the substantial volatility in the Russian political economy during the period since the changes were introduced. Real income has not recovered to its 1989 level, real GDP per capita plunged 50 percent between 1989 and 1999, and economic crises became recurrent. Despite massive loans from the World Bank, Russia's budget deficit became huge (e.g., between 1985 and 1991 it increased from 2 percent to 30 percent of GDP). There was hyperinflation (e.g., prices increased twenty-six-fold in 1992 alone), direct foreign investment dried up, and the value of the currency plummeted. Many people worked for months without being paid. Indeed, the economy had disintegrated to such an extent by the late 1990s that, by one estimate, about 80 percent of the country's business transactions were being conducted in barter trade (Goldman 1998).

The impacts on the citizens were severe. The state could no longer afford to provide social services to a population increasingly ravaged by unemployment and inflation. While only 2 percent of the Russian people were in absolute poverty in 1988, fully 40 percent were in poverty in 1999 (World Bank 2001). A significant increase in the inequality of wealth is reflected in the rise in the Gini inequality index (from 31.0 to 48.7) between 1990 and 1999. By 1999, the richest one-tenth of the Russian population was earning more than twenty-three times the wages of the poorest tenth.

By the late 1990s, many Russians felt that they must have experienced the worst effects of the economic transition and that things would begin to improve. Then another major economic crisis occurred in 1998, marked by a 70 percent loss of value of the ruble, a return of hyperinflation, and the imposition of stringent controls by the international financial community. The proportion of the Russian people living below the subsistence level increased from 22 percent to 35 percent (55 million people) in less than one year (July 1998 to June 1999).

Despite an overwhelming array of problems in Russian society at the end of the 1990s (e.g., severe political decay, corruption, crime, environmental degradation), it

TABLE 15.4
Changes in the Russian Economy, 1992–1995

	Year				
Types of Change	1992	1993	1994	1995	1999
Percent change in real income	−47%	+10%	+16%	−1%	N/A
Percent change in GDP	−14%	−9%	−13%	−4%	3.2%
Inflation rate	2,600%	94.%	320%	130%	63%
Unemployment rate	4.9%	5.1%	7.1%	8.2%	13.5%

Sources: World Bank 1996: A2; Harmon 1996: A6; Peterson 2001: 8; World Bank 2001.

Box **15.1** (CONTINUED)

is not surprising that the three top problems identified by the citizens were directly related to economic performance: price increases, rising unemployment, and the "crisis in the economy" (VCIOM 1999). People's daily lives and the political economy had been so negatively affected that four-fifths of those surveyed in 2001 said they wished the old Soviet Union still existed, and only one in four Russians (27 percent) disagreed on a survey with the conclusion that it would be better (for Russia) had "everything in this country remained as it was prior to 1985" [that is, when the country was still communist and authoritarian] (Peterson 2001; VCIOM 1999).

By 2003, many Russian leaders were expressing optimism that the worst conditions of transition had passed. GDP has been growing steadily since 1999, averaging about a 7 percent increase per year. The budget is balanced, wages are being paid, inequality has been reduced, and a 13 percent flat tax is generating considerably more revenue for government operations. Like most large countries, there are now several Russias. Prosperity and optimism are more evident among the population living in major cities, especially Moscow, and among the young; poverty and disillusionment are more common in the nonurban areas, especially in the villages, and among the older generations of Russians. Virtually all agree that the first decade of economic and political transition in post-communist Russia was a deeply painful experience. (This discussion based on Goldman 1998; McFaul 2001; Millar 1999; Roberts and Sherlock 1999; Schleifer and Triesman 2000).

Source: Danzinger, CARTOONISTS & WRITERS SYNDICATE/cartoonweb.com

TABLE 15.5
Prosperity Measures for Selected Transitional Developed Countries

State	GDP/Capita (PPP $U.S 2002)	Human Development Index
Taiwan	18,000	N/A
Slovenia	17,748	88.1
South Korea	16,465	87.9
Czech Republic	15,148	86.1
Hungary	13,129	83.7
Uruguay	12,118	83.4
Estonia	11,712	83.3
Argentina	10,594	84.9
Poland	10,187	84.1
Latvia	8,965	81.1
Chile	9,561	83.1
Malaysia	8,922	79.0
Mexico	8,707	80.0
Russia	7,926	77.9
Brazil	7,516	77.7
Bulgaria	6,909	79.5
Thailand	6,788	76.8
Venezuela	5,226	77.5
Ukraine	4,714	76.6

Sources: World Bank 2004; United Nations Human Development Program, 2003: table 1.

relative security and equality in their material lives, these growing inequalities and severe hardships are distressing and disruptive.

Third, the PCDCs must *ensure that the vigorous new group politics does not undermine economic policy making.* In a situation of economic hardship, many citizens have used their new democratic voting rights to reject each set of incumbent leaders and parties, whom they associate with the negative impacts from economic transitions. This results in substantial political instability and makes it difficult for any political leadership to implement tough economic policies and also retain popular support (Hanson 2001; Linz and Stepan 1996; but also see Weyland 1999).

Sustained economic development in most PCDCs requires an unlikely combination: farsighted economic policies, responsive social policies, hard work and tolerance from a citizenry receiving minimal rewards, cooperation and economic support from the more developed countries, and considerable good fortune. Achieving prosperity remains a substantial challenge.

GOAL: STABILITY

Under Communism

For communist political regimes, a basic assumption was: prosperity + equality = stability. That is, social and political stability would result because the people were pleased by the relatively equal distribution of abundant goods and services. This equation achieved only partial success. On the one hand, most of these countries had among the world's most equal wealth distributions, including 8 of the top 14 countries (World Bank 1999: table 5). Also, the state did provide free or subsidized education, food, and welfare goods, such as housing and health care, and people believed the system would take care of them in times of need. On the other hand, novelist George Orwell's ironic observation in *Animal Farm* (1945/1964) that "everyone is equal, but some are more equal than others" aptly applied to citizens in these states. Certain groups, such as professionals, urban citizens, and certain ethnic groups, were favored in the distribution of material goods and status. The greatest benefits were enjoyed by Communist Party members, especially those near the top of the hierarchy.

In terms of the stability equation, however, the key problem under communism was the insufficient *level* of prosperity, not the degree of inequality. The failure of the economy to generate greater material abundance was a major source of citizen dissatisfaction. These states promised far more material well-being than they could deliver, causing alienation in some of the population and undermining support for the political system.

Instruments of social control.   To ensure stability in the absence of prosperity, these states imposed a pervasive system of controls over many aspects of people's lives based on four key instruments:

- First, *rewards and sanctions* were a major part of order maintenance. Those who were obedient and supported the system could gain such benefits as Communist Party membership, higher priority for desired goods, job advancement, and status rewards such as plaques and public recognition. In contrast, an extensive system of surveillance was employed to ensure that those who failed to obey the rules of the communist system lost basic welfare benefits, and those who committed serious offenses were imprisoned.

- Second, the state used the agents of *political socialization* throughout a person's life to reinforce the values of loyalty, obedience, and service to the society. The educational system and mass social organizations (e.g., youth clubs), which people were required to participate in, were especially important. And the state owned all television, radio, and news media, which presented high-quality content intended to educate, entertain, and socialize.

- Third, *Communist Party* members, an honor extended to only about 10 percent of the population, were expected to encourage friends and workmates to support party policies and to report anyone's inappropriate behavior.

- Finally, the *governmental apparatus*, and especially the huge bureaucracy, the police, and the military, shaped many aspects of social and organizational life as it administered policy in day-to-day activities.

Performance.   These mechanisms of control resulted in a high level of stability under communist regimes. There were occasional outbreaks of collective violence, as in the uprisings in Hungary in 1956, Czechoslovakia in 1968, and Poland in 1956, 1968, and the 1980s. But such outbreaks were firmly suppressed, and the normal pattern of collective life was stable, with the party and the state in firm control.

Overall, the people behaved in accordance with the rules of the regime. This was partly because the mechanisms of control were effective and, at times, totalitarian. It was also because the people accepted a life that, although dull, was safe and secure. Violent antisocial behavior—that is, crimes against people (e.g., murder, rape, assault) and crimes against property (e.g., burglary, theft)—was at much lower rates than in the leading developed countries. This difference is shown in Table 15.6, which provides comparative crime data from 1987 for the United States and the Soviet Union, shortly before its breakup. While crime was low in such oppressively stable systems, individual frustration did manifest itself at the personal level. Substance abuse (e.g., alcoholism) and family problems (e.g., divorce, child abuse) were relatively high (Goldman 1998).

Opposition to the Communist Party became more open and personal freedoms expanded significantly during the 1980s, with an enormous boost from Soviet Premier Mikhail Gorbachev's policy of *glasnost*—a tolerance of public discussion and criticism of the political, economic, and social systems. By the late 1980s, it was evident that Gorbachev would not use the Soviet Union's military or economic power to support an unpopular political regime in any country in the region.

Box 15.2 details key events in the extraordinary year 1989. With the world watching, the streets of East Germany, Czechoslovakia, and other states filled with citizens demanding political and human rights. After decades of repression, the Communist Party leaderships capitulated in country after country, lacking either the will or the capacity to retain power. Except in Romania (where events corresponded to a revolution from above), the dramatic changes occurred in these countries with so little violence that they are best described as "democratic revolutions"

TABLE 15.6
Crime Rates in the Soviet Union and the United States, 1987

Type of Crime	Cases per 100,000 Population	
	Soviet Union	United States
Aggravated assault	13	350
Rape[a]	6	37
Property crimes	191	4,906
Violent robbery	4	N/A
Murder[a]	6	8
Overall crime rate	657	5,550

Source: Los Angeles Times, February 15, 1989, based on reports of the Soviet Foreign Ministry and the U.S. Federal Bureau of Investigation.
[a]Soviet figures include "attempted rape" and "attempted murder," while U.S. figures include only rape and murder.

BOX 15.2

That's the Way the Curtain Crumbles: 1989 in Central and Eastern Europe

In 1989 there was a series of tumultuous changes in Central and Eastern Europe. Events occurred at a dizzying pace, and each incident impacted other states. Some of the most notable events are described below:

January and February

Hungary's Parliament legalizes freedom of assembly, and the Communist Party allows the creation of legal, independent political parties. In Poland, tens of thousands of citizens openly insist on their political and economic rights, staging demonstrations and wildcat strikes.

March, April, and May

The pivotal event, again in Hungary, is the dismantling of parts of the barbed-wire fence that separated Hungary from Austria, the first physical break in "the Iron Curtain"—a system of travel restrictions, guards, walls, fences, and other obstacles that physically prevented East Europeans from free entry into Western Europe. The Soviets begin to cut their troop levels in Eastern Europe, and most people conclude that Gorbachev's Soviet Union will not interfere with reforms. Public protests intensify and broaden, particularly in Poland and Czechoslovakia.

June and July

In Poland the independent trade union movement (Solidarity) deals the Communist Party a devastating defeat in legislative elections, creating a formal political opposition in the legislature. Moderates take control of the Hungarian Communist Party and attempt to negotiate with opposition groups.

August, September, and October

Central and East Europeans, including more than 30,000 East Germans, flow into Western Europe via the new openings in Hungary's borders. There are massive demonstrations in East Germany, and the party chief (Erich Honecker) resigns after 18 years. In Poland, a new government is formed in which non-Communists are the majority. Hungary establishes a "free republic" and plans multiparty elections in early 1990.

November and December

East Germany removes restrictions on foreign travel in an attempt to discourage the massive illegal exodus. Then, on November 9, it opens the Berlin Wall, the most dramatic and notorious symbol of the Iron Curtain. A million East and West Germans begin an exuberant reunion in the streets of West Berlin. A new East German government is formed in which the interim president and one-fourth of the cabinet

BOX **15.2** (CONTINUED)

are non-Communists. Free elections are promised for May (and then changed to March) 1990. After massive demonstrations, several reformations of the Czech government are attempted, leading to the replacement of the Communist Party leader, the prime minister, and the president, and the installation of the first non-Communist-dominated government in 41 years. Public demonstrations in Bulgaria force the government to promise free elections by June 1990. Violence explodes in Romania as the state's security police kill hundreds of demonstrators. After a brief civil war, a reformist group takes political control in Romania and executes Nicolae Ceauçescu, the hard-line party leader since 1965.

(see Chapter 12). By December 1991, after a brief, failed coup attempt by Communist Party conservatives, even the Soviet Union had been transformed into 15 independent countries.

Post-Communism

In most countries, the new leaders who emerged after 1989 were committed to sweeping transformations of the political system as well as the political economy. These countries crafted and ratified new post-communist constitutions—ones that established democratic, multiparty political systems with widespread participation in place of one-party authoritarianism. But the mechanisms of social control that these states had relied on to maintain stability—the political culture, the Communist Party, a massive state bureaucracy, selectively totalitarian methods, and Soviet military power—were now discredited or gone. Under these changed conditions, the capacity of the new political institutions to maintain stability is subject to new challenges related to democratization, social order, nationality issues, and globalization.

Democratization.   Throughout the region, democratic political systems were formed to replace authoritarian systems that had been undemocratic but highly institutionalized (Anderson et al. 2002). Many of these new constitutional regimes are hybrids (Chapter 7) that distribute power between an elected president and a legislature-plus-prime minister selected mainly through mixed member electoral systems. In marked contrast to their communist predecessors, judiciaries are attempting to fulfill an independent role.

Many political parties emerged, trying to gain support. For example, Bulgaria, Poland, and Russia have each coped with more than two hundred parties and recently have had as many as forty parties with representatives in their legislatures. In most PCDCs, the number of parties has declined, although they are still numerous. These include liberal parties that support rapid transition to a market economy, nationalist parties that are especially focused on issues of ethnic identity, and "reformist" parties that advocate a market system with a "social face," retaining some communist-era state distribution of welfare and state control of key industrial sectors (Grzymala-Busse 2002).

Most of the more developed PCDCs have made a successful transition to liberal democracy. Eleven are classified as "free," three (including Russia) are "partly free," and only two are not free, according to Freedom House (2003). All are electoral democracies except the two "not free" states (Belarus and Kazakhstan). In contrast, of the less developed post-communist states (grouped with the developing countries in this book), only one is "free," four are "partly free," and three are "not free."

In the "free" countries such as the Czech Republic, Hungary, Poland, and the Baltic states, the processes of group politics are relatively stable. Political discourse is wide-ranging and unconstrained, and virtually all political parties and groups accept the outcome of actively contested elections among genuine alternatives. When the reform Communists won control of both Polish legislative houses in a democratic election in 2001, everyone was confident that the parliamentary process would operate normally and that the reform Communists would accept a future electoral outcome that ended the party's period of rule.

The governments and elites in the "partly free" and especially the "not free" countries have resisted democratization and an open group politics. Rather, these remain authoritarian regimes, although with more political rights and civil liberties than during the communist period (Schnetzer 2003). Faced with severe economic problems and intense public debates on economic and social policies, these more authoritarian political systems are experiencing recurrent patterns of stalemate, crisis, and government turnover. In Russia, for example, President Yeltsin dismissed four successive prime ministers in the 18 months before his resignation in 2000, and President Putin's regime is increasingly authoritarian. And in Georgia, extensive rioting after a flawed election forced the resignation of the president (Shevardnadze in 2004) and new elections. It is common for the public mood to swing against whichever parties are in power. Elections tend to produce a majority of votes *against* the parties in power, undermining strong mandates or cohesive party coalitions.

Socioeconomic disruption. The free-wheeling economic systems and disappearance of the mechanisms of communist social control have negatively affected stability. Some PCDCs, such as Russia, Georgia, and the Baltic states, now have substantial *inequalities in prosperity* and incomes. Russia, for example, shifted in less than a decade from having a more equal income distribution than 75 percent of the world's countries to having a more equal income distribution than only 20 percent of the countries, with virtually the same Gini inequality index as the United States. In contrast, other PCDCs, including Belarus, Hungary, the Czech Republic, and Bulgaria, continue to have among the highest levels of income equality in the world.

Increasing poverty and inequality are associated with rising *social disorder*, reflected in a decline in both social capital and obedience to laws and rules. Disorder is dramatically evident in the high incidence of crime. In many regions, the police are either ineffective or corrupt, and citizens live in fear of organized crime, random criminal violence, and even the police (McFaul 1998). Countries that were accustomed to minimal rates of violent crime under communism are now reeling from an explosion of crimes against both people and property. In the first five years of post-communism, for example, reported serious crimes increased 270 percent in Romania, 222 percent in Bulgaria, and 105 percent in Poland (Murphy 1995). In

Russia, more than four thousand mafia crime groups are engaged in widespread extortion, auto theft, drug peddling, burglary, and other criminal activities. In contrast to the data in Table 15.6, the Russian murder rate is now more than double that in the United States.

Nationality conflicts. A few nationality groups, such as the Poles and the East Germans (who were reunited with their West German brothers and sisters), now live in ethnically homogeneous states. In 1993, Czechoslovakia broke peacefully into two states based on its two main ethnic groups (Czechs and Slovaks). However, *ethnonationalism* (recall Chapter 5) threatens the stability of many PCDCs that have two or more significant nationality groups within their borders. In most of the countries, marginalized ethnic groups are increasingly active in demanding greater autonomy. The major nationality group has often responded by aggressively asserting its domination. Thus internal ethnic conflict has exploded into violence most extensively in the highly multinational Russia (e.g., in Chechnya and Dagestan) as well as in Georgia and the Ukraine. And Yugoslavia, a complex multiethnic state under communism, became a brutal battleground as different nation-based groups fought to define the boundaries of a set of new states (see Box 15.3).

BOX 15.3

Out of Many, One; and Then Many Again: Yugoslavia

Like many countries, Yugoslavia was forged from many nationalities by the heat of history, military might, and strong leadership. Historically, the Balkan area included several ministates that had been dominated by the Austrian Hapsburg Empire and the Ottoman Turkish Empire. The first Yugoslav state, formed after World War I had diminished the former imperial powers, was a royal dictatorship called the "Kingdom of the Serbs, Croats, and Slovenes," and was renamed Yugoslavia ("Land of the South Slavs") in 1929. The lack of shared national identity among the various ethnic groups became most obvious during World War II. In a brutal civil war, the Slavs killed more of one another in interethnic fighting than were killed in Yugoslavia by the invading Nazis. The area was divided among the Germans, Italians, Albanians, Hungarians, and Bulgarians; Croatia declared independence and became an ally of the Germans.

After the war, Josip Broz Tito, a shrewd and charismatic leader of the resistance to the Nazis, took political power. Tito united the various groups (six republics and two autonomous regions) into a federation that was fragile at first but eventually gained stability and relative prosperity. He installed a collective executive that shared power among the various ethnic groups. Although Tito was a communist, he established an economy that allowed substantially more enterprise and initiative than the command economies in other East European states.

(continued)

BOX **15.3** (CONTINUED)

Tito also established an independent foreign policy, making political and economic alliances with West European states as well as with members of the Soviet bloc.

The country remained stable after Tito's death in 1980, but then the turbulence in Eastern Europe in the late 1980s reawakened the nationalist animosities within Yugoslavia. The key protagonists were 9 million Serbs (generally Greek Orthodox, pro-communist), 4.5 million Croats (Catholic, non-communist), 2 million Slovenes (Catholic, non-communist, and the most prosperous group in the country), 4.5 million Bosnians (Muslim), 2 million Macedonians (Greek Orthodox, with strong links to northern Greece), and 600,000 Montenegrans (Greek Orthodox, pro-Serbian, and with a history under their own king).

In 1991 the Croats and the Slovenes each rejected the authority of the central government, located in Belgrade in the Serbian region, and each declared independence. Each group fought against the Serb-dominated Yugoslav armed forces, briefly in Slovenia and for nearly a year in Croatia, until the United Nations arranged a cease-fire in April 1992. The major foreign powers and the United Nations recognized the sovereignty of Croatia and Slovenia.

But Bosnia did not gain immediate recognition when it declared independence in March 1992. Serbs, about one-third of the population within Bosnia, launched a bloody civil war as Bosnians and Serbs each attempted to secure as much of the region of Bosnia-Hercegovina as possible for their emerging states. In devastating town-to-town fighting, Serbian and Bosnian paramilitary groups murdered and brutalized each other and many civilians. Eventually, a settlement was imposed by the United Nations and the developed countries, based on a complex three-person presidency representing all key ethnic groups.

The next explosion of violence was in Kosovo, an impoverished province in southern Serbia, in which 90 percent of the population are ethnic Albanians. The ethnic Albanians' desire for autonomy resulted in a revolutionary guerrilla war led by the Kosovo Liberation Army. Fighting with the Serb rulers became extensive in 1998, and once again the United Nations attempted to intervene. While this unsuccessful effort was under way, Serbian President Slobodan Milosevic encouraged the local Serbs to engage in another round of ethnic cleansing. Within months, the great majority of ethnic Albanians were either dead or in exile. NATO intervened with massive airstrikes in Kosovo and in Serbia. By late 1999, NATO reestablished the rights of the ethnic Albanians to inhabit the area, and they returned, turning their hostility on the Serbs in residence.

Virtually the entire Balkan region, as well as all the minicountries that emerged from the former Yugoslavia, is characterized by recent instability. Albania had its government overturned by a coup in 1997, lost control of its northern areas to rebel groups, and its reform communist government claimed parts of Macedonia as well as Kosovo. Bulgaria faced antagonism from the Serbs for cooperating with NATO in the Kosovo conflict. The multiple presidents of Bosnia-Hercegovina could not cooperate, as each sided with the ethnic group and country with which his group was associated. Croatia pursued an intensely nationalistic domestic and foreign policy under an authoritarian ruler. Macedonia is surrounded by hostile states with whom it has ethnic overlaps. Yugoslavia/Serbia is the region's major catalyst of vio-

BOX **15.3** (CONTINUED)

lence, but has been more conciliatory since Milosevic was arrested and tried by the International Criminal Court. Only Romania and Greece (entrenched in multi-issued conflict with Turkey) avoided the Balkan morass.

It is possible that this exceedingly complex turf war over the boundaries of new states-in-formation is reaching a resolution. The region has nearly completed an ethnic ordering in which borders coincide with nationality identity, although there are continuing bitter divisions in many locations where two ethnicities must try to coexist. This ethnic ordering might end most of the violent conflict that produced hundreds of thousands of refugees and more than one-quarter million people dead through brutal killings in the last decade (Brown 1999; Rupnik 1999).

Entry into Europe and the global system.   After decades of relative isolation, the PCDCs must establish new relationships with Europe and the global system. For Russia and most of the states emerging from it, preoccupation with the challenges of internal economic and social stability have deferred this issue. However, the states of Eastern Europe have actively sought full political and economic connections with the developed countries of Europe and the West. Among the most significant initiatives is membership in the European Union in 2004 for eight East European PCDCs, with two more in line for membership (recall Box 12.1). As conditions for membership, each PCDC must demonstrate, to the satisfaction of all existing EU member states, that: (1) its political institutions are stable and democratic, (2) it has an effectively functioning market political economy, (3) it will follow EU law, and (4) it will be integrated into the EU's political and economic frameworks. To meet this package of conditions, a PCDC is forced to eliminate nearly all of its communist elements and to operate politically, economically, and militarily like other developed countries in the global system. If these PCDCs are able resolve the many difficult policy issues resulting from their differences with existing EU states (e.g., agricultural subsidies, movement of labor, purchase of property) while they maintain political stability, they will achieve a notable transition, including their movement to Chapter 13 in this book!

Overall.   Most of the post-communist developed countries have established democratic political practices and institutions that seem to be functioning effectively. The speed and apparent depth of these changes is remarkable, given their conflicting political cultures and the economic and social instability that most have experienced since the end of communism. Many of the Central European states, including the Czech Republic, Hungary, Poland, and the Baltic states, seem to have attained suf-

Chechen rebels threaten Russian prisoners of war captured during a bloody battle in the Chechens' ethnonationalist struggle for regional autonomy.

ficient economic strength, political institutionalization, and nationality identity to maintain stability. And political leaders and citizens in many of the PCDCs accept the key elements of democracy—a limited mandate, active and open opposition, and so on—even in the face of destablizing conditions. A few, such as Belarus and Georgia, have been much less receptive to democratization, and the authoritarianism of the past has remained strong. And Russia, huge, financially challenged, and unstable, has continued to limit political rights and civil liberties (McFaul 2001). For these latter two groups of countries, the transition to a stable and effective postcommunist political system seems far more lengthy and uncertain and more prone to the kinds of political disorder and violence described in such analyses as Huntington's conception of political decay (Chapter 10).

GOAL: SECURITY

The fundamental goal of all states is survival. By that standard, the 1990s was a disaster for the Soviet Union and its allies in Central and Eastern Europe. In December 1991, the Soviet Union disappeared, replaced by 15 states that are based on historical ethnic and regional boundaries. East Germany, the economically strongest state, also disappeared, having merged with West Germany in 1990. Yugoslavia fractured into multiple states, and Czechoslovakia split in two. All this seems remarkable for a "Soviet Empire" that was judged an adversary equal to the powerful United States during the four-decade cold war. A brief consideration of the security situation in the Soviet Union and Eastern Europe during the cold war aids our understanding of the different security issues that these states now face.

Under Communism

History and geopolitics. Between its foundation in 1917 and its demise in 1991, the Soviet Union placed exceptionally high importance on security goals. In Halford John Mackinder's (1996) famous nineteenth-century geopolitical analysis, Eastern Europe and Russia were the essential "heartland"—control of that region would ensure world dominance. These areas have been battlefields for the last 200 years, including devastating invasions by the French under Napoleon and by the Germans under Hitler.

After World War II, the Soviet Union perceived itself to be surrounded by increasingly hostile, anticommunist threats to its survival. To the east, Japan, a historical military adversary, evolved into a major capitalist world power. To the southeast, China, with its huge population and alternative vision of communism, displayed growing combativeness. To the southwest, the militancy of Islamic fundamentalism presented a clear danger, given its antipathy to communism and the prevalence of Islamic peoples in the Soviet Union's southwestern regions. To the west were the major capitalist powers, with their own deep animosity to the communist systems and with NATO's devastating military (including nuclear) capabilities stretched along almost half of the Soviet bloc's border.

Military power.   To protect itself against all these real or perceived threats to its survival, the Soviet Union aimed for unchallengeable military power. In order to create a buffer zone between itself and its rivals, it gained control over territory on all sides, annexing some areas into the Soviet Union and creating a bloc of subservient states in Central and Eastern Europe. These states established the Warsaw Pact—a Soviet-centered collective security system. This bloc then built what was arguably the world's most powerful military for conventional warfare, and the Soviet Union was not far behind the NATO allies in air power and nuclear capabilities.

In the bipolar international system, the rivalry between the Soviet Union and the United States spawned a huge military buildup and arms race and resulted in the mutually assured destruction (MAD) discussed in Chapter 11. Soviet leaders from Stalin to Gorbachev opted for guns over butter, spending 9 percent to 15 percent of the GNP on defense in the late 1980s (compared with United States spending of about 6 percent). Such high military expenditure substantially reduced the societal resources available for economic growth and distribution of welfare and is arguably the main reason for the demise of the Soviet system (Medvedev 2000).

Post-Communism

The post-communist period has fundamentally altered the security situation for the states in the region. The region's collective security arrangement, the Warsaw Pact, collapsed. Ten former Warsaw Pact members from Central and Eastern Europe joined the old enemy, NATO, despite strong opposition from Russia. Some PCDCs fear Russia will attempt to reassert itself as the dominant regional power, using economic or military power to limit the autonomy of other states, reminiscent of its imperial style in the nineteenth century (Kurth 1999). On the international stage, Russia maintains its military machine, including a large standing army and the second largest nuclear arsenal in the world, with more than eight thousand six hundred strategic nuclear warheads (Bulletin of Atomic Scientists 2002). However, the actual capabilities of that military are in question. Russia's spending on its military dropped almost 85 percent between 1990 and 1999 (Petersen 2001). These changes have increased both the complexity of international relations in the region and the insecurity of Russia and other former Soviet buffer states that are outside of NATO.

In economic terms, some PCDCs are successfully participating in the global economy, and this integration should be accelerated by EU membership. But the states with less well developed economies, including some entering the EU, might become more dependent on the expertise, capital, and technology of the most developed countries, the multinational corporations, and the international financial community. As the discussion in Chapter 11 indicated, globalization results in reduced autonomy for every country since a country loses some control over the flow of goods, ideas, capital, and labor across its borders. This change is especially stark for these countries that, under communism, exerted tight control on all these elements.

In retrospect, the international system had become relatively secure under the strong bipolar security regime dominated by the United States and the Soviet Union. The breakup of the Soviet Union transferred control of its vast military capabilities from a single conservative and stable state to a dozen unpredictable and unstable states. Such shifts substantially increased the insecurity of all states, especially those within and adjacent to the region. According to balance-of-power analyses, the current evolution toward a more diffuse, multipolar international system will increase insecurity in the relations among states (see Chapter 11). In the post–cold war world, one of the major challenges for all countries, including the post-communist developed countries, is how to adapt to the end of the bipolar system.

THE NEWLY INDUSTRIALIZING COUNTRIES

During the past several decades, one group of countries has been particularly successful in achieving the transformation from developing toward developed countries. These countries have been labeled the NICs (some, such as the World Bank, also refer to them as the NIEs—the newly industrializing economies). A NIC is distinguished by its economic transition into a major exporter of manufactured goods and by its sustained high economic growth rate, relative to population growth.

To this point, only a few Asian NICs—South Korea and Taiwan—have been fully successful on both dimensions. (Indeed, one NIC—Singapore—has now been "promoted" to the developed countries group in this book, based on its levels of both economic and social development.) Certain Latin American countries, especially Argentina and Chile, have also advanced considerably toward achieving the level of development and sustained growth characteristic of the leading NICs. There is a larger set of countries, mainly in Asia (e.g., Malaysia) and Latin America (e.g., Brazil, Mexico, Venezuela), that seem to be reaching the levels of development that place them in this group. The NICs are clearly above most other developing countries in the analytic framework presented in Figure 13.1. This section discusses the key political and economic transitions that are occurring in the NICs. Although some commonalities are identified, the Asian and Latin American NICs are discussed separately.

POLITICAL CULTURE

Generally, the Asian NICs share a social and political culture that is influenced by such ethical-religious philosophies as Buddhism, Taoism, and most notably, Confucianism. Indeed, many analysts conclude that Asian cultural norms, and Confucianism in particular, are the critical factor that accounts for the notable success of the NIC approach in Asian countries compared to Latin America or other regions (Compton 2000; Fallows 1995; Huntington 1991; Pye 1985; but also see *The Economist* 1998). These norms emphasize hard work, acceptance of authority, and subordination of personal needs to collective goals. Box 15.4 explores the critical linkages between Asian political culture and economic development.

The political cultures in Latin American NICs have some similarities to those of the Asian NICs. The Catholic Church is an important institution that traditionally encouraged obedience to a hierarchical authority system and the subordination of current rewards to eventual benefits. Similarly, Latin American social structure has generally been based on hierarchical class strata and a dominant ruling class whose members are in charge of the economic and political systems. However, Latin American cultural norms generally place less importance than Asian ones

BOX 15.4

Confucius Says . . . : Culture and Development

Important scholars such as Max Weber (1958a) and R. H. Tawney (1938) have linked crucial elements of a society's cultural norms with its success in implementing capitalist economics. Recently, analysts have asked: How can we explain the particular recent success of the leading Asian NICs in achieving economic development, given a global system that seems to advantage the more developed countries (recall the dependency approach discussion in Chapter 10)? Many answers have emphasized the powerful positive influences of Confucian cultural norms (Compton 2000). Based on the teachings of a fifth-century B.C.E. Chinese intellectual, *Confucianism* stresses that individual action must be based on what is best for the group and for society as a whole. Harmony and cooperation are always to be sought, and disunity and conflict must be avoided. Society is shaped by a series of superior–subordinate relationships in which obedience must be offered: by subject to ruler, by child to parent, by younger to elder, and by female to male.

In political terms, Confucianism places the highest value on *order, stability, and discipline* within a framework of hierarchical authority. The ruler, the parent, and the boss must be obeyed unquestioningly. The individual's responsibilities and public duty have priority over his individual rights and interests. Such principles powerfully support a political system in which authoritarianism is natural and acceptable. The political elite is justified in taking any action that maintains harmony and order or that serves the broader interests of the society, regardless of the costs to individuals or interest groups (e.g., political parties, unions, students). Other key cultural norms include the beliefs that making and saving money are virtuous and that individuals (traditionally, males) should achieve the highest possible level of education and learning.

Analysts suggest that this combination of norms has encouraged behaviors that facilitated capitalist development in the late twentieth century. These behaviors include the discipline and loyalty of employees to the firm, the subordination of personal needs and prosperity to enhance the goals of the nation, the high propensity to save (and invest), and the acceptance of close linkages between the state and the economic elite (Fallows 1995). Obviously, many other factors are also critical for economic development, including the availability of necessary resources, the activities of economic competitors, the quality of economic and political leadership, the security of the country, and so on (The Economist 1998). But most agree that Confucian cultural norms have been a very positive force in the economic transition of the Asian NICs.

on mass education, hard work, and the pursuit of collective goals relative to familial advancement.

Both regions have considerable experience with authoritarian political leadership. The Latin American region is particularly associated with a popular acceptance of leaders, often with a military background ("caudillos"), who exert extremely strict control over the political system. Latin American political cultures have typically assumed that there would be political competition but that it would be hegemonic, involving the alternation between elites rather than open competition among truly opposing groups (Aguero and Stark 1998; Lozada 2003). In contrast, Asian political cultures have placed considerably less premium upon political competition and group struggle, given the value attached to consensus and hierarchy. Broadly, political authoritarianism has been consistent with the political cultures in both regions.

GOAL: PROSPERITY

The most successful NICs, particularly those in Asia, have pursued prosperity by employing variations on the *developmental-state strategy* outlined in Chapter 10: (1) an export-oriented market political economy, but with an activist state whose policies enable firms to be more profitable; (2) close cooperation between firms and government to target niches in which export goods can be sold; and (3) government support of the agrarian sector, including the redistribution of land and encouragement of commercial agriculture.

This strategy emphasizes the primacy of economic development (Fallows 1995; Johnson 1996; Simone 2001). Governments in the Asian NICs generally defer state policies likely to result in political or social development, except where such changes directly promote economic goals. State expenditures are directed toward development of the infrastructure for the economy (e.g., transportation systems, communications networks) and education of the labor force. Government policy encourages savings and investment rather than consumerism, and it limits wage rates for workers. Only as economic development reaches high levels is there a shift toward policies that allow citizens to acquire more consumer goods and that increase the level of welfare distribution to less advantaged citizens.

While the broad strategy of the Asian NICs is similar, there are significant differences within states. For example, the South Korean government supported the development of a few very large national firms called *chaebols* (e.g., Hyundai, Goldstar, Samsung), which produce a vast diversity of manufactured goods. In contrast, the Taiwanese government encouraged many small firms with specialized product bases. And Malaysia has allowed more extensive involvement of foreign multinational corporations, especially from the United States and Japan, as it focused on manufacturing, particularly electronics components. Government economic policies in most Latin American NICs have been less interventionist than those in Asia. For example, the governments have generally been less involved in firms' production decisions, less active in agrarian reform and rural land redistribution, and less controlling regarding the role of multinational corporations in their economies. Many Latin American countries abandoned statist strategies in the last several decades, adopting developmental-state or market-oriented approaches. Because most Latin American NICs have a more substantial endowment of natural resources and agricultural goods, their governments have generally attempted to balance their development policies to support not only manufacturing and service industries but also the extraction and processing of natural resources and foods. Additionally, the lengthier period of active electoral politics in the Latin American NICs has had numerous consequences, including more extensive distribution of social welfare goods by the state to secure votes and fewer restrictions on trade union activities. The Japanese economy has influenced development in the Asian NICs since World War II, and the vast economic system of the United States has had even greater impacts on economic development in Latin America, and for a much longer period.

Performance.   In general, all the NICs have enjoyed increases in both GDP per capita (Figure 15.1) as well as Human Development Index scores. Although the Latin American NICs generally began at higher levels than the Asian NICs in 1960, the Asian NICs have had more consistent increases on both measures and at a higher rate of improvement since that time. Table 14.3 reported GDP/capita growth rates for selected NICs. Figure 15.1 displays these growth patterns in more detail.

The leading Asian NICs sustained economic growth rates averaging about 7 percent annually during the period from 1980 to 1995, placing them among the fastest-growing economies in the world. They had positive trade surpluses and high levels of capital accumulation, and their firms became competitive in the international marketplace across a wide range of goods. Only a few Latin American NICs, such as Chile, approached this admirable rate of persistent growth over the same period. Most Latin American NICs tamed hyperinflation but had only sporadic periods of economic growth, averaging less than 3 percent annually (Hakim 1999).

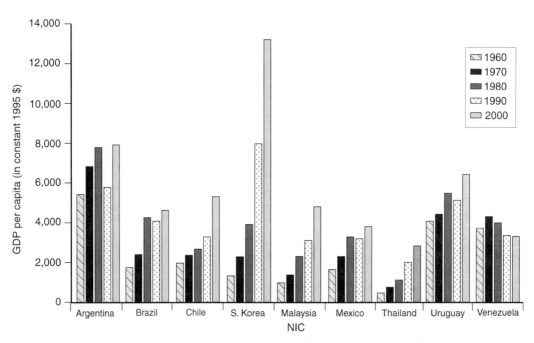

FIGURE 15.1   Changes in prosperity measures for selected transitional developed countries, 1960–2000

By the mid-1990s, not only the original Asian "tigers" (e.g., Singapore, South Korea, Taiwan) but also a second wave of "little dragons" (e.g., Malaysia, Thailand) seemed to be on a fast track of rapid and sustained economic development. Then in 1997, the economies of most Asian NICs experienced a severe and unexpected decline. Currencies lost value, stock markets collapsed, banks and other major firms went into bankruptcy, and direct foreign investment dried up. Within only 15 months, $1 trillion in loans had defaulted, $2 trillion in stock market value had disappeared, and $3 trillion of economic growth in gross domestic product was lost (Winters 1998). To limit the damage to the global economic order, the International Monetary Fund quickly sent more than $150 billion in rescue loan packages to the Asian NICs. The economic disruptions negatively affected almost every economy in East Asia and then spilled over into the economies in other "emerging markets," particularly in such transitional countries as Brazil and Russia.

Most Asian NICs recovered their economic momentum within a few years, and South Korea and Malaysia still averaged growth rates of 4 to 5 percent annually for the period 1990–2001. Measured as GDP per capita, these leading Asian NICs (especially Taiwan and South Korea) are comparable to some developed countries (Table 15.5). Standards of living in the leading Asian NICs have remained relatively high, with HDI scores over 80, placing them in the top fifth of the world's countries and with more equal distributions of wealth than most developing countries. However, the "magic" of the Asian NICs as invulnerable engines of economic growth and increasing prosperity had been debunked (Mahon 1999; Winters 1998).

Among the Latin American NICs, GDP per capita has been somewhat volatile, with Uruguay and Argentina generally highest (Table 15.5). Chile has had the most solid growth during this period, but most others averaged below 2.5 percent per year. In contrast to the Asian NICs, the Latin American NICs experienced recurring periods of economic decline and hyperinflation, rather like their less developed regional neighbors (recall Chapter 14). Mexico suffered a "peso crisis" in 1994, Brazil's economy has been highly volatile with a major currency devaluation in 1999 (see Box 15.5), and Argentina's economy experienced near collapse in 2002. The core causes of these economic problems in the Latin American NICs are disputed, but many analysts attribute them to the same sorts of weaknesses listed above for such PCDCs as Russia. Privatization, corruption, international competition, and exploitation by multinationals and "crony capitalists" have taken a severe toll in Latin America (Hakim 1999; Heredia 1997; Mahon 1999).

As the Latin America NIC economies have been buffeted by the forces of severe economic volatility and globalization, their governments have implemented structural adjustment programs required by the International Monetary Fund that have resulted in increased unemployment and reductions in government services. A proportion of the population enjoys an extremely high standard of living, material possessions, and services (e.g., health care, education), and Argentina, Chile, Mexico, and Uruguay have HDI scores in the 80s. However, many people in these and other Latin American NICs have suffered a serious reduction in their standards of living over the last two decades. Real income has declined in every country except Chile and so has the quality of most public services. Increasing numbers (and large proportions) of people remain very poor and experience a harshness of life comparable to that in many of the developing countries. In addition, the region's inequalities of income and wealth are the most severe in the world and are getting worse. Brazil has the fifth highest level of wealth inequality in the world among the 108 countries that were ranked. Chile is twelfth and Mexico is sixteenth in inequality (recall Table 14.4).

These are some of the reasons that strong and active opposition to neoliberalism and globalization is increasingly evident within the Latin American NICs. It is notable that the region's four most visible political "champions" of neoliberalism in the late 1990s—Argentina's Carlos Menem, Chile's Augusto Pinochet, Mexico's Carlos Salinas de Gortari, and Peru's Alberto Fujimori—were eventually subject to criminal charges, under house arrest, or exiled from their countries. Thus the conflicts associated with economic liberalization policies pervade not only the strategies of industrialization but also the dynamics of political stability and democratization in the NICs.

GOAL: STABILITY

The governments of the Asian NICs have been particularly concerned about maintaining a highly stable and orderly social system. As Box 15.4 indicated, conflictual politics, social disorder, and labor agitation are viewed as serious impediments to economic development as well as contrary to Confucian cultural norms about appropriate social relations. A further reason that the Asian NICs value stability is the assumption that the economic system thrives in an environment of order and predictability. Thus, until recently, governments in the Asian NICs have been centralized, authoritarian, and repressive (Simone 2001).

For example, Taiwan was under martial law from 1949 to 1987. In South Korea, the period from 1948 to 1987 was dominated by three autocratic presidents, Syngman Rhee, General Park Chung Hee, and Chun Doo Hwan. The less developed Asian NICs have been less successful in maintaining order and are characterized by more complex multiparty politics and less political stability. Thailand, for example, has suffered nearly twenty successful or attempted coups since 1932.

In the Latin American NICs, as previously noted, Catholicism and a well-entrenched social class system have had effects somewhat similar to Confucianism in encouraging obedience to authority and an acceptance of hierarchy. Strong leaders and extensive control of the political system by a hegemonic class elite were also characteristic of most of the Latin American NICs in the second half of the twentieth century. Chile, Uruguay (recall Box 11.2), and Argentina alternated between periods of rule by a civilian government and by authoritarian military regimes that, in most cases, came to power by violence and ruled repressively. Mexico was dominated nationally by a single, socially conservative political party, PRI, from 1929 until 2001. Even Venezuela, which has generally avoided authoritarianism, lost its democratic edge under Hugo Chavez.

Thus there has been a tendency for many NICs to have more the appearance than the reality of popular elections with multiple parties and genuine alternatives, tolerance of government opposition, civil liberties, and representative legislatures with significant power. However, by the late 1980s and early 1990s, all the NICs had begun a process of democratization that is proceeding at varying rates in different countries. In 1992, for example, Taiwan held its first truly competitive legislative election in the more than fifty years since the political elite had fled China after losing the civil war to Mao Zedong. In the same year, South Korea also held its first fair and actively contested presidential election with a genuine multiparty system. A vigorous and competitive democratic politics reemerged in the 1990s in the place of repressive regimes in Argentina, Chile, and Uruguay. With the 2000 election of Vincente Fox, even PRI in Mexico lost its one-party dominance of the national political system (recall Chapter 7).

Along with the positive effects, the combination of democratization, greater prosperity, and economic volatility has generated forces of instability in many NICs. In general, the NICs that have achieved the highest levels of economic development now seem most able to cope with these forces. They have adapted best to the expansion of political democratization and to the instability associated with competitive group politics, social change, and vigorous public debates over such issues as the allocation of resources and the shape of the political economy. There can be wide swings in the successes and setbacks associated with these efforts to maintain stability. These were evident in public protests driving Peru's President Fujimori from power (2000), rioting in Argentina (2002) resulting in the succession of five "presidents" in less than three weeks, a coup and counter-coup in Venezuela (2002), and in the recent history of Brazil described in Box 15.5 (Lozada 2003). In

BOX 15.5

Order and Progress in Brazil: Sometimes

The motto on the Brazilian flag is "Order and Progress." The vision of order and progress has guided much of Brazilian policy since the founding of the republic in 1889, but recent circumstances have cast doubt on its ability to realize this vision. Brazil is the fifth largest country (in area) in the world, with a population of 182 million and vast natural resources. In many ways Brazil reflects the promise of development in the twenty-first century—but it also epitomizes the troubles associated with that quest.

Progress

From the mid-1960s to the mid-1970s, the Brazilian state took the lead in guiding industrialization, both emphasizing import substitution and promoting exports. The involvement of international capital and foreign corporations was encouraged. The results were impressive. Brazil's economic development was praised worldwide as a "miracle," with yearly growth averaging 10 percent. Brazil's economy is larger

(continued)

BOX **15.5** (CONTINUED)

than that of all the rest of South America and is now the eleventh largest in the world. It is a leader among the developing countries in the production of many goods, including such agricultural exports as coffee, sugar, and cocoa; such minerals as tin, gold, iron ore, and bauxite; and such industrial goods as textiles, cement, automobiles, weapons, and machinery.

Order

Politically, Brazil is a constitutional democracy. The government is a federal republic, with an elected president who has dominant power over the bicameral National Congress. It has a multiparty system, universal and compulsory voting, an independent judiciary, and a relatively free press. The large state bureaucracy has maintained social and political order, with minimal class-based conflict, and Brazil is often cited as one of the world's most successful multiracial societies. A strong military ensures Brazil's security and sovereignty.

Progress?

The economic miracle was built on a weak, statist base, fueled by debt-led growth, and deeply dependent on external support for finance capital, technology, and markets. Much of the growth was in the 600 state-owned companies, many of which were extremely inefficient and eventually went bankrupt. The emphasis on industrial development has had many negative consequences: The agricultural sector has atrophied, resulting in 2 million landless peasants and the need to import basic foods; in urban areas, the upper and middle classes have received most of the benefits of uneven development, and there are large numbers of working poor and unemployed. More than 40 percent of Brazilians (60 million people) live in absolute poverty.

Brazil has the fifth widest gap between rich and poor in the world. After years of miracle growth, the economy came close to collapse between the early 1980s and the mid-1990s. The average annual growth rate for the period from 1985 to 1994 was 0.4 percent, coupled with hyperinflation. The inflation rate averaged about 370 percent per year during this period, reaching a staggering high of 2,864 percent in 1990. Despite new economic policies and the privatization of many state-owned enterprises since 1995, annual growth for the period 1990–2001 still averaged only 1.4 percent and inflation averaged 162 percent per year. Brazil's foreign debt is the largest in the transitional countries or developing world, more than $220 billion. Consequently, under structural adjustment pressures from the international banking community, reductions in social spending leave almost half of Brazil's huge population with a miserable standard of living.

Order?

Since 1930, the military has deposed six top political leaders from office. The military, supported by the middle class, seized power most recently in a 1964 coup against an elected government that was judged too sympathetic to the needs of the

BOX **15.5** (CONTINUED)

many rural and urban poor. The military government was repressive and ruthless, crushing leftist opposition, censoring the press, and compiling one of South America's worst records of human rights abuses. An elected president took office in 1985 after 21 years of authoritarian military rule, and a new constitution was implemented in 1988. Since that time, the recurrent economic problems have provoked a huge rise in social disorder. Crime rates have shot up; urban riots are frequent, especially in the huge shantytowns surrounding the cosmopolitan cities; and there is violence between peasants and landholders, who are disputing the government's announced but unfilled promises of land reform.

One recent president (Collor de Mello) was forced to resign due to a massive corruption scandal. When the next president (Fernando Henrique Cardoso) assumed office in 1995, the citizens reflected their disgust with government: One in three Brazilians abstained in the presidential election and blank (protest) votes outnumbered votes cast for any Senate candidate in 22 of the 26 states. Luiz Inacio Lula da Silva, a former metalworker and union organizer, was swept into power in October 2002. But the first leftist president in four decades faces a fractious legislature composed of 19 political parties whose members are primarily loyal to their regional political bosses. The Brazilian flag flaps ironically over the building where these politicians attempt to govern. (This discussion is based on Goodwin 2000: 64–70; Margolis 1992; World Bank 2003.)

Brazilian President da Silva promises land reform for 400,000 rural families in an emotional speech at a campsite of landless workers.

2002, between 79 percent (Brazil) and 95 percent (Argentina) of the citizens in these four countries declared that they were "not satisfied" with the way democracy was working in their country (Latinobarometro 2003).

Another source of instability is the groups who are most negatively affected by cutbacks in government welfare and by the recurring periods of economic crisis. Political violence has been the response from some economically and politically marginalized groups, such as the peasants in the Chiapas region of Mexico, students and labor union members in South Korea, and the Indian populations in Brazil. Moreover, instability that occurs outside the borders of an NIC can spill over into disruption and violence in that NIC, as in Chile (from Peru), Malaysia (from Indonesia), South Korea (from North Korea), or Venezuela (from Colombia).

The economic crisis that emerged during the late 1990s has impacted many NICs and is a strong test of political institutionalization: To what extent would governments in the NICs tolerate instability before implementing repressive policies? To what extent would citizens tolerate attempts by government to reduce their new economic and political liberties? While governments in the least advanced NICs, such as Malaysia, did restrict civil rights and political freedoms, most of the NICs in both regions displayed considerable tolerance and resilience in the face of difficult economic and political circumstances. The challenges to stability confronting these transitional countries will continue to be serious and persistent in the first decade of the twenty-first century.

GOAL: SECURITY

The borders of Latin American states were established in the nineteenth century and have been relatively stable for more than one hundred fifty years. While there have been occasional political disagreements between the Latin American NICs and their neighbors in recent decades, these rarely reach the level of militarized disputes (as described in Box 12.4). Interstate war involving these states was rare in the twentieth century. While the NICs' considerable military strength could be deployed for protection against neighboring states, it has been more actively engaged in maintaining internal order, either by supporting the political leadership or by overthrowing it and seizing political power.

Some of the most significant threats to security have been from the former colonial powers that limited the NICs' autonomy and freedom of action, particularly the United States, Spain, and Great Britain. Indeed, the most notable conventional war since 1950 that involved a Latin American NIC is the Falklands War between Argentina and Great Britain in 1982. This conflict resulted from the attempt by the Argentinean military government to seize islands off its coast that remained under the colonial dominion of Britain. Argentina's defeat in a short war, like the deep penetration into Latin American economies by the developed countries and their financial institutions, was a reminder that dependency and subordination persist in the postcolonial period.

Despite their effective policies for internal stability, the Asian NICs operate in a region where there are significant external threats to security. Japan occupied most of these countries in a brutal manner during World War II (and, in the case of Korea, from 1905). South Korea has the particular challenge of dealing with the huge differences in political economy and ideology in relation to its militaristic brothers and sisters in North Korea, a conflict that began with the Korean War from 1950 to 1953. Despite recent discussion of reunification, tensions have been high, with South Korean attacks on North Korean military ships and airplanes and the possible development of North Korean nuclear weapons capabilities. Taiwan is treated by much of the international community as a breakaway province that must ultimately be reunited with China, and a serious conflict between Taiwan and China would result in severe regional instability. And from a broader perspective, every Asian NIC perceives Japan, China, and/or Russia as major powers in the region that might have geopolitical designs on it. The Asian economic crisis was a clear indicator that these transitional countries are all extensively integrated into the global economy, resulting in considerable economic dependence on key actors such as the European Union, Japan, the United States, and the International Monetary Fund. With the exception of South Korea, none of the Asian NICs has sufficient military power to resist the advances of a strong country. Thus most have relied on the protection of an interested "big brother" (e.g., Great Britain, the United States) or the international security regime (e.g., the United Nations) to provide sufficient military power to protect their borders.

THE FUTURE OF THE TRANSITIONAL DEVELOPED COUNTRIES

While the two sets of countries discussed in this chapter are quite different from each other, most of these countries-in-transition share an uncertain future. Many are currently confronted with development dynamics that could disrupt the relative stability and whatever prosperity they have enjoyed.

The Post-Communist Developed Countries

The PCDCs are attempting to make the most dramatic transformations, having abandoned political institutions, a political culture, and a political economy that provided generations of citizens with stability and security, although with disappointing levels of prosperity. Unlike the Asian NICs, where economic development preceded political democratization, the PCDCs are engaged in a simultaneous transition to democratic politics and to a market economy. Coping with both forms of change at once can be overwhelming. And, perhaps even more than for most citizens in developing countries, the citizens in the post-communist developed countries have higher expectations for the standard of living their governments should provide. Thus there is a particular risk of an intolerable gap between expectations and reality in the achievement of prosperity, stability, and security.

Shifts to a market political economy and a democratic political system require extensive institutional adaptation and citizen tolerance. The most favorable prognosis might apply to those PCDCs that began the process with the highest levels of economic development and greatest population homogeneity and are "harmonizing" their systems with other countries in the European Union (Schnetzer 2003). This group joining the EU includes the Baltic states, the Czech Republic, Hungary, Poland, Slovakia, and Slovenia. The practices of liberal democracy seem to be functioning relatively well in these countries, the expansion of the private sector has been strong, and the probability of improvements in prosperity and quality of life seems high.

Political leadership and the political system are generally under more pressure in those countries where the levels of prosperity and stability have been particularly disappointing in the post-communist period. In most of the states emerging from the Soviet Union and Yugoslavia, the politics have been volatile or there has been a reliance on authoritarian leadership. Economic assets have not been distributed fairly. And the situation is compounded by a weakening of economic safety nets, which further heightens conflicts between groups. At this point, many citizens in all the PCDCs are struggling to achieve personal success in a setting of economic and social dislocation and hardship.

The NICs

The NICs are clearly in a more advantageous position. Several (e.g., South Korea, Taiwan, Venezuela) are approaching the levels of some of the more developed countries in prosperity, stability, and security. These leading NICs are also similar to the developed countries regarding the continuing challenges that they must address to sustain high achievement of these goals (recall Chapter 13).

For most of the emerging NICs, current efforts at transition to a fully developed economic system and to political democracy will result in a mix of positive and negative effects. Economic growth and development offer the promise of rising standards of living for a larger proportion of the population as more products are generated by the market and more welfare is distributed by the state. As their political economies become more diversified and resilient, the emerging NICs should also have increased control over their own destiny in the global economy. There is now a deepening democratization and a stronger civil society based on a community of interest groups. This provides support for the political system and resistance to a return to the kinds of authoritarian politics that have been prevalent in most of the NICs in both Latin America and Asia. Among the greatest challenges facing the NICs are sustaining solid economic growth and responding to the aspirations of the population, especially where poverty is widespread and inequality remains high.

The dynamics in the transitional developed countries are complex, and positive political, economic, and social outcomes are not inevitable. The sudden and precipitous decline in the economic fortunes of many Asian NICs in the late 1990s is compelling evidence that economic growth is reversible and that its foundations can be substantially less solid than they appear. Few of these transitional countries have escaped crony capitalism; overspeculation in currencies, property, and stocks; and dependency on the global economy.

There are many promising signs that democratic practices are becoming institutionalized and that economic growth can be achieved. However, the transitions to full democratization and economic development entail considerable disruption and dislocation. It is evident that no one fully understands how to sustain economic growth in the current international environment, and thus prosperity in the transitional countries is vulnerable to many forces that the leaders cannot control. Most of the countries examined in this chapter are likely to confront periods when false steps, disruptions from the external environment, or bad luck could severely challenge their pursuit of prosperity, security, and stability.

KEY CONCEPTS

communism
Confucian culture
crony capitalism
developmental-state strategy
egalitarianism
Marxism-Leninism

newly industrializing countries (NICs)
people's democracy
post-communist developed countries
   (PCDCs)
transitional developed countries
Warsaw Pact

FOR FURTHER CONSIDERATION

1. What seems to be the most serious obstacle in converting a command political economy into a market political economy in post-communist developed countries? How can this obstacle be reduced or overcome? In the absence of prosperity, is democratic politics doomed to failure?
2. Are the greatest threats to the security of the post-communist developed countries due to internal or external factors?
3. Develop an argument for or against including any of the NICs within the group of more developed countries considered in Chapter 13.
4. Is there any element in the NIC development strategy that seems particularly difficult to implement in countries outside of Asia?
5. Explore similarities and differences between Confucian culture and Latin American Catholic culture as mechanisms for social order.

FOR FURTHER READING

Alexander, James. (2000). *Political Culture in Post-Communist Russia: Formlessness and Recreation in a Traumatic Transition.* New York: St. Martin's Press. Based on detailed studies of two Russian towns, the author offers an illuminating explanation of the difficulties associated with the "traumatic transition" from authoritarianism to a more liberal democratic political culture and the continuing impacts of broader Russian cultural traditions.

Fallows, James. (1995). *Looking at the Sun: The Rise of the New East Asian Economic and Political System.* New York: Pantheon. A readable and insightful analysis of the interplay among political culture, politics, and political economy in the Asian NICs.

Flynn, Norman. (2000). *Miracle to Meltdown in Asia.* New York: Oxford University Press. The rise and sudden crisis in the Asian NICs are thoughtfully analyzed, with particular attention to the balance of power between the market, cronyism, and authoritarianism in governing the state and guiding the political economy.

Goldman, Marshall. (2003). *The Piratization of Russia: Russian Reform Goes Awry.* New York: Routledge. A revealing critique of the poor choices and political deals that have plagued the privatization of Russian assets.

Laquer, Walter. (1994). *The Dream That Failed.* New York: Oxford University Press. A renowned historian traces the rise and fall of the Soviet Union, from the Bolshevik revolution to the collapse of Mikhail Gorbachev's leadership.

McFaul, Michael. (2001). *Russia's Unfinished Revolution: Political Change from Gorbachev to Putin.* Ithaca, NY: Cornell University Press. The challenges facing Russian political leaders during the 1990s are thoughtfully explained within the context of the author's view that the period is best understood as one of revolutionary transformation without the use of revolutionary language or symbolism.

Medvedev, Roy. (2000). *Where Is Russia Going?* Trans. George Shriver. New York: Columbia University Press. A lengthy but insightful exploration of the difficulties during the Yeltsin era of what Medvedev, a key advisor to both Gorbachev and Yeltsin, believes has been a too-radical transition to a market economy.

Simone, Vera. (2001). *The Asian Pacific: Political and Economic Development in a Global Context.* 2d ed. New York: Longman. A thorough comparative study of the political and economic development of the 15 countries of East and Southeast Asia, with particularly strong treatment of China, Japan, and the Asian NICs.

True, Jacqui. (2003). *Gender, Globalization and Postsocialism: The Czech Republic after Communism.* New York: Columbia University Press. A rich combination of the study of the dynamics of change in a post-communist society with the way in which gender roles are affecting those changes and being changed by them, all within the context of globalization.

Thomas, Robert. (1999). *The Politics of Serbia in the 1990s.* New York: Columbia University Press. An interesting approach to understanding the political dynamics and power struggles in Serbia, the key protagonist in the chaotic Balkans, emphasizing an analysis of what was being said (as well as done) by the key actors, especially Milosevic.

ON THE WEB

http://www.aseansec.org/index.asp

On the official web site of the Association of South East Asian Nations, there are information and documents relevant to ASEAN, news about countries in the region as well as somewhat self-serving web pages constructed by each member state.

http://lanic.utexas.edu/index.html

The Latin American Network Information Center, hosted at the University of Texas, Austin, provides a vast number of Internet-based information sources about the politics, economics, culture, and other areas of the Latin American NICs.

http://www.ce-review.org/

The Central Europe Review provides detailed information regarding political and cultural issues relevant to these post-communist developed states.

http://www.russiajournal.com/

An online daily English-language newspaper published in Moscow that provides a perspective on the politics and society of Russia.

http://www.europeanforum.bot-consult.se/cup/country.htm

The European Forum for Democracy and Solidarity offers country-by-country information on politics and economics for the post-communist developed countries.

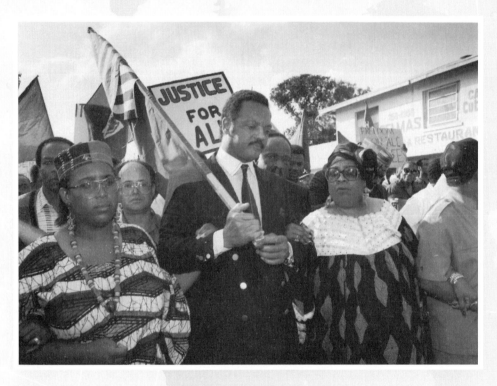

The Reverend Jesse Jackson marches in support of democracy in Haiti and in support of the broad goal of justice for all.

CHAPTER 16

The Last Chapter: Looking Backward, Looking Forward

Profound and powerful forces are shaking and remaking our world. And the urgent question of our time is whether we can make change our friend and not our enemy.

—Former U.S. President Bill Clinton

It is not easy to understand the political world.

First, the scale of political phenomena is vast. There is an international political system, at least one hundred ninety national political systems, and tens of thousands more local political systems. There are also the political beliefs and actions of the more than six billion individuals in all those political systems. How would you estimate the number of politically relevant actions on a single day? It is surely in the trillions.

Second, the range of political phenomena is immense. Politics affects every action or thought that touches on the authoritative allocation of values and meanings—in your life at school, in the workplace, at leisure, in your home.

Third, political phenomena are often complex, changeable, unpredictable, even paradoxical. The attempt to generalize about the political world is both fascinating and frustrating. Einstein's observation that politics is more difficult than physics is an apt characterization of the challenges facing those who attempt to understand the political world.

This book has provided you with some conceptual tools and substantive information aimed at improving your ability to understand the political world. It's basic premise has been that it is possible to formulate some generalizations about politics. Not every political event is unique, not every political system is one-of-a-kind, and not every person's political behavior is random. To this point, the study of politics, as political science, has mainly provided descriptive taxonomies and only a modest level of explanation. But the application of more systematic methods and more rigorous thinking does seem to improve our insights about politics. Most of our reflections on the political world have related to four essential themes: political outputs, political structures, political processes, and political change. Let's review them briefly.

POLITICAL OUTPUTS

What is the domain of politics? One crucial task is to define the essence of politics and the range of phenomena that are political. This book has employed this widely used definition: The political system is that set of activities through which values are authoritatively allocated for the collectivity. The main element in this definition is political outputs—those decisions and actions the political system makes that determine the differential distribution of rewards and sanctions to individuals and groups.

The first central issue is: *What values will be allocated?* All societies are generally concerned with achieving prosperity, security, and stability. In the pursuit of these broad objectives, which value allocations are appropriately handled through the political process? In each society, it is politics that defines *res publica*—things of the people. This definition sets the boundaries within which political action and decision are appropriate.

Some political systems assert extensive control over virtually every aspect of their citizens' lives, while others intervene only minimally. Thus different political systems reach dramatically different answers to political questions such as these:

What (if any) religious instruction will occur in the schools?

Who will decide the value of a person's labor?

What (if any) level of health care is the right of all citizens, and how will health care be financed?

Who owns land and what limits are placed on its use (abuse)?

How will people be protected from physical harm by others?

What things is a person forbidden to say, to read, to view?

The second central issue is: *Who will benefit from and who will be burdened by* the particular configuration of value allocations? Most values are scarce, and their very "value" is often subject to significant disagreement. Thus there are few value allocations by the political system that are truly *Pareto optimal*—an action that makes some individual or group better off and no one worse off. Usually an allocation that is favorable for some produces a negative outcome for others. In virtually all cases, the result of a particular value allocation is that some receive greater benefits (or lower burdens) relative to others.

For most individuals, politics tends to be personal. For them, the essential question regarding any value allocation is: *How does this decision affect me/my loved ones/my group?* The individual wonders if she will pay higher taxes, receive increased health care benefits, be protected from cultural works she perceives as offensive, and be given access to a broader range of imported products.

As a political analyst, you must also assess the broader effects of political decisions and actions on groups, on countries, and even on the international system. What groups or classes will experience a disproportionate share of the increased benefits or burdens from a public policy decision that increases the taxes on fuel, that restricts imports of a product, that alters eligibility rules for a welfare service, that decreases expenditure on nuclear weapons, that lowers the priority of prosecuting racial discrimination cases, or that implements collectivization of agriculture? Such concerns are at the core of the essential political question: *Who gets what?*

POLITICAL STRUCTURES

How do people organize themselves politically? In the early twenty-first century, there are only a few societies that continue to operate without explicit, complex political structures. To understand the political world, one must have a clear knowledge of the structural arrangements through which political decisions are made and implemented.

At the *formal-legal* level, the study of political structures focuses on the nature of the state, the basic actor in international politics. The state exercises sovereign power over its people and its territory; it has primary responsibility for making and carrying out political decisions. Among other things, the state formulates the basic laws, often embodied in a constitution, that define acceptable political behavior for individuals and groups as well as for the state itself. A state can decide to grant some of its legal power to another political entity, such as a regional federation or an international organization.

The *institutional approach* is explicitly concerned with the nature of political structures. This approach attempts to characterize different forms of executives, legislatures, judiciaries, bureaucracies, political parties and party systems, electoral systems, areal distributions of power, and the like. The key substantive interests of the institutional approach include explaining how political structures are organized, what responsibilities are associated with each role within a structure, and how the various roles and structures interact.

Finally, the more *analytic approach* to political structures attempts to develop conceptual models based on abstractions that represent the forms and relationships among those structures. The concept of a political system operating within an intrasocietal and extrasocietal environment has been the most widely used analytic framework for characterizing political structures.

POLITICAL PROCESSES

There are both micro-level and macro-level dimensions to the study of political processes. The *micro-level political processes* concern how the individual understands the political world and how the individual acts politically. First, a person's political beliefs can be characterized and the configuration of these beliefs can be summarized as her belief system. Similarly, the forms and frequency of political actions performed by individuals can be described. Second, these patterns of political beliefs and actions can be compared across individuals in the search for generalizations about micropolitical processes. Third are the explanations of these processes—attempts to identify the factors that cause individuals to hold certain political beliefs and to act politically in some ways rather than others. This process entails an analysis of the agents of political socialization, the cultural and political milieu within which the individual exists, and the individual's own physical and psychological characteristics.

Macro-level political processes are the politically relevant interactions among many individuals, groups, and organizations. The themes of power, authority, influence, bargaining, decision making, conflict, and conflict resolution are central. This is the "stuff of politics" for most of those who are interested in understanding the political world. These processes take many forms, as political groups emerge and attempt to influence the selection of political actors and public policies; as political demands, supports, and other types of political information are communicated; as value allocation decisions are made by the political system; as public policies are implemented; and as goods and services are produced and distributed in the political economy. When states interact in the international environment, these processes include the patterns of cooperation, equilibrium, domination and dependence, and violence. The elite, class, and group approaches are three general forms for explaining the fundamental dynamics of macro-level political processes.

POLITICAL CHANGE

At the beginning of the twenty-first century, the political world is changing more rapidly and constantly than ever before. Citizens and elites in every country are grappling with the implications of such trends as the globalization of the world economy, the evolution of democratic politics, and the explosion of scientific and technical knowledge. New technologies of production, communications, transportation, and warfare have created an interdependent global village in which every state is subjected to powerful forces of change. Key political questions concern the direction, rate, and controllability of change.

Direction

Chapter 10 explored the changes that occur when social mobilization, economic development, urbanization, and political development interact. In most states, the exposure to organizational and technological knowledge increases specialization, rationalization, and predictability in the structures and processes of the political system as well as other systems.

However, political development is more susceptible to reversal into political decay than are the "modernizing" transformations in the social, economic, and cultural systems. Democracy can break down, political leaders can trample constitutional restraints, bureaucracies can be wracked by inefficiency and corruption, party systems can collapse, and groups can resort to political violence. The last fifty years provide ample evidence that the direction of political change is not necessarily toward greater order and rationality.

Rate

Even in the early twenty-first century, there are still a few groups, such as the Bushmen of the Kalahari Desert in southern Africa and the Masai in Kenya and Tanzania, whose social and political lives have remained almost unchanged over hundreds of years. A few contemporary political systems, such as those of Britain and the United States, have changed only gradually over hundreds of years. But the rate of change in most current political systems is quite high. Sudden and fundamental (revolutionary) change has always been possible and has become far more likely today. Even in the absence of revolution, the dynamics of the modern world tend to transform most political systems at a very high rate. The impacts, structures, and processes of most political systems have changed more during the past fifty years than in the preceding five hundred. The rate of political change is likely to continue to accelerate. Can you think of circumstances that would slow the rate of political change in a particular state?

Controllability

The leaders of every political system attempt to use governmental policies to control the changes that occur both within the system and in its environment. Earlier chapters have provided dramatic examples of the capacity of strong political leadership to control such changes: Mao Zedong in China, Kemal Atatürk in Turkey, Pol Pot in Cambodia. To achieve its goals, a leadership needs some combination of political will, political skills, effective political structures, group support, relevant resources, and luck.

There are many reasons why the leaders of a political system usually have only modest capacity to control change. First, they may be deficient in such elements as will, skill, support, and resources. Second, in complex systems, powerful forces of inertia offer resistance to change. Third, unanticipated effects of action can be more significant than the intended changes. Fourth, the array of national and international actors can undermine change as they pursue their own objectives. The recent developments in countries that emerged from the former Soviet bloc provide dramatic examples of how these powerful forces can affect change.

Even with the extraordinary political leaders cited previously, changes ultimately evolved in ways that they neither anticipated nor desired. Despite the formidable powers that these leaders can harness, it is perhaps more remarkable that significant change can *ever* be controlled than that leaders often fail to achieve their objectives.

INTO THE TWENTY-FIRST CENTURY: UNDERSTANDING AND ACTION

Novelist Charles Dickens opens *A Tale of Two Cities* with his famous observation: "It was the best of times, it was the worst of times. It was the age of wisdom, it was the age of foolishness. . . . It was the spring of hope, it was the winter of despair." Many people might find this to be an apt description of the political world in the first decade of the twenty-first century. The danger of a nuclear war between the United States and the Soviet Union has become a historical anecdote, democracy has spread to more political systems than ever, technology enables us to produce a remarkable array of material products, and globalization increasingly connects us. More people live longer and with a higher quality of life than at any point in history.

At the same time, people also seem to accept the inevitability of widespread political violence, human suffering, and environmental degradation. While some are optimistic about changes in the post–cold war period, others see little evidence that it is going to be less violent or less destructive than in the past. As we move into the twenty-first century, three broad challenges loom especially large.

Challenge 1: The Quest for Harmony with Our Technology

Technology (i.e., applied knowledge) is the most remarkable change agent in the contemporary world. In its many forms, it has vastly expanded human powers of control and production. But new technologies are also closely linked to many substantial changes in personal and social life, in political and economic life, and in the environment. While many people assume that technologically driven change necessarily enhances the quality of our lives, the reality is considerably more complicated.

A computer can serve as the eyes and ears of a disabled person or as the guidance system of a missile. A therapeutic wonder drug can be distributed to all who need it or sold only to the wealthy few for a very high profit. Genetic engineering can develop a new breed of rice or a new breed of people. Moreover, major technologies often generate effects that were neither intended nor desired. A nuclear power plant is not built with the expectation that its radioactive materials will cause severe health problems to local residents. A commercial airplane is not designed to function as a massive bomb. Vast electronic networks can link us to a global community but also reduce our personal interactions with our friends and workmates. Extensive databases of personal information increase the efficiency of our transactions with business and government, but they also provide many actors with access to detailed information about our private behavior.

This huge expansion of technological capacity occurred during a century in which humans killed far more of their race than at any time in history. Do you think that this is a coincidence? In addition to the sheer efficiency of war technologies, can you think of other ways in which new technologies have contributed to the increase in political violence?

The fact is that every technology offers a variety of possible uses and impacts that are determined largely by human choices. Many of these choices are motivated by particularistic interests (e.g., domination, profit, convenience) rather than by concern for the collective good. Thus these choices are political, both because they affect public life and because they should be guided by wise public policy. Box 16.1 explores some of the political implications of communications technologies—arguably the most pervasive change agent in the contemporary world.

In most countries, few constraints have been placed on the development and application of advanced technologies. However, faced with the extraordinary range of technological impacts, many governments are intensifying their attempts to manage technology. Policies have been implemented in such areas as protecting individual privacy against electronic surveillance, improving the safeguards against technologically based accidents, limiting the use of environmentally destructive chemicals, and assisting those unemployed due to technological changes in the workplace. In some of the most dramatic examples, promising informal and formal international agreements have been reached to prevent the proliferation of nuclear weapons and the manufacture of chemical and biological weapons.

BOX 16.1

Will the Communications Revolution Revolutionize Politics?

Just one generation ago, the large majority of citizens in even the most technologically advanced countries did not have the types of media that you probably take for granted today—personal computers, DVDs, cell phones, PDAs, e-mail, and satellite communication systems. In many countries, even televisions and telephones were available only to a small proportion of the population. Given the astounding expansion of communications media during the last several decades, it is not unreasonable to talk of a revolution in communications technologies.

As these technologies have become more widely available, intriguing questions have emerged: What effect does all this technology have on politics? Has it revolutionized politics—that is, has it fundamentally transformed the manner in which political power is distributed and exercised? In a world of electoral campaigning via television ads, "sound-bite" news, "spin doctors," and "mediagenic" politicians, it is clear that the new communications technologies have substantially altered politics, even if the changes are not yet transformational (Neuman 1999).

First, the new communications media have greatly expanded the means of information exchange between political elites. Direct dialogue has been facilitated by multisite videoconferencing, electronic mail, and satellite technology. Elites can more easily assess the situation and attitudes of both allies and rivals by monitoring television and radio broadcasts. Sophisticated surveillance technologies have also vastly expanded the elite's capacity to monitor others, both within and outside the country.

Second, the emergence of global networks controlled by a few multinational corporations might be the dominant trend in the next several decades. Despite the proliferation of the media and media sources and the possibility for many individuals and groups to transmit information, the huge media conglomerates will likely shape the world of communications (recall Box 13.4 on Rupert Murdoch). Howard Frederick (1993: 124) predicts that soon "five to ten corporate giants will control most of the world's important newspapers, magazines, books, radio and television outlets, cinema, recording industries, and videocassettes." This concentration and globalization of major communication sources could have profound effects, creating a shared global culture and furthering the integration of economic and political life (Barber 1995).

Third, the media and the Internet have made far more information about politics easily accessible to the citizens than at any previous time. In some countries, an individual has access to hundreds of hours of "news" *every day.* Such news (not all of it political, of course) can be a rich source of information as well as analyses and criticisms regarding the political world. For example, as much as 40 percent of total television broadcast hours in many countries is devoted to news programming (e.g., Argentina, Canada, India, Poland, Russia, Zimbabwe) (Lippman 1992). Most of the democracies of Europe and North America now televise the proceedings of their national legislatures. The most dramatic recent expansion of information power has

(continued)

BOX **16.1** (CONTINUED)

particularly benefited those information-haves with access to the Internet and other multimedia resources. Through digital libraries, web pages, CD-ROMs, and the like, individuals can undertake precise searches for relevant political information in the vast, global information environment.

A key question is whether the recent changes—the enormous volume of information about politics and the greater diversity of sources—significantly increase citizens' knowledge and interest in the political world and encourage their more active participation in the political process (Bimber 2003). To this point, the evidence is mixed. Consistent with the adage that you can lead a horse to (a huge body of) water but can't make it drink, no clear linkage has yet been established between the explosion of sources of information and greater absorption of political knowledge by most citizens. And since virtually anyone can now construct a plausible web page, it is increasingly difficult to determine whether web-based information, the information source of choice for many young people, is reliable.

Fourth, the new information and communications technologies make it far more difficult for a government to control the information available to its citizens. From radio to cross-border television to regional satellite transmissions to the Internet, national borders have been obliterated as barriers to the movement of information (Franda 2002). When asked what had caused the remarkable collapse of communism in Central and Eastern Europe in the late 1980s, then-President Lech Walesa of Poland pointed to a television set and proclaimed, "It all came from there."

All political regimes attempt to manipulate information as a means of social control. When the citizenry has access to news and information broadcasts from other countries and when foreign media are persistently probing the situation within the country, even an authoritarian regime has reduced capacity to deceive its own population and to prevent outsiders from witnessing its repression and cruelty. The new media have been a key factor in the recent wave of democratization—enhancing citizens' ability to communicate with others within their society, increasing their awareness of the rights and privileges enjoyed in other countries, and emboldening them in the knowledge that "the whole world is watching" as they publicly demand their political and social rights.

Fifth, the new technologies open the possibility of "electronic democracy." Citizens can use computers to vote electronically. Television, interactive cable systems, and the Internet might be employed to enable government to convey facts and issues regarding a policy decision to citizens in their homes, for citizens to participate in questions and discussion, and then for citizens to register their approval or even to vote on a policy choice from their remote location (Becker and Slaton 2000). However, it is not obvious that government decision makers will facilitate the implementation of such systems, since their own decision-making discretion is reduced by such electronic plebiscites.

Sixth, the new communication technologies can affect the political and social values of many people, especially those in more traditional societies. The increasing availability of foreign media exposes people to information and ideas that challenge their cultural base, including their understandings about the political world. As each individual can choose among several hundred cable television channels,

BOX **16.1** (CONTINUED)

many are likely to find a reference group and a national identity (recall Chapter 5) whose values are at variance with the dominant values of their states.

Electronic networks, such as electronic mail, weblogs, and chat rooms, now extend this changing political identity even further. For those who are part of these electronic networks, the community, as a set of individuals with whom one has face-to-face interactions, might disappear. Instead, the high-tech citizen's group identity and interactions could be primarily with a network of individuals who are geographically dispersed and strongly reinforce one's own values (biases?) (Sunstein 2002). As a result, a very different form of globalized group politics might emerge in high-tech societies. Until now, groups have emerged through personal interactions and then taken their demands directly to political officials, government offices, or into the streets. Increasingly, action by "virtual" groups might dominate, existing primarily in blizzards of e-mail messages originating from isolated keyboards throughout the city, region, or world and directed at the mailbox of a political decision maker. Thousands of electronic political networks already exist, such as Green-Net based in London and MoveOn.org based in California. However, it is unclear whether these virtual groups will have the same capacity to effect change as the mass mobilization of people in direct political action.

Do you think government will be more or less able to control its citizens in a world with a huge proliferation of media sources and with individuals' own communications increasingly mediated by electronic technologies?

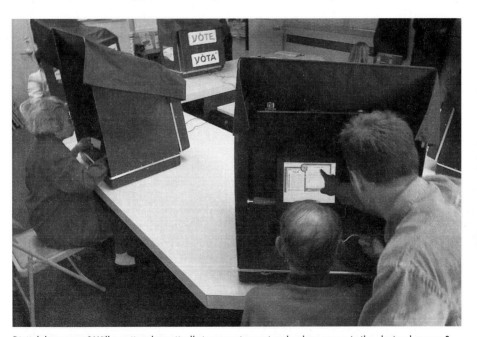

Digital democracy? Will e-voting dramatically increase turnout and reduce errors in the electoral process?

Despite these efforts, more countries than ever have the capacity to destroy using nuclear weapons and other technologies of war, more groups and even individuals can wreak havoc through pathological uses of various technologies, increasing numbers of workers are permanently unemployed, and we spend more time interacting with electronic equipment than with each other. Thus the key political challenge is to develop local, national, and international strategies that will guide important technologies to serve the collective good and to do minimal damage.

Challenge 2: The Quest for Harmony with Planet Earth

One central focus of this book has been to examine the efforts of political actors and political systems to control their environments, both internal and external. Political and economic development and contemporary technology have created increased capacity for control of the environment but also for its unparalleled destruction. Such "environmental degradation" includes both the poisoning of the ecosystem by generating more wastes than the earth can absorb and the consumption of the earth's resources at a high rate.

Global warming, massive oil spills, ozone-layer depletion, contamination from nuclear waste, rapid deforestation, and the like tend to elicit a resigned response of "so it goes." For a majority of people, especially those in the developing countries, protection of the environment remains a secondary goal relative to increasing material prosperity. For example, croplands are depleted through the attempt to grow too much too fast in a battle against hunger; air quality is sacrificed to ensure that export-oriented industries will produce at a profitable unit cost; the benefits of trees to the biosphere are sacrificed to meet the immediate need for fuel or shelter. Even most citizens in the developed countries, where there is more concern for environmental quality, are not prepared to reduce their high consumption levels or to pay the full costs of repairing the damage caused by their lifestyle.

Is there hope for the global ecology? Individuals and countries must agree to sacrifice their short-term benefits in order to improve the prospects for longer-term environmental health. Individuals must recognize that their own decisions and actions are linked to those of many other actors and produce cumulative impacts on the environment. There are now, both locally and globally, groups such as Greenpeace and the Green parties that promote more environmentally sensitive behavior.

Many countries are showing willingness to share responsibility in curbing certain practices, as in the 1985 international Convention on Prevention of Marine Pollution by Dumping of Wastes and Other Matter, the 1991 Protocol on ozone-destroying chlorofluorocarbons (the first international treaty to ban a non-military commodity), and the 1997 Kyoto Protocol reducing countries' levels of carbon emissions as a response to global warming. Such agreements are a hopeful sign, although they still cover only a few environmental risks, are sometimes violated, and are not supported by all countries.

More broadly, some UN agencies advocate a worldwide program of "sustainable development," which would require substantial restraints on growth and resource use by the developed countries and an expanded but limited use of resources to allow modest prosperity among the developing countries' poor (World Commission on Environment and Development 1987).

Drawing by Scott Willis. © Tribune Media Services, Inc. All Rights Reserved. Reprinted with permission.

Some observers are pessimistic about the willingness of people and countries to accept such restraints on their quest for material abundance. Richard Falk, an international relations scholar, asserts that the current system of states is incapable of generating the cooperation necessary to prevent environmental disaster. Thus Falk proposes the establishment of international agencies with wide-ranging powers: to set detailed standards for environmental protection; to monitor the behavior of countries, their citizens, and their corporations; and to enforce compliance (Falk 1975, 1995; Haas, Keohane, and Levy 1993). The most pessimistic analysts argue that *no* political arrangements will induce people to save the planet, except perhaps a worldwide authoritarian regime whose top priority is environmental issues (Hardin 2000).

Challenge 3: The Quest for Harmony with One Another

At the signing of the Declaration of Independence, Benjamin Franklin observed: "We must indeed all hang together, or, most assuredly, we shall all hang separately." Franklin was referring to the need for the separate states of the emerging United States to cooperate in the late eighteenth century. His insight applies with even greater force to the relations among individuals, groups, and states in the twenty-first century.

The globalization of communications and the economy are shrinking the planet. Economic enterprises, interpersonal networks, and personal reference groups are expanding beyond the boundaries of any political jurisdiction. These developments could increase our sense of common destiny and shared values, and, as a consequence, increase our capacity for cooperation across states and nations.

However, greater interaction among states and nations might also generate antipathy. Familiarity can breed contempt, as increased knowledge of other groups accentuates the importance of differences. For example, indifference could be replaced by a sense that the behavior or values of another group are a threat that requires a response. The possibility of conflict might also increase as groups that are extremely unequal in resources and power become more aware of each other. There is no compelling short-run evidence that either globalization or the end of the cold war has substantially reduced the overall level of political violence, and each might be a cause of increased nation-based violence.

At the height of the rioting in Los Angeles during the spring of 1992, Rodney King, the victim of the police beating that was the catalyst for the riot, made his first public appearance to ask: "Can't we all just get along?" This plaintive question applies equally to the groups, nations, and countries that are both the components of the social world and the source of continuing political violence. One hopeful sign is the increasing efforts of the United Nations and other multinational agencies to resolve conflicts and restore social peace. Clearly, the ultimate challenge is to develop both personal and global strategies for sharing benefits and burdens and for getting along.

CHOOSING A FUTURE

As we think about the political world, fundamental questions are never far below the surface. Many of these questions entail the conflict among such desirable values as individual freedom, social order, material abundance, social justice, democracy, and happiness. Each individual and each political system makes decisions about the importance they attach to these values and then attempts to create the political conditions under which they can achieve the values.

The comparison of different political systems has highlighted variations in collective judgments about the relative importance attached to major political goals and, perhaps even more, in the relative success of various political systems in achieving their objectives. The contrast can be dramatic when two bordering states employ different approaches in pursuit of their goals. The juxtapositions between North Korea and South Korea, Iran and Turkey, and the United States and Mexico provide particularly stark contrasts.

In the first decade of the twenty-first century, some people enjoy astonishing material abundance while one-fifth of the world's population lives on a subsistence diet and 15 million people each year die from the effects of hunger. Contemporary political systems spend more than $25,000 per soldier per year on the military and less than $1,000 per student per year on education (Sivard 1996: 6). Citizens in some countries enjoy almost unlimited personal freedom while in other countries they languish under totalitarian constraints. Political choices account for these circumstances.

There has never been such awareness of what is possible and such sensitivity about the gap between expectations and reality as in the current period. Global communications, a global economy, and a decline in authoritarian regimes have combined to make 6 billion people far more aware of what they have (and what they do not have) in comparison with others around the world.

Indeed, as more individuals, groups, and states increase their expectations and hence their demands, the possibility of satisfying everyone diminishes. A widely quoted statistic is that the United States, with about 5 percent of the world's population, has been accustomed to using about 25 percent of the planet's resources. Obviously, as even a few countries approach these consumption levels and as most countries try to consume their own "fair share," the worldwide consumption of resources will accelerate environmental degradation.

Ultimately, *political choices* will determine whether individuals, states, and the international system will implement public policies that ensure life, liberty, and happiness for most people; that constitute a more protective approach to natural resources; and that employ technologies safely and humanely.

Although people have become aware of what they want, the changing conditions do not necessarily increase their understanding of how to meet their wants or of the costs and trade-offs involved in pursuing their values. Thus one benefit you can receive from education in general and from the study of political science in particular is enhanced critical thinking skills. Such skills are now the key to personal and national success in goal achievement, according to Robert Reich, professor and Secretary of Labor in the Clinton administration. In *The Work of Nations: Preparing Ourselves for Twenty-First-Century Capitalism,* Reich (1993: 154) argues that the "standard of living of a nation's people increasingly depends on what they contribute to the world economy—on the value of their skills and insights." Thus citizens must be able to identify false assumptions and inadequate concepts, select significant information, and assess its longer-term consequences.

Many people look to their political system to provide solutions in a complex world. But many also seem to believe that political systems are a major source of obstacles preventing their achievement of goals. This book's central objective has been to increase your understanding of the political world through the discussions and many examples that have hopefully helped you (in Popper's expression from Chapter 1) "to see more clearly than before." You should now have a more informed opinion about whether political *science* is feasible. Even more importantly, you should have a clearer opinion about whether political analysis contributes to the pursuit of political good.

Voltaire observed, "If we believe absurdities, we shall commit atrocities." The political world is full of disagreement, hyperbole, and ruthless competition. Political science cannot necessarily make the world a better place; its primary role is to increase our understanding about how politics works. Such understanding can be the basis of insights: about different conceptions of how politics should be organized, about the basis of any real political disagreements that require response, about mechanisms for conflict resolution, and about how to organize ourselves in the pursuit of specific (private, group, or national) interests within a framework of the common good.

Can the young people who will take power in the twenty-first century provide the political understanding and leadership necessary to enable all of humanity to live in peace and prosperity?

As individuals, we often feel powerless in the face of the massive power mobilized in the political world. But every individual—even you!—can affect what happens. The democratic ideals that are widely celebrated in the political world are based on the assumption that people, individually and collectively, can make a difference. First, if you approach political questions with knowledge, insight, and sensitivity, you can better understand how to think and act in the political world. Second, you can communicate your own political demands and supports in order to influence the policies that are made by actors in the political system. Third, you can become a political activist as a shaper of public opinion, a leader of a political group, or a public official. The American novelist F. Scott Fitzgerald observed, "One should be able to see that things are hopeless and yet be determined to make them otherwise." In the political world, things are not yet hopeless unless people like you fail to think, to understand, and to act.

APPENDIX Political Analysis

The mind rests in explanation.

—Aristotle

This book began with the claim that, in a democracy, men are more likely to vote than women. You were encouraged in Chapter 1 to read this Appendix on political analysis as you considered this question about the relationship between gender and voting and as you assessed the data in Table 1.1. Chapter 1 defined *political analysis* as the attempt to describe and explain political phenomena. The following sections introduce you to some of the basic tools political theorists use for political analysis—that is, for conceptualizing, collecting, and analyzing data about actual political phenomena. After a brief discussion of such data, we shall consider how to read data like those in Table 1.1 and how to draw a tentative inference based on

FRANK & EARNEST reprinted by permission of Newspaper Enterprise Association, Inc.

those data. Most of the Appendix describes four broad approaches used for political analysis: taxonomic analysis, formal analysis, functional analysis, and relational analysis.

DATA IN POLITICAL ANALYSIS

Many political analyses rely on data assessment. Data can be defined as any observations, facts, statistics, or other forms of information that attempt to measure or represent some aspect of reality. The data used in political analysis can be characterized on different dimensions, including the style of measurement, the level of analysis, the composition, and the time dimension.

1. *Style of measurement.*
   a. *Nominal data* measure by applying names to phenomena that have some common characteristic. Examples: male voters or female voters; Conservative, Labour, or Liberal parties in Britain; democratic, authoritarian, or totalitarian governments.
   b. *Ordinal data* rank phenomena in an order, such as from higher to lower, bigger to smaller, greater to lesser. Examples: more developed countries or less developed countries; voters who are older than sixty-five, voters between thirty-five and sixty-five, or voters younger than thirty-five; political party systems that have one major party, two major parties, or many parties.
   c. *Interval data* are like ordinal data, but they also have a numerically equal distance between any two adjacent measures—the distance from 5 to 6 is the same as the distance from 81 to 82. Example: The Bush presidency of 1989–1993 (four years) was exactly half as long as the Reagan presidency of 1981–1989 (eight years).
   d. *Ratio data* are like interval data, but they also have a real zero point. Examples: a country's total expenditure on defense in a specific year; the number of citizens participating in antigovernment rallies; the percentage of seats in the legislature held by a particular political party.
2. *Level of analysis.* Political data can be measured according to a position in a scale or rank . Examples: at the individual level, the strength of a particular individual's loyalty to a political party; at the group level, the percentage of Asian-Americans who vote; for a geographic area, the number of parliamentary seats in Wales.
3. *Composition.* Data can measure a single phenomenon, such as a political leader's age or a country's percentage of yes votes on a set of related issues at the United Nations; or they can be aggregate measures that combine phenomena, such as the percentage of total votes cast for conservative political parties in an election or a country's average annual rate of inflation over ten years.
4. *Time dimension.*
   a. *Cross-sectional data* measure a single point in time. Example: a person's vote for president in 2000.
   b. *Longitudinal data* measure several points through time. Example: a person's votes for president in 1984, 1988, 1992, 1996, 2000, and 2004.

The example in Chapter 1 of voting in the 1976 presidential election uses data that are nominal (men versus women), ratio (percentages), and aggregated (for many people) in a cross-sectional analysis (only one election). You might think of data as dry statistics, but the data in political analysis are rooted in real-world events. If properly analyzed, relevant data can increase our political knowledge on an endless list of questions. Examples: Are countries that spend the greatest amount on military preparedness more likely to avoid war? Is religion or social class a better predictor of whether a Scot will vote for the Labour Party? How much longer is average life expectancy in rich countries than in poor countries?

ON READING TABLES

Table A.1 (which shows the same data as Table 1.1 in Chapter 1) provides data from selected presidential elections in the United States. Does this table help you to clarify the relationship between gender and voting level in democracies? Since political analysis often includes data presented in tables, it is useful to know the basic steps for reading them. When you examine a table such as Table A.1, the first thing is to establish precisely what the data are about. The title of the table and the names given to the variables (the key concepts measured in the table) indicate what the analyst who created the table thinks that it reveals. But the analyst can be misleading or

TABLE A.1

Analysis of Table 1.1: Participation of Eligible Voters in the 1976 and 2000 U.S. Presidential Elections by Gender

	1976	
	Men	*Women*
Voted	a. 77%	b. 67%
Did not vote	c. 23%	d. 33%

Yule's $Q = +.24$

	2000	
	Men	*Women*
Voted	a. 53%	b. 56%
Did not vote	c. 47%	d. 44%

Yule's $Q = -.06$

mistaken, so it is worthwhile to assess whether the phenomena measured by the data correspond to the labels given to the variables, whether the data seem relevant to the analytic question, and whether the data seem accurate.

Next you should examine the data in the table. What do the data measure? Table A.1 provides data on the percentage of men and women who did or did not vote in the election of the U.S. president in 1976 and 2000. How are such tabular data read? Are either of the two following statements supported by the 2000 data in the table?

1. Forty-seven percent of those who did not vote were men.
2. Forty-four percent of the women did not vote.

It is useful, especially when there are percentages in a table, to examine how the columns (up and down) and the rows (across) are formed. In the case of percentages, find any direction(s) in which the data add to 100 percent. In this table, the columns add to 100 percent. Thus statement 2 is supported by the table and statement 1 is not. Can you see why this is so?

In many cases, the analyst uses more sophisticated techniques than tables in order to assess the relationships between variables. Box A.1 discusses the relational modes of analysis and considers the use of statistical techniques to examine these relationships. It also explains the meaning of the Yule's Q statistics in Table A.1.

The use of statistics and other quantitative techniques can be helpful in political analysis. The more demanding task for the analyst is to use careful judgment to decide whether the relationship identified by such techniques has *substantive* significance. The key question is: Do the tables, statistics, and other data provide useful insights about political processes or about how political phenomena are associated?

MODES OF POLITICAL ANALYSIS

Chapter 1 indicated that political science has little theory in the strictest sense of the term; that is, it does not have a set of precise, systematically related generalizations. However, most contemporary political analysis does strive to make our understanding of politics more general, precise, and systematic by ordering empirical data with one of these four modes of political analysis: taxonomic, formal, functional, or relational.

Taxonomic Analysis

Aristotle (384–322 B.C.E.), the father of political analysis, was interested in distinguishing different types of Greek city-states. He classified them by using a concept derived from earlier work by Herodotus (c. 484–425 B.C.E.): the size of the ruling group. Aristotle defined three categories: The city-state might be ruled by one person, by a few people, or by many people.

This is an example of **taxonomic analysis:** the orderly arrangement of some political phenomena by developing a set of distinct categories. Most political analysis begins with a taxonomy—a set of categories that classify data into different types. The categories within a taxonomy establish the crucial concepts that define the analysis. The criteria for naming the types and for classifying phenomena into each type are arbitrary in the sense that they are established by the analyst on the basis

BOX A.1

Assessing Relations between Phenomena

To interpret most quantitative analyses in political science (and most other social sciences), you need to understand a bit about the meaning of the most commonly used statistics (e.g., Pearson's r, regression analysis, factor analysis). Ideally, you will take some statistics coursework so that you understand the logic and assumptions of the statistics being employed.

The simplest relational statistics (e.g., Pearson's r, *tau beta*, Spearman's *rho*) usually range in value between +1.00, which indicates a perfect positive relationship between the variables, and −1.00, which indicates a perfect negative relationship between the variables. Many of these simple statistics will also have a *significance* level—an indication of how likely it is that the observed relation between variables might have occurred by chance. This is normally measured in terms of this chance probability: .05, .01, .001. The smaller the probability of a chance relationship, the greater the analyst's confidence that the variables are actually associated.

In the case of two variables, a +1.00 correlation would look like graph *A* in Figure A.1: As one variable increases one unit in value, the other variable increases at a corresponding rate. For example, you would find a +1.00 correlation if each $100,000 spent on congressional political campaigns increased voter turnout by 1 percent. A −1.00 correlation would look like graph *B*. Rarely do real-world phenomena in political science come even close to a perfect positive or negative correlation.

A correlation statistic close to .00 means that there is virtually no linear relationship between the two variables, as in graph *C*. For example, you are likely to find that campaign expenditure levels have no consistent relationships with turnout rates. Political phenomena are often extremely complex and subject to many influences, so they typically have little or no systematic relationship with other factors that you might consider. Thus in many political analyses, the statistical associations are low or statistically insignificant. The strongest statistical relationships for interesting political data are usually at moderate levels of correlation, in the range of $\pm$ .10 to $\pm$ .35, as in graph *D*.

You can look at simple arrays of data, like those in Table A.1, and draw your own conclusions. Graphical representations (like the four scattergrams in Figure A.1) are another straightforward way to assess data. Each point in the figures represents one case, located at its appropriate value on each of the two variables in the analysis. This visual mapping of cases can provide useful insights about the nature of the relationship between two variables.

As the data become more complex, statistics can help inform your judgment. Table A.1 indicates that the correlation between gender and voting in the 1976 election data is $\pm$ .24, using a very simple correlation statistic for 2×2 tables called "Yule's Q." The correlation of $\pm$ .24 suggests that in these data there is a moderate, systematic relationship between male gender and higher probability of voting. In the 2000 data, the relationship between gender and voting appears less pronounced, and

(continued)

BOX **A.1** (CONTINUED)

this judgment is supported by the Yule's Q of –.06, which indicates that there is virtually no systematic relationship.

While most statistics of association require a calculator or a computer, you can calculate Yule's Q yourself for any 2 × 2 table: (1) multiply the values of the two cells on each diagonal: $a \times d$ and $b \times c$; (2) subtract the two products: $ad - bc$; (3) add the two products: $ad + bc$; (4) divide $ad - bc$ by $ad + bc$; (5) the result of this division should be a correlation score, ranging between +1.00 and –1.00. The formula for Yule's Q is thus: $(ad - bc)/(ad + bc)$. (Unlike the case for most correlation statistics, a positive Yule's Q means that the ad diagonal is stronger than the bc diagonal.)

Beyond simple statistics and graphs, political scientists have an array of sophisticated data-analysis techniques to examine questions using quantitative data. Most of the techniques are elaborations on the basic idea of examining whether the values on phenomena seem to be systematically related to each other.

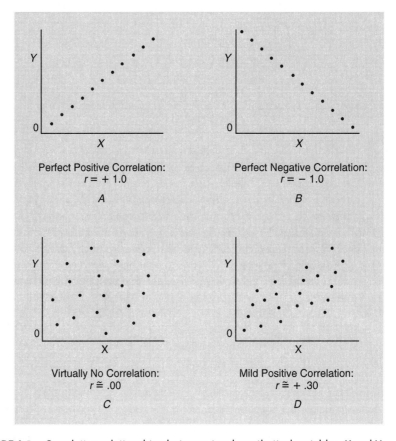

Perfect Positive Correlation:
$r = +1.0$

A

Perfect Negative Correlation:
$r = -1.0$

B

Virtually No Correlation:
$r \cong .00$

C

Mild Positive Correlation:
$r \cong +.30$

D

FIGURE A.1   Correlation relationships between two hypothetical variables, X and Y

Aristotle

of substantive concerns. But the categories ought to be exhaustive (all cases are classified), mutually exclusive (no case fits into more than one category), and comparable (all categories are distinguished by the same criteria). Relevant data might be of any type, although they are usually nominal or ordinal.

Aristotle's three categories of city-states are sufficient to create a taxonomy. But to enrich his analysis, Aristotle also employed a second concept: the group(s) whose interests the ruler serves. His two categories were (1) the ruler(s) could rule in the general interest, or (2) the ruler(s) could rule in self-interest. Thus Aristotle's taxonomy of governments had two central concepts, each based on nominal data, resulting in the six categories displayed in Table A.2. Aristotle then provided names for each category in the taxonomy. For example, he labeled as a **monarchy** any city-state in which one person ruled in the general interest; if a few ruled in their own interest, the system was called an **oligarchy.** Notice that Aristotle labeled the most perverse case, where many attempt to rule in self-interest, a *democracy!*

Aristotle used his taxonomy for political analysis by placing each Greek city-state in one of the six categories. Athens, for example, was classified as an aristocracy. Notice that a taxonomy organizes data, but it does not answer the *how* and *why* questions. To explore such questions (e.g., Is a prosperous middle class more likely in an oligarchy? Under what conditions does a polity transform into a democracy?), the analyst must move beyond taxonomic analysis.

> **TABLE A.2**
> Aristotle's Taxonomy of Political Systems

	In Whose Interest?	
How Many Rule?	*General*	*Self*
One	Monarchy	Tyranny
A few	Aristocracy	Oligarchy
Many	Polity	Democracy

Formal Analysis

Suppose you want to travel around New York City on the subway. If you are unfamiliar with New York, you will probably use a subway map, which indicates the spatial relationships among different subway stations and identifies the stations where one subway line connects with another one.

A subway map is an example of the product of formal analysis. A **formal analysis** specifies abstract forms that correspond to the reality in which the analyst is interested. The analyst attempts to "model" reality by defining and interrelating concepts so that the linkages among the concepts in the formal analysis reflect the dynamics and interactions among the actual phenomena. Some formal analyses have the same physical form as the actual phenomena being modeled, such as a miniaturized version of an automobile engine. But most formal analyses use symbol systems as abstract representations of the phenomena, such as a subway map, a schematic drawing of the circuitry in a radio, or a mathematical formula for the trajectory of an object moving through space.

Most formal analyses of political phenomena are recent. Some political scientists have attempted to devise schematic diagrams that represent how some aspect of politics works. In one well-known example, David Easton (1965) developed an abstract diagram, composed of boxes and arrows, that attempts to characterize the flow of activities by which decision makers in the political system establish public policies. Their decisions are influenced by the resources available in the environment and the pressures they experience from various groups. This "political system model" is explained in detail in Chapter 5.

An array of formal analyses called *rational choice theory* (or *public choice theory*) has become an important approach in political science. Applications of rational choice theory can be quite complex, but they share two basic features. First, they are attempts at representing political processes primarily by means of mathematical formulations or systems of symbolic notation. From the perspective of advancing a science of politics, such formal theories are given special prominence, because they aim to be general, systematic, abstract, and testable in actual settings.

Second, it is assumed that political actors (e.g., voters, legislators, political parties) behave purposefully. The approach does not assume that all political actors behave with complete rationality all of the time, but it does assume that their behavior is goal oriented and calculating. Both their preferences for various outcomes and their calculation of the costs, benefits, and likely success of different strategies to achieve those outcomes can be formulated as quantified indicators or as systems of symbols (Mueller 1993).

To introduce the rational choice approach in a nontechnical manner, we offer several simple examples grounded in the logic of the approach. In Box 4.1, the approach is employed to assess whether it is rational for an individual to vote in a U.S. presidential election. The following paragraph describes another brief example (without the mathematics) of how the approach is applied.

Political scientist William Riker (1962) has posited the theory of the "minimum winning coalition." This is a mathematical representation linked to the well-known saying, "To the victors go the spoils." That is, it assumes that the benefits of any policy decision in a legislature will tend to be distributed among those who have voted in favor of the decision. However, Riker argues, as the size of the coalition voting for the policy becomes larger, the benefits must be distributed among more people (or the groups each person represents) and thus there is a smaller share of benefits available to each coalition member. In order to assure each coalition member of the largest possible share of benefits, there is a tendency to create a coalition that has just enough participants to ensure victory—hence the idea of a minimum winning coalition. This concept is developed as a formal theory through specification of mathematical equations that relate the size of the decision-making group, the size of the coalition, and the amount of resources available for distribution. (For an empirical analysis of national legislatures that challenges Riker's theory, see Strom 1989.)

Functional Analysis

Suppose someone asks you how a car works. You are likely to discuss the key structural components of a car's engine and power train, such as its carburetor, pistons, and driveshaft. You might then detail the processes of the internal combustion engine, noting how an ignited fuel expands in an enclosed area, pushing a series of mechanisms into directed motion. This style of description and explanation is the basis of functional analysis. **Functional analysis** describes the contributions of a certain element (process or structure) to the activities of the phenomenon under study.

In political science, one widely used form of functional analysis identifies certain functions (i.e., processes) that occur within a political system, and it describes how and by what structures the functions are performed. Some scholars, such as Gabriel Almond and his colleagues (2004), have defined certain functions, including political communication, rule adjudication, and interest articulation, that must be performed in every political system.

Applications of functional analysis are described in Chapters 5, 10, and 11. As a brief example here, we can consider the interest articulation function. Individuals might want their government to spend more on preschool care or to protect their right to own handguns. The processes by which individuals communicate these specific interests to others in the political world are called *interest articulation.* According to functional analysis, this communication of political needs and wants is a necessary function in every effective political system. Most functional analysts also describe and explain how structures perform these types of functions. Thus interest groups emerge to amplify the shared interests of many individuals. For example, the National Rifle Association uses various strategies to promote many individuals' concerns about gun ownership to those who make and implement government policies on firearms.

Related to functional analysis is *constitutive analysis.* Constitutive analysis assumes that political functions can be explained primarily in terms of one fundamental concept. (Indeed, every scientific discipline strives to discover, ultimately, the fundamental structure or process that accounts for more complex phenomena.) Among the concepts that have been proposed as the central one to explain politics are the interactions between groups, classes, or roles.

Constitutive theories are discussed in various chapters, especially in Chapter 9, which presents the elite, class, and group approaches to explaining politics. As an example, Karl Marx's theory of politics pivots on one key concept: class. In every historical period, society is divided into a set of classes based on the distribution of economic power. The structure of classes determines political and social relations as well as economic relations. In political terms, the class structure determines who wields political power, for what purposes, and for whose benefit. The role of the state and the dynamics of political change are also explained in terms of class relations.

Relational Analysis

Box 1.3 (in Chapter 1) and Table A.1 consider the question of voting differences between men and women: Is there some relationship between an individual's gender and the likelihood that she or he votes? This is typical of the kinds of questions addressed by relational analysis.

The central goal of **relational analysis** is to discover and explicate the systematic connections between phenomena. The basic question is always: Are political phenomena linked? For example: Are democratic countries more stable than nondemocratic countries? Are older people more politically conservative than younger people? Are states dominated by Islam more warlike than states dominated by Hinduism? What conditions are associated with victory by revolutionary forces?

Both formal analysis and functional analysis also assume connections, but relational analysis tries merely to identify the connections between phenomena. It does not attempt to model or schematize the connections as does formal analysis. And it does not focus on crucial functions, as does functional analysis. There are two levels of relational analysis: (1) correlational analysis and (2) causal analysis. To determine whether there is a systematic association between variables, most correlational and causal analyses use various statistical techniques. These statistics provide a mathematical appraisal of the extent to which change in one phenomenon is systematically related to changes in one or more other phenomena. Box A.1 provides further information about such statistics.

Correlational analysis.   Correlational analysis determines whether there is a statistically probable relationship between two variables. It does not presume, as does causal analysis (discussed in the next section), that one variable actually is the agent that causes change to occur in another variable. It merely assesses the strength and direction of an association between variables. Many empirical attempts to understand politics begin with the establishment of a correlation between political phenomena.

For example, evaluation of the linkage between gender and voting in Table A.1 is an example of correlational analysis. The table and the Yule's Q statistic both seem to support the tentative conclusion that, for 1976 at least, there seems to be a modest correlation (i.e., a systematic, statistically probable association) between gender and voting. While this seems correct, there are obvious problems with using this election as the basis for a broader generalization about gender and voting. First, it examines only a single election. The relationship is not evident in the 2000 electoral data. In fact, women outvoted men in every U.S. presidential election after 1980. You might pursue this research on U.S. elections by asking: Is this a new trend or a temporary deviation from a 50-year pattern?

Second, a generalization about democracies might also consider elections other than the presidency and certainly should analyze other democracies. For example, any generalization might take into account an analysis of British and German national elections since 1970, in which there is no correlation between gender and voting rates (Walker 1988: table 1). A third problem with the evident pattern between gender and voting in the 1976 data will be explored later in this section.

Causal analysis. Causal analysis goes beyond correlational analysis because it explicitly identifies one phenomenon as the effective agent that brings about changes in another phenomenon. Much of the language in political analysis is loosely causal, implying that there is a cause-and-effect relationship between two variables. However, causal analysis is the only approach that attempts an explicit empirical test of cause and effect. Causal analysis presents the "if X, then Y" mode of explanation described in Chapter 1. Here X is the *independent variable* that, given a certain value, actually causes Y, the *dependent variable*, to change in a particular way.

An example of causal analysis links the electoral system and the number of political parties. In his book *Political Parties*, French political scientist Maurice Duverger (1954) contends that the type of electoral system *causes* the number of effective parties to increase or decrease. In particular, he hypothesizes the following:

1. Plurality electoral systems (in which the candidate who receives the most votes wins) reduce the number of major political parties toward two.

2. Electoral systems with proportional representation (in which candidates are elected to the legislature in proportion to their party's share of the total vote) and with multimember districts (more than one legislator per district) allow more than two major parties (recall Box 7.1).

Political analysts have tested Duverger's hypotheses using data from various electoral systems (e.g., Riker 1982; Taagepera and Shugart 1989: ch. 13). Table A.3 presents data from 20 democratic countries for the period from 1945 to 1965. Do you think the data in Table A.3 support Duverger's hypothesis? Why?

TABLE A.3
Relationship between Number of Political Parties and
Type of Electoral System

	Electoral System[a]	
Number of Parties[b]	Plurality	Other
Two	23	4
More than two	7	73
Yule's $Q = +.97$		

Note: Based on data from twenty Western democracies, in elections of legislative representatives, between 1945 and 1965.
[a]In plurality, or "first-past-the-post systems," the party/candidate with the largest number of votes wins a seat in the legislature, and all other parties/candidates gain no seats. In other systems there is some form of proportional representation or vote transfer.
[b]Number of political parties with at least 5 percent of the seats in the legislature.
Source: Rae 1971.

DRAWING CONCLUSIONS FROM EMPIRICAL ANALYSES

The purpose of empirical analysis is to increase our knowledge about politics. It is especially important that the analyst draw appropriate conclusions. In political analysis, as in politics, things are often not what they seem. Let us consider some of the potential problems, using the causal analysis of electoral systems and party systems as an example. You probably concluded that the data in Table A.3 support Duverger's hypothesis. Do we now know that the electoral system causes different types of party systems? Yes, maybe. . . .

YES: There is certainly some persuasive empirical evidence for such a conclusion. And, on logical grounds, it does seem reasonable that the electoral system might cause variations in the number of parties that survive over time.

MAYBE: However, the political analyst must always be cautious in drawing conclusions and making generalizations. Several questions should be considered:

1. Are the data and methods appropriate? Did the analysis use accurate, relevant data and the correct analytic techniques? Is the sample of nations or the time period examined typical? Does this generalization also hold for non-European nations? Were systems divided between "plurality" and "other" in a manner consistent with Duverger's hypothesis?

2. Are the analyst's inferences about cause and effect persuasive? Might the dependent variable (in this case the number of political parties) actually have a significant effect on the presumed independent variable (the electoral system)? That is, since the parties in most legislatures have the power to establish the electoral system, certain parties might try to implement an electoral system that perpetuates their power via the existing party system.

3. Are there plausible rival hypotheses? Is there another independent variable, not considered in this analysis, that might better account for the pattern of values on the dependent variable? It is possible that both the number of parties and the electoral system are related primarily because each is correlated with the third variable. For example, the number of fundamental issues that divide the

electorate might have the greatest effect on the number of major parties if one party emerges for each pattern of positions on the fundamental issues (Taagepera and Shugart 1989).

When political scientists use the scientific method, any of these kinds of "problems" with a conclusion might be raised by other analysts. The data, the methods, or the inferences might not stand up to such scrutiny. In our examination of Duverger's claims about the causal relationship between electoral systems and number of parties, none of the three problems just listed seems to undermine the analysis. Until one of these types of criticisms is supported persuasively, we can have some confidence that the generalization about the causal relationship is correct—that electoral systems do seem to cause certain types of party systems to evolve over time.

But the gender and voting analysis based on the 1976 election data in Table A.1 is an example of how an initial causal inference can be challenged. The three potential problems must be considered in an assessment of whether the data reveal that gender differences do cause different probability of voting:

1. The data and methods do seem appropriate. However, a generalization (even limited to the United States) would certainly require more than a single case.

2. The posited cause-and-effect relationship seems reasonable. This is the only possible direction of causality, since voting certainly cannot "cause" gender. Also there are reasonable explanations for why men might vote at higher rates than women. Can you think of at least one?

3. However, to make a compelling argument that the data reveal causality, it would be necessary to ensure that there is no other causal agent (i.e., no plausible rival hypothesis) that better explains voting levels or that creates the apparent relationship between gender and voting. While the analyst can never disprove every competing hypothesis, it is important to examine and reject the most plausible ones.

Let us reexamine the 1976 voter turnout data in Table A.1. Can you propose another explanation of the incidence of voting in the United States that is as plausible as gender? Among those you might suggest are age, social class, occupation, interest in politics, identification with a political party, and education level. Table A.4 provides the relevant data on one of these—education level—for our analysis of voting in 1976. Do these data alter your judgment about the importance of gender?

TABLE A.4

Participation of Eligible Voters in the 1976 U.S. Presidential Election, by Gender and Education Level

Education Level	Percentage Who Voted	
	Men	Women
Grade school	72%	50%
High school	69	64
College	86	84

One reasonable interpretation of Table A.4 is the 1976 election revealed that there is a considerable difference between men and women in the incidence of voting among those with minimal education but that there is virtually no difference in the level of voting between men and women who have a college education. In the absence of further analysis (and many further analyses could be attempted), these data about education seem to reduce the power of gender as an adequate causal explanation of voting. One might infer, at least on the basis of Table A.4, that both education and gender were important in 1976 but that gender impact was powerfully altered by education level. This closer look should suggest to you that if you were developing a causal theory of voter turnout, you would need to consider many variables and diverse data.

This example reveals a common challenge for most of the interesting questions addressed by causal analyses of politics: There are almost always clusters of plausible explanatory factors that seem interrelated. For example: What accounts for a person's decision to vote for the right-wing People's Party in Austria—class, education, family experiences, occupation, wealth, beliefs about society, attitudes toward governmental leaders, or something else? What factors lead a group to undertake revolutionary violence—political oppression, poverty, corrupt government officials, charismatic leadership, unequal distribution of wealth, foreign domination, or something else?

KNOWLEDGE AND POLITICS REVISITED

Chapter 1 suggested a number of ways it is possible to know things about the political world. Your understanding of politics does not need to be grounded in the scientific method and in empirical analysis. Insight and understanding about politics might be based on the method of authority or the method of personal thought, or they might be derived from other sources such as literature, films, or art.

In the attempt to develop precise and valid generalizations about politics, however, most contemporary political scientists use some form of the scientific method and some of the modes of political analysis described in preceding sections. Whatever types of data and modes of analysis they use, political scientists generally accept the notion that all aspects of their research should be subject to scrutiny and challenge by other analysts. Most also agree that their hypotheses, inferences, generalizations, and theories must be subject to some empirical test of validity. Although various sources of knowledge can provide you with insights about politics, this book emphasizes the modes of political analysis described in this Appendix as the best means for broad understanding of the political world.

KEY CONCEPTS

causal analysis	interval data
constitutive analysis	longitudinal data
correlation	nominal data
correlational analysis	ordinal data
cross-sectional data	ratio data
formal analysis	relational analysis
functional analysis	taxonomic analysis

Glossary

Adjudication: Every society creates and enforces rules and laws regarding the proper forms of behavior for individuals and groups. The adjudication function attempts to interpret and apply the relevant rules or laws to a given situation. Most political systems have established judicial structures (e.g., criminal courts) whose primary role is adjudication.

Administration: The general term used to describe the machinery and processes through which rules and policies of an organization are applied and implemented. It is a core function of political systems and is usually one of the four basic institutional structures (along with executives, legislatures, and judiciaries). (See also *Bureaucracy.*)

Assembly system: A form of collective leadership in which a large group, usually constituted as a legislature, is clearly dominant over the executive. Examples: the United Nations; the European Parliament.

Associational interest group: A type of political interest group organized specifically to further the political objectives of its members. Examples: the British Medical Association; Common Cause. (See also *Interest group.*)

Authoritarian regime: A political system in which the ruler is not constrained by a limited mandate to rule and has an absolute right to make policy decisions. The political rights of the population are severely restricted. However, nonpolitical aspects of life, including occupation, religion, and social life, are not under the extensive control of the political system.

Authoritarianism: (1) A political system generally characterized by little or no commitment to equality or democratic participation and by a strong emphasis on order and stability. The political behavior of the population is severely constrained. In many countries, authoritarian regimes are dominated by a military elite. (2) A personality syndrome, associated particularly with political and social attitudes and behavior, in which the individual tends to: revere strong leadership; draw sharp boundaries between the identity group and all others; be intolerant of unconventional behaviors; and exhibit considerable hostility toward minority groups.

Authority: (1) A source of knowledge about the political world. The method of authority involves the appeal to any document, tradition, or person that is believed to possess the controlling explanation regarding a particular issue. (2) The legitimacy attached to the decisions of the political system, in the sense that people willingly accept those decisions as binding, independent of their own self-interest.

Balance of power: A configuration of power among a set of states in which there is a broad equality in the power resources (political, economic, and especially military) that can be exercised by competing states. Through a system of shifting alliances, no state or group of states is able to achieve a preponderance of power. Thus stability and the status quo are usually sustained, since states will intervene to prevent a serious imbalance that might lead to domination.

Bureaucracy: Although often used as a synonym for administration, bureaucracy has been defined, especially by Max Weber (1956), as a particular structure and style through which administration can operate. Structurally, bureaucracy is characterized by hierarchical organization and a highly specialized division of labor. Members of the bureaucracy behave according to specific rules of action so that treatment of each case is relatively predictable and nondiscriminatory. (See also *Administration.*)

Capitalism: One of the great "isms," explicitly linking politics to political economy, capitalism is a system that corresponds loosely to a market economy. In this system, private economic actors are generally free from state constraints and the state engages in only limited efforts to shift resources among private actors. Capitalism is founded on the philosophy of laissez-faire economics. There is no assumption that capitalism requires a particular form of political processes to function efficiently.

Causal analysis : A type of relational analysis, causal analysis goes beyond correlational analysis because it explicitly identifies one phenomenon as the effective agent that brings about changes in another phenomenon. Causal analysis presents the "if X, then Y" mode of explanation where X is the independent variable that, given a certain value, actually causes *Y,* the dependent variable, to change in a particular way.

Civil war: A form of political violence that occurs when a significant proportion of the population within a region actively supports a separatist movement and political violence emerges on a large scale. Examples: Sudan (the late 1990s); U.S. Civil War (1861–1865).

Class approach: An analytic explanation of the value allocation process (politics) based on a core notion of stratification—structured inequality in the distribution of key values in society. The class approach centers on an examination of the tactics of class domination and the dynamics of class struggle. Class theory is particularly associated with the writings of Karl Marx (1867) and later forms of Marxist theories.

Classical liberalism: One of the major Western political ideologies. In classical liberalism, the highest value is placed on each individual's natural rights to life, liberty, and property and the freedom of the individual to pursue these rights as an independent actor. Government plays a very limited role under classical liberalism, which celebrates a laissez-faire economy and discourages government attempts to create material equality (although equality of opportunity is important). Political thinkers associated with classical liberal thought include John Locke (1632–1704), Adam Smith (1723–1790), and John Stuart Mill (1806–1873).

Colonialism: A situation of dominance and subordination in the relations between two states. One state asserts substantial power and control over the other, based on military, economic, and/or political power. The goals of the dominant state might include: to extract resources, to control a market for its products, to use the strategic location, to instill its own values into members of the subordinate state, or to obtain international prestige. Most areas that were colonial holdings became independent in the decades after 1945.

Command economy: A type of political economy in which the state assumes total control of virtually all significant factors of production. The state replaces or eliminates the role of private owners of land, labor, and capital; makes all production decisions; and determines the value of all goods. The state owns, plans, controls, and regulates all major economic activity. (Compare with *Market economy.*)

Communism: One of the major "isms" linking politics and political economy, communism is a system that is closely associated with the command political economy. Based on the theories of Karl Marx (1867) and others, the key to communism is the socialization of resources—the notion that the state must maintain control of society's land, labor, and capital. Although it is primarily an economic system, communism also emphasizes an ideological commitment to economic and social equality among all of its citizens. It also posits that until such equality is achieved, government and politics must be guided powerfully by a unified leadership. Examples: Cuba; the former Soviet Union.

Comparative politics: One of the four major subfields within political science, comparative politics focuses on the similarities and differences in political processes and structures, either cross-nationally or by comparing differences within a single system, such as comparing the welfare policies of the 50 American states. A few of the many subjects for comparison are public policies, legislatures, and political parties.

Confederation: A loose association of states. In a confederation, each state delegates some power to a supranational central government but still retains primary power, and its compliance is always conditional. Confederations are usually created when states decide that the performance of certain functions is enhanced by structured cooperation with other states. Example: the United Nations.

Conservatism: One of the major Western political ideologies, at the core of conservatism is the commitment to sustain traditional values and forms of behavior and to maintain social order. Tradition and religion, rather than reason, are viewed as the most reliable sources for guiding society. There is loyalty to the nation and antipathy to egalitarianism. The writings of Edmund Burke (1790) provide a good example of conservative thought.

Constitution: A set of statements that describes the fundamental rules of a political system, including a characterization of the core activities of major political structures. Most constitutions are a single, written document, such as the U.S. Constitution, but some are embedded primarily in major statutes, precedents, and legal decisions.

Constitutional regime: A political system that operates in terms of the rule of law, as defined within the constitution, and that ensures effective restraints on the power holders. The defining feature of a constitutional regime is that the state does attempt to fulfill the provisions of its constitution.

Core: Refers to the set of states, firms (especially multinational firms), and financial institutions that have enormous power and influence in the global system and the international political economy. The core, primarily located in the developed countries, dominates the world's "periphery," composed of institutions and peoples that have minimal power and are primarily located in the developing countries. Core is a crucial concept of the dependency approach, which is an explanation of both the relations between states and also the development process.

Corporatism: A corporatist state is characterized by extensive economic cooperation between an activist state and a set of large organizations that represent actors who control major productive resources. In the hope that there will be cooperation and consultation (rather than conflict) among the state, big capital, big owners, and big labor, the leaders of these groups are given great influence in working with the state to make and implement policy on key political economy issues.

Correlational analysis: A form of relational analysis that determines whether there is a statistically probable relationship between two variables. The analysis does not conclude that one variable is actually the agent that causes change to occur in another variable (as in causal analysis) but merely assesses the strength and direction of the association between variables. Correlational analysis is often a key step in any empirical attempt to understand politics.

Council systems: A political system in which a small group shares collective leadership and is responsible for both executive and legislative functions. All members of the council have relatively equal power, so decisions and actions are based on the will of the council majority or council consensus. Examples: mayor-council systems and boards of supervisors in many American local governments.

Coup: Occurs when the top political leader or leadership group is replaced by violence or the explicit threat of violence. A coup is a common form of leadership turnover in political systems that have no accepted and enforceable procedures for leadership succession. Examples: replacement of Wahid in Pakistan (1999); ouster of Aristide in Haiti (2004).

Democracy: A political system in which governance is accomplished by leaders whose authority is based on a limited mandate and who are elected by a universal electorate. Such an "electoral" democracy becomes a "liberal" democracy when the population selects among genuine alternatives and also has significant rights to political participation, expression, and opposition.

Democratic socialism: A variation of socialist ideology that treats greater egalitarianism as its primary goal but also assumes that its goals can and should be implemented by a government that comes to power and rules by democratic means, not by violence and repression. Under democratic socialism, the government might own some of the major economic resources and regulate much of the economy, but it does not attempt to plan and control all aspects of the economic system. (See also *Socialism.*)

Democratization: The effort to institutionalize democratic political regimes more fully and deeply, especially in countries with limited democratic processes. Analyses often try to measure the extent of democratic consolidation and to specify the political, economic, and social conditions conducive to further democratization.

Dependency approach: This claims that an economic and political hierarchy exists in which many actors take advantage of those with less power and resources. At the top are the most developed countries, and the poor people and the villages of the developing countries are at the bottom. Some analysts claim that many of the difficulties facing the less developed countries stem from their vulnerability to, and dependence on, the more highly developed countries and the transnational institutions they control.

Dependent variable: The *Y* variable whose value changes as a result of changes in some other specified (independent) variables. Causal analysis presents the "if *X*, then *Y*" mode of explanation, where *X* is the independent variable that, given a certain value, actually causes *Y*, the dependent variable, to alter in value in a particular way.

Dictatorship: A political system in which political leaders are not subject to a limited mandate but have absolute power and authority. The citizens have no regular and realistic opportunity to replace such political leadership in a nonviolent manner.

Dual executive: A political system in which one actor, the head of state, performs the more ceremonial aspects of top leadership and embodies the nation, while another actor, the head of government, is responsible for the more political aspects of the executive role. (See also *Executive.*) Example: The United Kingdom has Queen Elizabeth (head of state) and Prime Minister Blair (head of government).

Economic development: This occurs as more and more households and firms within a country are engaged in ever-higher levels of production and consumption. Based on greater control of the environment and resources, more (and more complex) goods are produced and exchanged, and the GDP gets larger relative to the number of people sharing in the market.

Electoral system: The framework by which the votes of citizens are converted into specific selections of candidates who have a mandate to hold office. There are many variations, some based on selection proportional to votes cast and others based on the selection of the candidate with most (plurality) or at least half (majority) of the votes.

Elite approach: An analytic explanation of the value allocation process (politics) in which the political world is characterized by political stratification, the segmentation of the population into separate groups with greater or less power. There are only two major strata—those that do more of what there is to do (in the policy process) and that get more of the resources that are available, and those that do less and get less. These two groups are called the political elite and the mass, respectively. Key elite theorists include Gaetano Mosca (1896) and C. Wright Mills (1956).

Ethnonationalism: A powerful attitude of identity with and support for others perceived to share a key nation-based trait (e.g., ethnicity, religion, common geography). There is often animosity between groups with different nationality identities. This animosity has become a particular problem that produces conflict and violence, both within and between states, because the nationality identities of many people are not coterminous with the borders of their state.

Executive: The branch of the political system composed of a leader or group of leaders who are responsible for defining and managing the implementation of public policy. A broad definition of the executive includes not only the chief executive (e.g., mayor, governor, prime minister, president, queen) but also the entire administrative system.

Fascism: A political ideology that places fundamental importance on the unity and harmony of government and society and is defined particularly by its opposition to forces that might weaken that collective unity. It further assumes that the top leader is the embodiment of the natural will and that all individuals and groups must obey the will of the leader. It is both antisocialist and antidemocratic. Facism had major impact on twentieth-century history and is particularly associated with such regimes as those of Adolf Hitler ("Nazism") in Germany (1932–1945) and Benito Mussolini in Italy (1922–1943).

Federation: A political system in which there is a constitutional division of power and functions between a central government and a set of regional governments, usually known as states, provinces, or cantons. Power is shared among the levels of government, and no level has legal power to dominate any other level in all policy domains. Examples: Brazil; Canada; Mexico; the United States.

Formal analysis: Specifies abstract forms that correspond to the reality in which the analyst is interested. The formal analyst attempts to "model" reality. Most formal analyses use symbol systems as abstract representations of the phenomenon under study, such as a subway map or David Easton's (1965) political system model.

Functional analysis: Describes the contributions of a certain element (process or structure) to the activities of the phenomenon under study. For example, one form of functional analysis identifies certain functions or processes (e.g., political communication, rule adjudication) that occur within a political system and describes how and by what structures the functions are performed.

Geopolitics: An analytical method that assumes that the geography of a state—its particular geographical location and also its physical characteristics, natural resources, and human resources—can significantly affect the domestic and foreign policy actions of the state.

Globalization: The increasing integration of diverse economic, sociocultural, military, and environmental phenomena by means of dense networks of action and information that span vast distances around the world. These networks dramatically increase interdependence among actors within the international system and within such environments as the economic system and the environmental system.

Group approach: An analytic explanation of the value allocation process (politics) that is grounded in the concept of the group—any aggregate of individuals who interact to pursue a common interest. Within this approach, politics can be understood as the interaction among groups that are pursuing their political interests, and policy decisions are the outcome of that group process. It is assumed that any particular individual can belong to many different groups and has some political resources that can be used in an attempt to influence policy decisions.

Guerrilla war: Violent opposition to an existing regime by means of a long, protracted campaign primarily from rural bases. Fighting is typically in a hit-and-run style, with extensive efforts to win the support of the peasants and the creation of new political institutions prior to collapse of the old regime.

Hegemony: The existence of an extraordinarily powerful group (a "hegemonic elite") or country ("hegemon") that sustains its domination over other actors for a long period of time.

Hybrid systems: A political system that attempts to blend the desirable aspects of both the presidential and cabinet systems of government. Hybrid systems have a prime minister and an elected legislature that can both enact and implement policies, but they also have a president who may have

relatively equal power with the cabinet or may have key specific, but limited, powers. Examples: France; Russia.

Hyperpluralism: A situation in which many effective groups are able to pressure the government to respond to their policy demands. As the government tries to satisfy them all, public policy can become contradictory or muddled. At worst, government may become paralyzed, unable to respond in the face of strong competing demands.

Independent variable: The variable in a cause-and-effect hypothesis or explanation that produces change in another variable. In the "if X, then Y" mode of explanation, X is the independent variable that, given a certain value, actually causes Y, the dependent variable, to change in a particular way.

Interest group: A group that directly attempts to influence the allocation of public values or other actions of those in the political system. It may undertake political action, provide goods or services to political actors, or provide data and information to those within the political system in its attempts to achieve its political objectives. It may also exert influence through compliance or noncompliance with the government policy process.

Intergovernmental organizations (IGOs): A political actor whose members are states, not private groups or individuals. IGOs can shape the cooperative relations among states, some or all of whom are their members. States form IGOs to provide a forum of communication among states, to enact international laws and treaties, and to intervene in disputes between states. Examples: European Union; NAFTA; NATO.

International law: A broad attempt to establish principles and rules that formalize and constrain the interactions among states. Positivist law, or written agreements between states in the form of international treaties or conventions, is the basis for international law.

International organization: A broad term that refers to many of the cross-national institutions whose objectives are to influence the behavior and policies of states. The two primary forms are NGOs (nongovernmental organizations) and IGOs (intergovernmental organizations). Examples: Amnesty International; the United Nations.

International regime: A set of norms, rules, and procedures that are accepted by many countries and guide their behavior with each other in a particular issue domain. Examples: the World Trade Organization on trade relations; the Nuclear Nonproliferation Treaty.

International relations: One of the four major subfields within political science that examines the political relations between countries and the dynamics within the worldwide system of states. Subjects of analysis include foreign policy, interstate conflict and conflict resolution, and international law.

Judicial review: In political systems where the judiciary is relatively independent, the judiciary can interpret or even revoke the policy decisions and actions taken by the other political structures, thus exercising the power of judicial review. In the United States, for example, the Supreme Court exercises the power of judicial review when it declares that a law passed by Congress is unconstitutional.

Judiciary: An important branch of most political systems, the system of courts and personnel that determine whether the laws of the society have been transgressed, and, if so, whether and what type of sanctions ought to be imposed on the transgressor.

Legislature: The political structure in which, typically, policy issues are discussed and assessed and public policies are enacted by a set of elected or appointed legislators. Although a particular legislature may not exercise these powers, most have three broad roles: (1) enacting legislation, (2) representing the citizenry, and (3) overseeing the executive.

Liberal democracy: A political system that is not only an electoral democracy (periodic elections, limited mandate) but also ensures extensive political rights (e.g., parties promoting genuine alternatives, opposition) and civil liberties (e.g., freedom of expression, religion, and the media).

Macropolitics: The politically relevant behaviors and interactions that occur among large groups, institutions, or states. These phenomena are distinguished analytically from those of micropolitics, which particularly focus on the political behavior of individuals and small groups.

Market economy: A type of political economy in which there is near-total private control of land, labor, and capital. Every actor has direct control over his or her own factors of production, and production decisions are essentially the sum of all private actors' decisions. The exchange value of goods is decided by the market. The state is generally quite passive in a market economy, enforcing rules and providing minimal protection to economic actors. (Compare with *Command economy.*)

Marxist-Leninist socialism: A variant of socialist ideology heavily influenced by the writings of Karl Marx and the interpretations by V. I. Lenin. It begins with three assumptions regarding the changes necessary to produce the key goals of equality and social justice: (1) it might be necessary to use violence to overthrow the old economic order, (2) a powerful government is necessary to restructure the economic system, and (3) a small dictatorial leadership group must manage the government and effect the economic and social changes. This group will be unnecessary when equality is achieved and can be replaced by decentralized citizen-run politics. (See also *Socialism.*)

Micropolitics: An analytic focus on individual and small group political processes, with a particular emphasis on how the individual understands the political world and how the individual acts politically.

Mixed economy: A political economy that attempts to combine the strengths of both market and command economies while also minimizing their shortcomings. Control of the means of production is shared between the state and private actors. The state's rules, actions, and direct involvement in the economic system guide some production, distribution, and pricing decisions and also moderate and limit the market behavior of private households and firms.

Monarchy: (1) A political system with a hereditary sovereign, often called a king or queen. (2) Analytically, a political system in which one person exercises a very large proportion of political control.

Nation: A sociopolitical unit defined by a deeply shared fundamental identification among a set of people based on shared ethnicity, language, descent, culture, religion, or geographic space. The nation is a major group, beyond the family, with whom the individual identifies very powerfully.

Nationalism: A strong affection and commitment to the well-being of the nation with which one identifies, in comparison with minimal concern for those outside the nation. Nationalism can become the underlying principle shaping people's loyalty and willingness to make sacrifices for the protection and enhancement of the nation and its collective interests.

Natural law: Refers to sensible, widely accepted norms of behavior that ought to guide the relations among states and individuals and that should restrain hostile or destructive interactions.

Neocolonialism: New forms of domination and dependence between states that have emerged in the decades (after World War II) since the end of colonialism. Although direct occupation by colonial powers was ended at independence, domination has been extended in some cases by the manipulation of such power resources as economic aid, technology transfer, military support, and economic intervention.

Neoliberalism: An approach to economic development that emphasizes a reliance on a local and global free market that is guided by entrepreneurs who shape decisions about production and distribution of goods. The state plays a minimal role in the political economy, and public spending is focused on infrastructure support (e.g., transportation, education) rather than welfare distribution.

Nonconstitutional regime: A political system in which there is persistent nonenforcement of crucial limits on the rulers and/or protection of the rights of the ruled, especially those limits and rights specified in a constitution and other key legal documents. Most authoritarian or totalitarian regimes are nonconstitutional.

Nongovernmental organizations (NGOs): National or transnational associations that are not part of the governmental/state apparatus but are committed to the promotion of an issue with national or international policy dimensions. (In the latter case, the association is called an international nongovernmental organization). Members are groups and individuals who combine their knowledge and financial and political resources to pursue a shared objective. Examples: Amnesty International's monitoring of human rights; Medecins sans Frontieres (Doctors without Borders) provisions of medical assistance.

Normative political knowledge: Answers questions about what ought to be rather than simply providing descriptions and explanations of what is. Examples of normative questions: "Should there be limits on free speech?"; "How much and what types of health care should the state provide?"

Oligarchy: Literally, rule by the few. Hence, a political system in which a small number of actors dominate the resource allocation process, usually serving their own interests.

Parliamentary (cabinet) government: A political system in which the executive and legislative functions and structures are fused. The people elect the legislature (parliament), whose majority empowers a cabinet, which then empowers one of its members to be the chief executive, usually called a prime minister or premier. The cabinet devises, drafts, and implements most policies, although they must be enacted by the legislative majority. Examples: Italy; the United Kingdom.

Participatory democracy: Democracy in its classic sense as government of and by all the people. There is active, direct participation by all citizens in the authoritative allocation of values.

Party system: The configuration of political parties in a political system. Party systems are generally classified according to the number of political parties and nature of the interactions among the parties in the governing process.

Political analysis: The attempt to describe and explain political phenomena that strives to make understanding of politics more general, precise, and systematic, and ultimately to generate and test theories.

Political belief system: The configuration of an individual's political orientations across an array of political issues. Many political beliefs are evaluative orientations, which synthesize facts (cognitive orientations) and feelings (affective orientations) into a judgment (evaluative orientation) about some political phenomena.

Political culture: The general configuration of a particular people's (e.g., a nation's or a country's) political beliefs. It characterizes those cognitive, affective, and evaluative orientations that are dominant among that people. Many explanations of political behavior and political processes are grounded in interpretations of political culture.

Political decay: The phenomena that occur when there is a decline in the capacity of the political system and especially its effectiveness in maintaining order. It can be manifest in such collective behavior as demonstrations, protests, rebellion, and other forms of political violence. It is often associated with extensive demands that the political system cannot meet and with the loss of citizen support for the political system. According to Samuel Huntington (1968), the probability of political decay increases as a state has a lower level of political institutionalization.

Political development: The specifically political aspects of development and modernization. It can refer either to a set of characteristics of the political system or the process through which those characteristics are increased. The key characteristics of more developed political systems can include: (1) the concentration of power in the central state; (2) "modern" forms of political organization, such as institutionalized party systems and effective bureaucracies; (3) complex and extensive forms of individual and group political behavior; and (4) expanded capabilities of the political system to maintain order, manage the environment, meet the demands of the citizens, and so on.

Political economy: The combination, in theory or in practice, of politics and economics. The political system and the economic system are inextricably intertwined, because many of the decisions made by the political system have significant impacts on the economy and activities within the economic system have major impacts on the state. Two ideal-type political economies are the market economy and the command economy.

Political elite: A general term for those individuals who have relatively high levels of power, influence, interest, knowledge, and involvement in political life and is the stratum of the population that does more of what there is to do (in the policy process) and gets more of what there is to get (in the allocation of values).

Political group: An aggregation of individuals who interact to pursue a common political objective—a policy or action that might be taken by a governmental or private actor (e.g., a legislature, a corporation). Examples: the National Rifle Association; Greenpeace.

Political idealism: A perspective, especially in international relations theory, that posits that human nature is basically good and thus states have a natural tendency to be cooperative and even altruistic. Political institutions can then be shaped to facilitate the emergence of these cooperative, nonviolent tendencies in the relations among states.

Political ideology: A comprehensive set of beliefs about the political world, including a specification of desirable political goals and the best way to achieve those goals, based on particular assumptions about human nature, the relation of the individual to society, and the desirability of equality.

Political institutionalization: The extent that political organizations and procedures have acquired value in the eyes of the population and the stability to withstand significant pressure. It is measured by the political system's capacity to regulate its citizens, respond flexibly to citizen demands, extract and distribute resources efficiently, and adapt to changing circumstances.

Political participation: The term applied to all modes of the political actions by individuals and groups. The broad goal is to influence the actions or selection of political rulers. Modes of political participation for an individual range from listening to political discourse to voting to taking part in a demonstration to holding political office.

Political party: An organized group that attempts to capture political power directly by placing its members in government office. The political party is the broadest institution in most political systems that links individuals and groups to the state, and it can organize the activities of those participating in government. It also aggregates political interests into a comprehensible set of policy goals.

Political realism: A perspective, especially in international relations theory, that assumes that people are naturally disposed to behave selfishly and that this self-interested orientation extends to the behavior of states. The fundamental goal of each state is to ensure its own security and survival by maximizing its power. Interstate conflict is likely to be a recurring event, and states sometimes use balance-of-power strategies to limit the frequency of major conflicts.

Political resources: Something that can influence the actions and decisions of political actors such as social status, money, legality, special knowledge or skills, ability to mobilize large numbers of people, visibility in the media, and control of productive capabilities. According to the group approach, political resources are of many forms and widely distributed. According to the class and elite approaches, one or a few types of political resources are critical, and control of those resources tends to be concentrated in a limited group.

Political science: A set of techniques, concepts, and approaches whose objective is to increase the clarity and accuracy of understandings about political phenomena. This academic discipline is labeled a "science" in the United States because most political scientists use the scientific method to establish shared knowledge about the political world.

Political socialization: The process through which individuals acquire their cognitive, affective, and evaluative orientations toward the political world. Some of the most important agents (sources) are the family, the schools, peer groups, the media, and culture.

Political society: Formed when individuals cede to the state a monopoly over the legitimate use of violence, sacrificing their own right to do violence to others in exchange for a similar sacrifice from others. This agreement among individuals is termed the "social contract" by Hobbes.

Political system: A (formal) theoretical concept that attempts to model the fundamental structures, processes, and institutions of politics. According to David Easton (1965), the defining feature is its authoritative allocation of values for the collectivity.

Political theory: A broad subfield of political science that focuses on the ideas and debates regarding major political issues. One central orientation is to address normative questions, such as the appropriateness of different forms of political leadership or the rationale for political authority. As well as normative approaches, it can also be understood more broadly as knowledge claims about political phenomena that are grounded in axiomatic thinking (e.g., rational choice theory) or the scientific method (e.g., empirical political theory).

Political violence: The use of physical violence, or very serious threats of such violence, to achieve political goals. The modes range from nuclear war to assassination to riots. Some analysts define as political violence other activities that do not entail physical violence, such as racial epithets or ethnic discrimination.

Politics: The process through which power and influence are used in the promotion of certain values and interests and the determination of who gets what, when, and how in a given society.

Positivist law: Explicit written agreements, often enacted by legislatures and interpreted by judiciaries, that specify appropriate and unlawful behaviors as well as the sanctions for the latter. In the form of treaties or conventions between states, positivist law is the basis of international law.

Power: Exercised when A (one actor) induces B (another actor) to behave in a manner in which B would not otherwise behave. One taxonomy classifying the forms of power includes force (coercive power), exchange (economic power), and mutuality (integrative power).

Presidential government: A political system in which there is a separation of executive and legislative power and structures. This is meant to ensure a system of checks and balances in the policy process, with the legislature taking primary responsibility for policy making and the president (the executive) taking primary responsibility for policy implementation (although in practice these distinctions may be blurred). The president and the members of the legislature are elected independently, for fixed terms. Examples: Mexico; the United States.

Privatization: The selling off of state-owned firms to private actors and/or the use of private firms to provide public goods and services.

Rational choice theory: An array of formal analyses that share two basic features: (1) they are attempts to represent political processes primarily by means of mathematical formulations or systems of symbolic notation, and (2) it is assumed that the behavior of political actors is goal oriented, based on self-interest, and calculating. Examples: game theory; minimum winning coalition theory.

Relational analysis: Approaches to political analysis that specify the systematic connections between sets of phenomena, revealing either patterns of association (correlation) or of causality.

Representative democracy: A form of electoral democracy in which citizens elect people to represent them in the governing process and to allocate values on their behalf for the collectivity. Also known as a republic.

Revolution: A rapid and fundamental transformation of the state organization and of the allocation of values in a society. A revolution often involves the use of force and violence to destroy the existing political system.

Social market system: A political-economic system in which the state encourages the operation of an extensive free-market economy but is also committed to social welfare distribution and some income redistribution, within the context of a democratic political process. Contemporary examples: Germany; Sweden.

Social movement: Interest group activities that emerge through a dispersed set of actors who develop shared identity, but only a loosely structured organization. Such movements typically focus on a single issue area and often have a protest orientation. Example: WTO protestors.

Social welfarism: A set of ideological orientations and public policies that aim to ensure that all citizens receive an adequate quality of life in such domains as education, health care, housing, and employment opportunities. Usually characterized by relatively high taxes, more extensive resource allocations (e.g., transfer payments or subsidized goods and services), and more active state intervention to protect citizens against the behaviors of those firms or others whose actions reduce the quality of life. Example: Sweden.

Socialism: One of the major Western political ideologies in which the most important goal is to provide a high-quality, relatively equal standard of living for all. Each individual is encouraged to increase the collective good of all in an environment that encourages cooperation and sharing. Government plays a crucial role as it attempts to use its allocation of values and control of resources to increase the material, social, and political equality of all citizens. Two major variations are Marxist-Leninist socialism and democratic socialism.

Sovereignty: The premise that each state has complete authority and is the ultimate source of law within its own boundaries. It assumes the equality before the law of all states and that each state has the right to protect its territory against any aggression or intervention.

State: (1) The legal notion of the state is that it is a "territorially bound sovereign entity." (2) In the general language of political science, "state" usually refers to the organizational units, institutions, and individuals that perform the political functions for a national territorial entity, such as France or Nigeria. (3) The state can also be defined as the entity with a monopoly on the legitimate use of violence to enforce the laws and decisions of the society.

Statism: A state-centered strategy for facilitating economic development. The statist approach emphasizes the importance of strong state action to support and guide the production and distribution of goods by the political economy. The state typically plans and regulates major aspects of the political economy and might own and operate key economic sectors.

Taxonomic analysis: Approaches to political analysis that establish the orderly arrangement of phenomena into a set of categories that classify those phenomena/data into different types. Categories should be exhaustive, mutually exclusive, and differentiated by consistent criteria. The categories of a taxonomy establish the crucial concepts that structure the analysis.

Territorial integrity: A concept closely associated with sovereignty, it is a premise of international law that holds that a state has the right to resist and reject any aggression, invasion, or intervention within its territorial boundaries.

Terrorism: Premeditated violence serving an underlying political objective, in which the target of violence is an "innocent." As a revolutionary strategy, terrorism involves selective acts of violence, usually by small organized cells of political activists.

Totalitarianism: A political regime that demands complete obedience to its extensive rules regarding not only politics but virtually all aspects of life, including culture, economics, religion, and morality. It might prescribe and proscribe the behavior and thoughts of its population in every domain of existence. Examples: contemporary North Korea; the Soviet Union under Joseph Stalin.

Transnationalism: A system of institutions and relationships in which key actors' loyalties and identities are not linked to any particular country. Many of these powerful actors are multinational corporations (MNCs) such as General Motors, Exxon, and IBM, and other important transnational actors include the International Monetary Fund, OPEC, NATO, and other IGOs and NGOs. Increasingly, MNCs and other transnational actors hold international economic power, shape global culture and communications, and operate outside the legal control of states.

Treaty: A formal agreement between states that they will cooperate or assist each other militarily, economically, or politically. A treaty carries a stronger expectation of compliance than an alliance. Example: NATO; Nuclear Nonproliferation Treaty.

Unitary state: A political system in which the central government holds all legitimate power. The central government may delegate power or functional responsibilities to territorial units (often called departments, regions, or prefectures), but those delegated powers and functions can be revoked at any time. Examples: China; France; Japan; the United Kingdom.

War: Interstate violence that is sustained, organized, and usually involves hostilities between the regular military forces of the states. War is the ultimate mechanism for attempting to resolve power struggles and conflict between states. Examples: Iran–Iraq War; Korean War.

References

Abrahamian, Ervand. (1993). *Khomeinism: Essays on the Islamic Republic.* Berkeley: University of California Press.

Achebe, Chinua. (1959). *Things Fall Apart.* New York: Fawcett.

Adorno, T. W., Else Frenkel-Brunswick, Daniel Levinson, and R. Nevitt Sanford. (1950). *The Authoritarian Personality.* New York: Harper & Row.

Agnew, John. (2003). *Geopolitics: Re-Visioning World Politics.* London: Routledge.

Aguero, Felipe, and Jeffrey Stark, Eds. (1998). *Fault Lines of Democracy in Post-Transition Latin America.* Miami, FL: North-South Center Press.

Allison, Graham. (1999). *The Essence of Decision: Explaining the Cuban Missile Crisis.* New York: Addison Wesley Longman.

Almond, Gabriel. (1987). "The Development of Development." In *Understanding Political Development,* ed. Myron Weiner and Samuel Huntington, pp. 437–490. Boston, MA: Little, Brown.

Almond, Gabriel, and Sidney Verba. (1963). *The Civic Culture.* Princeton, NJ: Princeton University Press.

———.(1980). *The Civic Culture Revisited.* Boston, MA: Little, Brown.

Almond, Gabriel, G. Bingham Powell, Kaare Strom, and Russell Dalton, Eds. (2004). *Comparative Politics Today: A World View.* 8th ed. New York: Longman.

Amnesty International (2004). Amnesty International Report 2003. http://web.amnesty.org/report2004.

Anderson, Richard D., M. Steven Fish, Stephen E. Hanson, and Philip G. Roeder. (2002). *Postcommunism and the Theory of Democracy.* Princeton, NJ: Princeton University Press.

Ardrey, Robert. (1966). *The Territorial Imperative.* New York: Atheneum.

Arendt, Hannah. (1963). *On Revolution.* New York: Viking Press.

Bachrach, Peter, and Morton Baratz. (1962). "The Two Faces of Power." *American Political Science Review* 56 (December): 947–952.

Banuazizi, Ali. (1987). "Social-Psychological Approaches to Political Development." In *Understanding Political Development,* ed. Myron Weiner and Samuel Huntington, pp. 281–316. Boston, MA: Little, Brown.

Barber, Benjamin R. (1995). *Jihad versus McWorld.* New York: Random House.

Barkan, Joel. (2002). "The Many Faces of Africa." *Harvard International Review* (Summer): 14–18.

Barnet, Richard J., and John Cavanagh. (1994). *Global Dreams: Imperial Corporations and the New World Order.* New York: Simon & Schuster.

Bastow, Steve, and James Martin. (2003). *Third Way Discourse: The Crisis of European Ideologies in the Twentieth Century.* Edinburgh: Edinburgh University Press.

Baumol, William. (2003). *Economics.* 9th ed. Fort Worth, TX: Harcourt College Publications.

Becker, Ted, and Christa Slaton. (2000). *The Future of Teledemocracy.* Westport, CT: Praeger.

Bennett, W. Lance. (2003). *News: The Politics of Illusion.* 5th ed. New York: Longman.

Bentley, Arthur. (1908/1967). *The Process of Government.* Cambridge, MA: Harvard University Press.

Bill, James, and Robert Hardgrave. (1981). *Comparative Politics: Quest for Theory.* Lanham, MD: University Press of America.

Bimber, Bruce. (2003). *Information and American Democracy: Technology and the Evolution of Political Power.* New York: Cambridge University Press.

Birnbaum, Jeffrey H. (1993). *The Lobbyists: How Influence Peddlers Get Their Way in Washington.* New York: Times Books.

Black, Cyril. (1966). *The Dynamics of Modernization.* New York: Harper & Row.

Blasi, Joseph R., Maya Kroumova, and Douglas Kruse. (1997). *Kremlin Capitalism: Privatizing the Russian Economy.* Ithaca, NY: Cornell University Press.

Boulding, Kenneth E. (1989). *Three Faces of Power.* Newbury Park, CA: Sage.

———. (1993). "Power." In *The Oxford Companion to Politics of the World,* ed. Joel Krieger, pp. 739–740. New York: Oxford University Press.

Brams, Steven J., and Peter Fishburn. (1983). *Approval Voting.* Cambridge, MA: Birkhauser Boston.

Bratton, Michael, and Nicolas van de Walle. (1997). *Democratic Experiments in Africa: Regime Transitions in Comparative Perspective.* New York: Cambridge University Press.

Brecher, Michael, and Jonathan Wilkenfeld. (1997). *A Study of Crisis.* Ann Arbor: University of Michigan Press.

Bremer, Stuart. (1980). "National Capabilities and War Proneness." In *Correlates of War, II,* ed. J. David Singer, pp. 57–82. New York: Free Press.

Brinton, Crane. (1957). *The Anatomy of Revolution.* Rev. ed. New York: Vintage.

Broomfield, John H. (1982). *Mostly about Bengal.* New Delhi: Manohar.

Brown, Justin. (1999). "Lowdown on a High Strung Corner of Europe." *Christian Science Monitor,* March 16: 12–13.

Brown, Lester R., Christopher Glavin, and Sandra Postel. (1992). *Saving the Planet: How to Shape an Environmentally Sustainable Global Economy.* Washington, DC: Worldwatch Institute.

Bulletin of Atomic Scientists (2002). "Global Nuclear Stockpiles: 1945–2002." Volume 58 (November/December): 103–104.

Burke, Edmund. (1790/1955). *The Works of Edmund Burke.* New York: Harper & Row.

Candar, Cengiz. (2000). "Redefining Turkey's Political Center." *Journal of Democracy*: 11 (July): 129–141.

Cantril, Hadley. (1965). *The Pattern of Human Concerns.* New Brunswick, NJ: Rutgers University Press.

Castells, Manuel. (2000). "Materials for an Exploratory Theory of the Network Society." *British Journal of Sociology* 5: 1 (January/March): 5–24.

Castles, Francis G. (1999). *Comparative Public Policy: Patterns of Post-War Transformation.* Northampton, MA: Edward Elgar Publishing.

Center for Media Education. (2001). Teensites.com: A Field Guide to the New Digital Landscape. http://www.cme.org/teenstudy/.

Center for Responsive Politics. (2003). www.opensecrets.org.

Central Intelligence Agency. (2003). *World Factbook 2002.* http://www.odci.gov/cia/ciahome.html.

Churchill, Winston. (1948). *The Second World War: The Gathering Storm.* Boston, MA: Houghton Mifflin.

Cimbala, Stephen. (2000). *Nuclear Strategy in the Twenty-First Century.* Westport, CT: Praeger.

Clarke, Ian. (1985). *The Spatial Organization of Multinational Corporations.* London: Croom Helm.

Clausewitz, Karl von. (1833/1967). *On War.* Ed. and trans. Michael Howard and Peter Paret. Princeton, NJ: Princeton University Press.

Colburn, Forrest. (2002). "Fragile Democracies." *Current History* 101 (February): 76–80.

Coles, Robert. (2003). *Bruce Springsteen's America: The People Listening, A Poet Singing.* New York: Random House.

Compton, Robert W. (2000). *East Asian Democratization: Impact of Globalization, Culture and Economy.* Westport, CT: Greenwood.

Conger, Lucy. (1998). "A Fourth Way?: The Latin American Alternative to Neoliberalism." *Current History* 97 (November): 380–384.

Connor, Walker. (1994). *Ethnonationalism: The Quest for Understanding.* Princeton, NJ: Princeton University Press.

Converse, Philip. (1964). "The Nature of Belief Systems in Mass Publics." In *Ideology and Discontent,* ed. David Apter, pp. 224–240. Glencoe, IL: Free Press.

Cruikshanks, Randall. (2000). "Conflict Resolution in the Other World." In *The Other World: Issues and Politics of the Developing World,* 4th ed. ed. Joseph Weatherby et al., pp. 78–109. White Plains, NY: Longman.

Cutright, Phillips. (1963). "National Political Development: Measurement and Analysis." *American Sociological Review* 20: 253–264.

Cyert, Richard, and James March. (1963). *A Behavioral Theory of the Firm.* Englewood Cliffs, NJ: Prentice-Hall.

Dahl, Robert. (1961). *Who Governs? Democracy in an American City.* New Haven, CT: Yale University Press.

———. (1967). *Pluralist Democracy in the United States.* Chicago: Rand McNally.

———. (1971). *Polyarchy: Participation and Opposition.* New Haven, CT: Yale University Press.

Dahl, Robert, and Bruce Stinebrickner. (2003). *Modern Political Analysis.* 6th ed. New York: Pearson.

Dahrendorf, Ralf. (1959). *Class and Class Conflict in Industrial Society.* Stanford, CA: Stanford University Press.

———. (1999). "The Third Way and Liberty." *Foreign Affairs* 78: 5 (September/October): 13–17.

Dalton, Russell. (2002). *Citizen Politics: Public Opinion and Political Parties in Advanced Industrial Democracies.* 3d ed. New York: Chatham House.

Davies, James C. (1971). "Toward a Theory of Revolution." In *When Men Revolt and Why,* ed. James C. Davies, pp. 134–147. New York: Free Press.

Davis, Richard. (1998). *New Media and American Politics.* New York: Oxford University Press.

Davis, Winston. (1987). "Religion and Development: Weber and the East Asian Experience." In *Understanding Political Development,* ed. Myron Weiner and Samuel Huntington, pp. 221–280. Boston, MA: Little, Brown.

Demick, Barbara. (2003). "U.S. Gets a Bad Name in South Korea." *Los Angeles Times* (July 12, 2003): A3.

Derbyshire, Denis with Ian Derbyshire. (2000). *Encyclopedia of World Political Systems* . New York: M.E. Sharpe.

Deutsch, Karl. (1961). "Social Mobilization and Political Development." *American Political Science Review* 55 (September): 493–511.

Diamond, Larry. (2000). "The Global State of Democracy." *Current History* 99 (December): 412–418.

Diamond, Larry, Marc Plattner, Yun-han Chu, and Mung-mao Tien, Eds. (1997). *Consolidating the Third Wave Democracies: Themes and Perspectives.* Baltimore, MD: Johns Hopkins University Press.

Domhoff, G. William. (2002). *Who Rules America? Power and Politics.* 4th ed. Boston, MA: McGraw Hill.

Donovan, John, Richard Morgan, Christian Potholm, and Marcia Weigle. (1994). *People, Power and Politics.* 3rd ed. New York: Random House.

Doyle, Michael W., and Nicholas Sambanis. (2000). "International Peacebuilding: A Theoretical and Quantitative Analysis." *American Political Science Review* 94: 4 (December): 779–801.

Dunleavy, Patrick, and Christopher Husbands. (1985). *British Democracy at the Crossroads.* London: Allen & Unwin.

Duverger, Maurice. (1954). *Political Parties.* New York: Wiley.

Easton, David. (1953). *The Political System.* New York: Knopf.

———. (1965). *A Framework for Political Analysis.* Englewood Cliffs, NJ: Prentice-Hall.

Eckstein, Harry. (1966). *Division and Cohesion in Democracy: A Study of Norway.* Princeton, NJ: Princeton University Press.

The Economist. (1998). "What Would Confucius Say Now?" *The Economist,* July 25: pp. 23–24, 28.

———. (1999). *The World in 2000.* London: Economist Press.

Edwards, George, Martin Wattenberg, and Robert Lineberry. (2004). *Government in America.* 11th ed. New York: Longman.

Ehrlich, Paul R., and Anne H. Ehrlich. (1990). *The Population Explosion.* New York: Simon & Schuster.

Elgie, Robert, Ed. (1999). *Semi-Presidentialism in Europe.* New York: Oxford University Press.

Elkington, John, and Seb Beloe. (2003). *The 21st Century NGO: In the Market for Change.* London: SustainAbility.

Erikson, Erik. (1958). *Young Man Luther.* New York: Norton.

———. (1969). *Gandhi's Truth.* New York: Norton.

Esping-Andersen, Gosta. (1990). *The Three Worlds of Welfare Capitalism.* Princeton, NJ: Princeton University Press.

Estes, Richard. (1988). *Trends in World Social Development.* New York: Praeger.

Evans, Emmit B., Jr., and Dianne Long. (2000). "Development." In *The Other World: Issues and Politics of the Developing World,* 4th ed. ed. Joseph Weatherby et al., pp. 53–77. White Plains, NY: Longman.

Evans, Peter. (1979). *Dependent Development: The Alliance of Multinational, State and Local Capital in Brazil.* Princeton, NJ: Princeton University Press.

———. (1987). "Foreign Capital and the Third World State." In *Understanding Political Development,* ed. Myron Weiner and Samuel Huntington, pp. 319–352. Boston, MA: Little, Brown.

Evans, Peter, Dietrich Rueschmeyer, and Theda Skocpol, Eds. (1985). *Bringing the State Back In.* New York: Cambridge University Press.

Fagen, Richard. (1964). *Cuba: The Political Content of Adult Education.* Stanford, CA: Hoover Institute.

Falk, Richard A. (1975). *A Study of Future Worlds.* New York: Free Press.

———. (1993). "Sovereignty." In *The Oxford Companion to Politics of the World,* ed. Joel Krieger, pp. 851–854. New York: Oxford University Press.

———. (1995). *On Humane Governance: Toward a New Global Politics.* University Park: Pennsylvania State University Press.

———. (1999). "The New Interventionism and the Third World." *Current History* 98 (November): 370–375.

Fallows, James. (1995). *Looking at the Sun: The Rise of the New East Asian Economic and Political System.* New York: Random House.

Federation of American Scientists. (2004). www.fas.org/nuke/guide.

Fendrich, James. (1993). *Ideal Citizen: The Legacy of the Civil Rights Movement.* Albany, NY: SUNY Press.

Flanigan, William, and Nancy Zingale. (2002). *Political Behavior of the American Electorate,* 10th ed. Washington, DC: Congressional Quarterly Press.

Franda, Marcus. (2002). *Launching into Cyberspace: Internet Developments and Politics in Five World Regions.* Boulder, CO: Lynne Reinner.

Frederick, Howard H. (1993). *Global Communication and International Relations.* Belmont, CA: Wadsworth.

Freedom House. (2001). *Freedom of the World: 2000–2001.* http://freedomhouse.org.

———. (2003). *Freedom of the World: 2002–2003.* http://freedomhouse.org.

Friedman, Thomas L. (1999). "DOScapital." *Foreign Policy* 113 (Fall): 110–127.

———. (2001). *The Lexus and the Olive Tree: Understanding Globalization.* New York: HarperCollins.

Fuller, R. Buckminster. (1970). *Operating Manual for Spaceship Earth.* New York: Pocket Books.

Galbraith, James K. (1999). "The Crisis of Globalization." *Dissent* 36 (Summer 1999): 12–16.

Global Exchange. (2003). "Top Ten Reasons to Oppose the World Trade Organization." www.globalexchange.org.

Gochman, Charles S., and Zeev Maoz. (1984). "Militarized Interstate Disputes, 1816–1976." *Journal of Conflict Resolution* 18 (December): 588–615.

Goldman, Marshall I. (1992). *What Went Wrong with Perestroika.* New York: Norton.

———. (1998). "The Cashless Society." *Current History* 97 (October): 319–324.

———. (2003). *The Piratization of Russia.* New York: Routledge.

Goodwin, Paul. (2003). *Latin America,* 10th ed. New York: McGraw Hill.

Graber, Doris A. (2001). *Processing Politics: Learning from Television in the Internet Age.* Chicago: University of Chicago Press.

———. (2001). *Mass Media and American Politics,* 6th ed. Washington, DC: Congressional Quarterly Press.

Grotius, Hugo. (1625/1957). *De Jure Belli et Pacis [On the Laws of War and Peace].* New York: Macmillan.

Grzymala-Busse, Anna M. (2002). *Redeeming the Communist Past: The Regeneration of Communist Parties in East Central Europe.* Cambridge: Cambridge University Press.

Gurr, Ted Robert. (2000). *Peoples Versus States: Minorities at Risk in the New Century.* Washington, DC: United States Institute of Peace Press.

Gutman, Roy, and David Rieff, Eds. (1999). *Crimes of War: What the Public Should Know.* New York: W.W. Norton.

Gwartney, James, and Robert Lawson. (2003). *Economic Freedom of the World: 2003 Annual Report.* www.freetheworld.com.

Haas, Peter M., Robert O. Keohane, and Marc A. Levy, Eds. (1993). *Institutions for the Earth: Sources of Effective International Environmental Protection.* Cambridge, MA: MIT Press.

Hachten, William A., and James Scotton. (2003). *The World News Prism: Global Media in an Era of Terrorism,* 6th ed. Ames: Iowa State University Press.

Hagopian, Mark. (1984). *Regimes, Movements and Ideology.* New York: Longman.

Hakim, Peter. (1999). "Is Latin America Doomed to Failure?" *Foreign Policy* 113 (Winter 1999-2000): 104–119.

Hanson, Stephen E. (2001). "The Dilemmas of Russia's Anti-Revolutionary Revolution." *Current History* 100 (October): 330–335.

Hardin, Garrett J. (1995). *Living within Limits: Ecology, Economics and Population Taboos.* New York: Oxford University Press.

Hastie, Reid. (1986). "A Primer of Information-Processing Theory for the Political Scientist." In *Political Cognition,* ed. Richard R. Lau and David O. Sears, pp. 83–112. Hillsdale, NJ: Lawrence Erlbaum Associates.

Hayes, Edward. (1972). *Power Structure and Urban Policy.* New York: McGraw-Hill.

Hechter, Michael. (2002). *Containing Nationalism.* New York: Oxford University Press.

Hearnshaw, F. J. C. (1933). *Conservatism in England.* London: Macmillan.

Hearst, Patricia. (1988). *Patty Hearst: Her Own Story.* New York: Avon.

Heilbroner, Robert. (1993). "The Multinational Corporation and the Nation-State." In *At Issue: Politics in the World Arena,* ed. Steven L. Speigel, pp. 338–352. New York: St. Martin's Press.

———. (1994). *Twenty-First Century Capitalism.* New York: W.W. Norton.

Hemphill, Michael R., and Larry David Smith. (1990). "The Working American's Elegy: The Rhetoric of Bruce Springsteen." In *Politics in Familiar Contexts,* ed. Robert L. Savage and Dan Nimmo, pp. 199–214. Norwood, NJ: Ablex.

Heredia, Blanca. (1997). "Prosper or Perish?: Development in the Age of Global Capital." *Current History* 96 (November): 383–388.

Heyne, Paul, with Peter Boettke and David Prychitko. (2003). *The Economic Way of Thinking.* 10th ed. New York: Prentice-Hall.

Hobbes, Thomas. (1651/1958). *Leviathan.* Oxford, England: Clarendon.

Holley, David (2001). "Kofi Annan Accepts Nobel Peace Prize." *Los Angeles Times,* December 11: p. A15.

Holsti, Ole, and James Rosenau. (1984). *American Leadership in World Affairs: Vietnam and the Breakdown of Consensus.* Boston, MA: Allen & Unwin.

Hunter, Floyd. (1953). *Community Power Structure.* Chapel Hill: University of North Carolina Press.

Huntington, Samuel P. (1968). *Political Order in Changing Societies.* New Haven, CT: Yale University Press.

———. (1987). "The Goals of Development." In *Understanding Political Development,* ed. Myron Weiner and Samuel Huntington, pp. 3–32. Boston, MA: Little, Brown.

———. (1991). *The Third Wave: Democratization in the Late Twentieth Century.* Norman: University of Oklahoma Press.

———. (1996). *Clash of Civilizations and the Remaking of the World Order.* New York: Simon & Schuster.

Huxley, Aldous. (1932). *Brave New World.* London: Chatto & Windus.

Inglehart, Ronald. (1989). *Culture Shift in Advanced Industrial Societies.* Princeton, NJ: Princeton University Press.

———. (1997). *Modernization and Post-Modernization.* Princeton, NJ: Princeton University Press.

Inkeles, Alex. (1997). *National Character: A Psycho-Social Perspective.* New Brunswick, NJ: Transaction.

Inkeles, Alex, and David Smith. (1999). *Becoming Modern: Individual Change in Six Developing Countries.* Cambridge, MA: Harvard University Press.

Inkeles, Alex, et al. (1985). *Exploring Individual Modernity.* New York: Columbia University Press.

International Food Policy Research Institute. (2003). http://www.ifpri.org/.

Isbister, John. (2004). *Promises Not Kept: Poverty and the Betrayal of Third World Development,* 6th ed. Bloomfield, CT: Kumarian Press.

Iyengar, Shanto. (1994). *Is Anyone Responsible? How Television Frames Political Issues.* Chicago: University of Chicago Press.

———. Ed. (1997). *Do the Media Govern? Politicians, Voters and Reporters in America.* Thousand Oaks, CA: Sage.

Jenkins, Barbara. (1993). "Multinational Corporations." In *The Oxford Companion to Politics of the World,* ed. Joel Krieger, pp. 606–608. New York: Oxford University Press.

Jennings, M. Kent, and Jan Ven Deth, Eds. (1989). *Continuities in Political Action.* Berlin: de Gruyter.

Jennings, M. Kent, Gregory Markus, and Richard Niemi. (1991). *Youth-Parent Socialization Panel Study, 1965–1982.* Ann Arbor, MI: Interuniversity Consortium for Political Research.

Jervis, Robert. (2002). "Theories of War in an Era of Leading-Power Peace." *American Political Science Review* 96 (1): 1–14.

Johnson, Chalmers. (1983). *Revolutionary Change.* 2d ed. London: Longman.

———. (1985). *MITI and the Japanese Economic Miracle.* Stanford, CA: Stanford University Press.

———. (1996). *Japan: Who Governs? The Rise of the Developmental State.* New York: W.W. Norton.

Kaplan, Morton. (1957). *System and Process in International Politics.* New York: Wiley.

Kapstein, Ethan, Robert Keohane, and Richard Haass. (1999). *Is Global Capitalism Working?* New York: W.W. Norton.

Karatnycky, Adrian. (2003). "The 2003 Freedom House Survey of Freedom." http://freedomhouse.org.

Karlekar, Karin Deutsch. (2003). "Press Freedom in 2002". http://freedomhouse.org.

Keck, Margaret, and Kathryn Sikkink. (1998). *Activists without Borders: Advocacy Networks in International Politics.* Ithaca, NY: Cornell University Press.

Kegley, Charles W., Jr., and Eugene Wittkopf. (1993). *World Politics: Trend and Transformation.* 4th ed. New York: St. Martin's Press.

———. (1995). *World Politics: Trend and Transformation.* 5th ed. New York: St. Martin's Press.

———. (1997). *World Politics: Trend and Transformation.* 6th ed. New York: St. Martin's Press.

———. (2001). *World Politics: Trend and Transformation.* 8th ed. New York: St. Martin's Press.

———. (2004). *World Politics: Trend and Transformation.* 9th ed. New York: Thompson Wadsworth.

Kellner, Douglas. (1990). *Television and the Crisis of Democracy.* Boulder, CO: Westview Press.

Keohane, Robert O., and Joseph S. Nye, Jr. (2000). "Globalization: What's New? What's Not? (and So What?)" *Foreign Policy* 115 (Spring): 1014–1119.

———. (2001). *Power and Interdependence: World Politics in Transition*, 3d ed. New York: Longman.

Kerpelman, Larry. (1972). *Activists and Nonactivists: A Psychological Study of American College Students.* New York: Behavioral Publisher.

Khalidi, Rashid I. (1993). "Intifada." In *The Oxford Companion to Politics of the World,* ed. Joel Krieger, pp. 463–464. New York: Oxford University Press.

Klare, Michael T. (1987). "The Arms Trade: Changing Patterns in the 1980s." *Third World Quarterly* 9 (October): 1257–1281.

———. (1988). "Low-Intensity Conflict." *Christianity and Crisis,* February: pp. 11–14.

———. (1997). "The New Arms Race: Light Weapons and International Security." *Current History* 96 (April): 173–178.

Kramer, John M. (1998). "The Politics of Corruption." *Current History* 97 (October): 329–334.

Krasner, Stephen. (1978). *Defending the National Interest: Raw Materials, Investments and U.S. Foreign Policy.* Princeton, NJ: Princeton University Press.

Kuhn, Thomas. (1996). *The Structure of Scientific Revolutions,* 3d ed. Chicago: University of Chicago Press.

Kurian, George Thomas. (1998). *The Fitzroy-Dearborn Book of World Rankings.* Chicago, IL: Fitzroy-Dearborn.

Kurth, James. (1999). "The Baltics: Between Russia and the West." *Current History* 98 (October): 334–339.

Larkey, Edward. (1990). "Rock Music and Cultural Theory in the German Democratic Republic." In *Politics in Familiar Contexts,* ed. Robert L. Savage and Dan Nimmo, pp. 215–224. Norwood, NJ: Ablex.

Lasswell, Harold. (1960). *Psychopathology and Politics.* New York: Viking.

———. (1977). "Propaganda." In *Harold Lasswell on Political Sociology,* ed. Dwaine Marvick. Chicago: University of Chicago Press. (Originally published in *Encyclopedia of Social Sciences,* 1934.)

Latinobarometro (2003). www.latinobarometro.org.

Lenski, Gerhard. (1966). *Power and Privilege: A Theory of Social Stratification.* New York: McGraw-Hill.

Lewis, Martin. (1999). "Is There a Third World?" *Current History* 98 (November): 355–358.

Lijphart, Arend. (1978). *Democracy in Plural Societies.* New Haven, CT: Yale University Press.

———. (1984). *Democracies: Patterns of Majoritarian and Consensual Government in Twenty-One Countries.* New Haven, CT: Yale University Press.

———. (1999). *Patterns of Democracy: Government Forms and Performance in Thirty-Six Countries.* New Haven, CT: Yale University Press.

Lindblom, Charles E. (1977). *Politics and Markets: The World's Political-Economic Systems.* New York: Basic Books.

———. (2003). *The Market System: What It Is, How It Works, and What to Make of It.* New Haven, CT: Yale University Press.

Linz, Juan J. (1993). "Authoritarianism." In *The Oxford Companion to Politics of the World,* ed. Joel Krieger, pp. 60–64. New York: Oxford University Press.

Lippman, John. (1992). "Tuning in the Global Village." *Los Angeles Times,* October 20, special supplement: pp. H1–H12.

Locke, John. (1690/1963). *Two Treatises on Government.* New York: New American Library.

Loveman, Brian. (1994). "'Protected Democracies' and Military Guardianship: Political Transitions in Latin American, 1978–1993," *Journal of InterAmerican Studies and World Affairs* 36 (Summer): 114–130.

Lovenduski, Joni, Rosie Campbell, and Jacqui Sampson-Jacent, Eds. (2003). *Women, Public Life and Democracy.* London: Pluto Press.

Lozada, Carlos. (2003). "Think Again: Latin America." *Foreign Policy* 135 (March/April): 18–26.

Lukes, Steven. (1997). *Power: A Radical Review,* 4th ed. London: Palgrave-Macmillan.

Lyman, Princeton (2000). "Globalization and the Demands on Governance." *Georgetown Journal of International Affairs* (Winter/Spring). http://data.georgetown.edu/publications/journal/1_11.htm.

Machiavelli, Niccolò. (1517/1977). *The Prince.* Trans. and ed. Robert M. Adams. New York: Norton.

Mackinder, Halford John. (1996). *Democratic Ideals and Reality.* Washington, DC: U.S. Government Printing Office.

Macridis, Roy, and Steven Burg. (1997). *Introduction to Comparative Politics: Political Regimes and Political Change,* 2d ed. New York: Addison-Wesley.

Mahon, James E. (1999). "Economic Crisis in Latin America: Global Contagion, Local Pain." *Current History* 98 (March): 105–110.

Mainwaring, Scott, and Matthew Soberg Shugart, Eds. (1997). *Presidentialism and Democracy in Latin America.* Cambridge, MA: Cambridge University Press.

Mander, Jerry. (1999). "Regarding the WTO." *International Forum on Globalization.* www.ifg.org/media.html.

March, James G., and Johan P. Olsen. (1989). *Rediscovering Institutions: The Organizational Basis of Politics.* New York: Free Press.

Margolis, Mac. (1992). "Black Is for Progress." *World Monitor,* December: pp. 38–43.

Marquand, Robert. (1996). "The Age of Anonymous Terrorism." *Christian Science Monitor,* July 29: pp. 1, 8.

Marx, Karl. (1867/1981). *Capital.* Trans. David Fernbach. New York: Vintage.

Marx, Karl, and Frederich Engels. (1848/1978). "The Communist Manifesto." In *The Marx-Engels Reader,* 2d. ed., ed. Robert Tucker, pp. 482–500. New York: Norton.

Maslow, Abraham. (1954). *Motivation and Personality.* New York: Harper & Row.

———. (1968). *Toward a Psychology of Being.* Princeton, NJ: Van Nostrand.

Masters, Roger D. (1992). "How Television Has Transformed American Politics." *Public Affairs Report,* November: pp. 7–9. Berkeley, CA: Institute for Governmental Studies.

———. (2001). "Biology and Politics: Linking Nature and Nurture." In *Annual Review of Political Science* 4 (June).

Maxfield, Sylvia. (1997). *Gatekeepers of Growth: The International Political Economy of Central Banking in Developing Countries.* Princeton, NJ: Princeton University Press.

McClelland, David. (1961). *The Achieving Society.* Princeton, NJ: Van Nostrand.

McCloskey, Herbert, and Dennis Chong. (1985). "Similarities and Differences between Left-Wing and Right-Wing Radicals." *British Journal of Political Science* 15 (July): 329–363.

McDonald, Forrest. (1979). *Alexander Hamilton: A Biography.* New York: Norton.

McFaul, Michael. (1998). "Russia's Summer of Discontent." *Current History* 97 (October): 307–312.

———. (2001). *Russia's Unfinished Revolution: Political Change from Gorbachev to Putin.* Ithaca, NY: Cornell University Press.

Mearshimer, John J. (2001). *The Tragedy of Great Power Politics.* New York: W.W. Norton.

Medvedev, Roy. (2000). *Where Is Russia Going?* Translated by George Shriver. New York: Columbia University Press.

Meisner, Maurice. (1999). *Mao's China and After,* 3rd ed. New York: Free Press.

Menkhaus, Ken, and John Prendergast. (1999). "Conflict and Crisis in the Greater Horn of Africa." *Current History* 97 (May): 213–217.

Mettenheim, Kurt von. (1997). *Presidential Institutions and Democratic Politics: Comparing Regional and National Contexts.* Baltimore, MD: Johns Hopkins University Press.

Mewes, Horst. (1987). "The Green Party Comes of Age." In *Comparative Politics* 87/88, ed. Christian Soe, pp. 110–118. New York: McGraw Hill.

Meyer, David S., and Sidney Tarrow, Eds. (1997). *The Social Movement Society: Contentious Politics for a New Century.* Lanham, MD: Rowman & Littlefield.

Meyer, David S., and Nancy Whittier, Eds. (2003). *Social Movements: Identity, Culture and the State.* New York: Oxford University Press.

Migdahl, Joel. (1974). *Peasants, Politics and Revolution: Pressures toward Political and Social Change in the Third World.* Princeton, NJ: Princeton University Press.

———. (1987). "Strong States, Weak States: Power and Accommodation." In *Understanding Political Development,* ed. Myron Weiner and Samuel Huntington, pp. 391–434. Boston, MA: Little, Brown.

Milbrath, Lester, and M. L. Goel. (1982). *Political Participation.* Lanham, MD: University Press of America.

Millar, James R. (1999). "The De-development of Russia." *Current History* 98 (October): 322–327.

Milgram, Stanley. (1974). *Obedience to Authority.* New York: Harper & Row.

Mills, C. Wright. (1956). *The Power Elite.* New York: Oxford University Press.

Mitchell, Jennifer D. (1998). "Before the Next Doubling." *World Watch* (January/February): 20–27.

Moore, Barrington. (1966). *The Social Origins of Dictatorship and Democracy.* Cambridge, MA: Harvard University Press.

Morgenthau, Hans J. (1993). *Politics among Nations.* Brief ed. Revised by Kenneth W. Thompson. New York: Knopf.

Mosca, Gaetano. (1896/1939). *The Ruling Class.* Trans. Hannah Kahn. New York: McGraw-Hill.

Mueller, Dennis. (1993). *The Public Choice Approach to Politics.* Northhampton, MA: Edward Elgar Publishers.

———. (2003). *Public Choice III.* New York: Cambridge University Press.

Murphy, Dean. (1995). "East Europe P.D. Blues." *Los Angeles Times,* February 28: pp. H1, H4.

Murphy, Kim. (2003). "Takeover of Polling Firm Causes a Stir." *Los Angeles Times,* August 23, 2003: pp. A3.

Nelson, Joan. (1987). "Political Participation." In *Understanding Political Development,* ed. Myron Weiner and Samuel Huntington, pp. 103–159. Boston, MA: Little, Brown.

———. (1993). "Political Participation." In *The Oxford Companion to Politics of the World,* ed. Joel Krieger, pp. 720–722. New York: Oxford University Press.

Neuman, W. Russell. (1999). *The Gordian Knot: Political Gridlock on the Information Highway.* Cambridge, MA: MIT Press.

Neuman, W. Russell, Marion Just, and Ann Crigler. (1992). *Common Knowledge: News and the Construction of Meaning.* Chicago: University of Chicago Press.

Niemi, Richard G., and Herbert Weissberg. (2001). *Controversies in Voting Behavior,* 4th ed. Washington, DC: Congressional Quarterly Press.

Nimmo, Dan, and James E. Combs. (1990). *Mediated Political Realities,* 2d ed. White Plains, NY: Longman.

Nordlinger, Eric A. (1987). "Taking the State Seriously." In *Understanding Political Development,* ed. Myron Weiner and Samuel Huntington, pp. 353–390. Boston, MA: Little, Brown.

Norton, Philip. (2001). *The British Polity,* 4th ed. New York: Longman.

Nugent, Neill. (2003). *The Government and Politics of the European Union,* 5th ed. Durham, NC: Duke University Press.

O'Connor, Karen, and Larry Sabato. (2004). *The Essentials of American Government.* New York: Longman.

O'Connor, Robert. (1978). "Political Activism and Moral Reasoning: Political and Apolitical Students in Great Britain and France." *British Journal of Political Science* 4 (January): 53–78.

Onwumechili, Chuka. (1999). *African Democratization and Military Coups.* Westport, CT: Praeger.

Organization for Economic Cooperation and Development. (2003). *Economic Outlook* 73 (microfiche) (June). Paris: OECD.

Orwell, George. (1945/1964). *Animal Farm.* Middlesex, England: Penguin.

———. (1949/1967). *1984.* Middlesex, England: Penguin.

Parenti, Michael. (1992). *Inventing Reality: The Politics of the Mass Media,* 3d ed. New York: St. Martin's Press.

———. (2002). *Democracy for the Few,* 7th ed. New York: St. Martin's Press.

Parker, Geoffrey. (2000). *Geopolitics: Past, Present and Future.* London: Pinter Publishers.

Pateman, Carole. (1980). "The Civic Culture: A Philosophic Critique." In *The Civic Culture Revisited,* ed. Gabriel Almond and Sidney Verba, pp. 57–102. Boston, MA: Little, Brown.

Peterson, Scott. (2001). "Jaded Hope: Russia 10 Years Later." *Christian Science Monitor* (August 17, 2001): 1, 7–8.

Physicians for a National Health Program. (2003). www.pnhp.org.

Popper, Karl. (1963). *The Open Society and Its Enemies,* vol. 2. New York: Harper & Row.

Population Institute. (1992, September). Untitled pamphlet. Washington, DC: Population Institute.

Poulantzas, Nicos. (1973). *Political Power and Social Classes.* London: Sheed and Ward.

Przeworski, Adam. (1985). *Capitalism and Social Democracy.* Cambridge, UK: Cambridge University Press.

———. (1993). "Socialism and Social Democracy." In *The Oxford Companion to Politics of the World,* ed. Joel Krieger, pp. 832–838. New York: Oxford University Press.

Putnam, Robert. (1993). *Making Democracy Work: Civic Traditions in Modern Italy.* Princeton, NJ: Princeton University Press.

Pye, Lucian W. (1962). *Politics, Personality and Nation-Building.* New Haven, CT: Yale University Press.

———. (1985). *Asian Power and Politics: The Cultural Dimensions of Authority.* Cambridge, MA: Belknap Press.

Rae, Douglas. (1971). *The Political Consequences of Electoral Laws.* New Haven, CT: Yale University Press.

Ramonet, Ignacio. (1999). "A New Totalitarianism." *Foreign Policy* 113 (Fall): 110–127.

Ramsey, Jeff. (1999). *Africa,* 8th ed. New York: McGraw Hill.

Randall, Vicky. (1998). *Political Change and Underdevelopment: A Critical Introduction to Third World Politics.* Durham, NC: Duke University Press.

Ranney, Austin. (2001). *Governing: An Introduction to Political Science,* 8th ed. Englewood Cliffs, NJ: Prentice-Hall.

Raymond, Nicholas. (1991). "The 'Lost Decade' of Development: The Role of Debt, Trade and Structural Adjustment." *The US National Committee for World Food Day,* October: pp. 1–14.

Reich, Robert. (1993). *The Work of Nations: Preparing Ourselves for Twenty-First-Century Capitalism.* New York: Vintage.

Reppy, Susan. (1984). "The Automobile Air Bag." In *Controversy,* 2d ed. ed. Dorothy Nelkin, pp. 161–174. Beverly Hills, CA: Sage.

Rigby, T. H. (1999). "New Top Elites for Old in Russian Politics." *British Journal of Political Science* 29 (July): 323–343.

Riker, William. (1962). *The Theory of Political Coalitions.* New Haven, CT: Yale University Press.

———. (1982). "The Two Party System and Duverger's Law." *American Political Science Review* 76 (4): 753–766.

Riker, William, and Peter Ordeshook. (1973). *An Introduction to Positive Political Theory.* Englewood Cliffs, NJ: Prentice-Hall.

Roberts, Cynthia, and Thomas Sherlock. (1999). "Bringing the Russian State Back." In "Explanations of the Derailed Transition to Market Democracy," pp. 477–492. *Comparative Politics* 39 (July).

Robinson, Simon. (2003). "Iraqi Textbooks: X-ing Out Saddam." *Time,* July 21, 2003, 18.

Rodrik, Dani. (1997). "Sense and Nonsense in the Globalization Debate." *Foreign Policy* 111 (Summer): 19–36.

———. (1999). *The New Global Economy and Developing Countries.* Washington, DC: Overseas Council.

Rokeach, Milton. (1960). *The Open and Closed Mind.* New York: Basic Books.

Rosenau, James N. (1997). "The Complexities and Contradictions of Globalization." *Current History* 96 (November): 360–364.

Rosenau, James, and Ole Holsti. (1986). "Consensus Lost, Consensus Regained?" *International Studies Quarterly:* 375–409.

Rosenberg, Shawn. (1988). *Reason, Ideology and Politics.* Cambridge, England: Polity Press.

———. (2002). *The Not so Common Sense: Differences in How People Judge Social and Political Life.* New Haven, CT: Yale University Press.

Royo, Sebastian. (2002). "A New Century of Corporatism?": *Corporatism in Southern Europe—Spain and Portugal in a Comparative Perspective.* Westport, CT: Praeger Publishers.

Rueschemeyer, Dietrich, Marilyn Rueschemeyer, and Bjorn Wittrock. (1998). *Participation and Democracy East and West: Comparisons and Interpretations.* Armonk, NY: M.E. Sharpe.

Ruffin, Roy, and Paul Gregory. (2000). *Principles of Economics.* 7th ed. New York: Addison Wesley Longman.

Rummel, R. J. (2004). *Death by Government.* www.hawaii.edu/powerkills/.

Rupnik, Jacques (1999). "The Post-Communist Divide." *Journal of Democracy* 10 (January): 57–62.

Russett, Bruce, and John R. Oneal. (2001). *Triangulating Peace: Democracy, Interdependence and International Organizations.* New York: Norton.

Russett, Bruce, Harvey Starr, and David Kinsella. (2003). *World Politics: The Menu for Choice,* 7th ed. New York: Thomson Wadsworth.

Rustow, Dankwart. (1967). *A World of Nations: Problems of Political Modernization.* Washington, DC: Brookings.

Rutland, Peter. (1999). "The Revolutions of 1989 Revisited." *Current History* 98 (April): 147–152.

Sabato, Larry. (1991). *Feeding Frenzy: How Attack Journalism Has Transformed American Politics.* New York: Free Press.

Sadowski, Yahya. (1998). "Ethnic Conflict." *Foreign Policy* 31 (Summer):12–23.

Safran, William. (2003). *The French Polity,* 6th ed. New York: Longman.

Salisbury, Robert H. (1990). "The Paradox of Interest Groups in Washington, D.C.: More Groups and Less Clout." In *The New American Political System,* rev. ed. ed. Anthony King. Washington, DC: American Enterprise Institute.

Salisbury, Robert H., John P. Heinz, Robert L. Nelson, and Edward O. Laumann. (1991). "Triangles, Networks and Hollow Cores: The Complex Geometry of Washington Interest Representation." In *The Politics of Interests,* ed. Mark P. Petracca, pp. 130–149. Boulder, CO: Westview Press.

Sassen, Saskia. (1996). *Losing Control?: Sovereignty in the Age of Globalization.* New York: Columbia University Press.

Savage, Robert L., and Dan Nimmo, Eds. (1990). *Politics in Familiar Contexts: Projecting Politics through Popular Media.* Norwood, NJ: Ablex.

Schattschneider, E. E. (1960). *The Semi-Sovereign People.* New York: Holt, Rinehart & Winston.

Schedler, Andreas. (1998). "What Is Democratic Consolidation?" *Journal of Democracy* 9 (January): 91–107.

Schelling, Thomas. (1960). *The Strategy of Conflict.* Cambridge, MA: Harvard University Press.

Schiller, Herbert I. (1976). *Communication and Cultural Domination.* White Plains, NY: Sharpe.

Schleifer, Andrei, and Daniel Triesman. (2000). *Without a Map: Political Tactics and Economic Reform in Russia.* Cambridge, MA: MIT Press.

Schmitter, Philippe C. (1993). "Corporatism." In *The Oxford Companion to Politics of the World,* ed. Joel Krieger, pp. 195–198. New York: Oxford University Press.

Schnetzer, Amanda. (2003). "Nations in Transit 2003: Milestones." www.freedomhouse.com.

Schumpeter, Joseph. (1950). *Capitalism, Socialism and Democracy,* 3d ed. New York: Harper & Row.

Scott, Bruce R. (2001). "The Great Divide in the Global Village." *Foreign Affairs* (January/February): 160–177.

Segre, Claudio G. (1993). "Fascism." In *The Oxford Companion to Politics of the World,* ed. Joel Krieger, pp. 294–296. New York: Oxford University Press.

Sesser, Stan. (1992). "A Nation of Contradictions." *New Yorker,* January 13: pp. 37–68.

Shawcross, William. (1991). Murdoch. New York: Simon &Schuster.

Shepsle, Kenneth, and Mark Bonchek. (1997). *Analyzing Politics: Rationality, Behavior and Institutions.* New York: W.W. Norton.

Shugart, Matthew Soberg, and John M. Carey. (1992). *Presidents and Assemblies: Constitutional Design and Electoral Dynamics.* New York: Cambridge University Press.

Shugart, Matthew Soberg, and Martin P. Wattenberg., Eds. (2001). *Mixed-Member Electoral Systems: The Best of Both Worlds?* Oxford: Oxford University Press.

Silone, Ignazio. (1937). *Bread and Wine.* Trans. Gwenda David. New York: Harper & Row.

Simon, Julian L. (1998). *The Ultimate Human Resource 2.* Princeton, NJ: Princeton University Press.

Simone, Vera. (2001). *The Asian Pacific: Political and Economic Development in a Global Context,* 2d ed. New York: Longman.

Singer, J. David. (1991). "Peace in the Global System: Displacement, Interregnum or Transformation?" In *The Long Postwar Peace,* ed. Charles W. Kegley, pp. 56–84. New York: HarperCollins.

SIPRI. (2003). *The SIPRI (Stockholm International Peace Research Institute) Yearbook 2002.* http://editors.sipri.se/pubs/yb02.html.

Sivard, Ruth Leger. (1991). *World Military and Social Expenditures 1991.* Washington, DC: World Priorities.

———. (1996). *World Military and Social Expenditures 1996.* Washington, DC: World Priorities.

Skidmore, Thomas E., Ed. (1993). *Television, Politics and the Transition to Democracy in Latin America.* Washington, DC: Woodrow Wilson Center.

Skinner, B. F. (1948). *Walden Two.* New York: Macmillan.

Skocpol, Theda. (1979). *States and Social Revolutions: A Comparative Analysis of France, Russia and China.* New York: Cambridge University Press.

Smith, Dan. (1997). *The State of War and Peace Atlas.* London: Penguin.

Sniderman, Paul M. (1975). *Personality and Democratic Politics.* Berkeley: University of California Press.

———. (1993). "The New Look in Public Opinion Research." In *Political Science: The State of the Discipline II.* ed. Ada W. Finifter, pp. 219–245. Washington, DC: American Political Science Association.

Sniderman, Paul M., Joseph Fletcher, Peter H. Russell, Philip E. Tetlock, and Brian J. Gaines. (1991). "The Fallacy of Democratic Elitism: Elite Competition and Commitment to Civil Liberties." *British Journal of Political Science* 21 (August): 349–370.

Snyder, Jack. (2000). *From Voting to Violence: Democratization and Nationalist Conflict.* New York: W.W. Norton.

So, Alvin Y. (1990). *Social Change and Development: Modernization, Dependency, and World-System Theories.* Newbury Park, CA: Sage.

Sophocles. (1967). *Antigone.* Trans. E. F. Watling. Middlesex, England: Penguin.

Sorensen, Georg. (1998). *Democracy and Democratization: Processes and Prospects in a Changing World,* 2d ed. Boulder, CO: Westview Press.

Spencer, William. (2000). *Middle East,* 9th ed. New York: McGraw-Hill.

Stearns, Jill. (1998). *Gender and International Relations: An Introduction.* New Brunswick, NJ: Rutgers University Press.

Steele, Valerie J., Ed. (1999). *Washington Representatives 1999.* Washington, DC: Columbia Books.

Stepan, Alfred, and Juan J. Linz. (1996). *Problems of Democratic Transition and Consolidation: Southern Europe, South America and Post-Communist Europe.* Baltimore, MD: Johns Hopkins University Press.

Stoessinger, John G. (2005). *Why Nations Go to War,* 9th ed. Boston, MA: Bedford Press.

Strauss, Leo. (1959). *What Is Political Philosophy?* New York: Free Press.

Strom, Kaare. (1989). *Minority Government and Majority Rule.* New York: Cambridge University Press.

Studlar, Donley T., Ian McAllister, and Bernadette C. Hayes. (1998) "Explaining the Gender Gap in Voting: A Cross-National Analysis." *Social Science Quarterly* 79:4 (Winter): 186–212.

Sunstein, Cass. (2001). *Designing Democracy: What Constitutions Do.* New York: Oxford University Press.

———. (2002). *Republic.com.* Princeton, NJ: Princeton University Press.

Taagepera, Rein, and Matthew S. Shugart. (1989). *Seats and Votes.* New Haven, CT: Yale University Press.

Tawney, R. H. (1938). *Religion and the Rise of Capitalism: A Historical Study.* Middlesex, England: Penguin.

Thompson, Leonard. (1966). *Politics in the Republic of South Africa.* Boston, MA: Little, Brown.

Thoreau, Henry David. (1849/1981). *Walden and Other Writings.* ed. J. W. Krutch. New York: Bantam.

Thurow, Lester C. (2003). *Head to Head: Coming Economic Battles among Japan, Europe and America.* New York: HarperBusiness.

———. (1997). *The Future of Capitalism.* New York: Viking-Penguin.

Tocqueville, Alexis de. (1835/1945). *Democracy in America.* New York: Knopf.

Todaro, Michael, and Stephen Smith. (2003). *Economic Development,* 8th ed. New York: Addison-Wesley-Longman.

Transparency International. (2003). http://www.transparency.org.

Truman, David. (1951). *The Governmental Process.* New York: Knopf.

United Nations Commission on Transnational Corporations. (1991). *Recent Developments Related to Transnational Corporations and International Economic Relations.* New York: United Nations.

United Nations Development Programme. (1999). *Human Development Report 1999.* New York: Oxford University Press.

———. (2003). *Human Development Report 2003.* www.hdr.undp.org/reports.

United Nations Population Division. (2003). http://www.un.org/esa/population/unpop.htm.

United Nations Peacekeeping. (2003). http://www.un.org/Depts/dpko/dpko/home.shtml.

U.S. Arms Control and Disarmament Agency. (1994). *World Military Expenditures and Arms Transfers, 1991–1993.* Washington, DC: U.S. Government Printing Office.

U.S. Department of State. (2003). *Patterns of Global Terrorism 2002.* http://www.state.gov/s/ct/rls/pgtrpt/2002/.

VCIOM (1999). Russian Center for Public Opinion and Market Research. "Russian Citizen Survey" (March): www.russiavotes.org.

Verba, Sidney, and Norman Nie. (1972). *Participation in America.* New York: Harper & Row

———. (1975). "Political Participation." In *Handbook of Political Science, vol. 4.* ed. Fred Greenstein and Nelson Polsby. Reading, MA: Addison-Wesley.

Verba, Sidney, Norman Nie, and Jae-on Kim. (1978). *Participation and Political Equality: A Seven-Nation Comparison.* London: Cambridge University Press.

Verba, Sidney, Kay Schlozman, and Henry Brady. (1995). *Voice and Equality: Civic Voluntarism in American Politics.* Cambridge, MA: Harvard University Press.

WABF. (2001). *World Almanac and Book of Facts.* Mahwah, NJ: World Almanac Books.

Walker, Nancy. (1988). "What We Know about Women Voters in Britain, France and West Germany." *Public Opinion,* May–June: pp. 49–55.

Wallach, Lori, and Patrick Woodall. (2004). *Whose Trade Organization?: The Comprehensive Guide to the WTO,* 2nd ed. New York: New Press.

Wallensteen, Peter, and Margareta Sollenberg. (1999). "Armed Conflict, 1989–98", *Journal of Peace Research* 36 (5).

Wallerstein, Immanuel. (1974). *The Modern World System.* New York: Academic Press.

———. (1980). *The World System II.* New York: Academic Press.

———. (1991). *Geopolitics and Geoculture: Essays on the Changing World System.* New York: Cambridge University Press.

Waltz, Kenneth. (1979). *Theory of International Politics.* Reading, MA: Addison-Wesley.

———. (1995). "Realist Thoughts and Neorealist Theory." In *Controversies in International Relations Theory: Realism and the Neoliberal Challenge.* ed. Charles W. Kegley, pp. 67–83. New York: St. Martin's Press.

———(1999). "Globalization and Governance." *PS Online* (December). http://209.235.241.4/PS/dec99/.

Weatherby, Joseph. (2003). "The Old and the New: Colonialism, Neocolonialism and Nationalism." In *The Other World: Issues and Politics of the Developing World,* 5th ed. ed. Joseph Weatherby et al., pp. 23–60. New York: Longman.

Weatherby, Joseph, Randall Cruikshanks, Emmit Evans, Reginald Gooden, Earl Huff, Richard Kranzdorf, and Dianne Long. (2000). *The Other World: Issues and Politics of the Developing World,* 4th ed. New York: Addison-Wesley-Longman.

Weatherby, Joseph, Emmit Evans, Reginald Gooden, Dianne Long, and Ira Reed (2003). *The Other World: Issues and Politics of the Developing World,* 5th ed. New York: Longman.

Weber, Max. (1951). *The Religion of China: Confucianism and Taoism.* ed. Hans H. Gerth. New York: Free Press.

———. (1958a). *From Max Weber: Essays in Sociology.* ed. Hans H. Gerth and C. Wright Mills. New York: Oxford University Press.

———. (1958b). *The Religion of India: The Sociology of Hinduism and Buddhism.* Trans. Hans Gerth and Don Martindale. New York: Free Press.

Weiss, Thomas, Ed. (1996). *NGOs, the UN and Global Governance.* Boulder, CO: Lynne Rienner Publishers.

Wen, Chihua. (1995). *The Red Mirror: Children of China's Cultural Revolution.* Boulder, CO: Westview Press.

Weyland, Kurt. (1999). "Neoliberal Populism in Latin American and Eastern Europe." *Comparative Politics* 31 (July): 379–400.

Wiarda, Howard J. (1997). *Corporatism and Comparative Politics.* Armonk, NY: M.E. Sharpe.

Wilber, Charles, and Kenneth Jameson, Eds. (1996). *The Political Economy of Development and Underdevelopment,* 6th ed. New York: McGraw-Hill.

Wilson, Edward O. (1978). *On Human Nature.* Cambridge, MA: Harvard University Press.

Wilson, Graham K. (1991). "American Interest Groups in Comparative Perspective." In *The Politics of Interests,* ed. Mark P. Petracca, pp. 80–95. Boulder, CO: Westview Press.

Wilson, William Julius. (1987). *The Truly Disadvantaged.* Chicago: University of Chicago Press.

———. (1996). *When Work Disappears.* New York: Knopf.

Winters, Jeffrey A. (1998). "Asia and the 'Magic' of the Marketplace." *Current History* 97 (December): 418–425.

Wolf, Edward. (1985). "State of the Earth 1985." *Natural History* 94 (April): 51–88.

Wolf, Eric. (1969). *Peasant Wars of the Twentieth Century.* New York: Harper & Row.

Wolin, Sheldon. (1960). *Politics and Vision.* Boston, MA: Little, Brown.

Woo-Cumings, Meredith, Ed. (1999). *The Developmental State.* New York: Cornell University Press.

World Bank (1996). *World Development Report 1996.* New York: Oxford University Press.

———. (1999). *World Development Report 1998–99.* New York: Oxford University Press.

———. (2001). *World Development Report 2000–2001.* New York: Oxford University Press.

World Bank Online. (2004). www.worldbank.org (subscription service). Also available in World Bank (2004). *World Development Indicators.* New York: World Bank.

World Commission on Environment and Development. (1987). *Our Common Future.* New York: Oxford University Press.

World Trade Organization. (2004). *What Is the World Trade Organization?* www. wto.org.

World Values Survey, 1995–1997. (2001). Ann Arbor, MI: Interuniversity Consortium for Political Research.

Worldwatch. (2003). *State of the World 2003.* Washington, D.C.: The Worldwatch Institute.

Woshinsky, Oliver. (1995). *Culture and Politics.* Englewood Cliffs, NJ: Prentice-Hall.

Wright, Erik Olin. (1998). *The Debate on Classes.* London: Verso.

Wright, Robin. (1999). "Wars of Identity." *Los Angeles Times,* April 3: p. A 15.

Wrong, Dennis. (1995). *Power: Its Forms, Bases and Uses.* Brunswick, NJ: Transaction Press.

Zakaria, Fareed. (1997). "The Rise of Illiberal Democracy." *Foreign Affairs* 76 (November/December): 23–46.

———. (2003). *The Future of Freedom: Illiberal Democracy at Home and Abroad.* New York: W.W. Norton.

Zaller, John R. (1992). *The Nature and Origins of Mass Opinion.* New York: Cambridge University Press.

Ziring, Lawrence, Robert E. Riggs, and Jack C. Plano. (2001). *The United Nations: International Organization and World Politics.* 3d ed. Fort Worth, TX: Harcourt.

Credits

Chapter 1   2: AP/Wide World Photos; 10: AP/Wide World Photos

Chapter 2   27: AP/Wide World Photos; 37: AKG/Photo Researchers Inc.; 39: ©Topham Picturepoint/ The Image Works; 40: © The British Library / Topham-HIP / The Image Works; 43: © The British Library / Topham-HIP / The Image Works

Chapter 3   50: AP/Wide World Photos; 56: Robert Harbison/2003 © The Christian Science Monitor; 62: AP/ Wide World Photos; 70: AP/Wide World Photos

Chapter 4   78: Greg Davis/ ZUMA Press. © 2000 by Greg Davis; 84: Frank Cotham; 88: AP/Wide World Photos; 98, left: Getty Images; 98, right: Mansell/Time Life Pictures/Getty Images

Chapter 5   108: AP/Wide World Photos; 124: John Spragens, Jr./Photo Researchers, Inc.; 131: Bob Daemmrich Photography, Inc./The Image Works

Chapter 6   149: AP/Wide World Photos; 155: Sidney Harris

Chapter 7   162: Getty Images; 167: AP/ Wide World Photos; 177: Library of Congress

Chapter 8   198: AP/Wide World Photos; 204: AP/Wide World Photos

Chapter 9   229: AP/Wide World Photos; 236: Mark E. Tetrault/Index Stock Imagery

Chapter 10   244: AP/Wide World Photos; 265: AP/Wide World Photos; 270: Sally Wiener Grotta/CORBIS

Chapter 11   274: Eagles Roar, Inc./CORBIS Sygma; 286: AP/Wide World Photos; 288, left: Shamil Zhumatov/Reuters/TimePix/Getty Images; 288, right: Karamallah Daher/Reuters/ TimePix/Getty Images

Chapter 12   306: AP/Wide World Photos; 314: Bettman/CORBIS; 315: © Susan Meiselas/ Magnum Photos; 319: AP/Wide World Photos; 328: Georges Gobet/AFP/Getty Images

Chapter 13   342: AP/Wide World Photos; 350: Pool Photo/Getty Images; 361: AP/Wide World Photos

Chapter 14   378: AP/ Wide World Photos; 403: James Danziger; 410: Photo by Carolyn Cole. Copyright, 2005, *Los Angeles Times*. Reprinted with permission.

Chapter 15   428: Hulton| Archive/Getty Images; 448: AP/Wide World Photos; 459: AP/Wide World Photos

Chapter 16   466: AP/Wide World Photos; 475: AP/Wide World Photos; 480: Kocatepe Gunes/GAMMA

Appendix   485: The Art Archive/Museo Nazionale Romano Rome/Dagli Orti (A)

Index

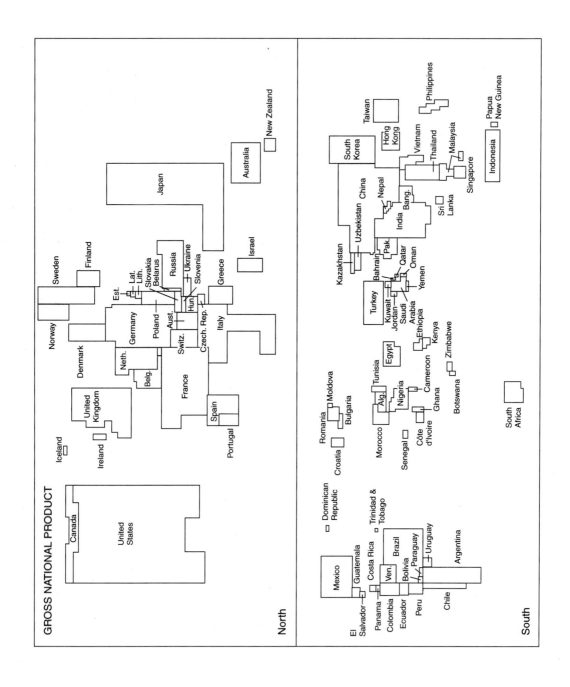

GROSS NATIONAL PRODUCT